ADVANCE PRAISE FOR *MAN OF DESTINY*

"No one has written with greater authority on American political leadership in the 1930s and 1940s than Alonzo Hamby. *Man of Destiny* is simply the best one-volume biography of FDR we have—a superb, clear-headed study based on a lifetime of research and hard thinking."

—Anthony Badger, author of *FDR: The First Hundred Days*

"FDR remains the most influential, enduring, and enigmatic leader of twentieth-century America. Alonzo Hamby's book offers a fascinating portrait of Roosevelt, brilliantly capturing his political prescience and strategic acumen, as well as his personal egotism and intellectual inconsistency. Hamby explains how a very human president contributed to seemingly superhuman outcomes. This book is a must-read for anyone interested in history, politics, and leadership."

—Jeremi Suri, author of *Liberty's Surest Guardian: American Nation-Building from the Founders to Obama*

MAN OF DESTINY

FDR and the Making of the
American Century

ALONZO L. HAMBY

BASIC BOOKS
A MEMBER OF THE PERSEUS BOOKS GROUP
NEW YORK

Designed by Jack Lenzo

Library of Congress Cataloging-in-Publication Data
Hamby, Alonzo L.
Man of destiny : FDR and the making of the American century / Alonzo Hamby.
pages cm
Includes bibliographical references and index.
ISBN 978-0-465-02860-3 (hardcover : alk. paper)—ISBN 978-0-465-06167-9 (e-book) 1. Roosevelt, Franklin D. (Franklin Delano), 1882–1945. 2. Presidents—United States—Biography. 3. United States—Politics and government—1933–1945. 4. World War, 1939–1945—Biography. 5. New Deal, 1933–1939. I. Title.
E807.H323 2015
973.917092—dc23
[B]
2015007617

10 9 8 7 6 5 4 3 2 1

For Joyce,
With thanks for so much,
for so long.

CONTENTS

PREFACE

I HAVE A HAZY MEMORY OF MY MOTHER AND FATHER, SEATED NEAR THE FAMILY radio, listening to a speech by Franklin D. Roosevelt, likely his last fireside chat, on January 6, 1945. I have a much clearer recollection of hearing the late-afternoon bulletin on April 12, 1945, announcing Roosevelt's death, and running to tell my mother.

Above that radio, for many years after the war, hung a wartime map of the world with pictures of Allied civilian and military leaders along its edges. Roosevelt at the top was the most prominently displayed. My parents taught me that he was the greatest of all American presidents. My mother always remembered his birthday and thought she knew his favorite song. (Could it really have been "Home on the Range"?) My father recalled that when his fortunes were at low ebb during the Depression, Roosevelt's speeches had bucked him up. As a teenager, I began a practice of making Christmas donations to the March of Dimes, Roosevelt's charity devoted to the treatment and eradication of polio. Some years later, as a professional historian writing about Harry S. Truman, I discovered that much of the controversy about HST revolved around a dispute over whether he was following the course FDR had charted.

A child of wealth and privilege, possessing unlimited will and ambition, Franklin Delano Roosevelt was destined to lead a nation large in population, rich in resources, and committed to a universalist ideology of liberal democracy. His twelve years in the White House culminated in the creation of what can justly be called an American century. This convergence of individual and national destinies created a large and complex story that remains essential to our understanding of the world in which we live today.

History is more than biography, but individual actors nonetheless chart its course. There are many accounts of Roosevelt's life, most of them either laudatory tributes or blandly noninterpretive narratives in which large themes get lost. No twentieth-century American lived a bigger or more consequential life. I have attempted to treat it fully but economically and from a point of view that acknowledges genuine achievements while recognizing large failures. I hope I have succeeded in bringing out its meaning without taxing the reader's patience.

A. L. H.
Athens, Ohio
January 2015

PART I

BECOMING FDR

Chapter 1

"The Best People"

Family and Identity, 1882–1896

My dear Mama.

Thank you so much for the lovly soldiers. Brother Rosy may take a picture of our gardans because it looks so nice. We are going to have a big bush in our gardans and it's nearly two feet high. I take my rest evry day but I am not out much We have battles with the soldiers evry day. And they are so nice. Good bye dear Mama Your loving little

Franklin
P.S. Give my love to papa and Uncle Frank and Aunt Laura.[1]

FRANKLIN DELANO ROOSEVELT WAS SIX YEARS OLD WHEN HE WROTE THIS letter to his mother, Sara Delano Roosevelt, in the spring of 1888. Franklin's birth on January 30, 1882, had been a near-run thing, accomplished only after his mother had undergone twenty-four hours of excruciating labor and the administration of chloroform; the ten-pound baby who emerged then required mouth-to-mouth resuscitation. The boy seems to have retained no buried sense of his precarious entry into existence. He lived contentedly in a safe, structured world, defined by the wealth and authority of his family.[2]

Roosevelts and Delanos, it seemed, had always been there, moneyed and prominent, quiet and steady, exemplifying the virtues of wealth, responsibility, and leadership. By the mid-nineteenth century, both families formed part of a well-defined, self-conscious stratum of the wealthy—"patricians," the "gentility," or the "Best People." They treated their inherited wealth as an annuity to invest carefully that it might produce sufficient income to sustain an affluent lifestyle. They served on boards of directors but rarely acted as hands-on managers. They supported charities. In politics, they generally advocated reform in the sense of honest, efficient, and frugal government. But few deigned to run for office.

Economically, by the mid- to late nineteenth century the American nouveau riche—the entrepreneurs and financiers who built empires, made tons of money, and flaunted their riches—had surpassed the Best People. The Astors, the Vanderbilts, the Carnegies, the Morgans, and slightly less luminous capitalists inevitably assimilated with them. Still, the distinction remained clear on both sides.[3]

The first of the American Roosevelts appears to have been a simple farmer from an island off the Dutch mainland, but his descendants prospered as merchants, bankers, investors in land, and sugar refiners. The Roosevelts maintained close family relationships throughout the eighteenth and nineteenth centuries. Possessing modest to substantial wealth, they enjoyed status and esteem as members of the oldest families in New York, the Dutch-based Knickerbocker society.[4]

The Delanos traced their ancestry to French Calvinists (Huguenots) who had fled to the safety of Leiden in the Dutch Republic. In 1621, one of them followed the English Calvinist Pilgrims, who a year earlier had left on the *Mayflower* for America. His descendants found prosperity as shipbuilders, whalers, and overseas traders. Like the Roosevelts, the Delanos exemplified how early settlement, old money, and entrepreneurial talent over several generations would lead to a special social standing. Warren Delano II made a fortune in what the family later delicately called "the China trade"—selling opium to the Chinese, a dangerous but extraordinarily lucrative business. He married eighteen-year-old Catherine Lyman in 1843 and fathered eleven children with her.[5]

A formidable man, Delano dominated his offspring and enforced his will strictly, inspiring, as Sara Delano Roosevelt later put it, "equal parts of awe and fear." Prospective husbands for his daughters had to possess a strong character and a "competence" of at least $100,000, the equivalent of $1.5 million or more in the early twenty-first century.[6]

Franklin's father, James Roosevelt, led a pedestrian life compared to that of Warren Delano. Yet their families had similar roots and shared values grounded in the seventeenth-century Calvinism that had migrated from England and the Netherlands to the northeastern United States. The Roosevelt fortune had been made well before James was born in 1828; though not as grand as Warren Delano's, it was sufficient to sustain a comfortable life among the American gentry.

The usually dutiful son of a nonpracticing physician who preached strait-laced morality, James had displayed traces of rebellion and self-assertion. He insisted on attending the University of New York (now NYU), failed mathematics and Latin courses, and was sent home. Shipped off to Union College in Schenectady, he joined a so-called secret society that held its meetings in a local tavern. He achieved distinction as a student; graduating in July 1847, he delivered the class oration. Demanding a grand tour of Europe, he arrived as the liberal revolutions of 1848 broke out across the continent. In Italy, he served briefly in Giuseppe Garibaldi's revolutionary army. He returned home in May 1849, after an exciting year and a half.[7]

Harvard Law School followed, and James graduated with the class of 1851. Two years later, Harvard's most prestigious eating club, Porcellian, made him an honorary member. His talent and family connections won him a place with a prestigious corporate law firm. He made his country residence at Mount Hope, a Hudson River estate inherited from his grandfather.

By then, American capitalism was approaching what later development theorists would call a takeoff point. The age of steel and steam, embodied in railroads and the coal that fired their boilers, had arrived. The Roosevelts, aligned with their relatives, the Aspinwall and Howland families, built formidable business combinations in both industries. James became a partner and made the relationship intimate by marrying his second cousin, Rebecca Brien Howland, in 1853. Hardly out of law school, he was elected a director of the Consolidated Coal Company of Maryland. Soon he was also general manager of the Cumberland and Pennsylvania Railroad. Other such ventures would follow throughout his life.

James Roosevelt measured risk carefully, never put all his eggs in one basket, and scrupulously limited his liability, but he was more than a fusty collector of dividends and directorship stipends. He thought big and promoted visionary enterprises, wagering that the America in which he had come of age would develop into a mighty nation with global reach. After the Civil War, he and his relations built on their coal operations, establishing the Consolidation Coal Company, the nation's largest producer of bituminous coal. Separately, he and others partnered with Tom Scott, president of the Pennsylvania Railroad and a would-be rail monopolist, to establish a holding company designed to buy a controlling interest in the major trunk lines of the old Confederacy; Scott

hoped to link these to his grand and ultimately unfulfilled project for a southern transcontinental Texas and Pacific Railroad. James made a substantial personal investment and was elected the company's president. The Panic of 1873
and the depression that followed put all these enterprises on the rocks.[8]

James's grandest and most daring speculation came in the 1880s and early
1890s: the Maritime Canal Company of Nicaragua proposed to build an
Atlantic-Pacific canal through that Central American nation. The extent of his
investment is uncertain. His greatest value to the company lay in his close relationship with Democratic president Grover Cleveland, whom he had supported
generously. He moved his family to Washington, DC, during the winter of 1887
to lobby for a federal appropriation. Although a rational alternative to a canal
through Panama, the plan ultimately ran afoul of the great depression of the
1890s and the vagaries of politics in both the United States and Nicaragua. Its
stock eventually became worthless.[9]

Through it all, James received a consistent stream of income from other investments. First among them was the Delaware and Hudson Canal Company, which
also operated railroads and anthracite coal mines. He served as one of its vice
presidents and often used a private railway car for personal and business trips.

He and Rebecca lived much of the year at Mount Hope, wintered at their
Manhattan town house, enjoyed long trips to Europe, exchanged visits with their
extended families, and attended glittering social events. Their only child, a son,
was born on March 27, 1854. His father, employing the Dutch equivalent of the
English "junior," named him James Roosevelt Roosevelt. Inevitably, he became
known inside and outside the family as "Rosy." Handsome, energetic, intelligent,
and unserious, he would become a dashing young man, marry into the Astor
family, and serve for a time as a junior member of the US diplomatic service.

In September 1865, Mount Hope burned to the ground while the family was away on a yearlong trip to Europe. James decided against rebuilding
and bought an estate two or so miles up the east side of the Hudson River at
Crum Elbow, just south of the small village of Hyde Park. It consisted of a
large house, outbuildings, and 110 acres of farmland. He had the house modernized and furnished it elegantly. Over several years, he acquired adjoining
land until he owned a thousand acres, some of it wooded, some of it pasture
for purebred horses and cattle, much of it devoted to commercial farming. The
house required eight to ten servants; the farming operation employed numerous additional workers. James called his little empire "Springwood." Rosy and
his wife would eventually occupy a comfortable country home ("the little Red
House") on the grounds.

James became a person of substance in the Hyde Park community and developed a life resembling that of an English squire. He took up membership in the local Episcopal congregation, St. James Church, where he was a vestryman and for a time senior warden. He also served as an overseer of the local public school and the county jail, won election to the town's board of supervisors, and became prominent for his charities. A fine horseman, he sponsored and led the annual Dutchess County hunt. As he moved into middle age, he looked the part of a man of distinction—fit but carrying a little extra weight, sporting mutton-chop whiskers, wearing tailored Scottish tweeds and a top hat. He became known to his employees and many of the townspeople as "Mr. James."

His politics were representative of those of the Best People with one exception—he was a Democrat. He had no truck with the radical Democrats of the West and the South who wanted to debase the dollar, attack business, and spend recklessly. Nor did he give more than token support to the Irish-based urban Democratic machines of the North, such as New York's Tammany Hall. Essentially, he was a Jeffersonian, believing in small, frugal government, low taxes, free trade, and sound money, even if he did not shy from federal subsidies for internal development. The New York politician he most admired, Grover Cleveland, epitomized this creed.

Mr. James and his Republican friends generally agreed on one point. Leadership in one's community was a gentleman's duty. Otherwise, politics was not a gentleman's business. He refused requests to run for Congress or the state legislature and even declined a diplomatic appointment from President Cleveland.

The Calvinist values James had learned as a child persisted. Thrift, hard work, and character, he declared in a talk to a church group, determined success in life. Only the poorest of the poor—the denizens of the Lower East Side in New York or the East End of London—born without a chance, living in squalor by necessity, were deserving objects of charity. It should come not simply from the rich but from those no more than a step or two above them, for with charity came redemption. This was classic Calvinism, characterized by a moral sense that all classes shared a common humanity. Mr. James's charitable works gave life to his admonitions and surely transmitted to his offspring some sense of the Best People's obligation toward the lower classes.[10]

James and Rebecca had hardly passed their fifteenth anniversary before her health broke. On August 21, 1876, her heart gave out. She was buried in the St. James Church cemetery at Hyde Park. After a long period of mourning, James began to look for a new wife. He was initially attracted to Anna ("Bamie") Roosevelt, the daughter of his fourth cousin and great friend, Theodore Roosevelt

Sr. An appealing and sympathetic young woman, she was, alas, less than half his age. As nicely as possible, she rejected his proposal.

Shortly afterward, at a small dinner party held by Bamie's mother, James met Sara Delano. Warren Delano's seventh child, she had been introduced to society in January 1873, at the age of eighteen, a striking and attractive young woman, just two inches short of six feet tall, her fair skin contrasting fetchingly with her dark brown hair and eyes. Like Bamie, she was half James's age. He was immediately smitten. Sara, not yet having received a proposal from a wealthy young man and uncomfortably close to being an old maid, was attracted to him. Warren Delano, a longtime friend and business associate, swallowed whatever doubts he may have had. James was a good man. He possessed an abundant competence. Sara was willing to accept him as a husband. They would live just a few miles away.[11]

The pair married on October 7, 1880. He was fifty-two, she twenty-six. They took an extended honeymoon in Europe. By the time they returned home ten months later, she was well along in her first and only pregnancy. In later years, she would claim that their son was "a Delano, not a Roosevelt at all." Genetically or otherwise she passed along her father's characteristics of enterprise, daring, and a strength of will that verged on the domineering.[12]

The boy to whom she gave birth with such difficulty was a product of generations of intermarriage among elites. He could claim relationship to several *Mayflower* passengers, eight former presidents, and two future ones. He was distantly linked to Jefferson Davis, Robert E. Lee, and a seven-year-old English aristocrat named Winston Churchill. Both his mother and father were related by marriage to the Astors. From an early age he would have a strong awareness of his membership in these two large and important extended families.

The boy was also a product of two centuries of Calvinist piety, thrift, and capitalist enterprise on both sides. He, however, would be neither pious, nor thrifty, nor a capitalist enterpriser.

WITH JAMES'S CONSENT, SARA DECIDED THE CHILD WOULD BE NAMED AFTER one of her uncles, Franklin Delano. On March 20, 1882, he was thus christened at St. James Church. One of his godfathers was Elliott Roosevelt, the youngest son of Theodore Roosevelt Sr. and soon-to-be father of a daughter named Eleanor.[13]

Franklin's parents stood at the center of a stable and carefree world. Rosy, functionally more an uncle than a half brother, was a frequent presence, as was his son, "Taddy," three years older than Franklin. The Delanos came often; their estate, Algonac, was almost a second home. Despite his large, supportive family, however, in some ways Franklin's childhood was lonely. Without siblings, he lacked the constant companionship of other youngsters his own age. As a young man, he would make it clear that he wanted to father a large family.[14]

Franklin's early upbringing combined an ethic of responsibility with a sense of authority and leadership. In the company of other children, he tended to have a take-charge attitude. Years later, Sara recalled that he organized his playmates and was always prone to issuing commands. "Mummie," she remembered him saying, "if I didn't give the orders, nothing would happen!"[15]

James and Sara appear to have been exemplary parents, providing abundant personal contact and affection, along with order and structure. Young Franklin always had a nurse, but Sara breast-fed, bathed, and dressed him regularly. "I felt," she commented years later, "that every mother ought to learn to care for her own baby, whether she can afford to delegate the task to someone else or not." Indeed, she was perhaps excessively dutiful about this. At the age of eight and a half, Franklin would remark in a letter to his father, "Mama left this morning and I am going to take my bath alone." In the mode of the time, he wore dresses until he was five. For a few years Sara frequently dressed him in kilts, which she called his Murray suits after a late-medieval Scottish ancestor, John Murray, the Outlaw of Fala Hill. The Murray costume gave way to sailor suits that recalled the Delano family's maritime heritage. When Franklin was four, he, on a pony, and his father, on a horse, began regular morning horseback rides around the estate, masters of all they surveyed. They sledded and ice-boated in the winter, sailed in spring and summer.[16]

Another male role model entered Franklin's life as he moved toward young adulthood. Theodore Roosevelt Jr. ("Teedie" to the family at that time) had become a national figure—New York legislator, US civil service commissioner, New York City police commissioner, author of a torrent of books, and a prominent naturalist. Vigorous and outspoken, Ted, increasingly known as TR, was an exciting model of Victorian masculinity.

James and Sara gave Franklin about anything he wanted—a dog, a pony, a gun to shoot local birds, money to have the specimens stuffed and mounted, a display cabinet for them, expensive cameras and photographic equipment— and indulged him in whatever collecting whim he developed, whether naval prints or stamps. But entitlement demanded responsibility. Franklin had to take care of his dog and pony, use his gun responsibly, kill only one example of each bird species, and employ his camera to document family life and travels. More generally, mother and father taught him that life was about work and achievement, not idle pleasure—that much of the Calvinist ethic remained alive and well.

Travel was a regular part of life. The winter social season required a residence in Manhattan—first a town house on Washington Square, then one
on Forty-Ninth Street, and finally an apartment in the Renaissance Hotel at
Fifth Avenue and Forty-Third Street. To escape the summer heat, the family
retreated to a large vacation cottage on the Canadian island of Campobello,
just off the coast of Maine. There, in the Bay of Fundy, James, Franklin, and
numerous guests sailed the family schooner *Half-Moon*.

Many years included an extended trip to Europe, accompanied by two or
three servants. Such cosmopolitan mobility ultimately gave Franklin a greater
firsthand knowledge of continental Europe than of the continental United
States. Mostly vacation, the trips also provided an opportunity for James to
pitch investment in the Nicaraguan canal project to wealthy acquaintances.
Some time in England was mandatory. On at least one occasion, the Roosevelts
visited the Duke of Rutland at Belvoir, with James riding to the hounds in the
annual hunt.[17]

Franklin accompanied his parents on their stay in Washington in early 1887.
James brought him to the White House to meet President Cleveland. As they
prepared to leave, the president heaved his considerable bulk out of his chair,
walked over to the boy, patted him on the head, and said in what must have
been a weary voice, "My little man, I am making a strange wish for you. It is
that you may never be President of the United States."[18]

UNTIL AGE FOURTEEN, FRANKLIN WAS EDUCATED ALMOST ENTIRELY AT HOME,
one-on-one, by a succession of seven governesses and tutors. They were com-
petent to superior teachers, instructing him in a wide range of topics—French
and German, Greek and Latin, history (ancient and modern), religion, science,
mathematics, geography, and literature—and prepared him excellently for the
elite schools he would later attend.[19]

The boy's only experience with public schooling came in Germany when he
accompanied his parents in the spring of 1891 on one of their annual trips to
the spa at Bad Nauheim. Sara sent her nine-year-old son to a *Stadtsschule*. "I go
to the public school with a lot of little mickies and we have German reading,
German dictation, the history of Siegfried, and arithmetic," he wrote to two of
his cousins. "I like it very much." The term lasted only six weeks. Franklin's language seems to indicate that he found it and his schoolmates mostly amusing.[20]

By then, Franklin understood that his father was in Bad Nauheim because
he was unwell. James had suffered a heart attack in late 1890. The best physicians could do no more than advise treatment at a spa. So he took the waters

year after year, invariably feeling better after a month of relaxation and warm baths. In reality, of course, his condition slowly worsened. Until the very end, however, he was not an invalid. He continued his horseback riding until his final weeks, ten years after his first attack.[21]

It is hard to say how his father's slow decline affected Franklin. His mother may have told him, or perhaps he simply sensed, that James required peace, quiet, and special consideration. His parents were the two people of consequence in his life. He tried hard to please them—concealing a broken tooth, for example, to avoid spoiling an outing or, on another occasion, hiding a nasty cut on his forehead to avoid upsetting them. He was far less solicitous of the feelings of others.

As his mother would admit, despite her depiction of him as practically the perfect boy, he was a prankster. The pranks were relatively harmless. He inflicted perhaps the most consequential on his first full-time tutor at Hyde Park, Fraulein Reinsberg, a high-strung German woman. Slipping into her bedroom, he put effervescent powder into her chamber pot. When she used the convenience in the middle of the night, the resultant bubbling and hissing sent her screaming down the hall. Mr. James discerned that Franklin, who was eight or nine years old at the time, was probably behind the incident. When the boy confessed, his father, convulsed with laughter, told him to consider himself spanked and sent him away. Fraulein Reinsberg left the Roosevelts' employ in mid-1891 and eventually suffered a nervous collapse. In later years, Franklin recalled her as the governess he had driven to the madhouse. Two years later, Sara wrote of a successor, "Poor little Mlle Sandoz had such an upset tobogganing that she came home . . . quite black & blue. Franklin seemed to think it rather a joke."[22]

The servants put up with Franklin's misbehavior, perhaps feeling that he needed a good spanking, perhaps dismissing his antics as minor and amusing. There was a dark side, of course—a sense that one's employees were there to be abused. Still, what might have been perceived as insufferable brattiness was mitigated by an intense charm. Years later, Sara recalled asking their beloved Scottish head housekeeper Elespie McEachan if "our boy" had been misbehaving. The housekeeper responded, "They tell me that he has faults, but I can not see them."[23]

The boy seems never to have been at a loss for a wisecrack, as when he wrote for Mademoiselle Sandoz about the Egyptian kings who starved their people "by jinks!" by the "quadrillions." For a time during his twelfth year he signed his name backward ("Tlevesoor D. Nilknarf") in communications to his mother. Such antics may have been a low-key protest against his highly structured life of tutoring, playdates, and meals for which one must dress appropriately. When vacationing with his parents at Campobello in September 1890, he demanded and received a day of freedom, took off on his own, and, as he or his mother recalled years later, returned in the evening dirty and hungry. The next day, he resumed the usual routine without protest. From a very early age, he had an astute sense of just how far he could stretch the limits.[24]

Young Franklin possessed remarkable confidence and self-reliance. At the age of fourteen in London, when his mother and father were unable to accompany him, he insisted on traveling alone by train to the Nottinghamshire home of Cecil George Foljambe (Baron Hawkesbury), a noted ornithologist. He enjoyed the baron's collection of mounted birds, had a fine visit with him, stayed overnight, and was more than a little annoyed when the great man insisted on having his housekeeper escort the boy back home. That same summer, he and his tutor, Mr. Dumper, employing Franklin's impressive gilt-edged membership card for New York's American Museum of Natural History, talked their way into its great British counterpart in London, although it was closed to host a reception by the prince of Wales. They went on to the Continent, where Franklin, speaking German and radiating a charming innocence, secured the lenience of ordinarily nonlenient local authorities when he and Dumper were detained for minor misdemeanors during a bicycle trip through the country.[25]

By then Franklin was about to be removed from his comfortable, sheltered life and sent to boarding school at Groton, where he would enter the third form (ninth grade). In mid-September, as Sara described it, "we turned over to the headmaster there a white-faced little boy whose pride kept him from admitting that he carried a heavy heart and whose parents found the parting no easier to bear."[26]

CHAPTER 2

YOUNG GENTLEMAN

SCHOOLDAYS, 1896–1904

THIRTY-SIX YEARS AFTER HIS PARENTS LEFT HIM AT GROTON TO MAKE HIS way without their loving supervision, Sara Roosevelt recalled that Franklin was "dry-eyed and resolute, if a little tremulous." Relatively unformed, at an age awkward for all young males, he had to undertake a process of self-definition while coping with all the physical and emotional changes that accompany adolescence, and he had to do it as a new boy in a small, rigid society. The wonder is not that he found it difficult but that he was so successful.[1]

Franklin's parents wanted him to do well in school and emerge a gentleman of style and substance along the lines of his father, a leader to whom ordinary people naturally looked for guidance. Groton, in many respects, established the mold, producing a young man who would glide easily through Harvard, take his place among the nation's elite, marry within his class, and undertake respectable, if unnecessary, employment.

GROTON WAS PERHAPS THE MOST PROMINENT OF A NUMBER OF EXCLUSIVE boarding schools established to prepare the sons of America's elite for entry into its best colleges while shaping leaders of high character and Christian fortitude. Explicitly based on England's Rugby, the Massachusetts school was the personal creation of its rector, Episcopal reverend Endicott Peabody, who dominated the small, self-contained educational community he had founded.[2]

Peabody envisioned a school that would realize the best ideals of the English system. He would brook no "fagging" (use of young boys to perform menial errands for the older ones), no flogging, and no snobbish class system among the students. Groton had six "forms," or grades, the final one mimicking Harvard's freshman year. His school would forge learned and moral young gentlemen from boys separated from indulgent parents and the diversions of urban life. Typically, they entered at age twelve and graduated at eighteen. The isolated campus—a little cluster of redbrick buildings two miles out of town—guaranteed a near total lack of distractions and enhanced Peabody's dictatorial presence. The curriculum emphasized ancient history and classical languages. The purpose of education, Peabody asserted, was not to prepare children narrowly for an occupation but to "develop in them the powers and interests that will make them in later life the masters and not slaves of their work."[3]

Tall and imposing, with an impressive head of brownish-blond hair, and an overpowering speaker, the rector left a deep impression on parents, students, and donors. He established high expectations for his charges, set rigid rules of behavior, and sanctioned harsh punishments. William Averell Harriman, who entered Groton in 1904, described Peabody memorably in a letter to his railroad-magnate father: "You know he would be an awful bully if he wasn't such a terrible Christian." The boys listened to him preach every day, shook hands with him before bedtime every night, cringed at the thought of appearing before him for misbehavior, and welcomed the sympathetic attention of his wife, Fanny.[4]

Franklin's new quarters consisted of a six-by-nine cubicle with a bed, bureau, study desk, and pegs on which to hang his clothing. Three of its walls stopped well short of a high ceiling; a curtain, drawn across the entry, served as a door. A student's day was long, busy, and closely monitored. Activity was constant, privacy minimal. The boys wore suits, stiff-collared shirts, black neckties, and glossily polished patent leather shoes. They were allowed spending money of only twenty-five cents per week and had to donate a nickel of it at Sunday church service.[5]

There was little or no snobbery at Groton because most of the students came from rich families listed in local social registers. At school, moreover, they could not differentiate themselves by dress, possessions, or spending money. Size and athletic prowess became the main sources of distinction, and Peabody encouraged participation in team sports, which in his view built courage, determination, and group fealty. He considered football "the most spiritual of all games" and therefore special: "It makes a man eat plain food and keep early hours. It keeps back our growing tendency to indulge in luxuries. It inculcates obedience."[6]

Peabody also demanded adherence to a rigid code of conduct. "There is a good deal of the soldier element in a boy," Peabody asserted, "and he will respect decided treatment, and firm discipline, and will yield his loyalty when they are consistently carried out." Masters (teachers) gave out "black marks" for misconduct and imposed penalties that had to be worked off. Six black marks in one week could lead to a dreaded interview with the rector. Senior students, empowered as prefects with disciplinary authority over lower-form boys, administered two frightening sanctions: "bootboxing," in which a boy would spend a night doubled up in the locker where his boots were stored, and "pumping," a procedure akin to what a later generation would call "water boarding." Peabody acknowledged neither of these practices but tolerated them and gave at least indirect assent to each pumping.[7]

ON THE SURFACE, THE FOURTEEN-YEAR-OLD FRANKLIN WOULD SEEM ILL equipped to deal with Groton's social environment. In September 1896, he stood only five feet, three inches tall and weighed about one hundred pounds. Entering the school in the third rather than the first form, he and one other new boy, Jimmy Goodwin, were interlopers who had to make their way among the fifteen others who had enrolled at age twelve and already formed firm relationships.[8]

In letters to his mother and father (a weekly requirement at the school), Franklin was lighthearted. The first set the tone: "Dear Mommerr & Popperr, I am getting on finely both mentally and physically." Subsequent missives hit the same note time and again. Franklin knew they expected him to be a little man. He also was surely aware of the precariousness of his father's health and determined not to be a source of stress for either parent.[9]

He coped with his outsider status, probably more out of instinct than conscious design, by discerning what those around him expected and acting accordingly. Once some fourth formers armed with hockey sticks cornered him, ordered him to dance, and began jabbing at his ankles. With hardly a hesitation, he performed vigorously and nimbly with a big smile on his face, seeming to enjoy the experience. After a few minutes, the bullies moved on.[10]

Franklin was never boxed or pumped. Neither was he especially popular. A poor athlete, he did not make the first-string football squad and rarely played in interscholastic games. At his father's insistence, he took some boxing lessons, went two rounds against another boy with whom he had a dispute, and was judged the loser. In his junior year, he was appointed assistant manager of the baseball team, and as a senior he served as manager. The position, which carried the duties of laying out the field and looking after the equipment, qualified him for an athletic ribbon.[11]

He competed seriously only in a silly and dangerous competition called "the High Kick," which required boys to kick at a tin pan hanging from the gymnasium ceiling, throwing themselves into the air and falling backward onto the floor. Franklin won the competition for smaller students during his first year. "At every kick," he reported to his mother and father, "I landed on my *neck* on the left side so the result is that the whole left side of my body is sore and my left arm is a little swollen." His parents do not seem to have been pleased. Nevertheless, he competed again the following year, finished second, and took away a sore elbow. Over his four years at Groton, he would suffer one minor injury after another, mostly from athletics.[12]

Sent to Groton with earnest entreaties to follow the rules faithfully and work hard, he was slow to understand that a determined effort to win the Punctuality Award did not earn him the goodwill of his classmates. Nor did a perfect behavior record for his first eight months. He finally got the point. He wrote to his parents on May 14, 1897, that he had worked off his first offense. "I am very glad I got it, as I was thought to have no school-spirit before." The artfully constructed sentence, transforming classmates' judgment about his personal spirit into one about his "school spirit," displayed developing manipulative skills.[13]

Eleanor Roosevelt recalled many years later that Franklin had said he had always felt an outsider at Groton. In her mind, he had never quite erased the traumas of separation from parents, adjustment to a challenging environment, and redefinition of his identity. Perhaps so, but more likely Franklin simply found his level in the new society into which he had been thrown. His life at Groton was neither entirely satisfactory nor miserable. As all boys do, he complained from time to time about the alleged arbitrariness of his teachers; occasionally he even expressed bitterness toward the rector. Yet in later years he thought the Groton experience a positive one and expressed nothing but veneration for Reverend Peabody. He insisted on sending all four of his sons there, entering each in the first form at the prescribed age of twelve.[14]

He was a superior student, never at the top of his class but close to it, and a strong participant in the junior and senior debating clubs. A surviving draft of an argument against annexing Hawaii, written just before his sixteenth birthday in January 1898, is impressive and literate. By then he had gained enough confidence to assume what fellow latecomer Jimmy Goodwin characterized as "an independent, cocky manner" and a tendency to be "very argumentative and sarcastic." He participated in the school's Missionary Society, assisting an elderly Negro woman who lived near the school, playing the organ at its services, and helping with a summer camp it ran for underprivileged boys. He also wrote a few insubstantial articles for the school magazine, *The Grotonian*. During his senior year, he landed a juicy supporting role in the sixth-form play.[15]

As a fifth former, Franklin was appointed a school mail clerk with the informal and inelegant title "mail nigger." The coveted job gave him the privilege of breakfasting with Reverend Peabody twice each term. In his final year, he was a dormitory prefect, by all accounts much admired by his younger charges. The rector gave him special recognition in the form of a spacious single study and living quarters. Much to his annoyance and strong resentment, however, Peabody did not name him a "senior prefect."

Groton had its disappointments, none of them horrendous, even if they may have seemed so at the time. It also delivered small triumphs. His admission to Harvard was a given; he easily passed entrance examinations that allowed him to skip freshman requirements and in effect enter as a sophomore. He graduated near the top of his form scholastically and received the Latin Prize, an honor accompanied by a forty-volume set of Shakespeare's works. Whatever his inner turmoil, he was to outward appearances a confident, self-possessed young man. He wrote to his parents during his last days as a student at Groton, "I can hardly wait to see you but feel awfully to be leaving here for good."[16]

Groton had given Franklin a first-rate education and instilled in him a degree of self-discipline that it seems he had not possessed before. Above all, it introduced a pampered boy to the experience of living and coping in a society of peers. He had managed the challenge well, developing a competitive personality and establishing himself as an achiever. He left the school as an ambitious young man determined to achieve recognition at his next stop. One of his teachers, the much respected Reverend Sherrard Billings, considered him a person of almost infinite promise. A few years later, he wrote to his former student, then probably a senior at Harvard or a first-year law student, "I pray with all my heart that men will say of you that he was a man sent from God to help the world in its dire need. I have faith to believe that years hence as they look back men will say just that."[17]

AT EIGHTEEN YEARS OLD, A STILL SLIM FRANKLIN HAD REACHED HIS ADULT height of six feet and achieved a sense of himself as an independent personality. An early indication of this had come in 1897 at the end of his first year away from home. Bamie Roosevelt had invited him to spend the Fourth of July weekend at the Oyster Bay, Long Island, home of her brother Theodore. For some reason his mother disapproved and declined for him. His response was curt: "As you told me I could make my own plans and as Helen [Rosy's daughter] writes me there is to be a large party & lots of fun on the 4th, I shall try to arrange it with Cousin B. next Wednesday. Please don't make any more arrangements for my future happiness." His brief stay with his famous cousin was a memorable experience.[18]

A year later, Theodore Roosevelt, having done what he could as assistant secretary of the navy to take the United States into war with Spain, became a military hero as commander of a volunteer regiment, then won the Republican nomination for governor of New York. Mr. James, abandoning his Democratic allegiance, openly supported his cousin's victorious campaign. During his last year at Groton, Franklin, given a vision prescription for nearsightedness, ordered pince-nez eyeglasses identical to those affected by the new governor. TR would be his hero for the next decade and an exemplar in many ways for his entire life.[19]

Theodore and Franklin possessed commonalities in their personal histories beyond their family name. Both were raised and influenced by fathers who overlaid their wealth and social status with a commitment to philanthropy and public responsibility. Both were expected in some fashion to be public leaders. Both would choose politics as their vocation. In the summer of 1897, no one could predict that Theodore Roosevelt would become president of the United States. Almost everyone, however, could agree that he was a man to watch. His charm, vigor, delight in the exercise of power, and professed devotion to good government and the interests of middle-class America all surely excited Franklin. TR's subsequent presidency—marked by struggles against "malefactors of great wealth" at home, strong assertions of American power abroad, a consummate mastery of public relations, and a willingness to stretch presidential power—would give Franklin a template for his own tenure in the White House.

By the time he left Groton, Franklin was confident and emotionally self-sufficient. His letters, still at times punctuated by a wisecrack, assumed the tone of communications written by someone older. His recreational reading was substantial and mature in content. At fifteen and sixteen, he was especially interested in Admiral Alfred Thayer Mahan's works on the relationship between naval power and national greatness. Fascinated with ships, he developed an encyclopedic knowledge of sea vessels. During his extended summer vacations at Campobello, he enjoyed nothing more than sailing his small yacht in the sometimes treacherous waters that surrounded the island. He also became an avid golfer, laid out a course, established the Campobello golf club, and served as its secretary.[20]

During his years at Groton, he faced one ominous development. His father's health declined noticeably despite the annual trips to Germany. Photographed holding his one-year-old son on his shoulder in early 1883, James Roosevelt had looked strong, smooth-faced, and younger than his years. A decade and a half later, photos taken by Franklin revealed a tired, wrinkled, elderly man in the late stages of congestive heart failure. Warren Delano had died in January 1898. It was increasingly apparent that James would not long survive him. By the summer of 1900, his health was so precarious that he and Sara decided not to make the trip to Groton for Franklin's graduation. In December 1900, as Franklin was nearing the end of his first semester at Harvard, his father's condition worsened. He rushed to New York, where his parents were staying at their hotel apartment. James died there in the early hours of December 8 with Sara, Rosy, and Franklin at his bedside. A special train, filled with mourners, took his remains to Hyde Park, where he was interred alongside his first wife at St. James Church.

James Roosevelt's estate amounted to just over $713,000, equivalent to between $15 and $20 million a century later. After taxes and expenses, Sara, Rosy, and Franklin each received approximately $229,000. James's will placed Franklin's portion in a trust fund until he reached the age of twenty-one and established a similar fund for Sara (who had already inherited $1.3 million from her father). The will left Springwood and about half of the surrounding property to her for her lifetime, providing that upon her death it would pass to Franklin. Rosy received the house he and his wife had long used and the surrounding property.[21]

Franklin, eight weeks short of his nineteenth birthday, was now the man of the family. He was also rich. The workers at Hyde Park would soon begin calling him "Mr. Franklin." From this point on, he would be the male representative of the family whose benefactions had meant much to the community and to his father's beloved St. James Church.

Sara accepted widowhood easily and graciously. Only forty-six and quite a catch for an eligible widower, she seems never to have contemplated remarriage. As she entered into the traditional six months of deep mourning, she had the consolation of Franklin. She now focused the affection and emotional dependence previously divided between husband and son entirely on him. Her greatest happiness, she told her son a month after his father's death, was "in thinking of you and of his pride in you."[22]

James's wish, expressed in his will, that Franklin should exist "under the influence of his mother" reinforced her strong controlling instincts. She tried too hard for a time, actually taking rooms in Boston to be close to him for much of the school year, yet seeing little of him all the same. He accepted her devotion smoothly while keeping his distance. His affection for his mother and need for her love were genuine, but so was his determination to assert his independence and achieve a transition to manhood. In the end, it would be he, not she, who controlled the relationship.[23]

THE HARVARD THAT FRANKLIN ROOSEVELT ENTERED IN 1900 WAS BOTH A finishing school for the sons of the social elite and the incubator of a meritocratic leadership class for the nation. President Charles Eliot, in his address to the freshman class of more than five hundred men, made a point of denouncing the "common error" that only moneyed young men attended Harvard; still, more than half the students came from families of above-average income. A full 7 percent were Jewish, many from prosperous families of northern European extraction. On campus, the class distinctions between the entitled rich and aspiring strivers were palpable.

The secondary institution most heavily represented among the newcomers was an elite public school, Boston Latin, which trained talented children of all classes. About 40 percent of Roosevelt's classmates had graduated from that or similar institutions, but they did not have a lot of visibility on campus. Harvard had the nation's richest system of scholarships, but the holders had to grind out top-quality work in order to maintain their financial aid. They might also be employed part-time. Many lived in Harvard Yard's decrepit dormitories, which were hardly a step above the mean tenements of lower-working-class Boston. With hard work and frugality, they might graduate with high marks, establish themselves in honorable professions, and move a rung or two up the social ladder. Harvard's Franklin Roosevelts paid them little heed as they glided through their classes, content with gentlemen's Cs, participated in a social whirl, and provided leadership in student activities.[24]

Roosevelt and a Groton friend, Jake Brown, leased a two-bedroom apartment on the off-campus "Gold Coast." They decorated their quarters with beer steins, Groton and Harvard pennants, and school athletic photos. All but two members of Roosevelt's Groton class entered Harvard with him that September. They gathered daily for breakfast, lunch, and dinner in a private dining hall at a designated Groton table. They also socialized with graduates of St. Paul's, St. Mark's, and other elite establishments. Franklin, like most of his comrades, learned to smoke cigarettes and appreciate good whiskey. It was all "great fun."[25]

Becoming a big man on campus in such circles required distinction in extra-curricular pursuits. Roosevelt tried out for several and displayed slender talent at most. Franklin's playing weight of just under 150 pounds disqualified him from serious consideration for the football squad. That fall, he captained an intramural scrub team aptly named "the Missing Links." He also sang with the freshman glee club and was elected its secretary. During his second semester, he acted as captain of the third-string crew in one of the private rowing clubs. He would work his way up to second string before dropping out after his second year.[26]

By then he was spending most of his energy on the campus newspaper, the *Harvard Crimson*. His first application to join its staff in the fall of 1900 was rebuffed, but he came back in February 1901 with a real scoop. He had learned that cousin Theodore, now vice president elect of the United States, had agreed to speak, without prior publicity, to A. Lawrence Lowell's class in constitutional government. After the *Crimson* broke the story on the morning of the event, an estimated 2,000 people mobbed the small theater in which the class was held. A few months later, Franklin was elected one of five new *Crimson* editors for the coming year.[27]

During his first semester at Harvard, Franklin had supported Theodore's vice presidential candidacy enthusiastically, right down to joining the university's Republican club and participating in an eight-mile march through Boston. He was doubtless elated at the Republican victory, and not simply for reasons of family. The Democratic candidate, William Jennings Bryan, struck both him and his father as a simpleminded prairie populist willing to destroy the national currency for the alleged benefit of downtrodden farmers. The following September, Franklin and his mother returned from a European vacation to discover that President William McKinley had succumbed to an assassin's bullet. Cousin Ted was now the nation's president.[28]

Franklin had pressed for the European trip to avoid facing the usual vacation period at Campobello without Mr. James. He and Sara, accompanied by a cousin, Teddy Robinson, steamed to Hamburg on the German liner *Deutschland*. (Two years later, Robinson, a nephew of Theodore Roosevelt, would marry Rosy Roosevelt's daughter, Helen.) There, in what Sara may well have planned as a matchmaking exercise, they linked up with Mrs. Alfred Pell and her tall, attractive daughter Frances, with whom Franklin had studied ornithology a few years earlier.

The quintet embarked for a leisurely sail up the Norwegian coast on the luxurious cruising yacht *Prinzessin Victoria Luise*. Their vessel entered the port of Molde to find anchored there the *Hohenzollern*, the royal yacht of Germany's

Kaiser Wilhelm II. His imperial majesty accepted the captain's invitation to tea, impressing the officers and passengers with his unsmiling, fiercely authoritarian demeanor. Franklin and Frances joined several other passengers in a visit to the *Hohenzollern*. Upon his return, Franklin cheerfully presented to his mother a pencil lifted from the kaiser's desk and bearing royal tooth marks.[29]

WHEN FRANKLIN RETURNED TO HARVARD THAT FALL, THE *CRIMSON* WAS HIS major interest; he devoted enormous amounts of time to it. By the spring of 1903, he was managing editor and in line to become president (editor in chief) for the 1904 fall semester. Taking the position would require his staying at Harvard for a year past his June 1903 graduation.[30]

Roosevelt's college transcript has never been released, but it is generally accepted that he collected gentlemen's Cs. He sought recognition and prestige through Harvard's complex and hierarchical club life rather than through grades. His ultimate goal was selection for Porcellian, the famous club that had extended honorary membership to his father, but its sixteen active members passed him over. He never understood why and resented the omission for the rest of his life. Although it is tempting to view the incident as a source of his later democratic politics, his only quarrel with the club system was more probably its failure to give him its ultimate recognition.[31]

On the surface, he remained genial, unruffled, and eminently clubbable. He was already a member of Hasty Pudding, the famous theatrical club, and would be elected to membership in Alpha Delta Phi ("Fly"), the Signet Literary Society, and the Memorial Society (guardians of the history of Harvard). He served as librarian for Hasty Pudding and Fly, buying collectible books for both, as well as rare volumes for himself and his mother. On top of this, he led a busy social life of lunches and dinners in Boston with family friends, numerous trips back to Groton, faithful attendance at Harvard home football games, and weekend excursions here and there.[32]

Of all the social occasions, the most memorable surely was a long weekend in Washington just after New Year's Day, 1902. He was one of many guests attending a gala ball at the White House marking the social debut of Alice Roosevelt, President Theodore Roosevelt's glamorous and vivacious daughter. Even more important to Franklin were two meetings with the president and a memorable lunch with Cousin Bamie.[33]

In the midst of all this, he found time for charitable activities. He made periodic visits to the Groton Missionary Society's St. Andrews Boys Club in Boston, where he taught classes and officiated at games. He also was a member of the Harvard Social Services Society. To all indications, he did useful, if super-ficial, work in the spirit of upper-class Christian charity but never began to think of the problem of poverty as endemic to a social system that had to be changed. He also made a public splash by heading up a committee to provide relief for South African Boers, confined to concentration camps after their mil-itary defeat by the British. The effort raised a meager $336 but won him fulsome commendation in the *Boston Globe*.

Well-prepared and smart enough to produce undistinguished but passable work with relatively little effort, he stayed afloat academically. Declaring a major in history, he took courses in the "softer" humanities and social sciences. Consciously or otherwise, he passed over opportunities to study under some great minds, among them Josiah Royce and George Santayana, the eminences of the most distinguished philosophy department on the North American con-tinent. Abstract and systematic thought held little appeal for him.

Relatively nontheoretical and fact grubbing, history was an attractive major taught by a distinguished faculty. Perhaps the most notable was a visiting pro-fessor from the University of Wisconsin with whom Roosevelt took a course in the spring of 1904—Frederick Jackson Turner. Taking a Caribbean cruise with his mother, he missed about a third of Turner's course on the history of the American West. Nevertheless, he could not have avoided Turner's central ideas: westward expansion had been the driving force behind the development of the United States; the end of a discernible frontier line in 1890 marked a new and potentially critical period in which America was likely to become a nation more like the European industrial countries, characterized by intensi-fied class conflict and uncertain economic growth. Roosevelt could not have imagined that these arguments would have policy resonance thirty years later as he began his presidency in the depths of the Great Depression.

During his three years as an undergraduate, free to study whatever appealed to him, he pursued a curriculum composed heavily of history, English, and government courses. In one of them he wrote a paper titled "The Roosevelts of New Amsterdam." Heavily genealogical in content, it praised the "demo-cratic spirit" of his ancestors but provided little evidence of such sentiments. The assertion revealed his developing political sensibility.[34]

He was not uncritical of TR's actions but, by and large, expressed his res-ervations privately. He especially disapproved of his cousin's interference in the anthracite coal strike of 1902, which had cast the coal operators—Roo-sevelts and Delanos among them—as arrogant plutocrats unwilling to negoti-ate a square deal with their men. He was also wary of Ted's expansive claims to presidential power: "His tendency to make the executive power stronger than the Houses of Congress is bound to be a bad thing, especially when a man of weaker personality succeeds him in office." The comment was shrewdly predictive of the presidency of William Howard Taft, if not of Franklin's own tenure in the White House a generation later.[35]

Such measured criticism aside, Theodore was irresistible. His political passion and raw energy appealed to a vast constituency. His conviction that American society required significant, but not revolutionary, change stirred the impulses of youth. In 1904, Franklin cast his first presidential vote for his famous Republican relative.

After taking his bachelor of arts degree at Harvard's 1903 commencement, he talked his mother into letting him celebrate his achievement somewhat as had his father—with a trip to Europe sans parental supervision. It was no grand tour, just a month in England and Switzerland with Charles Bradley, a Harvard friend, but it was his first major travel without his mother. Sara broke into tears as she saw him off on the White Star liner *Celtic*. He sent her a note to be taken back ashore by the harbor pilot: "Don't worry about me—I always land on my feet—but wish so much you were with me."[36]

Actually, being on his own was the real purpose of the trip, and he never came close to losing his footing. He found London invigorating, but the special highlight was a visit to the Roosevelts' old friend, Sir Hugh Cholmeley of Easton Hall, and a day excursion to Belvoir, the great house of the Duke of Rutland, whom he encountered riding on the grounds at the age of eighty-seven. Sir Hugh was an expansive and generous host, treating his young visitor to tennis, fishing, bridge, billiards, sumptuous dinners with fine wines, and "*some port* of about A.D. 1800 that made me almost weep for joy." Taken to a large house party and cognizant that the English seldom made introductions, he "walked up to the best looking dame in the bunch & said 'howdy?'" Switzerland's beautiful scenery failed to match the pleasure of mingling with the English elite.[37]

Roosevelt returned to Harvard in the fall as a graduate student in history, but his real major was still the *Crimson*. Its sole editorial writer, he revealed a lot about himself, especially when he admonished the incoming freshman class, "It is not so much brilliance as effort that is appreciated here—determination to accomplish something." Perhaps because Jake Brown managed the football team, he devoted editorial after editorial to calling for student support, school spirit, and team effort. He also crusaded for better walkways in Harvard Yard and strong fire-protection measures in the shabby university dormitories. An effective manager, he provided lubricant for his authority in the form of a weekly staff "punch night." "In his geniality," one of the staffers recalled, "there was a kind of frictionless command."[38]

Presidency of the *Crimson* made Roosevelt's reputation at Harvard, establishing him as a notable of the class of 1904 (of which he considered himself a member, his 1903 AB notwithstanding). He ran for one of three positions as class marshal but lost to a club ticket. He did, however, win election as chairman of the class committee.

As at Groton, his college years had not been without accomplishment, but neither had they given him everything he wanted. He surely had more friends than enemies, but some acquaintances had doubts that foreshadowed those of future critics. Was there phoniness behind all that surface geniality? Did his demeanor reveal him as a lightweight? Did his lack of athleticism denote a certain lack of masculinity? Teddy Robinson's sister, Corrine, called him "the handkerchief box young man," after the drawings of pretty boys that typically adorned such containers. His substance lurked behind a facade that appeared intentionally designed for concealment.

Groomed as a leader, Franklin revered the example his cousin, the president, had set. He was intent on establishing an independent life, yet deemed it important to preserve his close relationship with his mother. He would spend years juggling these ambitions.[39]

CHAPTER 3

ELEANOR AND FRANKLIN

MARRIAGE, FAMILY, JOB, 1904–1910

THE FRANKLIN ROOSEVELT WHO LEFT HARVARD IN THE SUMMER OF 1904 WAS twenty-two years old, immature emotionally, and still dependent on his mother. Withal, he was highly intelligent, possessed great charm, and harbored large ambitions underneath a lightweight exterior. He hungered for marriage, several children, wide popularity, and, driven by the example of Cousin Theodore, political acclaim.

AS AN ONLY CHILD, FRANKLIN HAD LIMITED EXPERIENCE IN DEALING WITH women his own age. In addition, he had to juggle any romantic prospects with a mother emotionally disinclined to share him with another woman. His first love may have been Alice Sohier, a beauty from a prominent Boston family. The two met during Roosevelt's freshman year at Harvard and saw each other frequently until she embarked on an extended European tour in the fall of 1902. Whether he actually proposed marriage is uncertain. As she recalled it, he told her he had been lonely without siblings and wanted to father a large family. "I did not wish to be a cow," she commented years later. (She would marry in 1910, have two children, and divorce her husband in 1925. After Roosevelt became president, she was outspoken in her scorn for him and his politics.)[1]

Roosevelt escorted other girls to parties but found himself increasingly drawn to one who seemed unlikely: Eleanor Roosevelt, daughter of his deceased godfather, Elliott Roosevelt. On November 19, 1903, he told his mother that the previous Saturday he had asked Cousin Eleanor to marry him, and she had accepted. He had not the slightest understanding that he had proposed to an emotional train wreck.

Two and a half years younger than Franklin, Eleanor was living proof that birth to wealth carried no guarantee of psychological well-being. Her father, Elliott, by common consent the most charming of all the Roosevelts, had also been ineffectual, an alcoholic, and a philanderer. Elliott cherished his daughter, who returned his affection and always remembered him as the brightest star of her youth. Eleanor's mother, the beautiful Anna Hall, hailed from two of the great families of New York, the Livingstons and the Ludlows. Cold and distant, she called her quiet, insecure, and inhibited daughter "Granny" and once told her, "Eleanor, I hardly know what's to happen to you. You're so plain that you really have nothing to do except *be good*." Anna Hall died of diphtheria in December 1892. Eight years old, Eleanor went to live with her grandmother, Mary Ludlow Hall, and saw her increasingly unstable father only rarely. In August 1894, Elliott Roosevelt died in a drunken accident.[2]

Eleanor spent five years with her grandmother, who despite her wealth was unable to provide much love. She had no regular playmates, was periodically terrorized by a harsh French nurse charged with her care, and experienced periods of depression, which she called "Griselda moods" after a patient and obedient but badly mistreated character in Boccaccio's *Decameron*. The moods foreshadowed a behavioral characteristic that would plague her own marriage: the sublimation of anger and self-doubt into passive aggressiveness.

Her struggles for self-worth bore fruit only after she enrolled in 1899 to Allenswood, an exclusive boarding school in Wimbledon Park, just outside London. Its headmistress, Marie Souvestre, was an educator of great renown and a presence in the lively intellectual life of turn-of-the century London. A charismatic and demanding teacher, as well as a freethinker and nonconformist, she may have had lesbian relationships with the two women who successively served as her main partners in her teaching ventures.[3]

Eleanor arrived at Allenswood a month short of her fifteenth birthday, tall, gangly, and full of self-doubt but equipped with excellent French, the school's required language of instruction and social discourse. She alone among the new students could communicate fluently with the headmistress. Mademoiselle Souvestre all but adopted her and transmitted to Eleanor a sense of self-worth. They took summer trips, for which Eleanor made the arrangements, through France and Italy, staying in simple hotels, eating the food and drinking the *vin de pays* of ordinary people. In the process, Eleanor learned that social classes below her own had value and dignity. She also blossomed among the students. Her cousin, Corrine Robinson, who entered Allenswood during Eleanor's final year there, recalled her as the object of numerous adolescent crushes, loved for her kindness, admired for her sophistication, and respected for her intelligence.

Eleanor was devoted to Mademoiselle Souvestre, but it is unlikely that their mutual affection ever reached a physical expression. In her letters, the headmistress, sixty-four when she first met Eleanor, always addressed her as "dear child"; she doubtless saw the girl as a protégé and hoped to impart to her an understanding of the wider meaning of life.

Eleanor wanted to remain for a fourth and final year at Allenswood, but her grandmother ordered her home for her eighteenth birthday and introduction to society in October 1902. The departure was hard. Her new life, the headmistress told her, would be difficult. She should enjoy the worldly pleasures it would bring but also "bear in mind that there are more quiet and enviable joys than to be among the most sought-after women at a ball or the woman best liked by your neighbor at the table, at luncheons and the various fashionable affairs." They corresponded for a time but never met again. Eleanor asked Mademoiselle Souvestre for a photo, which she kept at her desk for the rest of her life.[4]

WHEN ELEANOR RETURNED TO THE UNITED STATES, SHE HAD REACHED HER adult height of an even six feet; she was neither unattractive nor a standout beauty. Having been abroad for three years, she had few friends of either sex and was installed in New York City with her featherbrained Aunt Edith ("Pussie"), a fading belle who reminded her from time to time of her failure to measure up to the Hall-Livingston standard of feminine desirability. A third of a century later, Eleanor would recall as "utter agony" the incessant balls and receptions, the relative inattention she received from young men, and the early departures.[5]

After the first distasteful months, she began to recover her equilibrium. Many younger girls in her set admired her much, as had her Allenswood schoolmates. Robert Munro Ferguson, an esteemed veteran of Theodore Roosevelt's Rough Riders during the Spanish-American War, escorted her on social occasions and introduced her to a wide circle of acquaintances, many of them artists and literary figures. She also began to take charge of the care of her younger brother, Hall, who entered the first form at Groton in September 1903. With her grandmother and aunt financially unable to maintain their house in the city, Eleanor joined her godmother and maternal cousin, Susie Parish, and her husband, Henry, in their town house at Fifth Avenue and Seventy-Sixth Street. Aunt Pussie stayed next door with Susie's mother and Eleanor's great aunt, Elizabeth Livingston Ludlow. The arrangements were at least marginally more congenial.

By then, Eleanor was firmly committed to achieving a sense of self-worth by doing good in the larger world. Making a crucial transition from charity to social work, she taught classes at the Rivington Street Settlement House in Manhattan's crowded, sometimes menacing Lower East Side. She also became a member of the Consumers' League, an organization primarily concerned with achieving decent conditions for female workers.

In the summer of 1902, she encountered her cousin Franklin on a train. It was their first meeting in three and a half years and revealed an instant mutual attraction. She saw him at various events over the next several months as his interest in Alice Sohier played itself out. He in turn discovered the world of the Lower East Side as he learned about her Junior League work and social concerns. Invitations to Hyde Park followed—for Franklin's twenty-first birthday party, for the celebration of his AB degree, and then for a week in Campobello. A pattern was emerging.

Sara missed it, probably because Eleanor's seriousness and social concerns seemed much in contrast with her son's determined lightness of manner. But Franklin had never been obvious. Since he had begun reassuring his parents that all was going well at Groton, he had honed his skills of manipulation and deception to a scalpel's edge. Alice Sohier's brittleness possibly cast Eleanor's earnestness as appealing. Franklin's attraction to her revealed a fundamental seriousness that his demeanor was calculated to conceal.

Franklin failed to see a certain lack of maturity and a paucity of the adult skills one expected of a prospective wife. Eleanor's intelligence notwithstanding, she could not budget the allowance she received from her mother's estate until Henry Parish showed her how to keep rudimentary accounts. She had not the foggiest idea of how to manage a household and no experience with the rearing of children. More than thirty years later, she described herself as "a curious mixture of extreme innocence and unworldliness," possessing "painfully high ideals and a tremendous sense of duty . . . entirely unrelieved by any sense of humor or any appreciation of the weaknesses of human nature." She also had, she recalled, "very high standards as to what a wife and mother should be and not the faintest notion of what it meant to be either a wife or a mother."[6]

Eleanor also failed to perceive Franklin's own problematic traits: an only child's self-centeredness, a core of unquenchable ambition that would lead him to put career ahead of family, and a tendency to see the women in his life primarily as support mechanisms. None of this made any difference in the autumn of 1903. Franklin was a fine-looking, wealthy, charming young man less than three months from his twenty-second birthday when he proposed marriage. Eleanor was a sensitive and appealing young woman of nineteen, longing for a happier personal life. Youth and mutual attraction prevailed.

Sara's emotional attachment to Franklin and her clear reluctance to share him with another woman complicated her practical qualms. She asked him to reconsider, arguing that he and Eleanor were both young and needed to give the rest of their lives deliberate consideration. Franklin and Eleanor agreed only to push the marriage into the future and not to announce the engagement for a year. Time, Sara hoped, would change her son's mind.

Franklin and Eleanor persevered for nearly a year and a half, enduring Sara's obvious opposition, stealing a few moments alone now and then, and remaining unyielding in the conviction they had a future together. They exchanged many letters. None of his survive—Eleanor destroyed them. Franklin preserved Eleanor's, and they leave no doubt that the two were deeply in love. He sent her poetry, and she responded in kind. She had achieved, she told him, the greatest happiness of her life. For the moment, Eleanor's biographer Blanche Wiesen Cook has written, "their affinity was chemical, intellectual, total."[7]

In the fall of 1904, Franklin began law school at Columbia University, following a plan Sara had laid out in a letter he received at the beginning of his third year at Harvard:

> I still have a few friends of your dear father's who would take an interest in you when you come to New York, and I want you to think seriously of coming to the Columbia law school. . . . I know Brother Rosy feels that after your college course is over you ought to be in your own city and get to be known among the best men, also be nearer Hyde Park. I feel so very strongly. . . . I merely wish you to think seriously of it, and to realize how much it will be for you and for me, for you to be near your own home.[8]

After Franklin's matriculation at Columbia, Sara rented a town house on Madison Avenue. Eleanor, still living with the Parishes, continued to pursue her settlement work and other reform causes. Occasionally, Franklin escorted her back uptown. Once he helped her take a sick girl back to her apartment in a squalid tenement and came out shocked by the living conditions of the urban poor.[9]

Cousin Ted, easily elected to a second term as president in November 1904, agreed to attend their wedding and give the bride away. His scheduled review of New York's St. Patrick's Day parade determined the date, March 17, 1905, just thirteen days after Eleanor and Franklin were among the guests at his inauguration in Washington, DC. The wedding ceremony and reception were held in the adjoining town houses occupied by the Parishes and Mrs. Ludlow. Large sliding doors connecting the homes were opened to provide ample space.

By the standards of high society, the affair was a small one, with only about two hundred invitees, the majority just for the reception. Reverend Endicott Peabody officiated over the much smaller family wedding rites. Franklin's best man was Jake Brown; other Grotonians served as ushers. Eleanor, stunning in a long, white wedding gown, was attended by six bridesmaids, among them TR's daughter Alice. After the young couple had been pronounced man and wife and positioned themselves to receive congratulations, TR remarked, "Well, Franklin, there's nothing like keeping the name in the family." He then moved across to the reception buffet, followed, to the consternation of the bride and groom, by most of the guests. Late in the afternoon, the newlyweds departed for Hyde Park and a honeymoon week alone at Springwood, after which they returned to New York and lived in a hotel apartment provided by Sara while Franklin finished his first year of law school.[10]

That summer, they took a traditional honeymoon, a three-and-a-half-month grand tour of Europe, including Scotland, England, France, Germany, Switzerland, and Italy. Booked in London at Brown's Hotel, they found themselves identified as close relatives of the president of the United States. With his usual flamboyance, Franklin wrote to his mother, "We were ushered into the royal suite, one flight up, front, price $1,000 a day. . . . Our breath was so taken away that we couldn't even protest and are now saying 'Damn the expense.'" (The actual rate was £7, about $35 a day.)[11]

The trip was not without its frictions. Eleanor obsessed over correct etiquette in the British country homes they visited. Too flustered to give the welcoming talk at a local flower show in Scotland, she had to be rescued by Franklin. His refusal to let her use her superior Italian in bargaining with book dealers annoyed her. The coolest patch came in Cortina, Italy. After Eleanor decided against going on a climbing expedition with him, Franklin made the trek in the company of Miss Kitty Gandy, a thoroughly modern, cigarette-smoking New York milliner. "Though I never said a word I was jealous beyond description," Eleanor wrote more than thirty years later.

Franklin displayed stress of his own. A case of hives bothered him for much of their time abroad; he sleepwalked on ship and experienced nightmares. The dissatisfactions were ephemeral. The two returned to the United States after a long and generally happy trip, bringing back many purchases, including a

Scottish terrier puppy they named Duffy. To all appearances they were pleased with their life together.[12]

THE YOUNG COUPLE SET UP HOUSEKEEPING IN A RENTED TOWN HOUSE AT 125 East Thirty-Sixth Street, paid for and furnished by Sara, whose own Madison Avenue house was about three blocks away. Referring to the width of the front-age, Franklin called the place his fourteen-foot mansion. It was crowded from the beginning; Eleanor and Franklin employed at least three servants, a house-keeper, a cook, and a waitress. Soon there was a fourth, a nurse for their first child, Anna, born May 3, 1906. Three other children followed in quick succession: James, December 23, 1907; Franklin Jr., March 18, 1909; and Elliott, September 23, 1910. During this period, Eleanor continued to serve as a surrogate mother to her younger brother, Hall, by then a star pupil at Groton.

In 1907, Sara commissioned the construction of adjoining six-story town houses—one for her, one for Franklin and Eleanor—at 47 and 49 East Sixty-Fifth Street. In the style of the Parish-Ludlow homes that had hosted the wedding, large sliding doors connected the residences. Moving into them in the fall of 1908, the Roosevelt family was big, growing, rambunctious, and increasingly troubled. Franklin enthusiastically played with the two children he had fathered and looked forward to several more. (Cousin Theodore, after all, had brought six into the world.) Eleanor, however, was increasingly unhappy. She had come to her marriage with only the vaguest notions about sexual intercourse and unprepared for the realities of homemaking and motherhood. Many years later, her daughter Anna remembered her mother telling her that sex was a wife's burden to bear.[13]

Eleanor also felt a sense of impotence as her mother-in-law seemed to control her everyday life, arranging their living accommodations and engaging nurses for the children. In the beginning stages of her third pregnancy, she broke into tears in front of an uncomprehending Franklin. "I said I did not like to live in a house that was not in any way mine, one that I had done nothing about and which did not represent the way I wanted to live." He soothed her, telling her gently that she was "quite mad" and would be better after a bit. Feeling dominated and helpless, she dealt with her situation not by demanding more control over the details of her life but by resorting to "Griselda moods" of sullen, passive acquiescence.[14]

Recorded a quarter century later, her memories of those years were mostly of personal failure. She gave herself no credit for keeping track of the family expenses—after all, Franklin (and Mr. Parish before him) had taught her how to do it. Nor did she have a sense of achievement in handling numerous minor crises. She scolded herself for being unable "to manage an old-fashioned coal range and . . . cook a whole meal." She was both intimidated by the severe English nurses Sara hired and ineffective in managing her children by herself. Having picked up the idea that fresh air was good for them, she had them put in "a kind of box with wire on the sides and top" and hung it out a window for their naps. The practice came to an abrupt end when a neighbor, roused by Anna's frantic crying, threatened to report Eleanor to the Society for the Prevention of Cruelty to Children. Unable to control Franklin's horse at Hyde Park, she gave up riding for years rather than insist on having a separate mount. When she banged the family automobile into a gatepost, she foreswore driving. Induced to give up her settlement house work for fear that she might bring home one of the numerous diseases that raged through the crowded slums of the Lower East Side, she found herself miserable at home with the children.[15]

Franklin provided little in the way of sympathy or support. Away during the day, he spent frequent evenings out at club dinners and meetings, poker parties, and social gatherings with relatives. He was a convivial social drinker, and the smell of liquor on his breath horrified a wife who was the child of a tragic alcoholic. Their sharply contrasting attitudes toward the cocktail culture became a lifelong emblem of the gap between his self-indulgent, confident extroversion and her puritanical insecurity.[16]

The greatest trauma came when their cherished baby, Franklin Jr., died at only seven months old in October 1909. He was buried in the churchyard at Hyde Park. "How cruel it seemed to leave him out there alone in the cold," Eleanor wrote years later. Falling into a deep depression, she was convinced she somehow had been responsible. Franklin was more stoic. Bad things happen in life, he told her; one had to move on. His efforts merely persuaded her that he was uncaring and left her feeling "bitter" toward him.[17]

Albeit a terrible loss, an infant's death was not unusual at the beginning of the twentieth century. Eleanor and Franklin dealt with their grief as best as they could and got on with their lives. Eleanor soon became pregnant again with the boy they would name for her father, Elliott. Their happiest times seem to have been during the long summer vacations at Campobello, especially after they acquired their own thirty-four-room brick cottage, purchased for them in 1910 by Sara. More often, Eleanor suffered in silence. Without quite realizing it, she was moving toward a recognition that she would have to establish independence not only from her mother-in-law but also from her husband.[18]

THE PATTERN OF FRANKLIN'S LIFE WAS PREDICTABLE: LAW SCHOOL AND THEN the daytime practice of law, numerous evening social events, Hyde Park on weekends and long summer vacations at Campobello—more play than work with many more happy days than sad ones. Ultimately lacking was a sense of purpose and achievement. Although far from depressed—his capacity for enjoyment was too great—he had developing ambitions and an increasing need to work toward them.

He approached his law studies much as he had his Harvard education. Most courses were a bore. A Roosevelt did enough to earn a gentleman's C. Employment, if one desired it at all, would come through contacts. On the return leg of his honeymoon, he and Eleanor had checked into their Paris hotel to find waiting a letter from Columbia University Law School informing him that he had failed two of his spring semester courses. Unruffled, he cabled for his books to be sent to London. He crammed on the way back across the Atlantic and passed makeup exams with relative ease. In June 1906, at the end of his second year at Columbia, he took the state bar examination. In February 1907 he received official notice that he had passed. Wholly uninterested in finishing a final semester of classes and securing another diploma, he dropped out of law school.

A job came quickly thereafter, facilitated by a family friend who was a partner in the Wall Street law firm of Carter, Ledyard & Milburn, which primarily represented leading corporations and financial establishments. The terms of employment were as penurious as the firm was prosperous: no salary for the first year and only a small one for the second. The job was to begin in September 1907. His title would be "clerk" (not "associate"). Franklin had no illusions about the position. Writing to his mother, he told her, "I shall be a full-fledged office boy."[19]

He drafted a "handbill" advertising the range of his services. Aimed primarily at his mother, it lampooned several topics about which they disagreed: his habit of not attending to debts, his preference for hard-liquor cocktails over wine, Cousin Theodore's insistence that Anglo-Saxons were on the verge of "race suicide," Sara's fussy little canine and dominance over the care of their children:

FRANKLIN D. ROOSEVELT
COUNSELLOR AT LAW
54 WALL STREET
NEW YORK
I BEG TO CALL YOUR ATTENTION TO MY UNEXCELLED FACILITIES FOR
CARRYING ON EVERY DESCRIPTION OF LEGAL BUSINESS.
UNPAID BILLS A SPECIALTY.

BRIEFS ON THE LIQUOR QUESTION FURNISHED FREE TO LADIES.
RACE SUICIDES CHEERFULLY PROSECUTED.
SMALL DOGS CHLOROFORMED WITHOUT CHARGE.
BABIES RAISED UNDER ADVICE OF EXPERT GRANDMOTHER,
ETC., ETC., ETC.[20]

Franklin's legal career lasted three years and left no promise of greater things to come. He handled mostly small-claims cases. His greatest triumph came with his assignment by the criminal court to defend a ne'er-do-well accused of stabbing another ne'er-do-well. The judge directed a verdict of acquittal. On one occasion, after winning a case against a fellow lawyer of unpromising origins trying to support an impoverished mother, he gave his strapped opponent a sizeable personal loan. The adversary, who later became a prominent attorney, never forgot the generosity.

In the main, Franklin still seemed a lightweight; he was tall and handsome but not especially masculine, invariably well dressed, always sporting TR-style pince-nez eyeglasses, and much involved in the New York Yacht Club and other social organizations. To all appearances, he was the least serious of the firm's five clerks. Yet he managed to handle the assignments given him, and in his second year he was made managing clerk at a salary of $10 a week. Nonetheless, the senior managing partner, Lewis Cass Ledyard, seems to have found him annoying. Once, Roosevelt and a fellow clerk, Grenville Clark, took the better part of a spring afternoon off to watch a baseball game. When they got back to the office, they encountered Ledyard, who demanded to know where they had been. Franklin, his breath redolent with ballpark beer, began a response, which Ledyard cut off with a loud "Roosevelt, you're drunk!" He later told Sara that Franklin lacked the drive and concentration to be a successful lawyer.[21]

What then was the purpose of the three years at the firm? Franklin likely regarded it as a ticket to be punched along the way to other things. Years later, Grenville Clark, who had become a much esteemed leader of the moderate northeastern Republican establishment, recalled a conversation the five clerks had one afternoon when work was done at the office. Each talked about his plans for the future. Roosevelt told them he wanted to go into politics. He would start with election to the New York State Assembly, get himself appointed assistant secretary of the navy, then become governor of New York. The governor of New York always stood a good chance of becoming president of the United States. He expected to seize that chance. Clark recalled no grins or wisecracks. Something about Franklin invited caricature, but when he spoke seriously, he conveyed force and credibility.[22]

In 1910, Roosevelt entered his third summer as a Wall Street lawyer. He was twenty-eight years old and had endured enough of the practice of law. American politics from Washington down to the state and local level had become turbulent. Much of the country was dissatisfied with Cousin Theodore's Republican successor, William Howard Taft, and ready for a change. The time was right for an ambitious young Democrat to make his move.

CHAPTER 4

INSURGENT PROGRESSIVE

1910–1913

ON AN AFTERNOON IN AUGUST 1910, FRANKLIN ROOSEVELT CALLED ON TOM Leonard, a housepainter and local Democratic Party committeeman. Leonard responded to a warm "Hello, Tom" with a formal and deferential "How do you do, Mr. Roosevelt." His caller shook hands firmly and responded, "No, call me Franklin, and I'm going to call you Tom." With those words, the twenty-eight-year-old patrician crossed a social gap, openly embraced a consuming ambition, and indicated an intent to emulate his famous cousin, Theodore, against long odds.[1]

FRANKLIN POSSESSED NO INTEREST IN LAW AS A PROFESSION AND REJECTED opportunities his Delano relations could have provided in one of their enterprises. Largely adopting his father's role as a local squire, he acquired land adjoining his own, some of it worked by tenant farmers, some of it producing evergreen trees periodically harvested and sold at Christmastime. He dabbled in community activities, including involvement with the volunteer fire department and the local ice-boating club, became a director of the Bank of Poughkeepsie, and served as a vestryman at St. James Church. None of these activities satisfied an expansive ambition.[2]

Theodore Roosevelt's example was clearly a driving force, and 1910 was a propitious year to enter politics. TR had become the leading figure in the multifaceted push for social and political reform that was beginning to be called the progressive movement. A reaction against big finance, large corporations, militant labor unions, and traditional political machines, progressivism respected educated expertise in public policy and maintained an attitude of benevolence toward the nation's large impoverished class of unskilled and semiskilled workers. TR established its tone and policy with advocacy of reasonable concessions to workers, government oversight of the "trusts," support of conservation, an arm's-length stance toward political machines, and espousal of a "square deal" for all Americans.

TR's successor, William Howard Taft, had proven inept, unexciting, and seemingly dominated by Republican regulars representing the interests of trusts and big bankers. "Insurgents" in both parties fought with machine regulars. Wanting to return control of government to the people, they advocated direct democracy in the form of the initiative, the referendum, the recall, the direct primary, and the direct election of US senators.

Who would lead the people? TR provided a compelling family example. Franklin's Groton and Harvard educations explicitly prepared young men for leadership. By the summer of 1910, Franklin was plotting a run for a two-year term in the New York State Senate. True to his father's legacy, he would do it as a Democrat, hoping to capitalize on the bitter Republican split between the Roosevelt and Taft factions.

Franklin requested Ted's benevolent neutrality through Theodore's sister Bamie. In August, she relayed the former president's response: "Franklin ought to go into politics without the least regard as to where I speak or don't speak." Though not exactly ironclad, it was assurance enough. (TR would speak in the district that fall and make no mention of either Franklin or his opponent.)[3]

The heavily rural senate district, covering three counties located between the Hudson River and the Connecticut border, was normally solidly Republican. The local Democratic leaders were happy to have a candidate who would finance his own race and provide some extra money to the party coffers. Roosevelt adapted easily and energetically to the demands of campaigning. He spent only a few days at Campobello with Eleanor; pregnant with their fourth child, she vacationed there with the children, their nurse, and Sara. Returning to New York, she gave birth on September 23 to the baby boy they named Elliott. Preoccupied with her children, she remained aloof from the campaign.

On October 6, a party committee formally nominated Roosevelt for the state senate seat. He spent the next month barnstorming the district, often accompanied by Democratic candidates for other positions. They traveled in a fire-engine-red Maxwell touring car, which Roosevelt hired for $20 a day. The auto had neither top nor windshield, forcing the passengers to wear dusters over their suits and to keep rain slickers at the ready on cloudy days. The rutted rural roads were unwelcoming and the pace grinding: they stopped wherever a group of a few people could be found and usually attended a planned rally in the evening.

Roosevelt was good at "retail" one-to-one politics. Shaking every hand he could reach, he spoke to farmers, small-town shopkeepers, and immigrant railroad workers with an unforced geniality. He began every speech with the phrase "my friends" and kept his oratory short. Spending freely, he blanketed his district with campaign buttons, posters, and newspaper advertisements.[4]

In a normal year Franklin's wealth and intensity might have been irrelevant. But Theodore Roosevelt, calling for a "New Nationalism" that would establish the power of the people over trusts, bosses, and reactionary judges, was bringing progressivism to a high tide and splitting the Republican Party. Franklin seldom missed an opportunity to declare, "I'm not Teddy," but he made ample use of TR's favorite exclamation: "Bully!"[5]

He not only did a fair TR impression but also talked like a nonpartisan independent opposed to machine rule and its abuses, determined to restore integrity to democratic government: "I am pledged to no man; I am influenced by no special interests, and so I shall remain." His rejection of political machines and the corruption they generated, along with his espousal of "honesty & economy & efficiency in our State senate," resonated with both the tone of the progressive movement and the respectable Democratic conservatism of Grover Cleveland. Appealing to Republican progressives, he praised New York's chief executive, Charles Evans Hughes.[6]

As the campaign entered its last weekend, an exhausted Franklin was perhaps not in his best speaking form. Eleanor, who had not yet heard him make a political speech, came to his last two major appearances. She recalled the occasions vividly:

> He spoke slowly, and every now and then there would be a long pause, and I would be worried for fear he would never go on. . . .
>
> He looked thin then, tall, high-strung and, at times, nervous. White skin and fair hair, deep-set blue eyes and clear-cut features. No lines as yet in his face, but at times a set look of his jaw denoted that this apparently pliable youth had strength and Dutch obstinacy in his make-up.[7]

He gave his final talk to a crowd of friends and well-wishers at Hyde Park. "You have known what my father stood for before me, you have known how close he was to the life of this town, and I do not need to tell you that it is my desire to follow always in his footsteps." The next day, he won, polling nearly 52 percent of the 30,276 votes cast and benefitting from a national trend of Republican malaise that threw control of the legislature and the governorship to the Democrats in New York and numerous other states.[8]

Franklin had displayed energy and earnestness, as well as shrewdness in identifying himself with dominant political sentiments, but it remained to be seen whether this young Galahad was a man of destiny or soon to be yesterday's story.

ROOSEVELT TOOK A FOUR-MONTH LEASE AT $400 A MONTH ON A LARGE THREE-story Albany house a few blocks from the capitol. The $1,600 in rent alone exceeded his $1,500 annual legislative salary. Eleanor rented out their New York town house and supervised the move of the household—the three children, an English nurse, a "German girl," a wet nurse "who spoke no language known to us," and three other servants. Pleased that her son had won election to "a really fine & dignified position," Sara came up for his legislative debut but had no intention of staying. For nearly three more decades, she would always be just over the horizon in the lives of her son and daughter-in-law, seldom an intrusive day-to-day presence.[9]

January 2, 1911—inauguration day for the new governor, John Alden Dix—was loud and happy. After the ceremony, Senator Roosevelt returned to his residence, already swarming with as many as four hundred visitors from his district. They consumed large quantities of chicken salad, sandwiches, coffee, beer, and cigars before Franklin and Assemblyman Ferdinand Hoyt marched with them to the railroad station and saw them off.[10]

The New York Democratic Party was, like all American political parties, a large, complex aggregation, but it was easily lumped into two factions—the respectables (old stock, northern European, High Church Protestant, affluent, well educated, conspicuously high-minded, with a small cadre of prosperous German Jews at the fringe) and the rabble (more recent immigrant stock, southern and eastern European, mostly Catholic or Jewish, mostly poor and working-class, ill educated, notably pragmatic in their social and political values). In Roosevelt's world, respectables generally considered themselves the class fit to run things and resented their usurpation by a rabble that sold its votes to roguish machine grafters. The chief rogue in New York politics was Boss Charles Francis Murphy of New York's infamous Tammany Hall.

The machines mobilized the votes of the poor and the working classes by providing small favors and rudimentary social services. The men at the top tended to be from older waves of immigration, usually Irish. They invariably parlayed their organizing skills into considerable wealth for themselves. They might often aspire to the role of gentlemen but maintained power by force and fraud when necessary, stuffing ballot boxes, utilizing street thugs, and financially ruining opponents. They tolerated a chain of graft all the way down the line from the mayor's office to the lowliest license clerk or policeman, while taking the biggest cuts for themselves. Such was the system in one American city after another. Politics was about transactions, not ideals. The organization provided for its followers—jobs, cash handouts, food baskets, buckets of coal—and the followers returned the favor with votes.

The gulf between a Roosevelt and the bosses involved not just civic idealism; it extended to religion and ethnicity, inviting latent snobbery on Roosevelt's part and palpable resentment on Murphy's part. A Sara or Eleanor Roosevelt might dismiss Tammany grandees such as Tom Grady or Big Tim Sullivan with such adjectives as "horrid." They might think of Murphy—a former shipyard worker, streetcar conductor, and saloon keeper who affected the appearance of a middle-aged gentleman and maintained a large estate on Long Island—as a lace-curtain Irishman with pretensions beyond his social pedigree. Kinder and gentler than most of his peers, Murphy kept aloof from organized vice and crime, but everyone knew that many lucrative municipal contracts and other favors required his approval and assumed its bestowal was the source of his considerable wealth. Men like Franklin Roosevelt, who genuinely believed in Yankee Protestant high ideals of civic virtue, found the bosses intolerable. Franklin also knew well that Cousin Ted had gotten his start in politics by fighting them.[11]

Ted was clearly Franklin's model during his first year in Albany. There is a story that at the opening legislative session, as the tall young patrician walked down to the well of the senate to present his credentials, Tammanyite Big Tim Sullivan told his colleague Tom Grady, "Well, if we've caught a Roosevelt, we'd better take him down and drop him off the dock. The Roosevelts run true to form, and this kid is likely to do for us what the Colonel is going to do for the Republican Party, split it wide open."[12]

Boss Murphy wanted strong leaders in Albany. He had given the nod to Alfred E. Smith for Speaker of the assembly. For Democratic senate leader, he backed Robert F. Wagner, a Tammany loyalist widely respected for his talent, relative independence, and breadth of view. Roosevelt confided to his diary that Wagner "has good intentions; the only obstacle is the pressure of his own machine."[13]

The first task of the legislature, with assemblymen and senators voting together as a committee of the whole, would be to choose a new US senator. (The

Seventeenth Amendment to the US Constitution, providing for direct popular election of senators, was two years away from adoption.) The New York State Assembly comprised 114 Democrats and 86 Republicans. The Democratic caucus would name the party's candidate by binding majority vote. The reality then was that fifty-eight legislators, mobilized by the machine, would choose New York's new senator. Murphy let it be known that he backed William F. Sheehan.

Roosevelt saw Sheehan ("Blue-Eyed Billy" to his friends) as a big, provocative red flag. A wealthy and influential New York corporate attorney, Sheehan was a partner in a prestigious law firm and director of several railroad and public utility companies. Thirty years earlier, as an up-and-coming politician on the make in Buffalo, he had displayed (or so his enemies asserted) flexible political morals and had tangled acrimoniously with then mayor (and later governor) Grover Cleveland. So far as Franklin was concerned, Sheehan had been a political enemy of his father. He joined a fragile and decidedly motley coalition of twenty-one Democratic dissenters—enough in combination with the Republicans to block Sheehan's election. They backed Edward Shepard, a much respected old Cleveland associate with a reputation for independence but little different from Sheehan in his social and economic views.[14]

Roosevelt quickly became the movement's chief spokesman and public ringleader. He had an attention-grabbing name and, like Theodore before him, was righteously spoiling for a fight. "There is no question in my mind that the Democratic party is on trial," he wrote in his diary. The insurgents gathered at his house each morning, marched to the capitol to cast their votes against Sheehan, returned in the afternoon after the session adjourned, went their separate ways again for dinner, then came back for late-evening talk that Roosevelt described as mostly sitting and swapping stories "like soldiers at the bivouac fire."[15]

Franklin had far less to lose than most of his comrades, but he had no illusions that the fight would be easy. The insurgents faced mortgage foreclosures, loss of government contracts, and deprivation of patronage. Roosevelt himself was chair of the Senate Forest, Fish and Game Committee; the senate leadership fired a friend he had appointed as committee clerk. Tammanyites, including Al Smith, freely charged the insurgents with anti–Irish Catholic prejudice, although at least three of them were practicing Catholics. The Catholic bishop of Syracuse joined in the attack.[16]

Similar battles played out across the country. In New Jersey, Woodrow Wilson was locked in a senate election struggle with the machine that had nominated and elected him. There was a principle greater than loyalty, Wilson declared: that of respect for democracy and duty to support the winner of the nonbinding senatorial primary. By the end of January, Wilson had prevailed, crushing the power of Democratic boss James Smith; in the process, he electrified progressives all over the country.

So, to a lesser extent, did Franklin Roosevelt. His name, youth, good looks, articulateness, and leadership-class demeanor attracted national attention. A *New York Globe* writer sketched a man "physically fit to command" with "a glow of country health in his cheeks." She noted especially his stubborn, aggressive chin and firm lips that "part often in a smile over even white teeth— the Roosevelt teeth."[17]

Always polite and conciliatory, Franklin stood firm and resolute in pursuit of fundamental principles. Were he and his fellows bolting from the Democratic Party? Of course not; they were simply trying to save it from a disastrous mistake. Had the dispute become too personal? Roosevelt went out of his way to maintain cordial relations with Murphy, Wagner, Smith, and other Democratic leaders. He shrugged off personal attacks obviously directed from the top. At the same time, he consistently returned to the theme of fundamental conflict. Tammany was "an insurmountable obstacle in the way of party success." The row was between principled men and machine hacks. Was he the leader of those principled men? "Leader? I should not claim that title. There really is no leader." And what of his "uncle-in-law," the former president? "I am sure that any fight for principle would have his blessing and approval."[18]

This was a difficult act, but one with great appeal to a middle-class public tired of machine mediocrity and unthinking partisanship. Profiled in newspapers and magazines across the country, Franklin Roosevelt had become a household name. Gratifying as all the articles must have been, he probably most cherished a handwritten note he received at the end of January:

Dear Franklin,

Just a line to say we are really proud of the way you have handled yourself. Good luck to you! Give my love to dear Eleanor.

Always yours,
Theodore Roosevelt[19]

Despite wide recognition by the end of January that his candidacy was hopeless, Sheehan refused for weeks to withdraw. The dissenters held together, but the pressure to break ranks grew increasingly stronger. Murphy suggested replacing him with a respected judge, Victor Dowling. The insurgents agreed. Dowling, however, refused and endorsed Judge James Aloysius O'Gorman, a former grand sachem of the Tammany organization, actually closer to Murphy than Sheehan, but possessing a clean, if undistinguished, record. The rebels had been smoothly baited and switched.

Half the insurgents proceeded dutifully to the final Democratic senate caucus and voted for O'Gorman. The rest, led by Roosevelt, stayed away but attended the legislative session necessary to ratify the caucus decision. Amid the jeers and catcalls of the Tammany loyalists, Roosevelt struggled to explain his position: "We have followed the dictates of our consciences and done our duty. . . . We are Democrats—not irregulars, but regulars. I take pleasure in casting my vote for the Honorable James A. O'Gorman."[20]

By any objective standard, the insurgency had ended, not with a bang but with a whimper. A sharply critical *New York Times* editorial observed that Sheehan had been considerably better qualified and far more independent of Tammany. It accused the insurgents of a "miserable surrender" that had rendered Murphy more powerful than ever. The judgment made a lot of sense. At the time, no one could predict that O'Gorman would be far more independent than expected.[21]

Roosevelt responded by declaring victory. "I have just come from Albany and the close of a long fight which lasted sixty-four rounds," he told a YMCA dinner in New York a day after O'Gorman's election. "Some got battered, but you can see by me that there were few scratches on the insurgents." Much depended on whether the insurgency had been about defeating Sheehan or beating Tammany. Roosevelt chose the first version, struck a good pose, and came out of the fight looking strong and confident.[22]

However dubious his triumph, he had displayed impressive skills as a spokesman and conciliator. It had been an achievement to hold so disparate a group together for three months. He and his fellows, if outfoxed in the end, had made their point and put themselves on the side with momentum in American politics—that of popular democracy. But how could an anti-Tammany Democrat with a bare majority in a Republican district move beyond a short legislative career in the world of New York politics?

IN 1912, FRANCES PERKINS, A YOUNG SOCIAL WORKER, LOBBIED FOR STATE legislation to limit the work of women and children to fifty-four hours per week. She had met Roosevelt socially before he was elected to the state senate and written him off as just another Harvard fop. What she saw of him in Albany confirmed that impression: "I have a vivid picture of him operating on the floor of the Senate: tall and slender, very active and alert, moving around the floor, going in and out of committee rooms, rarely talking with the members, who more or less avoided him, not particularly charming (that came later), artificially serious of face, rarely smiling, with an unfortunate habit—so natural that he was unaware of it—of throwing his head up. This, combined with his pince-nez and great height, gave him the appearance of looking down his nose at most people." Young Roosevelt, she thought, "really didn't like people very much," lacked humility, and displayed a self-righteous certitude. Many legislators heartily disliked him. He did not display the warmth and human sympathy of a Tim Sullivan or Tom Grady. A gap existed between his public democratic persona and his private hauteur.[23]

Roosevelt's progressivism seemed more procedural than reformist. He and his rural constituency displayed no interest in labor laws. Farmers, their wives, and their children worked from dawn to dusk at least six days a week; they saw no reason why factory workers should not do the same. Members of Roosevelt's own class expected their employees to keep long hours. Tammany leaders generally thought of themselves as self-made men and understood that state agencies providing for the needs of the poor could displace them. Franklin Roosevelt nonetheless quietly voted for the fifty-four-hour workweek after Frances Perkins persuaded Tim Sullivan to push it through the legislature over Boss Murphy's opposition.[24]

Roosevelt continued to denounce Tammany in general and Boss Murphy in particular. He also spoke out in favor of the direct primary, conservation legislation, administrative efficiency, and ballot reform. Striking a pose against waste and excessive expenditures, he actually rejected public works appropriations for his district. He generally deferred to the moral conservatism of his constituents, voting, for example, against Sunday baseball games. Yet, probably because Theodore Roosevelt had raised the issue earlier, he sponsored a legislative resolution in favor of a federal divorce law that would soften the rigid New York rules.[25]

His identity as a progressive increasingly clear, he groped toward an underlying philosophy. Speaking to the People's Forum in Troy, New York, on March 3, 1912, he advocated "liberty of the community." Drawing on ideas popularized by Theodore Roosevelt, the phrase pointed toward a cooperative regulatory society in which the rights and interests of the many would prevail over the greed and irresponsibility of the few. Liberty of the community would mean, among other things, strong conservation programs and popular control of irresponsible trusts and monopolies.[26]

Theodore Roosevelt remained a decided influence; Woodrow Wilson drew increased interest. In the course of a year, Wilson had put an impressive reform program through the New Jersey legislature: direct primary election

for all political party nominations, an anti–corrupt practices act, a public utility commission, and a workman's compensation program. Near the end of
1911, Franklin went to Trenton and spent the better part of an afternoon with
him. Reserved, austere, and dominating, the governor probably reminded
the younger man of Endicott Peabody. Roosevelt returned to New York and
pledged to support Wilson for the 1912 Democratic presidential nomination.[27]

During the legislative session of 1912, Roosevelt fought hard, and with some
success, for bills to protect fish and game from overhunting, to preserve clean
water resources, and to save forests from clear-cutting. Here he was especially
influenced by Gifford Pinchot, the great scientific conservationist and close
adviser to Theodore Roosevelt. Slowly, he was also learning the necessity of
compromise in legislative politics. To many working politicians, he remained a
loose cannon. He preferred to think of himself as a high-minded independent.[28]

WHEN THE 1912 LEGISLATIVE SESSION ENDED AT THE END OF APRIL, ROOSEVELT's
political situation was at once enviable and tenuous. He was known throughout
New York, in demand as a speaker, and a rising star in his party. He also had
the active enmity of the state's major Democratic machine, perceived a distinct
lack of enthusiasm from the organization in his own district, and feared a serious attempt to deny him renomination.

The times still favored the identity he had crafted. Nationally and at the state
level, the Republican Party was fatally divided between Taft and Theodore Roosevelt. TR was running hard for the Republican presidential nomination and a
third term. His candidacy generated wide enthusiasm that was partly personal
but also indicative of the growing support for progressivism and reform. The
Republican split established a setting for a sweeping Democratic victory if the
Democratic Party could produce a compelling progressive leader.

Franklin Roosevelt became one of the most visible and vocal figures among
a motley group of mainly upstate reform Democrats supporting Woodrow Wilson. Tammany controlled the Democratic state convention with an iron fist,
froze out the reformers, and named a subservient delegation to the Democratic
convention bound by the unit rule to vote unanimously for the candidate of the
majority. The convention met in Baltimore on June 25. Roosevelt attended as a
spectator, worked for Wilson, and promoted himself in the process. Among the
leading politicos upon whom he left a lasting impression was the North Carolina progressive Josephus Daniels.

Eleanor, still a novice at politics, watched the proceedings from the galleries with increasing incomprehension and outright moral indignation when

backers of Wilson's chief rival, Champ Clark of Missouri, marched with their candidate's attractive daughter on their shoulders. After a few days, she and the children left for Campobello, wondering if Franklin would miss them.[29]

Wilson came to the convention trailing Champ Clark, a shrewd Missouri congressman who represented a rural district near St. Louis and was adept at appealing to both farmers and urban politicians. When the Democrats had taken control of the House of Representatives in the election of 1910, they had named him Speaker. His folksy demeanor and personal background seemed to make him a natural successor to the party's venerable leader and three-time candidate for president, William Jennings Bryan.

Unlike Bryan, Clark presented a hazy ideological profile. He had vanquished Wilson in numerous midwestern presidential primaries and come to the convention as the leading candidate. But since Andrew Jackson's nomination in 1832, Democratic presidential nominees had required a two-thirds majority at the national convention. Wilson's cause was not hopeless. Roosevelt and many northeastern reformers saw him as far and away the party's best choice. Wilson's background—born in Virginia, raised in Georgia—also brought him strong support from the then solidly Democratic South.

Boss Murphy instructed his delegation to vote for Clark. The ploy backfired badly. Bryan, never a friend of Tammany, denounced Clark as a tool of disreputable urban machines and Wall Street financiers. When Tammany staged a floor demonstration for Clark, Roosevelt and several dozen Wilsonians muscled in and seized the New York standard. As the convention deadlocked, Clark's support ebbed. Wilson prevailed on the forty-sixth ballot. Elated, Franklin telegraphed Eleanor, "Wilson nominated this afternoon all my plans vague splendid triumph."[30]

The New York Wilsonians, Roosevelt prominent among the leadership, returned home to establish the Empire State Democracy, a progressive alternative to Tammany. The organizational meeting featured vituperative attacks on Boss Murphy and his minions and declared an intention to run a reform Democratic ticket in the fall.

Insurgent politics, then as now, was a combustible blend of absolutist principle and ego-fed ambition. Cooler heads—among them Wilson's closest New York backers—understood that a Democratic split would likely throw New York to Theodore Roosevelt, running as the candidate of the new Progressive Party. Recognizing the need for party solidarity, Franklin Roosevelt resigned from the Empire State Democracy, pleading his selection as a regular Democrat to the state convention. Several other notables did the same. Murphy pledged maximum support for the Wilson candidacy. The New York

Democrats thereupon closed ranks in the common pursuit of victory. Roosevelt's own move from hotheaded dissent to calibrated regularity signaled the lessons he had learned.[31]

He had to work for his own reelection. In what was becoming a career pattern, the weeks-long summer vacation at Campobello dwindled to patches of days snatched here and there. His role as an insurgent had not gone down well with Democratic regulars in his district, especially those who expected the state senator to find them public jobs. He scoured the territory by automobile, making his case to good effect. Ed Perkins and other Poughkeepsie Democrats resented how he had damaged relations with Tammany, but in the end the district committee nominated him without opposition.[32]

The race, he knew, would be hard, but the Republican split gave him a good chance. In mid-September, back in New York City, he and Eleanor came down with typhoid fever. She recovered rather quickly. He did not, although it was his second encounter with the dreaded disease (the first had come when he was seven, and it had taken him a long time to get better then). The infection lingered, leaving him run-down and feverish for weeks. It became clear that he would be unable to do much, if any, campaigning. Desperately, he looked for someone who could organize the effort and serve as a trusted advocate.

During the insurgency, he had from time to time drawn on the advice of Louis McHenry Howe, a veteran journalist with long-standing ties to anti-Tammany Democrats. A shabby little man who eked out a living as a stringer for the *New York Herald* and other newspapers, Howe was eleven years older than Roosevelt. Shrewd and seemingly practical to the point of cynicism, he was by conviction an idealist who understood that a successful political career required programmatic compromise, organizational talent, and reliable funding. Slightly built with a face scarred by a childhood accident, asthmatic with a weak heart, and a chain-smoker invariably appearing to be in ill health, he seemed the stereotypical incarnation of an ink-stained wretch—or, as he became known, a "medieval gnome." By conventional standards, he was a ne'er-do-well, hard-pressed to support his wife and daughter, and increasingly unable to spend much time with them. Eleanor at first found him impossibly off-putting; Franklin quickly came to see him as an indispensable adviser and political manager.[33]

Appointed Roosevelt's campaign manager at $50 a week plus expenses, Howe traveled the district, promising jobs to local influentials, buying advertisements in local newspapers, authoring letters to be sent with his candidate's signature to constituent groups, and developing appeals to gain the crucial farm vote. Devoted to Roosevelt, he addressed his boss as "Beloved and Revered

Future President." On Election Day, the Beloved and Revered One defeated his Republican opponent 15,590 to 13,889, with 2,628 for the Progressive Party's candidate. Although less than an absolute majority, the victory was nonetheless impressive.[34]

The statewide and national results mirrored Roosevelt's fortunes. Thanks to the Republican split, the Democrats swept New York. Woodrow Wilson took the presidency, Theodore Roosevelt finished second, and the hapless President Taft came in third. The Democrats won firm control of Congress. Franklin Roosevelt might go back to Albany for another term as an insecure state senator, or he could look to Washington.

IN JANUARY 1913, FRANKLIN ROOSEVELT CONFERRED WITH PRESIDENT-ELECT Wilson and William Gibbs McAdoo, the prominent New York attorney, banker, and street railway manager whom Wilson already had designated as his Treasury secretary. Then, or perhaps later, they offered him a choice between two visible and powerful positions: assistant secretary of the Treasury or collector of the Port of New York. The Treasury post would have made him a key operative in the development of the most important financial legislation in American history, the Federal Reserve Act; the collector post would have placed under his control a huge mass of federal patronage jobs and given him the opportunity to build a strong personal political organization. Declining both, he returned to Albany, armed with a raft of bills designed to establish him as a zealous guardian of the interests of New York farmers. However, he almost certainly indicated to Wilson and McAdoo his interest in becoming assistant secretary of the navy, the department's second-ranking civilian and chief operating officer.

On the surface, Wilson took his time building a cabinet, and many backroom discussions likely preceded public announcements. His letter formally inviting Josephus Daniels of North Carolina to be his secretary of the navy was dated February 23; Daniels's response was dated February 25. Inauguration Day arrived with no designee for assistant secretary. According to Daniels in his autobiography, he and Wilson had not discussed the post. Daniels had met Roosevelt at the Baltimore convention and found him engaging and impressive—it was "love at first sight," he recalled. Another meeting in New York during the campaign reinforced the impression. There can be little doubt that Roosevelt got across his interest in naval affairs. They ran into each other again at the Willard Hotel in Washington just hours before Wilson was due to take the oath of office. Daniels got right to the point: "How would you like to come to Washington as Assistant Secretary of the Navy?" Roosevelt answered, as Daniels remembered, "How would I like it? I'd like it bully well. It would please me better than anything in the world."[35]

Franklin Roosevelt had come a very long way in a short time. He had made his share of blunders as a working politician, but they paled before his other, special qualities—good looks and a fine voice, energy, undeniable talent, and the appearance and presence of a leader. Washington would be a crucial test.

CHAPTER 5

RIDING IN FRONT

ASSISTANT SECRETARY OF THE NAVY, 1913–1914

AFTER RECEIVING PRESIDENT WOODROW WILSON'S ASSENT TO FRANKLIN Roosevelt's appointment as assistant secretary of the navy, Josephus Daniels asked the New York senators for their support. James Aloysius O'Gorman delivered a chilly agreement. The other Empire State senator, Elihu Root, one of the nation's most respected Republicans, had no objection, but he delivered a warning: "You know the Roosevelts, don't you? Whenever a Roosevelt rides, he wishes to ride in front." Daniels told his diary, "I listened and replied that any man who was afraid his assistant would supplant him thereby confessed that he did not think he was big enough for the job."[1]

Josephus Daniels had risen from humble beginnings to become one of the South's leading Democrats and the publisher-editor of one of the region's most influential newspapers. He knew that he had brought aboard an ambitious, first-rate young man of a wholly different background. He may not have realized how much of a handful he had taken on. Roosevelt certainly did not fully appreciate that he had come to work for a formidable and resourceful boss.

DANIELS AND ROOSEVELT ASSUMED OFFICE AT A PIVOTAL TIME IN THE HISTORY of the US Navy. Torpedo-armed submarines had just become a part of every national fleet. New dreadnought-type battleships powered by fast turbine engines and carrying large, accurate guns had relegated their predecessors to near obsolescence. The new technology required an ambitious and expensive building program in those nations that aspired to preeminence on the high seas. At the beginning of 1913, Britain, with twenty-six dreadnoughts, and Germany, with seventeen, were the world leaders. The US Navy had eight, Japan four. Each country had additional dreadnaughts under construction.[2]

In Washington Franklin followed very much in the footsteps of Uncle Ted. He envisioned the United States becoming a global power with a naval reach beyond the Western Hemisphere. He had little concern about Britain, which had sought good relations with the United States for nearly two decades. By contrast, episodic tensions with Germany and Japan had created adversarial attitudes on both sides. Well read in naval affairs and international relations and convinced that the United States was destined for world leadership, the new assistant secretary was determined from the time he took office to push aggressively for a big navy.

Roosevelt's post was the culmination of a lifelong love of ships and the sea. He relished the formal ceremonies of boarding a vessel, receiving a seventeen-gun salute, and inspecting the crew. He was also an avid sailor, curious about whatever vessel he was on, far more knowledgeable than most civilian officials, and generally liked and admired by professional navy officers.[3]

Josephus Daniels, twenty years older than Roosevelt and a head shorter, had come of age in hardscrabble post-Reconstruction North Carolina. Amiable in manner and appearance, he spoke with the accent of the upper South and dressed in a style his son would later describe as "slightly archaic." A devout Methodist and ardent prohibitionist, he forbade the consumption of alcoholic beverages in the officers' mess on naval vessels. Roosevelt recalled years later that his new chief initially struck him as "the funniest looking hillbilly" he had ever seen. Daniels was nonetheless tough and accustomed to command.[4]

As editor and publisher of the *Raleigh News and Observer*, Daniels had aligned himself with populist and progressive forces within the state, protesting the supposed depredations of railroads, bankers, and big corporations. But his progressivism was for whites only. Racism floated in the air he had breathed from childhood on, but his brand was relatively benign. In the world of the early twentieth century, most northern Democrats, Franklin Roosevelt included, did not object.

Daniels's political hero was William Jennings Bryan, the Nebraska populist-Democrat for whom the Roosevelt family had maximum low regard. A paladin of the outlook and values of rural America, Bryan combined a socially conscious Christian Protestant fundamentalism with advocacy of prohibition of alcoholic beverages and a fiery political radicalism. Attuned to the interests of rural debtors, he had long advocated a drastic monetary inflation. A few days short of his fifty-third birthday when he joined Wilson's cabinet, he was rapidly balding and had developed a considerable paunch. Of average height, he somehow seemed taller and more imposing with his booming golden voice, carefully developed oratorical skills, and devotion to the needs of the common people.[5]

In deference to Bryan's preeminence within the Democratic Party, President Wilson had appointed him secretary of state, despite his lack of qualifications for the post. At heart, Bryan was an isolationist. Temperamentally a Christian pacifist, a critic of post–Spanish-American War imperialism, and an advocate of universal disarmament, he had no desire to see American military power and global influence expanded. Within the cabinet, he and Daniels constituted a two-man bloc at odds with Roosevelt's most fundamental opinions about America's mission in the world and the imperative of a strong military.

Worst of all, from Roosevelt's perspective, Bryan knew next to nothing about the navy. In later years, he told of the secretary of state rushing into his office excitedly and declaring, "White people are being killed in Haiti, and I must send a battleship there within twenty-four hours." When the assistant secretary responded that it would be impossible to move a battleship so rapidly, but a gunboat could be quickly dispatched, Bryan agreed that would be sufficient and added, "Roosevelt, after this, when I talk about battleships don't think I mean anything technical."[6]

Roosevelt's sense of superiority to Bryan and Daniels verged on arrogance. He openly criticized the secretary's evangelical pacifism and hostility to drink. At dinner parties, he sometimes entertained guests by doing an impression of his hayseed boss. On one such occasion, Roosevelt's closest friend among the cabinet members, the easygoing secretary of the interior, Franklin K. Lane, had had enough: "You should be ashamed of yourself. Mr. Daniels is your superior and you should show him loyalty or you should resign your office." The rebuke had an impact. Roosevelt in later years told the story approvingly.[7]

Roosevelt and Daniels, by all accounts, instinctively liked each other, but they came from enormously different backgrounds and had conflicting visions of America's future. Daniels surely got wind of Roosevelt's scorn. He appears to have simmered quietly from time to time but always decided against any action. His young subordinate, long on confidence and often short on tact, was fortunate to have so patient a boss. Only years later would Roosevelt come to understand that millions of voting Democrats idolized both Bryan and Daniels and that any prospective leader of the party would have to appeal to their constituency.[8]

The US Senate confirmed Franklin Delano Roosevelt as assistant secretary of the navy on March 16, 1913. The next day, his eighth wedding anniversary, he took the oath of office. Soon afterward, he was at his desk in the State, War, and Navy Building, the great, rococo Gilded Age structure just west of the White House that a later generation would know as the Executive Office Building. He wrote a typically flippant note to his mother: "I am baptized, confirmed, sworn in, vaccinated—and somewhat at sea! For over an hour I have been signing papers which had to be accepted on faith—but I hope luck will keep me out of jail." He ended with a slightly more serious thought: "I will have to work like a new turbine to master this job—but it will be done even if it takes all summer."[9]

Roosevelt, of course, had no doubt about his ability to handle a complex and difficult job. As the one and only assistant secretary, he was the service's chief civilian operating officer, tasked with a bewildering assortment of responsibilities, including oversight of navy shipyards around the country and all the jobs they performed. Daniels was the chief policy-making official. Guarding his prerogatives zealously, the secretary dealt with numerous long-serving desk admirals, whom he perceived as potential obstructionists, by transferring them to sea duty. He bluntly rejected repeated reorganization plans that would have put all consequential decisions in the hands of senior uniformed officers. He sought in various ways to make the navy more democratic, most notably by setting aside a few US Naval Academy appointments every year for outstanding enlisted men. He handled effectively the southern Democratic congressmen who wielded much of the power on Capitol Hill. The assistant secretary did whatever the secretary did not want to do. Roosevelt accepted the numerous assignments and did his determined best to influence policy.

On many matters, he could rely on the recommendations of a seasoned career staff, headed up by Charles McCarthy, a professional civil servant. Louis Howe came down to Washington as his other chief aide. Howe handled a multitude of duties capably, but unlike the careerists, who had dedicated their lives to the department, he devoted himself solely to the advancement of Franklin D. Roosevelt. Frequently abrasive and sometimes downright disruptive, he was not liked by the rest of the senior staff. Roosevelt overlooked his faults, appreciated his loyalty, and considered him indispensable.[10]

Following the example of Theodore Roosevelt, the assistant secretary fully intended to speak his mind, get noticed, and advance his career. He consistently sided with big navy admirals and developed close ties to the Navy League, a private organization of corporate leaders (many of whom had direct interest in navy contracts), retired naval officers, foreign affairs experts, and miscellaneous boosters of the service. The admirals and the Navy Leaguers had one primary objective: rapid expansion of the battleship fleet over a decade to forty-eight dreadnoughts. Daniels, positioning himself between big navy advocates and peace-minded economizers, wanted only a measured and economical expansion of US naval strength. President Wilson and Secretary Bryan shared his skepticism toward the expansionists.[11]

International crises that seemed to validate Roosevelt's push for a stronger navy erupted during his first year and a half in office. In 1913, Japan responded with outrage to discriminatory actions against Japanese immigrants by the state of California. Some military officials worried, not for the first time, about the vulnerability of the Philippines and perhaps Hawaii to attack and seizure. They recommended dispatch of the navy's small Asiatic Squadron, based off Shanghai, to the Philippines. Roosevelt quietly backed them.[12]

Daniels and Wilson, however, rejected any movement of the squadron as potentially provocative and ultimately useless in the face of Japan's vastly superior regional naval power. Roosevelt privately feared war but was careful in his public comments. Visiting the Boston Navy Yard on May 19, he declared, "We are not mobilizing our ships to fight Japan."[13]

In fact, he feared pressures from California to send half the battleship fleet from the East Coast to the Pacific. In May 1913, Theodore Roosevelt wrote to him, "We shall be in an unpardonable position if we permit ourselves to be caught with our fleet separated." Fourteen months later, Franklin privately asked Theodore and the great naval strategist Admiral Alfred Thayer Mahan to publish articles on the importance of concentrating the fleet. Both did so.[14]

The exchange with Mahan touched off a correspondence on naval strategy and world politics. Roosevelt floated the idea of a squadron of heavy, well-armed cruisers assigned to one ocean and a dreadnought fleet assigned to the other, on a rotating basis, with the new Panama Canal providing relatively quick access between the Pacific and the Atlantic. The case for a cruiser fleet, which would likely be destroyed quickly in an engagement with dreadnought-class battleships, was dubious. Mahan was nonetheless sympathetic and seems to have been impressed with the young assistant secretary. It was unfortunate that they never had a chance for a personal meeting before Mahan's death in late 1914.

Fears of Japanese imperialism remained in the back of Roosevelt's mind and foreshadowed the authorization of a genuine two-ocean navy during his presidency. More immediately, the crisis with Japan sputtered out with no increase in the modest US naval construction program.[15]

By the spring of 1914, revolutionary chaos in Mexico had become a more urgent problem. Roosevelt openly expected hostilities and worried about the support capabilities of his service. In April, he traveled across the country by train to inspect West Coast naval installations. On April 21, Wilson ordered the marines to occupy the Mexican port of Vera Cruz. In tune with the president's determination to provide democratic guidance to the Mexicans, Roosevelt told a reporter, "If it means war, we are ready."[16]

Wilson pulled back, accepted mediation, and eventually withdrew from Vera Cruz. By mid-July, Mexican dictator Victoriano Huerta was compelled to resign, but his successor, Venustiano Carranza, could not pacify an increasingly anarchic country. The navy would be called on episodically to evacuate US citizens from Mexican ports. Attacks on American interests and numerous cross-border raids by Mexican insurgents would finally lead to an American intervention commanded by General John J. Pershing in the spring of 1916.[17]

Haiti was another nearby trouble spot. In July 1915, Wilson ordered the marines to occupy the chronically unstable island, where they quickly found themselves facing a nasty and fanatical insurgency. About a year later, marines were deployed to the Dominican Republic. By virtue of his office, Roosevelt oversaw both endeavors. Although more distractions than significant naval operations, they stretched American capabilities.

Almost from the beginning, Franklin was the Wilson administration's most vociferous advocate of a greatly enlarged navy. Although at clear cross-purposes with Daniels here, he minced no words. Correctly dismissing arguments that gunboats were sufficient for coastal defense, he warned that the United States possessed only sixteen battleships capable of standing up against the numerically superior first-line fleets of Britain or Germany. "Any petty officer of a foreign country, if our first fleet was destroyed, could effect a landing on the East Coast of the United States," he warned a New York audience. In Milwaukee he declared, "The policy of our congress should be to buy and build dreadnoughts until our navy is comparable to any other in the world."[18]

Daniels and Wilson could not have been pleased with Roosevelt's behavior, but they neither reprimanded him nor gave serious consideration to dismissing him. Possibly they felt that so high profile a firing would create more trouble than it was worth. Moreover, Roosevelt was in many respects an outstanding assistant secretary. Only Wilson could have sacked him—the post of assistant secretary was a presidential appointment—and Wilson may have seen him as a useful counterpoint to Daniels. Above all, Roosevelt and Daniels continued to like each other, often meeting at the end of a busy day for a relaxing chat.

Roosevelt spent his first six months as assistant secretary living alone in hotels. Eleanor remained in New York with the children, dividing her time between their Manhattan town house, Hyde Park, and, for much of the summer, Campobello, with Sara usually in close proximity. Franklin spent as many weekends with them as possible.

He never lacked company in Washington. Among his many friends were TR's daughter Alice and her husband, Nicholas Longworth, a prominent Republican congressman; Eleanor's Aunt Bamie and her husband, retired admiral William Sheffield Cowles; and Lathrop Brown, his Harvard roommate, now a Democratic congressman from suburban Long Island. He also socialized with numerous Harvard or Groton acquaintances. He quickly joined the prestigious Metropolitan Club, the Army and Navy Club, and the Chevy Chase Club, where he pursued his addiction to golf on a near daily basis.

Month by month, his associations grew richer, many of them facilitated by his connection to Cousin Ted. He was soon a guest at periodic Sunday lunches given by Justice Oliver Wendell Holmes for prominent young men in government. Sir Cecil Spring-Rice, the British ambassador and long a chum of TR, became a good friend. So did the French ambassador, Jules Jusserand. Henry Adams, a direct descendant of John and John Quincy Adams, an eminent historian, and a longtime mordant observer of the Washington scene, was another prominent acquaintance. ("Young man," Adams once told Franklin as they dined at the old man's residence on Lafayette Square, "I have lived in this house many years and seen the occupants of that White House across the square come and go, and nothing that you minor officials or the occupants of that house can do will affect the history of the world for long.") Roosevelt also enjoyed a good relationship with Senator Henry Cabot Lodge of Massachusetts (another close friend of TR) and Lodge's son-in-law, Representative Augustus Peabody Gardner.[19]

Reunited in September 1913, the Roosevelts rented the Washington house of Aunt Bamie and Admiral Cowles at 1733 N Street. (The Cowles removed to their home in Connecticut.) The commodious four-story structure, just south of DuPont Circle, had a tiny front lawn and a small walled garden in the rear. Having been a guest there before her marriage, Eleanor found their new home comfortable and reassuring. Still, it was barely adequate for a household that included three children, four servants, a nurse, a governess, and a Scottish terrier.

The neighborhood was heavily populated by political policy intellectuals, retired senior military officers, and civil servants, many of them listed in the local social register. Connecticut Avenue and Eighteenth Street intersected at the west end of the block, where the most prominent building was the large and imposing British embassy. Nick and Alice Longworth lived close by at 2009 Massachusetts Avenue. Roosevelt customarily walked to work.[20]

Eleanor, to her dismay, learned that a complex Washington etiquette imposed manifold social obligations on her, including introductory calls on the wives of public officials and diplomats and the hosting (or cohosting with Mrs. Daniels) of various receptions. She found it all daunting but went about her duties with determination. Chauffeured by one of the servants in the family car, she spent weeks making calls all over Washington: "I am Mrs. Franklin D. Roosevelt. My husband has just come as Assistant Secretary of the Navy." With those ladies who were at home, she exchanged some pleasantries but kept the visit short; her rule was no more than six minutes. However trying, the experience helped her overcome a still strong shyness and left her more confident in her ability to deal with a wide variety of people.

Few evenings were free. Among the brighter stars in Washington's "smart, young set," the Roosevelts customarily attended dinners at least three or four nights a week. Acceptance of invitations from eminences such as Justice Holmes, from high-ranking administration officials, and from the established leaders of Washington society was mandatory. Eleanor and Franklin reserved two Sunday nights a month for close friends, to whom they served light suppers. They also were expected to give their own elaborate dinners for up to two dozen people at a time. Other functions—balls, receptions, garden parties—required their presence. Socializing lubricated the inevitable political conflicts and rivalries that permeated the government. Invitations had to be sent and answered; carefully devised seating charts reflected the rank and importance of each guest at events one hosted.[21]

Eleanor understood that she had to accept social responsibilities as a wife's obligation, but she clearly found them unsatisfying. The pressures may have contributed to painful migraine headaches that periodically plagued her during the first decade of her marriage. In the spring of 1914, she engaged a young woman from a good but impecunious family to work three mornings a week as her social secretary. The new employee, Lucy Mercer, six years younger than Eleanor, was well-bred, efficient, beautiful, and vivacious. Anna, eight years old when Lucy was hired, recalled a "warm and friendly manner and smile" that made people happy. In March 1915, with Franklin and Eleanor away on an extended trip, Sara stayed at the house on N Street to take care of the children. "Miss Mercer is here," she reported in a letter, "she is *so* sweet and attractive and adores you Eleanor."[22]

The family continued to grow. On August 17, 1914, Eleanor gave birth to a baby boy, the second to be christened Franklin Delano Roosevelt Jr. Their last child, named John Aspinwall Roosevelt for Franklin's paternal uncle, arrived on March 13, 1916. Both children thrived, but Eleanor seems to have become increasingly dissatisfied. She would recall with ill-concealed ruefulness in her autobiography, "For ten years I was just getting over having a baby or about to have one."[23]

She had given Franklin the large family he had always wanted and may have decided that she had done her duty. Every mainstream religious denomination, including the Roosevelts' Episcopal Church, forbade artificial contraception, which was illegal in most jurisdictions. Abstinence was the only option, even for married couples. Eleanor and Franklin may have begun to sleep in separate beds, at least when they were at Hyde Park. Many middle- and upper-class marriages of the time took the same course. They continued to have an affectionate relationship, but their union was in peril. Eleanor was happy enough to put the sexual/childbearing phase of her life behind her. Franklin was in his mid-thirties, handsome, prominent, and more attractive to women than ever.[24]

ROOSEVELT'S NEW POST HEIGHTENED HIS PUBLIC VISIBILITY AND WIDENED the range of his political contacts. He probably got more public attention than any other number two person in the cabinet. The position frequently took him out of Washington on inspection trips and other navy department business, mostly to large coastal states. Local newspapers were invariably interested, and Franklin, as adept at self-promotion as TR, usually provided a good story.

Roosevelt controlled or strongly influenced a wide variety of jobs and promotions in the shipyards. As an important Wilson Democrat, he had input into the allocation of many New York federal jobs, but patronage had to be shared with the locals—reformers and machine regulars. The president knew he could not ignore Tammany and cultivated Senator O'Gorman, whose relationship with Roosevelt seems to have grown frostier. Secretary of the Treasury William Gibbs McAdoo fancied himself the New York reform leader and aspired to succeed Wilson in the White House. He won not only a fair share of appointments but also one of Wilson's daughters, whom he married on May 7, 1914. Both friends and enemies began to call him "the Crown Prince." The president's closest informal adviser, Colonel Edward M. House, a Texan resident in New York, helped block the candidacy of Roosevelt's longtime backer, Poughkeepsie mayor John Sague, for collector of the Port of New York. Wilson's secretary and chief aide, Joe Tumulty, grabbed many jobs and promotions in the Brooklyn and Philadelphia shipyards. Thanks in no small measure to Howe's hard work and acumen, Roosevelt laid claim to most of the fourth-class postmaster jobs in Republican upstate New York, but the big-city post offices generally went to other grandees.[25]

Although far from insubstantial, the jobs and favors available to the assistant secretary of the navy were not enough to build a truly impressive organization capable of advancing a fledgling political career. For this endeavor, Roosevelt had to rely on his considerable personal assets, avoid overconfidence, and pick his fights carefully.

His duties brought him into close contact for the first time in his career with a working-class constituency that was usually Democratic in local elections but less so at the national level. Put off by the populist inflationary policies and rural ethos of William Jennings Bryan, workers had found the patrician conservatism of Grover Cleveland Democrats such as James Roosevelt equally repellant. At the turn of the twentieth century, Republicans persuasively marketed themselves as the party of prosperity, a sound dollar, stable prices, and, especially under Theodore Roosevelt, a "square deal" for the working man.

Franklin Roosevelt's experience with labor unions and the skilled and semi-skilled workers who constituted most of their membership was scant. Louis Howe understood their importance and provided a lot of guidance. Roosevelt picked up the lessons quickly, speaking with groups of workers and conferring with union leaders, who protested irregular work schedules and work "speed-ups" by navy bosses who invoked the principles of efficiency expert Frederick Taylor. Roosevelt renounced "Taylorism" and typically met labor demands halfway. The union bosses usually settled for that, valued their relations with the assistant secretary, and broadcast their successes to the membership. Roosevelt could present himself as following in the tradition of his famous cousin, working for the welfare of all and sympathetic to the legitimate needs of workers. He could boast of few major work stoppages on a watch of more than seven years.[26]

To his newfound affinity with labor, Roosevelt added an adversarial attitude toward "the trusts" with which the navy did business. Political progressivism, whether rural-populist or urban-middle-class in its origins, had long condemned huge corporations as killers of opportunity for individual enterprisers, oppressors of workers or farmers, and monopolistic price fixers. Theodore Roosevelt had condemned them as "malefactors of great wealth." In their attitudes toward big business, Franklin Roosevelt and Daniels agreed. They discovered, however, that low bids were not necessarily the best bids and that fighting even blatant price fixing by resorting to foreign suppliers was both politically and practically problematic.[27]

As a first-rank industrial power, the United States supplied arms to other nations. One of these was Argentina, a potential great power in the early years of the twentieth century and an aspirant to naval hegemony in the South Atlantic. In 1909, Bethlehem Steel had secured a contract to build two dreadnoughts for the Argentines. At the beginning of 1915, the first, the *Moreno*, had been completed, but the builder, a Bethlehem subsidiary, demanded payment of $3 million beyond the contract price of $12 million for unforeseen work and expenses. By mid-February, a thousand Argentine sailors were quartered at the US government's Philadelphia shipyard, waiting to take possession. At the request of the Argentine ambassador, Secretary Daniels sent Roosevelt to settle the controversy.[28]

Roosevelt found himself dealing primarily with Charles Schwab, the great captain of industry who had founded Bethlehem Steel. Tactfully but forcefully, he left no doubt of who possessed overriding authority. He told Schwab that the government, having taken "such an active part in obtaining the contracts," had a strong interest in a timely delivery to Argentina. He also suggested that Bethlehem had an equally strong incentive: "It is probably no secret to you that the Argentine Government has been thoroughly dissatisfied over the seizure of a number of its ships and munitions of war being constructed in Europe at the time of the outbreak of war last Summer, and if the Argentine Government can be made to feel secure in this country I have no doubt that there will be many opportunities given us for increased business." Within days, the dreadnought was floated from its Camden berth and turned over to the Argentine crew.[29]

Daniels, congenitally suspicious of large corporations, strongly favored taking as much business as possible away from big interests and doing naval construction in government shipyards. Roosevelt was far more equivocal and, as his letter to Schwab demonstrated, open to the idea that government and big business could enjoy a mutually beneficial relationship. He thereby followed the example of TR, who believed that the trusts required regulation for the common good but were nonetheless examples of productive efficiency. Interested in a strong US Navy above all, Franklin Roosevelt wanted the service to have some manufacturing capacity, which could be expanded in time of war, but he equally desired a strong private shipbuilding industry. Appreciating the huge overhead costs of heavy manufacturing, he also thought it useful to have a measure of the "actual cost of manufacture" against which to assess the pricing practices of private enterprise. In the much different context of electricity production twenty years later, he would speak of the need for a "yardstick."[30]

THE MOVE TO WASHINGTON HAD NOT LESSENED ROOSEVELT'S NEW YORK political ambitions. He stayed with his game plan of gaining Washington experience, then running for a major elective office in his home state. Largely successful in establishing himself as a strong and effective assistant secretary of the navy, he remained a significant presence in the New York reform Democratic movement. With Theodore Roosevelt's example in mind, he was palpably impatient for a shot at statewide elective office, but he faced a complex and difficult environment.

In the 1912 elections, Democrat William Sulzer, an erratic, Tammany-backed "populist," had won the governorship largely because the Progressive Party had split the Republican vote. Having broken with the machine and failed to get backing from reformers, Sulzer was impeached and ousted from office. His successor, Martin H. Glynn, possessed little popular appeal. By early 1914, the tide of opinion in the state strongly favored the Republicans.

Roosevelt impulsively threw himself into this unpromising political situation. The governor's office seems to have interested him at first, and some reform Democrats promoted him for it, but President Wilson shied away from an open endorsement and patronage backing. By midyear, Franklin had decided to try for the US Senate seat being vacated by Elihu Root. The Seventeenth Amendment, ratified in 1913, required popular election of US senators, and New York had adopted primary elections for party nominations. He would be able to make full use of his campaigning skills.[31]

Initially hoping for a Democrat-Progressive coalition, he told Eleanor, "I *might* declare myself a candidate for U. S. Senator in the Democratic and Progressive Primaries." TR, determined to take one last shot at establishing his new party as a stand-alone force, gave him no encouragement. Josephus Daniels told him flatly that he probably could not win the Democratic primary and, if he did, would likely lose in the general election. Nonetheless, Franklin entered the Democratic primary, scheduled for September 28. New York, he said, would have to decide whether the state would be "on the side of reactionary politics and politicians, or on the side of intelligent progress and honest administration of government."[32]

Roosevelt no doubt hoped that Tammany would run a machine hack against him or perhaps put up no candidate at all. But, as O'Gorman had demonstrated, the organization had respectable friends. On September 7, Tammany announced its candidate, James W. Gerard, a much esteemed attorney and jurist who was US ambassador to Germany.

Citing the diplomatic urgencies of the full-scale European war that had just broken out in August, Gerard stayed in Berlin. Roosevelt, who also faced considerable official responsibilities, spent two and a half weeks barnstorming through upstate New York. He got no encouragement from President Wilson, who remained concerned with party unity. Pressed to define just what kind of a Democrat he was, Roosevelt tried once again to plant a foot in both camps: "I am a regular organization Democrat of Dutchess County, a New York State Democrat and a National Democrat. I am not an anti-Tammany Democrat, but, in this campaign, as in many others, I have taken a consistent position against the control of the Democracy of this State by Charles Francis Murphy, believing that he is a handicap to our Democracy."[33]

On Election Day, 1914, the voters chose Gerard 210,765 to 76,888. Roosevelt could only pretend he had made an important point, swallow hard, smile, and give the winning ticket his wholehearted endorsement. In November, Republicans swept the statewide races. TR's efforts notwithstanding, the Progressive Party vote was insignificant. Henceforth, Franklin Roosevelt would avoid open jousting with Tammany, which had proven itself an indispensable reservoir of Democratic votes.

Tammany itself had begun to move toward alliances with reformers on social welfare legislation. Murphy empowered progressive-inclined Tammany loyalists such as Al Smith and Robert Wagner to join social reformers in a common cause. Roosevelt got with the program. In 1915, he delivered a florid endorsement of Smith's candidacy for sheriff of New York County (Manhattan). The following year, he facilitated an offer of the city's postmastership to Wagner, who declined it to pursue, and win, a seat on the state supreme court. By 1917, Franklin Roosevelt was keynote speaker at Tammany's annual July Fourth celebration.[34]

The 1914 debacle may have convinced Roosevelt that progressives would have to develop a power base within one of the established parties. He quite probably also grasped that a progressive-dominated party needed the votes of urban workers, and Tammany and other big-city machines were vehicles for delivering them. But the content of his own progressivism remained hazy.

The Wilson administration had accomplished great things: a general lowering of the protective tariff, an income tax, the Federal Reserve System, a major strengthening of the antitrust laws, and an agricultural extension service to provide assistance to farmers. More would come in 1916, with the appointment of Louis Brandeis to the Supreme Court, outright farm subsidies, a workman's compensation program for federal employees, an eight-hour day for railway employees, and a federal anti-child-labor law. Roosevelt supported all these measures. But he engaged with none of them.

He remained in Washington, with the navy as his primary, increasingly important responsibility. The vast war on the European continent would quickly spill over into the high seas, consume most of his attention, and provide him with new causes.

CHAPTER 6

ARMAGEDDON

THE GREAT WAR, 1914–1919

FRANKLIN ROOSEVELT'S POLITICAL CAREER HAD BEGUN AGAINST WHAT seemed a remote international background of great-power tension. The European order unwound rapidly and catastrophically in the summer of 1914 following the assassination of Austro-Hungarian archduke Franz Ferdinand in Sarajevo by a Serbian extremist. After a month of diplomatic maneuvering, ultimatums, and counter-ultimatums, most of Europe was at war, with a Central Power alliance of Germany and Austria-Hungary poised against Serbia, Belgium, France, Britain, and Russia. Turkey would quickly join the Central Powers. Japan would declare war against Germany with an eye to acquiring German concessions in China. So, eventually, would Italy, with its interest in acquiring the Austrian Tyrol. In the beginning, few imagined the catastrophic four-year bloodletting that lay ahead.

Roosevelt was one of them.

AS WAS CUSTOMARY, ELEANOR HAD TAKEN THE CHILDREN TO CAMPOBELLO— both parents feared the summer infantile paralysis epidemics that ravaged large American cities. Franklin, managing a wide range of routine business while keeping a watchful eye on the chaotic Mexican Revolution, spent a few days with his family toward the end of July. On July 28, he got the news that Austria-Hungary had declared war on Serbia. On July 31, he delivered a speech in Reading, Pennsylvania. On August 1, returning directly to Washington by train, he penned a brief note to Eleanor, predicting "the greatest war in the world's history."[1]

The following day, he wrote at greater length, betraying impatience and perhaps arrogance, but also displaying keen insight into the threat the European war posed to American interests and prescience about the future. He had found the Navy Department "asleep and apparently utterly oblivious to the fact that the most terrible drama in history was about to be enacted." Secretary Josephus Daniels felt "chiefly very sad that his faith in human nature and civilization and similar idealistic nonsense was receiving such a rude shock." Daniels and Secretary of State William Jennings Bryan, he thought, were under the delusion that the country could declare neutrality and pursue business as usual, with no understanding that the war would inevitably "give rise to a hundred different complications in which we shall have a direct interest." It was critical to concentrate the navy's fighting power and have it ready for use. He rejected predictions that the war would end soon because the bankers on both sides would refuse to finance it. "Money in spite of what the bankers say is not an essential to the conduct of war by a determined nation." He could not resist a final thought that reflected both his personal sentiment and a sense that the war would be fought to a finish: "Rather than long drawn-out struggle I hope England will join in and with France and Russia force peace *at Berlin!*"[2]

Roosevelt's attitude was out of step with the dominant strain of progressivism in the Democratic Party. Bryan and Daniels, representing the mostly rural South and West, were neutralist-pacifist and quasi-isolationist in their worldviews. The big-city Democrats, mostly led by predominantly Irish and viscerally anti-British machine bosses, provided no strong counterpoint.

Franklin, by training and background, was far more in tune with Uncle Ted's sense of the United States' unavoidable involvement in world politics. Both men were receptive to an alliance with the world's other great English-speaking nation, Great Britain. Theirs was in many ways a conservative viewpoint with a dark view of human nature, accepting conflict as inevitable in the affairs of nations. Franklin's outlook stemmed not just from the influence of TR but also from the beliefs of his father and mother, the Calvinist values that remained a presence in his family, and the preaching of Reverend Endicott Peabody.

THOUGH PRO-BRITISH IN SENTIMENT, PRESIDENT WOODROW WILSON REACTED immediately by proclaiming neutrality. War on the European continent posed no obvious threat to American interests. Moreover, the polyglot ethnicity of

America's population discouraged taking sides. The president urged Americans to remain neutral in thought as well as in deed.

Roosevelt made no attempt to do so, but he largely kept his preference to himself. Instead, for the next two and a half years he made himself the point man within the administration for naval expansion and preparedness. The endeavor brought him to cross-purposes with Daniels. He walked a fine line, maintaining his good personal relationship with the secretary while pulling the United States toward an unfamiliar and hitherto unwanted level of naval power. Seizing every opportunity, he conveyed one basic message: the American navy was too small and weak to defend the national interest against the world's major powers and required a drastic enlargement. Without openly criticizing Wilson or Daniels, he managed the task with a sustained barrage of statements, congressional testimony, and public speeches.

He sent a copy of one statement to Eleanor: "The enclosed is true and even if it gets me into trouble I am perfectly ready to stand by it. The country needs the truth about the Army and Navy instead of the soft mush about everlasting peace which so many statesmen are handing out to a gullible public." The navy, he asserted, although it had the full strength in personnel authorized by Congress, was 18,000 men short of being able to staff all its ships. Of the service's thirty-three first- and second-line battleships, only twenty-one could actually be deployed. Two more first-line battleships under construction would require an additional 1,000 men each. He proposed the establishment of a 50,000-man naval reserve force.[3]

Speaking to the prestigious National Civic Federation in December, he asserted, "We must have warships, and the phrase 'the control of the sea' represents what must be accomplished by a people who would hold their own against an enemy." The Civic Federation adopted a resolution supporting the establishment of a Council of National Defense.[4]

Testifying before the House Naval Affairs Committee a week and a half later, he reiterated the need for a major naval expansion, impressing many of his listeners with his grasp of the elements of naval power. His strongest congressional supporter was his friend Republican representative Augustus Peabody Gardner of Massachusetts, a son-in-law of Senator Henry Cabot Lodge and longtime gadfly to both parties on defense issues. From time to time, Roosevelt supplied Gardner with information on the navy's weaknesses. Employing a take-no-prisoners style of rhetoric, Gardner regularly pilloried President Wilson while singling out Roosevelt for extravagant praise.[5]

For the next two years, Roosevelt strongly advocated a big navy before groups such as the Navy League. On one such occasion, the crowd erupted into hisses at the mention of Daniels's name. The fault, he argued, lay not with the administration but with a pacifistic and tight-fisted Capitol Hill. Moreover, he consistently asserted, ship for ship and man for man, the US Navy ranked with the world's best; the problem was quantity, not quality. Rhetoric of this sort allowed him to stay on good terms with Daniels while disputing his chief's policies.[6]

During much of the first year of the war, the United States found itself at odds more with Britain than with Germany. The British navy ruled the Atlantic, seizing German flag vessels and searching neutral ships carrying goods to the Reich. Employing a steadily expanding definition of "contraband," the British confiscated cargoes from many American freighters and effectively cut off German-American commerce. The Wilson administration protested the British blockade but did not see it as a cause for war.[7]

In early 1915, Germany played its only strong naval card—the submarine. Declaring the seas around the British Isles a war zone, the Reich warned that the German navy reserved the right to torpedo any ship flying an enemy flag within the war zone and stated that, given the possibility of misuse of neutral flags, it could not guarantee the safety of any vessel. President Wilson, working with State Department counselor Robert Lansing, responded with a sharp note that Bryan signed reluctantly and Roosevelt must have silently applauded. It demanded observance of neutral rights and promised to hold Germany to "strict accountability."

On May 7, a German U-boat sunk the great British passenger liner *Lusitania*, with the loss of 1,198 lives, including those of 128 Americans. Most of the neutral world considered the event a war atrocity. Wilson, much to the outrage of Theodore Roosevelt and surely to the dismay of Franklin, declared in a speech on May 10 that there was such a thing as a man being too proud to fight. All the same, the president and Lansing, again working around Bryan but getting his signature, prepared a sharp note to the German government, demanding an end to the sinking of merchant ships and liners. When the response proved unsatisfactory, they drew up another tough communication, which this time Bryan refused to sign. One month to the day after the sinking of the Lusitania, the secretary of state resigned; Wilson promptly named Lansing his successor.

"What d' y' think of W. Jay B.?" Roosevelt asked in a letter to Eleanor, who was at Hyde Park. "It's all too long to write about, but I can only say I'm disgusted clear through. J.D. will *not* resign." Daniels clearly felt war could be avoided and was determined to steer the president in that direction. Wilson was still intent on neutrality. Germany provided him a victory by informally agreeing to stop sinking passenger ships, but then negated much of the goodwill its new policy might have generated by pursuing clumsy espionage and sabotage activities in the United States and Canada. Still sympathetic toward Britain and increasingly hostile to Germany, the president and Secretary Lansing clung to neutrality through 1916 and even hoped to mediate an end to the war.[8]

ROOSEVELT SENT A WHIMSICAL MEMO TO JOSEPHUS DANIELS PROBABLY TOWARD the end of 1915:

> Secnav—
>
> 1. I beg to report
>   (a) That I have just signed a requisition (with 4 copies attached) calling for purchase of 8 carpet tacks.
>
> Astnav.

Daniels returned it with the following notation: "Why this wanton extravagance? I am sure that two would suffice."[9]

The document had a larger meaning, readily apparent if one substitutes the word "dreadnoughts" for "carpet tacks." It revealed the good-natured way in which the two men handled their growing fundamental differences of opinion. Throughout 1915 and into mid-1916, Daniels continued to support naval growth at the rate of two new dreadnoughts per year, even as the submarine menace and the high-handed enforcement of the British blockade created heavy pressures for a stronger navy program. On February 3, 1916, in the middle of a major speaking tour through the isolationist Midwest, President Wilson asserted that the United States needed "incomparably the greatest navy in the world." By the end of March 1916, Roosevelt had progressed from advocating four dreadnoughts a year to an impossible eight.[10]

Relations with Germany ranged from difficult to grave. For a time, war seemed likely after a U-boat sank the French packet *Sussex* on March 24, 1916, killing several Americans. Germany pledged no more such attacks, and the crisis passed. Secretary of War Lindley Garrison developed a plan for a major expansion of the regular army and the replacement of state National Guard forces with a large, nationalized "Continental Army" reserve. Naval expansion drew substantial support, and Daniels reluctantly fell in line. In state after state, however, the bulk of Democratic progressives and influential National Guard officers bitterly opposed Garrison's program.[11]

On February 10, with his proposal blocked in Congress, Garrison resigned. Franklin Roosevelt was prominent among those mentioned as his possible successor. A *Washington Post* story declared, "No appointment would be welcomed with greater joy on the part of War Department officials." On March 7, Wilson named former Cleveland mayor Newton D. Baker, who acquiesced in a far more modest military expansion. Roosevelt continued, more safely and freely than ever, to be the leading big-navy advocate in the administration.[12]

One of his projects had been the establishment of a naval reserve program, a modest effort at best that drew a relatively small but enthusiastic group of volunteers, many of them upper-class young men. Roosevelt spoke to a group of them at a dinner in New York on June 23, 1916. In introducing him, the master of ceremonies drew raucous cheers by remarking, "I know it would not hurt your feelings if the word 'Assistant' were crossed out of this man's title." Preparedness had acquired a mass following. Roosevelt had become one of its most visible proponents.[13]

After intense debate and negotiation, Congress on August 15, 1916, gave Wilson the huge naval program he had requested. Roosevelt's advocacy had been significant in providing an initial impetus, but Daniels's loyalty to Wilson and his effective lobbying of the southern Democrats in the House were more vital in securing its passage. Contracts had to be awarded and price disputes settled. Daniels would secure funding for a government armor plant in 1917, but it had to be built. The navy program called for ten new dreadnoughts and a substantial increase in cruisers, destroyers, and submarines. The potential of the American economy for military manufacturing was almost unlimited; the existing capacity was heavily strained. When the United States entered the war in April 1917, other priorities would force postponement of construction of all but one of the dreadnoughts. Only three would ever be completed, none in time for wartime duty.[14]

Twenty years later, looking at a foreboding world from the vantage of the Oval Office, Roosevelt would remain skeptical of wishful thinking about peace, still believe strongly in a big navy, and understand the difficulties of dealing with complacent public opinion and antimilitary congressmen.

DURING THE LAST HALF OF 1916, ROOSEVELT FOUND HIMSELF CAUGHT UP NOT just in issues of naval preparedness but also in Woodrow Wilson's hard fight for reelection. The president's achievements were impressive by any standard. He had maintained US neutrality and kept the nation at peace in a war then generally recognized as the most costly and horrible ever fought. His program of military preparedness, if less aggressive than the defense hawks wanted, had put the United States on a course that would enable it to defend its interests in a hostile world. His record of domestic reform eclipsed Theodore Roosevelt's achievements. With the economy recovered from the initial shocks of the European war, he presided over a roaring prosperity buoyed by war orders from Britain and France. Still, his policies were controversial, and the Republicans were the nation's normal majority party. They had nominated a formidable candidate in Charles Evans Hughes, the former governor of New York and respected Justice of the Supreme Court. Theodore Roosevelt, who had hoped for the Republican nomination, folded his Progressive Party, supported Hughes, and delivered speech after speech denouncing Wilson's diplomacy as weak and ineffective.

Franklin Roosevelt played a relatively minor role in the campaign. He spoke only in the Northeast and confined his talks to defending the administration's management of the navy. He seems never to have mentioned the administration's domestic progressivism, which was outside his own area of responsibility and perhaps not an attractive issue with audiences who came to listen to an assistant secretary of the navy.

On election night, Roosevelt, like almost all Democrats, went to bed thinking that Hughes had won. Two days passed before Wilson emerged as the victor, primarily because he had carried Ohio and California by paper-thin margins. The tightness of the results obscured the potential they held for the Democratic Party, which until 1916 had been primarily a coalition of the South and the West. By positioning himself as a progressive president and a friend of organized labor, Wilson had taken the initial steps toward a political realignment that would achieve its final shape under his assistant secretary of the navy twenty years later. However indefinite the specifics in his mind, Roosevelt remained attached in at least a general way to the cause of reform. Writing to Eleanor, he declared, "I hope to God I don't grow reactionary with advancing years."[5]

Wilson's success in keeping the country out of the European war while trying to mediate an end to it had a lot to do with his victory. But even after suffering hundreds of thousands of casualties at the Somme and Verdun, the Allies and the Central Powers seemed determined to fight to a finish. Germany flirted with the possibility of unrestricted submarine warfare; Britain still interfered with American maritime commerce and confiscated cargoes. Still, the president decided that peace deserved one last effort.

On January 22, 1917, Wilson delivered a dramatic address to the US Senate, calling for a "peace without victory" as the prelude to a reformed world order built around principles of natural rights, self-government, and free commerce.

The speech won widespread praise but had no practical effect. Nine days later, Germany informed the United States that it would begin sinking any and all shipping entering the war zone around the British Isles. The United States immediately severed diplomatic relations. The nation suddenly found itself on an irreversible slide.

Wilson initially responded by arming American merchant ships. Roosevelt soon became involved. Only the government could provide the big six-inch guns required to destroy a submarine, and federal law forbade their sale. Roosevelt quickly obtained a legal opinion that they "may be *loaned* provided a suitable bond be given." A Senate filibuster in the waning days of the Fifty-Ninth Congress blocked legislative authorization, but on March 9, five days after beginning his second term, Wilson permitted the armament loans by executive order. The president, Secretary Daniels, and Roosevelt all surely realized that a deck gun would provide scant defense against torpedoes launched from beneath the surface. Daniels confided to his diary that he feared he was signing a death warrant for young Americans and moving the nation toward war.[16]

That March, Roosevelt made visits to the navy yards in Boston and New York. In New York, he spent an hour with Wilson's close adviser, Colonel Edward M. House, outlining the "principal weaknesses of [the] Navy," which included Daniels's procrastination, the anti-British attitudes of Chief of Naval Operations Admiral William Benson, and the failure to initiate immediate joint planning with Britain and France. He then visited the Brooklyn Naval Yard and deemed it ill prepared for war. Dining that evening with TR, General Leonard Wood, J. P. Morgan, Elihu Root, and other notables not known for their friendliness toward the administration, he got a sense, especially from his cousin, that the government might be moving in the right direction but needed to act with more vigor and clarity. "I backed T.R.'s theory—left for Wash[ington]. Told J. D. things not satisfactory Boston & worse N.Y. He said nothing."[17]

On March 18, three armed American merchant vessels steamed into the war zone and were promptly sunk with the loss of many seamen. By then, British intelligence had intercepted and given to the United States a secret German diplomatic cable offering an alliance to Mexico and promising the return of Texas and other territory lost to the United States in the Mexican-American War of the 1840s. The March revolution in Russia forced the abdication of the czar and established a democratic government. It was now possible to think of the war as a contest between the forces of popular democracy and those of militaristic reaction.[18]

Roosevelt was among those present on the evening of April 2, 1917, when Wilson appeared before a joint session of Congress to ask for a declaration of war. Understanding that the American public expected a grand rationale, the president asserted that joining the European conflict was necessary to make the world safe for democracy. His appeal rang with authenticity. It also gave Roosevelt a deep and lasting impression of what was necessary to bring the American people into a war and keep them behind it.

THE WAR MADE ONLY MINOR DIFFERENCES IN THE LIVES OF THE ROOSEVELTS. In the fall of 1916, they had left Aunt Bamie's comfortable old house on N Street for a more commodious one at 2131 R Street, just a few blocks away on the other side of DuPont Circle. Franklin frequently brought associates to the house for lunch and discussed confidential business with them, allowing servants to enter the dining room only when summoned with a small silver bell.

Eleanor continued to preside over a busy household and an intense social schedule. She seems to have struggled with bouts of depression. Many years later, Elliott recalled her breaking down in tears just before she was to receive guests at a dinner party. "I just can't stand to greet all those people," she told Franklin. "I know they think I am dull and unattractive. I just want to hide."[19]

She threw herself into war work, organizing knitting groups to make sweaters, scarves, and gloves for servicemen, helping to manage a Red Cross canteen at Union Station, and making hospital visits to sick and injured naval personnel. One of her coworkers was Lucy Mercer, no longer regularly employed by the family but still a presence in the Roosevelts' life. During the summer of 1917, when Eleanor and the children were away at Hyde Park and Campobello, Franklin frequently mentioned her in his letters as part of a group with whom he enjoyed his free Sundays.[20]

At home Eleanor instituted rules to conserve food that the War Food Administration adopted as a model for American households. The *New York Times* wrote a small piece on the achievement. Unfortunately, her choice of words made the project vulnerable to parody: "Making the ten servants help me do my saving has not only been possible but highly profitable." Franklin could not pass up the opportunity to rib her: "I am proud to be the husband of the Originator, Discoverer and Inventor of the New Household Economy for Millionaires. Please have a photo taken showing the family, the ten cooperating servants, the scraps saved from the table and the hand book. I will have it published in the Sunday Times."[21]

Such mortifications aside, Eleanor undoubtedly found her exhausting duties fulfilling. Dutiful but (by all indications) cool as a wife, she was also a remote mother, perhaps demonstrating the maxim that people are prone to repeat even unhappy aspects of their upbringing. "When I was young I determined that I would never be dependent on my children by allowing all my interests to center in them," she wrote nearly two decades later. She achieved self-validation by throwing herself into good causes for the benefit of humankind.[22]

She found some solace in contrasting herself with Cousin Alice. After her marriage to Nicholas Longworth had turned sour, Alice had increasingly become known for her vituperative wit. Writing in mid-1916 to her friend Isabella Ferguson, Eleanor confided her feelings about TR's eldest daughter: "She's a born hostess and has an extraordinary mind but as for real friendship and what it means she hasn't a conception. . . . I sometimes think that the lives of many burdens are not really to be pitied for at least they live deeply and from their sorrows spring up flowers but an empty life is really dreadful."[23]

THE DECLARATION OF WAR LEFT ROOSEVELT WITH AN OVERWHELMING SENSE of urgency and frustration that his feelings were not widely shared. He did not understand that both the Allies and the Central Powers were on the brink of exhaustion, each vulnerable to a final, last-gasp blow from the other. Clearly, he had a vivid appreciation of America's comparative naval weakness vis-à-vis a potentially victorious Germany. He doubtless understood that Berlin expected unrestricted submarine warfare to strangle Britain and France before the United States could achieve the mobilization necessary to tip the balance in the other direction.

From the beginning, he involved himself in everything and anything that he might influence. His drive led once again to friction with Secretary Daniels, who had come down in favor of war with great reluctance. Roosevelt possessed perhaps less wisdom and emotional depth about the horrors to come, but his impulses were better suited to the needs of the moment. His impetuous and sometimes insubordinate behavior was the flip side of a drive and energy that addressed multitudinous problems and got things done. As Daniels's son, Jonathan, put it many years later, his father "wanted Franklin to remain because he not only liked him, but he trusted him and depended upon him."[24]

An extraordinarily hectic year and a half followed. Roosevelt was involved in every phase of naval management and operations: finding office space for a greatly expanding bureaucracy, approving contracts, overseeing ship construction and the building of new military encampments, hammering out agreements with labor unions. Seeing himself as the Navy Department's take-charge man and chief cutter of red tape, he liked to tell friends that he often made decisions for which he risked imprisonment. Never timid about exercising his authority, he commandeered civilian resources when necessary—on one occasion he seized electrical generators destined for a large new Manhattan hotel and delayed its opening by three months. In all this, Louis Howe, to whom he delegated large responsibilities, and the solid professional staff he had inherited backstopped him.[25]

The pace was grueling, with long days, much paper pushing, and travel to shipyards or naval bases. Many mornings began at 7:00 a.m., participating with other subcabinet officials in group calisthenics. Their trainer, legendary football coach Walter Camp, described Roosevelt as "a beautifully built man, with the long muscles of the athlete." When he could, Roosevelt indulged in exhausting bouts of recreation. "A very busy day, consisting of steady golf, 36 holes, from 9 a.m. to 6 p.m. with an hour out for sandwich and rest," he wrote to Eleanor (off again with the children at Campobello) in mid-1917.[26]

Supervising the routine operations of the US Navy was an enormous job. Roosevelt was also immersed in war planning. Sometimes smashingly right, sometimes egregiously wrong, he pushed his preferences to the hilt. Possessing only minimal respect for the chain of command, he was instinctively drawn to new, experimental, and daring ideas, which rarely came from the highest seniority levels. He regarded costs as irrelevant.

The British navy had succeeded in bottling up Germany's surface force, but the Allies faced defeat from the Reich's submarine campaign. The British Admiralty, seemingly unable to think past traditional doctrine, sought to get supplies across the North Atlantic by dispersing merchant ships in the hope that enough would get through. When the United States entered the war, U-boats were sinking 350 vessels a month, a rate that surely would force surrender before the United States could mobilize. Roosevelt, fully as much a product of the dominant way of thinking as the leading American and British admirals, nevertheless backed tacticians who revised it radically. Once the leading civilian exponent of the dreadnought, he almost overnight became a backer of small, agile, and comparatively lightly armed antisubmarine craft.

The preeminent such vessel was the destroyer, three hundred or so feet in length, equipped with machine guns, three-inch artillery pieces, and depth charges. Roosevelt approved the assignment of the bulk of the American destroyer force to transatlantic convoy duty. By September 1917, sinkings had declined sharply. By then the navy had also stopped work on new dreadnoughts and devoted American shipyard capacity to destroyers and other more immediately needed ships.

Naval engineers also developed a new class of antisubmarine vessel: the wooden submarine chaser, a small boat fitted with light artillery pieces and depth charges that could be turned out quickly in large numbers. There were two models: a 110-foot ship capable of roaming dozens of miles into the ocean in search of enemy craft and a 55-foot ship designed for shore patrol only. The first, towed across the Atlantic in large numbers and often operating in tandem with destroyers, was highly effective. The second, too small to function in any but the calmest waters, was of little use even in guarding American beaches. Roosevelt pursued both projects with tenacity and enthusiasm.[27]

His most audacious project was the North Sea mine barrage, a difficult and complex plan to stretch mine-laced nets to a depth of two hundred feet some 230 miles across the North Sea from Scotland to Norway, penning in the German submarine force. The plan displayed yet another enduring, if typically American, Roosevelt characteristic: the lack of a sense of limits. The British thought it was too expensive and problematic. Roosevelt bulldogged it through the Allied military bureaucracy. Utilizing 80 million feet of wire rope and 100,000 antenna-detonated mines at a cost of perhaps $80 million, the barrage was substantially completed just weeks before the end of the war. It destroyed only three to six German submarines, but had the war gone on, it might well have achieved its objective. Roosevelt's critics depicted it as a stupendous waste of money; he would continue to see it as a constructive example of imaginative leadership prevailing over small minds.[28]

By mid-1918, those on the inside knew that the tide was beginning to turn. Naval convoying limited the effectiveness of German U-boats. The Allied navies ruled the waves. A huge, fresh American army was streaming into France. Roosevelt had done his part to make all this happen.

Like all politicians, he underscored his accomplishments and did not hesitate to exaggerate them. If he was not the secretary of the navy, he often behaved as if he were. He went directly to the White House for support when he needed it, most notably for the North Sea mine barrage. Too prone to believe that much of the navy bureaucracy was lazy and incompetent, he enlisted the popular American novelist Winston Churchill (no relation to the British Winston), a friend of Wilson and a graduate of the US Naval Academy, to do an investigative report for the president on the department's shortcomings.[29]

As ham-fisted and ambitious as he sometimes was, he had been the person pushing for readiness before the war. When war came, he was a first-rate administrator. A wide impression inside and outside Washington held that his accomplishments far outweighed his missteps. In 1917, when he broached the possibility of resigning to join the army or navy, General Leonard Wood declared, "It would be a public calamity to have him leave at this time." Who was the man pushing things along? asked the *Wall Street Journal* not long afterward. "That's easy: Franklin D. Roosevelt."[30]

In 1925, when someone suggested that the war effort had been the work of a united people, Roosevelt responded that Wilson and his cabinet had led public opinion, created emergency war agencies, and recruited the right men to staff them. "The American organization for war was created *from the top down, NOT from the bottom up.* This is most important." It was, he declared, the major lesson of war leadership.[31]

ROOSEVELT'S ONE REGRET WAS HIS LACK OF MILITARY SERVICE. THE EMOTION had a very personal dimension. Uncle Ted had offered to raise a volunteer division—a large-scale counterpart of his Spanish-American War Rough Riders—and personally lead it in France. President Wilson, with the near unanimous backing of the military establishment, had rejected the request. TR's four sons, however—Theodore Jr., Kermit, Archibald, and Quentin—all made their way to France as uniformed officers. So did Eleanor's younger brother, Hall. Theodore made no secret of his belief that Franklin should join them.[32]

By mid-1918, the assistant secretary was being talked up, with the apparent acquiescence of Tammany, as a possible Democratic candidate for governor of New York. Relinquishing that honor to Al Smith, Roosevelt had a different plan. After he made repeated requests, Secretary Daniels gave in to his proposal for a long inspection trip to Europe, where he would examine naval and marine forces, look into bases and contracts, and see the front lines for himself. After returning home and filing a report, he expected to resign and accept a command in the US Navy or Marine Corps. The political advantages were obvious, but he also felt a moral obligation. Writing to Eleanor from France that August, he said, "The more I think of it, the more I feel that being only 36 my place is not at a Washington desk, even a Navy desk. I know you will understand."[33]

The manner in which he crossed the Atlantic exemplified his attitude. He left the United States on July 9, 1918, on a new destroyer, USS *Dyer*, accompanying a convoy of supply ships. For a week and a half he was tossed around on rough waters, a submarine attack always a possibility. He found the experience exhilarating. "I have loved every minute of it," he wrote eleven days later as the craft approached Portsmouth.[34]

Considering that he was a subcabinet official, his reception in Europe was remarkable. This had something to do with his name, but it also was extremely unusual for important American officials to visit Britain. In London, he set up headquarters at the Ritz and proceeded to meet, formally and informally, with practically the entire British establishment, dealing especially with First

Lord of the Admiralty Sir Eric Geddes. He quickly discovered that he had a preference for one-on-one talks. On July 29, he had a forty-five-minute personal audience with King George V and was delighted by one of the monarch's remarks: "You know I have a number of relations in Germany, but I can tell you frankly that in all my life I have never seen a German gentleman."[35]

That evening, he and the Italian ambassador were guests at a formal dinner held at Gray's Inn in honor of the war ministers. He found Lord Curzon and sundry other speakers impressive but made no mention in his diary of the minister of munitions, Winston Churchill. Churchill quickly forgot the event and Roosevelt's presence at it. Twenty-one years later, in conversation with Joseph P. Kennedy, Roosevelt would recall Churchill as having "acted like a stinker" toward him.[36]

The next day he lunched at the American embassy with Britain's wily, charismatic prime minister, David Lloyd George, as the guest of honor. Roosevelt found him fascinating: "Thick set; not very tall; rather a large head; and rather long hair; but what impressed me more than anything else was his tremendous vitality."[37]

On July 31, Roosevelt and his party dashed across the English Channel on a British destroyer. After inspecting American bases and construction in the Dunkirk-Calais area, they made for Paris, based themselves at the Crillon, and undertook a round of meetings with civilian and military officials. The highlight was an audience with the nation's tough old premier, Georges Clemenceau. Roosevelt described him as a force of nature: seventy-seven years old, yet tireless, seemingly in constant motion, and dedicated to total victory against a hated enemy. "I knew at once that I was in the presence of the greatest civilian in France."[38]

He also took time for brief visits with his Aunt Dora (Sara's sister) and TR's sons Archie and Ted Roosevelt, both recuperating from serious war wounds. By then he had received the bitter news that their brother Quentin had been shot down and buried in France. Their example doubtless reinforced his sense that he, too, should be in uniform and redoubled his determination to see the front lines.[39]

On August 4, he started for the front. The American naval attaché who had planned the trip, doubtless under orders to bring Roosevelt back unscathed, presented him with an itinerary that "called for late rising, easy trips and plenty of bombed houses thirty miles or so behind the front." Roosevelt scrapped the plan and ordered his party farther north toward Chateau-Thierry and Belleau Wood, the battlefield where just weeks earlier American marines had pushed back the last big German offensive against Paris. He described the scene vividly:

We had to thread our way past water-filled shell holes and thence up the steep slope over outcropping rocks, overturned boulders, downed trees, hastily improvised shelter pits, rusty bayonets, broken guns, emergency ration tins, hand grenades, discarded overcoats, rain-stained love letters, crawling lines of ants and many little mounds, some wholly unmarked, some with a rifle stuck bayonet down in the earth, some with a helmet, and some, too, with a whittled cross with a tag of wood or wrapping paper hung over it and in a pencil scrawl an American name.

They reached the headquarters of army general Hunter Liggett, whose marine forces were part of a painful Allied offensive, then moved forward through marching troops and supply convoys, past the sight and stench of dead horses dragged to the side of the road and dead Germans laid out in a field for burial. Finally they got to Mareuil, a village that had been under German control the previous night, and were just three or four miles away from the actual fighting. With night falling, they returned to Chateau-Thierry for a late dinner and billeted themselves in a deserted house.[40]

Rising before six the next morning, they were soon on the road again, traveling east to Nancy, just south of a German bulge against which the Allies were massing for an attack. Here they linked up with marine general John A. Lejeune, inspected troops, and again stayed up until 1 a.m. with their host. On August 6, they got another early start, moving back around the German lines to Bar-le-Duc, then up the Voie Sacrée to Verdun, for a conference with the French commandant there and a tour of the killing fields that had claimed at least a half million lives. Spotted by a German observation balloon, they motored to safety ahead of a quickly incoming artillery barrage. On August 8, they were back in Paris.[41]

Although he never got all the way to the front, Roosevelt had come closer than a senior civilian official probably should have and exposed himself to some danger. At the very least, he had gathered a firsthand understanding of the conditions under which American and Allied soldiers labored. Most of all, he had satisfied his need for self-respect. He could, if need be, look Cousins Ted, Ted Jr., and Archie in the eye and tell them he had experienced war. A later generation might call the trip quixotic; in his world, it was gallant.

On August 9, Roosevelt left for Rome, where his main goal was to persuade the Italians to deploy their battleship fleet against the Austro-Hungarian navy. Instead he obtained a symbolic Allied staff committee, chaired by British admiral Sir John Jellicoe. The Italians would never commit the fleet to battle. (They would follow the same policy in World War II.) Roosevelt's assumption of authority on this matter irritated Daniels, Secretary of State Lansing, and President Wilson. Still, none of them could quarrel with his purpose, and the offense was relatively minor. He seems to have received no reprimand.[42]

Back in Paris on August 13, Roosevelt launched into another grueling tour of American installations around the country. At Sainte-Nazaire a few days later, he inspected another of his unorthodox pet projects, the Naval Railway Guns—fourteen-inch battleship guns mounted on a large, enclosed platform car—conceived as a response to German long-range artillery. Each weighed ninety tons and had to be accompanied by a dozen or so railcars carrying men, ammunition, and supplies. The guns fired a 1,400-pound shell eighteen to twenty-three miles. They were powerful and effective, but production and transportation difficulties resulted in only five seeing action in France. The commander of the operation was Rear Admiral Charles Plunkett, a salty old officer who already had rebuffed army objections to the navy markings that would be displayed prominently on the vehicles.

Roosevelt confided his desire for active military duty and expressed an interest in commanding one of the guns. The fifty-four-year-old Plunkett was probably taken aback by the idea of an inexperienced civilian taking over a sophisticated piece of heavy artillery, but he was politic enough simply to ask his young superior if he could swear in French. Roosevelt unleashed a string of Gallic invectives, some authentic, some contrived. The admiral thereupon said he would take the younger man on with the rank of lieutenant commander— the equivalent of a major in the army or marines. Roosevelt appears to have planned to hold him to the promise.[43]

He spent several more days in France, always, it seemed, in constant motion. A press conference he held for the editors of leading Paris newspapers was something of a sensation. He sat on the edge of a table, addressed the journalists in what he called "Roosevelt French," and assured them that the war effort was "over the hump." Wholly won over, they wrote glowing reports of the event.[44]

Returning to Britain on a destroyer, Roosevelt got his closest taste of war yet. Zeppelin bombers targeted the vessel twice but failed to score a hit. In Scotland, he inspected progress on the North Sea mine barrage and managed a free day or two with old family acquaintances. The late Scottish summer was cold and wet. Refusing to moderate his standard pace of long working days and nights with little sleep, he spent one free morning fishing in a pouring rain, fortifying himself with Scotch whiskey.

He needed less Rooseveltian activity and more rest. The deadly Spanish influenza pandemic of 1918 and 1919 had engulfed much of the world and impacted areas hit by the war with special ferocity. Roosevelt probably contracted the virus in France, where he had begun to run an intermittent fever. The pace, the foul weather, and the lethal contagion all caught up with him. On September 12, back across the channel in Brest, he boarded the US liner *Leviathan* for New York. For three days he worked on his report, then collapsed and was confined to his bed for the rest of the trip. Influenza gripped the ship, felling many other passengers. There were numerous deaths; some of the deceased among the crew were buried at sea. Eleanor received word from the Navy Department that a doctor and an ambulance should meet Franklin at the dock. She and Sara were both there as he was carried out on a stretcher and transported to Sara's Sixty-Fifth Street town house, suffering from influenza and pneumonia in both lungs.[45]

One high point of a long, dreary convalescence was a note from TR, dated September 23:

Dear Franklin,

We are deeply concerned about your sickness, and trust you will soon be well. We are very proud of you.

With love,
Aff. Yours
Theodore Roosevelt
Later Eleanor will tell you of our talk about your plans.[46]

Franklin spent two weeks in the city, then two weeks at Hyde Park. After a time, he was able, with considerable help from Eleanor, to return to work on his report; a valuable document with numerous substantive suggestions, it would receive fulsome praise from both Daniels and Wilson.[47]

The postscript at the end of TR's note had referred to his insistence that his cousin should join the military. Franklin was by then more than eager to do so, but returning to Washington on October 18, he found himself a full-time acting secretary of the navy as Daniels stumped the country in the crucial midterm elections, supporting President Wilson's request for a Democratic Congress as a vote of confidence. On October 31, Roosevelt was finally able to see Wilson and request release for military duty. It was too late, the president told him. Germany was asking for peace terms. The armistice came eleven days later.[48]

As Eleanor remembered it, "Washington, like every other city in the United States, went completely mad. . . . The feeling of relief and thankfulness was beyond description." Franklin regretted never making it into uniform. From time to time in the future, he would become unnecessarily defensive about it—as when he complained about his name being omitted from a Groton monument to those who had served in the armed forces during the war. Still, he could be—and was—justifiably proud of his civilian role.[49]

By THE TIME OF THE ARMISTICE, THE ROOSEVELT MARRIAGE HAD PASSED through a crisis. The story comes to us through sources that are secondhand at best and frequently speculative. Franklin left no account of it. Eleanor left nothing in writing but did discuss her version of events with her daughter and with some close friends, including her biographer to be, Joseph Lash. Within the extended family, the episode was a matter of closely held gossip. Aside from the occasional, easily discredited rumormonger, no one wrote openly about it during Eleanor's lifetime.[50]

As Franklin lay in his sickbed after returning from Europe, Eleanor unpacked his luggage. She found a number of letters to him from Lucy Mercer. It is unlikely that anyone other than Eleanor and Sara read them before they were destroyed. They revealed a strong romantic relationship and constituted convincing evidence that Franklin had been, at the very least, emotionally unfaithful, probably sexually also. They left no doubt that, writing to Eleanor the previous summer, he had been blatantly deceptive in his casual references to Lucy as an escorted member of weekend outing groups.

Always the Puritan, Eleanor felt betrayed and retained an anguished bitterness over the affair for the rest of her life. She took the letters to Sara, who in many ways had stepped into the emotional space that Eleanor had reserved for her own long-dead mother. The two women met with Franklin. It is unlikely that anyone else was involved in the discussions that followed, and it seems certain that Sara was the dominant force.

There was talk of divorce—how serious and whether first broached by Franklin or Eleanor is uncertain. Lucy Mercer, a devout Catholic at a time when the church did not recognize marriages to divorcées, probably never could have married Franklin. But Sara surely would have been less concerned with practicalities and more with the concepts of honor and duty to family and children. Family lore has it that she played her trump card, telling Franklin that if he divorced Eleanor, she would cut him off financially, an act that would force a sharp trimming of his lavish lifestyle and write "finis" to his political career. Just perhaps Eleanor sensed that her own cool remoteness had been part of the problem.

In the end, Franklin and Eleanor agreed to stay together, and not simply as a matter of convenience or "for the sake of the children." It is doubtful that

Franklin ever wanted to get rid of her; he simply wanted Lucy to be part of his life also. Eleanor likewise probably would have found it difficult to leave him and the stability she had found among the Hyde Park Roosevelts. The two seem to have attempted to revive their marriage, spending more time together, sharing activities, and avoiding friction.[51]

Their relationship was nevertheless not free of speed bumps. Alice Roosevelt Longworth recounted with malicious glee the story of Eleanor leaving a dance at the Chevy Chase Club when Franklin, moving from one attractive woman to another, displayed no interest in an early departure. Finding that she had forgotten her house key when she got home, she sat on the front step in long-suffering Griselda fashion until her husband showed up shortly before dawn. In the wake of her wartime work, she clearly resented the resumption of a frivolous social role as wife, hostess, and less-than-elegant ornament.

The contrast with Lucy Mercer continued to gnaw and seems never to have left her. At times she drove out to Rock Creek Cemetery to the gravesite of Henry Adams and his wife, Clover. There she communed with *Grief*, the moving memorial to Clover sculpted by Augustus Saint-Gaudens.[52]

Franklin seems to have been puzzled and annoyed by her behavior but also willing to do what he could to satisfy her. When he obtained an assignment to return to France and oversee the winding down of the American naval presence there, he took her along. He had insisted on making the trip, arguing that the termination of contracts and sale of property were ultimately his responsibilities and that the potential for fraud and theft required his personal scrutiny. He surely was at least equally drawn by the spectacle of the peace conference in Paris. The Allies were undertaking the most important attempt to stabilize Europe since the Congress of Vienna a century earlier. He wanted to see the process firsthand.

Received with near hysterical adulation by the victorious populations, President Wilson had arrived in Europe on December 13, 1918, and held preliminary talks with Allied leaders on the shape of the world to come. Behaving almost like a disinterested neutral, he advocated a settlement based on broadly liberal principles (democracy, free trade, self-determination for formerly oppressed ethnic groups, an end to traditional imperialism). Everything, he believed, hinged on US acceptance of a League of Nations that would subject selfish nationalism to the imperatives of a liberal internationalism. His European allies, consumed with fear of a resurgent Germany, wanted full compensation for their enormous losses in men and money.

At home, the Republicans had won control of Congress in the midterm elections. Henry Cabot Lodge, long hostile to Wilson, would chair the Senate

Foreign Relations Committee. Theodore Roosevelt was another strong critic of the president and, despite his precarious health, seems to have seriously contemplated a run for the 1920 Republican nomination. Both fierce partisans with a personal dislike of Wilson, both TR and Lodge also held a view of foreign relations that stressed the primacy of national self-interest and balances of power. A similar worldview had animated Franklin when he joined the Wilson administration. Publicly, he had to support the president; privately, he must have shared to some degree his cousin's skepticism. His subsequent foreign policy thinking would attempt to reconcile TR's realism with Wilson's idealism.

On January 1, 1919, the Roosevelts boarded the USS *George Washington*, a renamed German passenger liner impressed into the US Navy as a transport ship headed for Europe. Commanded by Captain Edward McCauley, Roosevelt's aide on his trip to the Continent six months earlier, it had taken President Wilson to France. On January 6, the ship received word by radio that Theodore Roosevelt had died suddenly. Eleanor and Franklin both realized that, as she put it, "a great personality had gone from active participation in the life of his people."[53]

In France and briefly in Britain, Roosevelt inspected installations, toured the front lines, and handled some major negotiations on the sale of facilities and equipment. Eleanor visited military hospitals and traveled with him, except when he went to war zones from which women were still banned. Mostly, they were in Paris, established at the Ritz, socializing with friends, family, and various eminences involved in the peace conference. On the surface, they were a dynamic, still-young couple, united in affection and purpose. The French capital was for the moment the world's most exciting city. "It is full beyond belief and one sees many celebrities and all one's friends," Eleanor wrote to her mother-in-law. "People wander the streets unable to find a bed and the prices are worse than New York for everything."[54]

On February 15, she and Franklin, along with President Wilson, boarded the *George Washington* for the return trip home. The president carried with him the initial draft of the Treaty of Versailles; embedded within it was the covenant of the nascent League of Nations. Wilson understood that Senate ratification would be difficult. Determined to fight, he declared, "The United States must go in or it will break the heart of the world."[55]

Franklin must have sensed that he was nearing a new chapter in his life. His time with the Navy Department would likely be behind him in a year. The next challenge was beyond prediction.

The return to the United States was his twenty-fourth Atlantic crossing. He could never have imagined that he would not make another for twelve years.

CHAPTER 7

VICTORY IN DEFEAT

1919–1921

AT 11:15 P.M. ON JUNE 2, 1919, AS THEY RETURNED FROM ONE OF THEIR MANY social engagements, Franklin and Eleanor heard a powerful explosion, followed by sirens. Still two or three blocks from home, they ran frantically and found Attorney General A. Mitchell Palmer's house, directly across the street from theirs, seriously damaged, its front door blown out and its walls buckled. The bloody pieces of an unlucky bomber littered the pavement. The blast had shattered all the Roosevelts' front windows but inflicted no bodily harm. Police were just arriving at the scene. James, eleven years old, stood barefoot at his bedroom window in his pajamas, broken glass all around him. In later years, he recalled his father grabbing him and administering a hug that almost cracked his ribs, then his flustered, nearly hysterical mother asking him why he was up at so late an hour. Franklin hurried across the street and found the Palmers unscathed.

Anarchist leaflets, apparently carried by the bomber, lay amid the gore. The bomb was one of eight set off at approximately the same time in eight different cities across the country. They caused only one death—that of the Washington perpetrator—but the terror factor far overshadowed the actual outcome.[1]

The Roosevelts had returned from France a few months earlier with what could only be a sense of triumph about victory in the war, President Woodrow Wilson's leading role at the peace conference, and the safer future that lay ahead. The Palmer bombing reflected a grimmer reality: an overheated economy at home, labor strife, race riots, specters of bolshevism and anarchy, and bitter partisan division over the president's cherished League of Nations. During the next year, Palmer would head an indiscriminate federal effort to arrest and deport radicals. A downward spiral was beginning. The collapse of the Wilson administration would be the first event in a decade of challenge and adversity.

FOR THE REST OF 1919 AND THE FIRST HALF OF 1920, ROOSEVELT WORKED ON the transition from war to peace with the goal of strengthening a navy that he hoped would become second to none. The United States, he claimed with a straight face, had to be able to face down Great Britain if necessary, although he was more likely worried about Japan. Determined to restart suspended dreadnought projects as quickly as possible, he displayed no patience when the large steel companies submitted identical high bids for armor plate. Using still effective war powers, he requisitioned 14,000 tons of armor plating at a market price to be determined later. Confronted with labor restiveness as postwar price inflation took off, he professed sympathy for the real problems of shipyard workers but also opposed strikes and advocated compulsory arbitration.[2]

Identifying himself as a progressive more vociferously than ever, Roosevelt publicized some of the lessons he thought he had learned from Washington's conduct of the war. Most notably, he argued in favor of a centralized budgeting system for the entire government and establishment of a Bureau of the Budget. He also commended the British system of maintaining respected, nonpartisan, permanent undersecretaries in government departments. At heart, he remained a TR progressive who had not yet reconciled the values of the more forward-looking elements of a northeastern elite with those of a Democratic Party still rooted geographically in the South and the West and intellectually in Jeffersonian localism. He also loyally supported President Wilson on the Treaty of Versailles and its most visible provision, the League of Nations. This stand ruptured his cordial, if distant, relationship with Wilson's primary antagonist, Senator Henry Cabot Lodge.[3]

Like the senator (and Theodore Roosevelt), Franklin Roosevelt had long believed that military power and national interests were the decisive forces in international relations. This maxim constituted the basis for Lodge's "reservations" about the treaty; the senator was determined to make it part of a revised agreement. TR had favored a league that would enforce the peace and serve as an adjunct to American power. Franklin probably shared these sentiments and would have been amenable to a compromise. As a member of the administration, however, he backed the president to the hilt.

Neither Lodge nor Wilson displayed an interest in compromise. Their mutual hostility dwarfed much larger questions of national policy. In September 1919, Wilson, already visibly unwell, embarked on a nationwide speaking tour designed to secure Senate ratification of the treaty without Lodge's desired revisions. Three weeks into the trip, he suffered a stroke and was rushed back to Washington partially paralyzed. His wife and his physician provided no information about his condition while keeping him secluded not only from the public but from most administration officials and Democratic leaders. On November 19, the Senate rejected the treaty by a 38–53 vote. By the end of the year, the administration was rudderless, with a semirational president locked into a rigid no-compromise position.

Writing to a friend, Eleanor said, "I wish the President had been more willing to accept reservations. Still I do wish he could have had the League. I want it behind us & a free hand for all the many domestic problems." She probably relayed Franklin's feelings as much as her own. The Roosevelts did not improve their popularity with Wilson by entertaining the eminent British diplomat Sir Edward Grey when he was in Washington on a mission to persuade the president to accept the Lodge reservations. "F D R persona non grata with W," Josephus Daniels recorded in his diary on February 21, 1920.[4]

Daniels's entry came just a week after Wilson had dismissed Secretary of State Robert Lansing—who had been denied communication with the president—for calling and presiding over cabinet meetings without his consent. The incident intensified a widespread sense that the administration was adrift. In late 1919 and early 1920, many of the men who had managed the war resigned.[5]

Turmoil across the country underscored a widespread sense of national malaise: a police strike in Boston, a general strike in Seattle, crippling work stoppages in the coal and steel industries, bombs sent through the mail, the establishment of the Communist Party of America, Palmer's mass roundups of radicals. Passage of the Eighteenth Amendment to the Constitution and its enforcement mechanism, the Volstead Act, outlawed the manufacture and sale of alcoholic beverages, injecting another bitterly contested issue into American politics and dividing Democrats far more than Republicans. In March 1920, with Wilson holding firm to his no-compromise position, the Senate again failed to muster the required two-thirds majority for the Treaty of Versailles and the League of Nations.

Roosevelt, Daniels, and others who stayed on in their posts surely felt they were on a sinking ship. In fact, the secretary of the navy and the assistant secretary spent much of 1919 and 1920 encircled by hostile Republican congressmen and offended naval officers who hoped to bring down one or both of them on charges that ranged from unpreparedness for the war to corruption, waste, mismanagement, and tolerance of vice. Daniels was their primary target, but Roosevelt, as the department's chief operating officer, was an increasingly tempting secondary objective.

Over a two-year period, Franklin faced investigations that centered on three charges: improper navy deals with oil companies; mismanagement of the navy prison at Portsmouth, New Hampshire; and personal approval of an investigation of "vice" (homosexuality) in the service that authorized investigators to provide irrefutable proof by actually engaging in sex with the men they subsequently arrested. Nothing much came of any of the inquiries. The vice investigation was potentially the most explosive; Roosevelt vehemently denied knowledge of its methods. In July 1921 a Senate Naval Affairs subcommittee issued a report censuring him and Daniels but produced no evidence that either man had behaved improperly. The partisan tone was obvious; the report was a one-day sensation, quickly forgotten.[6]

The most imposing challenge came from Admiral William S. Sims, commander of US naval forces in Europe. At the beginning of 1920, Sims dispatched a long and bitter seventy-eight-point memorandum to Secretary Daniels. Leaked to the *Washington Post*, the document depicted a Navy Department mired in bureaucratic lassitude, ignorant of the requirements of transatlantic warfare, reluctant to cooperate with allies, and generally unprepared for a major conflict. The Senate Naval Affairs Committee launched an investigation.[7]

Sims's angry manifesto made many of the points that Franklin Roosevelt had voiced semipublicly for years. For a time he and the admiral had been quiet allies. On February 1, 1920, Roosevelt delivered an address in Brooklyn expansively describing the nation's lack of naval preparedness at the beginning of the war and the steps he had taken to deal with it. In the absence of clear authority, he declared, he had "committed enough illegal acts to put him in jail for 999 years" and evaded impeachment only because he had made the right guesses. He further claimed that Admiral Sims had been sent to London as the American head of the Allied naval effort at his recommendation.[8]

Many of Roosevelt's assertions contained kernels of truth, which he grossly magnified in an honest belief that he had been the only dynamic force in the Navy Department. His enormous confidence and self-regard irked many but seemed perfectly natural to him. His attitude also demonstrated a tendency toward the dramatic that, throughout his life, had a way of breaking free of reality. Daniels was understandably outraged and may have considered asking the president to fire him. Roosevelt, for his part, quickly understood that there was no payoff for abandoning Daniels and dropped whatever impulse he may have had to align himself with Sims, who, after all, near the end of his lengthy letter, had obliquely attacked the North Sea mine barrage as an expensive diversion of valuable resources.[9]

Attacking the Senate investigation in early June, Roosevelt defended civilian control, denounced "holier-than-thou" critics, and declared, "Frankly, what is the most serious trouble with the Navy now, as it has been in the past, is Congress." By then, he had not only repaired relations with Daniels but positioned himself as a strong and effective spokesman for the administration. His charm, physical profile, and articulateness all created more admirers than detractors. By early 1920, he seemed more than ever a man born to govern and a potential candidate for national office.[10]

In May 1919, the NEW YORK SUN—conservative and Republican but edited by Charles A. Dana, an old friend of Franklin's parents—suggested Roosevelt as a possible successor to Wilson. A New York friend, Judge Henry Heyman, probably acting with the assistant secretary's knowledge, had anonymously sent materials promoting his qualifications for the office to numerous metropolitan newspapers. When one recipient publication pointedly noted that Heyman's packet bore a Washington postmark and implied that it had been generated in the Navy Department, Roosevelt asked Heyman to cease.[11]

Roosevelt surely saw the Oval Office as his ultimate goal, but he also understood that 1920 was too soon to run. A vice presidential candidacy, however, had allure, offering national attention, a chance to get acquainted with leading Democrats across the country, and little chance of blame if he performed well in a losing cause. He may for a time have envisioned himself as a running mate for wartime food administrator Herbert Hoover, a political independent who had won nearly universal acclaim for his service. The two men had a remote but politically friendly relationship, facilitated by Hoover's support of TR's Progressive Party candidacy in 1912. "I wish we could make him President," Franklin wrote privately at the beginning of 1920. Shortly afterward, Hoover publicly declared himself a Republican, thereby making it impossible for the Democrats to nominate him.[12]

Through the spring of 1920, Democratic prospects steadily shrank. Prohibition sharply divided the party. The continuing deadlock over the League of Nations demonstrated the administration to be incapable of compromise and accomplishment. President Wilson remained sick, isolated, and nearly invisible to the public. Postwar inflation drove up the cost of living. By the end of June, as the party's convention met in San Francisco, the postwar economic boom was turning into a painful bust.

Roosevelt came to the City by the Bay as the most notable member of the New York delegation. He established headquarters on the battleship *New York*, anchored in the harbor, and entertained various VIPs there. Although his relations with Tammany had become relatively cordial, he ostentatiously demonstrated his independence, leading a successful fight against the organization's attempt to impose a unit rule on the New York delegates. When the convention erupted into a demonstration after the unveiling of a huge portrait of President Wilson, the anti-Wilson Tammanyites who dominated the New York delegation remained glued to their seats. In an altercation newspapers described as a "near fist fight," Roosevelt seized the New York standard and joined the pro-Wilson marchers. When the proceedings reached the nominating stage, however, he seconded Bourke Cockran's oration in favor of Al Smith.[13]

Smith, just finishing his first term as governor of New York, was one of many contenders for the nomination. Wilson, out of touch with political reality, refused to take himself out of contention. By rule of the Democratic Party since 1836, a nomination required a two-thirds majority. William Gibbs McAdoo quickly stalled out. Governor James Cox of Ohio, a popular chief executive in the critical swing state that already had given the Republicans Senator Warren G. Harding as their nominee, emerged as a favorite of bosses and party leaders. The voting continued through July 3 and, after a recess for Independence Day, went on through July 5. Roosevelt, after Smith withdrew, cast votes for McAdoo until he too quit the race. Then he voted for John W. Davis, ambassador to Great Britain and a family friend; Davis's backers in turn mentioned Roosevelt as a probable vice presidential selection. At 1:39 a.m. on July 6, the forty-fourth ballot gave Cox the nomination. The convention recessed with a vote on the vice presidential choice scheduled for early afternoon.[14]

Roosevelt had come to San Francisco with his eye on a race for the US Senate in the fall, but friends and admirers talked him up for the vice presidential nomination. Perhaps sensing the political tide in his home state and by no means certain of full-hearted Tammany support in a Senate contest, he did not call them off. That both regular machine elements and self-described progressives widely deemed him acceptable was a tribute to his carefully crafted persona. Cox's floor manager, Edmund Moore, telephoned his chief in Ohio, suggested Roosevelt, and found the governor amenable if Tammany boss Murphy signed off. Murphy told Moore that he did not like Roosevelt but appreciated the courtesy of being asked for his assent and declared that he would vote for the devil if Cox requested it.

Ohio Judge Timothy Ansberry was delegated to make the nominating speech. It suddenly occurred to him that Roosevelt just might be under the constitutional age requirement of thirty-five. He found his man on the convention floor and recalled their conversation a few days later:

"How old are you?"

"Thirty-eight. Why do you want to know?"

"I'm going to nominate you."

"Do you think I ought to be around when you do?"

"No, I'd leave the hall."[15]

Roosevelt became the party's vice presidential choice by acclamation.

Cox, a strong and capable governor, was a good selection, but Roosevelt was even more popular. "When parties can pick a man like Frank Roosevelt there is a decent future in politics," Walter Lippmann told the nominee. Herbert Hoover declared, "I consider it a contribution to the good of the country that you have been nominated." The *New York Times* called Roosevelt a man who had united "unusual intelligence with sterling character" and who, if called upon to assume the presidency, could do so "without causing the country a tremor of apprehension."[16]

On his trip back east, Roosevelt stopped in Columbus, Ohio, to meet with Governor Cox. They quickly agreed to make the League of Nations the dominant issue in the campaign. Roosevelt, clearly determined to be an activist vice president, also suggested that he should participate in cabinet meetings. Cox, probably correctly smelling a bid to be copresident, brushed the idea off.[17]

On July 16, they met again at the White House to pay their respects to President Wilson. Wilson's spectral appearance and inability to engage in a sustained conversation stunned both men. Cox fought back tears and assured Wilson they would be "a million per cent with [him]." Roosevelt, apparently unaware that Wilson continued to nurse an intense resentment of him, described the event to Eleanor as a "very wonderful experience."[18]

Franklin tendered his resignation as assistant secretary of the navy on August 6. Secretary Daniels presented him with a silver loving cup on behalf of the department employees. A vice president of the master mechanics union described him as "a fellow worker and friend, a man who has endeared himself to every one connected with the great naval establishment." Roosevelt sent a wireless message to all officers, sailors, and civilian employees, expressing his pride in them and their work. He gave Daniels ("My dear Chief") an affectionate handwritten letter that belied the very real conflicts and tensions of their relationship. Daniels would send him an equally fulsome response. In his diary later that day, the secretary wrote of the letter, "[It] made me glad

I had never acted upon my impulse when he seemed to take sides with my critics."[19]

IN THOSE DAYS, CANDIDATES RECEIVED OFFICIAL NOTIFICATION OF PARTY nominations and delivered acceptance speeches at their homes. Roosevelt attended the ceremony for Cox at Dayton the day after he left the Navy Department. On August 9, he accepted the vice presidential nomination on the front porch of his home at Hyde Park and spoke to a crowd of 5,000 people spread out across the large lawn. The event, the *New York Times* declared, "resembled that of an admiring but not overawed community being addressed by a super-valedictorian at commencement exercises in a local school."[20]

The speech, mostly written by Roosevelt himself, laid out the themes of the campaign. Effective and well delivered, it revealed that he had substantially mastered the art of crafting a political appeal, developed a sense of timing, and understood that the moment required more than old-fashioned partisan oratory. The united efforts of Democrats and Republicans, he declared, had won the war, but the Democrats had the broadest vision for a postwar world that required internationalism and "organized progress at home."

In line with the promise he and Cox had made to President Wilson, the speech emphasized the Treaty of Versailles and the League of Nations. America had a choice: to live in hermit-like isolation, armed to the teeth against possible aggression, or to join the international order. At home, progress meant better management in government, "a systematized and intensified development of our resources and a progressive betterment of our citizenship." Cox, the "engineer-statesman," not the bumbling Harding, was the man for the task.

The campaign proceeded with a strenuousness that Cousin Ted would have appreciated. Roosevelt assembled a first-rate team, two members of which would later serve him in the White House. Former navy public relations man Marvin McIntyre traveled with the candidate as a publicity and speech-writing aide. Stephen Early, a tough, shrewd newsman who had covered the navy beat for the Associated Press, acted as advance man, making arrangements with local party leaders, sending back intelligence on themes to stress in speeches, and warning of local rivalries and sensitivities.[21]

Roosevelt left New York on August 10 to undertake a speaking tour that began in Chicago and took him to the West Coast and back, spanning eighteen days, covering twenty states, and averaging seven talks a day. He spent most of September campaigning in New York and New England. A foray into the West and Midwest, followed by a final swing through the northeastern states, consumed much of October. During all this time, he took just three days off, one of them for the funeral of his uncle, Warren Delano III. He made a strong personal impression at every stop.[22]

The Republicans assigned Theodore Roosevelt Jr. to follow FDR through his initial western tour and contest his implicit claim to the TR mantle. Determined to duplicate his father's path all the way to the White House, Ted did so with gusto, telling audiences that the maverick Franklin did not wear the family brand. Thus began a rivalry—relatively good-natured at first, but less so with each passing year.[23]

Franklin's one conspicuous gaffe came at Butte, Montana, on August 18. He defended the League of Nations against the Republican charge that Britain and her semi-independent dominions would have six votes against one for the United States. The Caribbean and Central American nations, which regarded the United States as a guardian, totaled twelve; Franklin asserted they would invariably vote with the United States. Then, referring to the marine presence in Haiti and the Dominican Republic, he went on to say that he had controlled two of them himself. Piling fantasy on top of indiscretion, he continued, "The facts are that I wrote Haiti's Constitution myself, and if I do say it, I think it a pretty good Constitution."[24]

This was not much of an issue, but the Republicans jumped on it. Roosevelt, having let his inner imperialism show, claimed he was misquoted. Harding actually apologized. Later, after stenographic evidence confirmed the story, FDR took refuge in the politician's last resort: categorical outright denial for the remainder of the campaign and his life.[25]

The three months of constant movement and frenetic speech making all came back, time and again, to the League of Nations, which by late 1920 was a fading issue. One wonders if Roosevelt really believed his assertions that membership in the League would bring a world of lasting peace. Republicans depicted it as a threat to American sovereignty and independence. Harding posters carried the slogan "America First." Voters were receptive to the charge that membership would bring more unwelcome foreign entanglements.

The Democrats had nothing else. The economy was deteriorating in the worst possible way. Crashing agricultural commodity prices alienated much of the farm vote; urban consumers still complained about the wartime high cost of living. President Wilson might remain a hero to many Democrats, but much of the nation saw him as sick and ineffective and simply wanted to be rid of him. German Americans, who had mostly been against the war, and Irish Americans, who saw England as a hated oppressor, held special grudges. Ethnic Democratic constituencies in general resented Prohibition.

The Democratic leadership had blocked out western itineraries for Roosevelt in the hope that he would appeal to Republican and independent progressives, an important force in the region's politics. But many western progressives were also anti-League. Roosevelt tried to assure audiences in California that Cox was "the Hiram Johnson of the East." Johnson—their former governor, running mate of Theodore Roosevelt in 1912, and by 1920 one of their senators—was irreconcilably opposed to the League. Charges that the Republicans had amassed a huge and somehow illegitimate campaign fund had no impact. Neither did Roosevelt's persistent efforts to remind the electorate that a senatorial cabal had selected Harding in a smoke-filled room at two o'clock in the morning.[26]

On Tuesday, November 2, Warren Harding and Calvin Coolidge buried the Democratic ticket, polling 61 percent of the vote in, to that date, the most impressive landslide in post–Civil War American political history. Never again a candidate for public office, Cox spent the rest of his life expanding his newspaper business into a major media empire. Roosevelt was a long-run winner. He, at least as much as Cox, was the star of the campaign on the Democratic side. His name had attracted attention. His articulateness, vigor, and good humor had won him friends just about everywhere he campaigned.

In 1936, Steve Early would remember the Roosevelt of 1920 as a "playboy" who let others write his speeches and spent his spare time at card games. Playboys, however, do not spend three exhausting months making six to eight speeches a day, seven days a week. Early's memory is a tribute to how effortless his chief made the grinding tedium of the campaign seem. As never before, Roosevelt absorbed the political geography of the northern and western states, made hundreds of face-to-face contacts, and brought back a card file of names for future use. Only the then Solid Democratic South remained mostly unknown territory for him. In all, he had won a victory in defeat.[27]

On November 3, however, he could do nothing but send a telegram of congratulations to Coolidge. He returned to the New York law partnership he and two associates had begun in 1911. He also accepted a lucrative offer to become a vice president and head of the Manhattan office of the Fidelity and Deposit Company of Maryland, a surety bonding company interested in enlarging its New York business. Its chief executive officer and controlling shareholder, Van Lear Black, also owner of the *Baltimore Sun*, admired Roosevelt and envisioned him as a client-attracting acquisition. No informed observer expected these jobs to monopolize his time. At the end of 1920, he and Eleanor moved back to their New York residence on East Sixty-Fifth Street, both understanding that their ultimate objective was the White House.

CHAPTER 8

PARALYSIS AND PHILANTHROPY

1921–1928

FRANKLIN ROOSEVELT RETURNED TO NEW YORK AT THE BEGINNING OF 1921 solidly established as a coming force in the Democratic Party. He planned to make a little money, wait for the right political opportunity, win election as governor or senator, and then make a dash for the presidency. The design was plausible until tragedy struck that summer. For most politicians of the day, paralysis from the waist down would have been a career-ending event. Roosevelt was a man of means with a supportive family, generous friends, and devoted helpers. He was also a person of Nietzschean will and determination, capable of turning a devastating handicap into an asset.

HE DIVIDED HIS TIME BETWEEN THE FIDELITY AND DEPOSIT (F&D) OFFICE IN lower Manhattan and his law practice. In both enterprises, he probably saw his role primarily as attracting clients. He was successful at "good old F& D"; after all, meeting people and making a sales pitch was not much different from political campaigning. His friend and boss, Van Lear Black, valued his name on the firm's letterhead, admired him greatly, and hoped to become a political backer. F&D paid Roosevelt a generous $25,000 a year, the rough equivalent of at least $500,000 in early-twenty-first-century dollars.

His enthusiasm did not extend to his law office, in which he had been inactive since before going to Washington. To the distress of his partners, Langdon Marvin and Grenville Emmett, he brought in little business and spent most of his time there engaged in an extensive correspondence with Democratic Party contacts.[1]

Roosevelt also devoted a lot of time to uncompensated charitable and public service activities, including the Harvard Board of Overseers, the Boy Scouts, the National Civic Federation, the Lighthouse for the Blind, the Manhattan Navy Club, the New York State Forestry Association, and the Netherlands-America Foundation. He was especially prominent in the Woodrow Wilson Foundation, a nonprofit organization established to honor the legacy of the former president and a nearly mandatory affiliation for Democratic politicians with national aspirations. All these activities involved business meetings, rallies, fund-raisers, and dinners.[2]

His ventures and political aspirations required a full-time staff. As Roosevelt's administrative assistant at F&D, Louis Howe aided in his boss's rainmaking endeavors while continuing as an indefatigable political operative. Unable to afford suitable accommodations in Manhattan, Howe settled his wife and son in Poughkeepsie, where his daughter was a student at Vassar. Howe himself became a member of the Roosevelt household, rendering his relationship with his family a matter of weekend visits—when possible.[3]

Roosevelt also acquired a personal secretary, Marguerite LeHand. The type that people of the time described as a "nice-looking, perky girl," LeHand came from a modest Boston-area family. Twenty-two years old in 1920, she had landed a job on Roosevelt's vice presidential campaign staff. Capable, discreet, and skilled beyond her years in human relations, she quickly established herself as indispensable. Promised that she would not work as a legal aide, she accepted Roosevelt's offer to stay on with him after the election. Soon she was also an honorary member of the family. Finding it difficult to say "Miss LeHand," the younger Roosevelt boys inadvertently nicknamed her "Missy."

Clever, pleasant, and flirtatious, Missy became unconditionally devoted to Roosevelt. He would increasingly depend on her emotionally as on no other woman. Eleanor surely realized the developing closeness but would never feel the resentment she had felt for Lucy Mercer—perhaps because Missy came from a different social class, perhaps because Franklin never complained about Eleanor's own developing and intense relationships.[4]

ROOSEVELT'S SCHEDULE WAS STRENUOUS, BUT HE ENJOYED HIS VARIOUS activities and doubtless valued the attention they garnered. On July 10, 1921, he joined Eleanor and the children at Campobello, hoping for a restful two months there. Instead he found himself called back to Washington to prepare a response to Republican charges that he was responsible for the Newport homosexual "morals scandal."[5]

He returned to New York and stayed there several days to catch up with correspondence and other business. On July 28, acting in his capacity as president of the Boy Scout Foundation of Greater New York, he and some fifty other officials steamed up the Hudson to Bear Mountain to visit summer Scout encampments. He clearly found the day long and satisfying, joking with his fellow dignitaries, relishing his role as benefactor to the mostly earnest boys he met, giving short speeches, and enjoying a campfire dinner. Someone took a photo of him and two fellow Scout officials marching in front of an American flag. Despite the heat, he wore a dark jacket and tie. Sporting a beribboned badge and taller than his comrades, he looked every inch the dashing, important man he was.[6]

It would be the last photograph of him walking unassisted.

HE RETURNED TO CAMPOBELLO ON AUGUST 7 ABOARD VAN LEAR BLACK's imposing yacht, which he personally steered through the Bay of Fundy's difficult waters. For the next three days, he vacationed in his customary mode of nonstop activity. On August 10, he, Eleanor, James, and Elliott got into his small craft, *Vireo*, to sail around the bay. They found a fire on a nearby island and spent an exhausting hour or so beating it out with evergreen boughs. Then, back on Campobello, he and the children got into swimwear, ran two miles across the island, and took a dip in a large pond, followed by a plunge into the icy bay. After that, he raced the boys back to the cottage. By dinnertime, he was extraordinarily tired and shivering. Unable to eat a decent meal, he went to bed early.[7]

The next morning, he was running a 102-degree fever; his left leg gave way under him. The island's only doctor, a rural general practitioner, examined him and concluded that he had a bad cold. Roosevelt's right leg quickly also became useless. An aged eminent physician brought up from his vacation in Maine guessed that a blood clot in the spinal area had temporarily blocked the nerves to Roosevelt's lower limbs. He prescribed torturous daily massages of the patient's tender legs. The paralysis spread. For a time, Roosevelt's hands were partially immobilized. His bladder and bowel stopped functioning and had to be cleared with catheters and enemas. He found breathing difficult. His fever continued at dangerously high levels. Eleanor and Louis Howe, whose family had been visiting, gave him round-the-clock care that may have saved his life.

Howe, increasingly dubious of the physician's advice, wrote a long letter describing Franklin's symptoms to Sara Roosevelt's younger brother, Frederic A. Delano, an esteemed business executive and public servant who had taken a close interest in his nephew's career. Delano quickly arranged a visit from Dr. Robert W. Lovett, a leading Boston physician and an authority on paralytic diseases. Lovett visited Campobello on August 25 and quickly diagnosed polio. He ordered a stop to the massages at once—they were doing no good and might actually damage muscles. A quick first examination suggested that the lasting damage would be minor.

Roosevelt spent three more weeks at Campobello as an utter invalid in constant pain. Word got out that he had fallen ill. Howe developed a story line that attributed his indisposition to bathing in the cold waters surrounding the island, always ending with a reassuring refrain: the patient was recovering rapidly. Finally, on September 13, Franklin was put on a boat to Eastport, Maine, and there loaded into a private railroad car for New York. Reporters, kept at a distance, looked through the window and saw him propped up in a sleeping berth, appearing relaxed with a lighted cigarette at the end of a long holder, his Scottish terrier at his side. In fact, every jostle and bump between Campobello and New York was acutely painful.

The train arrived in New York early on the afternoon of September 15. Immediately transferred to an ambulance and taken to Presbyterian Hospital, Roosevelt came under the care of Dr. George Draper, a noted physician, a protégé of Lovett, and an old Grotonian acquainted with the patient since their school days. It was no longer possible to conceal the true character of Roosevelt's illness, which, given his prominence, became a front-page news story. Draper, based on Lovett's diagnosis, told the press, "You can say definitely that he will not be crippled." After an examination, however, Draper could not promise that Roosevelt, whose back muscles were still weak and atrophied, would even be able to sit upright in a chair.[8]

Some years later, Roosevelt told Frances Perkins that he had experienced the darkest despair during the first few days of his illness and felt that God had deserted him. Then, knowing that he would live, he came to feel he had been spared for some purpose. Taking refuge in extreme denial, he convinced himself that intensive physical therapy would allow him to walk unassisted. Draper, in the mode of most physicians of the day, allowed him to be optimistic. It was important to maintain the patient's spirits and make what progress one could: "He has such courage, such ambition, and yet at the same time such an extraordinarily sensitive emotional mechanism," Draper wrote to Lovett, "that it will take all the skill which we can muster to lead him successfully to a recognition of what he really faces without crushing him."[9]

Roosevelt spent six weeks at Presbyterian in quasi-isolation; most visitors outside his immediate family were turned away. His wife and children and the few close friends admitted to his room all remembered his gaiety and optimism. Most left feeling more cheerful than when they had arrived. The fever that had wracked his body for a month disappeared for good, and exercise began to reconstitute his lower back and hip muscles. He became able to pull himself up to a sitting position by a strap that hung down over his bed. On October 28, he left the hospital for the family house on Sixty-Fifth Street.

JIMMY, IN HIS SECOND YEAR AT GROTON, RETURNED HOME FOR CHRISTMAS vacation, apprehensive about meeting a sick father he had not seen since September. He found him propped up in a bed over which hung "trapezes and rings"; Franklin had already strengthened his upper body considerably with them. "Come here, old man!" his parent commanded. As soon as the boy was within reach, Roosevelt administered a bear hug, slapped him on the back, and led him into a conversation about dear old Groton and the doings of its immortal headmaster. Jimmy quickly learned that his father was still immobile below the waist but able to wrestle and roughhouse with the younger children. Franklin made it easy for them to believe they were playing a happy game.[10]

Still, the overcrowded household was not happy. The large family had already filled the home's available space to the limit. Louis Howe, who tended to Franklin's correspondence and other duties at F&D, had taken over Anna's spacious third-floor bedroom and private bath. (Franklin's day nurse used Howe's room as a sitting area while Howe was at the office.) Anna and Elliott had bedrooms on the fourth floor. The two younger boys and their round-the-clock nurse used connected fourth-floor rooms in Sara's house next door. As for Eleanor: "I slept on a bed in one of the little boys' rooms. I dressed in my husband's bathroom. In the daytime I was too busy to need a room."[11]

Anna, who had turned fifteen in May, was at a difficult time of life for any girl. The boys were boisterous, resistant to structured learning, and cared for by a series of severe nurses straight out of Grimm's fairy tales. Sara, who wanted to stay close to her son and manage his future, was often on the scene. She lobbied single-mindedly for Franklin to abandon his political career, remove to Hyde Park, and live the life of a country squire. Wanting to get rid of Howe, she relentlessly fed Anna's resentment at being evicted from her former quarters.

Roosevelt himself must have had doubts. His recovery was slow and erratic. In January 1922, his hamstring muscles began to contract, causing his legs to double up. They had to be put in casts and straightened with wedges over several excruciating weeks. In the end, however, denial and determination prevailed. That summer Franklin and his family went up to Hyde Park, not to stay but to redouble his efforts at recovery. His nurse also came along, as did the first in a series of sturdy valets on whom he would rely from that point forward to assist him in all the routine tasks of life. He exercised intensively. Using rings hung over his bed and parallel bars set up on the lawn, he developed the arms and upper body of an athlete. A physical therapist came up from New York three times a week to supervise routines for his hips and legs; they may have had some effect in restoring the hips, but the legs remained numb and atrophied.

By now, he was wearing steel braces that belted on at the waist, locked at the knees, and fully encased his legs. They weighed fourteen pounds. Slowly he mastered the use of crutches. The task required strength, stamina, and a sure sense of balance. That summer and through the fall, he worked hard, usually in vain, to make it unassisted from the house down the quarter-mile driveway to the Albany Post Road. On perhaps the only occasion that he managed the distance, he was so worn down that he was unable to exercise for four days.

Dr. Lovett, who continued to monitor his progress, had long since lost his early optimism; he now believed that his patient would never regain the use of his legs. Roosevelt, maintaining the stubborn denial that allowed him to retain a sense of purpose and destiny, was convinced that exercise could rebuild his withered limbs and make them functional again. The buoyancy of water, the warmer the better, allowed movement. Two or three times a week, he took advantage of the heated "swimming tank" on the Rhinebeck estate of his wealthy cousin and admirer Vincent Astor. The illusion that he was actually using his legs strengthened his determination and kept alive the hope that some day he might again walk unassisted. Recalling his last enervating swim in the Bay of Fundy, he told his chauffeur, "Water got me into this fix, water will get me out again!"[12]

Roosevelt stayed at Hyde Park well into the fall. On October 22, 1922, he was driven down to New York on his first trip back to F&D since he had left for Campobello fifteen months earlier. His car stopped right at the door. With his driver's assistance, he easily negotiated the one step up to the front door of the building, but halfway to the elevator, one of his crutches slipped on the slick marble floor, and he fell backward. On the floor, surrounded by a curious and concerned crowd, he quickly erased whatever anger or disappointment might have flitted across his face, smiled, joked, and asked a couple of solid-looking younger men to assist the chauffeur in getting him up. He proceeded to his office, spent the afternoon there, went back to Hyde Park, and did not return for two months.

The Roosevelts moved back into their New York house in early December. Franklin hoped to spend at least two days a week at the office. Reality was dispiriting; bad weather made it nearly impossible for him to go out. He felt cold temperatures more keenly than in the past and must have found exercise more difficult. The household remained crowded and hectic. Deciding to get away to warmer climes, he traveled to Florida, rented a houseboat, the *Weona II*, and for three weeks cruised around the tip of the peninsula with old friends indulgent of his fun-loving streak. Eleanor spent only a few days with him.[13]

Appointing himself "admiral," he kept a log that documented a carefree vacation of skimpy dress, skinny-dipping, fresh-caught fish dinners, and abundant bootleg booze. He produced a versification, entitled "Community Life," for the boat's log. One stanza captured the tone of the journey:

When they first come on board they think it's so nice—
With staterooms and bathtubs and comforts sans price—
Till they suddenly realize that every partition
Sounds intimate echoes of each guest's condition
Of mind and of body—For whispers of details
The wall in its wisdom with great gusto retails.

He returned to New York at the end of March, deeply tanned, feeling fit and happy, and sporting long, well-developed sideburns that his mother found eerily similar to his father's.[14]

For the next three years, late-winter excursions to Florida and aimless cruises on a happy houseboat were an annual event. Roosevelt and a good friend, John Lawrence, a semi-invalid with weak legs, jointly purchased a beat-up Florida-based houseboat and renamed it the *Larooco* (Lawrence, Roosevelt & Co.). Its temperamental engines, peeling paint, and leaky deck did little to discourage the low-level bacchanal atmosphere in which he gloried.[15]

On each of these voyages, which lasted from two to three months, Roosevelt brought along Missy LeHand. Far more than a scheduler of appointments, taker of dictation, and handler of his personal finances, she had become his closest female companion. Eleanor cared little for Franklin's diversions and found his cocktail hours especially off-putting. Missy was always at his side, adding gaiety to every social occasion and increasingly becoming a frank, valued confidential adviser on political matters. Roosevelt needed her. His efforts at madcap amusement were reactions to bouts of dark depression. Years later, Missy told Frances Perkins that on some days he stayed in bed until nearly noon before he managed to pull together the buoyant manner to which his guests had become accustomed.[16]

Eleanor accepted Franklin's relationship with Missy without complaint, possibly because she thought they did not have a sexual relationship. On the surface, her attitude toward her husband's secretary would always be one of unreserved warmth. Sara displayed the same attitude.

If the *Larooco* provided a lot of pleasure, it was not without its frustrations. Maintenance was expensive, and the waters off Florida provided minimal opportunities for the exercise Roosevelt needed in his quest for further recovery. By the spring of 1925, he wanted to get rid of the boat. When he and Lawrence could find no takers, he used it again in 1926. That fall, a major hurricane ravaged South Florida. *Larooco* was swept far inland and deposited in a pine forest. After a vain attempt to market it as a hunting lodge, the owners sold it for scrap. By then, Roosevelt had turned his attention for recovery and psychic fulfillment elsewhere.

NOTED PHILANTHROPIST AND BANKER GEORGE FOSTER PEABODY INTERESTED Franklin in a thermal pool at Bullochville, Georgia, eighty miles south of Atlanta. A native Georgian who affected a large mustache and a goatee, Peabody was an enormously successful businessman and financier who generously supported the development of the post-Reconstruction South and promoted better race relations. He had acquired a run-down Victorian-era resort hotel, the Meriwether Inn, which a Georgia state historian has described as "a large, rambling building with gingerbread on its roofline, curlicues in its woodwork to shame an old-fashioned penman, gables galore and contours unclassifiable in architecture." Fourteen freestanding cottages, also in need of rehabilitation, flanked the inn. A hot thermal spring fed its swimming pools. Peabody had initially hoped to redevelop the battered old resort into a health spa, but by 1924 he was mostly interested in selling it to someone who might preserve it.[17]

Franklin and Eleanor arrived for a visit on the evening of October 3, 1924. In hopes of luring more visitors, Bullochville was about to change its name to Warm Springs, but there was little to attract outsiders. The town was tiny (population 470) and shabby. The surrounding countryside reflected the general poverty of rural pine country Georgia. Roosevelt was long acquainted with the straitened circumstances of Hudson Valley farmers; some of his own tenants lived in substandard housing. What he found in Georgia was worse. On their first morning there, he and Eleanor awoke to sunlight shining in through cracks in the walls of their cottage. They quickly learned that, as Eleanor later put it, "for many, many people life in the South was hard and poor and ugly."[18]

Eleanor, who would never much care for Warm Springs, spent only a day there before heading back to New York and John W. Davis's futile Democratic presidential bid against Calvin Coolidge. In a dramatic role reversal, she devoted more time to the campaign than her husband. Franklin tarried with Missy for more than three weeks. The inn was closed for the season, and he had the pool all to himself. The eighty-eight degree water made long stretches of invigorating exercise possible two or three times a day. The locals, seeing him as a potential patron who could bring money and business to the community, went out of their way to be hospitable. Democrats from around the state extended speaking invitations.

A reporter from the *Atlanta Journal* came down to interview him and penned a widely disseminated article titled "Franklin D. Roosevelt Will Swim to Health." A photo pictured Roosevelt in a swimsuit at poolside, displaying matchstick legs without a hint of self-consciousness. The article quoted him as saying he was contemplating a complete cure and observed that he had "made a great hit with the people of Warm Springs." Writing to his mother, Roosevelt said, "I feel that a great 'cure' for infantile paralysis and kindred diseases could well be established here."[19]

Returning to Warm Springs at the beginning of April 1925, he found that stories about his enthusiasm for the thermal waters had attracted numerous "polios" (as victims of the disease preferred to be called) from around the country. Some left after learning that the inn had no physicians, therapists, or treatment plan. Others insisted on staying. Roosevelt had a nearby doctor give them a cursory examination to ensure they were healthy enough for vigorous exercise. Then he improvised: "I undertook to be doctor and physiotherapist, all rolled into one. . . . I taught them all at least to play around in the water." Soon he was glorying in his role as "Old Doctor Roosevelt," examining the muscles of his new charges, exercising with them, and taking them on picnics. He moved easily between leadership and comradeship, always maintaining a gay and happy facade. Involving himself in the efforts to restore the resort, he became, he wrote to a friend, "consulting architect and landscape engineer . . . giving free advice on the moving of buildings, the building of roads, setting out of trees and remodeling the hotel."[20]

Still, he hesitated to invest financially, probably because neither his wife nor his mother thought his pocket could sustain the burden of his transformational vision. He spent more than three months, from late August through early December 1925, in Marion, Massachusetts, under the care of Dr. William McDonald, a neurologist who subjected his patients to rigorous exercise and advised them to work without their braces as much as possible. In early December, wearing a brace on only one leg and using crutches, he managed to "walk" about a block. He spent the summer of 1926 under McDonald's care, but he also plunged ahead with his plans for Warm Springs.

Like his father, Franklin Roosevelt was willing to take financial gambles—so long as the stakes were relatively small and the risks carefully contained. During the 1920s, he got involved in a number of speculative business ventures, the most daring being an investment company formed to trade against fluctuations in the German mark. As Eleanor recalled it, he lost money in almost every such enterprise, but never very much. Now he was preparing to bet most of his modest fortune on Warm Springs. His wife made a final argument with him, expressing her worry that the project might make it impossible to educate the children. He responded, no doubt accurately, "Ma will always see the children through."[21]

After his final cruise on the *Larooco*, Roosevelt returned to Warm Springs and closed the purchase. The transfer, concluded on April 29, 1926, for $195,000, conveyed to him the resort grounds, the Meriwether Inn, the guest cottages, the springs, and approximately 1,200 adjoining acres. Roosevelt gave Peabody a mortgage with no fixed payment schedule to cover the purchase price. It alone obligated about two-thirds of Roosevelt's net worth. Development of the property would cost tens of thousands more. The deed done, Eleanor gamely told him, "I'm old and rather overwhelmed by what there is to do in one place and it wearies me to think of even undertaking to make new ties. Don't be discouraged by me; I have great confidence in your extraordinary interest and enthusiasm. It is just that I couldn't do it."[22]

In January 1927, Roosevelt established the nonprofit Georgia Warm Springs Foundation, to which he assigned the property. The foundation was to manage it, pay off the mortgage, raise money for its operations, and return Roosevelt's personal investment to him. It gave him a note for the full amount of the mortgage, by then more than $201,000, and made periodic payments on it for the rest of his life. He served as the foundation's president and de facto chief fundraiser. His new law partner, Basil O'Connor, became its primary legal counsel and secretary-treasurer with day-to-day administrative duties. Peabody, a loyal political supporter as well as a philanthropist willing to back a good cause, seems never to have pressed for the money owed him.

Roosevelt had initially hoped to combine a luxury resort with a polio treatment center. It soon became clear, however, that affluent guests who wanted a relaxing vacation found the sight of the crippled depressing; some even worried about contracting polio themselves. The Warm Springs complex became solely a hydrotherapy facility for polios. Its new owner, moreover, was determined that it should be made available, regardless of ability to pay, to all comers. Roosevelt encouraged service or fraternal organizations to underwrite the costs of indigent clients. From time to time, he personally covered their expenses.[23] Rosy Roosevelt died in May 1927, leaving Franklin a welcome financial cushion with a bequest of $100,000.[24]

Warm Springs became a remarkably successful philanthropic enterprise. The improvisational, chaotic atmosphere over which Old Doctor Roosevelt had presided in the spring of 1925 gave way to a thoroughly professional routine staffed by skilled physiotherapists and lubricated by Rooseveltian joviality. During its first year of operation, the foundation treated eighty polios. Only a few would be able to throw their crutches away after extended stays there, but the waters allowed for concentrated exercises to restore muscles not rendered totally useless. The staff trained patients to cope with their handicap. Most left better able to function in society and more confident of their powers.[25]

Roosevelt's return to politics in 1928 would greatly increase his visibility and give him fund-raising leverage with constituents who hoped to gain favor or simply to bask in his goodwill. The clientele, staff, and facilities grew rapidly. In 1928, one large pool was enclosed in glass for year-round use, courtesy of a $25,000 gift from Edsel Ford. Even after the Great Depression set in, Roosevelt managed to raise approximately $1.25 million. The ramshackle inn was demolished after new purpose-designed buildings had been erected. In 1934, 267 individuals received therapy. By then, the White House had given the Old Doc a unique platform for his dearest cause. Money flowed in freely.

The foundation, appropriately recognizing Roosevelt as its greatest asset, insured his life for $500,000 for its own protection and to compensate his survivors for any unreimbursed investment he had made in it. It managed the polio center and expanded its work to treatments other than hydrotherapy. During his years as governor of New York, Roosevelt forgave $18,500 of the principal. As president, he would give the foundation a cottage his mother had built there (valued at $3,000) and just over $9,500 in royalties from his published personal papers. At his death, the foundation still owed him $93,341.68 in principal and $44,621.73 in interest, all of it covered by the insurance on his life.[26]

In 1938, Roosevelt would establish the National Foundation for Infantile Paralysis—the March of Dimes—to fund the increasingly large and complex operations of Warm Springs and also to undertake the mission of finding a cure for what remained a dreaded disease that annually blighted the lives of tens of thousands of children. The payoff, the eventual eradication of polio in America, would come a little more than a decade after his death. If Franklin Roosevelt had done nothing more with his life, this alone would have established him as a historical figure.

IT IS FAR EASIER TO TRACE THE COURSE OF ROOSEVELT'S REACTION TO POLIO than to gauge its impact on his life. The surface manifestations were clear enough to those close to him. The avid golfer would never walk the links again. The fine young horseman was now very occasionally put up on a placid mount for a publicity photo, but his paralyzed legs were incapable of controlling a steed at a normal canter.

Only his intimate companions knew that he spent much of his time in a wheelchair, that he had to be lifted out of it into a bed or a chair, carried up steps or around other obstacles, and assisted in dressing or undressing, that he was in fact utterly dependent on the round-the-clock assistance of his valets. After years of effort, he managed to create the illusion of walking over short distances. Actually, he was swinging rigidly braced legs with his hip muscles, grasping a sturdy companion's right arm with his left hand, and steadying his right leg with a cane. As he increasingly regained a sense of balance, he made it look relatively easy.

In the beginning, concealment of his true condition from the larger world was a product of the widely perceived unseemliness of displaying a handicap in public, firmly reinforced by his deep denial that the condition was permanent. By the beginning of the 1930s, denial had become deception. As he prepared to run for president during his second term as governor of New York, his office would baldly assert that he did not use a wheelchair and claim that horseback riding was a regular recreation for him.

Polio produced far more than denial. Years later Eleanor thought that the long, hard struggle, especially the need to commit to a course of treatment and stay with it over the long haul, had given her husband deep reserves of self-control and patience. He had developed, she said, an understanding that "once you make a decision you must not worry about it."[27]

Polio increased the range of Roosevelt's experiences and the depth of his emotions; it may well have transformed his own sense of class identity by bringing him into contact with a wide range of fellow sufferers. Earlier in his life, he had caught only fleeting glimpses of how most Americans lived. At Warm Springs, he found himself sharing a common physical disability with ordinary people who had no experience of privilege and little money. He made himself their benefactor and leader, and he seems to have felt vividly that they all shared a common experience and a common humanity. He genuinely enjoyed splashing in the pool with them and gloried in providing whatever amateur therapy he could. Wheeled to the edge of the pool, commanding the attention of his charges, he would ask at the top of his lungs, "Have you been good boys and girls while Papa was away?" Most of all, he enjoyed his role as chief turkey carver at the Warm Springs Thanksgiving dinner, which he missed only twice between 1927 and 1939.

Warm Springs also provided close contact with the deep poverty and backwardness of the rural South. He first visited the town only sixty years after Sherman's march through Georgia and less than fifty years after the end of Reconstruction. Sharecropping, hardscrabble farming, a one-crop economy based on the chronic overproduction of cotton, industrial underdevelopment, dirt roads, lack of electricity—all characterized a rural world at least half a century behind that of the Northeast.

Roosevelt frequently drove himself through the countryside in a modified Ford with hand controls that operated accelerator, clutch, and brake. Talking with local farmers and townspeople along the way, he got a keen sense of how hard their lives were. Years later he recalled discovering the limitations of the rural education systems when a young man he took to be eighteen or nineteen invited him to be the graduation speaker at a nearby high school. Asked if he was president of the senior class, the visitor replied, "No, I am the principal of the school." He had completed only his freshman year at the University of Georgia and was being paid $300 a year.[28]

In addition to the Meriwether Inn property, Roosevelt purchased 1,700 acres of his own, hired local help to farm it, and prohibited the cultivation of cotton. He took a local country squire's interest in the community and its people. In 1932 he built a new cottage to the south of the polio center on a slope that afforded a beautiful view of the countryside. A modest bungalow with a tiny kitchen, three small bedrooms, and a living-dining area with a fine stone fireplace, it would later become famous as the "little White House."

By 1928, Franklin Roosevelt had established himself as a philanthropist of national reputation, and he remained a prominent Democratic Party leader. He was also a person of importance in Georgia, a benefactor of the Warm Springs area, and an honorary southerner. Without ever rejecting his attachment to the Hudson Valley, he now gloried in a second identity. Warm Springs had brought him great personal satisfaction and established an important base for his future political career.

CHAPTER 9

THE YOUNG PRINCE RETURNS

1922–1928

AT THE 1924 DEMOCRATIC NATIONAL CONVENTION, FRANKLIN D. ROOSEVELT spoke not only to the delegates but also to a huge radio audience. Suddenly, the felled young prince of the Democratic Party was back, sounding strong and fit. He also was in the company of a wife who was making herself an independent force in American politics. The destinies of the man and his party were converging.

BEFORE POLIO STRUCK, ROOSEVELT HAD ESTABLISHED A GAME PLAN OF calculated public prominence by way of civic activities and policy pronouncements, cultivation of state and local party leaders across the country, an eventual successful run for governor of New York, and finally a campaign for the White House. His courage and guile made the disease that had crippled him seem insignificant. Almost from the day he came home from the hospital, he created an illusion of constant and varied activity to convey the impression that he remained busy and concerned with the public good. He was especially visible in the New York Boy Scouts organization and the Woodrow Wilson Foundation and in fund-raising for St. John the Divine Cathedral.[1]

In 1923, he accepted, without pay, the presidency of the American Construction Council, a trade association for which he functioned as external spokesman and internal mediator but not day-to-day manager. Like Secretary of Commerce Herbert Hoover, he became a vocal advocate of voluntary, long-range business planning. The poorly funded organization achieved little authority over the fragmented construction industry, but it left Roosevelt with a concept of government-fostered industrial self-regulation that would prove attractive in the crisis days of his early presidency.[2]

He was about as obvious an heir-apparent for a Democratic presidential nomination as anyone else. The party's 1920 nominee, James Cox, had withdrawn from politics. Woodrow Wilson's secretary of the Treasury and son-in-law, William Gibbs McAdoo, moved from New York to California, aligning himself with the southern and western wings of the party. New York's Al Smith was the major northeastern urban Democrat.

Roosevelt surely understood that he had outshone Cox in 1920 and transcended the regional appeals of McAdoo and Smith. Many boosters already saw him as the party's ultimate hope. He probably also realized that with the economy making a strong recovery from the postwar recession, the Democrats were unlikely to prevail in the 1924 presidential election. His task was to bide his time, appear to overcome polio, and promote himself as the party's hope.

The Democratic Party, from its inception in the 1790s, had been a tenuous coalition of southern agrarian forces allied with northern big-city machines. From 1860 through 1920, it had won only four of sixteen presidential elections, two with Grover Cleveland and two with Woodrow Wilson. During the 1920s, its regional split was especially intense. Southern and western Democrats were mostly old-stock, Anglo-Saxon, Protestant, pro-Prohibition, anti-immigrant, and tolerant of a strong and revived Ku Klux Klan. The northeastern faction was predominantly urban, dominated by bosses who drew their support from newer immigrant groups, heavily Catholic and Jewish, vehemently anti-Prohibition, and hostile to the Klan. The regional division created a political minefield for aspirants to national leadership.

Polio gave Roosevelt an excuse to avoid a premature run for office while involving himself deeply in party affairs. Hardly home from the hospital at the beginning of November 1921, he had written to the newly elected chairman of the Democratic National Committee (DNC), Tennessee congressman Cordell Hull. The letter extravagantly (although not necessarily insincerely) praised the DNC for selecting a leader with Hull's "soundness of judgment and ability to get results," asserted the need to reorganize the committee into a more effective political force, advocated a "yearly get-together conference" (at which Roosevelt would doubtless figure prominently), and offered his services. It was the work of a man not simply willing, but expecting, to lead his party out of the wilderness.[3]

In New York politics, Roosevelt possessed a special status as an upstate Protestant Democrat who had made a strong reputation in Washington, run on a national ticket, and established tolerable relations with Tammany while keeping the machine at arm's length. His old acquaintance from the legislature, Al Smith, was the state's leading Democrat. Elected governor in 1918, Smith had served with distinction, only to be swept under in the Republican landslide of 1920. Roosevelt and numerous other party leaders wanted him to make another run in 1922. Smith, heading a trucking company and making more money than ever before in his life, was genuinely reluctant, but the most likely alternative was a bitter enemy, the wealthy and demagogic publisher William Randolph Hearst.

Tacitly admitting that no other New York Democrat possessed Roosevelt's appeal and visibility, Smith asked him for a public letter urging another gubernatorial candidacy. Upon receiving it, he responded with a "Dear Frank" missive announcing his availability. Sara congratulated her son for taking an action that "will save us from Hearst." She was hardly the only Democrat to give him exaggerated credit. Nominated that fall, Smith went on to a resounding victory in November.[4]

Unable to campaign, Roosevelt was a bystander; still, he had given Smith a real boost. It was easy to believe at the time that the two men were partners who strongly admired each other. In fact, they were simply allies of convenience. Smith had never much liked Roosevelt from their first meeting in Albany and never quite got past the idea that Roosevelt was a dilettante, but he understood that a Roosevelt endorsement mattered upstate.

Roosevelt conversely needed Smith as a vital link to Tammany in a relationship that remained uneasy even after the sudden death of Boss Charles Murphy in March 1924. Respecting Smith's accomplishments as governor and appreciating his political skills in the context of New York politics, he also surely realized that Smith was a hard sell nationally. He unquestionably knew that Smith was the one New York Democrat standing between him and a presidential nomination.

Thus the two began a wary pas de deux that would last for a decade.

Smith, back in Albany and emerging as a possibility for the 1924 Democratic nomination, asked Roosevelt to serve as his campaign manager. Roosevelt accepted with alacrity. After the death of Bourke Cockran, a grand old orator who had placed Smith's name in nomination on other occasions, Smith asked Roosevelt to perform the task at the national convention. Once again, he received hearty agreement. Working honestly for Smith, Roosevelt displayed himself to party notables around the country as an attractive personality back in the fight.

Ultimately a drama that played out at Madison Square Garden for two weeks in late June and early July told the nation as a whole of Roosevelt's return. The Democratic convention of 1924 became an epic battle between the Smith and McAdoo wings of the party. Tempers flared inside the sweltering arena as the delegates fought over the platform. A plank that refrained from condemning the Klan by name carried by a single vote out of more than 1,000 cast. McAdoo led in the balloting but could not come close to the two-thirds majority he needed. Smith trailed hopelessly but was determined to deny McAdoo a victory. Finally both men withdrew, and on the 103rd ballot, the nomination went to John W. Davis, the eminent attorney and former ambassador to Great Britain who had been an outside possibility in 1920. Davis was especially esteemed by Sara and liked by Franklin, but realists understood he had no chance of victory in November. Franklin wished him well but surely knew that defeat was likely, leaving him with a clearer path to the presidency.

The 1924 national party conventions were the first broadcast to much of the nation by radio. Twenty-one stations from Boston in the North to Atlanta in the South and Kansas City in the West, many with powerful transmitters, carried the proceedings. The nation's first great national radio announcer, Graham McNamee, described the event to audiences ranging from families in their living rooms to crowds listening to loudspeakers at storefronts or in public parks. Radio could be an enormous asset for personalities who possessed good voices and shrewd instincts about its use.[5]

Roosevelt's role at the convention is mostly remembered for his speech nominating Smith, but every day, before and after his time on the podium, he made the walk to his seat in the New York delegation from which he operated as Smith's floor manager. He drew on his son Jimmy, tall and strong at age sixteen, to act as his aide and human prop. For two weeks, he got out of his car and into a wheelchair; he was then pushed to the arena floor entrance closest to his seat and helped to a standing position, legs locked, crutch under his right shoulder, left hand gripping Jimmy's arm. Slowly, wearing smiles that belied the difficulty of the task, they made their way toward the New York standard.

At first, the spectators in the galleries watched silently from above. After a few days, they began to applaud and cheer. Announcer McNamee, prompted by the noise, described the scene to his national audience. Most listeners surely believed they were hearing an account of a determined and courageous man considerably farther along in recovery from polio than he actually was.

Roosevelt made the nominating speech for Smith at noon on June 26, proceeding by wheelchair with Jimmy from the floor to the rear of the platform, then tensely waiting to be introduced. A minute or two in advance, he was helped to his feet and assumed his customary stance, crutch on his right side, son on his left. (Jimmy recalled, "His fingers dug into my arm like pincers.") He asked one of the dignitaries to test the strength of the rostrum and got assurance he could safely lean on it. Then, when the time came, he took a second crutch from Jimmy and deliberately walked the fifteen feet to his speaking position. Thirty-five years later, Jimmy vividly recalled the scene: "As he slowly swung himself forward he saluted the crowd—since he could not lift his arms—with his big smile. Then, as he reached the rostrum, came the tremendous, roaring ovation. At that moment I was so damned proud of him that it was with difficulty that I kept myself from bursting into tears."[6]

Roosevelt "placed both hands on the speaker's desk and stood with head erect, a vigorous and healthful figure, except for his lameness," wrote *New York Times* reporter Elmer Davis. He spoke for thirty-four minutes, making the expected attacks on the Republicans as the party of corruption and special interests, presenting the Democrats as the party of the people, and extolling Smith as a Lincoln-like leader of the common folk. Roosevelt's strong, assured voice and patrician accent, which denoted authority in the America of his day, distinguished the address from routine convention oratory. Its partisanship was strong but seemed neither angry nor extreme; it focused more on Smith's virtues than on the defects of his prospective Republican opponent. Oddly, the line everyone remembered was one that Roosevelt had wanted to delete. It came six paragraphs before the conclusion: "He is the Happy Warrior of the political battlefield."[7]

The address reestablished Roosevelt as a major presence within the Democratic Party. He remained on the platform while Smith's supporters staged a riotous demonstration, then, after an hour and a quarter, assisted the chair, Senator Thomas J. Walsh of Montana, in quelling it. According to Elmer Davis, a careful and much esteemed journalist, Roosevelt was able to stop that and one other outburst simply by raising a hand high in the air. His oratory buoyed the Smith forces without offending the McAdoo supporters. Many delegates were moved by his appearance and determination to overcome his handicap. Kansas City's tough, unsentimental boss, Tom Pendergast, told a friend, "Had Mr. Roosevelt . . . been physically able to have withstood the campaign, he would have been named by acclamation. . . . He has the most magnetic personality of any individual I have ever met." The *Times* called him the most popular man at the convention. The *New York World*, the nation's most important Democratic newspaper, said he was "the real hero" of the gathering, commended the "fine courage that flashes in his smile," and pronounced him "the one leader commanding the respect and admiration of delegates from all sections of the land."[8]

John W. Davis, the first choice of almost no one, the candidate of a party in disarray, went through the motions of a campaign in the fall against President Calvin Coolidge and Senator Robert La Follette Sr., the leader of a Progressive Party insurgency. Coolidge won handily. Davis got only 28 percent of the vote and returned to his lucrative law practice. Who better to pick up the pieces than Franklin D. Roosevelt?

While Roosevelt was in the early stages of physical rehabilitation and developing a political identity as the next leader of the Democratic Party, Eleanor was rapidly becoming a major Democratic figure. Louis Howe had suggested to her that she might deliver talks to various groups as a stand-in for her husband. Still afflicted with insecurity and prone to stage fright, she agreed reluctantly. With Howe's diligent coaching, she learned how to suppress a chronic nervous twitter, speak extemporaneously without awkward pauses, and deliver a prepared text with authority. Her name—"Mrs. Franklin D. Roosevelt" was the universal style then—demanded attention and presumed a position of leadership. The onset of women's suffrage opened large new opportunities for female political participation. Soon she was a party activist, speaking at dinners, hosting teas, writing articles, driving voters to the polls, and pushing hard in party councils for more recognition of women.

She established her credentials as a tough fighter in the fall of 1924, when Al Smith faced a hard reelection fight against Theodore Roosevelt Jr. Warren G. Harding had appointed Ted to TR's old office of assistant secretary of the navy. Every bit as much as Franklin, Ted had his eyes on the presidency, with election as governor of New York the primary stepping-stone.

A formidable challenger to Smith, Ted had one big vulnerability. At the direction of Secretary of the Navy Edwin Denby, he had signed off on the transfer of the Naval Oil Reserves at Elk Hills, California, and Teapot Dome, Wyoming, to the Department of the Interior. Secretary of the Interior Albert B. Fall had then leased the properties to private oil companies in return for huge bribes. "Teapot Dome," uncovered after Harding's sudden death in August 1923, was an epic scandal. Ted, although an innocent bystander, was left holding the political bag. That October, Eleanor, standing in for Franklin and accompanied by Louis Howe, followed him around the state by automobile, campaigning for Smith. On the roof of her vehicle they mounted a huge teapot that puffed steam on command. Smith won handily. Ted never ran for elective office again. Looking back a quarter century later, Eleanor admitted that she was guilty of "a rough stunt."[9]

Eleanor's partisan attachment to the Democratic Party was only one dimension of an emerging career as a social activist in the liberated feminist-intellectual world of New York City. Drawn especially to peace causes, she was a vocal promoter of such projects as US entry into the League of Nations and adherence to the World Court. Another enthusiasm was the New York Women's Trade Union League, with which she worked closely in pursuit of better labor conditions, evening educational opportunities, and social welfare legislation for women workers. She even persuaded her reluctant mother-in-law to cohost a tea that would raise money for the Women's Trade Union League. The day after the event, Sara wrote to Franklin, "600 invitations sent out about 30 came!!! Hardly worthwhile was it?"[10]

By then Eleanor was a major Democratic figure in her own right, helping to establish a monthly party magazine aimed at women, spearheading a drive to organize youth through a new Junior Democratic League, speaking to women's groups, writing articles, and giving occasional radio talks. She was among the most prominent of the women who succeeded in persuading party leaders to grant females full status as members of the state committee. She advocated a woman nominee for at least one important state office. "Women must learn to play the game as men do," she told the readers of *Red Book* magazine in 1928. "Our means is to elect, accept and back women political bosses."[11]

Also active in a larger world of women's reform politics, she participated in the League of Women Voters and the Women's City Club of New York. Serving on the board of the City Housing Corporation, a private developer of cooperative housing projects for wage earners, she learned about the possibilities of planned communities. By 1928, she had involved herself in enough controversy that a group of radicals headed by Clarence Darrow sent her a whimsical invitation to a "blacklist party" of notables barred from speaking at gatherings of the Daughters of the American Revolution (of which she was a member).[12]

In September 1926, a *New York Times Magazine* profile described her manner as "that of the young suburban mother," but she was also an emerging practical politician. Despite her own leanings toward Prohibition, she readily acquiesced in omitting the issue from the state party platform. Criticized for dodging the need to enforce the Eighteenth Amendment to the Constitution, she shot back that her critics might give thought to enforcement of the Fourteenth and Fifteenth amendments (which purportedly had given full rights of citizenship to blacks).[13]

Socially and culturally distant from Al Smith's Irish Catholic identity and possessing personal qualms about his ample consumption of alcohol, she believed his social progressivism trumped all else. Speaking to the ladies of the

Flatbush Democratic Club in 1928, she declared that Uncle Ted had been a foe of religious bigotry who looked forward to the day when a Catholic or a Jew might become president—and she claimed to have letters to prove it. Her speeches and radio talks, delivered in a high-pitched, excruciatingly correct patrician voice, had a tone of the upper-crust lady talking down to common people. But her concern for the less privileged and a sense that socioeconomic issues were more important than cultural controversies won over many Democrats.[14]

THE CLOSEST AMONG ELEANOR'S MANY NEW FRIENDS AND ASSOCIATES WERE Nancy ("Nan") Cook, who worked for the Women's Division of the New York Democratic Committee, and Marion Dickerman, a teacher at the Todhunter School, an upscale Manhattan academy for girls. Both were college-educated reformers.[15]

In 1926, Eleanor, Nan, and Marion pooled their funds to build a fieldstone country cottage at Val-Kill, just a few miles from the Roosevelt Springwood estate on land that Franklin had acquired; he let them have the property with the understanding that it would revert to him or his estate at their deaths. A retreat for Eleanor and a primary residence for Nancy and Marion, the house was planned for the three of them right down to a communal bedroom. Franklin called the house "the honeymoon cottage" but lent the venture his moral support and actually designed it. The dwelling indicated the understood, perhaps explicit, agreement he and Eleanor had reached to lead substantially separate personal lives on a basis of mutual respect and political collaboration.

The three women quickly established Val-Kill Industries, a small furniture factory near the cottage to provide work for underemployed rural craftsmen who, they believed, would find the enterprise a liberating alternative to mass-production industry. The business also produced some pewter items and marketed local woven goods. The products were of high quality but the customers few. Franklin and Eleanor probably purchased more Val-Kill products than anyone else. Never profitable, the enterprise closed in 1937.

In 1927, Eleanor and her two friends pooled their resources again to purchase the Todhunter School from its retiring headmistress. For ten years, they all taught there. Eleanor, strongly influenced by theories of progressive education, specialized in American history, literature, and current events. She wanted the school to prepare girls for active citizenship in the here and now.

It is easy to conclude from her deep relationships with other females that Eleanor had crossed over into the world of lesbianism. Clearly she was more comfortable in personal relationships with women than with men. One can only guess whether her intensely affectionate attachments had a physical dimension—and wonder if it really matters.

Not particularly attractive to men, she possessed a magnetic appeal to many women. Her commanding height, intelligence, energy, emerging confidence and authority, and willingness to lead all made her stand out as she had at her old preparatory school, Allenswood. Franklin possessed many of the same characteristics. For the duration of their lives as national political leaders, both he and Eleanor exuded a charisma that aroused strong feelings, negative as well as positive. In their personal lives, admirers surrounded both, jockeying like jealous suitors for their affections.

Eleanor became something more than a female Democratic partisan. A large public found her intriguing and wanted her opinions on social issues involving marriage and the family, the role of women in a modern urban society, and the upbringing and education of children. She welcomed the opportunity, delivering often thoughtful answers that attempted to find a balance between the traditional and the progressive. The nineteenth-century family, she wrote, had been an economic unit, held together by necessity as much as affection. Modern technology had liberated women from many of the traditional functions that had confined them to the home, and higher standards of living forced many of them to work. Children no longer had to perform the various farming tasks expected of them by a bygone rural society. They had to be raised by sympathetic example rather than arbitrary command and encouraged to work out problems themselves.

Addressing the increasing number of divorces, she conceded that some were inevitable. But, arriving at a conclusion more autobiographical than most of her readers or listeners realized, she attributed many to a lack of self-discipline when the first romance of marriage gave way to dissention. Husband and wife had a duty to discipline themselves and achieve a better, more firmly cemented relationship. She surely felt she had done that in her own life.[16]

IN THE IMMEDIATE AFTERMATH OF THE 1924 ELECTION DEBACLE, FRANKLIN had wasted no time in making an implicit bid for a leading position within the party. A letter to every delegate at the Madison Square Garden convention asked for the recipient's "counsel and thought." It laid out "certain fundamental truths" that Roosevelt saw as a starting point: (1) the Democratic National Committee should function continuously, not just in election years; (2) it should work much more closely with state Democratic organizations; (3) its activities should be "put on a . . . businesslike financial basis"; (4) its publicity and public information operations "should be greatly extended"; and (5) "party leaders from all sections should meet more frequently in order to exchange views and plan for united party action." The Republicans, he went on, were the party of conservatism, standing "for the control of the social and economic structure of the nation by a small minority." The Democrats were "unequivocally the party of progress and liberal thought" but prone to squabble over prospective presidential candidates rather than "organizing for party principles." If the party could present a "logical and progressive program," it could gain the confidence of the country.[17]

Cynics who saw the letter as a launching pad for Roosevelt's own ambitions could claim accuracy as a defense. It was less a quest for useful information than an attention-getting device. The numerous responses provided no useful consensus. Still, his advice was fundamentally sound and long overdue. In terms of finance and organization, the Democratic Party was in many ways mired in the nineteenth century.

The communication was also a plea for a party identity defined by a coherent programmatic ideology, "progressivism," that rejected cultural politics. McAdoo and Smith were both progressives, but their common identity was submerged in a poisonous brew of regional, religious, and ethnic hostilities. Roosevelt undertook a calculated effort to show that he, waving the banner of progressive politics, could transcend the party's divisions.

By then, he had forged a friendship and political alliance with Montana senator Thomas Walsh, a leader of the western Democratic progressives. The two called for a meeting of 150 to 200 Democratic leaders in the spring of 1925 with the objectives of revitalizing the party's organizational structure and preparing a coherent manifesto of its principles. DNC chairman Clem Shaver, perceiving a challenge to his leadership and unwilling to cooperate in a progressive attempt to seize control of the party, blocked the plan.[18]

Numerous party eminences feared that any kind of a national meeting would quickly reopen all the unhealed wounds of Madison Square Garden. Three-time nominee and former secretary of state William Jennings Bryan opposed the idea as both premature and an effort to establish top-down control of what should be a bottom-up party. He and Roosevelt met in Florida, where Roosevelt was cruising on the *Larooco*, and had an amicable, inconclusive discussion.[19]

First and foremost, Roosevelt believed that the Democrats had to be the nation's progressive party. But what did the term "progressive" mean and how could he sell it to his fellow partisans? Heavily inspired by the Republican example of Theodore Roosevelt, Franklin had come into politics as an advocate of good government, a foe of political machines, and a promoter of conservation. Democrats in general tended to be Jeffersonian decentralizers uneasy with TR's "New Nationalist" vision of progressivism administered by a strong central government in Washington.

Roosevelt's gropings for a progressivism congruent with the examples of both Bryan and TR remained at the stage of generalization. In a typical communication, he declared that progressives were, above all, opposed to "the industrial and commercial interests and the privileged classes which now run the government." They favored "development of our natural resources by the whole people and not by the privileged few." Encouraging farm life, they wanted to make agriculture profitable enough "to start the flow of population away from, and not to, the cities." They sought "the reduction of taxes by elimination of unnecessary and wasteful government activities." They wanted to help the other nations of the world, without entering into entangling alliances, through the encouragement of world trade and opposition to high tariffs imposed for the benefit of "a privileged few."[20]

Following TR, he disdained the Republican Party's leading insurgent, Senator Robert La Follette Sr., whose Progressive Party candidacy in 1924, he argued, was a futile exercise that blurred the line between sound progressivism and extremism. "The Democratic Party is *the* Progressive Party of the country, but it is not the ultra-radical party of the country," he told a correspondent. "We cannot surely progress unless each advancing footstep is placed on firm and tried ground."[21]

Prohibition sharply divided the country. Roosevelt understood its difficulties firsthand. He had developed a love for the cocktail hour and seems always to have maintained his access to good whiskey. His mother favored banning hard liquor. Eleanor, the child of an alcoholic, semipublicly supported prohibiting all alcoholic beverages. The issue sharply divided urban and rural New York. In 1922, Roosevelt lamely suggested to an upstate Democratic candidate that it might be possible to argue that 3 or 4 percent beer could be classified as nonintoxicating, but "I would go a little slow on the question of light wines."[22]

Roosevelt eventually discovered a way to reformulate his sense of progressivism along distinctly Democratic partisan lines in a rather unlikely place. Toward the end of 1925, Claude G. Bowers, editor of the *New York Evening World*, a popular historian, and a Democratic Party intellectual, asked him to write a feature review of Bowers's latest book, *Jefferson and Hamilton: The Struggle for Democracy in America*. Roosevelt leaped at the offer, using the opportunity to deliver a message to the newspaper's predominantly Democratic audience. He probably genuinely discovered a quite different Thomas Jefferson from the figure introduced to him through neofederalist lenses at Groton and Harvard; scorned by Theodore Roosevelt and Republicans generally, that

Jefferson had been depicted as an exponent of states' rights, individual liberty, small frugal government, and national weakness.

Northern urban Democrats vehemently opposed to federal Prohibition enforcement might find the idea of states' rights attractive; later on, moreover, Roosevelt and New Deal policy intellectuals would discover a Jeffersonian resonance in such concepts as grassroots democracy and regional planning. All the same, Jeffersonian ideas would most likely serve as arguments against top-down social reformism and as a rationale for a limp foreign policy. It was not by chance that the brunt of early-twentieth-century progressivism had been Republican; the party's tradition of Hamiltonian nationalism enabled Washington-administered reform. Woodrow Wilson's administration, characterized by a vast expansion of federal authority, had suggested a reinterpretation of his party's adherence to states' rights. Still, well into the 1920s, Democrats who took Jefferson seriously were more likely to invoke him in arguing against anti-child-labor acts or maximum-hours laws.

Bowers's book focused on the Jefferson-Hamilton rivalry and the development of political parties in the 1790s. Where it had been the habit of progressive intellectuals to picture Jefferson along Hamiltonian lines as a decentralizer and the leader of an essentially reactionary agrarianism, Bowers depicted him as the American nation's first great democrat, the master political organizer of a struggle against greedy special interests, and a tribune of the common man. This interpretation appealed to Roosevelt's conception of himself as a country gentleman with an interest in the welfare of his community, his instinct for activist reform, his sense of progressivism as the promotion of democracy, and his increasing inclination to be critical of the business and financial interests that seemed to be running the country ("malefactors of great wealth," Uncle Ted had called them two decades earlier). His review in fact revealed a politician whose sense of himself and his mission had changed.[23]

The *Evening World* published Roosevelt's eulogistic piece on December 3, 1925. An American patrician, born to wealth, accustomed to a lavish lifestyle, trained to lead, once scornful of Bryanite populism, and all too cognizant of his superiority, now found himself denouncing Alexander Hamilton's identification with "the organized compact forces of wealth, of birth, of commerce, of the press." Jefferson, by contrast, was "a veritable Westerner" attempting to organize "the working masses" and solicitous of what Hamilton "thought of as the rabble—the poor, the uneducated, the average human being who, even then, made up the masses of the country." In the end, Roosevelt concluded, "Jefferson's faith in mankind was vindicated; his appeal to the intelligence of the average voter bore fruit; his conception of a democratic republic came true."

Jefferson and Hamilton, Roosevelt declared, had left him with a "breathless feeling" about the young nation's escape from the clutches of wealth and aristocracy in its early years. "But I have a breathless feeling, too, as I wonder if, a century and a quarter later, the same contending forces are not again mobilizing," he concluded. "Hamiltons we have to-day. Is a Jefferson on the horizon?" Whether from the crippling experience of polio, from his contact with the impoverished rural South, or from sheer political ambition, an American aristocrat was now ready to lead a populist crusade that Bryan, who had died four months before the review appeared, would have appreciated.[24]

ROOSEVELT INDEED DIRECTED MUCH OF HIS POLITICAL EFFORT OVER THE NEXT few years at Bryan's old constituency, the residual progressives of the hinterland South and West, among them men such as the still influential Josephus Daniels, with whom he maintained a fond relationship, and Senator Walsh, perhaps the foremost advocate of a modernized version of Bryan's populism. This meant giving attention to the grievances of a primarily rural, small-town constituency largely unintelligible to an Al Smith but comprehensible to the country squire Roosevelt imagined himself to be. Early on, he was committed, if a bit vaguely, to some sort of relief for farmers struggling with low commodity prices. He would become a champion of rural electrification and a critic of the private electrical utilities.

None of this damaged him in New York, where he kept one foot in the city and the other upstate. He had reached enough of a modus vivendi with Tammany that the machine probed his interest in running for mayor of New York in 1925. He wisely turned that possibility aside, then found the state party eager to draft him for a US Senate candidacy in 1926. Thinking the time still not right and still pursuing greater physical rehabilitation, he declined. The Senate nomination and eventual victory in the general election went to an old acquaintance of his days in the state legislature, state supreme court judge Robert F. Wagner—like Smith, a Tammany man much admired for his rectitude and ability.

Roosevelt had also determined that the Senate was not a goal he wished to pursue. "I am temperamentally unfitted to be a member of the uninteresting body known as the United States Senate," he told a correspondent. "I like administrative or executive work, but do not want to have my hands and feet tied and my wings clipped for 6 long years."[25]

In 1927, he found another issue in the great Mississippi River flood, which inundated vast areas along the river's route to the Gulf of Mexico. Secretary of Commerce Herbert Hoover headed a major relief effort that won widespread

praise, but Roosevelt found it far short of what was needed. Denying any intention of criticizing his "old friend" from the Wilson administration, he nonetheless dismissed Hoover's estimates of relief costs as much too small. He called
on President Coolidge to meet with leaders of both parties, fashion a nonpartisan "constructive rehabilitation plan" for the Mississippi Valley, and convene a
special session of Congress to enact it.

Coolidge ignored Roosevelt's plea for a special session, but in the spring of
1928 the Republican Congress satisfied most Mississippi Valley residents by
voting an enormous appropriation for rebuilding and strengthening the river
levees. Roosevelt incurred neither harm nor political advantage from the episode. It did demonstrate, however, certain characteristics that would resurface
in the future and serve him well: an interest in river valley development, a tendency to think big in terms of money and planning, and a zeal for immediate
action rather than extended deliberation.[26]

By 1928, Roosevelt had not only preserved but in many respects broadened
his status as an important Democratic politician. He had cultivated ties to all
major groups in his party. Eleanor's contacts with practically every reform
movement of the 1920s were especially helpful. His struggle against polio had
brought him to rural Georgia, given him a second identity as a part-time southerner, and made it easy for him to relate to Dixie Democrats. In the spring of
1927, the South's leading newspaper, the *Atlanta Constitution*, fingered him as
"an ideal candidate" for president.[27]

Maintaining an ambiguous stance on Prohibition and the other cultural
controversies of the decade, Roosevelt had taken positions on economic issues
with wide appeal throughout the party. To this, he added a magnetic personality and an appearance of physical vigor that belied his difficulty walking. He
may have begun to accept that, whatever his hopes, he had come about as far as
possible in his long fight to reverse his paralysis.

He realized that 1928 was not the year to make a bid for the White House.
The esteemed Hoover, as the Republican candidate, would be riding a wave of
booming prosperity. On the Democratic side, McAdoo declined another candidacy, guaranteeing an easy nomination for Smith. The Democrats convened
in Houston that June, two weeks after the Republicans had named Hoover.
There was no hundred-ballot brawl this time; otherwise much seemed a repeat
of 1924. As then, Roosevelt came to the convention as Smith's floor leader and
made the nominating speech. He used his own skills to maximum effect to
promote himself as well as Smith.

He knew that at least sixty radio stations from coast to coast would carry the
proceedings. He estimated, probably conservatively, that 15 million listeners

would hear his voice. He shrewdly understood that his task was to persuade beyond the convention hall and that shouted convention oratory was not the best way to communicate with ordinary people sitting in their living rooms. He told Walter Lippmann several weeks later, "I tried the definite experiment this year of writing and delivering my speech wholly for the benefit of the radio audience and press rather than for any forensic effect it might have on the delegates and audience in the convention hall."[28]

This time, Elliott, a strong, handsome young man three months short of his eighteenth birthday, assisted his father to the podium. Roosevelt's left hand grasped his son's right arm. His right hand held a cane. His progress was measured and deliberate but more confident than at Madison Square Garden four years earlier. As in 1924, a large, spontaneous cheer followed him to the microphones. Much of it was in anticipation of the speech for Smith, but a fair amount was a tribute to him. Grasping the podium with his left hand, he waved to the crowd with his right.

Delivered to a receptive audience, the address struck a nice balance between the old-fashioned and the modern, tossing in enough partisan shots to satisfy the crowd while emphasizing Smith's greatness of character and maintaining something that approached a conversational tone for the radio listeners. It ended, as all nominating speeches must, with the candidate's name: "Victory is his habit—the happy warrior, Alfred E. Smith!" The inevitable noisy demonstration ensued, followed the next day by Smith's equally inevitable nomination.

The speech had played well and demonstrated an appeal that went beyond conventional partisanship. The *New York Times* said that Roosevelt had "proceeded like a gentleman speaking to gentlemen" and declared, "It is seldom that a political speech attains this kind of eloquence." Will Durant, in the *New York World*, called Roosevelt "beyond comparison the finest man that has appeared at either convention." Colonel Robert McCormick, one of Roosevelt's Groton schoolmates and publisher of the solidly Republican *Chicago Tribune*, delivered what was for him the ultimate tribute, calling him "the only Republican in the Democratic party."[29]

The *Tribune*, of course, was guilty of wishful thinking, but the general reaction to the second "happy warrior" speech and to Roosevelt's entire presence demonstrated broad hunger for a type of leadership that neither Smith nor Hoover could provide. For seven years, Franklin Delano Roosevelt had been the lost prince of the Democratic Party. He would soon begin to claim his due.

CHAPTER 10

CHIEF EXECUTIVE

POWER IN ALBANY, 1929–1932

GIVEN LITTLE REAL RESPONSIBILITY IN AL SMITH'S 1928 PRESIDENTIAL campaign, Franklin Roosevelt went to Warm Springs in mid-September. Beneath his surface loyalty and enthusiasm, he was privately dismayed. Downplaying his progressivism, Smith had named as chair of the Democratic National Committee John J. Raskob, a wealthy director of General Motors, a Catholic, and a vocal critic of Prohibition. In so doing, Smith had sacrificed a progressive identity with some national appeal and emphasized a cultural one that would harm him outside metropolitan America. For all his genuine merits, the New York governor was an urban provincial unable to connect with the American heartland and little interested in the farm distress at the heart of 1920s progressivism. Conversely, the Republicans claimed credit for the nation's widespread prosperity. Their candidate, Herbert Hoover, was among the most esteemed public leaders in the country.[1]

Smith wanted Roosevelt to run for governor of New York, but FDR was loath to swim into a Republican riptide. Moreover, he was fervently devoted to developing the Warm Springs polio treatment center and perhaps believed that his legs could improve with intensive treatment there. On October 1, the eve of the state Democratic convention, Smith and Raskob got him on the telephone and met every objection he raised. Raskob agreed to underwrite the fledgling Georgia Warm Springs Foundation. Smith assured Roosevelt that the esteemed

Herbert Lehman would serve as lieutenant governor and handle as much of the work of the governor's office as Roosevelt cared to delegate. Roosevelt, after talking with Lehman, never quite agreed to accept the nomination but left himself wide open for a draft.[2]

Twenty-four hours later, he was the Democratic candidate for governor of New York.

ONE CAN SURMISE THE CALCULATIONS THAT RAN THROUGH HIS HEAD. He had been dodging nominations since 1922; the Democratic Party would not come after him forever. An alternative candidate might win and block his own advancement. If he refused and a substitute lost, he would take the blame. If he lost, he would likely have campaigned well, appear a casualty of the Hoover undertow, and be able to claim another shot in 1930. A win in either 1928 or 1930 would put him in a prime position for a Democratic presidential nomination.

Roosevelt, with his nearly two decades of political experience, national reputation, and deep reservoir of goodwill, was in fact the best nominee the Democrats could have chosen. Much of the initial Republican commentary complimented his character and argued against him only on the basis of fragile health. The *New York Herald-Tribune* asked, "Who can defend the risking of another's health and whole future career in the cause of one's own vanity and ambition?" Such comments reduced the campaign to a fitness contest and handed Roosevelt an opportunity that he exploited to his advantage by campaigning nonstop, giving a major speech each evening except Sunday, along with numerous small talks, and making several hand-shaking stops each day.[3]

The itinerary was not easy. Getting out of an automobile was awkward. He had to swing his legs out and lock his braces before he could be pulled to his feet. His driver or another companion had to provide a strong right arm with which he steadied himself, then, cane in his right hand, he moved painstakingly forward. From time to time, the lack of an elevator required that he be carried up stairs—once even up a fire escape and through an open window. He took it all with aplomb. News reports, following the era's standards of good taste, rarely mentioned his infirmity. His endurance vindicated Al Smith's remark that "a Governor does not have to be an acrobat."[4]

Roosevelt established the major themes of his campaign in his acceptance speech and hammered away at them day after day: a general commitment to good government and social change, a special interest in public development and control of hydroelectric power, reform in the administration of civil and criminal justice, attention to the problems of New York farmers, and reorganization of county and local governments for greater economy and efficiency. On an issue that in general divided Democrats from Republicans, Prohibition, he tried to stay as vague as possible but felt obliged to support Smith's veto of a state enforcement bill, asserting that having been established by constitutional amendment, Prohibition was a federal responsibility. By Election Day, he had clearly run a good race, but few disinterested observers saw him as a distinct front-runner. The Republican candidate, state attorney general Albert Ottinger, was a respected public servant and the favorite in the eyes of many political oddsmakers.[5]

As the returns came in that evening, it became obvious early on that Smith, although the beneficiary of a huge margin in New York City, was polling well behind Hoover in the state and most of the country. He would concede defeat at midnight. Roosevelt, on the other hand, had a city margin only slightly smaller than Smith's and was stronger in rural precincts. As the night wore on, about 1,000 upstate voting districts seemed to be holding back their returns. Roosevelt personally called several county sheriffs. One of his managers, Democratic Bronx boss Edward J. Flynn, publicly declared that the very next day he would lead a delegation of "a hundred lawyers ready to resist or prevent any fraud which might be attempted." Whether prompted by the statement or not, the missing precincts began to disgorge their tallies. Shortly before dawn, the late edition of the *New York Times* declared Roosevelt the victor.[6]

The final returns gave him the election by a margin of 25,564, less than 1 percent of all votes cast. A hairsbreadth victory, it was nonetheless impressive. Roosevelt led the Democratic ticket, running only about 32,000 votes behind Smith in New York City while leading him by 73,000 upstate. Nationally, Smith, drawing on the near-tribal loyalty of recent immigrant groups, carried the nation's ten largest cities for the Democrats but lost badly among the rural and small-town voters. Disappointed and bitter, he announced his retirement from politics. His urban breakthrough had been impressive, but as a practical matter, the Democratic Party needed a leader who could appeal to both constituencies. It now had an indication that his name might be Franklin D. Roosevelt.[7]

THE ROOSEVELTS WHO MOVED TO ALBANY AT THE BEGINNING OF 1929 WERE empty nesters. Anna had married three and a half years earlier and given her parents their first grandchild, a daughter born in 1927. James, a junior at Harvard, was prominent in class activities, an indifferent student, and secretly engaged to Betsy Cushing, the lovely daughter of a prominent surgeon; they would wed in June 1930. Elliott was in his final year at Groton, Franklin Jr. was in the third form there, and John was in the first.

A quarter century later, Eleanor recalled the Governor's Mansion as "a very nice old home" located in a once fashionable part of Albany that had become an Italian working-class district. During the hot summer the residents held "frequent, long, and noisy" festivals. Eleanor and Franklin spent holidays and as many weekends as possible at Hyde Park. Each Christmas season, they continued Al Smith's custom of hosting a party for the children of a nearby orphanage. Each January, Louis Howe scripted an elaborate birthday celebration for Franklin, complete with costumed theatrical skits.[8]

Roosevelt found the governorship fun, but the position also had a frightening side. That April, postal authorities intercepted a lethal explosive device addressed to him. One wonders if the thought crossed his mind that the Palmer bomb ten years earlier might have been intended as the Roosevelt bomb. Just days later, an arsonist, who was never apprehended, burned to the ground a luxurious new mansion built by his son-in-law, Curtis Dall, in Westchester County, New York. Prominence produced resentment as well as admiration; charisma bred hatred as well as devotion.[9]

Eleanor transformed the position of First Lady, minimizing its purely ceremonial duties while maximizing its public policy possibilities. She held as few teas and receptions as possible and acted as a behind-the-scenes adviser to her husband. She also continued almost all of her previous activities: teaching at the Todhunter School three days each week, delivering speeches and radio talks, publishing magazine articles, maintaining her activities in reform organizations, and solidifying her status as the most important woman in the New York Democratic Party.

Sometimes her causes spelled trouble for Franklin. Few New York Democrats were enthusiastic about Prohibition; yet Eleanor appeared publicly at meetings of "dry" prohibitionist organizations. Franklin countered with his own carefully crafted image as "moderately damp."

A far more combustible debate—one on which Eleanor, perhaps due to her own experience, gave little ground—surrounded birth control, an issue fundamental to feminists, important to many Protestant and Jewish social reformers, and sacrilegious to Roman Catholics. An early scare in Roosevelt's 1932 campaign for the presidency would involve his receipt of a letter warning that influential "radio priest" Father Charles Coughlin was planning a broadcast that would denounce Eleanor for allegedly preparing a book advocating birth control. Coughlin, based in Detroit, preached coast to coast every Sunday on a nationwide network, mixed politics with his religious message, and had millions of followers. A gubernatorial missive to the good father assured him that the story was false and concluded, "I do hope if you come East you will stop off in Albany to see me. I want to talk with you about many things." A personal meeting shortly afterward apparently mollified Coughlin.[10]

Eleanor developed a fond relationship with her state trooper bodyguard, Earl Miller, a tall, handsome man with the lethal fists of a champion amateur boxer. A dozen years younger than his charge, Miller possessed a roughhewn charm and take-charge practicality epitomized on the silver screen by the young Clark Gable. A ladies' man never quite able to settle down with one woman, he would marry and divorce three times.[11]

Miller was a constant presence in Eleanor's private life for a time, whether teaching her how to dive into a swimming pool or use a firearm. (In later years, Eleanor often carried a loaded revolver in her purse when she traveled alone.) Their relationship was affectionate; whether it was motherly, sisterly, or romantic remains speculative. It quickly became the subject of widespread gossip. When the Roosevelts moved to Washington in 1933, Miller stayed behind, but Eleanor still saw him frequently.

However separate Eleanor's career might be, it was irretrievably linked to Franklin's. Their social outlooks and policy objectives were nearly identical, differing only in the priority he attached to his sense of the politically possible. Her husband valued her thoughts, especially as he put together a staff for his administration.

Both soon realized that the most critical issue he faced was the assumed continuance of Smith lieutenants—and, indirectly, of Smith himself—in positions of power. Smith actually reserved a hotel suite in Albany with the clear intention of remaining a not-so-behind-the-scenes presence at the highest levels of state government. He did not fathom the hard inner core that lay at the center of Roosevelt's superficially lightweight persona.

Two of Smith's appointment suggestions were especially telling. He recommended Robert Moses, an overbearing aggregator of power, as secretary of state. As chair of the Long Island State Park Commission and the State Council of Parks, Moses had already established himself as a maestro of public works, constructing magnificent parks interlaced with broad expressways. Partly because he had dismissed Roosevelt's proposal for a Taconic state park/parkway system between Dutchess County and New York City, the new governor heartily disliked him. Eleanor concurred. Franklin instead appointed Edward Flynn, the Bronx Democratic leader who had played a key role in his campaign. The selection had much merit; it also signified both Roosevelts' preference for an Irish politician with, as Eleanor remarked many years later, "a very intellectual side." Flynn would continue his leadership of the Bronx Democratic Party and serve as Roosevelt's primary political representative in New York City, thereby establishing a degree of separation between the governor and Manhattan's Tammany machine.[12]

The other nominee, even dearer to Smith, was Belle Moskowitz, a remarkable social worker and political activist who had become Smith's political manager, speechwriter, and major adviser. Influential social worker and Democratic activist Frances Perkins recalled her as "vigorous and domineering"; Eleanor thought her "ruthless." Tough and manipulative, Belle was to the outgoing governor what Louis Howe had long been to Roosevelt. Working with Smith, she had been the state's most powerful female Democrat. Smith recommended her appointment as secretary (chief aide) to the governor and handed him a Moskowitz-composed draft of an inaugural address.[13]

Eleanor was wary from the start. "Don't let Mrs. M. get draped around you," she wrote to Franklin. "It will always be one for you and two for Al." Louis Howe gave his chief the same message. Roosevelt, displaying what would become an administrative characteristic, delayed as long as possible. Finally, the day before his inauguration, he told Smith he was going to appoint as his secretary a political nonentity named Guernsey Cross. "You know I need a great, big strong man as secretary. I need someone whom I can lean on physically, if necessary, and I think it will be better, Al."[14]

Smith, stunned by the confident independence of an associate he had considered little more than a playboy with a gift for public speaking, suddenly found himself an outsider of scant influence dealing with an improbable man of power. Thus began a personal alienation that would become political and ideological.

LOUIS HOWE CONTINUED AS ROOSEVELT'S NUMBER ONE. HE WOULD SPEND most of the next four years in New York City at the Roosevelt town house, promoting the governor's presidential ambitions. He came up to Albany once a week for a day or two of conferences with his boss and stayed in a Governor's Mansion guest room set aside for his use.[15]

Missy LeHand remained as close to Roosevelt as ever. To assist her, he chose Grace Tully, an attractive young convent-educated woman who had been secretary to the Catholic cardinal of New York before being released to work with Eleanor on Smith's presidential campaign. Efficient and discreet, she moved seamlessly into the office. Lieutenant Governor Herbert Lehman, son of a founder of the Lehman Brothers investment firm, was a Jewish patrician with a strong sense of public duty, deeply held progressive principles, and considerable executive talent. Capable and not hesitant to assume responsibility, he was happy to serve as, in Roosevelt's words, a "good right arm"; he was certainly perceptive enough to know he was establishing himself as the probable successor in Albany.

As industrial commissioner, a cabinet-level office concerned with labor relations and working conditions, the new governor picked Frances Perkins, whom he had known slightly in 1911 and 1912 as a member of the legislature. An effective and loyal member of Smith's state industrial commission, she had been a noted advocate of protective legislation for workers. Eleanor backed her strongly, although the two women were never personally close. Perkins herself considered Roosevelt a transformed personality who had cast off the arrogance and superficiality of his years in the legislature. Polio, she believed, had brought depth to his character and given him sympathy for the trials of ordinary people. She would be a mainstay of his administration.[16]

To address the problems of New York farmers, Roosevelt tapped his friend Henry Morgenthau Jr. The son of an eminent New York businessman, philanthropist, and diplomat, he was the proprietor of a large farm in Dutchess County. His wife, Elinor, was one of Eleanor's closest friends. A "gentleman farmer" and publisher of a regional weekly magazine, *The American Agriculturist*, Morgenthau possessed a deep and genuine interest in agricultural science and the problems of farming as a vocation. Ten years younger than Roosevelt, he admired the governor enormously. Roosevelt, perhaps inspired by the memory of Uncle Ted's presidential Country Life Commission, made him chair of an Agricultural Advisory Commission charged with developing a program to assist New York farmers.

As counsel to the governor, Roosevelt picked Samuel I. Rosenman. The son of Russian Jewish immigrants, Rosenman was an American success story. A star student in the New York City schools and at Columbia University, he had served in the army during World War I, graduated from Columbia Law School, established a practice, and won election to five one-year terms in the state assembly. Assigned to the Roosevelt campaign in 1928, he displayed quiet competence, sound judgment, capacity for hard work, and proficiency as a speechwriter. He would spend much of the next decade and a half in the service of his new boss.

Roosevelt inherited as a political manager James A. Farley, secretary to the state Democratic committee and its chairman after 1930. A popular presence and a superb political tactician unencumbered by ideology, Farley had built his life largely around Democratic politics. He would remark to an associate some years later, "After my country, my family, and my church, my party comes next."[17]

ROOSEVELT'S INAUGURATION ON JANUARY 1, 1929, TOOK PLACE IN AN ATMO-sphere of amiable celebration. Sketching in general terms the progressive program he had espoused in the campaign, he disavowed mindless partisanship and called for a new "era of good feelings" in state politics. That sentiment quickly collided with reality. The new governor faced a Republican legislature inclined toward the traditional mission of the opposition—to oppose. He knew from the start that he faced a brawl and went at it determined to establish himself as a tough and effective chief executive.[18]

Smith had bequeathed to his successor new "executive budget" procedures that gave the governor responsibility for presenting and enforcing a unified state spending plan. The process was very much in keeping with the early-twentieth-century progressive bias toward orderly, "scientific" public management and in line with Roosevelt's advocacy, as assistant secretary of the navy, of similar procedures for the national government. Arcane and remote to most citizens, the budget issue spoke to perhaps the most perennial conflict in popular government: the struggle between the legislature and the executive for control of expenditures and the accompanying political power.

The legislature inserted provisions in its appropriation bills that effectively gave its majority leaders a veto over gubernatorial discretion. Roosevelt, bypassing his Republican attorney general, appointed a special counsel to mount a legal challenge. In October 1929, the state's highest judicial body, the Court of Appeals, issued a decision that largely upheld the governor's position. Declaring that the court had vindicated a "sacred time-honored American principle," he had demonstrated that he was not a chief executive to trifle with.[19]

No large public issue was more important to Roosevelt than public control of the state's hydroelectric sources. Tactically, the issue united Democratic and Republican progressives, enhancing the political coalition he wanted to build. He also thought that breaking the private corporate stranglehold on electricity distribution was a moral imperative.[20]

By 1929, electricity was available in all cities and many smaller towns throughout the nation. It still had not penetrated far into the countryside, where widely separated farmhouses and low rural incomes presented private utility companies with daunting economic prospects and consumers with high rates. A source of energy for lights, refrigerators, washing machines, radios, phonographs, and other conveniences, electricity had changed the quality of life for a majority of Americans.

Those without it felt dispossessed. Those who enjoyed its benefits received them from a franchised monopoly and found it easy to believe they were being overcharged. In an age of widespread corporate mergers, the large electric utilities presented progressive politicians with a big, visible target. Roosevelt was surely aware of the political implications of a power policy that, in addition to burnishing his progressive credentials, would connect him with both urban consumers and farmers. All the same a sincere faith in public power seems to have motivated him at least as much as political opportunism.

In his inaugural address and first message to the legislature, the new governor made clear his belief that New York waterpower resources "should belong to all the people." In a *Forum* magazine article at the end of 1929, he asserted that public hydroelectric power could provide a "yardstick" for the regulation of private utility rates. He forced the resignation of the chairman of the state Public Service Commission under threat of impeachment for pro-corporation bias, denounced rate increases, and vainly attempted to block a J. P. Morgan–financed merger of the state's three largest electric utilities. He and his utility advisers, all unabashed supporters of public electricity, frequently cited the low rates charged by the socialized electrical authority of the neighboring Canadian province of Ontario. Franklin also advocated shared Canadian-American St. Lawrence River hydroelectric development as a key element in the much larger proposal for a St. Lawrence Seaway.[21]

Roosevelt's position on the utilities was more ideological than economic. In the spirit of Uncle Ted, he denounced what he considered antisocial corporate behavior. In the spirit of Woodrow Wilson's decentralizing progressivism, he decried corporate consolidation. He peremptorily dismissed other viewpoints, even when offered by supportive and nonpartisan observers such as his uncle Frederic Delano, a governor of the Federal Reserve Bank of Richmond, a former member of the Federal Reserve Board, and primary author of a US Chamber of Commerce report on the utilities.

A contentious exchange between Franklin and his uncle in late 1929 underscored the gap between Fred's cautious business-minded progressivism and his nephew's ideological politics. "Nobody claims that government operation with all factors properly balanced is more businesslike than that of a private company," Franklin declared in a letter to his uncle, "but the fact remains that where there is government operation the household consumer pays less in his monthly bills." Delano's response was conciliatory but firm: "If it is true that the Government pays no taxes, pays little or nothing for the cost of financing, and assumes no interest during construction, and therefore is able to [charge] lower rates for electric power," he wrote, "the general public must pay the equivalent in taxes in some other way, and what is perhaps more serious, all private development in that field ceases."[22] For the next fifteen years, uncle and nephew would agree to disagree on the topic.

Separate US-Canadian negotiations for a St. Lawrence development treaty progressed slowly, with Roosevelt largely frozen out of the discussions by President Hoover. (A pact signed near the end of the Hoover administration would not come before the Senate until 1934, at which time it was, to the disappointment of President Franklin D. Roosevelt, rejected. The St. Lawrence Seaway would not come to full fruition until the presidency of Dwight D. Eisenhower.)

ROOSEVELT PURSUED AN AMBITIOUS LEGISLATIVE PROGRAM THAT HAD MUCH in common with the agendas of progressive governors all over the United States. By mid-1930, as he planned his reelection campaign, he had managed to extract from a Republican legislature a fairly extensive program of "farm relief" (farm-to-market road improvements funded by a two-cent gasoline tax, aid to rural schools, and increased agricultural research), an old-age pension program for the indigent elderly, approval of a bond issue to fund state prisons and hospitals, and continued extensive park construction. He had also made a significant dent in Republican dominance upstate by virtue of his program and a vigorous push for stronger Democratic organizing efforts there.[23] The governor, wrote journalist Ernest K. Lindley in September 1930, had not simply continued in, but moved well to the left of, the progressive tradition of Al Smith. He was also a formidable tactician, "a staunch partisan, frankly diligent in strengthening the party organization, [who] enjoys immensely the game of 'practical' politics."[24]

Yet he likely spent more time out of the state than any of his predecessors, with a month to six weeks in Warm Springs after the end of the legislative session each April, followed by a similar break each fall. (Herbert Lehman filled in capably, even handling a major prison riot during one such absence.) The daily schedule prescribed by his doctor and reported by the *New York Times* seemed more tailored to a gentleman of leisure than the governor of a big state: "He should go to bed not later than 10 or 10:30 o'clock and should rise about 9:30 o'clock. He ought to have an hour's rest lying down after lunch and he should have his regular exercises. And, above all, he ought to try to keep away from . . . handshaking and that sort of thing." Yet his administration became known for its activism, and he personally developed a reputation for physical stamina.[25]

Each summer he spent the better part of a month on "inspection tours" of state facilities, usually traveling by water on a small state-owned houseboat that he named *The Inspector*. Eleanor accompanied him, functioning as his legs, eyes, and ears; she thought in later years that they must have traversed every mile of waterway in the state. She did the actual inspecting while he met with local notables or gave informal talks. Goodwill and party building were major objectives of the tours, but the governor took the inspection mission very seriously. He sent Eleanor to local prisons and hospitals with a mandate to snoop around: look for signs of overcrowding such as folding beds stashed away in closets or behind doors; read the menus, then go to the kitchens and see what was really cooking on the stoves. The tours did not uncover much in the way of flummery or corruption but did reveal a lot of unavoidable overcrowding and provided a basis for demanding appropriations from the legislature for new facilities. They also served as a politically valuable show of gubernatorial concern for the entire state.[26]

The tours also validated Roosevelt's claims to good health and extraordinary vitality. "He has proved himself not only a prodigious worker but one of the most mobile governors in the history of the State," Ernest Lindley wrote in September 1930, during the governor's run for reelection. "He has surmounted his handicap so handsomely that it can no longer be a feature in his campaign."[27]

Roosevelt indeed approached the reelection campaign with justified optimism. He had proven himself a strong, effective, and popular governor, developing a constituency in normally Republican upstate areas and winning a fulsome endorsement from the state branch of the American Federation of Labor. With Albert Ottinger uninterested in another race, the Republican opposition was lackluster.[28]

The campaign aimed as much to establish a strong national profile as to win another two years in Albany. Roosevelt devoted about two-thirds of a public letter laying out his accomplishments to the issue on which he had temporized throughout the 1920s: Prohibition. His statement demonstrated a clear sense that the once bitterly divisive liquor question was becoming irrelevant a year after the great stock market crash of 1929. It cleverly established a stance in favor of moderate change instead of outright repeal. Each state should be empowered to establish its own rules for intoxicating beverages, right down to continuing a total ban. Local option provisions should give the same discretion to individual cities and towns. State agencies should manage the sale of alcohol. The return of the old-time rowdy saloon should be barred. The formula was yet another application of the Jeffersonian decentralization that Roosevelt had embraced as consistent with the heritage and character of the Democratic Party. It won him widespread praise.[29]

As had been the case two years earlier, Roosevelt spent much of October on a speaking tour around the state. He also made effective use of radio, taking partisan shots while stressing a willingness to work with Republicans and claiming tangible improvements in state services. Inevitably he drew national attention.

Signaling the campaign's broader significance, three members of President Hoover's cabinet, Secretary of State Henry L. Stimson, Secretary of the Treasury Ogden Mills, and Secretary of War Patrick J. Hurley, made major speeches attacking him. Roosevelt responded sarcastically, dismissing Hurley as an Oklahoma carpetbagger and Stimson and Mills as politicians whose earlier bids for the New York governorship had been rejected.[30]

On November 4, 1930, the governor swamped his hapless opponent, former US Attorney Charles Tuttle, by 725,000 votes—nearly doubling Al Smith's record victory margin of 1922 and carrying the upstate counties by almost 168,000 votes.

HIS EYES INCREASINGLY ON THE PRESIDENCY, ROOSEVELT HAD NO PLAN FOR major new programs during his second term. Faced with a dramatically collapsing economy, however, he moved to ameliorate its worst effects.

When the stock market crashed in October 1929, Roosevelt, very much in line with most financial watchers, believed the debacle a hiccup that would have mild, transitory effects. In early 1930, with the economy apparently stabilizing, his son-in-law, Curtis Dall, purchased a seat on the New York Stock Exchange at the auction price of $398,000. Roosevelt apparently had no qualms about helping to finance Dall's transaction with a $50,000 personal loan; Dall got another $250,000 from Eleanor's cousins and benefactors, Henry and Susie Parish. The transaction did not seem much of a gamble at the time, but the markets and the price of an exchange seat would soon begin a sharp downward trajectory. Dall found himself moving from one firm to another in possession of a debt-laden white elephant. It is unclear whether he was ever able to reimburse the Roosevelts or the Parishes.[31]

By the fall of 1930, the economy was beginning the protracted collapse that would come to be called the Great Depression. The need to assist the jobless had been a talking point in Roosevelt's reelection campaign. In December, the collapse of New York City's Bank of the United States, an institution with hundreds of thousands of small depositors, laid bare the fragility of the banking system and made the governor, who to this point had given scant attention to the problem, a proponent of stronger state banking regulations.[32]

Roosevelt seems basically to have agreed with President Hoover that government could do little more than enforce elemental honesty within the financial system. He trusted the judgment of many respectable Wall Streeters, including Lieutenant Governor Lehman, that a strong government hand in the industry was likely to be clumsy and do more harm than good. The idea of insuring depositors' accounts, moreover, seemed extraordinarily radical to him and, in the state context, may not have been feasible.

It was not until January 1932, with a banking crisis spreading across the nation (and his bid for the presidency assuming a high national profile), that Roosevelt asked the legislature for a strong regulatory program. The relatively mild legislation he got established a state banking board to share oversight authority with the state superintendent of banks. The president who would become the scourge of Big Finance loomed nowhere on the Albany horizon.

IN NEW YORK, AS ELSEWHERE, UNEMPLOYMENT GREW TO CRISIS PROPORTIONS. Widespread distress, disorderly demonstrations, and Communist Party "hunger marches," frequently broken up by truncheon-wielding police, revealed a growing cache of social dynamite. State and federal statistics on the jobless in those days were tenuous, but plausible estimates by economic historians suggest that unemployment nationally moved above 10 percent in November 1930, continued up relentlessly through 1931, broke through 20 percent in early 1932, and was above 25 percent by midyear. The New York experience was likely close to the national trend. Increasingly, the Depression was a major humanitarian and political challenge.[33]

No one was more important in keeping the governor focused on the jobless than Frances Perkins. From her post as industrial commissioner, she could measure with considerable accuracy employment declines in all major lines of business within the state. Convinced, probably correctly, that she had a firmer grip on the issue than US functionaries, she regularly issued news releases that questioned rosy estimates from Washington and documented increasing layoffs in one New York industry after another. Her figures provided a rationale for strong efforts to stabilize the economy and provide help to those out of work.[34]

Roosevelt moved slowly. In the early spring of 1930, he had appointed a Committee to Suggest a Plan for Stabilization of Industry. The guiding assumption behind its creation seemed to be that careful planning by business leaders and public officials, lubricated by useful public works, could smooth out the business cycle and reduce unemployment meaningfully. By the fall, however, the sharply declining economy was overwhelming the committee's efforts. Renewing its mandate, the governor designated it as primarily "an emergency commission" with the task of coordinating reemployment and relief efforts. The longer-range concept of a progressive government-business partnership, discussed in many circles as the Depression set in, would remain firmly embedded in Roosevelt's mind.[35]

Speaking to the New York Federation of Labor convention in August 1930 and laying down a marker for his fall reelection campaign, Roosevelt called for replacement of the dole with an unemployment insurance system in which "the State, the employer and the employee would all be joint premium payers." Over the next year, strongly seconded by Perkins, he pushed the plan against legislative recalcitrance, getting nowhere with it but burnishing his credentials as a progressive with an interest in the problems of workers.[36]

By mid-1931, the Depression was generating intense hardship. On the national scene, progressives of all stripes were calling for federal relief and work programs. President Hoover responded that the government would try to speed up planned public works projects, but relief was primarily a state responsibility. Roosevelt, surely sensing both a moral need to do more for the unemployed and a political need to grapple with the crisis, called a special session of the legislature to authorize $20 million for a Temporary Emergency Relief Administration (TERA). He couched the project in ways to disarm conservatives: It met Hoover's request for states to accelerate their own public works agendas. It required labor from recipients. It would be fully paid for by a 0.5 percent increase in the state income tax. The state, Roosevelt asserted, possessed a "definite obligation to prevent . . . starvation or dire want." Threatening to keep the Republican legislature in session until it capitulated, he got everything he wanted.[37]

Organized that fall and effectively beginning activities in November, TERA was the first state relief agency created to cope with the Depression. Compatible with Hoover's guidelines, it also placed the governor in the vanguard of progressive activism. To head it up and serve as its public face, Roosevelt selected Jesse Straus, a much respected Democratic businessman. Straus picked as executive director and chief operations officer Harry L. Hopkins, a leading New York social worker. The agency cooperated with and at times subsidized local relief programs, including the very large municipal one in New York City. Hopkins took charge aggressively, organizing a strong staff, rapidly developing work projects, and wheedling discounts from food wholesalers. His energy and improvisational skills caught the governor's attention. When Straus resigned in the spring of 1932, Roosevelt named Hopkins his successor.[38]

By the time TERA began operations, New York State's unemployed totaled more than 1 million workers, the majority with families to support. As the Depression steadily worsened, so did the numbers. In early 1932, the agency estimated 1.75 million jobless. TERA's $20 million equaled perhaps $500 million in early-twenty-first-century dollars; cities, counties, and private charities provided an additional $19 million. Still, Hopkins estimated that he was able to put to work only 30 percent of the able-bodied unemployed. TERA hired mostly manual labor for the construction and maintenance of roads, parks, and playgrounds. It also had limited funds for various white-collar jobs, mostly clerical in nature.

Hopkins's first report to the public, covering the period from November 1, 1931, to June 1, 1932, asserted that 85 percent of the initial $20 million appropriation had gone toward wages. Nearly $7 million of the combined state and local money went to "home relief" (direct welfare payments). He claimed that the program had saved 130,000 families from starvation. Roosevelt secured another $5 million from the legislature. Resistance to higher taxes forced him to back a proposal for a $30 million bond issue that would keep the agency going through 1933.[39]

One idea that Roosevelt pressed on Hopkins was more an indication of his own values than a practical method for coping with the Depression. Bothered by what he saw as a population imbalance, the governor advocated the resettlement of unemployed workers onto subsistence farms. TERA helped several hundred families make such a transition. But few unemployed workers possessed either the skills to make a living at farming or the desire to make it a lifetime pursuit. TERA also funded many "subsistence gardens" in urban areas.[40]

The agency, for all its limitations, succeeded in providing much needed help to tens of thousands of families. Roosevelt was its foremost cheerleader. All of the program's facets—work relief, direct welfare, the back-to-the-land scheme, and the inevitable deficit financing—provided models for the national efforts that lay in the future.

FRANKLIN ROOSEVELT'S LAST ANNUAL MESSAGE TO THE NEW YORK LEGISLAture in January 1932 ranged across a broad swath of issues: land-use planning, criminal justice reform, new taxes to maintain state solvency, and the nationwide Depression and crises in banking and employment, as well as new departures that included public hydroelectric power, old-age pensions, and wage and hours legislation for workers. Acknowledging the crisis enveloping the nation, but trying to depict himself as a man of the progressive center, he said, "Let us not seek merely to restore. Let us restore and at the same time remodel."[41]

By about any standard, Roosevelt had been a successful governor. Politically, he had aligned himself with forces of modernization and progressivism while taking care to avoid being typed as a flaming radical. He had transcended the deep divide between urban and rural cultures that had all but wrecked the Democratic Party during the 1920s. No other major northern Democrat was so well liked in the South. Most New Yorkers realized that he was to some degree crippled, but he conveyed an image of energy that overwhelmed the reality of his withered legs and circumscribed work schedule. No other American politician had employed radio so effectively. He had positioned himself as the most likely Democratic nominee for president of the United States.

CHAPTER 11

DESTINY CALLS

THE QUEST FOR THE PRESIDENCY, JANUARY–JULY 1932

"IF IT IS THE DESIRE OF OUR PARTY LEADERS IN YOUR STATE THAT MY NAME BE presented at your coming primaries as a candidate for the Democratic nomination for the Presidency, I willingly give my consent," Franklin Roosevelt declared in an open letter to the secretary of the North Dakota Democratic Party on January 22, 1932. He would, he said, remain at his post as governor of New York, devoting himself to the interests of the people of his state while hoping that his party would give the nation "candidates who stand for progressive ideals of Government, who represent no mere section, no narrow partisanship and no special class."[1]

Roosevelt was clearly the leading contender for his party's nomination. He possessed a famous name, was a well-regarded political personality with a national profile, and governed a state that possessed forty-seven electoral votes, about 18 percent of the total needed for victory. Radio listeners across the country recognized his voice. His part-time residence in Georgia made him an adopted son in the South. He had assiduously maintained contacts in the western United States dating to his vice presidential campaign in 1920.

Though formidable, these advantages carried no guarantees. He faced the biggest obstacles within his own state: his increasingly tenuous relationship with Tammany Hall and Al Smith's reawakening ambition.

AFTER LOSING THE PRESIDENTIAL ELECTION TO HERBERT HOOVER IN 1928 and "retiring" from politics, Smith had become president of the company that built and managed the Empire State Building. The position made him wealthy, but with Herbert Hoover lurching toward defeat in 1932, Smith's thoughts and emotions all ran in the direction of another try for the White House. His relationship with Roosevelt had always been one of convenience rather than personal affection. He, not inaccurately, took Roosevelt's breezy bonhomie as social condescension. Roosevelt found it difficult to find the right tone and body language in communicating with a rough-edged man of Smith's servant-class origins. When the two got together socially, the conversation was congenial and the liquor flowed. Beneath the surface, the relationship was tense.

Word, perhaps accurate, got back to Smith that Roosevelt had accused him of leaving a mess in Albany. Smith then vocally opposed a state constitutional amendment to fund one of Roosevelt's pet projects: reforestation. The amendment carried. Roosevelt pointedly recalled that he had kept his mouth shut about occasional disagreements when Smith was in office.[2]

On November 18, 1931, the two men discussed the state budget over lunch in New York, smiling broadly and behaving genially, but most observers understood, as the *New York Times* put it, that the meeting had been arranged "purely for its pictorial effect on disturbed Democratic minds throughout the country." The next day, Roosevelt left for his customary year-end trip to Warm Springs. There he received a letter from his friend and warm supporter Clark Howell, owner of the *Atlanta Constitution*. Howell recounted a meeting with Smith during a trip to New York, during which he had asked for a candid talk about Roosevelt. Smith had given it to him: "Do you know, by God, that he has never consulted me about a damn thing since he has been Governor? He has taken bad advice and from sources not friendly to me. He has ignored me! By God, he invited me to his house before he recently went to Georgia and did not even mention to me the subject of his candidacy." Revealing an astonishing detachment from the economic crisis all around him, Smith told Howell that the main issue before the country was Prohibition, not the Depression, and accused Roosevelt of dodging it.

Roosevelt was surely correct in understanding that with unemployment at 20 percent, most Americans were more concerned about jobs and food than about beer. Smith's tirade, however, had less to do with policy disagreements than with resentment at one perceived slight after another. Howell believed Roosevelt could repair the damage. Roosevelt seems never to have tried.[3]

On February 7, 1932, Smith, claiming the continuing leadership of the Democratic Party, announced his availability for the presidential nomination. His chances were almost nil, but he remained a formidable presence. Two of his closest allies controlled the Democratic National Committee: John Raskob, still national chairman, and Jouett Shouse, the party's executive director.[4]

The next day, Smith and Roosevelt met again and talked for about an hour. Roosevelt later quoted Smith as saying he had thrown his hat in the ring only at the urging of bitter Massachusetts Democrats and had not countenanced a "stop Roosevelt" movement. His dissembling notwithstanding, the long, uneasy partnership was over, the fight to a finish begun.[5]

The rift with Smith underscored Roosevelt's still tenuous relationship with Tammany Hall and by extension other big-city Democratic organizations. Tammany and similar machines operated in an ethical twilight zone where the sale of positions and favors at best violated strict standards of morality and at worst degenerated into grand larceny. Such machines functioned in most American metropolitan areas during the 1920s, fueled by a general prosperity, bootleg booze, the rise of organized crime, and a widespread rejection of old moral standards.

As the nation's largest city, New York provided a conspicuous example, with judgeships and judicial decisions for sale, prosecutors uninterested in prosecuting obvious targets, police vice squads more prone to extortion than enforcement, and cops who occasionally hired out as underworld hit men. Presiding over it all was Mayor James J. ("Jimmy") Walker, dapper, charming, roguish, and conspicuously enjoying a high life far beyond his known financial means.

So long as the 1920s roared, New Yorkers did not seem to care. The forces of reform—respectable Republicans, the Socialist Party, and assorted independent liberals—had little basis for a common alliance and no organization capable of mobilizing voters. They could, however, make noise, which no one did better than their strongest political candidate, Congressman Fiorello La Guardia. Napoleonic in both stature and ambition, determined to become mayor of New York, and ideologically a social democrat, he ran as a Republican against Walker in 1929, mobilizing all the forces for honest government save the Socialists.

Walker crushed him, winning by nearly 500,000 votes. Governor Roosevelt got the message. Exuberant crusaders might fight the good fight to the last ditch. A working, ambitious politician with big goals had to keep the machine at arm's length while striving for a modus vivendi. Hard-eyed and realistic, the assessment exposed Roosevelt to damaging contrasts between the good Franklin, the youthful crusader against Boss Charles Murphy, and the bad Franklin, a pussyfooting pol playing winks and nods with Murphy's successor, Charles Curry.

The most sensational example of Roosevelt's acquiescence to Tammany may have been his appointment of Joseph Force Crater to the New York Supreme Court. Crater, who for a time served as secretary to Robert F. Wagner before Wagner's election to the US Senate, appears to have purchased the Tammany endorsement for the going rate of $20,000, then used his position to recoup his investment rapidly. A familiar figure in the New York nightclub scene, invariably accompanied by the showgirl du jour, he was last seen in Midtown Manhattan on the evening of August 6, 1930. Probably the victim of a gangland assassination, the judge was never found.[6]

The Crater episode was embarrassing but not lethal for Roosevelt, who covered himself by requesting three separate inquiries into New York judicial corruption. He surely expected the wheels to grind slowly and take the issue out of the 1930 election campaign. Few voters held him personally responsible for Tammany's misbehavior, and the gathering Depression was a far more immediate concern.[7]

THE ISSUE WOULD NOT DIE, HOWEVER. IN 1931, THE REPUBLICAN LEGISLATURE established a special committee to investigate New York City corruption. Its chairman, Senator Samuel Hofstadter of Manhattan, designated Samuel Seabury as committee counsel. Seabury, like Roosevelt, was a Democratic blueblood of impeccable ancestry, but unlike the governor he was a crusading reformer determined to expose sin wherever he found it. The city reformers cheered him on.

The ultimate target of the reformers was Mayor Walker, hard-pressed to explain the large sums of money that gravitated toward his person and his frequent appearances after hours with a Broadway beauty who was not his wife. Walker, a former Tin Pan Alley lyricist, was quick-witted and smart enough to avoid hypocrisy. When Al Smith advised him against running for reelection in 1929, he countered that Smith, puritanical in his marital attitudes, was against him "because I have a girl."[8]

Seabury submitted a list of charges to the governor in early 1931, but it was difficult to show that Walker, who defended his right to receive "beneficences" from friends, had crossed the line between impropriety and outright illegality. Colonel Edward M. House, once Woodrow Wilson's grey eminence and now a political adviser to Roosevelt, told the governor that he had no choice but to reject Seabury's bill of offenses. On April 28, to the reformers' dismay, Roosevelt issued a categorical dismissal, gratuitously remarking that he had debated whether Seabury's indictment merited his comment.[9]

The governor's efforts at artful dodging created a hail of journalistic criticism. In early 1931, *Time* magazine accused him of "buck-passing." An extended acrimonious correspondence followed between its publisher, Henry Luce, and Roosevelt's secretary, Guernsey Cross, who signed letters drafted by his boss.[10]

Responding to a harsh attack from the *New York World-Telegram* while on vacation at Warm Springs in late 1931, Roosevelt indeed passed the buck: "I am not pleading the constitutional fact that Herbert Lehman is the Acting Governor of the State and that when outside the State I have absolutely no jurisdiction as Governor, but I may suggest that at this distance I have just about as much knowledge of what is going on in the Seabury investigation as if I were in South America. . . . May I suggest also that if the World-Telegram wants some kind of action immediately you take it up with the Acting Governor of the State."[11]

In June 1932, just before the start of the Democratic convention, the *World-Telegram* on five consecutive days published a series of articles, written in a prosecutorial muckraking tone, condemning Roosevelt as subservient to Tammany Hall and calling him a disgrace to his family name. Roosevelt no doubt told himself that he had to move ahead in the world that existed rather than the one that he would prefer, but his earlier identity as an anti-Tammany crusader kept getting thrown in his face. Devoted supporters would stand by him. A larger public and an emerging critical commentariat with the ability to sway middle-class independent voters might see indecision and weakness.[12]

No member of that commentariat was more influential than Walter Lippmann, America's most important independent syndicated news columnist. On January 8, 1932, newspapers across the country carried his thoughts on Roosevelt's presidential aspirations. Lippmann viewed the New York governor as an opportunist adroit at carrying water on both shoulders with no strong underlying convictions. He was "highly impressionable" and "an amiable man with many philanthropic impulses" but "not the dangerous enemy of anything," careful "to offend Tammany just as little as he dared," constant only in the pursuit of his own ambition—"a pleasant man who, without any important qualifications for the office, would very much like to be President."[13]

Lippmann's column appeared just days after Roosevelt received a report from the Hofstadter committee documenting that Sheriff Tom Farley of New York County (Manhattan) had during his seven years in office accumulated at least $250,000 that he could not explain. Many observers believed the money represented payoffs from illegal gamblers, one of whom openly ran games in Farley's Tammany clubhouse. Roosevelt took his time going over the charges, asked Farley for a written reply, then conducted a public hearing, which left no reasonable doubt of Farley's impropriety. On February 24, Roosevelt removed him from office but did not press for criminal charges and promptly accepted Tammany's recommendation for a successor.[14]

Independent observers failed to perceive a profile in courage. Reform movement leaders John Haynes Holmes and Rabbi Stephen S. Wise submitted to Roosevelt a petition for the removal of the sheriff of Kings County (Brooklyn) and in a separate communication requested the ouster of the chief clerk of the Queens County Surrogates Court. Seabury delivered a radio speech asserting Tammany influence over an unnamed candidate for president of the United States, leaving his listeners to decide whether he was talking about Roosevelt or Smith. Roosevelt rejected the Holmes-Wise demands with a barbed response that charged them with "rushing into print early and often with extravagant and ill-considered language [that] causes many of our decent citizens to doubt your own reliance on law, on order and on justice."[15]

In May 1932, Seabury questioned Mayor Walker under oath about more than $1 million traced either to Walker or to a bookkeeper who used the money to pay Walker's bills. The mayor's answers were unconvincing. Another request for removal made its way to Albany, accompanied by a more damning bill of particulars. Roosevelt, attempting to maintain a frayed relationship with Tammany, resented the pressure. "This fellow Seabury is merely trying to perpetrate another political ploy to embarrass me," he told Colonel House just weeks before the opening of the Democratic National Convention.[16]

COMPARED TO THE UNTIDINESS OF NEW YORK POLITICS, ROOSEVELT'S DRIVE for the presidential nomination was a model of efficiency. Louis Howe, playing the role of "Mr. Inside," ran a small office in New York; it produced pamphlets and other literature, carried on a wide correspondence, and facilitated a first-rate campaign biography, *Franklin D. Roosevelt: A Career in Progressive Democracy*, by respected journalist Ernest K. Lindley. State Democratic chairman James Farley (no relation to the sheriff) was "Mr. Outside." He traveled widely, made friends easily, tirelessly promoted the Roosevelt candidacy, and kept in touch with Democratic Party leaders from coast to coast.[17]

In mid-1931, Farley, using the excuse of attending the national convention of the Benevolent Order of Elks in Seattle, traveled across the country and back, covering eighteen states in nineteen days, sounding out sentiment for a Roosevelt candidacy. It would have been indiscreet to send an Irish Catholic from New York into the South, where Roosevelt relied on such friends as Josephus Daniels, Clark Howell, and Tennessee senator Cordell Hull. Farley was perfect for the rest of the nation. There was little of the clichéd Irishman about him.

Tall, imposing, genial, and discreet, he was a teetotaler and as good a listener as a talker.

Meeting with Democratic officials, he found widespread sentiment for Roosevelt, most of it based on limited personal contact, a few radio speeches, and two gubernatorial wins in New York. South Dakota's national committeeman told him, "Farley, I'm damned tired of backing losers. In my opinion, Roosevelt can sweep the country, and I'm going to support him." Farley returned to Washington with 1,100 names and addresses of state and local Democratic officials, most of whom he had met personally. The trip persuaded him that his man was the only candidate with a truly national appeal and that a groundswell of historic proportions was building.[18]

The trick would be to develop a mood of inevitability that would overwhelm the one remaining barrier to nomination: the Democratic Party's rule requiring two-thirds of the delegate votes at the convention for nomination. Roosevelt had to go into the gathering with a strong simple majority, hoping that favorite sons and waverers would accept him as inevitable. At the beginning of April 1932, the Roosevelt camp disseminated a slightly optimistic tally that claimed 701 of the 770 votes the two-thirds rule required.[19]

Roosevelt still faced a gaggle of favorite sons and party princes. None were plausible candidates, but all seemed capable of controlling their delegations. Most appeared motivated by delusional egos and the faint hope that lightning might strike if the convention deadlocked. A few were genuine heavyweights: Speaker of the House of Representatives John Nance Garner of Texas; California party leader William Gibbs McAdoo; Ohio's Newton D. Baker, Wilson's secretary of war; and Owen D. Young, chairman of the board of General Electric and the most progressive business leader in the country.

McAdoo, Baker, and Young neither announced as candidates nor got around to declaring an unequivocal withdrawal. McAdoo controlled the California Democratic Party. Ohio's fifty-two votes were Baker's for the asking. William Randolph Hearst, whose communications empire included more than two dozen newspapers, a dozen and a half magazines, several radio stations, and the popular Movietone newsreels seen weekly across the country by regular filmgoers, backed Garner, who had his state's forty-six votes in his pocket. Young seems never to have attempted even a covert campaign.

Considered one by one, these rivals mostly paled beside Roosevelt. As a collective mass, united solely by their opposition to him, they could block his nomination. But doing so would involve a replay of the bitter deadlock of 1924 and sow widespread doubts about whether the Democrats were capable of governing a nation in crisis.

AMPLE CASH FUELED ROOSEVELT'S DRIVE. AMONG THE EARLY BIG CONTRIBU-tors were Frank Walker, a prominent New York attorney; both Henry Mor-genthau Sr. and Jr.; William Woodin, president of a large corporation that manufactured railway equipment; Macy's department store head Jesse Straus; Robert Bingham, publisher of the *Louisville Courier-Journal*; and Massachu-setts financier and movie producer Joseph P. Kennedy.[20]

Roosevelt was a consumer of ideas. Colonel House, seventy-three years old at the beginning of 1932, may have fancied himself as reprising his role as clos-est confidential adviser to Woodrow Wilson. In fact, Roosevelt valued him chiefly as a prestigious ornament and instead drew on a new class of university intellectuals actively seeking public service and ambitious to take their exper-tise beyond the classroom.[21]

Professor Felix Frankfurter of the Harvard Law School had been a close friend and informal adviser to Roosevelt since 1917, when he had come to Washington to chair the War Labor Board. He was especially important on the electrical utilities issue during Roosevelt's terms as governor. A protégé of the great "people's lawyer," Supreme Court Justice Louis Brandeis, and a major scholar in his own right, Frankfurter operated behind the scenes and avoided publicity.[22]

Proximity conferred power and attention to three New Yorkers, all associated with Columbia University: Raymond Moley, Adolf A. Berle Jr., and Rexford G. Tugwell. All were men of progressive inclinations, as were others who seemed to flit in and out of the advisory group, most notably General Hugh S. Johnson and Henry Morgenthau Jr. As these policy advisers gained visibility, journalists grasped for a label that would explain their function. A *New York Times* reporter came up with the phrase "brains department," then, even better, "brains trust." The latter phrase, often modified to "brain trust," would stick.[23]

Moley, forty-six years old and perceptibly balding, was a political scientist best known as an eminent authority on criminal justice. Often pictured puffing reflectively on a bent-stem pipe, he was at heart a man of moderation attuned to the need for gradual change. Berle, the youngest of the three at thirty-seven, was a law professor deeply concerned with and troubled by the political and legal implications of the modern corporation's separation of ownership from manage-ment. The forty-one-year-old Tugwell was the only professional economist of the trio. A radical critic of capitalism in his younger days, he had imprudently writ-ten poetry about rolling up his sleeves and remaking America. More recently he had journeyed with a number of political pilgrims to the Soviet Union. From the beginning, Roosevelt admired his unorthodoxy. For the moment, all agreed that the Great Depression was the result of a chaotic laissez-faire economy requiring a degree of rationalization and organization that only government could impose. Roosevelt was more than receptive to their message.

IN THE EARLY TWENTIETH CENTURY, CANDIDATES GENERALLY DID NOT CAMpaign intensively for a presidential nomination. Instead, supporters and proxies shepherded their causes through state conventions or spoke on their behalf in primary elections. This saved Roosevelt from arduous travel but deprived him of his best asset, his personal presence, and required the construction of a mostly fictional image of a vigorous man ready to seize the reins of the presidency.

As early as the spring of 1930, publicists had distributed photos of the governor on horseback and planted the story that his treatments at Warm Springs had restored his ability to ride at a vigorous trot. The *New York Evening Journal* published one such picture with captions that read, "Roosevelt's Rough Ride" and "Governor Wins Health Fight." The campaign maintained a clipping service that ranged far and wide, enabling a riposte to an editor in Huron, South Dakota: "My physical condition is about 100%, with the exception, of course, that after catching Infantile Paralysis in the epidemic in New York a good many years ago, I still have to wear braces on my legs and my locomotion is slow!" Roosevelt also "corrected" the editor of the *Butte Standard*: "I don't use a wheel chair at all except a little kitchen chair on wheels to get about my room while dressing, before I am dressed, and solely for the purpose of saving time. . . . [I]n my work in the Capitol and elsewhere I do not use one at all."

In the spring of 1931 and again in 1932, eminent physicians issued public statements certifying Roosevelt's robust health and continuing recovery from the effects of polio.[24]

ROOSEVELT TOOK ADVANTAGE OF A FEW PROMINENT SPEAKING OPPORTUNIties to convey a general sense of what he might do as chief executive. Convinced that issues of foreign policy had for the moment become irrelevant, he focused solely on the domestic crisis of the Depression and aligned himself with the party's radical wing.

On February 2, 1932, speaking to the New York State Grange, he established policy positions guaranteed to please the nation's isolationist mood. Asserting that the League of Nations had failed to live up to the vision of Woodrow Wilson, he rejected American membership in it. Criticizing the efforts of President Hoover to postpone or scale down the massive war debts owed to the United States, he declared, "Europe owes us. We do not owe her." Both stances revealed a heavy streak of cold political realism. His shift on the League simply recognized the reality that it had become a debating society, without admitting that Wilson's vision had been flawed. Still, the statement dismayed many progressive Democrats who remained devoted to Wilson's legacy. One of the most ardent was Eleanor, who would not speak to her husband for several days. His position on the war debts, which imposed an enormous burden on the international economy and had contributed mightily to the worldwide economic slump, pandered blatantly to popular sentiment. On this issue, Hoover was far more clear-eyed and courageous.[25]

Tactically, the Grange speech removed a distraction. It also got rid of an impediment to support from an important but heretofore unlikely source: Roosevelt's old nemesis, the fiercely isolationist publisher William Randolph Hearst. Before the Grange speech, Hearst's publications criticized Roosevelt bitterly; after it, the comments softened and paved the way for a détente.[26]

Three important addresses at the height of the nominating season established Roosevelt's tone toward the collapsing economy. The first, on April 7, 1932, was a ten-minute coast-to-coast radio talk. President Hoover, Roosevelt conceded, had substantially increased spending on public works, but the government could not raise the money to provide indefinite employment for the 7 to 10 million jobless. The administration's recent creation of a Reconstruction Finance Corporation with a $2 billion fund to support large banks, railroads, and corporations would do nothing to help farmers and urban homeowners facing mortgage foreclosure. The rural and small-town economy had to be revived through the restoration of farm prices. The Republican Smoot-Hawley tariff had to give way to a plan to "revise our tariff on the basis of a reciprocal exchange of goods." "These unhappy times," Roosevelt declared, "call for the building of plans that put their faith once more in the forgotten man at the bottom of the economic pyramid." Recalling his own service in 1917 and 1918, he said, "It is high time to admit with courage that we are in the midst of an emergency at least equal to that of war. Let us mobilize to meet it." Forever remembered as "the forgotten man speech," the talk delighted Democratic radicals and horrified conservatives.[27]

To the surprise of many, Al Smith joined the latter camp. Speaking to a Jefferson Day dinner in Washington on April 13, he declared he would "take his coat off" and fight any candidate who "persists in a demagogic appeal to the working classes." Smith's declaration excited northeastern conservative Democrats, but conservative southerners, rooted in an environment steeped in anti-Catholicism and Prohibition, could never embrace him. Democratic progressives, who had once favored him, were more drawn to Roosevelt than ever.[28]

The governor followed up the forgotten-man talk with his one campaign trip of the primary season. On April 18, he keynoted a Jefferson Day observance in St. Paul, just days after he had swept the Wisconsin presidential primary. Minnesota and Wisconsin were centers of midwestern radicalism with independent left-wing parties he hoped to attract to the Democratic side. His St. Paul speech reprised his interpretation of Thomas Jefferson as a large-visioned apostle of American democracy who would have favored "economic planning, not for this period alone but for our needs for a long time to come." Presenting itself as "an agency of national unity," the Democratic Party needed to labor for "a widespread concert of thought, capable of concert of action, based on a fair and just concert of interests."[29]

Editorialists across the country characterized the talk as platitudinous. Ordinary people did not seem to care. At one stop after another on his way home, waiting crowds cheered him as the likely next president. In Chicago, he met with party leaders to appeal for Illinois's large bloc of votes at the Democratic convention. Over the next two weeks, however, Al Smith's supporters would show that the enthusiasm was premature as they won solid victories in Pennsylvania, Massachusetts, and Connecticut.[30]

During his usual long vacation at Warm Springs, Roosevelt delivered his last major pronouncement of the primary campaign, a commencement address on May 22 at Oglethorpe College in Atlanta. Some of the newsmen who covered him had twitted him about the perceived blandness of the St. Paul speech. He had challenged them to write something better. Ernest Lindley accepted, and Roosevelt liked the result. It appealed to his instinct for activism and provided more widely quotable phrases.

The Oglethorpe speech surveyed at some length the devastation of the economy, criticized speculative greed, rejected the idea that capitalism was inherently unstable, and boldly asserted the need for government planning to provide a steady income and a fair share of purchasing power for the average citizen. Most memorably, it made a virtue of its lack of specificity:

> The country needs and, unless I mistake its temper, the country demands bold, persistent experimentation. It is common sense to take a method and try it: If it fails, admit it frankly and try another. But above all, try something. The millions who are in want will not stand by silently forever. . . .
>
> We need enthusiasm, imagination and the ability to face facts, even unpleasant ones, bravely. We need to correct, by drastic means if necessary, the faults in our economic system. . . . We need the courage of the young.[31]

THROUGH THE SPRING, STATE PRIMARIES AND PARTY CONVENTIONS GAVE Roosevelt a clear majority of votes for the presidential nomination. On April 30, however, Jim Farley conceded that, as Al Smith had in 1928, Roosevelt would fall short of the needed two-thirds on the initial roll call. But as in 1928, he predicted, favorite sons would then shift to the front-runner before the convention chairman declared the count final, thereby providing a first-ballot victory. This seemed a reasonable estimate until, one week later, John Nance Garner, with the support of William Randolph Hearst and the acquiescence of William Gibbs McAdoo, defeated the Roosevelt slate in the California primary.[32]

Eighteen states had yet to hold their primaries or conventions. Farley accurately predicted that fifteen would go to Roosevelt, but all were small to medium in size. Garner, on the other hand, had the forty-four votes of California and the forty-six votes of Texas. Smith would go to the convention with the votes of Massachusetts, Connecticut, Rhode Island, and New Jersey pledged or instructed to him and with large blocs from split delegations in New York and Pennsylvania. The main purpose of favorite-son candidacies in Illinois and Ohio, where big-city organizations were based on largely Catholic immigrant constituencies, was to avoid a choice between the two New Yorkers. Of the ten largest states in terms of votes at the convention, Roosevelt could count on only a unit vote from Michigan, about half of Indiana and Pennsylvania, perhaps a third of New York, and a quarter of Illinois. The "stop Roosevelt" movement seemed to have a fair shot at success.[33]

Roosevelt's precarious situation made seizing control of the convention by electing a friendly permanent chairman imperative. He backed Senator Thomas J. Walsh of Montana, an esteemed progressive, a reliable supporter, and a Catholic. Because Farley's public prediction of a wave of vote changes at the end of the first ballot now seemed less likely, the Roosevelt camp began to plan a controversial rule change: a motion to abandon the two-thirds rule in favor of a simple majority for nomination. Both moves were dangerous, exposing their candidate to an early reversal on procedural matters rather than on his merits.

Jim Farley, Ed Flynn, and Louis Howe led the Roosevelt team in Chicago when the convention opened on Monday, June 27, in the Chicago Stadium. They hoped to steamroll the gathering but were soon relieved of their illusions. Numerous interests within the party, the South especially, cherished the leverage that a supermajority rule gave them. With near certain defeat in the offing, Roosevelt sent a message asking his backers to withdraw the proposal for nomination by a simple majority. A subsequent floating of a rule for a simple majority after six nominating ballots drew few converts. It was as if the convention were a gathering of amnesiacs with no memory of 1924.[34]

The backdown was embarrassing but not disastrous. On Tuesday, Senator Walsh defeated Jouett Shouse for the post of permanent chairman by a 626–528 vote. The tally confirmed Roosevelt's majority but also showed him well short of the 769.3 votes needed for nomination.[35]

The next contentious item of business was the party platform on Prohibition, an issue that sharply divided Roosevelt's supporters. He staked out a position they could swallow: repeal of the amendment accompanied by a provision for state and local control of intoxicating beverages. The democratic localism resonated with the party's Jeffersonian outlook and was a natural compromise.

By mid-1932, the Depression had hit Chicago hard. Bread lines could be found within blocks of the convention. Banks were failing daily. The city could not pay schoolteachers. Inside the stadium, however, demon rum moved the delegates. The galleries, which Mayor Anton Cermak's machine had packed with Smith supporters, nearly booed Cordell Hull off the platform when he advocated a go-slow approach to repeal. In a nearly unprecedented move by a declared candidate, Al Smith, who was a New York delegate, came to the stage to deliver a sharp retort. The crowd roared its approval. "The Sidewalks of New York" blared from the sound system. A stampede was in the offing, but it was for repeal, not for Al. The Roosevelt managers made no attempt to instruct their delegates. Smith's short, clear plank for simple repeal was the wish of the majority; Roosevelt embraced it.[36]

The repeal plank aside, the rest of the platform was brief. It was also self-contradictory, promising on the one hand a balanced budget and on the other increased public works programs, aid to farmers, and a lower tariff.[37]

Farley and Flynn did what they could to hold wavering delegates in line and round up new ones. They reported to Howe, who never left his suite in the Congress Hotel, followed the convention on the radio, and kept in touch with his chief in Albany. Several years later, Farley vividly recalled the scene: "Louis was lying on the floor in his shirt sleeves, his shirt open at the throat, and his head resting on a pillow. He had two electric fans blowing on him to bring relief from the oppressive heat." Appearing almost at death's door, he seemed determined to live only for "Franklin."[38]

On Thursday, June 30, a day behind schedule, the nominating speeches, nine altogether, finally began. The three serious candidates were Roosevelt, Smith, and Garner. Finally, in the wee hours of Friday morning, the Roosevelt forces, still convinced they had momentum, pressed for an immediate ballot. At 4:28 a.m., the first roll call began.

The state-by-state voting proceeded slowly, interrupted by polling to verify the counts of several delegations, including the big one from New York, where Roosevelt managed only 28.5 of the state's 94 votes. Farley remembered the delegates themselves as "wan and weary, petulant and ill-humored," some sound asleep, others in advanced states of exhaustion. He was still confident that Roosevelt would emerge with so large a lead that the favorite sons would switch to him.

The tally, finally announced two hours later, showed Roosevelt with 666.25, Smith with 201.75, Garner with 90.25, and the remainder scattered among favorite sons and dark horses. Roosevelt was 103 votes short of two-thirds but far ahead of his nearest rival. No state moved to change its votes.

The second ballot followed immediately. Farley now authorized a few votes from delegates he had told to abstain from the first ballot. The result was even more overwhelming: Roosevelt, 677.75; Smith, 194.25; Garner, 90.25.

Still no break.

Farley desperately searched for more votes. On the third ballot, he managed to net only five more. Roosevelt remained eighty-seven shy of victory with no more support in sight. At 9:15 a.m., everyone in the arena had had enough. The convention adjourned until the evening.

Was there a viable alternative in the shadows? Smith had established himself as a spoiler, seemed interested only in the divisive cultural politics of Prohibition, remained unpopular outside metropolitan America, and was no longer the progressives' hero. Garner, much esteemed in Washington, was a provincial politician unlikely to resonate with most of the country and not perceptibly different from Hoover in his social outlook. Newton D. Baker was a real-life possibility.

A widely respected keeper of the Wilsonian flame, Baker could satisfy all wings of the party. Fervent supporters, among them a young utility executive named Wendell Willkie, had come out of the shadows to work the delegates personally. Thousands of telegrams supplemented their efforts. Eighty noted internationalists, headed by Walter Lippmann, circulated a petition endorsing him. Maryland's favorite-son candidate, Governor Albert Ritchie, was prepared to withdraw in his favor. Yet Baker's approach to the Depression was hard to discern from Hoover's. His highest elective office had been as mayor of Cleveland, seventeen years in the past, and he was known to have at least a mild heart condition.[39]

From Roosevelt's perspective, the situation was grave. Mississippi was ready to break for Baker. North Carolina was restive. Farley and Howe in Chicago and Roosevelt in Albany all realized that it was time for a deal with Garner, McAdoo, and William Randolph Hearst.

At the convention, Farley approached Texas congressman Sam Rayburn. In Boston, Joseph P. Kennedy and Mayor James Michael Curley made phone calls to Hearst, who saw Roosevelt as a lesser evil than Baker. The Texas delegation was willing to swallow Roosevelt if Garner would be his running mate. Garner, a political pro and consummate realist, would not assume responsibility for a stalemate and possible general election loss. Despite emotional resistance from some die-hard Texans, the deal was done.

The convention reassembled at 9:00 p.m. At the beginning of the fourth ballot, Alabama, Arizona, and Arkansas all, as on the earlier ballots, voted for Roosevelt. It was California's turn. McAdoo strode to the podium, jeered by the Smith supporters in the galleries, until Mayor Cermak finally quieted them. McAdoo was blunt: "California came here to nominate a President of the United States. She did not come here to deadlock this convention. . . . California casts forty-four votes for Franklin D. Roosevelt!" The balloting rolled on with one favorite son after another falling in line. Only Smith refused to release his delegates. The final tally: Roosevelt 945, Smith 109.5, others 13. The organist struck up the victor's campaign song, "Happy Days Are Here Again!"

After the Roosevelt demonstration subsided, one party leader after another urged unity and support for the candidate. Chairman Walsh then made a dramatic announcement. Governor Roosevelt, breaking with previous practice, would fly to Chicago to accept the nomination in person. The delegates, now mostly cheering and optimistic, felt that their party had reached a dramatic turning point.

At 7:30 a.m. on Saturday, July 2, Roosevelt boarded a Ford Trimotor, the best passenger aircraft of the day, but light, painfully slow by later standards, and incapable of flying at altitudes that would put it above bad weather. Eleanor, Anna, James, Elliott, and John were with him; so were his secretaries—Missy LeHand, Grace Tully, and Guernsey Cross—along with his personal bodyguard, a burly New York police detective named Gus Gennerich, and Eleanor's protector, Earl Miller.

The trip was a thoroughly unpleasant experience. Strong prevailing headwinds buffeted the aircraft all the way to Chicago. The nation followed its progress through radio reports of it landing for refueling in Buffalo and Cleveland. Roosevelt had never flown before; he would not do so again for another ten years. Finally, at 4:30 p.m., two hours behind schedule, the Trimotor touched down at Chicago airport.

Roosevelt transferred to a waiting motorcade that took him to his suite at the Congress hotel. After a brief time there, he was driven to the convention through streets lined with curious and hopeful spectators. Louis Howe was at his side, basking in the latest triumph of their long association. To his surprise, Howe gave him a draft acceptance speech, even though he knew that Roosevelt, Moley, and Rosenman had prepared one in Albany. "Dammit, Louie, I'm the nominee!" he said, but he took the manuscript and glanced through it while waving to the crowds. By the time they reached the stadium, he had decided that he could not disappoint the wizened little man who had served him so faithfully for two decades. He would begin with Howe's first page, then switch to the Albany text.[40]

By the time Roosevelt arrived, the convention had nominated Garner for vice president by acclamation, passed numerous resolutions of gratitude and appreciation, and endured impromptu entertainment from local singers. Seated near the rostrum, the governor received formal notification of his nomination from Chairman Walsh, then listened to a recitation of the party platform, delivered by its primary drafter and his old colleague from the Wilson administration, A. Mitchell Palmer. At last, he rose to take the few steps to the rostrum, his left hand gripping James's right arm just as it had at Madison Square Garden eight years earlier. Delegates and spectators stood also, applauding, cheering, and producing what journalist Arthur Krock called the illusion of a great surge upward.[41]

Roosevelt moved quickly to the serious and the partisan. His journey to the convention, he said, was "unprecedented and unusual," but so were the times. "Let it be from now on the task of our party to break foolish traditions." The Republicans were the party of broken promises, economic mismanagement, and concern only for the privileged few; the true progressives among them should join with him in a common cause. The "nominal Democrats" who looked backward had to get into step with the progressive majority. "Ours must be a party of liberal thought, of planned action, of enlightened international outlook, and of the greatest good to the greatest number of citizens."

Next came a list of objectives: attention to the problems of the nation based on the assumption of an interconnectedness of economic interests, cutting the cost of government, repeal of Prohibition, full disclosure in the marketing of securities, widespread and large-scale public works, aid to agriculture, mortgage relief, and tariff revision to restart world trade. What did the American people want more than anything else? "Work and security—these are more than words. They are more than facts. They are the spiritual values, the true goal toward which our efforts of reconstruction should lead." He would not cast aspersions on the Republican Party, he told the crowd, but he would call out its leaders, who had demanded observance of sacred economic laws while men and women were starving. He would, he promised, bring America back from disaster: "I pledge you—I pledge myself to a new deal for the American people. . . . Give me your help, not to win votes alone, but to win in this crusade to restore America to its own people."[42]

Eloquently crafted and forcefully delivered in that distinctive voice that bespoke authority and demanded respect, the rhetoric was that of a charismatic leader promising secular salvation. In Chicago, a partisan crowd roared its approval. Radio listeners across the country heard a formidable personality. A great campaign, near certain victory, and enormous challenges lay ahead.

CHAPTER 12

MUCH TO FEAR

ELECTION AND INTERREGNUM, JULY 1932–MARCH 1933

A DOZEN YEARS EARLIER, FRANKLIN ROOSEVELT HAD ADMIRED HERBERT Hoover as a Democratic presidential possibility and indicated a willingness to run on his ticket as the vice presidential candidate. Hoover had maintained his family's traditional Republican affiliation and, as "the Great Engineer" in the cabinets of Warren G. Harding and Calvin Coolidge, had spearheaded efforts ranging from industrial planning to Mississippi River flood relief. He had won the White House easily in 1928 but struggled subsequently to deal with the Great Depression. By previous standards, he was an activist in his efforts to deal with an economic calamity. By Roosevelt's standards, he was a clueless do-nothing. The two would face off in a bitter and intensely personal campaign fight.

AN EARLY INDICATION OF JUST HOW PERSONAL THE BATTLE WOULD BE CAME on April 28, 1932, when Hoover hosted a White House dinner for state chief executives at the conclusion of the national governors conference in nearby Richmond. Newspapers played up an impending confrontation. Rearranging the protocol for such occasions, the White House devised a seating order that put a wide distance between Governor Roosevelt and the president.[1]

Appearances meant even more than usual, making Roosevelt's denial of his disability an urgent necessity. He arranged to use the south entrance to the executive mansion in order to avoid negotiating steps and to enter close to an elevator that would take him to the second-floor reception room. He requested a sturdy chair at the dinner table and a strong man to hold it as he took his seat. He and Eleanor approached the White House a bit early, posing for a photo in which he held a stylish straight cane in his right hand and steadied himself by unobtrusively holding Eleanor's arm with his left hand. His big smile exuded relaxed joviality; Eleanor displayed the wide-eyed apprehension of a deer caught in the headlights.

The two joined a gathering crowd minutes before the president's scheduled appearance—and waited, with everyone standing for twenty to thirty minutes. The experience strained Roosevelt's fragile legs to the limit, and it showed. Twice White House servants offered him a chair. Twice he refused. Finally, the president appeared, and Roosevelt moved to his place at the table. White House butler Alonzo Fields held his chair at a prescribed 45-degree tilt. The sit-down, as Fields recalled it, was more a fall-down in which Roosevelt collapsed into the chair, legs straight out until he could unlock his braces. The White House subsequently attributed Hoover's delay to Minnesota governor Floyd Olson's unexpected failure to show up. Franklin and Eleanor suspected a dirty trick and never forgot about it.

Hoover himself thought that Roosevelt was neither physically nor temperamentally up to the demands of the presidency. He surely remembered the breezy young man in the Wilson subcabinet, attractive but lacking depth and oblivious to the experience of advancement through hard work. An orphan who had pulled himself to wealth and success, blunt and matter-of-fact, the president valued exhausting, incessant effort. He did not yet suspect that steel lay behind his rival's soft, smiling exterior. Roosevelt more shrewdly intuited that Americans preferred a sunny optimist to a dour workaholic.

The downturn that began with the Wall Street collapse in October 1929 had become a full-fledged depression by the end of 1930. Waves of bank failures, collapsing prices, and accelerating unemployment had produced the worst economic catastrophe in forty years. The malaise was worldwide and especially bitter in the industrial nations. By 1932, international trade, hampered by unstable currencies, widespread tariff protectionism, and the evaporation of savings around the globe, was less than a third of its 1929 total, and US gross national product was down by about 40 percent. By the time Roosevelt accepted the Democratic nomination, unemployment had idled one in every four American workers—approximately 15 million people altogether.

Governments in the past had done little to deal with economic crises beyond taking measures to protect the dollar and maintain the public credit. President Hoover had, by those precedents, been unusually active. More than any of his predecessors, save perhaps Theodore Roosevelt, he believed the American economy could benefit from government organization. He stepped up federal public works, but the employment generated was small. He established a Federal Farm Board to boost agricultural prices by buying and storing major commodities, but endless surpluses overwhelmed the Farm Board's appropriation. For a time he secured the voluntary cooperation of corporate leaders in maintaining employment, production, and capital expansion plans, but as the economy worsened, even the strongest corporations had to cut output and lay off workers. In 1932, Hoover established a Reconstruction Finance Corporation (RFC) to prop up shaky financial institutions, but its appropriation of $500 million and authorized borrowing authority of $2 billion, although massive by the standards of the time, were insufficient. Other administration policies— the high protective tariff, a sharp increase in income tax rates, higher interest rates—protected the dollar and contained the federal budget deficit but also got in the way of economic recovery.

What, then, to do about the armies of unemployed and the tens of thousands of farmers facing bankruptcy and foreclosure? Progressives called for big federal make-work programs, large agricultural subsidies, and, by one means or another, federal control of farm production. Perhaps out of a sense that the government simply could not afford such expensive ventures, or possibly out of a deeply held ideological conviction that they would be morally wrong, Hoover, the onetime progressive organizer, became a conservative rugged individualist. Relief, he insisted, was a local function that the national government might facilitate but could not, as a matter of principle, take over. Not until the eve of the 1932 campaign did he give in and sign a bill empowering the RFC to lend up to $1.5 billion to finance state and local public works. In the meantime, the ranks of the destitute and dispossessed grew frighteningly. On the fringes of one city after another, shantytowns began to appear, providing pitiable shelter for the broke and the evicted. The president's critics called them "Hoovervilles."

By the summer of 1932, the most nationally visible of these settlements was in Washington, DC, on the flats next to the Anacostia River, peopled by homeless veterans of the World War and their families. They were the remains of the Bonus Expeditionary Force (BEF), or Bonus Army, which had pressured Congress for early payment of a service bonus scheduled for 1945. The cause was dubious: the Depression affected veterans no more severely than it did other Americans. After an emotional debate, Congress rejected the request. Perhaps as many as 15,000 veterans stayed on in the fetid and hazardous encampment next to the river. Others took over two vacant federal buildings, scheduled for demolition, on Pennsylvania Avenue. A few camped in DC parks.

In the context of the times, the BEF was a tempting propaganda target for both protofascist and Communist Party agitators, but they seem to have made few inroads. Only a fevered imagination would envision a coup d'état, but it was not unreasonable to see the displaced veterans as a disorderly, somewhat menacing element in the life of the city. On July 28, police evicted squatters from the Pennsylvania Avenue structures amid fighting and gunfire. Hoover ultimately agreed to call out the army. Personally commanded by Army Chief of Staff Douglas MacArthur, a detachment that included machine-gun-equipped infantry, mounted cavalry, and light tanks cleared the buildings and parks. As darkness fell, the soldiers attacked the Anacostia encampment; employing tear gas and fixed bayonets, they drove its inhabitants—men, women, and children—before them and burned their shacks.

The rout of the Bonus Army split the nation along class and ideological lines. Hoover justified the drastic action as a necessary suppression of "overt lawlessness." Many Americans, quite a number of them Democrats, agreed, if samples of contemporary press commentary are representative. Many others were outraged.[2]

Roosevelt, Rexford Tugwell recalled, was privately furious. Hoover, he said, should have met with a BEF delegation. He should have sent the veterans coffee and sandwiches. Instead, he had harbored an absurd fear of revolution. He had once seemed a great man; now it seemed he had nothing left inside but jelly; maybe there had never been anything there. Having vented his feelings privately, Roosevelt made no public statement and spent the rest of the year dodging the issue of whether he favored payment of the bonus. Thus began a campaign to redefine the American future.[3]

FIRST, HOWEVER, ROOSEVELT HAD TO DEAL WITH THE FESTERING SORE OF New York City corruption and the problem of its mayor, Jimmy Walker. For progressives of both parties, the Walker case would serve as a litmus test of Roosevelt's courage. For Tammany, it would provide the ultimate indicator of Roosevelt's party loyalty. The governor opted to preside personally over a public hearing on the many charges against the mayor, then decide whether to remove him. This was a bold course that at worst could alienate Tammany and lose him New York State in the general election. To a larger national audience, however, it could display him as a fearless, decisive chief executive.

The hearings began on Thursday, August 11, in the large paneled executive chamber of Albany's old capitol building. Beneath the portraits of former New York governors, including Grover Cleveland and Theodore Roosevelt, Roosevelt presided as judge-interrogator. Legislative investigator Samuel Seabury laid out the case against the mayor. Walker, assisted by his attorneys, proved an agile and articulate defendant. The proceedings lasted for two weeks, with Seabury and his associates laying bare the multiple ways in which Walker had received kickbacks and payoffs for official favors.

Roosevelt dominated the scene, displaying an especially firm hand with Walker's counsel and not hesitating to speak sharply to Walker himself, as he probed, for example, the mayor's apparent indifference to his personal accountant's flight to Mexico. The proceedings dragged on, with the governor taking time off to give two major speeches. On September 1, Walker abruptly resigned his office and issued a bitter statement in which he depicted himself as the victim of an "inquisition."[4]

Angry Tammanyites threatened to knife the governor and his preferred state-level candidates in the fall. In the end, the wobbling machine had to settle for blocking Sam Rosenman's candidacy for the state supreme court, a move that required the organization to endorse its chief Republican critic, Senator Samuel Hofstadter, for the position. Whatever his intentions, Roosevelt had empowered the New York reform movement and fatally weakened Tammany's grip on the city. Congressman Fiorello La Guardia and the civic reformers awaited the 1933 mayoral election with eager anticipation.

VICE PRESIDENTIAL CANDIDATE JOHN NANCE GARNER CAME UP TO NEW YORK in mid-August for ritual Democratic unity meetings with Roosevelt and Al Smith. Aside from renouncing religious bigotry and proclaiming support for repeal of Prohibition, he had one central piece of advice: "Sit still and keep quiet." Widespread popular reaction against President Hoover's failure to deal with the Depression would sweep the Democrats into power in November. Garner would follow his own advice and contribute little to the Democratic campaign.[5]

Roosevelt intended to do much more. He wanted to convince the electorate that he would be a strong, vigorous agent of change. He needed to persuade Democrats across the country that he had spearheaded their impending electoral victory and deserved their loyalty. Most of all, he wanted to redefine his party as more than an uneasy alliance of seamy northern urban machines and reactionary southern ruralists.

Moved in large measure by the example of Uncle Ted, through the 1920s he had advocated a party with a strong national organization, annual leadership meetings, and a continuing national platform that transcended the quadrennial convention document. He had argued for a reinterpretation of Jeffersonianism as faith in democracy and the common people. Perceiving that the shock of the Depression rendered ethnic rivalries and cultural issues largely irrelevant, he saw an opportunity to remake his party as an activist force and carve out a new political majority. He wanted the support, and eventual migration to the Democratic Party, of independent progressives, most of them nominal Republicans.

His first national campaign speech on July 30—a radio address delivered not in an arena to a cheering crowd but from the governor's mansion in Albany, in, Roosevelt said, a "quiet of common sense and friendliness"—forecast the future not through its content but through its character. The talk itself was a bland exposition crafted to cast the party platform and the speaker as safe and moderate exponents of tight budgeting and sound money. What counted was the Roosevelt presence projected across the airwaves into living rooms across the country and the dual impressions of intimacy and authority it conveyed.[6]

Roosevelt's first speech to a large campaign rally on August 20 in Columbus, Ohio, presented a nine-point program for reform of the financial markets that pretty accurately forecast what he would do in office. Once again, however, tone was the critical feature. He hit hard at Hoover and the Republicans, decried their alleged protection of selfish concentrated wealth, and reasserted his determination to champion "the forgotten man."[7]

A week later, speaking to a crowd in New Jersey, he slammed Republican dithering on Prohibition, called for modification of the Volstead Act to permit the production of beer, and pledged himself to repeal of the Eighteenth Amendment. He made his position more palatable to the party's still substantial southern and western dry faction by stressing his belief that states and localities should enjoy a local option, and he sweetened the prospect all around by reminding his audience that the customary taxation of alcohol would yield much needed revenues for stressed government budgets.[8]

The campaign began in exhausting earnest after Labor Day. Roosevelt wanted to prove his stamina, and he quite simply enjoyed the train, the crowds, and the firsthand observation of the nation. He set out on September 12 for an 8,000-mile "swing around the circle" that took him through the American heartland, down the West Coast, then up through the mountain states and back to the Midwest before returning to New York on October 3. The schedule was grueling, but he thrived on it. All Americans knew that to some extent he was crippled, but he left behind an overwhelming impression of unquenchable vigor. It was easy to think that he had more strength and energy than the dour Hoover.[9]

He delivered his first important speech, on farm policy, in Topeka. Approximately 22 percent of the US population worked and lived on farms. Agricultural prices impacted perhaps an equal number in hinterland towns and cities. The Depression had dealt rural America a staggering blow. Iowa dairy farmers were dumping or giving away milk not worth the expense of bringing to market. For the same reason, wheat, corn, and other commodities rotted in fields. Hoover's attempts to prop up prices, although unprecedented, had failed.

Farm leaders and economists floated plans for massive export subsidies or acreage restrictions or ever-higher tariffs on foreign-grown commodities. As on most other issues, Roosevelt refused to make a firm choice. A presidential campaign was about getting elected, building coalitions, displaying concern, and showcasing leadership qualities. The development of specific, coherent public policy could wait.

Before audiences in Topeka and Sioux City, he touted his own experience as a farmer in New York and Georgia. Charging that Republican tariff policy had destroyed agricultural export markets, he talked generally about national planning, strong federal land-use policy, fairer taxes, farm mortgage relief, and reciprocal agricultural trade agreements. More vaguely, he suggested giving agricultural commodities consumed in the United States "a benefit equivalent to a tariff." These addresses hinted at what he might do without making specific commitments. They showed his listeners that he felt their pain and intended to bring them relief.[10]

The other notable speech of the tour came in San Francisco, where he appeared before business and civic leaders at the Commonwealth Club. The talk dropped more clues as to his thinking about the Depression and his future course than any other pronouncement of his campaign. Primarily the work of Adolf Berle, the speech began with assumptions that Roosevelt may well have recalled from his Harvard course with Frederick Jackson Turner. It asserted that with the settlement of the West and the end of "free land," an era of economic expansion had ended. It then moved on to the issues of corporate concentration and control that preoccupied his Brains Trusters. "We are steering a steady course toward economic oligarchy, if we are not there already," he charged. The public good demanded a reappraisal of values. The day of the great tycoon who built industrial empires was over. The contemporary task was "the soberer, less dramatic business of administering resources and plants already in hand," reestablishing foreign markets, dealing with underconsumption, adjusting production, and distributing wealth and products equitably. "The day of enlightened administration has come." Signaling the uncertainty of the times, his audience of business leaders gave him a standing ovation for an address that clearly pointed toward unprecedented government control over their activities.[11]

The long campaign tour was a triumphal procession. Everywhere, Roosevelt drew friendly crowds, whether speaking to huge audiences or making off-the-cuff rear-platform appearances at small junctions. He displayed the rare gift of empathetic communication, however fuzzy the specifics. His press coverage was sympathetic, due partly to his winning personality but also to the deft facilitation of Steve Early, a loyalist since he had covered Roosevelt as a reporter during the 1920 campaign. By the time the candidate returned to New York, his victory seemed all but certain.

Walter Lippmann ratified a growing consensus. Recanting his caustic put-down at the beginning of the year, he declared that Roosevelt had managed the Walker hearing brilliantly, displayed prudence in avoiding promises that he could not keep, and demonstrated independence from outside manipulation. As for Hoover, Lippmann believed the president would be unable to govern in the face of a Democratic Congress. "I shall vote cheerfully for Governor Roosevelt," the columnist announced.[12]

Other fence-sitters fell into line. Most predictable were the independent progressives. Senator George Norris, the most beloved of the group, appeared jointly with Roosevelt in Nebraska and tendered a fulsome endorsement. Almost all the rest followed, including Senators Hiram Johnson of California (TR's 1912 running mate), Bronson Cutting of New Mexico (like FDR, a Grotonian), and Robert La Follette Jr. of Wisconsin.[13]

As the campaign entered its final month, the raw breach with Al Smith was healed. Smith remained bitter, but he was too good a party man to take a walk. At the New York Democratic state convention, he and Roosevelt exchanged a cordial handshake. Too honest to endorse the increasingly discredited Tammany leadership, Smith aligned himself with Roosevelt by backing Herbert Lehman for the gubernatorial nomination. During the campaign, he delivered addresses for the ticket. "Radio priest" Father Charles Coughlin's strong support for Roosevelt also helped mightily with Smith's Irish Catholic constituency.

Although his general inclinations were pretty clear, Roosevelt still made vague and sometimes conflicting pronouncements. He blatantly evaded the issue of the veterans bonus and regularly condemned the Smoot-Hawley tariff while promising some measure of protectionism for agriculture. Presented with drafts of a speech, one advocating freer trade, the other strongly protectionist, he airily told his writers to weave the two together. Having intimated the need for large-scale and costly government programs, he delivered a speech at Pittsburgh in the waning days of the campaign that promised to balance the budget. With some justice, Hoover roused a crowd in Indianapolis by comparing his opponent's position on the tariff to that of a "chameleon on Scotch plaid."[14]

HOOVER, ASSUMING THAT THE PUBLIC WOULD AGREE WITH HIS DISPARAGING evaluation of Roosevelt and appreciate his tireless engagement with the problems of the Depression, had planned to remain hard at work in the White House. By October he realized that he had miscalculated badly. He spent much of the month making several major speeches and numerous rear-platform talks. He fired up partisan audiences at rallies in Republican strongholds such as Des Moines and Indianapolis, but in Detroit hostile demonstrators booed him at the railroad station and lined his four-mile route to the arena. In his last effort of the campaign, a nationally broadcast speech at Madison Square Garden on October 31, he warned that if the Democrats won the election and repealed the Smoot-Hawley tariff, "grass will grow in a hundred cities. . . . [T]he weeds will overrun the fields of millions of farms." By then, much of the electorate had tuned him out.[15]

Millions of voters had personally experienced joblessness and financial ruin. On October 31, Roosevelt reached out to them with his own nationally broadcast address, timed to follow Hoover's, from a packed arena in Boston. Declaring that "grim poverty stalks throughout our land," he asserted that the government owed "a positive duty that no citizen shall be permitted to starve." Calling relief for the unemployed "the immediate need of the hour," he also promised "a tariff benefit" for farmers.[16]

Election Day was November 8. That evening, Roosevelt, in the company of family and close friends in a small suite next to the Democratic headquarters at New York's Biltmore Hotel, listened to the radio as returns came in from across the country. By 11:00 p.m., it was clear that he was the beneficiary of an enormous landslide. Louis Howe opened a twenty-year-old bottle of sherry, filled glasses, and proposed a toast. The victor accepted congratulations, listened to returns from the West, and finally left for his Sixty-Fifth Street town house. When he arrived at around 2:00 a.m., he found his mother, now two months past her seventy-seventh birthday, waiting for him. Putting her arms around him, she said, "This is the greatest night of my life."[17]

Final returns confirmed triumph by more than 7 million popular votes. Roosevelt had won forty-two of the forty-eight states; Hoover took only one big prize, Pennsylvania, an industrial and manufacturing powerhouse wedded to a high tariff. The winner now had a little less than four months to prepare for the daunting task of governing a nation in a time of economic prostration.

ROOSEVELT REMAINED GOVERNOR OF NEW YORK THROUGH THE END OF THE year but handed off most of his responsibilities to his successor, Herbert Lehman, probably the most capable and active lieutenant governor in the state's history. The president-elect had to build an administration that would exceed Hoover's failing efforts to deal with an ever-worsening economy. Neither he nor his advisers could have imagined how much worse it would get over the next 115 days as the nation edged toward total collapse. Major bank failures wiped out the deposits and savings of millions of Americans, removing large reserves of credit and financing essential to the functioning of a sound economy. Agriculture and industry came close to paralysis. By the end of February 1933, governors had attempted to stem the financial crisis by temporarily closing banks in thirty-two states. Almost everywhere else, banks were subjected to strict limitations on their transactions. Unemployment was somewhere between 25 and 30 percent. American capitalism was on the verge of shutting down.

Hoover, although he had lost badly, remained convinced that his course of defending the dollar and protecting the government's credit was right. He hoped that with the election campaign in the past, he could persuade Roosevelt to fall in with his policies. At his request, the president-elect, accompanied by Raymond Moley, met with him and Secretary of the Treasury Ogden Mills at the White House on November 22 for an excruciating two hours and twenty minutes.

The atmospherics alone would have prevented a meeting of the minds; the two comrades from the Wilson administration had passed the point of no return in their hostility toward each other. They had also developed radically different understandings of the Depression. Hoover deemed it an international phenomenon that demanded international stabilization measures. Most salient among these was continuation of a moratorium on war debt payments to the United States, which he had accepted in June 1931. The debt payments constituted a serious drain on the economies of several European nations, endangered the stability of their currencies, and impaired their potential for economic recovery. Hoover feared that a wave of sovereign debt defaults would have catastrophic consequences. He hoped, in addition, that a World Economic Conference, scheduled for mid-1933, could effect an agreement on international financial stabilization. His acceptance of the debt moratorium and the pending conference, widely unpopular at home, had rightly received acclaim abroad as an act of statesmanship. (Somewhat inconsistently, however, Hoover was unwilling to press for a mutual lowering of tariff barriers that were strangling foreign trade. Neither was Roosevelt.)

Roosevelt, along with most of his advisers, viewed the Depression as a domestic issue requiring domestic solutions. The president-elect also wanted to preserve absolute freedom of action and surely felt that linking his name to a Hoover policy would be politically poisonous. The nation, he believed, could have only one chief executive at a time; he had no constitutional authority to take joint action with Hoover. Rejecting further delays on war debt payments, he expected them to resume as scheduled on December 15, 1932, whatever the damage to the Europeans. (As it turned out, two of the four largest debtors, Britain and Italy, paid on schedule; the other two, Belgium and France, did not. The end was near for the debt repayment system.)

Roosevelt and Hoover would meet again at the White House on January 20. The disdain they felt for each other enveloped the room. The meeting made no progress, ended with intensified ill feelings, and unavoidably contributed to the pervasive sense of drift afflicting the country.

THROUGH ALL THIS, ROOSEVELT FOUND SOME TIME FOR TWO BRIEF VISITS TO Warm Springs, a satisfying Christmas holiday at Hyde Park, and, at the beginning of February, a relaxing cruise on Vincent Astor's luxurious yacht, *Nourmahal*. The cruise—beginning in Jacksonville, Florida, proceeding to the Bahamas, and concluding in Miami—gave him time to think about numerous serious matters. It ended in Miami on the evening of February 15.

A large crowd gathered at the waterfront to greet him. Sitting on the top of the back seat in an open car, Roosevelt told his audience of the fine fishing he had enjoyed, lamented the ten pounds he had gained on the trip, and promised to return. He then slid down into a normal seated position. As he did, Chicago mayor Anton Cermak, who had come to Florida to meet with the president-elect about assistance to his desperately strapped city, came over to talk.

Suddenly, there were pistol shots.

Cermak slumped to the ground. A Secret Service bodyguard took a round through the hand. Three bystanders were hit. The driver started the car and began to move it forward. The shooting stopped after police, members of the crowd, and a woman who had grabbed his arm as he emptied his revolver subdued the would-be assassin. Roosevelt ordered the car backed up, had Cermak put in next to him, and told the driver to get them to the nearest hospital. "Tony, keep quiet—don't move. It won't hurt if you keep quiet."[18]

The shooter, an inconspicuous little man named Giuseppe Zangara, defiantly told the world that he was an anarchist who hated all presidents. In all, he wounded five people, Cermak gravely. In critical condition when he got to the hospital, the Chicago mayor rallied but then developed an infection that took his life. The state of Florida swiftly tried Zangara, who almost certainly had acted alone, convicted him of first-degree murder, and executed him on March 20, 1933.

Zangara's confession must have stirred in Roosevelt's mind memories of the 1919 bombing of A. Mitchell Palmer's house and of the bomb mailed to him, perhaps also by an anarchist, shortly after he became governor of New York. His calm demeanor greatly impressed those closest to him. He returned to the yacht that night, Raymond Moley recalled, utterly unfazed, even after having had time to take it all in and understand how close he had come to death. The attitude, Moley thought, was "magnificent." It also likely revealed a man who had become convinced after the ordeal of polio that God, or perhaps simply destiny, had marked out a plan for him.[19]

ROOSEVELT HAD BY NOW ACCUMULATED A LARGE ENTOURAGE OF SUPPORTERS and advisers pursuing power, recognition, and policy influence. Three were millionaires—Wall Street operator and World War I industrial mobilizer Bernard Baruch (often with his close aide, General Hugh Johnson, at his side), industrialist William Woodin, and speculator-financier Joseph P. Kennedy. Baruch, the largest contributor to the campaign, leaked to the press that he would like to be secretary of state or the Treasury or perhaps some sort of economic czar. Testifying before Congress after the election, he urged economic policies that struck progressives as positively Hooverian. Woodin, the second-largest contributor, was a registered Republican but nonetheless close to Roosevelt and a trustee of the Warm Springs Foundation. Kennedy hoped to play a big role in financial regulation.[20]

Many of the rest were politicians, attracted in various measures by Roosevelt's personality, electability, and ideology. Among them were Governor George Dern of Utah and Senators Cordell Hull of Tennessee, Thomas J. Walsh of Montana, and Claude Swanson of Virginia. Independent progressives had organized for him; the most eminent, after George Norris, were Harold Ickes of Chicago and Henry A. Wallace of Iowa. Finally, in the innermost circle were personal loyalists with attachment rooted in the sands of time: Ed Flynn, Jim Farley, Louis Howe, Frances Perkins, Harry Hopkins, Henry Morgenthau Jr., Steve Early, Marvin McIntyre, Missy LeHand, and Grace Tully.

The assembly of an official family involved a strategy of recognizing Democratic Party notables, then appealing to the independent progressives. The White House staff, still quite small, would consist of tried-and-true Roosevelt loyalists, indebted to no one else.

The incoming administration rolled out the cabinet choices a week after the assassination attempt. For secretary of state, Roosevelt selected Hull, much esteemed on Capitol Hill and a political friend with whom the new president had long enjoyed a cordial relationship. Baruch would have to settle for status as a friend and confidential adviser. With some misgivings, Roosevelt first offered the Treasury to Virginia senator Carter Glass, a primary author of the Federal Reserve Act and for two years secretary of the Treasury under Wilson. When Glass demurred, the post went to William Woodin. For secretary of war, the president-elect designated George Dern, a valuable preconvention backer. For secretary of the navy, he picked Senator Claude Swanson of Virginia, a valuable link to the southern Democrats.[21]

The attorney general was to be Senator Thomas Walsh of Montana, a longtime ally and reliable progressive. On March 2, while traveling by train to Washington with his new bride, Walsh died of a heart attack. Roosevelt replaced him with Connecticut Democratic leader Homer Cummings. As secretary of commerce, Dan Roper of South Carolina was probably the most conservative member of Roosevelt's cabinet and a conduit to the business community. He would have scant influence on policy.

As expected, Jim Farley became postmaster general and chief patronage dispenser. Postmasters in those days had to pass a basic qualifying examination but otherwise served at the pleasure of the president; a change of party in the White House signaled a wholesale turnover in post offices across the country. Farley would also exercise informal authority over many other nonmerit federal positions reserved not just for Democrats but for Roosevelt Democrats.[22]

Roosevelt named Frances Perkins as secretary of labor, a stunning selection not simply because she would be the first woman cabinet officer but also because she was a social worker with a direct relationship only to women's trade unions. The American Federation of Labor (AFL) openly lobbied against her appointment. She herself tried to turn it down. Never hostile to unions as such, Perkins would be more interested in promoting broad-gauged reform programs aimed at ordinary working people, first and foremost social security.[23]

Two key slots went to independent progressives. Henry Morgenthau Jr. had hoped to become secretary of agriculture but had no support among southern and midwestern farm leaders. The appointment went to Henry A. Wallace, scion of a noted family of Iowa farm leaders and the third member of his clan to edit *Wallace's Farmer*, an influential Corn Belt weekly founded by his grandfather, "Uncle Henry" Wallace, who in his day had turned down an offer to become secretary of agriculture. Henry A.'s father, Henry C. Wallace, had served unhappily in that office under Harding and Coolidge. A plant geneticist of genuine distinction, Henry A. had played a major role in the development of hybrid corn, thereby qualifying as a pioneer in the struggle against world hunger. Although a registered Republican, he had endorsed Al Smith for president in 1928 and Roosevelt in 1932. Forty-four years old at the beginning of 1933, Wallace seemed a more or less practical, orthodox midwestern farm advocate; stylistically, he was a bit rustic. No one discerned the strains of mysticism and collectivist radicalism within his multilayered personality.

Two progressive Republican senators, Hiram Johnson of California and Bronson Cutting of New Mexico, declined appointment to the Interior Department, long a focus of suspicion and concern among conservationists. Roosevelt then fixed on Harold Ickes, a crusty old Chicago progressive Republican who had backed TR in 1912 but supported Cox and Roosevelt in 1920. Anathema to the Chicago machine, he had the warm support of Johnson and Cutting. Roosevelt learned how to pronounce his name ("Ik-ees," not "Iks"), spent perhaps five minutes with him, and gave him the job.

Just a few weeks short of his fifty-ninth birthday, Ickes would bring to his post, in the words of historian Linda Lear, "unsurpassed energy, ego, and administrative virtuosity." He also possessed a hair-trigger temper, a near paranoid suspicion of others' motives, and a voracious appetite for territorial aggrandizement. From the day he took office, he schemed to wrest control of the Forestry Service from the Department of Agriculture, and he forever resented that Roosevelt (and Senator Norris) established the Tennessee Valley Authority as an independent agency. No other member of Roosevelt's cabinet would offer a resignation so many times. Roosevelt always rejected the tenders, seeing him, warts and all, as a sound administrator and a valuable token of independent progressivism.[24]

That left the personal White House staff, tiny by post-1945 standards. In 1932, Congress had provided for three "secretaries" who served as aides to the chief executive. (Woodrow Wilson had gotten by with only one.) Roosevelt's selections were largely predictable. He named Louis Howe, Steve Early, and Marvin McIntyre.

Howe's duties were at once broad and vague. Age had reduced his energy; nothing in his experience had prepared him for the Depression. In the end, Howe was in the White House because he had been a devoted loyalist for more than two decades. Roosevelt still valued his political instincts, and his presence must have provided a reassuring sense of continuity. Above all, the appointment was an act of friendship. Early and McIntyre were known and reliable actors who had flitted in and out of Roosevelt's life since his days in the Navy Department. From the beginning, Early's primary responsibility would be press relations; McIntyre would function as appointments secretary.

It went without saying that Missy LeHand and Grace Tully would make the move to Washington. Just thirty-four years old when Roosevelt assumed the presidency, Missy controlled the flow of paper to the president's desk, drafted letters for his signature, answered many routine queries herself, and did not hesitate to contribute political or policy opinions. More than ever, her relationship with Roosevelt was uniquely personal. Having power of attorney, she managed his finances, right down to controlling his checkbook. She was a regular at late-afternoon cocktail parties, frequently dined with the first family, and might be called on to serve as hostess in Eleanor's absence. Tully worked with her smoothly and tirelessly as assistant and understudy.

What to do with the Brains Trusters, for whom no appropriate White House positions were available? Roosevelt placed them officially as assistant secretaries in cabinet departments but actually utilized them as personal policy aides. Moley accepted designation as assistant secretary of state, Tugwell as assistant secretary of agriculture. Berle opted to remain in New York.

Two valued personalities seemed more or less left out. Morgenthau received assignment only as caretaker head of Hoover's Federal Farm Board. Harry Hopkins was left behind in New York. Both likely expected that bigger things awaited them.

HOOVER PERSISTED IN ATTEMPTING TO GET ROOSEVELT TO SIGN ON TO HIS economic program. The president-elect continued to balk. The financial system continued to collapse. Across the country, people rushed to withdraw their bank deposits. Available funds exhausted, banks, large and small, shut their doors. Those unable to reopen took with them the savings of ordinary people and effectively closed down thousands of business enterprises. Financial speculators, expecting a dollar devaluation, sold the American currency short and hoarded gold. With the British pound already off the gold standard, the consequences of American abandonment were uncertain, but the prospect of an international commerce conducted in currencies with no precious-metal backing seemed potentially dire.

On February 18, Hoover handwrote a long letter, delivered by courier to Roosevelt in New York the same day. It requested a public pledge that Roosevelt would defend the dollar by preserving its gold valuation and balancing the budget, even at the cost of higher taxes. Compliance would, as Hoover privately commented, close off most of Roosevelt's policy experimentation. Annoyed and still determined to preserve his freedom of action, the president-elect dallied in answering. A second urgent letter from the president finally got a response just days before the inauguration. Roosevelt demurred, leaving an angry Hoover convinced that his successor, by pursuing a policy of monetary uncertainty, wanted to create as bad a situation as possible.[25]

In Washington on March 3, the eve of the presidential transition, Roosevelt, accompanied by Eleanor, Jimmy, and Jimmy's wife, visited the White House for a customary ceremonial tea with the Hoovers. When they arrived, the outgoing president was waiting with his Treasury secretary, Ogden Mills. The president-elect immediately called for Raymond Moley to join him. After a tense hour-and-a-half wait, a policy discussion began. Hoover wanted to issue a proclamation declaring a bank holiday throughout the country under the 1917 Trading with the Enemy Act but was unsure of his authority. Would his successor join in?

Roosevelt replied that he believed Hoover had the legal power and should go ahead and issue the order on his own. If not, he probably would do so the day after his inauguration. As the meeting came to its awkward end, the president-elect remarked that, given the emergency decisions Hoover faced, there was no need for him to follow what Roosevelt understood to be the custom of the outgoing president returning the visit the following morning. As he recounted it, an enraged Hoover responded, "Mr. Roosevelt, when you are in Washington as long as I have been, you will learn that the President of the United States calls on nobody."[26]

Amid the economic ruins of the country, Franklin Delano Roosevelt was eighteen hours from his date with destiny.

ROOSEVELT HAD LEFT WASHINGTON TWELVE YEARS EARLIER, A DEFEATED BUT promising vice presidential candidate who considered his losing effort a first step toward an eventual campaign for the presidency. Everything he had undertaken, with the possible exception of the Warm Springs rehabilitation center, related to that long-term project. Even Warm Springs had broadened his political horizons by allowing him to develop ties to the southern wing of his party and by putting him in close contact with ordinary people who faced great difficulties beyond their control.

He had demonstrated invincible determination, developed a compelling personal presence, and learned to project his powerful personality over the radio. Yet many of his fellow partisans wrote him off as a light-minded opportunist. The appearance was a mask, worn by a man who valued his lineage and breeding, had confidence in his talents, and was skilled in the politics of democracy. Whether talking face to face with Georgia farmers, splashing in the pool at Warm Springs with his fellow polios, or delivering conversational radio talks to unseen mass audiences, he excelled at combining authority with a common touch.

No politician was better at identifying himself with broad common denominators in the American experience. Roosevelt told a reporter who asked about his political philosophy, "I am a Christian and a Democrat, that's all." All who knew him closely agreed that his religious convictions were both sincere and simple, little influenced by doctrinal controversies. Responding to a query about his ancestors from the editor of the *Detroit Jewish Chronicle*, he wrote, "In the dim distant past they may have been Jews or Catholics or Protestants. What I am more interested in is whether they were good citizens and believers in God. I hope they were both."[27]

Speaking to students at the Milton Academy in 1926, he declared he had learned from Endicott Peabody that human history was a cycle of ups and downs with a constant trend line of progressive change. The assertion reflected the optimism of the Victorian world in which he had grown up and been educated.[28]

His Democratic allegiance was likewise both a legacy from his father and a practical implement in the service of a larger vision. A political leader had to begin by belonging, Roosevelt told Rexford Tugwell shortly before the 1932 election. Rex's friends, the independent progressives, were a decent bunch, but they were individualists and political hobbyists, lacking organizational cohesion, possessing no comprehensive program, and bereft of the organizational skills to guide a legislative program through Congress. A president at the head of a party, equipped with a strong popular mandate, could deal with fellow partisans and get most of what he wanted. Roosevelt's "new deal for the American people" would be a Democratic program.[29]

Such comments laid out an insight Roosevelt had possessed about himself at least since he had turned down opportunities to run for the US Senate. He was an executive, not a legislative type. He wanted to run things, not debate them, to give directives rather than engage in protracted discussion. He knew that administration required powers of motivation and persuasion. He understood the power of his personal charm and magnetism when linked to the majesty of high office and popular acclaim. And he realized full well that subordinates were there to be used, with few personal considerations, for larger ends. Like his father, who had once fired a butler who applied for a position with another gentleman, he was capable of cutting off aides who left without his consent.

Franklin Roosevelt clearly had two presidential role models: Theodore Roosevelt and Woodrow Wilson. Like both, he saw himself as a "progressive," struggling for fairness and social justice against entrenched privilege. This self-image validated an appetite for power and responsibility. Like both of his larger-than-life predecessors, he believed that a president could make himself into the dominant, driving force in American politics. TR had once privately remarked that William Howard Taft was "a far abler man than I but he don't know how to play the popular hero and shoot a bear." FDR understood that a successful president had to be a self-dramatizer. Wilson had vividly displayed the power of oratory and seen himself as akin to a British prime minister, actively leading his party in Congress and pushing through a legislative program. The new president would draw heavily on both examples.[30]

Charming, inspirational, and calculating, Roosevelt was on the verge of remaking the American presidency. On the morning of March 4, 1933, the nation awaited him with an anxiety unmatched since Abraham Lincoln's first inaugural.

Part II

The New Deal

CHAPTER 13

NOTHING TO FEAR

CREATING A NEW DEAL, MARCH–JULY 1933

This is a day of national consecration. . . . [T]he only thing we have to fear is fear itself. . . . [W]e must move as a trained and loyal army. . . . I assume unhesitatingly the leadership of this great army. . . . The people of the United States . . . have asked for discipline and direction under leadership. They have made me the present instrument of their wishes. In the spirit of the gift I take it.[1]

UTILIZING A FAR-REACHING PROGRAM OF RELIEF AND REFORM AND DRAWING on a unique talent for speaking to millions of his countrymen, Franklin Roosevelt was about to bring the national government, the New Deal, and above all himself into every part of the American nation.

AMERICANS LISTENING AT RADIOS ON SATURDAY, MARCH 4, 1933, HEARD A now-familiar voice, radiating strength and patrician authority, promising strong leadership in desperate times. A majority wanted just that. "You felt that they would do *anything*—if only someone would tell them *what* to do," Eleanor remarked later. Skeptics feared dictatorial ambition. But most of the new president's countrymen, although living in desperate circumstances, had given no sign of being ready for another Benito Mussolini. They wanted assertive democratic direction, not authoritarian dictation. Roosevelt understood the difference.[2]

His inaugural address was far more than a declaration of personal strength. It expressed a classic progressive ideology in its attack on "the unscrupulous money changers" who had "fled from their high seats in the temple of our civilization," in its claim that "our true destiny is not to be ministered unto but to minister to ourselves, to our fellow men," and in its call for "an end to speculation with other people's money." It laid out a policy direction: "Our greatest primary task is to put people to work." A majority of the listeners probably nodded appreciatively at these sentiments. Above all, they wanted action. Over the next three months, in the first hundred days of the New Deal, Roosevelt pushed through Congress a legislative program that would change America forever.

INAUGURAL FESTIVITIES CONSUMED THE REST OF THAT SATURDAY. SUNDAY would not be a day of rest. As Roosevelt recalled it, he arose early, ate breakfast, and had himself wheeled to the Oval Office. Alone and seated at the presidential desk, he surveyed bare surfaces, opened empty drawers, and looked around in vain for a call button with which to summon aides. After a moment, he let out a shout that brought Marvin McIntyre and Missy LeHand scurrying into the room. The story remains a serviceable parable of the helplessness that afflicted the nation and of the new president's determination to get beyond it.[3]

Action came fast and hard. Roosevelt called an afternoon cabinet meeting at which he informed the department heads gathered around him that Treasury functionaries, most of them Hoover holdovers, were at work drafting legislation for federal inspection of every bank in the country and preparing a proclamation mandating a national bank holiday. The proclamation was issued shortly after midnight on Monday morning. A second proclamation summoned Congress to Washington for a special session to begin on Thursday, March 9.

Franklin and Eleanor found time for a birthday visit to retired justice Oliver Wendell Holmes on March 8, the great jurist's ninety-second birthday. Holmes doubtless remembered the president as one of the bright young men for whom he had hosted luncheons during the Wilson administration. The conversation was as pleasant as the champagne procured for the occasion (Prohibition notwithstanding) by Holmes's former law clerks. After Roosevelt left, the old justice delivered an evaluation that would ring through the ages: "A second-class intellect, but a first-class temperament!"[4]

Roosevelt seems never to have been told of Holmes's comment—some writers doubt that the justice ever uttered those words; others believe he was referring to TR—but the new president understood that the economic crisis demanded temperament above all else. During his first week in office, he managed a display of strength, decision, and concern that brought a strong majority of the nation behind him.[5]

BEFORE CALLING ON JUSTICE HOLMES, ROOSEVELT HAD PRESIDED OVER HIS first press conference. The newsmen were generally delighted that the president was executing a radical departure from the previous practice of chief executives, who had spoken off the record and frequently required advance submission of written questions. Roosevelt's rules were astonishingly liberal by comparison: direct attribution allowed, direct quotation with permission, everything on the record unless otherwise specifically stipulated. The exchange was informal to the point of parody: Eleanor came in during the middle of the proceedings to deliver a whispered message; Elliott staged another interruption a bit later to bid his father good-bye before leaving town. The president welcomed photographers and posed for pictures.

On the surface, the questions and answers seemed remarkably frank. In fact, Roosevelt pleased his audience and conveyed a sense of things without saying much more than that banking legislation was on the way. As a *New York Times* header put it the next day, "Enjoys Jokes, Allows Cameras." At the end of the conference, the press applauded. No president, the *Times* declared, had been as open with reporters since Theodore Roosevelt. Many of the White House reporters leaned in a liberal Democratic direction; the personal bond that Roosevelt established provided reinforcement. From time to time, the relationship might fray a little, but even those who knew that a charmer was playing them generally enjoyed the experience.[6]

Roosevelt's first working week was a hectic but carefully orchestrated whirl of activism. Motivated in part by the public relations imperative of providing a contrast to Herbert Hoover's apparent paralysis, it also demonstrated a new attitude toward the potential of government to manage the economy. Congress was not in a mood to block executive initiatives. The president met with legislative leaders, requested their advice, sometimes took cues from them, and mollified them when necessary. He also ostentatiously conferred with progressive Republicans. Over the next hundred days, Capitol Hill accepted a stunning agenda of legislation largely drawn up by the White House. Secretary of the Treasury William Woodin and Raymond Moley emerged as the president's chief financial advisers.[7]

On Thursday, March 9, Congress was back in session. The banks had been closed since March 3. Businesses and ordinary people were trying to make do with little or no ready cash, frequently exchanging non–legal tender promises to pay. An emergency banking bill was ready for consideration. Roosevelt had been up past 1 a.m. that morning, selling it to the legislative leadership. It provided for federal inspection of every bank in the United States, certification of those that were sound, and liquidation of those that were not. He had persuaded the congressional nabobs of both parties that there was no time for committee consideration or lengthy debate.

House Banking and Currency Committee chair Henry Steagall walked down the aisles of his chamber holding the only copy of the bill, complete with penciled corrections. "Here's the bill! Let's pass it!" he announced. House Republican leader Bertrand Snell seconded him. The chamber shouted a voice-vote approval. The Senate then began immediate consideration. A few mavericks talked back, but Carter Glass of Virginia, drawing on his renown as a legislative founder of the Federal Reserve System and former secretary of the Treasury, took the bill through the upper house with dispatch. That evening, Roosevelt signed it into law before a phalanx of press photographers and newsreel cameramen, then met with congressional leaders until past midnight.[8]

Over the next week, the Treasury Department, working closely with the district Federal Reserve banks, would undertake quick examinations of nationally chartered banks across the country, closing down many but allowing most to resume business, frequently with loans from the Reconstruction Finance Corporation. The administration extended similar support to state-chartered banks that appeared fundamentally sound. The calls were sometimes close. Woodin decided to reopen the Bank of America, the largest bank on the West Coast, against the contrary advice of the San Francisco Federal Reserve Bank. It surely helped that Bank of America's head, A. P. Giannini, could muster the support of California's two senators, William Gibbs McAdoo and Hiram Johnson, as well as the goodwill of William Randolph Hearst. The gamble paid off. Bank of America thrived, and Giannini became a vocal Roosevelt supporter.[9]

Even a quick-and-dirty evaluation of institutions across the country would take more than a few days. The nation needed to be informed and reassured. The White House requested and received a radio slot for a brief talk to the nation on Sunday evening, March 12, during prime time, 10:00 p.m. Eastern, 7:00 p.m. Pacific. Using skills he had honed as governor of New York, the president imagined himself talking to ordinary people seated in their living rooms around the radio. He visualized them at work the next day, on a farm, behind a counter, laying brick on a construction project, all insecure about their bank deposits and their employment.

Even more than his masterful inaugural address, which had been formal and traditional, this first "fireside chat"—a network announcer invented the phrase on the spur of the moment—was a milestone in American democratic rhetoric. Despite the availability of radio for nearly a decade, neither American nor European politicians (with the exception of Britain's Stanley Baldwin) had tried to use it as a mode of intimate contact with constituents. Roosevelt's instincts were those of a visionary who grasped the future of political communications.[10]

The opening phrase, "My friends," would become a trademark Roosevelt opening intended to diminish the distance between himself and the humble citizen. In this first chat he acknowledged the confusion most people felt, then sketched in the simplest terms the workings of a banking system that accepted deposits, loaned most of the money out, and could not possibly meet demands for mass withdrawals. The government was rehabilitating that system through regulations that would provide for continuity. Most banks were sound. They would reopen, cushioned with ample supplies of money issued by the Federal Reserve. The reopening would have to be phased. Listeners should not worry if their own bank was slow to open. Any bank that reopened was sound; their money was safer there than under a mattress. "You people must have faith; you must not be stampeded by rumors or guesses. Let us unite in banishing fear. We have provided the machinery to restore our financial system; and it is up to you to support and make it work."[11]

The delivery was perhaps a trifle fast, but the voice was firm and authoritative, the contrast with the glum-sounding Hoover great. As banks resumed business over the following weeks, customers flocked to them, making deposits that far exceeded withdrawals. Roosevelt had established a new and formidable mode of presidential leadership.

On March 10, in a bow to fiscal conservatives, he sent an economy bill to Congress. Warning that "too often in recent history liberal governments have been wrecked on rocks of loose fiscal policy" and raising the specter of national bankruptcy, he expressed alarm at a national debt headed toward $5 billion and called for broad authority to make drastic spending cuts. He got the legislation ten days later. It cut veterans benefits—half the national budget—by 50 percent and prescribed significant decreases in salaries for most federal employees. The pain thus inflicted was real and perhaps necessary, but it would not prevent the president from making enormous emergency expenditures.[12]

In order to raise revenues and redeem a promise of real significance to the urban wing of the Democratic Party, the president also sent up a bill permitting the sale of beer and wine of "such alcoholic content as is permissible under the Constitution" and establishing federal taxes on the legalized beverages. Congress quickly complied by specifying that a 3.2 percent alcoholic content was permissible under the Eighteenth Amendment, thereby clearing the way for a new stream of federal revenue. A few months later, state conventions would adopt the Twenty-First Amendment to the Constitution, repealing Prohibition and enabling a complex patchwork of state and local regulations on the subject. A divisive distraction vanished from American politics.

THESE EARLY MOVES ESTABLISHED SOME BASELINES FOR THE NEW PRESIDENCY: change, unorthodoxy, a willingness to lead, and a patina of fiscal caution. Roosevelt had won the confidence of a solid majority, but he had yet to address the fundamental problems of Depression and mass joblessness. Unemployment was at 25 percent, farm prices at all-time lows, mortgage foreclosures peaking, business plumbing new depths, and extreme hardship a way of life for millions of Americans. All this required far more than a banking act and government economy. The president and the people around him began rolling out a program that Roosevelt would later characterize as one of relief, reform, and recovery. It kept Congress in session for the rest of the spring and transformed the nation's political economy.[13]

Relief came most visibly and quickly. Two and a half weeks after the inauguration, the White House sent Congress a bill to establish a Civilian Conservation Corps (CCC), akin to the agency he had authorized in New York. Ten days later, he signed the act into law. Over the next ten years, the CCC would cycle two volatile sources of social instability—250,000 rootless World War I veterans and 3 million young unemployed men between the ages of eighteen and twenty-five—into quasi-military camps run by the US Army. The Department of Labor recruited the enrollees. The Departments of Agriculture and the Interior selected conservation projects: reforestation, erosion control, dam construction, and park maintenance and development. Robert Fechner, a vice president of the American Federation of Labor, served as the CCC's civilian director.

The camps, typically located in rural areas near small towns, instilled discipline in their inhabitants, who usually wore army-style uniforms when off base. The work, mostly manual labor, was healthy, the food simple and plentiful. The experience provided structure and basic skills. The CCC's mission embodied the passion for conservation that Roosevelt's own rural background and the example of TR had stoked within him. It also appealed to a national sense that America's natural heritage must be preserved. The CCC was probably the most popular of all the New Deal programs. In 1934, Congress established it as a permanent agency and authorized an increase to 360,000 enrollees.[14]

On May 12, Roosevelt signed into law an act establishing a Federal Emergency Relief Administration (FERA). To administer the new program, he called to Washington his old New York relief impresario, Harry Hopkins. A relentless pragmatist, Hopkins attacked problems head-on. Arriving at his new, still unfurnished Washington office, he found a desk in the hallway, sat down at it, and quickly authorized $5 million in expenditures.[15]

The agency's then large appropriation of $500 million went mostly to state relief programs, which usually made direct payments to the destitute. The FERA also provided funds for public works projects, some paid for entirely with federal money, others funded jointly with states. Hopkins, from the beginning, favored work relief. The "dole" might work for England, Hopkins conceded, but it deprived its recipients of "their sense of independence and strength." The FERA pursued primarily small-scale projects, such as road improvements and modest public buildings. It would be the main conduit of help to the poor and the unemployed for the first two years of the Roosevelt presidency until superseded by the Works Progress Administration and the Social Security Act in 1935.[16]

A chain-smoking obsessive, Hopkins fashioned projects for unemployed artists, professionals, and manual laborers alike. He attempted, not very successfully, to fend off politicians who saw the FERA as a patronage vehicle. The nation's foremost advocate for the jobless and the face of New Deal relief, he was on his way to becoming indispensable to the president.[17]

On May 18, Roosevelt signed the Tennessee Valley Authority (TVA) Act, the legislative embodiment of a promise to Nebraska senator George Norris to establish a regional development agency that would not simply harness the electrical generating capabilities of the World War I dam on the Tennessee River at Muscle Shoals, Alabama, but also pursue conservation programs, produce cheap electricity, tame the flood-prone Tennessee, and engage in economic development.

The most imposing public planning project in American history, TVA affected seven states and envisioned the construction of an additional sixteen dams. It converted a raging river into a navigable waterway, established planned communities, produced fertilizers marketed by the government, and generated inexpensive electricity that would attract industry to a largely agricultural region. Headquartered in Knoxville, Tennessee, it seemed a major example of the Jeffersonian decentralization that remained important to many Democrats. Its founders proudly, and with some exaggeration, touted it as an example of "grassroots democracy." Over the next several years, it provided jobs aplenty, but from the beginning, it also challenged traditional notions about the baseline importance of private enterprise in American society, especially corporate capitalism as embodied in the electrical utility industry.[18]

Relief also meant mortgage assistance. Farmers, who had suffered from depressed commodity prices since the end of World War I, had taken a beating in the twenties. The Depression turned all but the most efficient farm operations into money losers; mortgage foreclosures mounted ominously. On March 27, Roosevelt signed an executive order merging nine separate federal rural credit agencies into one Farm Credit Administration (FCA) and appointed his loyal friend Henry Morgenthau Jr. to head it. On June 16, the Farm Credit Act equipped the FCA with broad authority to refinance farm mortgages, issue new loans, establish local debt-adjustment committees, and assist agricultural cooperatives.[19]

Since the beginning of the Depression, foreclosures had blighted not just the countryside but also the urban neighborhoods of middle-class America. Roosevelt and the New Dealers had not taken office with a master plan to enlarge homeownership in the United States, but their efforts moved almost irresistibly in that direction. The Hoover administration had established a network of Federal Home Loan Banks to underwrite mortgages. Roosevelt greatly enlarged the system with the establishment of the Home Owners Loan Corporation (HOLC), which became law on June 13. The HOLC subsequently acquired approximately 75 percent of the total value of nonfarm home mortgages in the United States. The establishment of the National Housing Administration in 1934 would provide federal underpinning for long-term mortgages financed through federally chartered and insured savings and loan associations.[20]

The first hundred days provided relief from the ravages of the Depression on an unparalleled scale. For those at the receiving end, the New Deal was all about government assistance; this was the primary source of allegiance for many voters. Roosevelt and his advisers were more expansive in their ambitions. The Depression, as they saw it, provided an opportunity to reshape the American economy.

The president and the people around him believed that government needed to play a much bigger role in the economy as regulator, promoter, and balance wheel. The general idea was not new. During the last comparable national emergency, the World War, the government had assumed active management of agriculture through Herbert Hoover's Food Administration and of industry through Bernard Baruch's War Industries Board. Roosevelt and the New Dealers downplayed Hoover's past as an economic manager but wanted to build on his rudimentary efforts in the 1920s to organize the American economy, first as secretary of commerce, then as president. The state, as they saw it, could partner with business, labor, and agriculture. Reform, they had no doubt, would facilitate, not hinder, recovery. From that perspective, the centerpieces of the New Deal were not the relief efforts, worthy though they might be, but the agricultural and industrial programs.[21]

FARMING HAD BEEN THE SICK MAN OF THE AMERICAN ECONOMY SINCE THE END of the World War. From the earliest days of the republic, agriculture had comprised two socioeconomic strata: impoverished operators, struggling for a bare subsistence on marginal land they frequently did not own, and middling to large operators, often heavily in debt, producing for a market over which they had no control. Most New Deal legislation for agriculture targeted the latter group.

The marginal farmers, pursuing hard lives that provided no promise of prosperity, were mostly relief problems. The larger farmers constituted a necessary agricultural adjunct to an industrial economy. Especially in the South they might be exploiters of the marginals, whom they employed as sharecroppers or tenants. Nonetheless their production fed and clothed a nation and attracted the attention of congressmen and federal officials. Large organizations—the Farm Bureau Federation, the National Farmers Union, and the National Grange—spoke for them in Washington and developed local followings through cooperatives that sold insurance, processed crops, and ran retail farm supply operations. The Department of Agriculture was already a sprawling bureaucracy, centered in Washington but reaching out to the state and county levels through the land-grant agricultural and mechanical college system that could be traced back to Lincoln and the county agent program established under Woodrow Wilson. The still-powerful Jeffersonian folk belief that tilling the soil was a uniquely virtuous occupation deserving of national support reinforced this highly organized web of political power.

Nearly half of all Americans depended economically on agriculture, either as farmers or as residents of small towns and cities in rural areas. Agricultural regions were palpably overrepresented in Congress. (The Supreme Court mandate for equalization of legislative districts was decades in the future.) The South, the core region of the Democratic Party, was heavily agrarian in its politics and economy.

For all its organization and emotional support, agriculture had enjoyed scant success in its drive for assistance during the 1920s, achieving only some minor legislative victories during the presidency of Warren G. Harding before slamming into the free market ideology of Calvin Coolidge. American farming was deeply divided between five basic commodities—wheat, corn, cotton, rice, and tobacco—predominant in different areas of the country and subject to different market conditions. In addition, many agriculturalists produced specialized crops that ranged from hops and barley to citrus fruit, or they derived their income from milk or raised livestock for slaughter. Nor was there one single farm ideology or political agenda. The farm organizations proposed remedies ranging from price supports to export subsidies to Bryanite currency inflation.

Two things were certain: the Depression had flattened about every variety of farm income, and the unrest in rural America was nearly revolutionary. Here and there, armed bands of farmers blocked foreclosure sales. In Iowa, a spontaneous movement, the Farmers' Holiday Association, headed by a firebrand named Milo Reno, set up roadblocks manned by shotgun-wielding dairy farmers to intercept and dump milk on the way to processing plants. The movement, although illegal and ineffective, enjoyed widespread local support.

Against this background of armed agrarians attempting to stave off personal and financial ruin, Congress and the administration labored to put together an agricultural relief and recovery program. The effort consumed ten weeks following Roosevelt's inauguration.

Secretary of Agriculture Henry Wallace, aided by Rexford Tugwell and the department's Bureau of Agricultural Economics, developed a new approach to the problem of chronic surpluses. Farm leaders had wanted the government to buy excess production and dump it overseas, but such an exercise would generate ever-greater surpluses and require unsustainable funding. Wallace and his advisers believed that a farm program had to consist primarily of payments for cutting production. Their system, "domestic allotment," would have large components of decentralization and individual choice. Administered by local committees organized by the Agricultural Extension Service and its county agents, the program would assign to farmers in every county a certain number of acres to be withdrawn voluntarily from production in exchange for a generous government payment. The resulting drop in production would swing supply into balance with demand, increase commodity prices sharply, and bring prosperity back to the countryside. Rotation of fallow acreage over a cycle of years would moreover serve as a conservation measure.

The concept was attractive to academic planners. But would it actually reduce production? Might it instead encourage farmers to use their allotment payments to finance equipment, fertilizers, and hybrid seed that would get more from less soil? Was it moral in a time of widespread want to restrict production? What kind of big-brother government would be needed to police the plan?

A surprising number of politicians and farm leaders argued for full production and lavishly subsidized exports. Others fell back on the old agrarian nostrum of currency inflation. John A. Simpson, president of the National Farmers Union, advocated a government guarantee of the "cost of production," which of course was easier to talk about than to determine. Rural legislators led by Senator George Norris lined up to support the proposal. Roosevelt, determined to keep the costs of farm support within reasonable bounds, got it killed.[22]

On May 12 the congressional sausage grinder finally sent the president an omnibus bill that combined three major strands of legislation: mortgage relief, agricultural organization, and monetary expansion. The heart of the bill provided for the establishment of an Agricultural Adjustment Administration (AAA) built around the domestic allotment concept but containing far-reaching authority to limit production by other means, including subsidization of agricultural exports. Its first head, George N. Peek, had spearheaded the drive for full production and export subsidies during the previous decade. The monetary provisions gave the president wide authority to devalue the dollar by adjusting the official Treasury price of gold, establishing silver as a basis for American currency, or simply printing greenbacks. They established much of the legal basis for Roosevelt's monetary experiments over the next year.

ON MAY 7, WITH PASSAGE OF THE AGRICULTURE BILL IMMINENT AND ENACT-ment of an industrial recovery bill within sight, Roosevelt delivered a second fireside chat. Laying out as nonthreateningly as possible his vision of the administration's mission, speaking in measured and authoritative cadences, and ad-libbing frequently to make the formal text more conversational, he declared it "wholly wrong" to characterize his program as one of government control of farming, industry, and transportation. "It is rather a partnership."[23]

The linchpin of the emerging "partnership" for industry was the National Industrial Recovery Act (NIRA), passed on June 16, just before the special session of Congress adjourned. The industrial economy far outstripped agriculture in importance and long had been the dynamic source of economic growth in the country. The New Deal would stand or fall as an economic recovery program on this legislation.

Like other major New Deal programs, the NIRA had divergent sources. But as with the agricultural measures, it drew on a common theme: the perceived need for centrally administered organization of the American economy. Like the agriculture community, the "business community" was divided between large corporations with a global reach and small to midsize enterprises whose operations were local to regional in scope. The lines of business themselves were multitudinous. As in agriculture, the large players were the truly important objects of a recovery program.

Herbert Hoover had favored voluntary industrial self-government with government acting in an advisory capacity. Roosevelt and his advisers wanted to build on this vision. But what limits or mandates did self-regulation require?

Would "reform" lead to price fixing, division of marketing territories, and similar cartel-like practices?

Organized labor, a growing voice in the Democratic Party, wanted strong federal backing for unionization, arguing that this would ensure fairness and decent wages for workers. Senator Hugo Black of Alabama sponsored legislation for the establishment of a thirty-hour workweek that would presumably spread employment around. The unions backed it. On April 6, the Senate passed the Black bill, forcing the administration to formulate and push through an alternative.

Drawing on the experience of the War Industries Board and Hoover's own efforts during the 1920s, White House drafters, legislators sympathetic to the labor movement, and a few business leaders developed a bill that provided for the organization of business into self-governing trade associations, akin to the construction industry association Roosevelt had headed for a time in the 1920s. Each would adopt "codes of fair competition" with the force of law. The codes would dictate pricing and marketing, provide workers with minimum wages and maximum hours, and recognize their right to bargain collectively. The codes and the trade associations would function under the aegis of a National Recovery Administration (NRA) with wide supervisory and enforcement authority. The NRA, the administration believed, would foster a healthy reform of industry.

Title II of the NIRA established a Public Works Administration (PWA) with a huge appropriation of $3.3 billion, equal to the total outlay of the federal government just three years earlier. The PWA would become known for large-scale enterprises—great hydroelectric dams, suspension bridges, spacious auditoriums, and port facilities—but during its first two years it pursued many modest projects. The PWA also undertook many state-level projects, but these required matching funds, were slow to get under way, and were often too dispersed to have much of an economic impact. Conceived as a part of the economic recovery program, the PWA actually operated more as a conventional construction program that concentrated on high-quality work and scrupulously honest management. Over a ten-year history, it would provide a lot of employment and produce such national ornaments as New York's Triborough Bridge and the Grand Coulee and Bonneville dams.[24]

It seemed reasonable to assume that a single administrator with the authority to coordinate their activities would run both agencies. Instead Roosevelt picked retired General Hugh S. Johnson, one of the bill's primary formulators, to head the NRA and named Secretary of the Interior Harold Ickes to run the PWA. Perhaps he thought the two jobs were too much for any one appointee. Perhaps he simply did not want to give one person so much power and authority.

In addition to legislation related to relief and economic restructuring, the president promoted and Congress delivered a Railroad Transportation Act, which would attempt with scant success to revive major rail lines bogged in bankruptcy; a Truth in Securities Act, which would lay the groundwork for the establishment of the Securities and Exchange Commission a year later; and the Glass-Steagall Act, which established the Federal Deposit Insurance Corporation and separated retail and investment banking.

Congress adjourned 104 days after Roosevelt's inauguration. Americans had witnessed history racing at top speed before their eyes. Roosevelt had been at the center of it all, making the key decisions in negotiations with Congress, swaying the public with his radio talks and press conferences, and overwhelming Washington in a fashion that eclipsed even the example of Uncle Ted.

It was natural to feel that a strongman president had executed a major departure in American politics. But how drastic was it? How radical? On the one hand, the emerging New Deal seemed to be building huge new bureaucracies to run the economy. On the other, it made much of its Jeffersonian Democratic roots. The agricultural program was organized at the county level, and participation was optional. The National Recovery Administration declared that most of its codes would be written at a regional level, would be minimal, and, although they had the force of law, would rely on voluntary compliance rather than strict enforcement. Some critics grumbled that this was all a smoke screen for progressive centralism and large-scale government compulsion of a sort that would have delighted Uncle Ted (or Stalin or Trotsky). But key personnel the president had chosen—Woodin at Treasury, Johnson at the NRA, Peek at the AAA—seemed safe and conservative.

Even the government expropriation of the nation's gold supply was not out of line with emergency measures taken in other nations. For every person who feared a devaluation of the dollar, a dozen or more others would, for various reasons, welcome such an event. Above all, the nation saw a magnetic president who had taken bold action in attacking a major crisis.

After signing the final pieces of legislation and turning implementation over to his subordinates, Roosevelt left Washington for a much deserved vacation. He traveled by train to Boston, where an estimated 250,000 people lined the streets to cheer him, then continued to Groton to pay respects to the revered old rector, and then went on to Buzzards Bay, where a rented forty-five-foot schooner, *Amberjack II*, awaited him. Accompanied only by his sons, James and Franklin Jr., he sailed some four hundred miles up the coast of Maine, shadowed by a small press boat and the US Navy cruiser *Indianapolis*. To surface appearances, the sailing was quiet and carefree. Inwardly, the president pondered whether the New Deal was compatible with efforts to reconstruct an international economic order that had largely collapsed in the chaos of the Depression.

BEFORE THE DEPRESSION, THE INTERNATIONAL ECONOMY HAD HINGED ON A gold standard in which the major currencies—the French franc, the German mark, the American dollar, and, above all, the British pound—participated. Central banks issued currency redeemable in gold and accumulated the reserves of the precious metal to back up their paper. The gold standard inhibited monetary expansion and enforced stability to the point of a deflationary bias. Debtors, whether nations, business, or individuals, shrank from it; creditors embraced it.

The dollar had always been backed primarily with gold, but the United States had periodically flirted with unsecured greenbacks and issued some currency based on silver. These policies encouraged growth and speculative investment but also gave rise to fluctuating prices and economic instability. After the victory of William McKinley over William Jennings Bryan in 1896, both political parties accepted that US currency would be based on gold at $20.67 to the ounce, the issuance of a relatively small amount of "silver certificates" notwithstanding.

The World War had shaken the European economic order to its roots, leaving the preeminent European powers with huge debts and making an outsized creditor of the United States. Attempts by the European nations to reestablish their currencies had been fraught with difficulty. France and Germany had to undertake dramatic devaluations. Britain resumed gold payments at the prewar rate in 1925 but was forced to abandon the gold standard in 1931, when it also dropped free trade for protectionism. German efforts to defend the mark catastrophically deepened the Depression and facilitated the rise of Hitler. Italy, under the dictatorship of Benito Mussolini, stayed with gold. So did France.

Currencies redeemable in gold might signify economic strength, but they also made their countries' goods expensive in international trade. The obligation to redeem paper currency or bonded indebtedness in gold limited the amount a country could issue. During hard times, an inability to expand the money supply depressed price levels and made it difficult to manage formerly rational levels of debt. Whether democratic or authoritarian, the remaining gold standard nations hung on with caveats, arcane economic management, and a tolerance for pain.

By the time Roosevelt took office, world trade had all but collapsed, and the monetary system that served as its basis was in a shambles. In 1931, Great Britain had shaken the international financial community by suspending redemption of pound sterling obligations in gold. At the insistence of much of the rest of the world, President Hoover had declared a one-year moratorium on war debts owed the United States. Economists and practical businesspeople alike agreed that a revival of world trade and prosperity would require at least a long-term suspension of war debt payments, a general lowering of tariffs, and a reformed international monetary system that would peg currencies to each other at reasonable valuations.

By mid-1933, only the United States among the large economic powers maintained a truly convertible gold standard. At his first press conference, Roosevelt had made much of presumably temporary European restrictions on gold payments. He surely realized also that continued embrace of the gold standard and defense of the dollar would sharply curtail his ability to engage in the deficit spending that his recovery plan would require.[25]

Roosevelt undertook a series of actions to establish a federal gold hoard that could be used to defend the US dollar but also suspended redemptions of dollar obligations in gold. An act nullified gold clauses (payment in gold or its equivalent) in private business contracts. The administration suspended international transfers of gold. Most controversially, it moved to establish a government monopoly on ownership of commercial gold. On April 5, the president issued Executive Order 6102, requiring delivery of all gold coins, bullion, and gold certificates to the government in exchange for Federal Reserve notes backed only by the full faith and credit of the United States. The order made exceptions only for collectibles, jewelry, industrial needs, and foreign commercial ownership or obligation.[26]

For nearly two years, governments had been planning a World Economic Conference in the hope of establishing a stable system that would restart world trade by addressing the three major international issues of the Depression: currency stabilization, tariffs, and war debts. The active collaboration of the United States was essential. The problem was that the United States would need to make most of the concessions on all three topics. Roosevelt found himself forced to make time during the hundred days to meet with high-level European officials who urged him to make these sacrifices. For the most part, they left feeling encouraged.

The conference convened in London on June 12, just as the National Industrial Recovery, Home Owners Loan, Farm Credit, Emergency Railroad, and Glass-Steagall bills were all nearing passage on Capitol Hill. The American delegation itself was split and, in the absence of a firm mandate from Roosevelt, lacking in direction. It arrived in London with no clear negotiating positions. Its formal leader, Secretary of State Cordell Hull, presided over a motley group that included currency inflationists, sound-dollar men, internationalist free traders, and nationalist protectionists. The personal conflicts were even worse than those over policy. Nevada senator Key Pittman, a single-minded advocate of his state's silver-mining interests and also known for his attraction to good whiskey, pursued delegation staffer Herbert Feis through Claridge's hotel with a hunting knife. Hull resented the presence of his nominal subordinate, Assistant Secretary of State Raymond Moley.[27]

In theory, the delegates to the meeting could agree to the essentials necessary to revive the world economy. In fact, a self-enforcing general agreement was impossible. State planning, protectionism, and competitive currency devaluations had become common. No rational observer could believe that authoritarian nations such as Germany, Italy, or Japan would embrace open trade. It was reasonable to doubt that Britain, France, or other democracies would do much better. In the United States, both political parties were committed to the proposition that war debts must be paid to the US Treasury in full, and at American insistence the possibility of rescheduling payments had been removed from the agenda. The Democratic Party remained committed in principle to lower tariffs, but Roosevelt had pointedly refused to ask for a revision of Smoot-Hawley and seemed well on the way to initiating a system of national planning that might require trade barriers. It did not help that since being decoupled from gold, the dollar had been in free fall against the British pound. On April 1, it had taken just $3.42 to buy one pound; by June 30, the price would be $4.26. This collapse reflected a wide expectation that Roosevelt was planning a sharp devaluation.[28]

What then, in the end, was the purpose of the London conference? At best, it might set the table for trade deals and promote a sense of common interests among the shrinking number of liberal democratic powers in attendance. Bilateral negotiations between the British and American representatives raised the strong possibility of a reasonable dollar-pound ratio in a range centered on $4.00. Whether a trade agreement might follow was more speculative. Such accords would have possessed great value but would also have required determined leadership and heavy political lifting in both Washington and London.[29]

Roosevelt, despite a surface affinity for low tariffs and an attraction to international leadership, simply was not interested. Neither were most of his advisers. They distrusted Europeans in general, leaned toward national planning and economic management as the road to prosperity, and valued freedom of action above all else. The British and other Europeans were not much different. The American response to the conference would harden their attitudes.

On Friday, June 29, after hours of fighting a thick fog, Roosevelt piloted *Amberjack II* into the harbor at Campobello, just as he had done with similar small craft in happier years. An enthusiastic crowd awaited him, including much of the island's year-round population, the premier of New Brunswick, Canadian Mounties in dress uniform, and Scottish bagpipers. It was his first visit since he had been carried away on a stretcher twelve years earlier. He spent a pleasant three days at the old vacation house, departing on Sunday, July 1.

There, isolated from most of his economic advisers, he sent a personal, decisive message to the London conference: It would be a catastrophe if the meeting allowed itself "to be diverted by the proposal of a purely artificial and temporary experiment affecting the monetary exchange of a few nations only." The "sound internal economic system of a nation" was more important than "the price of its currency." He went on to say that the "old fetishes of so-called international bankers are being replaced by efforts to plan national currencies with the objective of giving to those currencies a continuing purchasing power which does not greatly vary in terms of the commodities and need of modern civilization." The United States, he continued, wanted to stabilize every nation's currency and restore world trade, but just how remained a mystery.[30]

The great British economist John Maynard Keynes, perhaps because he desperately wanted to influence Roosevelt, praised the president as "magnificently right" for refusing to accept old nostrums. The president, he bravely asserted, had not foreclosed a cooperative relationship with the British government. But Roosevelt had done just that. As both Keynes and the president surely understood, general currency stabilization in the world of 1933 could not take place without an agreement among leading gold bloc nations and the two great economic powers that had renounced gold, Britain and the United States.[31]

The letter blew up the economic conference, which staggered along for a few more weeks, then adjourned devoid of accomplishment. Roosevelt had chosen to go it alone economically, just as had most other national leaders. In the circumstances of mid-1933, the decision was easy, driven in substantial measure by the emotional isolationism embedded in the political DNA of most Americans. The shrinking number of liberal, democratic nations that looked to America for leadership learned a hard lesson. The British chancellor of the

Exchequer, Neville Chamberlain, was inclined from that point on to consider Roosevelt untrustworthy.

In the United States, there was scant popular dissent and a wide understanding that Roosevelt had told the rest of the world that the United States would pursue recovery at home, unhampered by international constraints. It was now up to the New Deal to restore the economy.

CHAPTER 14

UNLIMITED AMBITIONS, LIMITED ACHIEVEMENT

THE FIRST NEW DEAL, JULY 1933–NOVEMBER 1934

FRANKLIN ROOSEVELT'S PROMISE OF A NEW DEAL REQUIRED TRANSFORMATIVE expansions of both the government and the Democratic Party. Like all presidents, he could bring a few loyalists to Washington, but mostly he had to staff his administration with individuals who possessed independent identities and ambitions. They managed big new programs that sought comprehensive organization of the economy. Roosevelt welcomed the challenge, but inevitably the achievements of both the people and the programs were mixed. The assumption was that reform and recovery were inextricably linked. But were they? Or would one get in the way of the other? The result would be the First New Deal, whose performance failed to match its promise.

THE FIRST IMPERATIVE REMAINED RELIEF FOR THOSE STILL JOBLESS OR DESTI-tute after the economy began its slow recovery. With the Public Works Administration (PWA) perhaps unavoidably moving slowly, Roosevelt gave Harry Hopkins $400 million from the PWA and Federal Emergency Relief Administration (FERA) appropriations to set up a new agency, the Civil Works Administration (CWA). Established at the beginning of November 1933, by January

1934 it had funded 4 million jobs. The CWA established a template for federal work relief during the 1930s, exhibiting in abundance both the shame and the glory of such efforts. The glory showed amply in the improvement of roads and highways; the construction and refurbishment of schools; the employment of teachers; the building of public parks, swimming pools, sidewalks, and sewage systems; and the commission of murals and other works of public art. Some projects, created almost overnight, were shoddy, but most held up fairly well. Others, such as the raking of leaves in public parks, were evanescent, but even leaf raking needed to be done.

The shame grew out of the inevitable difficulties of administering a hastily conceived and lavishly funded program that reached into practically every county in the country. The CWA had to appoint state "reemployment directors" (who might have little or nothing in the way of staff resources) and rely largely on them to coordinate local committees that did the hiring and supervised the projects. From the beginning, local Democratic politicians took charge and behaved as American politicians always had when handing out money and jobs. They took care of friends and, following a still common practice, often exacted kickbacks as the price of employment or business relationships.

Critics, mostly Republicans, railed against waste and corruption, scoring points with Americans who could locate themselves in the secure middle class. Hopkins did what he could to stop such practices, even bringing in army officers to act as state and regional supervisors, but the political system was well entrenched. Members of Congress, who controlled the appropriations, almost unanimously viewed a jobs program as a patronage vehicle and fought to be certain that it benefited them and their supporters. The New Dealers could not overcome them. In the spring of 1934, the administration terminated CWA as a distinct agency, although the FERA carried on some of its projects. Recovery, Roosevelt hoped, was just around the corner; large-scale federal relief would soon be unnecessary.

The Public Works Administration began to establish itself as a major force. Its head, the pugnacious and incorruptible progressive Republican Harold Ickes, had witnessed too many dubious examples of public contracting in his hometown of Chicago. He insisted on vetting large-scale projects with extreme care. The imperative of honesty overrode the need for a quick economic stimulus.

The PWA picked up a few big ongoing endeavors, including the huge dam already under construction on the Colorado River, christened Hoover Dam by Ickes's predecessor, Ray Lyman Wilbur. Ickes, with typical peevishness, changed the name to Boulder Dam, a designation that stuck until the Republicans regained the presidency two decades later. Looking for jobs that could get under way quickly, the PWA outraged congressional progressives by invest-ing $238 million in a pet Roosevelt cause: a major naval building program that implemented plans for two aircraft carriers, a heavy cruiser, three light cruis-ers, four submarines, and twenty-two destroyers. Roosevelt probably imagined the ghost of Admiral Alfred Thayer Mahan nodding approvingly. The PWA also made loans to hard-pressed railroads.[1]

Most PWA projects were developed at the state level, required matching funds appropriated by legislatures, and ranged from monumental engineering chal-lenges to modest public buildings and bridges. The projects included construc-tion of rural roads, huge hydroelectric dams, municipal sewage systems, great bridges, and transportation tunnels, as well as naval construction and work on rivers, harbors, and flood control. In July 1934, the agency estimated that it directly employed 600,000 persons and indirectly funded 1.2 million more.[2]

Ickes, sixty in 1934, presided over these commitments with fierce, curmud-geonly integrity. He personally examined major contracts, fought bureaucratic turf battles with other New Deal stalwarts, and often behaved with egregious self-righteousness. Despite these faults, he revitalized the Department of the Interior and ran an extraordinarily honest program of public improvements. He was unremittingly loyal to Roosevelt, who in turn considered him an invaluable political and administrative asset.[3]

Other relief programs appeared on the fringes of the New Deal: rural reha-bilitation, subsistence homesteads, planned communities built from the ground up, farming co-ops. The Resettlement Administration (RA) consolidated these various endeavors under the directorship of Rexford Tugwell in 1935. Whether just outside large cities (Greenbelt, Maryland) or in remote Appala-chia (Arthurdale, West Virginia), RA projects aimed to help long-term jobless workers and impoverished subsistence farmers. They assumed that Americans in need would shed their traditional individualism and embrace cooperative principles such as shared ownership and group responsibility. But, implicitly rejecting no-fault welfare liberalism, the RA chose its clients carefully through a rigorous application process.

The co-op programs were comparatively small but, when measured on a cost-per-recipient basis, expensive. Ickes constantly fretted over the cost of PWA-funded community projects pushed by the First Lady. (One planned West Virginia town was actually named "Eleanor" in her honor.) The president suppressed any doubts he may have harbored. Speaking at Arthurdale in May 1938, he justified the outlays as development costs in a pioneering venture that would ultimately "save human lives and human happiness as well as dollars in this march of progress that lies ahead of us."[4]

All the same, the cooperative communities went against the American grain of individual ownership and self-reliance. New Deal programs that extended a helping hand or provided a salary in exchange for work were popular. But most Americans either recoiled from, or simply found incomprehensible, arrangements that, however comfortable, involved an administered collectivism. The Resettlement Administration would establish numerous farming cooperatives, providing cozy cottages, up-to-date mechanized equipment, and medical care programs, supervised by a team of project managers. Conservatives overheatedly denounced these exercises in benevolent paternalism as Stalinist collectivism. The beneficiaries themselves frequently grew restless and perhaps annoyed at being told what was best for them. Interviewing one on a successful RA plantation in Arkansas, Tugwell's aide, Will Alexander, asked for a candid reaction. The grizzled hardscrabble farmer, probably better off than at any time in his life, said, "I believe a man could stick around here for five or six years and save enough money to go off and buy himself a little hill farm of his own."[5]

By mid-1934, the New Deal had thrown unprecedented sums of money at the dual tasks of relief and recovery. Yet the economy remained weak. Harry Hopkins's deputy, Aubrey Williams, estimated that 13 percent of the population was already on the relief rolls and that the number would increase as winter set in. A gathering drought in the midsection of the country added to the distress. He warned that a "gigantic relief task" lay ahead.[6]

The president himself preferred to change the subject. Speaking in Montana at Glacier National Park that August, Roosevelt denounced the "selfish few" who sought to appropriate national resources for private gain. He extolled "the splendid public purpose that underlies the development of great power sites, the improving of navigation, the prevention of floods and of the erosion of our agricultural fields, the prevention of forest fires, the diversification of farming and the distribution of industry."[7]

Who dared argue against such causes? All the money thrown into efforts to help the unemployed and downtrodden had failed to bring back prosperity, but it had carried millions of people through a time of extreme desperation. Help from Washington, direct and personal, was the essence of the New Deal. Roosevelt was its face. His relief programs overshadowed efforts to impose the guidance of a reformist state on the underprivileged and the entire American economy.

WITH MORE THAN ONE-FIFTH OF THE POPULATION LIVING AND WORKING ON farms, there was general agreement on the necessity of large-scale government intervention in what had been a catastrophic free market for more than a decade. But no consensus existed on how to divide that aid between middling to large producers and the impoverished subsistence operators at the bottom of the heap.

Just forty-four years old in March 1933, Secretary of Agriculture Henry A. Wallace came to Washington with the enviable record of an eminently practical man who had excelled as an agricultural scientist and farm journalist. His material achievement concealed a restless, sometimes quixotic spiritual quest. He was, as hostile columnist Westbrook Pegler put it, a "spiritual window shopper." He aligned himself with a small theosophic sect, the Liberal Catholic Church, neither smoked nor drank, sporadically practiced vegetarianism, and exercised vigorously. A Thirty-Second Degree Mason, he sought meaning in one of the order's most mysterious symbols: the unfinished pyramid below a hovering triangle-enclosed eye that appears on the reverse side of the Great Seal of the United States. He successfully lobbied for its inclusion on the new $1 bill issued in 1935.

He was also a disciple of Nicholas Roerich, a magnificently bearded White Russian exile artist and theosophist, whom he addressed as "Dear Guru" in a series of letters that might conservatively be characterized as eccentric. Utilizing a term that appeared in his correspondence with Roerich, Wallace told FDR in the fall of 1933, "Mr. President, you can be the 'flaming one,' the one with the ever-upward surging spirit to lead us into the time when the children of men can sing again." Roosevelt's reaction to this exhortation is not known. Clearly, however, he saw Wallace as a link to progressive Republicans, appreciated his good judgment on agricultural policy, and valued his unqualified personal loyalty.[8]

Wallace surrounded himself with a motley group of aides and assistants, ranging from established champions of commercial farming who had fought for subsidies throughout the 1920s to younger, progressive-minded, sometimes glaringly urbanite lawyers and social scientists with broader agendas. The informal leader of the latter group was Rexford Tugwell, assistant secretary of agriculture until June 1934, when he became undersecretary.

Tall, handsome, and urbane, Tugwell conveyed a certain masculine glamour. Women flocked to his tumultuous Senate confirmation hearing. The *Washington Post* called him "the Administration Adonis." *Time* magazine described him as "a connoisseur of dress [and] . . . an amateur of wines." Like Raymond Moley's in the Department of State, Tugwell's assistant secretaryship was largely a post of convenience from which he could advise the president, but as a reformer-economist he saw agriculture as a free market system that required systematic planning. He got along well with Wallace, whom he rightly saw as a man of similar sympathies, without quite realizing the extent to which the secretary also felt bound by the practical limitations of the old order in agriculture.[9]

As Moley's star faded after the fiasco of the London conference, which he presumably had been dispatched to save, Tugwell drew increasing attention from political observers. The most radical of the first-rank New Dealers, he operated as a wide-ranging advocate of the idea that government had to gain far more control over an economic system run by big business. Competition, he bluntly declared, was wasteful and inefficient. "Using the traditional methods of a free people we are going forward toward a realm of cooperative plenty, the like of which the world has never seen," he declared in the spring of 1934. "If this be Socialism, let our enemies make the most of it!"[10]

Tugwell's promotion to the new post of undersecretary placed him in a position usually reserved for a chief operating officer, not a policy intellectual, and exposed him to vocal skepticism from critics of the administration. He won Senate confirmation only after testifying that as a young man on the farm (primarily a fruit-growing operation for the family canning business), he had "followed the plow," gotten mud on his boots, and raised a prize-winning calf. His interests in reshaping the American political economy, resettling the poor in cooperative communities, and pushing tough new food and drug regulation through Congress made him a lightning rod for attacks from the right.[11]

Tugwell drew wide attention, but the most important early appointment involving agriculture was that of George N. Peek, a veteran fighter for farm aid with immense standing among agrarian activists, to head the new Agricultural Adjustment Administration (AAA). The AAA would support commodity prices through acreage allotments assigned by local committees. Having served on the War Industries Board (WIB) during the World War, he had won the patronage of Bernard Baruch and developed strong credentials as an economic planner. Yet, in the end, he was a poor choice. Like most other advocates of farm relief in the 1920s, he wanted to support commodity prices through subsidized exports. He saw production controls as at best a temporary and ultimately immoral expedient. A friend of Wallace's late father, he was not inclined to recognize the son's authority.

When Peek demanded complete autonomy for his agency, Wallace rebuffed him and proceeded to appoint Jerome Frank as its general counsel. One of the great legal intellectuals of the twentieth century and a New York Jew, Frank put together a strong staff of young lawyers—quite a few also Jews—from leading law schools. A few were closet members of the Communist Party. All reeked of the big city, saw themselves as reformers, and worried that the agriculture program was hurtful to the toilers at the bottom of the heap. It did not help that one of them, Lee Pressman, cluelessly expressed concern for "macaroni growers" at a staff meeting.

Peek characterized the bright young men scathingly: "They all claimed to be friends of somebody or other and mostly of Felix Frankfurter and Jerome Frank. They floated airily into offices, took desks, asked for papers, and found no end of things to be busy about. I never found out why they came, what they did, or why they left." Using his own funds, he hired a personal legal adviser.[12]

By the time the AAA could be staffed, cash crops were well into the growing season, and acreage allotments had to be enforced retroactively through a program of systematic crop destruction. Only wheat, sharply curtailed by a great drought affecting the midsection of the country, was spared. In the South, farmers plowed up every third row of cotton. In the Midwest, corn-fed piglets were slaughtered. The policy, a onetime improvisation, was the only way of cutting supply. Many Americans nonetheless found the destruction of food and fiber in a time of extreme want offensive.

Peek was among the dismayed. Moreover, he was appalled by efforts, emanating primarily from Jerome Frank's office and supported by Tugwell, to control the pricing of goods produced by processors of agricultural commodities. Unhappy with acreage restriction, he searched relentlessly for foreign markets. In December 1933, he announced a plan to dump heavily subsidized American butter in Europe. Tugwell, acting secretary during Wallace's absence from Washington, blocked it, telling Peek that "our agricultural trade cannot possibly be improved by selling abroad at a lower price than the market at home." Wallace backed Tugwell, and Peek resigned. Accepting the resignation, Roosevelt effectively sided with Wallace and Tugwell. With Wallace's acquiescence, the National Recovery Administration assumed the AAA's industrial code authority. Tugwell and Frank had scored an important victory.[13]

Roosevelt appointed Peek a "special assistant to the president" with the mission of pursuing foreign agricultural trade agreements in coordination with the Department of State. For a time, it seemed that he might wield considerable influence, but Secretary of State Cordell Hull, a dogmatic free trader, had little use for subsidized commerce. Peek would leave the administration in December 1935 and shortly reemerge as one of its harshest critics.[14]

The new AAA administrator, Chester Davis, had been a close ally of Peek but was more open to the domestic allotment strategy, less combative, and confident he could reach an accord with Frank. Instead, the very success of AAA in implementing subsidized allotment agreements created new problems. In the politically crucial South, a region that produced an abundance of important high-seniority Democratic congressmen and senators, landowners generally refused to share allotment payments with tenants or sharecroppers. They often evicted those whose acreage now lay fallow. Davis and other agrarian traditionalists viewed this as simply an unfortunate by-product of the new way of doing business. To Tugwell, Frank, and the urban radicals in the counsel's office, it was rank social injustice that had to be dealt with, all the more so because many of the dispossessed were black.

Partly due to internal conflicts over policy, partly because it was launched out of sync with the farm calendar, the AAA failed to provide immediate relief to its constituency. By the fall of 1933, with the general economy slumping after what had appeared a burst of recovery, agricultural prices were declining. In Iowa, the Farmers' Holiday movement reemerged as shotgun-wielding farmers once again stopped dairy trucks and dumped the milk they carried. The administration established a new agency, the Commodity Credit Corporation ("farm CCC"), which purchased surpluses from farmers at above-market prices and was especially critical in propping up cotton. For the remainder of the 1930s, the farm CCC, in tandem with the AAA allotment program, brought a significant economic recovery to commercial farming. But the course was choppy, the cost great, and the accumulating surplus enormous.

The New Deal had made American agriculture a ward of the government, dependent upon direct and indirect price supports. Most of rural America, its vaunted "individualism" notwithstanding, accepted the bargain. As the decade progressed, commercial farming would become profitable, and stored surpluses of nonperishable commodities would grow apace. Ironically, the return of rural prosperity would highlight the persistence of the still grievously impoverished subsistence farmers, tenants, and sharecroppers.

THE WEIGHT OF THE AMERICAN ECONOMY LAY IN INDUSTRY AND MANUFACturing. The primary organizer and regulator of those sectors was the new National Recovery Administration (NRA), which had to balance the wildly diverse interests of consumers and producers, businessmen and workers, large and small operators. The closest thing in the American experience to the NRA was the 1917–1918 War Industries Board, headed by Bernard Baruch, who had clearly thought himself the natural choice to run the new agency. Roosevelt, more than willing to tap Baruch's largesse in campaign contributions, feared his likely freewheeling exercise of any power that might be given him. Instead FDR selected a Baruch aide since the WIB days, General Hugh S. Johnson (ret.), who had helped draft the National Industrial Recovery Act.

Baruch had his doubts. "I think he's a good number-three man, maybe a number-two man, but he's not a number-one man," he told Frances Perkins. "He's dangerous and unstable. He gets nervous and sometimes goes away for days without notice. . . . [D]o tell the President to be careful." Johnson confirmed Baruch's assessment when, learning at the last moment that he would not have control of the Public Works Administration, he blurted out, "I'm ruined, I'm ruined," and threatened to reject the appointment. Roosevelt, with no fallback available, told Perkins, "Keep him sweet. Don't let him explode." She took the general on an hours-long drive all over the District of Columbia and persuaded him to accept.[15]

On the surface, Johnson was a military cliché: a hard-riding, hard-drinking, chain-smoking, womanizing, profane old cavalryman. His tough exterior, however, hid a mass of insecurities. From the beginning it was an open question whether the bull within him would gore special interests that needed taking down or wander into a china shop.

The War Industries Board had left him with an extensive knowledge of the industrial economy. Just weeks short of his fifty-second birthday, he radiated energy and a sense of mission. But he was no irresistible force. He doubtless understood that Baruch's accomplishments as the head of the WIB had been fragile, enabled by a sense of crisis and a talent for mediation. Beginning with a keen awareness of the slenderness of his authority and the paucity of resources at his disposal, he increasingly attempted to achieve his agency's mandate by hard work and self-assertion.

State organization of the economy, heavy-handed by American standards, existed to one degree or another in most European countries, whether democratic or authoritarian. Johnson, like many Americans in the early 1930s, particularly admired Benito Mussolini's Italian "corporate state," which in its idealized form amounted to government planning of the national economy for the benefit of all. Mussolini, who had been in power for a decade by 1933, promoted this guiding vision with imposing public works and strong dictatorial leadership. The parallels to Roosevelt and his New Deal were oft-cited during the 1930s. Perceptive journalist John Franklin Carter described the NRA regime as akin to fascism but lacking "its political aggressiveness and accidental intolerance." Actually, the differences between Italy's thuggish police state and America's sometimes unruly democracy overrode the similarities.[16]

Drawing on the example of the War Industries Board, Johnson used its appeals to patriotism and duty. He adopted as the NRA's symbol a blue eagle against a white background, wings spread, holding lightning bolts in one talon and an industrial cog in the other. Ubiquitous posters displayed the blue eagle and added in big red letters the agency's slogan: "We do our part." The creative red-white-and-blue graphic, identifying patriotism with government guidance, was not in itself fascist; still, it possibly stirred a certain envy in the hearts of Mussolini and his recent German counterpart, Adolf Hitler.

Far from a foreign import or a Johnson hobby, national planning, carried out by disinterested experts in pursuit of the public interest, had deep roots in early-twentieth-century American progressivism. "The breakdown of the old economy has forced us to consider as never before the responsibility of the government," declared Secretary of the Interior Ickes. "We know now that we must build a new social order." As much an expression of Jeffersonian Democracy as of European fascism, the NRA embraced regionalism and localism as primary virtues and even touted voluntarism. In the spirit of many New Deal initiatives, it reflected Roosevelt's instinctive quest to reconcile a strong national government with the historical ideology of the Democratic Party, to bring together Theodore Roosevelt and Thomas Jefferson. (Uncle Ted, who had considered Jefferson a weak and ineffective president, never entertained the illusion that this was possible.)[17]

Representative bodies from within each industry would draw up short and simple "codes of fair competition." When approved by the president, they would have the force of law, but the government would rely on voluntary compliance. Most of the codes would provide for regional differences in standards of production, work hours, and wages. All had to specify basic rights for labor, including the right to organize and bargain collectively. They might also establish prices, production quotas, and marketing territories.

The NRA's launch on a wave of optimism that it could manage the world's largest and most diverse economy said much about the desperation of the Depression and the allure of government management in the 1930s. Johnson's energetic propaganda asserted that the agency could establish prosperity and justice for all. With characteristic overpromise, he asserted that he would put 5 million men back to work by the end of the summer of 1933.[18]

The NRA staged rallies and parades all over the country. The biggest occurred that September in New York City, where Johnson spoke to a large crowd at Madison Square Garden. The next day, the city administration, businesses, and labor unions mobilized 250,000 marchers, who paraded from Washington Square up Fifth Avenue to Seventy-Second Street. Halfway along the route, they passed a reviewing stand on which stood Eleanor Roosevelt, Johnson, the mayor of New York, and the governors of New York, Connecticut, and New Jersey. The event started at 1:30 p.m. The last marchers reached the termination point around ten hours later. The participants, the reviewers, and the estimated 1.5 million people who lined the way felt they had witnessed the wave of the future passing before them.[19]

As it turned out, it became clear that efforts to organize a continental industrial economy had a chance of succeeding only if backed by authoritarian methods. The initial steps—defining an "industry," reconciling the interests of large and small enterprises, and establishing rules for wages, prices, and marketing areas—were difficult enough.

Enforcement was extremely problematic. For example, three large companies—General Motors, Ford, and Chrysler—and several smaller outliers dominated the auto industry. Although the NRA could deal with an auto industry trade association already in place, negotiating development of an industry code nonetheless took three months. Henry Ford agreed verbally to abide by the new rules but refused to sign the code. Johnson responded by threatening a consumer boycott; Ford ignored him with impunity.[20]

Yet, for a time in the late summer and fall of 1933, the code regime expanded rapidly on a wave of mass enthusiasm. One by one, large core industries—oil, coal, steel, shipbuilding, lumber, apparel, and textiles among them—signed on. If the agency had limited its focus to manufacturing behemoths, it might have enjoyed a measure of success. Instead, small, family-run enterprises got caught up in the wave: micro-manufacturers who employed only a few dozen operatives, operated out of small buildings, subsisted on tiny margins, used out-of-date equipment, and could offer their employees only meager pay; retail grocers or dry cleaners with a clientele that in a large city might only span a few square blocks and a workforce that routinely included family members. Such enterprises often proudly displayed the blue eagle, only to get caught up in a maze of regulations beyond their ability to cope. A few states established "little NRAs" of their own, easily confused with their federal counterpart, that frequently practiced ham-fisted enforcement policies. Among the real-life unfortunates were a dry battery manufacturer who employed a dozen or so men in a converted garage behind his house and a befuddled immigrant tailor who ran afoul of the New Jersey NRA and did brief jail time for charging a nickel below the minimum price for pressing a pair of pants. Johnson and NRA enforcers saw such types as "chiselers." Many others viewed them as little guys trying to survive. Their cases, not those precipitated by large corporations, would decide the fate of the NRA.[21]

The corporate world did rather well under the NRA regime. Trade associations controlled by the big operators drew up the industrial codes, invariably meeting the general specifications stipulated in the law but often inserting details that froze out small competitors. Provisions that set prices and divided up marketing territories effectively nullified the antitrust laws. From Roosevelt down, the New Dealers fixated on stopping a deflationary price spiral, only to discover that raising prices, which the NRA did in many lines of business, created not economic recovery but more hardship for the consumer.

By early 1934, the NRA had become a large, unwieldy bureaucracy administering hundreds of codes, setting prices, establishing marketing regions for items ranging from cigars to petroleum, and becoming mired in a multitude of controversies. Johnson, whose forte was not delegation, seemed in perpetual motion, as cheerleader for the cause, adjudicator, and chief responder to complaints. At the end of February, he held hearings in Washington that provided a field day for the agency's critics. (One of them was Eleanor Roosevelt, who requested more consideration for the problems of small bookshops.) A hostile speaker asserted, "It will not be many years before the big monopolies will control the entire business of the United States and we will all be working for them."[22]

In early 1934, Roosevelt, pressured by Congress, appointed a National Recovery Review Board and named as its chair old progressive and renowned defense attorney Clarence Darrow. An ideological socialist and visceral foe of big business, Darrow issued a series of scathing reports. He and his staff seemed uncertain whether they wanted to restore capitalistic competition or institute Soviet-style state socialism. Nevertheless, their fusillade exposed serious shortcomings.[23]

A determined organizing drive by major labor unions added to the emerging sense of industrial chaos. Nonunionized businesses countered the NRA endorsement of collective bargaining by claiming that their "employee representation plans" were the equivalent of independent unions. In 1934, labor actions created spasmodic turmoil around the country. San Francisco endured a four-day general strike; Minneapolis experienced a bloody confrontation between the Teamsters union and local law enforcement; Toledo endured an ugly and unsuccessful attempt to organize the Autolite sparkplug company; the East Coast from New England to Georgia witnessed an effort, put down hard by local authorities, to unionize the textile industry.

Whether closet Communists like Harry Bridges of the West Coast longshoreman's union or registered Republicans like John L. Lewis of the United Mine Workers, labor leaders employed the slogan "President Roosevelt wants you to join the union." Lewis, whose union already had a strong presence in its industry, achieved some success. But more often than not, organizing efforts failed miserably in the face of opposition from local political establishments and law enforcement, as well as many workers' clear doubt that unions would do much more than tap their meager paychecks for dues.

By the fall of 1934, the NRA administered more than five hundred codes that attempted to dictate production, marketing, and pricing decisions in about every major line of business. Their rigidity brought at least one large industry, lumber, to a standstill. Other codes regulated items ranging from Atlantic mackerel to celluloid buckles. The task was too complex for any administrative bureaucracy and more likely to tie the economy in knots than to stimulate a recovery.[24]

For a year and a half, Johnson attempted to exercise control as if he were a battlefield commander, working himself to physical and emotional exhaustion, using bluster and braggadocio to compel dispute settlements, disappearing from time to time just as Baruch had predicted, and finding solace either in whiskey or in the arms of his attractive administrative secretary. He claimed that the NRA had put 4 million men to work, but joblessness had barely improved from the 20 to 23 percent range of two years earlier, when Roosevelt was campaigning against Herbert Hoover. In less than two years, the NRA had become an object of denunciation among progressives and conservatives alike.[25]

Johnson was confused, fatigued, incapable of rational discussion, and reflexively dictatorial in attitude. His personal peccadilloes verged on becoming public scandal. Roosevelt tried to ease him out as deftly as possible. On August 20, 1934, Johnson met at the White House with the president and several "witnesses": Frances Perkins, Harold Ickes, and Deputy NRA Administrator Donald Richberg. Roosevelt was uncharacteristically formal and stern. After Johnson turned down reassignment to a commission to evaluate European economic recovery, the president bluntly told him he had become a problem and must resign immediately.

Roosevelt, Perkins later reflected, liked to consider himself an astute handler of people, but he had humiliated Johnson by firing him in front of his peers. Johnson sent over a bitter letter of resignation, to which, he later wrote, Roosevelt responded with a letter "so affectionate, kind, considerate, understanding, and long-suffering, that I felt lower and more ashamed of myself than ever." As things turned out, he stayed on as administrator for a month, with Richberg actually running the NRA. On October 1, Johnson finally departed with an emotional speech to NRA employees, ending tearfully with the final words of his favorite opera character, Madame Butterfly.[26]

Roosevelt replaced him with a collective board mainly concerned with scaling the agency's activities back to manageable proportions. Richberg became its executive director and, briefly, the administration's presumptive strongman. The president still believed in the concept of an economy organized by a powerful executive for the benefit of all and hoped to preserve the agency in some fashion. By then, however, the NRA had resorted to the courts for enforcement, and its constitutionality was in wide doubt. In the spring of 1935, the Supreme Court heard arguments in the matter of code violations by the Schechter Poultry Corporation. The fate of an immense federal program suddenly hinged on a kosher butcher's sale of an allegedly sick chicken.

THE FIRST NEW DEAL HAD BECOME AN ECONOMIC FAILURE OF MAJOR PROPORtions. It succeeded only in bringing the economy back from the utter collapse of March 1933 to about where it had been on Election Day, 1932—from perhaps 28 percent unemployment to about 23 percent. Its relief efforts nonetheless brought tangible benefits to millions of people, winning their allegiance despite the persistence of hard times. They would support the president and a drive for fundamental reforms in American society that was about to enter a new phase.

CHAPTER 15

PRESIDENTIAL GOVERNMENT

THE POLITICS OF MAXIMUM LEADERSHIP, 1933–1934

WHATEVER THE NEW DEAL'S POLICY CONSEQUENCES, FRANKLIN ROOSEVELT'S overpowering personality was a hard fact, fully as important as the benefits he distributed. Speaking directly to the nation, communicating empathy in a way no other president had, he established a presence that eclipsed his programs. He *was* the New Deal. Exploiting the personal presidency to its limits, he enjoyed the adulation of a large public. He was leading a political revolution, but the economic recovery he promised remained tantalizingly over the horizon. It was uncertain whether he could deliver or how long the people were willing to wait.

THE AMERICAN DEPRESSION WAS AN ACUTE MANIFESTATION OF A GLOBAL phenomenon. Yet Roosevelt had indicated his lack of interest in a cooperative international economic policy by wrecking the World Economic Conference in 1933. The United States was the planet's largest creditor and greatest industrial power, but the president nonetheless seems to have shared with most Americans a belief that the debtor European powers remained financial and industrial giants and far more devious than the innocent and virtuous United States. The British Empire still seemed in the eyes of Americans—and Roosevelt—the superpower that had existed at the high noon of Queen Victoria's reign rather than a beaten-down island nation with an obsolescing industrial plant and a shaky currency.

The United States, as Hoover, for all his failings, had understood, had a special responsibility and a unique capability to provide economic leadership. But perhaps it was inevitable that as long as the nation-state was the basic unit of world politics, each country would move against the economic crisis in its own way. The New Deal chose to treat the global Depression as a zero-sum game in which players jockeyed for advantage in the areas of tariff policy and currency valuation. Such policies preserved the nation's (and the president's) freedom of action but did nothing to alleviate its economic malaise.

In the wake of the London fiasco, the dollar attracted the most attention. Here Roosevelt resorted to a common stratagem of the 1930s, the competitive devaluation, and ironically found himself following along the same path for which he and his parents had once scorned William Jennings Bryan. From the beginning of his administration, he had faced pressure from rural progressives to increase farm commodity prices by resorting to the old populist panaceas of greenbacks or free coinage of silver. During the first hundred days, he had suspended gold backing of the dollar, which fell sharply in value against gold-backed currencies and the British pound.

By the late summer of 1933, an initial mood of optimism was giving way to the hard reality of a continuing economic slump. Agriculture seemed at the brink of a violent explosion, with the prices of major commodities still falling. A push for more inflation via continued manipulation of the dollar could seem a reasonable response, as well as a politically expedient one.

Roosevelt had no obvious adviser on monetary policy. Raymond Moley and Rexford Tugwell handled the structure of the economy, not the currency. Secretary of the Treasury William Woodin, able and highly esteemed, developed grave health problems just months after taking office; returning to New York for medical treatment, he had no effective input into monetary issues. Instead, an outsider, Professor Charles Warren of Cornell University, influenced the president most heavily.

Warren's entrée to the administration rested in part on his deserved eminence in the field of monetary economics and in part on his identity as a former teacher of Farm Credit administrator Henry Morgenthau Jr. A further devaluation of the dollar, Warren believed, would increase price levels markedly and thereby fuel a recovery. The simplest way to do this would be for the government, acting through a special corporation funded by the Reconstruction Finance Corporation (RFC), to undertake a program of buying large quantities of gold at prices considerably higher than the still legally prescribed $20.67.

The theory was controversial but plausible; it had Morgenthau's backing and appealed to Roosevelt's penchant for dramatic action. In September 1933, the president decided to move ahead. To his consternation he found himself at loggerheads with Acting Secretary of the Treasury Dean Acheson.

Forty years old in 1933 and inexperienced in finance, Acheson nonetheless possessed formidable credentials for his unexpected role. Son of a prominent Episcopal cleric and born to moderate wealth, he had attended Groton (where he was a perpetual discipline problem), Yale, and Harvard Law School. His favorite law professor (and informal Roosevelt adviser), Felix Frankfurter, had secured him a clerkship with Supreme Court Justice Louis Brandeis. An association with the influential Washington law firm Covington, Burling & Rublee followed.[1]

A tall man of imposing demeanor, sporting a prominent black mustache and favoring tailored English-cut suits, Acheson was a rising star in the Washington community. Politically, he had defined himself as a Democrat. Frankfurter recommended him to Roosevelt for solicitor general; that post being unavailable, he was appointed undersecretary of the Treasury. A man of firm opinions and invincible confidence, coming roughly from the same class as Roosevelt, he seemed to be a rising star in the New Deal.

Put in charge of negotiating payment of British war debts, Acheson raised hackles by displaying sympathy for Britain's financial problems. Inside the administration, he balked at the gold-buying program, arguing that the law did not allow it. He doubtless also thought the policy unsound and realized that it would reduce the value of government securities already outstanding. Morgenthau produced an opinion from Farm Credit Administration counsel Herman Oliphant asserting that it would be legal. Attorney General Homer Cummings agreed orally but stalled on delivering a written opinion. RFC chair Jesse Jones suppressed private doubts. Roosevelt, fearing disorder in the countryside, presided over one last heated argument, then ordered Acheson to move ahead. The undersecretary, accompanied by Morgenthau, proceeded to a meeting of the RFC board to announce, red-faced and visibly angry, "I have just come from the President. You know that I am opposed to our buying gold. The President has ordered me to do it. I will carry out his orders."[2]

On October 22, Roosevelt concluded his fourth radio fireside chat with the declaration that the government would "take firmly in its own hands the control of the gold value of our dollar" through a policy of buying newly mined gold in the United States and buying or selling gold on the world market. "Government credit will be maintained and a sound currency will accompany a rise in the American commodity price level."[3]

Three days later, he began the first of a series of daily meetings with Morgenthau at which they determined the twenty-four-hour price of gold, changing it a bit every day in order to fool money speculators. The initial price, $31.36, would trend upward until the president felt the revalued dollar had reached an optimum point. The process left loyal and stolid Morgenthau a bit queasy. He confided to his diary, "If anybody ever knew how we really set the gold price through a combination of lucky numbers, etc., I think they would really be frightened."[4]

Wrongly suspecting Acheson of leaking his opposition to the press, Roosevelt wanted to fire him outright. At the insistence of Secretary Woodin, appallingly frail and back in Washington to arrange his own departure from the administration, the president agreed to accept a resignation. Acheson wrote the letter promptly, thanking the president for the opportunity to serve him, and went to the White House the next day to attend the swearing-in of his successor, Morgenthau. Roosevelt beckoned him to his side: "I have been awfully angry with you, but you are a real sportsman. You will get a good letter from me in answer to yours."[5]

The letter never came. Roosevelt's suspicions of Acheson returned when someone gave internal documents to the press. More than two decades later, Acheson recalled the counsel of his father, who quoted St. Paul: "Think not on those things which are past, but on those which lie before us." He returned to his law practice. Morgenthau would be appointed secretary of the Treasury upon Woodin's resignation at the beginning of 1934.[6]

The episode said much about Roosevelt, who deprived himself of the frank and honest advice of a talented naysayer and surely discouraged persistent dissent from other aides. Something deeper was at work also. Acheson, not unreasonably, considered himself the president's social equal. He also conceived of governance as an occupation that required mutual respect and dignity among its participants. Roosevelt habitually addressed others by their first name and devised comic sobriquets for them, such as "Henry the Morgue" for Morgenthau. The president deserved deference and respect; his lieutenants merited the same. "It is not gratifying," Acheson recalled, "to receive the easy greeting which milord might give a promising stable boy and pull one's forelock in return."[7]

Perhaps, however, Roosevelt learned something. At the beginning of 1941, with the world in crisis, he would bring Acheson back into the administration as an assistant secretary of state.[8]

GOLD BUYING AND DOLLAR DEVALUATION PUT MORE DOLLARS INTO CIRCULA-tion, but not enough to ignite an economic resurgence. Commodity prices remained stubbornly low. General price levels were unaffected. John Maynard Keynes would call the tactic akin to a thin man trying to get fat by buying a bigger belt. "The chief result of the policy," Rexford Tugwell later wrote, "was to import quantities of gold at a high price in dollars." The policy thereby subsidized the foreign speculators it attempted to discourage.[9]

By mid-January 1934, what had begun as an exuberant and hopeful exercise was clearly a dud. With administration encouragement, Congress passed the Gold Reserve Act, which restated the gold policy of the president's April 1933 executive order making it illegal for American citizens to own or trade in gold bullion, gold coins, or gold certificates. It gave the president authorization to fix the value of the dollar in gold within a range of $20.67 per ounce to $41.34 per ounce. The following day, Roosevelt issued a proclamation pricing gold at $35 per ounce, a substantial devaluation that reduced the currency to 59.06 percent of its old gold value.

The administration had held off the advocates of free coinage of silver. The precious metal, however, had great appeal throughout the old Bryan strongholds in the South and West. The influential "radio priest" Father Charles Coughlin joined the crusade. Silver mining interests, most strongly represented by Nevada senator Key Pittman, threw their resources behind the cause. The Treasury was already purchasing practically the entire national output of silver and issuing $1 bills as "silver certificates." In the spring of 1934, the White House agreed to accept a bill, the Silver Purchase Act, which effectively committed the government to buying huge amounts of the metal at prices well above market value. The financial cost of this enormously expensive subsidy to an industry that employed about 5,000 people was more than that of the agricultural program.[10]

With that, the monetary revolution was over. Debasing the currency would not bring prosperity internally; nor would it make much of a dent in the price deflation that obsessed the administration. Would it restart world trade?

No member of the administration was more dedicated to that mission than Secretary of State Cordell Hull. Sixty-two years old in the fall of 1933, six feet tall, white haired with piercing eyes, distinguished in appearance, and esteemed throughout the Democratic Party, Hull embodied all one might expect a secretary of state to be. Throughout the 1920s, he and Roosevelt had enjoyed a warm and friendly correspondence.

Hull had expected to be an activist manager of American foreign relations, but he soon discovered that Roosevelt intended to take charge of the big issues, often bypassing him to work directly with personally selected assistant secretaries. Hull, all the same, valued his position, saw it as a possible launching pad for a post-FDR presidential bid, and stayed with it. He knew that, given his prestige within the Democratic Party, firing him would be almost impossible. If a Roosevelt man within the department made a slip, Hull would push him out with no remorse, as he had Raymond Moley in the wake of the 1933 World Economic Conference fiasco.

The secretary pursued his one passion, free trade, with ardor, although it was incompatible with the administration's pursuit of national planning and difficult to achieve at a time when most countries had turned to economic nationalism. The World Economic Conference had demonstrated the impossibility of a general lowering of tariffs or an international currency-stabilization agreement. Trade agreements with individual countries on a basis that could be sold to Congress and the public as a good bargain all around, however, did seem possible. There was little reason to believe that a new trade policy would have a transformative impact. But Roosevelt had no problem with the idea and probably saw it as a political sop to the powerful bloc of southern Democrats.

In 1934, Congress passed the Reciprocal Trade Act, permitting the president to enter into agreements with specific nations without the need for treaty approval by two-thirds of the senate. Over the next six years, the State Department negotiated twenty-two such pacts, usually relatively narrow in scope, but at times opening the way to greatly expanded trade. The signatories pledged to levy on each other's goods only those rates they charged "most-favored nations." A 1936 agreement with Canada was an important first step in linking the fortunes of the British Commonwealth with those of the United States. Other agreements solidified relations with Latin American countries.[11]

These results trickled in over the remainder of the decade, were modest at best, and fell far short of restarting the world trading system. Smoot-Hawley remained the nation's basic trade law. In the end, the United States did not behave much differently than most other large nations, which looked inward, managed their trade carefully, sometimes sought autarkic self-sufficiency, and generally avoided the risks of open trade and fixed currencies. The overall volume of US foreign trade would not rise above that of 1929 until 1940.

One galling issue complicated relations with the major economic powers. By 1934, almost every nation that owed the United States debts from World War I had defaulted. The Depression, along with Nazi Germany's renunciation of reparations payments to the European Allies, made this development inevitable, but it still met with outrage in the United States. In the spring of 1934 Congress passed the Johnson Debt Default Act, forbidding both public and private loans to defaulting nations. The legislation expressed the widespread American opinion that the Europeans had cynically renounced their obligations to an innocent and well-meaning nation. Roosevelt was not ready to defy public opinion on the issue. The war debts grievance became in many ways the keystone in a wall of economic isolationism that the administration found itself constructing.

BY NOVEMBER 1934, THE NATION HAD BEEN THROUGH TWENTY MONTHS OF precedent-breaking legislation and government programs. The New Deal to many people seemed so at variance with the American past as to be positively disorienting. Washington was paying farmers not to produce and effectively taking over management of the agricultural economy. The federal government, through its manifold work-relief projects, was the nation's largest employer and a presence in about every county in the United States. Business and labor functioned under a blue eagle regime that was either the salvation of capitalism or the beginning of fascism.

Roosevelt was at the center of it all, larger than life. In less than two years, he had presided over dozens of press conferences, delivered six radio fireside chats, and established himself as a frequent presence in movie newsreels that gave Americans the illusion that they were getting a firsthand look at their leaders. Acting from an expansive definition of presidential power, he had summarily fired an obstructionist Republican member of the quasi-independent Federal Trade Commission, William E. Humphrey. His carefully choreographed film and photo events, along with his authoritative radio voice, conveyed assurance, strength, and command.[12]

Roosevelt conducted even his vacations on a grand scale. After staying close to Washington in the first year of his presidency, he took several weeks in the summer of 1934 for a voyage on the navy cruiser USS *Houston*, sailing to the Caribbean, through the Panama Canal (where he received the president of Panama), to Pearl Harbor, Hawaii, and then to the West Coast, where he transferred to a train and visited the huge Public Works Administration hydroelectric projects at Grand Coulee and Bonneville. The trip reminded the American people that their leader presided over a great power that exercised a benign hegemony in the Western Hemisphere and extended its reach far into the Pacific while developing mighty public projects at home.

FDR's penchant for imperial display notwithstanding, no president had been so much loved and so adept at the common touch. Somehow he had achieved a blend of patrician authority and egalitarian appeal. Journalist Martha

Gellhorn, reporting to Harry Hopkins on the mood of the country, declared that beaten-down southern mill workers revered the president almost as if he were a god who knew, understood, and cared about them. The sentiment was common across the country and surely had something to do with Roosevelt's earnest attempts, over many years, to learn about the lives of ordinary people.[13]

In public, he was a jovial quipster, exuding a happy optimism, whether as the first president to participate in a skit at the Gridiron Club or as he carved the Thanksgiving turkey for the polios at Warm Springs. Yet he understood Machiavelli's axiom that it is better for a prince to be feared than loved. He left even his most devoted aides uncertain about where they stood with him and was adept at engineering the exits of those who had outlived their usefulness. What other president had, within the space of a year and a half, jettisoned his chief policy adviser (Raymond Moley) and seen off the top operating officers of his agricultural and industrial programs (George Peek and Hugh Johnson) without a disastrous collapse of his own support? In that respect, he was as cold as a professional assassin. He joked about having appointed as a US marshal a convicted killer in a vain attempt to appease South Carolina senator Ellison D. ("Cotton Ed") Smith. He would not hesitate to authorize prosecutions of political enemies such as former secretary of the Treasury Andrew Mellon or of supporters whose excesses negated their usefulness, such as Kansas City boss Tom Pendergast.[14]

Roosevelt's popular support was broad, deep, and fervent and the ultimate source of enormous political power that he exploited with cool calculation. Democratic members of Congress, normally independent and district minded, realized that he usually elicited more reverence than they in their home precincts. They voted accordingly and frequently found themselves in a love-hate relationship with him.

Yet objective measures of the economy yielded an inescapable conclusion of failure. The Depression had scarcely abated. Unemployment clearly remained about as bad as it had been at its worst. But at least a quarter, perhaps even half, of those out of work were receiving, or had received, some degree of relief from the government, in the form of either direct payments or temporary work.

During his first year Roosevelt had advanced a program of unparalleled change, and he had become even more radical in his specific agenda and in the tone of his rhetoric, whether speaking publicly or in private. The persistence of the Depression goaded him to look for culprits. As early as October 1933, he told the cabinet that bankers were engaged in a conspiracy to block recovery by refusing to lend. Just why they would forego profitable opportunities he did not say, but the instinct to personalize policy differences was clear.[15]

The president's annual message to Congress in January 1934 underscored objectives that went well beyond recovery to far-reaching reform. The value of the National Recovery Administration (NRA) lay not just in the economic improvement it had husbanded, he declared, but in its abolition of child labor and setting of national standards for wages and hours. It had initiated a governmental industrial policy that would steer the nation between the extremes of "ruinous rivalries" and monopoly. Agriculture, conservation, flood control, electric power development, and land use, he believed, all required national planning.

During its second session, from January to June 1934, the Seventy-Third Congress passed nearly two dozen pieces of legislation elaborating on and extending the framework of federal relief and regulation enacted during the first hundred days of early 1933. These included the establishment of the Securities and Exchange Commission and the Federal Communications Administration. The Railroad Retirement Act, establishing a contributory retirement system for railway workers, exemplified New Deal efforts at both a systematic transportation policy and a comprehensive old-age assistance program.

Yet the New Deal was more slogan than coherent plan. Conflicts within the Agricultural Adjustment Administration and the NRA mirrored complex social divisions—labor versus management, small business versus big business, commodity farming versus subsistence farming, social reformers versus political opportunists—that could not be suppressed in a democracy. Roosevelt, for all his authority, could do little more than stand above these struggles and hope for good outcomes. Inevitably, conflict and unclear objectives were the by-products of major structural reform. "The objectives were experimental and not clearly stated," Henry Wallace recalled years later. "Therefore, there was certain to be, from the White House down, a certain amount of what seemed to be intrigue. I did not think that this situation would be remedied until the president abandoned to a considerable extent his experimental and somewhat concealed approach."[16]

ROOSEVELT'S DECISION TO ADOPT A STYLE OF MODERN-DAY POPULISM WAS both tactical and sincere. It expressed a sense that had been gnawing at him for well over a decade and was possibly related to the leveling impact of polio. The handsome, young pre-1921 patrician-politician may always have had progressive convictions, but the elite society in which he moved so easily and found most of his significant relationships had tempered them. Polio placed him at an awkward remove from many of that society's events. Increasingly, he found himself marginalized and at Warm Springs in the company of ordinary people struggling as he had, but without his wealth, to come to grips with an equalizing disease. Polio had brought him to rural Georgia and the routine poverty that was part of its atmosphere. Roosevelt's surface geniality usually overshadowed the harshness that increasingly crept into his speeches, but he seems to have developed real anger at smug elites.

For most of his life, he had lived on inherited wealth and the episodic generosity of a few friends. His only real managerial experience had come during his service as assistant secretary of the navy. He seems to have had few contacts among the entrepreneurial rich. Perhaps his closest comrade among the idle rich was his cousin by half-brother Rosy's marriage, Vincent Astor, a socially conscious philanthropist who fancied himself a dashing yachtsman and gloried in being photographed in his naval reserve uniform. Financially sustained by the proceeds of an enormous family trust, Astor all but worshiped his relative in the White House. Both men found it easy to disdain money-grubbers.

The president's emerging rhetoric must also have entailed some cool calculation. By 1934, with the Depression far from licked and tens of millions living in misery, a radical tide was gathering. Venerable socialist author Upton Sinclair staged a spectacular, if unsuccessful, campaign for governor of California. The demagogic governor of Louisiana, Huey Long, began to establish himself as a national presence with his Share the Wealth clubs. Father Coughlin promoted a populism of the Right. Left-of-center progressives began to assay the feasibility of a third party. Violent strikes raised the possibility of a revolutionary labor movement.

Against this background, Roosevelt's shots at the rich became more prominent. "I am speaking of individuals who have evaded the spirit and purpose of our tax laws," he declared in his 1934 annual message to Congress, "of those high officials of banks or corporations who have grown rich at the expense of their stockholders or the public, or those reckless speculators with their own or other people's money whose operations have injured the values of the farmers' crops and the savings of the poor." He especially focused on "tax evaders," a carefully chosen phrase evoking images of the notorious gangster Al Capone, who had landed in Alcatraz for failing to pay income taxes.[17]

His prime target was Andrew Mellon. Enormously wealthy from a banking empire headquartered in Pittsburgh, Mellon had been secretary of the Treasury under Warren G. Harding, Calvin Coolidge, and Herbert Hoover, who, finding him too opposed to government intervention in the Depression, had packed him off as ambassador to Great Britain. A stalwart advocate of hard money and low taxes who had believed in letting the business cycle take its course whatever the price, Mellon sported a large mustache and a dour demeanor that made him the clichéd image of a Union League reactionary. Among Democrats, he was a leading villain of the 1920s. He also had expended millions of his personal fortune in amassing one of the world's foremost Renaissance art collections, which he intended to make the core of a great national museum.

The Roosevelt administration's examination of his income tax returns suggested that Mellon had engaged in transactions with family members and with a trust that owned much of the art in ways that minimized his actual income and hence the taxes he paid. Under Republican administrations, the Bureau of Revenue, a division of the Treasury Department, had ruled such dealings within the law. To Roosevelt, Henry Morgenthau, and most liberal Democrats, taking advantage of loopholes in the law was unethical and presumptively illegal. (The question of ethics cut both ways. Roosevelt openly admitted that he personally had reviewed Mellon's supposedly confidential tax returns.)[18]

Attorney General Homer Cummings was reluctant to prosecute tax avoiders who had complied with the formalities of the law, as he believed that such cases stood little chance of success. Roosevelt and Morgenthau were not. The administration dispatched Assistant Attorney General Robert Jackson to pursue a criminal indictment before a federal grand jury in Pittsburgh. The grand jury refused to indict.[19]

The administration thereupon pursued a civil suit for $6.5 million against Mellon in federal tax court. Mellon shot back with a statement alleging "politics of the crudest sort." The case proceeded slowly. In late 1936, the dying tycoon offered his art collection to the government, along with financing for a grand building on the Washington Mall to be called the National Gallery of Art. The administration had little choice but to accept. The National Gallery, completed after Mellon's death, still houses at its main entrance a dedication plague engraved with his name along with those of Roosevelt and Morgenthau.[20]

The tax court ruled after Mellon had passed away, finding that his estate owed the government approximately $400,000 due to errors in his return. It also pointedly declared that he "did not file a false and fraudulent return with the purpose of evading taxes" and observed that the law extended to every taxpayer the presumption of good faith in his business dealings. Lawyers for both sides agreed on a settlement of $480,000. Over the next several years, the administration pursued other prominent individuals on tax charges with mixed success.

Republicans charged that Roosevelt and Morgenthau were waging demagogic class warfare for political gain. In fact, the merits of the various tax cases varied, but the administration had allowed moral indignation at Mellon's legal tax avoidance to lead it on a course more morally problematic than the behavior it condemned. The Mellon case was but one example of how the New Deal was reshaping American politics along deeply felt ideological lines and of Roosevelt's unattractive inclination to employ the government's police powers against political foes.

HERBERT HOOVER HAD BEEN AMONG THE MORE ACTIVIST PRESIDENTS IN American history with his own attempts to cope with the Depression. Roosevelt's efforts dwarfed his. In the first full year of his administration (fiscal year 1934), the president had increased the federal government's expenditures by 43 percent and created huge bureaucracies to control a largely unregulated economy. His efforts generated understandable shock at the scope of change and created a backlash of outrage among Republicans and conservative Democrats.

Republicans especially found the partisan temptation to denounce waste, fraud, and abuse (inevitable in such programs) overwhelming. While the Republican Party had long been one of activist economic development, its dominant wing had advocated subsidies and tariffs, not restraints on business behavior. The Democratic Party for an equal period had possessed its own conservative establishment, made up of sound-money men like Roosevelt's father, who differed from the Republicans mainly on the tariff. This wing still existed in the 1930s, linked to moneyed families such as the du Ponts and establishment pillars such as the party's 1924 candidate, John W. Davis. Most southern Democrats, moreover, possessed an inbred fear of federal bureaucracy and coercive regulation that dated at least to the not-so-long-ago days of Reconstruction. All found Roosevelt's innovations exotic and ultimately threatening.

By early 1934, with the NRA floundering, a new American Right was forming to oppose the president and his New Deal. Republican Representative Hamilton Fish Jr., a longtime antagonist who represented Roosevelt's own congressional district in New York, wielded a rhetorical flamethrower: "This administration has copied the autocratic tactics of fascism, Hitlerism and communism at their worst." Ogden Mills, who as outgoing secretary of the Treasury had collaborated with the administration on the Emergency Banking Act, compared Roosevelt to the Roman emperor Diocletian, who he claimed had debased gold coinage, fixed commodity prices, regulated all wages, decreed the plowing up of one-third of the vineyards of Italy, instituted a vast program of public works, and taxed to the limit.[21]

In August 1934, a group of conservatives, many of whom had bankrolled the struggle against Prohibition, formed the American Liberty League. Some were Republicans but most noticeable were the Democrats: Jouett Shouse, John

W. Davis, and Al Smith. The league declared that its objectives were to defend the Constitution and preserve liberty. It especially deplored the NRA, the new militancy of labor, and above all what Smith called "the baloney dollar" after the devaluation of 1934. The Liberty League seemed to be raising large sums of money and looked to be a force in the midterm elections. In September, Herbert Hoover issued an angry manifesto, *The Challenge to Liberty*, which called for a reassertion of the ethic of "rugged individualism" in American life. As with Smith's apparent about-face, the book's message seemed at odds with Hoover's past as a cautious progressive and advocate of government-led economic organization.[22]

The Liberty League provided the administration with the enemies it needed and facilitated a form of political jujitsu that rendered Republican conservatism more an object of comic scorn than a looming presence in American politics. Roosevelt himself established the Democratic line at a press conference. He allowed that the primary objective of the organization seemed to be "love thy God but forget thy neighbor," adding that "God" seemed to be property rights. He went on to enumerate other rights—to a job, a home, and an education—implicit in the commandment to love thy neighbor as thyself. He had, he told the newspapermen, been convulsed with laughter for ten minutes after reading a *New York Times* article characterizing the league as the answer to a Wall Street prayer. The next day, Democratic National Committee chairman Jim Farley, no firebrand but a shrewd politician, urged a Democratic rally in New Jersey to support the president's fight against "the selfish forces of money, power, and greed."[23]

Widely characterized as the epitome of avarice, the Liberty League became a liability to candidates it supported and a millstone around the neck of the Republican opposition. Despite all the attention and high-profile support it attracted, it was not equipped to play an active role in electoral politics beyond staging a few speeches. What might have been a serious dialogue about the capabilities and limitations of government became a farce.

The midterm congressional election campaigns amounted to a referendum on Roosevelt and the New Deal. Across the country, Democratic candidates for national office depicted themselves as the president's steadfast followers. Roosevelt himself made a conscious decision to stand above the fray. He made his only nationally broadcast speech, billed as a fireside chat, six weeks before the election. It made no concession to his critics; nor did it engage in Republican bashing. Hailing the NRA as an achievement that had facilitated the reemployment of 4 million workers, he admitted that it was an experiment requiring some refinement. To those who suggested that Britain's coalition National government, dominated by the Conservative Party, had been more successful in stabilizing the island's economy, he responded that British conservatism, far more socially reformist than its American cousin, was somewhere to the left of the New Deal. Most tellingly, he underscored his commitment to full recovery and greater social equity. "I am not for a return to that definition of liberty under which for many years a free people were being gradually regimented into the service of the privileged few."[24]

THAT SEPTEMBER, PERCEPTIVE JOURNALIST ANNE O'HARE MCCORMICK wrote of the change the president and his entourage had wrought. Washington had replaced Wall Street as the source of national energy and speculative enterprise. Roosevelt had supplanted the titans of finance and industry as America's hero. "When before in this country, except during campaigns, have photographs of a living President been hung in shops and homes, restaurants and gas stations? How often has a President evoked such emotion from a hard-pressed people as greeted Mr. Roosevelt in his recent trip across the continent? . . . [I]t has little to do with policies or reason. The President is more widely questioned and criticized than he was a year ago—and also more popular."[25]

On Election Day, Roosevelt cast his vote at the town hall in Hyde Park, performing with ease for newsreel cameras as he went through the motions of identifying himself to the election board clerk. ("Name, please?" "It's still Franklin D.") He spent half a minute with the voting machine, posed again for the cameras, then left for the family mansion, where he would spend the evening listening to returns.[26]

No intelligent observer expected a Republican victory. Jim Farley, as always cautious but prescient, had as early as August predicted that the Democrats would maintain their strong margins in both houses of Congress with gains balancing some losses. As the results came in, he found himself presiding over an even bigger sweep than he had expected. By the time all the returns were final, the Democrats had increased their representation in the Senate from 60 to 69 and in the House from 310 to 319.[27]

How was such a result possible in the wake of so inadequate an economic recovery? Part of the answer was clearly Rooseveltian charisma and guile. No president had so fully and effectively exposed himself to a mass media now capable of directly conveying his charm, command, and concern for ordinary people. On all counts, Roosevelt eclipsed any visible Republican leader. The other part of the answer was simple pragmatic calculation. The nation might still be in the grip of a terrible depression and unemployment might still be at disaster levels, but millions of Americans were better off than they had been two years earlier—with direct government relief, temporary public works jobs, and refinanced mortgages. The Republicans, a few progressive dissenters aside, had nothing to offer but criticism and a return to Hooverism.

The election amounted "almost to a political revolution," in the words of a *Cleveland Plain Dealer* editorial. The old Kansas progressive Republican William Allen White remarked that, although "the forgotten man is still forgotten," Roosevelt had been "all but crowned by the people." If the Republican Party were to survive, White admonished, it would have to redefine its conservatism as somewhere in the "middle left" and prepare for a comeback when an inchoate New Deal, built around the idea of taking away from the rich and giving to the poor, foundered.[28]

White's commentary astutely dissected both the president's success and the specters looming in the future. Roosevelt had given the nation leadership, hope, and near-term succor. But he had not restored prosperity, and his attraction to sweeping reform got in the way of his doing so. The administration's failures had left it vulnerable—if the Republicans could get beyond right-wing naysaying.

CHAPTER 16

TOWARD "A NEW ORDER OF THINGS"

ORIGINS OF THE SECOND NEW DEAL, 1935

ROOSEVELT COULD SAVOR THE DEMOCRATIC VICTORY IN THE NOVEMBER 1934 congressional elections as a vote of confidence in his charismatic activism. But the present remained bleak economically and uncertain politically. Unemployment still hovered close to 20 percent. A drought was turning much of the Great Plains into a giant dust bowl, adding thousands of farmers to the relief rolls. The New Deal faced criticism from both the disgruntled Right and the ideological Left and, most urgently, from an emerging populist opposition strengthened by charismatic leadership that obscured its impractical nostrums. In addition, the president's programs seemed to hang by a slender, fraying thread, threatened by their ineffectiveness and challenged in the courts.

As the First New Deal struggled for survival, Roosevelt responded with a second.

HE FACED A BEVY OF DISSENTING POLITICIANS FROM THE LEFT. THEY HAD LITtle criticism for what the New Deal had done and much for its failure to pursue possibilities for transforming the United States into a cooperative commonwealth. Several were of Republican-progressive background: Senator Robert

La Follette, his brother Governor Phillip La Follette, Representative Thomas Amlie (all of the Wisconsin Progressive Party), Minnesota's Farmer-Labor governor Floyd B. Olson, progressive Republican senator Gerald Nye of North Dakota, and recently elected Fusion Party mayor of New York Fiorello La Guardia. Others were independent Democrats: Senator Burton K. Wheeler of Montana, Senator Edward Costigan of Colorado, and Representative Maury Maverick of Texas. Utopian socialist and best-selling author Upton Sinclair snagged the Democratic nomination for governor of California in 1934 and attracted national attention with his EPIC (End Poverty in California) platform before losing the general election. An ideological cousin, Socialist Party leader Norman Thomas, gathered few votes in his tries for the presidency but enjoyed wide respect for his melding of Marxian socialism with a larger Christian reform tradition.

A broad spectrum of intellectuals and activists had established the League for Independent Political Action in 1929. They advocated a collectivist democracy, awaited the near-certain failure of the New Deal, and anticipated Roosevelt's defeat in 1936. That, they believed, would set the stage for the long-overdue collapse of the incoherent Democratic Party and the rise of a new Left-liberal party that would capture the government in 1940. In early 1935, with the New Deal floundering, their belief that the time was ripe for a new force in American politics had considerable plausibility.

FROM THE PERSPECTIVE OF THE WHITE HOUSE, THE RADICALS' CHALLENGE was less intimidating than one emanating from another set of extremists far more skilled at disseminating a message and arousing resentments. Their leading representatives were Dr. Francis Townsend, Father Charles Coughlin, and Senator Huey Long.

Townsend, a sixty-eight-year-old retired physician, advocated a generous pension system for old folks, to be funded by a national transactions tax (similar to what later would be called a value-added tax in Europe). The plan would boost a weak economy, he argued, because the recipients would be obligated to spend their stipend in full each and every month. The aged doctor's often desperate constituency embraced his panacea with quasi-religious intensity.[1]

The Townsend plan became a national movement with local clubs spanning the nation, a weekly newspaper with 200,000 subscribers, and its own anthem. Yet it did not stand up to close scrutiny. The transactions tax would have punished the poor while doing incalculable damage to any economic recovery. It probably would have been insufficient to finance a proposed benefit of $200 a month, a sum that exceeded the salaries of most workingmen. Still, Townsend's sincerity came through and persuaded others. By early 1935, the Townsend organization, with about 500,000 dues-paying members, was a potentially decisive political force in California and a few other states.[2]

If the Townsend movement possessed the air of a Protestant revival, Father Charles Coughlin's crusade had much of the flavor of a Catholic renewal. Based in suburban Detroit, Coughlin had begun broadcasting locally in 1926, then nationally on the fledging CBS network. Increasingly he talked about wider issues of "social justice" stemming from the Depression. In 1931, rejecting a CBS demand to review his scripts, he organized his own network. It reached millions of listeners from coast to coast, allowed him to shed whatever inhibitions he had possessed about speaking his mind, and made him a power in American politics.[3]

Vague in specifics, Coughlin stressed social harmony over class conflict and advocated a "Christian deal" for the benefit of all classes. He initially declared the National Recovery Administration (NRA) to be a step in that direction. In the atmosphere of the day, Coughlin seemed to point toward a benign form of fascism. Whether out of caginess or haziness, he rejected the term. He likewise rebuffed accusations of anti-Semitism. The ideological theme that he tapped into most clearly was a mainstay of the American populist tradition: a loathing of the "money power" that dominated the American financial system, a general distrust of all bankers, and a belief that a sharply inflationary devaluation of the dollar would take the country out of the Depression. During the first year of the New Deal, he differed little from Roosevelt, save in level of rhetoric and extremity of proposal. Two of his causes extended his appeal into the old populist areas of the West and Midwest: free coinage of silver and abolition of the Federal Reserve System in favor of one government-owned central bank with unfettered power to tinker with the money supply. He was, observers sensed, more "radical" than the president, but whether his radicalism was of the Right or the Left was unclear.[4]

So was his relationship with Roosevelt. The president had brought Coughlin into camp in 1932 and enjoyed his support during his first year in the White House. Their programmatic differences seemed reconcilable, but the clash of two large egos presented a fundamental problem. Roosevelt would brook overt political pressure from no one. Coughlin had surged to national importance as an oppositionist and could not remain a loyal lieutenant.

At the beginning of 1934, Coughlin seemed firmly in camp. He called the New Deal "Christ's Deal" and told his loyal audience it was "Roosevelt or ruin." In April, Secretary of the Treasury Henry Morgenthau Jr., hoping to head off or soften the Silver Purchase bill making its way through Congress, published a list of major purchasers of silver futures contracts, speculators who would benefit from rising prices if the bill became law. Coughlin's secretary and treasurer of his radio league figured prominently. Coughlin responded with a sharp attack against Morgenthau. He maintained contact with the White House but also appeared to outdo Roosevelt as an inflationist and insinuated that the New Deal was insufficiently radical.[5]

A break finally came on Roosevelt's request for the Senate to ratify US adherence to the World Court. Depicting the Court as a vehicle for selfish foreign interests and an intolerable impingement on American sovereignty, Coughlin tapped into a powerful strain of traditional American isolationism. At his urging a deluge of telegrams descended upon Capitol Hill. Enough skittish senators voted in the negative to deny the two-thirds majority the administration needed. Numerous partisan Republicans, the Hearst press, and several isolationist progressives were also against the Court, but Coughlin's big radio voice seemed to galvanize the opposition.

By 1935, Coughlin had established the National Union for Social Justice to promote his point of view. Contributions flooded in from tens of thousands of listeners, financing the radio sermons, a weekly newspaper (*Social Justice*), and a huge expansion of his parish church. Some Catholic prelates denounced him, but his immediate superior, Bishop Michael Gallagher of Detroit, tolerated and encouraged him. On March 3, 1935, in his regular Sunday afternoon broadcast, Coughlin made a clean break with Roosevelt, denouncing the New Deal as "two years of compromise, two years of social planning, two years of endeavoring to mix bad and good, two years of surrender, two years of matching the puerile, puny brains of idealists against the virile viciousness of business and finance—two years of economic failure."[6]

The White House avoided a strong counterattack. Former NRA administrator General Hugh Johnson, apparently acting on his own initiative, delivered a counterblast. Coughlin called Johnson a "chocolate soldier" but also said that, while reserving the right to air constructive criticism, he supported the president. That September, Joseph P. Kennedy, by then chair of the new Securities and Exchange Commission, brought the radio priest to Hyde Park for an off-the-record lunch that Roosevelt later described to a press conference as a "nice visit."[7]

For all the studied ambiguity, the president and the cleric were obviously veering away from each other. Increasingly, political observers speculated about the possibility of a third party, a grand coalition of the followers of Coughlin, Dr. Townsend, and the most impressive national rabble-rouser of them all, Senator Huey Long of Louisiana.

A PRODUCT OF LOUISIANA'S IMPOVERISHED HILL COUNTRY, HUEY LONG WAS A force of nature, capable of extravagant oratory, possessing a genuine concern for his state's underdogs, adept at class politics, and less prone than most of his southern colleagues to be a race-baiter. He expressed the bitter anger of poor whites against a political establishment that ran the state in the interests of big business, finance, and delta planters, while taking its own cut in the form of bribes and payoffs. Not just another redneck yahoo, he had argued legal cases before the US Supreme Court; Chief Justice William Howard Taft had deemed him a brilliant advocate.

As cynical and self-interested as he was altruistic, Long assumed that the ends justified the means and made sure he was taken care of. Elected to the State Railroad Commission (later the Public Service Commission) in 1918 at the age of twenty-five, he waged a one-man war on the objects of its oversight: railroads, oil companies, and public utilities. Ten years later, he won the governorship and embarked on a program to funnel large appropriations into education, good roads and bridges, and public hospitals, all to be paid for by a tax on the oil companies. Surviving an impeachment attempt, he used his control of the state police and judiciary to establish an effective dictatorship. Constantly surrounded by a retinue of armed bodyguards, he relentlessly intimidated the opposition. His mastery of the state was sometimes rough—serious observers questioned whether its people had been deprived of their constitutional right to a "republican form of government"—but did not differ much from the dominance of numerous other political bosses in the 1930s.[8]

Long was entertaining, whether as a governor spoofing Germany's local counsel and the commanding officer of one of its warships by receiving them in pajamas, a dressing gown, and slippers or as partier about town getting into an altercation in a nightclub restroom by attempting to urinate between the legs of a customer in front of him. He adopted as his nickname "The Kingfish," the sobriquet of a clownish character on the popular *Amos 'n' Andy* radio show. His entertainment value was a decided asset in a state that had never cottoned to straitlaced Puritans.

As governor, he delivered the benefits he had promised to an impoverished constituency: better roads, free schoolbooks, and charity hospitals. He produced increased funding that made Louisiana State University into a first-class educational institution, while catering to a mass public by seeming to care only about the school's football team and marching band. Although he was low-key about it, the state's black population got a share of his beneficences. Some observers, then and later, saw him as a southern politician who had broken through the shabby romanticism of white supremacy to the underlying realism of economic politics.[9]

In 1930, his second year as governor, he ran for the US Senate and won hand-ily, then proceeded to complete his four-year term as Louisiana's chief execu-tive before going to Washington to claim his seat at beginning of 1933. He left behind as his successor an obedient crony.

Long's national vehicle was his Share the Wealth plan, a redistributionist scheme that theoretically amounted to a social revolution. It would provide every American family with a stake of at least $3,000, the money to be confis-cated from the rich, who would be allowed to keep no more than $3 million of their wealth. The plan would also provide old-age pensions of $30 a month to every needy person over the age of sixty, prevent industrial overproduction by mandating a limited workweek, restrict agricultural output, provide for war veterans, and underwrite college, professional, and vocational education for all students. Like most plans for social amelioration, it grossly overestimated the amount of money that even the most draconian blueprints for taxation and confiscation could raise.

As a young man, Long had peddled patent medicine for a time. He liked to tell a story about a drummer who came into a small town, put on a little entertainment show, then launched into a pitch for his two all-purpose reme-dies, Highpapalorum and Lowpapahiram. When asked the difference between them, he explained that one was made from the bark at the upper end of the eucalyptus tree, the other from the bark at the lower end. Share the Wealth was the political equivalent.[10]

Long established his own national Share the Wealth Society and proclaimed as its slogan "Every man a king." Share the Wealth soon claimed 27,431 local clubs with nearly 7.7 million members. The numbers were grossly inflated, but no one could deny that Long was emerging as a formidable national force. Using his Senate mailing frank, he sent copies of his speeches to each club, in effect forcing the postal service to distribute, free of charge, his campaign material for a possible presidential run.

Long had been crucial to Roosevelt's nomination in 1932, when he prevented defections in the Mississippi delegation. In 1934, he had intervened in the Arkan-sas Democratic senatorial primary, campaigning decisively for Hattie Caraway, an inconsequential widow standing for her deceased husband's seat. Huey made it no secret that he intended to target Arkansas's other senator, Joe Robinson, the Senate Democratic leader, and Mississippi's Pat Harrison, the Senate Dem-ocratic whip. Democratic National Chairman Jim Farley worried that he could attract 6 million votes if he ran as a third-party candidate for president.[11]

The administration investigated Long for income tax evasion. It secured several indictments against his associates but was unable to come up with anything on him. Inevitably, the attempts poisoned Roosevelt's already deteriorating relationship with his onetime ally. The third-party candidacy seemed more likely than ever in mid-1935 and acquired increasing potency against the prospect of a floundering New Deal.

It was not uncommon to characterize Townsend, Coughlin, and Long as protofascists, but they were no more "fascistic" than the early New Dealers. They owed more to the sometimes unlovely heritage of American populism, with its sense of an intolerable gap between rich and poor, resentment of the "money power," embrace of inflationary solutions, and fringe anti-Semitism. None of the three movements fit neatly into simple categories of "Right" or "Left"; nor did they develop anything that might be described as an ideology. Each offered a superficially attractive panacea, and each had real appeal to specific followings: Townsend to the elderly, Coughlin to Catholics, and Long to southern whites.

In the uncertainty of early 1935, speculation arose as to whether these three forces could combine to mount a credible third-party challenge to Roosevelt. Long would be the inevitable presidential candidate, Townsend being disqualified by age and Coughlin by his Canadian birth and priestly vocation. But how well would Long play to the ethnic big-city constituencies so vital to victory? What would the average middle-class voter make of a platform with the possibility of culminating in Weimar-style currency inflation? The only sure bet seemed to be that Americans would answer these questions in 1936.

ROOSEVELT HAD LAID OUT AN AMBITIOUS DOMESTIC PROGRAM IN HIS ANNUAL message to Congress at the beginning of January. Radio listeners and movie newsreel audiences across the country heard and saw a man concerned about an obstinately struggling economy with persistent mass unemployment and determined to remake America. Rejecting the distinction between recovery and reform, the president asserted that piecemeal reform led to confusion, frustration, and the loss of ultimate goals. Most fundamental among these goals was the eradication of "old inequalities." Americans had to "forswear that conception of the acquisition of wealth which, through excessive profits, creates undue private power." Without abolishing the profit motive or striving for absolute equality of condition, society should provide its members "a proper security, a reasonable leisure, and a decent living throughout life." His legislative program would include conservation and development of the nation's natural resources, jobs for the unemployed, social security against the major hazards of life, and better homes for the people. To the greatest extent possible, it would eliminate the character-destroying narcotic of direct relief payments to those who were employable.[12]

The speech was as radical as any that Roosevelt had ever given. It clearly anticipated the continuance of the National Recovery Administration and the agricultural program, while advocating a big new agenda: a massive work-relief bill, social security legislation, a banking bill that would enhance the power of the Federal Reserve Board and concentrate control of monetary policy in Washington, a holding company bill designed to break up large and putatively unwieldy electrical utility combines, a labor relations act that would give federal protection to labor unions, and a tax bill that would impact high-income Americans. That few mainstream observers saw all this as a sharp turn to the left says much about the political climate of the day. Walter Lippmann interpreted it as a move away from an overly ambitious effort to manage the economy in favor of "a system of free enterprise compensated by government action."[13]

Lippmann was on to something. Of the original Brains Trust, only Rexford Tugwell was still in Washington, and he was increasingly at the margins of large-scale policy making. In the White House, two new advisers stood out: Benjamin V. Cohen, a modest Jewish bachelor, and Thomas Corcoran, a charming, dominating Irishman who was the life of every party and, when necessary, the president's arm-twister with members of Congress or uncooperative bureaucrats. Sharing a house in Georgetown, they drew considerable attention for how their relationship reflected the uneasy Catholic/Jewish alliance that was part of the political coalition Roosevelt was building.

Their primary sponsor was Roosevelt's old friend, cheerleader, and policy tutor, Professor Felix Frankfurter of Harvard. Frankfurter in turn was something of an agent for the great icon of American liberalism, Supreme Court Justice Louis Brandeis, Progressive Era foe of corporate concentration and formulator of Woodrow Wilson's "New Freedom" program. Widely admired for his rectitude and projecting a prophetic aura, Brandeis was known to Roosevelt and other admirers as "Isaiah." Because he did not profit personally from his indirect relationship with the president, he saw nothing improper in it.[14]

Roosevelt likely did not see himself as making a sharp turn. In neither his public rhetoric nor his private attitudes, as nearly as they can be discerned, did he abandon the NRA and its ethic of organizing the private economy. The New Deal, as he and most of the people around him conceived it, was less about organization than about creating a society that distributed wealth more equally and circumscribed the abuses of large interests (primarily corporations).

Roosevelt's impulses took on various manifestations: a sense that the government had to control agricultural production in order to maintain farming as an occupation peopled by small to midsize producers; a sentimental bias for "the little fellow" in business, frequently with scant understanding of either his limitations or the problems he faced; a conviction that government could manage some natural monopolies, foremost among them hydroelectric power, more efficiently than private enterprise; and a romanticization of the working class as the truly productive segment of society and as an indispensible political ally. These attitudes more or less reflected Roosevelt's personal thinking, but they fell well short of a blueprint for a socialistic state with comprehensive five-year plans. They were bases of a liberal belief that reform was the road to recovery, not a detour that might lead to a dead end.

ROOSEVELT ALSO RESPONDED TO A SENSE THAT THE NEW DEAL SEEMED IN important ways to be coming apart at the seams. Internal divisions plagued the farm program especially. Social reformers in the Department of Agriculture were concerned primarily with the desperately poor; price stabilizers were attuned to the economic plight of middling to large farmers who produced for the market. In the end, the conflict came down to a question of political power.

The poor were most heavily concentrated in the South. Black sharecroppers or tenants had suffered seven decades of racial repression. Their white counterparts were often excluded from voting by the still common poll tax and scorned by the planter-landlord class. Agricultural Adjustment Administration (AAA) payments went to landowners; toilers who complained could expect eviction. The picture was not pretty, but nor was it inconsistent with the ethic of capitalist enterprise, which accepted no obligation to support redundant workers. The major farm organizations represented the interests of landowners. AAA administrator Chester Davis needed their support and respected their clout.

At the beginning of 1935, AAA counsel Jerome Frank, leader of the department's reformers, acting while Davis was away in Iowa, put out a regulation prohibiting eviction of unneeded sharecroppers and tenants. He persuaded Davis's second in command, Victor Christgau, to send a form telegram announcing the change to AAA local offices under the signature of Secretary Henry Wallace. Frank and his associates saw themselves as attempting to impose simple justice on an oppressive neofeudal system. The landowners, and likely most ordinary farmers, perceived a challenge to long-recognized rights of employers and property owners. The flabbergasted Wallace resented being blindsided. Davis returned to Washington livid and threatened to resign unless allowed to purge the radicals in his agency. Wallace, practical enough to understand the firestorm of criticism gathering among southern Democrats on Capitol Hill, acquiesced. In short order, Davis demoted Christgau, dismissed Frank, and sent three others packing with him.

Asked about the "purge" in a press conference, Roosevelt professed not to know about it and called it "purely an internal matter of law." Rexford Tugwell, who had been unaware of Frank's order but surely favored it, left a few months later to head the newly established Resettlement Administration (RA). Designed to foster a better life for the agrarian underclass, the RA received only scorn from most conservatives, for whom Tugwell remained a lightning rod. Nor was it a priority for a liberalism increasingly centered in labor unions and the urban intelligentsia. Tugwell would resign in 1937.[15]

WITH THE AGRICULTURAL PROGRAM IN DISARRAY AND THE INDUSTRIAL recovery program staggering toward either internal collapse or a court-imposed shutdown, Roosevelt's reform agenda inched its way through Congress with little prospect of producing an economic recovery. Only the jobs bill, the Emergency Relief Act of 1935, proceeded on a fast track. Its political benefits were obvious to every Democrat on Capitol Hill; almost all would vote for it, then scramble to gain control over the jobs it would create. The legislation appropriated $4.88 billion, a sum that exceeded the entire federal budget during the last year of the Hoover administration, to be spent over the next two years. The president signed it into law on April 8 and became, in the words of columnist Raymond Clapper, the Santa Claus of American politics.[16]

At first glance, the new program seemed to vindicate a fairly widespread view that the president was greatly influenced by the British economist John Maynard Keynes, who had long advocated vigorous public spending as the best remedy for bringing his own country out of its economic malaise. Keynes, perhaps the most eminent policy intellectual in the English-speaking world, had met with Roosevelt on May 28, 1934. The conversation was pleasant, the communication less than complete. Roosevelt told Felix Frankfurter that it had been a "grand talk" but complained to Frances Perkins that Keynes presented him with "a whole rigamarole of figures." Keynes privately remarked that he had found the president economically illiterate. (Keynes regularly observed the hands of men he met. He later described Roosevelt's as "firm and fairly strong, but not clever or with finesse.")[17]

A week after their meeting, Keynes received an honorary degree at Columbia University. In his acceptance speech, he praised the New Deal effusively. Shortly after that, he published an "agenda for the president." Its key recommendation was extraordinary public spending at a rate of $400 million a month. He surely had said as much to Roosevelt in plain English. The Emergency Relief Appropriation a year later authorized spending at about half that pace but did not require the disbursement of funds in equal monthly installments. Perhaps Keynes had achieved more than he realized.[18]

The rest of the president's "must list"—the labor bill, social security, holding company restriction, and banking regulation—lingered in Congress. All in one way or another affected powerful interests and posed genuinely complex issues of public policy. Moreover, they presented no obvious political dividend for most representatives and senators. On April 28, Roosevelt attempted to give them some momentum with a fireside chat, delivered from the White House.

Only the seventh such address of his administration, the talk was technically pitch-perfect. The voice was masterful, the delivery flawless. Numerous ad-libs smoothly made a somewhat formal prepared text more conversational. Proclaiming his pursuit of "the general good" over "individual self-interest and group selfishness," Roosevelt declared that the administration had initiated an "already unmistakable march toward recovery." The new work-relief program would provide employment for many. Social security would allow the elderly to withdraw from the labor force; its provisions for unemployment insurance would sustain workers' purchasing power in tough times. The elimination of unnecessary public utility holding companies would do away with inefficient, capital-draining structures in the electric utility industry and bring the operating companies closer to their customers. A major transportation bill would create a coherent national policy for the regulation of buses, trucks, river barges, and railways. A strengthened Federal Reserve System would stabilize banking and credit in the public interest rather than in the narrow interests of large financial institutions. In sum, these measures would enrich the nation's life with "a sound and rational ordering of its various elements and wise provisions for the protection of the weak against the strong."[19]

The speech was notable for failing to endorse the labor relations bill, sponsored by Senator Robert F. Wagner, with whom Roosevelt continued to have rather distant relations. Hoping for congressional renewal of the National Recovery Administration, the president was less interested in empowering labor as an independent force than in establishing the federal government as the arbiter, perhaps the ultimate organizer, of the economy. He was confident that he and his agents understood the public welfare better than either business or labor. Legislators on Capitol Hill found these forces less easy to discount.

The fireside chat heartened Roosevelt's supporters and confirmed his stature as a master communicator, but it failed to rally a Congress that dragged its feet as it deliberated.

As the president tried to mobilize wary senators and representatives, he found himself presented with a major challenge from the Supreme Court. Whether in dictatorships or in democracies, judicial systems are, to one degree or another, extensions of politics. Roosevelt, just the second Democratic president since Grover Cleveland left office in 1897, faced a federal judiciary well stocked with Republicans, only a few of whom could be called political progressives. Moreover, the New Deal's unprecedented measures raised genuine, serious questions of constitutionality. By the spring of 1935, decisions issued by lower federal courts against many New Deal programs were making their way to final judgment by the Supreme Court.

The Court that Roosevelt inherited had no ideological cohesion but leaned toward the status quo. Its personal dynamics were tenuous. Until the completion of a freestanding Supreme Court building in the fall of 1935, the justices and their clerks worked from their own offices, scattered all over Washington, meeting only for regular conferences, formal arguments, and issuance of decisions. These arrangements encouraged neither congeniality nor mutual respect. Willis Van Devanter, James McReynolds, George Sutherland, and Pierce Butler, bedrock conservatives all, became known as "the Four Horsemen." Louis Brandeis, Harlan Fiske Stone, and Benjamin Cardozo took a fluid view of the law and harbored varying degrees of sympathy for the New Deal; liberals would come to think of them as "the Three Musketeers" fighting for the just cause. Chief Justice Charles Evans Hughes and Owen Roberts possessed ability and moderation but lacked direction.

In January 1935, the Court, by an 8–1 vote, had voided the NRA petroleum code as the product of an unconstitutional delegation of legislative power to the executive branch. The ruling, it seemed, could apply to all of the several hundred NRA codes. But able to enact individual codes directly, Congress had promptly done just that for petroleum and likely would do so in many other such cases.

Two weeks later, the Court ruled 5 to 4 against challenges to the administration's revaluation of the gold content of the dollar. The plaintiffs, holders of private contracts that provided for payment at the old ratio of gold to the dollar and holders of government bonds issued at that ratio, had sued for compensation at $1.69 in revalued dollars. The Constitution clearly allowed the government to establish and regulate a national currency; it also prohibited impairing the obligation of contracts. Emotions ran high on both sides. The Court's majority ruled that the government could change the gold content of the dollar and cited a failure to demonstrate loss of purchasing power. Chief Justice Hughes's majority opinion walked a fine line between conservative and liberal factions. The most vocal dissenter, Justice McReynolds, compared Roosevelt's monetary policies to the excesses of the Roman emperor Nero.[20]

On May 6, 1935, the Supreme Court declared the Railroad Retirement Act of 1934 unconstitutional in a 5–4 decision. Roberts, joining the Four Horsemen, wrote the majority opinion. Hughes, siding with the Three Musketeers, crafted the dissent. The emotional emphasis with which both Roberts and Hughes read their opinions revealed a fundamental split over basic issues of constitutional interpretation. The conservative majority sweepingly rejected the contention that the congressional power to regulate interstate commerce extended to the provision of a pension system for workers' welfare. Moreover, it asserted that the law violated constitutional guarantees of due process by taking mandatory contributions from one group (owners and active workers) for the benefit of another (retired workers). Hughes castigated the majority for its narrow definition of the interstate commerce powers and disregard of legal and political precedent. The case indicated strong differences of opinion on the Court itself and likely foreshadowed difficulties ahead for the New Deal.[21]

Just three days earlier, the Court had heard arguments in a long-awaited test case on the NRA, *Schechter v. United States*. The Schechter brothers owned a live poultry and butcher shop operation in New York City and seem to have done no selling outside Brooklyn. Their clientele consisted exclusively of Orthodox Jews who kept kosher. The enterprise, which appears to have been the largest of its kind in the borough, secured many of its chickens from neighboring states. All the same, it was a relatively small business with a strictly local clientele.[22]

The Schechters were appealing a conviction for violating several provisions of the NRA live-poultry code, including submission of false records and the sale of diseased chickens. Despite tenuous evidence for the last charge, the government and much of the press labeled the proceedings the "sick chicken case." The Schechters admitted to clearly violating only one code provision: the prohibition against customers picking out their chickens. The code mandated "straight killing"—the sale of the nearest fowls at hand. Kosher rules required customer choice.

From the government's perspective the case seemed promising. Poultry slaughtering was at best a shabby business, and the Schechters were recent immigrants who spoke broken English and displayed little couth. In an era of white, Anglo-Saxon ascendancy, they seemed easy marks. Nonetheless, they also appeared to vindicate the argument that the NRA existed to protect big operators and persecute little guys.

Solicitor General Stanley Reed and NRA administrator Donald Richberg, given a temporary appointment as an assistant attorney general, argued for the government. Conservatives provided the Schechters with the services of an esteemed white-shoe law firm, but their personal lawyer, one Joseph Heller, stole the show with his discussion, delivered in a tone appropriate to a Shakespearean tragedy, of the "straight killing" rule: "A customer came into the store and asked for eleven chickens. Ten chickens were taken from the coop. The rabbi's assistant stood there and killed them as they were taken out. Then we came to the eleventh. The customer said he didn't want that one, but another one. My client said, 'The code says you've got to take that one. . . . They've got inspectors watching me. . . . Well, the customer said 'All right, if I've got to take that chicken then I don't want any of them.' He walked out on us." The justices suppressed broad smiles. The room, according to a *Washington Post* reporter, "rang with laughter." Justice Sutherland added to the fun by asking, "What if the chickens are all at one end of the coop?" No good could come of this for the administration.

On May 27, just three and a half weeks later, the Court convened to announce three rulings. The first was on Roosevelt's summary removal of William Humphrey, a die-hard right-wing Republican, from the Federal Trade Commission. Humphrey had died, but his executors pressed the case to secure his back pay and score a legal point. Just nine years earlier the Court had held that presidents could summarily dismiss postmasters, but it now ruled unanimously that the same authority did not apply to members of quasi-independent regulatory bodies. Justice Sutherland articulated the opinion in strong language that all but accused the president of a lawless attitude. A second decision also unanimously held unconstitutional the Frazer-Lemke Mortgage Relief Act of 1934, which allowed farmers to reclaim already foreclosed property. Brandeis wrote the Court's opinion. Both decisions were blows to the administration, but not very serious ones.

Justice Hughes then announced that he would read the unanimous decision in *Schechter*. He was blunt and categorical. The National Recovery Act was unconstitutional on two counts: Congress could not delegate to the executive branch the power to write codes that had the force of law; moreover, while Congress could get around that objection by itself enacting codes, it could not use the interstate commerce power to control businesses that were fundamentally local in their scope, such as the Schechter operation. Cardozo joined in with a concurring opinion that declared the NRA code mechanism a case of "delegation running riot" and asserted that Congress could give neither the president nor private trade groups "a roving commission" to legislate. These opinions killed the NRA beyond resuscitation.[23]

With three decisions in which liberals, conservatives, and moderates joined, the Court sent Roosevelt a clear message that his agenda exceeded the bounds of a wide constitutional consensus. As if to underscore the point, Brandeis sent a page to summon Ben Cohen and Tom Corcoran after the session had adjourned. The two men found the great liberal hero, arms up as an attendant removed his robe, looking like an avenging angel in the service of a style of liberalism that abhorred concentrated power and stressed the virtues of localism. The president, he told them, had been living in a fool's paradise. They had to get Felix Frankfurter to tell Roosevelt that the Court would not let the government centralize everything, he said. The young New Dealers should go back to the states and do their work there. After they left, the justice turned to his former law clerk, Paul Freund, and said with evident satisfaction, "This was the Black Monday of the New Deal."[24]

ROOSEVELT RECEIVED THE NEWS WITH DISMAY, SHOCK, AND ANGER. ON MAY 31, 1935, at his next press conference, he read from telegrams and letters, all from small enterprisers who asserted that the NRA had saved their livelihoods and that they now faced ruin: "Unless the use of loss leaders by chain store vultures is prohibited the small independent merchants will be the biggest sufferers. . . . All good citizens are looking to you to exercise whatever power is at your command to prevent business chaos. . . . Chiselers already at our throats and have begun choking us. Need immediate action."[25]

Nobody should resent a Supreme Court decision, he told the newsmen, but it was fair enough to deplore one and to point out its negative consequences. The Court had held that extraordinary emergency conditions could not enlarge executive power. What did it think had happened during the emergency of World War I, when the executive branch had taken control of the nation's life? The Court held that while the Schechters had imported their chickens from out of state, their customers were all local. Thus the "stream of interstate commerce" had ended. This was a concept from "the horse and buggy age" that made no sense. If the Court applied its strict interpretation rigorously, most economic activity would be immune from federal regulation. The nation would "go back to a government of 48 states." Enterprisers would find themselves in a competitive race to the bottom over wages, working conditions, and prices.[26]

Whatever the Court might have expected, Franklin Roosevelt was not about to retreat passively. He was more determined than ever to get his legislative agenda enacted—even if Congress had to fight it out through a Washington summer that promised to be steamier and more intense than ever.

CHAPTER 17

RENDEZVOUS WITH DESTINY

THE SECOND NEW DEAL AND THE TRIUMPH OF 1936

ON JUNE 7, 1935, A WEEK AFTER HIS ANGRY MONOLOGUE TO THE PRESS ON THE *Schechter* decision, Roosevelt met again with reporters. What, asked one, was the social objective of his administration? His response was expansive:

> To do just what any honest government of any country would do; to try to increase the security and the happiness of a larger number of people in all occupations of life and in all parts of the country; to give them more of the good things of life; to give them a greater distribution, not only of wealth in the narrow terms but of wealth in the wider terms; to give them places to go in the summertime—recreation; to give them assurance that they are not going to starve in their old age; to give honest business a chance to go ahead and make a reasonable profit.[1]

"Places to go in the summertime": while perhaps too revealing of his privileged background, the phrase expressed concern for ordinary people and a determination to make their lives better. A sense that the New Deal was not exhausted, that indeed it had hardly begun, lurked behind the declaration.

A week after that, Roosevelt received Democratic leaders of the House of Representatives. Asking the president to give his blessing to the usual adjournment ahead of the steamy Washington summer, they encountered a "desk-pounding" chief executive unhappy that his legislative program remained stalled on Capitol Hill. A Democratic Congress, he told them, could not ignore a Democratic president.[2]

Faced with a floundering program, a hostile Supreme Court, and a lethargic Congress, Roosevelt had opted for a new reform agenda. Would it "increase the security and happiness" of the American people? Or would it get in the way of a desperately needed economic recovery? The second hundred days had begun.

THE PRESIDENT HAD ALREADY DISPLAYED HIS EXASPERATION WITH CONGRESS on May 22 when he vetoed a revived veterans bonus bill. For many Democrats and not a few Republicans, the legislation was, as in 1932, a quick and easy way to play to a large and politically powerful constituency. Breaking yet another precedent, Roosevelt came to the Capitol and read his message to a joint session of Congress. Millions listened at their radios across the country as he argued that the bonus was both inequitable and unaffordable. The House had overridden the veto by the time the president arrived back at the White House. As expected, however, the Senate sustained him and thereby underscored his leadership of party and nation.[3]

A "must list" Roosevelt gave House leaders three weeks later remained a bit vague. It clearly included social security, public utility holding company curbs, transportation regulation, and strengthening of the Federal Reserve. He had already called for passage of Robert F. Wagner's labor relations bill on May 24. Bringing all these measures to a vote over the next several weeks would be a daunting task.

Then, without warning, on June 19 the president sent a message to Congress demanding a new priority: a comprehensive revenue bill that would sharply elevate taxes on large inheritances, high incomes, and the net profits of corporations. Social justice, he declared, required these changes; the redistribution of wealth, moreover, would stimulate the economy. Huey Long strutted up and down the aisles of the Senate chamber as a clerk read the message. Most congressmen, wanting only to get out of town, were shocked. The president had displayed little interest in soak-the-rich taxation during his first two years in office. Was the message an ideological manifesto or a strategic ploy?[4]

It probably was a bit of both, expressing at once Roosevelt's alienation from a social and economic elite that mostly scorned him and his disdain for those Theodore Roosevelt had called "malefactors of great wealth." It equally reflected a cool political calculation that he needed to move in a populist direction. If that meant following a course that appealed to him anyway and shoving aside

Huey Long and Father Charles Coughlin in the process, so much the better. A careful reading of his message revealed the sensibility of an individual of modest wealth outraged at the lavish lifestyles of the very rich but far from ready to lead mobs of ragged peasants with pitchforks. Where Long proposed wholesale confiscation, Roosevelt quoted Andrew Carnegie on the virtues of thrift and industry, cited Uncle Ted on the deleterious effects of generational transmissions of vast wealth, and specifically suggested high taxation only on incomes exceeding $5 million a year, a level well in excess of that sustaining his country squire/small yachtsman lifestyle.

Democratic leaders in Congress promptly passed the word that the president was not insisting on immediate action; the White House did not contradict them. Twenty-two senators, most of them from the progressive bloc led by Robert La Follette Jr. of Wisconsin, responded by signing a manifesto calling for immediate consideration of the White House proposal. Roosevelt had long courted their support. Huey Long, not one of the signers, backed them up: "Don't give us the voice of Jefferson and the hand of Mellon and Morgan." The White House got the message. The president demanded quick passage of his still vague tax proposal.[5]

The bill that took shape over the next several weeks provided a template for Roosevelt's larger "must list." More than any other item, it gave thematic coherence to an agenda that had been a mishmash of relief programs, attempts to organize sectors of the economy, and bits of selective socialism. It addressed the economic need to deal with a mounting national debt and also served the political purpose of scapegoating the wealthy. Consistent with the New Deal's occasional prosecutions of rich and prominent figures for income tax evasion or other varieties of financial malfeasance, it was far more potent because it implicitly indicted an entire class. Thus the bill began its way through the legislative process, jostling with other items aimed at specific constituencies and adding to the irritability of a discontented Congress.

THE FIRST PIECE OF LEGISLATION TO CLEAR CONGRESS WAS THE WAGNER ACT, to which the Supreme Court invalidation of the National Recovery Administration (NRA) had given momentum. Signed into law by Roosevelt on July 5, the new act effectively wrote into law the NRA's labor provisions. It established as national policy the right of workers to organize and bargain collectively, provided for a National Labor Relations Board to administer the statute, and specified a series of unfair labor practices. Conceptually, it was a continuation of the NRA tendency to see the economy in "corporatist" terms of labor and management rather than as an aggregation of individuals pursuing personal interests.

Politically, the Wagner Act was a masterstroke. Since the early twentieth century, organized labor and the Democratic Party had been growing closer at the state and local levels. A certain ideological affinity existed between Democratic urban machines and the unions; the fact that the leaders of both often had Irish names and were Roman Catholic helped. Unions could provide campaign money and election workers; the government could provide protection in return.

American Federation of Labor president William Green hailed the bill as a "Magna Carta" for the union movement. Roosevelt declared, "By preventing practices which tend to destroy the independence of labor, it seeks for every worker within its scope, that freedom of choice and action which is justly his." Everyone with an interest in the legislation realized that its viability would ultimately rest on court decisions about the extent of the government's interstate commerce authority.[6]

The rest of the president's program simmered through a steamy July into the first two weeks of August, with representatives and senators of both parties displaying increasing crankiness. Congressional leaders toyed with the idea of a unilateral adjournment but knew that Roosevelt likely would call them back to a special session. They could do nothing but grind out the most hotly contested legislative program since Theodore Roosevelt and Woodrow Wilson had imposed their wills on Washington.[7]

THE SOCIAL SECURITY ACT CLEARED CONGRESS ON AUGUST 10. THE NEW program represented a triumph for a generation of progressives, inspired by social insurance programs already enacted in Britain and several European countries. The bill provided for a federal system of old-age and survivors insurance to be funded by a payroll tax levied on workers and employers. It also authorized federal subsidies to state plans for unemployment compensation, old-age pensions, and welfare payments to the needy, including dependent children. It laid the basis for what was to become an American welfare state.

The administration tried to sell the various Social Security provisions as adding to mass purchasing power and thus fostering economic recovery. Actually, the new taxes took money out of the private economy, and the levy on employers acted at least as a marginal deterrent to hiring new employees. The money that went into the Social Security trust fund could be invested only in US securities, making the government the major beneficiary. Conveniently, no taxes were to be levied until 1937. Old-age and survivors benefits were scheduled to begin in 1942, after the accumulation of a sizeable trust fund: (Four years later, Congress would vote to begin payments in 1940.)

Politically, Social Security was a response to the radical equalizing solutions proposed by Dr. Francis Townsend and Huey Long, who in turn attacked its benefits as insignificant and told a radio audience that the president was a "liar and a faker." Many of the act's formulators, however, saw it as establishing the foundations of a social welfare state that could provide succor for all the underprivileged in American society. "This law," Roosevelt declared, "represents a cornerstone in a structure which is being built but is by no means complete."[8]

NINE DAYS LATER, THE PRESIDENT AFFIXED HIS SIGNATURE TO THE BANKING Act of 1935. The bill the White House sent to Congress was primarily the work of Treasury economist Laughlin Currie and Federal Reserve Board chairman Marriner S. Eccles, a Utah businessman and banker who had worked briefly in the Treasury Department. An advocate of a strong federal spending program who might more appropriately have served as secretary of the Treasury, Eccles wanted from the beginning to bring focus to a Fed that was a loose confederation of twelve government-blessed but privately controlled and financed regional banks. In practice, the central board had limited power and tended to be dominated by the head of its largest and strongest constituent, the Federal Reserve Bank of New York. Possessing a westerner's suspicion of Wall Street, Eccles was determined to effect a reorganization that would allow Washington to control Federal Reserve policy in what he saw as the public interest.[9]

The statute greatly centralized the fragmented Federal Reserve System and enhanced the president's influence over monetary policy by empowering his key appointee, the chairman of the Federal Reserve Board, who also served as chair of the interest-rate-setting Open Market Committee. Now more visibly the nation's chief monetary official than ever, the chairman would increasingly be able to count on support from both the board and the Open Market Committee out of fear that dissent would undermine confidence in the dollar. The Banking Act paved the way for such later monetary czars as William McChesney Martin, Paul Volcker, Alan Greenspan, and Ben Bernake.

The act effectively transformed the Federal Reserve into a central bank with strong powers akin to those of the Bank of England. Eccles nonetheless used his authority sparingly. Persuaded that the administration should address the Depression through federal spending policy rather than by manipulating the money supply and interest rates, he was more interested in policing the banking system than addressing the wider economy. Perhaps also wary of Secretary of the Treasury Henry Morgenthau Jr.'s close relationship with the president, he was careful in his policy choices. As the Fed's subsequent monetary policy would demonstrate, he had more in common with the conservative banking establishment than most observers understood.

FIVE DAYS AFTER SIGNING THE BANKING ACT, ROOSEVELT PUT HIS NAME ON the Public Utility Holding Company Act. Ostensibly designed to curb abusive corporate consolidation, the new law powerfully expressed a long-held progressive conviction that utilities, necessities of life for those with access to them, should be publicly owned or at the least intensively regulated by government. Electricity had been one of the great American growth industries of the 1920s, requiring huge investments to build generating facilities and string lines. Utilities first serviced population centers, often charging initial high rates that usually declined as local markets used more and more of the product. By 1930, cities and most towns of any size were electrified. In general, the countryside and many small villages were not. They had too few paying customers.

Generating piles of cash, the electric utilities had attracted corporate buccaneers and empire builders. The most famous, Samuel Insull, established holding companies to buy out profitable operating companies and establish new ones. The process was messy, involving takeover bids and battles for control. The empires that emerged were rarely territorially coherent and often complex, with holding companies piled on top of each other to as many as six or seven levels. They also tended to have high levels of debt. The largest such group, headed by Insull, collapsed into bankruptcy under the weight of the Depression.

Defenders of the holding company empires discounted cumbersome corporate structures and speculative excesses. They saw the holding companies as an effective way of raising capital for the maintenance and expansion of the electrical capacity that the nation needed. Progressives, distrustful of the entire ethic of private investment, saw the whole process as parasitical. Utilities, they argued, were natural monopolies that government should operate. In particular, they thought public ownership or cooperative investment provided the best means of bringing electricity to American farms and small towns.

Roosevelt had long agreed with the progressive viewpoint. In May 1935, he set aside a large portion of the $4.2 billion relief appropriation to establish the Rural Electrification Administration (REA), which subsidized local rural electric cooperatives. The nonprofit character of the co-ops and generous government subsidies allowed the REA to distribute power to widely scattered customers. The rates were seldom cheap, but the lure of electricity was strong; most farmers found ways to pay. Over the next decade the REA would lead much of rural America out of the darkness.

The Tennessee Valley Authority (TVA), taking shape by mid-1935, was built on the promise of cheap, government-generated electricity. It sold some of its power production directly to consumers in its area and the rest to the Commonwealth and Southern Company, the region's dominant private electrical utility. TVA's clear long-run intention was to take over electrical distribution for the entire Tennessee Valley. Wendell Willkie, president of Commonwealth and Southern, emerged as its chief critic. What Willkie saw as a dastardly socialistic attack on private enterprise, Roosevelt and most New Dealers saw as a noble enhancement of the lives of ordinary people.

The holding company bill, as originally introduced in Congress, would have outlawed all public utility holding companies, in effect reducing private operations to local enterprises servicing contiguous geographical areas and rendering many vulnerable to competition from or takeover by the government-financed enterprises that progressives wanted to encourage. The bill's sponsorship represented the emerging Democratic coalition that the president needed for a reform program: in the Senate, Burton K. Wheeler of Montana, a progressive maverick; in the House, Sam Rayburn of Texas, a protégé of Vice President John Nance Garner popular among the regulars but also an heir to the populist tradition of the 1890s.

Envisioning themselves in a struggle for survival, the utilities mounted a strong opposition. Taking advantage of the fact that Washington lobbying, although constitutionally protected, possessed a malodorous reputation, administration forces in the Senate secured the establishment of a special committee to investigate the utility lobby. Headed by Alabama populist Hugo Black, it had the overt purpose of pillorying the opposition. The committee sent subpoena-armed investigators unannounced to the Washington offices of the Committee of Public Utility Education. They took its chief operating officer into custody for an immediate appearance before the Senate committee, then searched the files for evidence of skullduggery. Not surprisingly, they found some transgressions, among them the deployment of thousands of telegrams sent under names picked from city directories. It was easy to demonstrate that the companies were spending millions of dollars in the effort to preserve their existence.

Black's methods were rough at best. The American Civil Liberties Union denounced them. The *New York Times* characterized the rifling of files and publication of private documents as akin to intercepting private correspondence from the postal service. A US Court of Appeals ruled that the summary seizure of documents was illegal, but it could not prevent a coequal branch of government from publishing them.[10]

The bill laid bare fissures opening within the Democratic Party. The most prominent legal spokesman for the utilities was 1924 Democratic candidate for president and Roosevelt family friend John W. Davis. Other old Wilsonians joined him in opposition: Joseph Tumulty, Newton D. Baker, Bainbridge Colby, and A. Mitchell Palmer. Black denounced them all as members of a "five million dollar lobby" that threatened democratic government.[11]

Black spoke the feelings of a progressive coalition with a clear majority in the Senate. Harry S. Truman of Missouri, a freshman senator with strong populist inclinations, later remembered the bill as an effort "to destroy the cartels through which the power trusts were able to maintain exorbitant rates." He voted for it despite having received an estimated 30,000 letters and telegrams in opposition. "I knew the 'wrecking crew' of Wall Street was at work behind the scenes." On this issue, the Senate was more radical than the House, which refused to accept a categorical death sentence despite intense lobbying from the administration.[12]

Signed into law on August 28, the Public Utility Holding Company Act allowed holding companies to exist only at one level above that of consumer operations if they could be justified to the Securities and Exchange Commission. It also gave the Federal Power Commission extensive authority over the operations of the electrical utilities, paving the way for a system of integrated regional power grids. It may have complicated capital formation in a still expanding industry, and it made mergers very difficult. Contrary to the hopes of many of its backers, it did not clear the way for the general establishment of government-owned and -operated electrical energy. As is often the case in American politics, the act's results were not commensurate with the noise it generated.

TWO DAYS AFTER AFFIXING HIS SIGNATURE TO THE HOLDING COMPANY ACT, Roosevelt signed the bill that more than any other set the tone of the long, contentious summer, the Wealth Tax Act. Hammered out under pressure by a resentful Congress, the legislation elevated class sentiment to an intensity disproportionate to the act's actual effects.

To counter the appeal of Huey Long, Roosevelt had privately remarked, "it may be necessary to throw to the wolves the forty-six men who are reported to have incomes in excess of one million dollars a year." The president probably did not expect much in the way of actual legislation, but congressional progressives picked up his tax request and ran with it. The bill finally sent to the president increased federal taxes on estates, corporations, and individuals, but did so relatively narrowly. The new maximum rates seemed draconian: 79 percent on that portion of personal income in excess of $5,000,000; 70 percent on that portion of estates in excess of $50,000,000. To this the bill added relatively small increases in corporate taxes. It was generally understood that the only American taxpayer likely to find himself in the 79 percent bracket was John D. Rockefeller Sr. A $50 million estate was almost as rare. The new tax program significantly impacted less than 1 percent of taxpayers.[13]

The bill did of course result in some tax increases for many individuals and businesses; to that extent it was a drag on the economy. Politically, it stole much of Huey Long's thunder and established Roosevelt as an enemy of a callous upper crust. As the historian Mark Leff puts it, the administration had enacted a wealth tax without sharing the wealth. At most, Roosevelt set in motion a trend in which the government would rely increasingly on personal and corporate income taxes and less on excise taxes invisibly added to alcohol, tobacco, and various luxury goods. At the time, however, excise levies remained the primary source of federal revenues.[14]

OTHER LAWS THAT IN NORMAL CIRCUMSTANCES WOULD HAVE BEEN CONSIDered of primary importance accompanied the five big acts of the second hundred days. The Motor Carrier Act subjected commercial passenger bus and trucking companies to comprehensive regulation by the Interstate Commerce Commission. (In 1938, Congress would establish a Civil Aeronautics Authority to perform the same function for the emerging airline industry.) A new Farm Mortgage Relief Act and a new Railroad Retirement Act sailed through Congress; both were purportedly tailored to meet Supreme Court objections. The Guffey-Snyder Coal Act baldly reinstated the NRA regime for the coal industry.

The Motor Carrier Act was firmly rooted in Congress's power over interstate commerce. The other three bills, however, presented a direct challenge to the Supreme Court. As a group, they signaled a New Deal determination to bring government supervision of the economy to an unprecedented peacetime level.

Roosevelt did not get everything he wanted. By one count six "major" bills had failed to clear Congress. Nonetheless, one thing was certain: he was the dominant force in American politics. By about any measure, he had surpassed his two great exemplars, Theodore Roosevelt and Woodrow Wilson, in personal popularity, the deployment of presidential power, and mastery of the legislative process. He seemed always on the offensive, constantly pressing for transformative reform. Charisma, charm, and above all a pervasive impression of his concern for the trials of ordinary people were his most prominent soft assets. He supplemented them as necessary with hardball tactics. The White House traded favors for votes freely, twisted arms when it could, and accepted half loaves when necessary. *New York Times* correspondent Arthur Krock stated it bluntly: "Civil service regulations have been evaded or ignored, and to the politicians have been given great bags of patronage. Politics has suffused every word and act."[15]

Roosevelt likely read the Krock column with more amusement and satisfaction than annoyance. TR and Wilson had made their own compromises with the real world. He had achieved objectives in Congress that he believed were well worth whatever moral price they had exacted. He was ready to go to the source of his ultimate strength, the people, and begin his long fight for reelection.

A HARD STRUGGLE SEEMED IN THE OFFING. AT THE BEGINNING OF AUGUST, the Democrats lost a special congressional election in Rhode Island. Republicans attacked the New Deal as a lawless failed recovery program. Herbert Hoover declared, "It would be better for Liberty to commit suicide in the open rather than to be poisoned by indirection in the Capital of the Nation."[16]

In a process of bitter polarization, Hoover had moved well to the right, while Roosevelt had shifted steadily toward the left. Democrats painted Hoover, once widely thought a great humanitarian and a progressive advocate of an organized economy, as a coldhearted reactionary. Republicans saw Roosevelt, once considered a charming and relatively inoffensive lightweight, as a malevolent, psychologically unstable would-be dictator.[17]

Roy W. Howard, chairman of the important Scripps-Howard newspaper chain and generally supportive of the New Deal, wrote to Roosevelt on August 26, 1935, "Many business men who once gave you sincere support are now not merely hostile, they are frightened." Business and the country, he declared, needed a "breathing spell." Roosevelt responded with a firm but conciliatory communication, claiming a developing economic recovery. The administration's program, he concluded, "has now reached substantial completion and the breathing spell of which you speak is here—very decidedly so." It is impossible to know whether Franklin Roosevelt actually believed those words and necessary to remember that the phrase "breathing spell" implies a resumption of vigorous activity.[18]

AS THE CONGRESSIONAL SESSION GROUND TOWARD ITS END, HAROLD ICKES visited the Capitol and watched Huey Long hold forth: "He waved his arms, he contorted, he swayed, and at all times he talked in a very loud voice. I must admit, however, that he was clever. . . . He has a sharp, quick wit, even though he is a blatant and unconscionable demagogue." No senator posed a bigger political threat to the president. With the help of ghostwriters, Long had just finished a book-length manuscript forecasting a run for the presidency and titled *My First Days in the White House*.[19]

A week later, he was back in Louisiana tending to political business. Late on the evening of September 8, he walked through the state capitol building at the front of a retinue of aides and armed bodyguards. An inoffensive-looking little man in an immaculate white suit walked over to him, produced a small pistol, and shot him in the abdomen. The assassin, a dentist named Carl Adams Weiss, quickly lay dead in a pool of blood. Long lingered in the hospital for thirty hours. On the morning of September 10, he was pronounced dead.[20]

Roosevelt surely took no joy in the event. Still, he must have felt at least a glimmer of relief that the Louisiana senator would not be around to harass him in 1936. Father Coughlin and Dr. Townsend remained, but neither was a credible presidential candidate, and there was little likelihood that the more conventional progressives would mount a challenge from the coherent left.[21]

With Congress adjourned, the president followed what was becoming a natural pattern. First, he took a working vacation at Hyde Park. Next came a train trip across the continent, punctuated by major speeches and enthusiastic welcomes from large crowds. He proclaimed the success of the administration's agricultural policy at Fremont, Nebraska; underscored the need for regional development and the benefits of public electrical power at the dedication of the Boulder Dam (without mentioning that Hoover had begun the project); and trumpeted a gathering economic recovery, which he linked to his reform program in addresses in Los Angeles and San Diego. Then he once again boarded the USS *Houston* for another leisurely cruise through the Panama Canal and around to the East Coast.[22]

By late October, he was back at the White House, ready to meet Canadian prime minister MacKenzie King and sign a trade agreement with his northern neighbor. Then he was in Warm Springs for the traditional Thanksgiving dinner with the polios, who remained so important to him. In the run-up to Christmas, he delivered speeches in Atlanta and Chicago, once again hitting the themes of recovery and reform. The presidential campaign of 1936 was on the horizon.

THE PRESIDENT BEGAN THE NEW YEAR WITH HIS ANNUAL MESSAGE TO CONgress, delivered once again in person and, for the first time, at an evening hour—9:00 p.m. Eastern, 6:00 p.m. Pacific—designed to capture a peak radio audience across the nation. Significantly, he devoted about half the talk to foreign relations, decrying "those nations which are dominated by the twin spirits of autocracy and aggression," while promising to preserve America from war through "a well-ordered neutrality."

Then he asserted that the forces of autocracy were at work in the United States. Small but powerful "financial and industrial groups," dominant in the previous decade, were fighting his effort to achieve democracy at home. Seeking to subvert "the people's liberties," the money changers were back and strove for "autocracy toward labor, toward stockholders, toward consumers, toward public sentiment." In thirty-four months, he declared, his administration had built new instruments of public power. The economy was recovering, and ordinary people were receiving protection. It was up to Congress "to wage unceasing warfare" against reactionary fearmongers.[23]

The speech, which the president renamed as his "message on the state of the union," was unmistakably the first shot of his reelection campaign. It revealed that the contest would be among the most polarizing in American history. Liberals and Democratic loyalists cheered him as "heroic" and "eloquent." Conservatives and nearly all Republicans responded with "dirty campaign," "cloud of propaganda," and "wretched taste."[24]

On January 6, the Supreme Court made itself part of the controversy with a devastating decision in *U.S. v. Butler* (also known as the Hoosac Mills Case). A six-justice majority—the four conservatives and the two moderates—ruled unconstitutional the federal tax on agricultural processors that financed the Agricultural Adjustment Administration (AAA) acreage-restriction program, primarily because the management of local agricultural production was a state responsibility, not a national one. The majority seemed to assume that it was of no consequence that a crop would likely enter the stream of interstate commerce once produced or that, in any case, a national market would set its price.[25]

The conservative justices had taken the narrow definition of interstate commerce enabled by *Schechter* and run with it. The decision suggested that Roosevelt now faced an opposition majority of at least five horsemen determined to strike down the New Deal. Writing for the dissenters, Justice Harlan Fiske Stone accused the majority of "a tortured construction of the Constitution" and declared, "Courts are not the only agency of government that must be assumed to have capacity to govern." He undoubtedly spoke the feelings of the White House.[26]

The majority justices had struck at an unpopular target. The AAA enjoyed scant support except among the farmers who received its subsidies. For them, subsidized allotments spelled the difference between poverty and relative well-being. The Soil Conservation Act of 1936, signed by the president on February 29, perpetuated the crop allotment system under another rationale. But why would the Supreme Court consider soil depletion more of a national problem than agricultural production?[27]

It took little foresight to understand that if Roosevelt were returned to office, there would be a political showdown with the Court. Two and a half weeks after the *Butler* decision, Harold Ickes summarized Roosevelt's remarks to a cabinet meeting: "He is not at all averse to the Supreme Court declaring one New Deal statute after another unconstitutional. I think he believes that the Court will find itself pretty far out on a limb."[28]

WITH THE PROCESSING TAX DEAD, THE ADMINISTRATION HAD TO FIND MONEY to maintain the new soil conservation program. Revenue issues became even more pressing when, just weeks later, Congress responded to election-year exigencies by overriding Roosevelt's veto of a new veterans bonus bill. Both the president and Secretary of the Treasury Morgenthau, moreover, were sensitive about the 30 percent increase in the national debt since 1933. They developed legislation primarily designed to tap undistributed corporate profits, which they considered yet another unsavory way in which the wealthy avoided taxes.

In June legislation emerged from Congress establishing a graduated tax of 7 to 22 percent on undistributed profits. New Dealers argued that the tax would actually stimulate economic recovery by forcing money (presumably unproductive) out of corporate coffers—a stance emblematic of the vast gulf in perception between New Deal liberalism and conventional business conservatism. Conservatives argued with considerable justice that businesses required large reserves for expansion and unforeseen contingencies. Producing approximately $800 million a year in new revenue, the bill met the government's urgent fiscal needs. But how could pulling so large a sum out of the private economy contribute to the economic recovery that the administration still sought after three years in office?[29]

At least payment of the veterans bonus did put several hundred million dollars, most of which would be rapidly spent, into the economy. Harold Ickes's Public Works Administration (PWA) continued in charge of expensive high-visibility, large-scale public works projects. The new Works Progress Administration (WPA), under Harry Hopkins, put as much as 90 percent of its funds into salaries; it would tackle thousands of small projects designed to generate maximum employment in about every locality and provide much needed assistance to millions of unemployed workers.

By mid-1936, the WPA would have nearly 2.25 million employees. The PWA and other federal projects employed another 1.4 million. The stimulus to the economy was impressive and rapid. In those days, most projects really were "shovel ready," and laborers often actually worked with shovels. By then, Franklin Roosevelt was officially a candidate for reelection.[30]

THE NEW DEAL HAD BEEN CONTROVERSIAL. SIGNATURE PROGRAMS LIKE THE NRA and AAA had drawn a lot of disapproval. Considerable concern existed within the middle class, still the center of gravity in American politics, about the cost of jobs programs and general relief. Nonetheless, the president was a strong personality, his agenda had helped a lot of people, and his radio talks had established a personal bond with a large segment of the citizenry.

Elmo Roper, one of the best practitioners of the new art of public opinion research, conducted a poll for *Fortune* magazine in late 1935. Nearly a third of the respondents were strong Roosevelt supporters; almost another third thought the president had done more good than harm. A sitting president with the approval of two-thirds of the country had reason for confidence. He may have been getting similar signals from Democratic National Committee pollster Emil Hurja. "We will win easily next year," Roosevelt told cabinet members on November 9, 1935. "We are going to make it a crusade."[31]

By the time the Democratic convention gathered in Philadelphia on June 23, 1936, the Republicans had already named Roosevelt's opponent, Governor Alfred Landon of Kansas. A capable chief executive, Landon had roots in the progressivism of Theodore Roosevelt, prospered in the oil and gas business, and effectively managed his state's beleaguered finances. The Republican platform, moreover, was by no means a manifesto of rugged individualism. Denouncing many administration programs as egregious examples of government overreach, it declared its fealty to their objectives and contained some generalities that sounded positively New Dealish.[32]

Still, envisioning Landon as president required a hearty imagination. At his best, he was a down-to-earth everyman, a representative of Main Street whose nomination had been facilitated by the impossibility of a Hoover rerun and the reluctance of such GOP heavyweights as Michigan senator Arthur Vandenberg and Chicago publisher Frank Knox to go head-to-head with Roosevelt. A Republican banner, attempting to take advantage of Jim Farley's brush-off of the candidate as "a typical prairie governor," bravely declared, "Abraham Lincoln . . . a typical prairie lawyer. Alfred M. Landon . . . a typical prairie governor." The pitch was ludicrously counterintuitive. The upcoming campaign would show that the Republican Party had become, in reaction to the New Deal, a party of passive, minimalist government.[33]

On the heels of the Landon nomination, a new force announced its presence. Father Coughlin, Dr. Townsend, and the receiver of Huey Long's Share the Wealth movement, Reverend Gerald L. K. Smith, proclaimed a new Union Party. Its nominee, Representative William Lemke of North Dakota, was a neopopulist Republican known primarily for his sponsorship of farm mortgage relief. Earnest and plodding, Lemke was no Huey Long. The party leadership, moreover, was increasingly marginalized, Coughlin by overexposure, Townsend by the Social Security Act, and Smith by a vulgar anti-Semitism.

The Democratic Party's well-scripted convention in Philadelphia went off without a major hitch, but certain blips revealed important transformations. Al Smith and four other party notables sent an open message to the convention urging it to repudiate the New Deal, pass over Roosevelt, nominate "some genuine Democrat," and return to the principles of Thomas Jefferson, Andrew Jackson, and Grover Cleveland. Virginia's two major Democrats, Senators Carter Glass and Harry F. Byrd, ostentatiously refused committee assignments that would require them to endorse a New Deal platform. Senator Ellison D. ("Cotton Ed") Smith of South Carolina, declaring that he would not support "any political organization that looks upon the Negro and caters to him as a political and social equal," walked out after a black clergyman opened one of the sessions with a prayer.[34]

Roosevelt's nomination was unanimous. He delivered his acceptance speech, scheduled for the prime radio time of 10:00 p.m. Eastern time on June 27, before a crowd of over 100,000 at Franklin Field. His motorcade entered the stadium at 9:37 and made its way to a platform erected at one end of the playing field. He exited his car, steadying himself on James's arm, surrounded by guests and well-wishers. Suddenly someone lurched into him, a leg brace gave way, and he was on the ground. Aides quickly lifted him to his feet, recovered his speech, and brushed off his suit. He later recalled, "I was the damnedest, maddest white man at that moment you ever saw." A scene that fifty years later would have replayed incessantly on national television went unnoticed in the relative darkness by everyone except those immediately around the president. Roosevelt was quickly composed, on his feet, and walking with James to the platform as the crowd delivered a thunderous ovation.[35]

Powerfully delivered, his words echoed throughout the stadium and traveled across the country via perhaps 250 radio stations. The nation, he declared, had conquered the fear of 1933, but it still had far to go. Americans had to come to grips with a predatory economic royalism that exploited other people's money, took the fruits of their labor, and denied them true liberty. The collapse of 1929 had exposed it. The election of 1932 had been a mandate to end it. He was struggling, however imperfectly, to achieve that mandate.

> Governments can err—Presidents do make mistakes, but the immortal Dante tells us that divine justice weighs the sins of the cold-blooded and the sins of the warm-hearted in different scales.
>
> Better the occasional faults of a government that lives in a spirit of charity than the consistent omissions of a government frozen in the ice of its own indifference.
>
> There is a mysterious cycle in human events. To some generations much is given. Of others much is expected. This generation of Americans has a rendezvous with destiny.
>
> . . .
>
> . . . [H]ere in America we are waging a great war. It is not alone a war against want and destitution and economic demoralization. It is a war for the survival of democracy. . . .
>
> I accept the commission you have tendered me. I join with you. I am enlisted for the duration of the war.[36]

A roar went up from the crowd. The band struck up "The Stars and Stripes Forever." Joined by his mother, Eleanor, and four of their children, the president acknowledged the cheers. After several minutes, he called for "Auld Lang Syne." He and James returned to his automobile, circled the field to "Happy Days Are Here Again," and left the stadium in a state of exhilaration and optimism.[37]

THE SPEECH WAS MORE INSPIRATIONAL THAN INSTRUCTIVE. WAS IT A DECLARATION of class warfare? Just what was the rendezvous with destiny? Even many Democrats had their reservations, among them Raymond Moley, who had counseled a moderate and conciliatory tone and been derided unmercifully by Roosevelt at a White House dinner for the speechwriters. The president was determined to follow through on his resentment of the American elite and confident that he had found a winning issue.[38]

He faced the campaign with a different team. Louis Howe had died in April after a yearlong illness. The president had ordered a state funeral for him and traveled with his remains to their final resting place in Fall River, Massachusetts. Jim Farley mobilized state and local party organizations. Principal speechwriters included Sam Rosenman, Tom Corcoran, and liberal Republican Stanley High.

Eleanor, by 1936, was almost as prominent and controversial as her husband. Commuting to New York weekly, she continued to teach at the Todhunter School, but, devoted to interests far broader and more important than the instruction of daughters of the privileged, she was about to end her partnership with Nancy Cook and Marion Dickerman. She had taken on a daily newspaper column and a weekly radio program. Much in demand as a speaker, she traveled extensively. She was also developing other close attachments—to her own private secretary, Malvina "Tommy" Thompson, to journalist Lorena Hickok, and to dancer Mayris Chaney. Conservative Democrats grumbled about her; liberals increasingly saw her as an ideological lodestar. FDR probably viewed her, correctly, as a political asset.

Early polls, nonetheless, were not encouraging. Gallup gave Roosevelt just a 52 to 48 percent lead in national popular preference, listed only twenty-four states as safely Democratic, and put Landon ahead in the pivotal electoral states of Ohio, Illinois, Pennsylvania, and New York. Landon, he proclaimed, was leading in electoral votes by a razor-thin tally of 272 to 259. Emil Hurja's private polls for the Democratic National Committee were similar.[39]

Gallup's July snapshot was probably not far off the mark. Many New Deal policies and outcomes—a restrictive agricultural program, all-embracing NRA regulation, debasement of the dollar, an increasingly cozy relationship with labor unions, big spending, handouts to WPA workers often unfairly typed as politically connected slackers, and a rising national debt—were broadly unpopular. Yet Roosevelt himself remained very popular. The country might take a look at Landon, but the charisma gap between him and Roosevelt was a yawning chasm. In the end, the election was about the president himself. As from the beginning, he *was* the New Deal, and he relished nothing more than a campaign built on that premise.

The president was content to let Landon, whom he thought a weak candidate, enjoy a mini-surge in the polls. He realized that genuinely undecided voters would not make up their minds until well after Labor Day. Avoiding overt political activity in the weeks after the convention, he spent much of his time outside Washington, boating with his sons off the coasts of Nova Scotia and New Brunswick, spending a few days at Campobello with his mother, making a brief visit to Quebec City (exciting an audience by delivering his greetings in French), relaxing at Hyde Park, and inspecting Pennsylvania flood areas. In a "nonpolitical" address at Chautauqua, New York, he covered his foreign policy flank with assurances that he hated war.[40]

At the end of August, he began a train tour through drought-ravaged farm areas of the Midwest, where he delivered promises of federal assistance. He also found time to visit the still unfinished presidential shrine at Mount Rushmore. Back in Washington just before Labor Day, he broadcast his only fireside chat of the year, a nearly flawless talk in which he promised government aid for the needy. The American nation, he told his listeners, was built on principles of economic democracy that rejected the class conflict and consequent dictatorships that plagued much of Europe. "Labor Day belongs to all of us."[41]

In September, Roosevelt made another foray into the Midwest to meet with drought-state governors (including Landon), then embarked on a "nonpolitical" trip south. Along the way, he announced federal awards, grants, and work projects, even as he proclaimed a rapidly returning prosperity. On September 30, he delivered his official campaign kickoff to a cheering crowd at the New York State Democratic Convention. He followed up by spending much of October on the road and delivering a series of hard-hitting speeches that drew huge, friendly crowds.

The esteemed *Literary Digest* poll consistently showed him trailing Landon, but in mid-October Gallup gave him 54 percent of the popular vote and 390 electoral votes. The steel and auto industries were running at near capacity; port facilities were at their busiest in years. Industrial and manufacturing cities were enjoying an economic boom. Agricultural prices were strong. Unemployment remained high but was expected to decline as factories returned to full schedules. The recovery, global in scope, could not simply be attributed to the New Deal, but the United States, more than any other nation, drove the world economy.[42]

Clearly, administration policies had contributed to the rebound. Yet an army of the unemployed remained; estimates of its size ran from 6 to 10 million workers. The American Federation of Labor, a widely accepted source, put the number at 8.2 million that October. (The government did not yet produce monthly employment statistics.) Pessimists, Harry Hopkins included, assumed these numbers would stay high. The WPA and other work-relief programs, which that October employed 3.3 million people, sustained many of the jobless. All told, an estimated 15.7 million Americans, about one-eighth of the population, were receiving some kind of federal relief benefit. Most were grateful and willing to acknowledge the president as its ultimate source.[43]

Roosevelt's strong personality and the emerging recovery gave rise to a new and powerful political force that was transforming the Democratic Party: the "Roosevelt coalition." The old party had been an amalgam of the (then) Solid South, nursing grievances against Republicans that went back to the Civil War, and northern big-city political organizations, most often headed by men with Irish names. Under the leadership of William Jennings Bryan, the party's association with radicalism alienated patricians like FDR's father. Woodrow Wilson had associated it with a more sedate, if still aggressive, brand of reform. From the 1890s onward, the party's big-city constituencies had grown with each wave of immigrants. In 1936, they and their children were disproportionately beneficiaries of the New Deal.

New Deal programs in fact dished out benefits to almost every group of Americans whose economic status was below the national median. Negroes were grateful for the First Lady's open concern and for fairer treatment than they had received from the federal government since Reconstruction. The time had come, declared a prominent black journalist, to turn Lincoln's picture to the wall. Labor unions, representing workers of diverse backgrounds, contributed heavily to the president's campaign. The upstart Congress of Industrial Organizations (CIO), headed by the volatile mine workers leader, John L. Lewis, gave the Roosevelt campaign the then enormous sum of $500,000.

Roosevelt's appointment to high office of Catholics and Jews, such as Joseph P. Kennedy to head the Securities and Exchange Commission and Henry Morgenthau Jr. as secretary of the Treasury, heartened relatively well-off elites among the minorities. (Morgenthau was only the second Jew to be appointed to the cabinet; Theodore Roosevelt had named the first.)

Although a powerful political force, the coalition was also filled with contradictions. It included Negroes and white supremacists; Protestants, Catholics, and Jews; and multiple ethnic groups that wanted little to do with each other. Some members were already reflexive Democratic partisans; many were direct beneficiaries of a WPA job, a mortgage refinancing, an acreage allotment subsidy, or support for labor unions. Others were simply ready to reward a radio-communicated expression of presidential concern. Their diversity guaranteed eventual internal dissention; for the moment, however, the coalition members shared a temporary solidarity.

To this polyglot amalgam, Roosevelt added an ideological grouping: independent progressives, many with Republican backgrounds. A National Conference of Progressives, chaired by Senator Robert La Follette Jr., made the endorsement official. Its personalities ranged from urban radicals such as Mayor Fiorello La Guardia of New York to venerable agrarians such as Senator George Norris of Nebraska. Roosevelt himself would go out of his way to endorse Norris for reelection against a Democratic challenger. He wanted to make the Democratic Party the nation's progressive party and indelibly brand the Republicans its reactionary alternative.[44]

IF FOR THE DEMOCRATIC PARTY DEMOGRAPHY WAS DESTINY, ROOSEVELT'S overwhelming persona was a triumph of individual will. Of all the larger-than-life national leaders of the 1930s, he alone maintained himself in office by democratic procedures. Yet, for all his charm and appeal, he also displayed the off-putting characteristics of the charismatic leader: a palpable appetite for power, a resentment of restraint from such institutions as the Supreme Court, an ideological outlook that removed politics from the realm of divergent interests and compromise to one of grand principle, and a tendency to personalize differences of opinion and ambition. These attitudes, while reassuring to his followers, appeared autocratic and menacing to those who opposed him.

In the emergency of 1933, Walter Lippmann had encouraged Roosevelt to act the dictator. In 1936, Lippmann accused him of personal rule and an authoritarian temperament, worried out loud about the perils of an overwhelming Democratic victory, and pronounced Landon an acceptable alternative. The *Baltimore Sun* and *Washington Post*, both usually reliable Democratic newspapers, withheld backing for either candidate. The *Post* gave Roosevelt credit for good intentions but warned of "dictatorship by default." The leading voice of midwestern progressivism, the *St. Louis Post-Dispatch*, charged Roosevelt with big-government overreach and endorsed Landon. In contrast, *The Economist* (London), published in a nation accustomed to big government and high tax rates, saw the New Deal as a moderate program led by a president addicted to extreme language. "The qualities which inspire loyalty in a crisis," it observed, "are not those best calculated to inspire confidence in a calmer period."[45]

The angry Right—typified by the Liberty League, the Hearst newspapers, and the *Chicago Tribune*—portrayed Roosevelt as a would-be dictator inspired by Stalin, predicted a regime that would require its citizens to wear dog tags engraved with their Social Security numbers, and warned that the American way of life was at stake. Landon, trying to get some traction, increasingly veered in the league's direction.[46]

By the end of October, most seasoned observers realized that Roosevelt was moving toward a convincing victory, even if the *Literary Digest* persisted in predicting a Landon upset. Jim Farley predicted that the president would carry every state except Maine and Vermont.[47]

Roosevelt was riding a strong economy. He was the greatest popular communicator in the history of the office. His dominating personality contrasted vividly with Landon's blandness. His party was sure to maintain control of Congress. In such circumstances, many leaders might have dialed down partisanship and talked of national unity. But charismatic leadership fed on conflict and crisis. It was, above all, personal.

On October 31, at the last big rally of the campaign, Roosevelt made his way to the rostrum at Madison Square Garden and reached for the flamethrower. He told his listeners that he and they stood at the head of an army that for four years had been fighting against the exploitative forces of "business and financial monopoly, speculation, reckless banking, class antagonism, sectionalism, [and] war profiteering."

> They had begun to consider the Government of the United States as a mere appendage to their own affairs. We know now that Government by organized money is just as dangerous as Government by organized mob.
>
> Never before in all our history have these forces been so united against one candidate as they stand today. They are unanimous in their hate for me—and I welcome their hatred.
>
> I should like to have it said of my first Administration that in it the forces of selfishness and of lust for power met their match. I should like to have it said of my second Administration that in it these forces met their master.[48]

The crowd, a *Washington Post* reporter wrote, seemed to sway expectantly, waiting for the next verbal body blow to the opposition. Then "their pent-up force would crash to the roof-footlights in terrific noise."[49]

Three days later, the nation went to the polls.

ROOSEVELT WAITED FOR THE ELECTION RESULTS AT HYDE PARK, SURROUNDED by family and close aides. The first returns showed clearly that an epic landslide was in the making. He polled 60 percent of the popular ballot and ran 11 million votes ahead of Landon. The electoral college tally was 523 to 8. Lemke got less than 1 million votes. The Democrats won majorities of 331 to 89 in the House of Representatives and 76 to 16 in the Senate. The people had decided overwhelmingly that the president and the New Deal had more to offer them than did Landon and a return to yesterday.

Tommy Corcoran played his accordion for a joyful party. At Democratic gatherings all over the country, bands struck up "Happy Days Are Here Again." No president since George Washington had received so overwhelming a mandate from the American people. For a brief moment, all things seemed possible.

CHAPTER 18

"PANIC AND LACK OF CONFIDENCE"

THE ECONOMIC AND POLITICAL CONSEQUENCES
OF THE SECOND HUNDRED DAYS, 1937–1939

ON JANUARY 6, 1937, FRANKLIN ROOSEVELT DELIVERED HIS ANNUAL STATE OF the Union message two weeks before his second swearing in. The Depression, he declared, was rapidly coming to an end. An age of reform remained in its early stages. The economic crisis, he asserted, had laid bare a long neglect of the needs of the underprivileged. It thereby presented a challenge that American democracy had met with "first, economic recovery through many kinds of assistance to agriculture, industry and banking; and, second, deliberate improvement in the personal security and opportunity of the great mass of our people."[1]

Roosevelt admitted that the National Recovery Administration had been too ambitious in its effort to manage the economy, but, he added, controlling the evils of overproduction, underproduction, and speculation, achieving decent working conditions for labor, and creating just returns for agriculture remained necessary. Above all, "the deeper purpose of democratic government is to assist as many of its citizens as possible, especially those who need it most." This goal required a national housing program, extensive assistance to the rural poor, and a far more comprehensive Social Security system.

In remarks clearly directed at the Supreme Court, Roosevelt declared that governments, prevented from meeting the necessities of the day, had been replaced by militaristic authoritarianism. The framers of the Constitution had possessed an expansive interpretation of its powers; contemporary judges should follow their example. He followed this assertion by signaling yet another departure: "This task of Executive management has reached the point where our administrative machinery needs comprehensive overhauling. I shall, therefore, shortly address the Congress more fully in regard to modernizing and improving the Executive branch of the Government."

On January 20, Roosevelt took the oath of office, barely sheltered from a driving rain mixed with sleet, his hand on the two-hundred-year-old Dutch-language family Bible. Radio carried his inaugural address to tens of millions of listeners across the continent. Shortwave transmission conveyed it to millions more in Europe and Latin America. Firmly delivered against a background of pattering raindrops, the speech told the world that the New Deal was far from over.[2]

Utilizing quasi-religious symbolism to the utmost, the president recalled his determination, during his 1932 campaign, "to drive from the temple of our ancient faith those who had profaned it." Evoking the Founding Fathers and the constitutional mandate to promote the general welfare, he pledged to use his office to consolidate a "new order of things," characterized by social justice and economic morality, over the opposition of "private autocratic powers" and "heedless self-interest." "One-third of a nation," he estimated, was "ill-housed, ill-clad, ill-nourished." The democratic ideal demanded better: "The test of our progress is not whether we add more to the abundance of those who have much; it is whether we provide enough for those who have too little. . . . Today we reconsecrate our country to long-cherished ideals in a suddenly changed civilization."

The State of the Union and the second inaugural established a tone of militant progressive ambition. The second term, whatever else it might become, would not be an era of good feelings.

ROOSEVELT HAD ALREADY SHAKEN WASHINGTON WITH HIS EXECUTIVE reorganization plan, submitted to Congress a week before the inauguration. The proposal, developed by a committee of largely apolitical academics and professional administrators, drew on European examples of career public service. Presented as an effort to streamline a ramshackle federal administrative structure, it advocated a comprehensive extension of merit-based civil service positions to all the nonpolicy positions of the bureaucracy. It would consolidate all the agencies of the federal government, including regulatory bodies that operated quasi-independently of both the executive and legislative branches, into an enlarged cabinet that would have two new departments devoted to social welfare and public works. The plan also called for the addition of six administrative assistants (akin to top-level British civil servants) to the presidential staff and for an enlarged Bureau of the Budget reporting directly to the president.

The proposal won the enthusiastic support of most progressives and New Dealers who applauded its promise of professionalism and efficiency. To conservatives, it raised the specter of an unaccountable administrative apparatus with quasi-judicial authority, largely independent of legislative oversight, controlled by an enlarged and powerful presidency. To opposition partisans and a fair number of independent observers, the plan reflected Roosevelt's overweening desire for personal power. The few Republicans left in Congress would oppose it. So would most of the still powerful Democratic barons, jealous of their own prerogatives.[3]

Almost from the beginning, however, the president's hectoring of the Supreme Court in both his message to Congress and the inaugural address drew more attention than executive reorganization. Actually, the Court itself had read the election returns and was beginning to soften its hostility to the administration's agenda. On January 4, its first decision day of the year, it unanimously upheld a federal statute banning the interstate shipment of goods produced by convict labor. Interstate commerce and the power to regulate it now presumably extended to local processes of production. Surely the same principle would apply to child labor and other contingencies.[4]

The case perhaps indicated that the justices were groping for an accommodation with the administration. Clearly, however, the conservative opposition saw the courts as its last hope and was determined to reverse the New Deal through litigation. Roosevelt, fortified by his overwhelming electoral victory, was ready and eager to take up the challenge. Rumors circulated of draft legislation requiring a supermajority of perhaps 7 to 2 for a finding of unconstitutionality.[5]

On February 5, the president dropped his biggest bombshell since he had scuttled the London World Economic Conference. In a message to Congress he requested legislation "to maintain the effective functioning of the Federal judiciary." Recent crises had made the load of the courts especially heavy, he declared. The increasing age of the judiciary added to the problem. Asserting the need for younger blood, he requested authority to appoint additional judges at all levels to supplement those who had reached the age of seventy and declined to retire. In the case of the Supreme Court, that meant up to six new members.[6]

Roosevelt undoubtedly realized the proposal would generate bitter opposition but thought his electoral mandate and congressional majorities would carry the legislation through. The opposition erupted with the intensity of a wildfire on a sun-parched prairie. Herbert Hoover gave the proposal an indelible label when he asserted that the president was trying "to make changes by 'packing' the Supreme Court." Numerous personalities from Woodrow Wilson's presidency opposed the bill. Raymond Moley made his first open break with the administration. Walter Lippmann wrote one piece after another depicting the plan as yet another assertion of Roosevelt's lust for personal rule. The members of the Court were unanimous, if silent, in their opposition. One of the most vehement was Justice Louis Brandeis.[7]

Embodying the attitude of most conservative southern Democrats, the chairman of the House Judiciary Committee, Hatton Sumners of Texas, refused to hold hearings on the proposal. He did, however, agree to sponsor a bill providing retirement at full pay for justices who had reached the age of seventy and served for at least ten years. Congress passed the legislation quickly, and the president signed it on March 1.[8]

With Sumners balking, the Court-packing bill had to originate in the Senate. There, Judiciary Committee chairman Henry Fountain Ashurst, a colorful party regular, displayed minimal enthusiasm. The maverick Montana Democrat Burton K. Wheeler emerged as leader of the opposition; most of the western and midwestern progressives joined him. Wheeler was a Democrat by convenience, an independent by conviction. He had supported Roosevelt for the presidential nomination in 1932, backed most of the New Deal, and sponsored the Public Utility Holding Company Bill. Senate Republicans retreated into the woodwork, understanding that their open and vehement opposition could only alienate wavering Democrats.[9]

Wheeler declared that while he deplored the trend of recent Supreme Court decisions, the president's proposal could destroy the independence of the judiciary. A future right-wing chief executive could pack the Court in the other direction; progressives would then rightly charge that he was attempting to establish a dictatorship. He reflected the sense held by many Americans who neither hated nor loved their president that FDR, like his cousin Theodore, possessed an authoritarian streak.[10]

The Court-packing bill required the unequivocal support of Senate Majority Leader Joseph Robinson of Arkansas, a much admired moderate prone to support his president and known to covet appointment to the Supreme Court. As a southerner, however, he consistently voiced the regional orthodoxy of strict constructionism and states' rights. Robinson had a good chance of getting the legislation through if the president signaled he would be one of the new justices. But Roosevelt had reason to doubt that the senator would be a reliable liberal.

As a determined opposition formed on Capitol Hill, Roosevelt realized he would have to fight for a Court bill in the way he knew best: using his powerful presence and compelling voice. On March 4, he tried to rally the party faithful with a speech to a Democratic "Victory Dinner" in Washington, broadcast to 1,000 such events all over the country. He asserted that democracy could succeed in the United States only if the branches of government functioned as a three-horse team that pulled together.[11]

A few days later, he took his case directly to the people with the ninth fireside chat of his presidency. As always, he delivered the speech well, but at thirty-three minutes, it was on the long side; it was also complex to the point of being internally contradictory, peevish in tone, and perhaps too self-referential. Maybe because the Court's two most important invalidations—of the National Recovery Administration (NRA) and the Agricultural Adjustment Administration (AAA)—likely reflected popular opinion, he did not discuss them. Instead he singled out the Gold Clause Cases, which had ended with a 5–4 ruling in the administration's favor, and deplored the close vote. He assured his listeners that he wanted an independent judiciary. Obviously, however, it had to be an independent judiciary that agreed with him.[12]

The fireside chat did not move public opinion an inch. Gallup found the nation divided on the bill before the talk—38 percent for, 39 percent against, 23 percent for some vague modified plan—and essentially unchanged after it. Sentiment in Congress was not much different. With only a minority in either chamber enthusiastic about court packing, the administration faced defeat. Far more than the president realized, constitutional principles of checks and balances, along with anxiety about an all-powerful executive, were embedded in the nation's political culture. Roosevelt himself remained popular among nearly two-thirds of the public, but, reflecting the tendency of charismatic leadership to elicit strong feelings, much of the other third positively loathed him.[13]

The controlling force, as it turned out, was the Supreme Court itself. On March 21, Senator Wheeler released a letter he had received from Chief Justice Charles Evans Hughes. It demolished Roosevelt's argument that the ravages of age mandated an enlargement of the Court. Hughes documented a heavy workload of petitions read, arguments heard, and judgments rendered. There was no backlog. Additional members would mean "more judges to hear, more judges to confer, more judges to discuss, more judges to be convinced and to decide." To underscore the unanimity of feeling among the justices, Hughes closed by revealing that both the liberal hero Louis Brandeis and the archconservative Willis Van Devanter agreed with his letter.[14]

Eight days later, the Court began to issue a series of decisions that confirmed the early indications of a move to the left. Each was a 5–4 verdict in which Hughes and Roberts sided with the three liberals against the Four Horsemen; the new coalition upheld an Oregon minimum wage law, the Wagner labor relations act, and the Social Security Act. It appeared a sure thing that the social reform authority of the federal government would encounter few limits.

On May 18, Justice Van Devanter submitted a letter of retirement to the president, giving Roosevelt a Supreme Court appointment that likely would ensure liberal dominance. Here was an opportunity to make a strategic retreat. Instead, Roosevelt, uncertain about the permanence of the Court's change, rejected compromise. Hughes might stay in line, but Roberts was less certain. So, for that matter, was Robinson, and pressure from the Senate to nominate Senator Robinson as Van Devanter's replacement was intense. Roosevelt dallied on naming a successor, thereby signaling that Robinson would make the Court only if he could deliver legislation.

Robinson, sixty-four years old and in poor health, struggled to do so—until the morning of July 15, when a maid found him in his apartment, dead of a nighttime heart attack. Court packing thereafter was also dead. Many senators believed Roosevelt had pushed their much-liked leader into an early grave. In an atmosphere of bitterness, the Democrats voted for his successor as Senate majority leader in a close contest between Pat Harrison of Mississippi, a conservative-leaning representative of the Deep South, and Alben Barkley of Kentucky, a liberal-leaning border-stater. The administration threw all the muscle it could command behind Barkley, who won by one vote.

It remained only to designate a confirmable successor to Van Devanter. The president passed over such eminences as Felix Frankfurter for Senator Hugo Black of Alabama, a militant liberal in the tradition of southern populism. Black was easily confirmed. Shortly thereafter, it came out that in the early years of his political career, he had been a Ku Klux Klan (KKK) activist. Black responded with a radio address saying that he had put the KKK behind him. As a Justice, he would be a militant civil libertarian, but the temporary embarrassment, to both him and the president, was considerable.[15]

Black was the first of many appointments Roosevelt made. One by one, justices—conservatives, liberals, and swing voters—retired or died until, by April 1945, of the original nine Roosevelt inherited, only Roberts remained on the bench. The replacements—Stanley Reed, Felix Frankfurter, William O. Douglas, Frank Murphy, James Byrnes, Robert Jackson, and Wiley Rutledge— were mostly reliable New Deal supporters. In 1941, upon Hughes's retirement,

Roosevelt would appoint the liberal Harlan Fiske Stone chief justice. The new justices rarely questioned economic regulation but squabbled over issues of civil liberties and civil rights.

In September 1937, Roosevelt delivered a speech, broadcast nationally, observing the 150th anniversary of the Constitution, which he characterized as "a layman's document, not a lawyer's contract." In June 1938, he adopted the line that the Court fight had been "a lost battle which won a war." But many timorous congressmen knew now that they could defy and beat him. His years of near absolute mastery were ending at a time of grave challenges at home and abroad.[16]

THE 1937 SESSION OF THE SEVENTY-FIFTH CONGRESS NONETHELESS GAVE ROOsevelt pieces of legislation that at the time seemed progressive milestones but later called into question the judgment of their creators.

In April, the Guffey-Vinson Act effectively reestablished a regulatory regime of price fixing and planning for the coal industry. Critics feared it was the first step in the construction of a new NRA-style economic order. Actually it was a wobbly and unsatisfactory bureaucratic attempt to achieve equilibrium in an unstable industry. It and similar attempts to establish government-imposed "counter-organization" in chaotic, fragmented industries would not survive the eventual return of prosperity.[17]

In July, Congress passed the Bankhead-Jones Farm Tenant Act. An attempt to aid impoverished southern tenant farmers and sharecroppers and reestablish a class of small yeoman farmers, it established the Farm Security Administration (FSA), which assisted in the purchase and operation of 160-acre properties. The FSA also operated camps for migrant workers and pursued an ambitious program of photographic documentation of rural life (especially poverty). Expressing the missionary idealism of New Dealers, it had scant political support and little economic impact. Revolutions in agricultural technology, along with the New Deal farm subsidies that financed them, were already making small farms obsolete.

The Wagner-Steagall Housing Act, a landmark attempt to establish an ongoing federal housing program for the urban poor, created a US Housing Authority. The agency could boast of some achievements in the years to come, especially in providing shelter for war workers, but its adoption of the high-rise apartment building model proved dysfunctional. By the 1960s, many of the residential structures financed by the agency would be widely scorned as slums more dangerous and less livable than the neighborhoods they supplanted.

WITH THE COURT-PACKING ISSUE OUT OF THE WAY, ROOSEVELT BELIEVED HE could get more from Congress. But the controversy had graphically demonstrated the limitations of his power. Worse yet, labor-management discord wracked what had seemed a rapidly recovering economy, which was suddenly sliding toward a new abyss.

At the end of 1936, the United Auto Workers (UAW), a key component of the new Congress of Industrial Organizations (CIO) under John L. Lewis, staged a series of sit-down strikes at strategic General Motors (GM) plants. To the outrage of much of middle-class America, workers and union activists occupied the properties, brought assembly lines to a halt, and disobeyed court orders to vacate the premises. Sit-downs had already occurred in France, where they were a favored tactic of Communist trade unions. Some of the GM strike leaders were also Communists; others, including future auto union chief Walter Reuther, were left-wing socialists. But the effective director of the strike, Lewis, was a pragmatic, hard-nosed labor chief driven by a personal ambition to become the leader of the American working class and to secure high wages and good benefits for his followers. (When asked about his use of Communists as organizers, Lewis is widely reputed to have replied, "Who gets the bird, the dog or the hunter?")

Michigan's Democratic governor, Frank Murphy, refused to deploy his National Guard to evict the strikers. General Motors, fearing serious damage to the seized facilities, did not push very hard for force. Six weeks of negotiations followed, involving Murphy, Lewis, Secretary of Labor Frances Perkins, and, occasionally, Roosevelt himself. In mid-February, GM, having watched Ford, Chrysler, and lesser competitors produce at capacity for what seemed a recovering economy, agreed to limited recognition of the UAW. The decision led inexorably to full union representation of the company's blue-collar workforce over the next decade. The UAW quickly organized Chrysler, Packard, Studebaker, Hudson, and many of the larger parts suppliers. Only Ford, forewarned and well prepared with what amounted to a private police force, held out.

At the beginning of 1937, it seemed that sit-down strikes would metastasize throughout the economy, but a strong public backlash developed against them. Administration officials avoided stating an opinion until a federal circuit court upheld a finding that sit-downs were illegal. Secretary Perkins thereupon accepted the court's judgment and condemned the tactic as "unsuited to the temperaments and conditions of our modern life."[18]

Using more traditional methods and determined to pursue the opportunities conferred by the Wagner Act, the CIO engaged in strong organizing drives. Its biggest target was the nation's basic industry: steel. On March 2, 1937, America's largest steel company, United States Steel Corporation, recognized the CIO Steel Workers Organizing Committee (SWOC) as the sole representative of its workers. As in GM's case, business considerations dictated the decision. Domestic demand was high, and big contracts from the British navy, then beginning a major expansion, depended on guarantees of labor peace. For the union, this was an enormous coup: US Steel accounted for nearly 40 percent of the nation's steel capacity.

The remaining companies, collectively known as Little Steel, included Bethlehem, Republic, Youngstown Sheet & Tube, National, American Rolling Mill (ARMCO), and Inland. None had the special inducement that had motivated US Steel. All were hard targets. Many had matched their wages to US Steel's settlement with the SWOC, leaving workers doubtful that they had anything to gain by joining the union. Strikes nonetheless began that spring and dragged on for much of the year. Traditional picketing, given the belligerent stance of both sides, inevitably generated rough confrontations.

The toughest of the Little Steel companies was Republic, headed by self-professed "rugged individualist" Tom Girdler. Its Warren, Ohio, plant became a small fortress in which workers lived around the clock and ate food flown in by small aircraft that occasionally took gunfire from pickets. In Monroe, Michigan, only 10 percent or so of the Republic workers attempted to strike. When the union brought in outside picketers, local vigilantes (some of them reputedly workers) chased them out of town. In South Chicago, Illinois, local police permitted only limited picket lines. On Memorial Day, Sunday, May 30, after a pro-union rally, a large crowd marched on the plant gate. Someone threw a tree branch at the police line; other missiles followed. Untrained in crowd control and perhaps trigger-happy, the police opened fire, killing ten and wounding thirty. The unionists would call the incident the Memorial Day Massacre. The strikes ran on into the fall, with only Inland agreeing to recognize the union. The toll on the steel industry as a whole was relatively small, but the immense polarization of politics carried potentially grave consequences for the administration.

Other unions attempted to organize workers ranging from retail clerks to stevedores. Their heavy-handed tactics probably created more resentment among middle-class Americans than did the frequently rough responses of corporate management. Unionists saw the Memorial Day shooting in Chicago as a wanton massacre instigated by bloodthirsty management and fascistic police. Many newspapers, however, depicted the event as a "riot" initiated by militant strikers. Roosevelt was caught in the middle.[19]

That April, the president had made his own attitude reasonably clear to an off-the-record gathering of newspaper publishers and editors. Unionization, he said, was experiencing growing pains fueled by an emotional movement mentality. The organization of labor reflected progress but would inevitably involve bloody turmoil in its early years. Eventually, a postconflict generation of leaders would institutionalize new relationships between capital and labor. The process, he implied, was messy but unavoidable and ultimately for the best. He was willing to see it through.[20]

At the end of June, in an atmosphere of increased tension, Roosevelt was mindful of a growing backlash. Asked to comment on escalating labor-management hostilities, he replied that the majority of Americans were saying just one thing: "A plague on both your houses." He authorized a direct quotation.[21]

John L. Lewis's fierce and offensive response two months later, during a Labor Day weekend radio speech, insinuated that the CIO's hefty 1936 campaign contribution amounted to a purchase of Roosevelt's support. Using the deep, booming voice that had once made him an effective amateur actor, Lewis accused the steel companies of having killed eighteen strikers, then asserted, "It ill behooves one who has supped at labor's table and who has been sheltered in labor's house to curse with equal fervor and fine impartiality both labor and its adversaries when they become locked in deadly embrace. . . . Those who chant their praises of democracy, but who lose no chance to drive their knives into labor's defenseless back must feel the weight of labor's woe."[22]

The president did not respond. He needed the labor vote. The relationship with Lewis had never been easy; now the political had become personal. Two massive egos were facing off in a conflict that would wax and wane over the next several years.

THROUGH THE FIRST HALF OF 1937, DESPITE LABOR STRIFE, THE ECONOMY seemed to be booming. At midyear, the steel industry, despite its union problems, was operating at 85 percent of capacity. Auto production was at full tilt. It seemed reasonable enough to shift the emphasis of the New Deal from relief and recovery to long-term reform. But how hospitable would a climate of prosperity be to further reform? And what would the consequences be if the economy backslid?

It seemed obvious to many observers and administration officials that it was time to balance the federal budget. Within the administration, the chief advocate of tightening, primarily through spending cuts, was Secretary of the Treasury Henry Morgenthau Jr. The major skeptics were Works Progress

Administration (WPA) administrator Harry Hopkins, highly motivated to defend his huge clientele and enormous budget, and Federal Reserve chairman Marriner S. Eccles, increasingly a convert to Keynesian ideas about the importance of stimulative public spending. The strong economy gave the advantage to Morgenthau. So did political calculation. The WPA had made its substantial contribution to Roosevelt's reelection and could legitimately seem less needed economically. With the president's nod, the administration began to slash its rolls and those of other federal relief programs in early 1937; they were sharply lower at the beginning of the new fiscal year on July 1.[23]

The recovery also brought a disturbing whiff of inflationary price increases. General price levels were still below those of 1929, but the long Depression had established a new normal that made any increases seem menacing. The Treasury "sterilized" new gold inflows by refusing to use these as a basis for printing more money; the Federal Reserve mandated higher bank reserve requirements. Both policies tightened the nation's money supply and thereby bit into the economic upsurge. At the same time, higher federal taxes—Social Security contributions, the wealth tax levies, the undistributed-profits tax—all began to take hold. Although they did not carve huge amounts from the private economy, collectively they had an impact. Slumping agricultural prices, stemming from the limitations of the new soil conservation subsidies and increased production as the Dust Bowl drought ended, pinched farmers.

The currents of politics remained conducive to business-government conflict. Senators Burton K. Wheeler and Harry S. Truman conducted a scathing investigation of the mostly bankrupt railroads, charging with scant evidence that Wall Street financiers had looted the lines. Progressives hoped to nationalize all or most of the rail corporations. Roosevelt himself was interested enough to float the idea in a November 12 cabinet meeting.[24]

The government's conflict with the electrical utilities accelerated rapidly. The Tennessee Valley Authority (TVA) pressed hard for exclusive control of electrical power in its region. Major federal hydroelectric projects in the West challenged established generating companies. The Rural Electrification Administration expanded into underserved farming and small-town areas. The private utilities, slow to move into marginal markets and dependent on private financing, had themselves to blame for some of their difficulties. But government financing did give TVA and other public enterprises a big edge. And what was one to make of the administration's efforts to get congressional approval for seven more regional development authorities patterned on TVA and nearly certain to get into the electricity business? Was nationalization of the industry an unspoken New Deal objective?

In September 1937, the economy suddenly crashed. By the end of the year, capacity utilization in the steel industry had plummeted to below 25 percent. Unemployment, which had bottomed at approximately 7.5 million people, according to the widely accepted American Federation of Labor (AFL) estimates, was 9.3 million. For the first time, a strong scent of economic failure attached itself to the administration.[25]

With these trends just beginning to take shape in the weeks after Congress had adjourned, Roosevelt remained focused on his legislative program and pursued tactics that had worked well for him in the past. He got out of Washington and took a two-week rail tour of the heartland, from Chicago to the Pacific Northwest. The large and friendly crowds that greeted him reassured the president that the people remained firmly behind him. Back in Washington, he resorted to his other successful tactic, the fireside chat. Announcing a special session of Congress beginning November 15, he laid out an ambitious legislative agenda: wage-and-hours legislation, stabilization of farm prices, new regional planning and development authorities, the executive reorganization bill, stronger antitrust statutes, and encouragement of foreign trade. All this was far too much for any special session. On December 21, Congress dealt the president a serious blow by adjourning without having enacted one significant item on his must list.

Even more ominous for the future were indications that Republicans and anti–New Deal Democrats were beginning to talk to each other and vote together in an informal "conservative coalition." Most right-wing Democrats came from the South. A deep-seated racism aghast at the New Deal solicitude for Negroes and a wide conviction that the economically backward region could develop a manufacturing economy only if exempted from national wage and hours legislation increasingly countered traditions of populist insurgency. Vice President John Nance Garner, never a Roosevelt loyalist but usually a reliable aide on Capitol Hill, was getting notice as a leader of the conservatives and possibly their candidate for president in 1940. To liberal-minded aides like Harold Ickes and Tom Corcoran, Roosevelt himself seemed dangerously passive in the face of increasingly bad economic news. As 1937 ended, the president, so triumphant just twelve months earlier, faced an out-of-control legislative branch, a deepening economic slump, and a serious loss of personal authority.[26]

FROM ACROSS THE ATLANTIC, JOHN MAYNARD KEYNES VIEWED THE ECONOMIC crisis and the political drift in Washington with alarm. He had received too much credit as the mastermind behind the New Deal's 1935–1936 spending program, but he surely knew that it had roughly followed his public prescription. A political centrist who aligned himself with the nearly defunct British Liberal Party, he favored a mixed political economy, was temperamentally aligned with the New Deal, and admired FDR's charismatic leadership. He was also managing director of an insurance company, a member of other corporate boards, and a sometimes daring speculator in currencies and commodities. He understood the mentality of business enterprise and finance capital. Confidence and buoyant "animal spirits," he knew, were essential to a durable business recovery. He was determined to try to move events.[27]

Privately and publicly in late 1937 and 1938, he assessed the New Deal recovery program as incomplete. It had done little or nothing to restore the railroads to health, taken a negative attitude toward the utilities, and pursued a weak housing program. With these capital industries still suffering, a setback was inevitable once the government cut back its spending. In October 1937, he unburdened himself to Leonard Elmhirst, a British reformer whose American wife, Dorothy Whitney Straight, owned the *New Republic*, the most important organ of American liberalism. The Elmhirsts were personal and ideological friends of Eleanor Roosevelt. Keynes doubtless expected that his thoughts would find their way to her and then to the president.[28]

His words were sharp and direct: "I think the President is playing with fire, if he does not now do something to encourage the business world, or at any rate refrain from frightening them further. If one is purporting to run a capitalist system, and not something quite different, there are concessions which have to be made. The worst of all conceivable systems is a capitalist one kept on purpose by authority in a state of panic and lack of confidence." Elmhirst quoted Keynes's admonition to Eleanor in a letter dated December 11. If, as seems likely, she passed it along to Franklin, he disregarded it.[29]

At the end of 1937, Assistant Attorney General Robert Jackson (head of the Antitrust Division) and Secretary of the Interior Harold Ickes stepped up the rhetoric of class warfare with radio speeches denouncing "monopoly" and the "sixty families" that they believed controlled the American economy. Asserting that monopolistic pricing had caused the recession and warning that the nation faced the specter of "big business fascism," Ickes declared that big capital was engaged in a sit-down strike against the administration. The talks won ecstatic praise from political progressives; conservatives denounced them as demagoguery. Revealing a deep political polarization that could only get in the way of economic recovery, they must have confirmed Keynes's worst fears.[30]

On February 1, 1938, Keynes wrote an eight-page letter to the president. The New Deal, he said, had been guilty of "an error of optimism" in believing it had created the conditions for a sustainable recovery. Keynes recommended "a large-scale recourse" to public works and other investments, but the burden of his letter advised changing the tone of American politics through a détente with the financial and business establishments.

Drawing on England's experience, which under its conservative National government had pursued a strong program of subsidized worker housing and low-cost private homes, he declared, "The handling of the housing problem has been really wicked." So, for that matter, he went on, had the administration's approach to the utilities. The crusade against the holding companies was ill conceived; the real criminals were long gone. Public ownership was fine in situations where it could be achieved; otherwise, "make peace on liberal terms, guaranteeing fair earnings on new investments and a fair basis of valuation in the event of the public taking them over hereafter." Avoid a self-defeating policy of establishing plants to compete with viable private companies, simply ensuring losses all around. As for the railroads, they had to be made solvent. "Nationalize them if the time is ripe. If not, take pity on the overwhelming problems of the present managements." Above all, reach out to the business community. "You could do anything you liked with them, if you would treat them (even the big ones), not as wolves and tigers, but as domestic animals by nature, even though they have been badly brought up and not trained as you would wish. . . . If you work them into the surly, obstinate, terrified mood, of which domestic animals, wrongly handled, are so capable, the nation's burdens will not get carried to market; and in the end public opinion will veer their way."

Asking Roosevelt to forgive his candor, Keynes listed one New Deal policy that he supported after another. "But I am terrified lest progressive causes in all the democratic countries should suffer injury, because you have taken too lightly the risk to their prestige which would result from a failure measured in terms of immediate prosperity." That need not happen, he assured the president. "But the maintenance of prosperity in the modern world is extremely *difficult*; and it is so easy to lose precious time."[31]

Roosevelt had disregarded advice to consult Keynes in the past. Mentioning the Keynes letter to Harold Ickes, Roosevelt remarked that spending lavishly on relief had been the thing to do when the water had been near the bottom of the well, but he doubted that it was the right course when the water was within 25 or 30 percent of the top. Ickes disapprovingly confided to his diary that the president "knows that unemployment is increasing, that business is falling off, but he doesn't seem to me to know just what he can or should do about it."[32]

Roosevelt sent a bland reply to Keynes. The economist, who knew a brush-off when he saw one, could not resist a riposte. "You are treading a very dangerous middle path. . . . Your present policies seem to presume that you possess more power than you actually have."[33]

Through the 1937–1938 winter, joblessness had escalated steeply. At the time of the Roosevelt-Keynes exchange, the AFL put the figure at over 11 million, or 16 to 17 percent of the workforce. Horror stories about hunger and homelessness were common.

In mid-April 1938, Roosevelt finally announced a major spending program, mostly for the upcoming fiscal year, with sharp increases in public works. The WPA, which a year earlier had seemed a candidate for termination, would receive strongly increased funding. The Federal Reserve would lower its bank reserve requirements. The Treasury would monetize a whopping $1.4 billion of its gold reserve. The national debt, the president admitted, would increase by $1.5 billion, but it was a basic responsibility of government "to put idle money and idle men to work."[34]

With monetary policy eased and spending ramped up, the economy stabilized over the next several months. By AFL estimates, unemployment, which peaked at 11.4 million in May and June, was down to 10.3 million by the end of 1938. The downward spiral was stopped, but economic improvement would remain sporadic and unsatisfactory into 1939. Roosevelt returned to his confrontation with an increasingly rebellious Congress and now faced a public increasingly skeptical about deficit spending.[35]

THE PRESIDENT HAD DELIVERED HIS LARGER LEGISLATIVE AGENDA TO CONgress in person at its opening session on January 3, 1938: an agricultural program that would essentially revive the old AAA; minimum-wage/maximum-hours legislation for industrial workers, with no allowance for regional (i.e., southern) differentials; and adoption of the still pending executive reorganization proposals. He declared he would strive for a balanced budget, subject to the understanding that the government would make adequate provision for the unemployed, that budget cuts must not endanger national safety (i.e., cut defense expenditures), and that the overriding priority must be to "raise the purchasing power of the Nation."[36]

To this, Roosevelt added a sharp attack on monopoly, wealth, and economic power, citing a long list of abuses: tax avoidance, excessive capitalization, security manipulation, price rigging, collusive bidding, abuse of patent laws, intimidation of local or state government, and shifting of production in pursuit of cheaper wages. Invoking Andrew Jackson and Woodrow Wilson, he declared that these and other offenses "arise out of the concentration of economic control to the detriment of the body politic—control of other people's money, other people's labor, other people's lives." These words, coming on top of the Jackson and Ickes speeches, heralded a revived antitrust campaign that would coexist uneasily with his palpable nostalgia for the NRA and its regime of top-down "corporatist" control.

With administration encouragement, Congress established a Temporary National Economic Committee (TNEC), with members from both the executive and legislative branches to investigate monopoly and economic concentration in America. Over the next three years, the TNEC busied itself with hearings, frequently prosecutorial in tone, and the production of numerous staff studies—all devoted to demonstrating the curse of bigness. Its final report would come in the spring of 1941, when, as defense industries ramped up, it seemed more likely that large-scale industrial capabilities were a blessing.

In March 1938, Roosevelt appointed Yale Law School professor Thurman Arnold to head the antitrust division of the Justice Department, replacing Robert Jackson, whom he made solicitor general. Jackson, sincerely devoted to breaking up large corporations, had begun a suit to dismember Aluminum Corporation of America, which was overwhelmingly dominant in the aluminum industry. Arnold had no illusions that big business could be broken up, but he believed the antitrust laws could serve as an effective disciplinary tool. He was more concerned with preventing or punishing price fixing and other forms of collusion that damaged consumers. His preferred method of pursuing an antitrust charge was to arrive at a court-approved consent decree in which a defendant agreed to cease the offending action. The approach lacked the drama craved by one-hundred-proof populists but may have been more effective in dealing with real abuses while preserving the efficiencies inherent in large, well-capitalized corporate structures. At best, it served Roosevelt's political objectives while avoiding real damage to the manufacturing capabilities that would be so sorely needed in World War II. Arnold's style of attack, however, did nothing to deescalate a hostility between the administration and the business-financial establishment that could only get in the way of recovery.[37]

The presidential legislative agenda moved through Congress with more dispatch than might have been expected. A new Agricultural Adjustment Act cleared Congress in February, institutionalizing subsidies as a continuing essential of life for most medium- and large-scale farmers. A big Naval Expansion Act gave Roosevelt the increased defense capabilities he wanted, while supplying lots of jobs for shipyard workers. A Revenue Act established a basic corporate levy and abolished the much derided undistributed-profits tax. A Pure Food, Drug, and Cosmetic Act strengthened existing statutes. The

Fair Labor Standards Act established the wage and hour provisions Roosevelt had requested and definitively outlawed child labor. Executive reorganization remained stalled, and some of the other bills failed to provide everything the president had requested. He could easily have declared victory. Instead, openly affronted, he went to war with a substantial segment of his own party.

In mid-December 1937, the *New York Times* had reported that a group of conservative-leaning senators, mostly Democratic, had drafted a "manifesto" that criticized lavish spending. It advocated lower taxes, a balanced budget, an end to "coercion and violence" in labor relations, cessation of government competition with private enterprise, encouragement of capitalist investment, and extensive cutbacks in federal regulations. Hailing the "spiritual values" of democracy and capitalism, it asserted that only individual ambition and self-reliance could produce abundance, security, and happiness. The story associated six senators with the proposed statement: Josiah Bailey (D-NC), Harry Byrd (D-VA), Edward Burke (D-NE), Royal Copeland (D-NY), Millard Tydings (D-MD), and Arthur Vandenberg (R-MI).[38]

Although never signed or officially proclaimed by its drafters, the manifesto, which the *Times* published verbatim, was a telling indication of an uneasiness that knew no geographical bounds and was remarkably widespread among Capitol Hill Democrats. If almost all Democrats had voted for the greater part of Roosevelt's program, quite a few had done so only on final votes after maneuvering to kill or dilute the president's recommendations. Much of this sentiment stemmed from the instinctive reactions of men who had prospered politically under a traditional order that the New Deal challenged. Some of it was personal, however, reflecting resentment of a presidential command style that took loyalty for granted and seldom displayed appreciation. It was most discernible among southerners, who were deeply apprehensive about the administration's tentative challenges to white supremacy and fearful that pro-union, high-wage policies would destroy their region's one advantage in economic development.[39]

The president and his aides resented what they saw as an obstructionist effort to negate one of the greatest electoral mandates in human history. Roosevelt was especially offended that his executive reorganization bill remained stalled in Congress amid mutterings of his alleged dictatorial ambitions. On March 30, 1938, he released to the press a letter he had written to an unnamed friend. It began with a disavowal: "(A) I have no intentions to be a dictator. (B) I have none of the qualifications which would make me a successful dictator. (C) I have too much historical background and too much knowledge of existing dictatorships to make me desire any form of dictatorship."[40]

On June 24, just after the adjournment of Congress, Roosevelt delivered his thirteenth fireside chat. He blamed business leaders who kept prices high and wages low for the economic recession, then went after their allies on Capitol Hill. Congressional Democrats, he declared, had been elected on the liberal national platform of 1936. A few had given lip service to that platform while in practice embracing conservative principles that would take the nation back to the 1920s. "I feel I have every right to speak in those few instances where there may be a clear-cut issue between candidates for a Democratic nomination involving these principles, or involving a clear misuse of my own name."[41]

The president and his aides had already compiled a hit list of senators who had blocked or watered down important legislation and might be beatable in primary elections. Newspaper leaks appeared about the project's initial scope, then gradual whittling down. Some right-leaning legislators, such as Pat McCarran of Nevada, Bennett Champ Clark of Missouri, and Harry Byrd of Virginia, were too well entrenched to challenge. In the end, the hit list contained only five incumbents: Guy Gillette of Iowa, Frederick Van Nuys of Indiana, Walter F. George of Georgia, Millard Tydings of Maryland, and Ellison D. ("Cotton Ed") Smith of South Carolina.[42]

Even in Britain, where parties were organized from the top down, prime ministers could not routinely jettison unreliable members of the House of Commons. In the United States, parties were organized from the bottom up; local politicians saw themselves as advocates for their districts, not for national platforms, and resented interference from Washington. In Iowa that June, Gillette cruised to a primary victory against a more liberal Democratic congressman. In normally Republican Indiana, which chose nominees at a party convention, the instincts of party regulars were for party unity. Van Nuys, who had incurred Roosevelt's wrath mainly by opposing Court-packing, won easily at the state Democratic gathering in early July.

The president also endorsed some incumbents who faced primary challenges. His biggest and clearest win was Senator Alben Barkley's solid victory over Governor A. B. ("Happy") Chandler in the Kentucky primary. But accusations that Barkley's organization had tapped WPA workers for contributions and campaign work would later besmirch even that victory. A Senate committee, headed by Morris Sheppard of Texas, documented similar abuses in several other states. Reminding Americans that in many areas the WPA was, in roughly equal parts, a relief agency and a political patronage vehicle, the controversy left the New Deal morally tarnished.[43]

By early August, with much of the nominating season over, Roosevelt was down to George, Smith, and Tydings. He had worked largely behind the scenes and accomplished little. He either had to abandon what observers were calling a purge (after Josef Stalin's bloody remaking of the Soviet Communist Party) or double down and take an open lead. His combative instinct prevailed.

Dedicating a rural electrification project in the little town of Barnesville, Georgia, on August 11 before a crowd estimated to be in excess of 30,000, with Senator George just a few feet away on the platform, the president recounted his long association with the state and his commitment to the struggle against southern poverty. He assailed legislators who had "listened to the dictatorship of the small minority of individuals and corporations." Walter George was "a gentleman and a scholar," but "I am impelled to make it clear that on most public questions he and I do not speak the same language." Neither did another candidate, the popular and demagogic Herman Talmadge, who "would contribute little to practical government." The president openly endorsed Lawrence Camp, a capable and liberal former state attorney general. The cheers of the crowd conveyed goodwill for Roosevelt but also produced loud shouts of "Hurrah for Senator George!" The next day, speaking from the rear platform of his train in South Carolina, Roosevelt declined to directly endorse Governor Olin D. Johnston against Senator Smith but did ask the crowd to vote for strong supporters of the New Deal. A couple of weeks later, he proclaimed his strong preference for the South Carolinian who thought in terms of the present and future instead of the distant past.[44]

Roosevelt followed that pronouncement up with a press conference denunciation of the Democratic primary candidacy of Senator Tydings and added to it one important House race, that of Representative John J. O'Connor of New York, chairman of the House Rules Committee (and brother of FDR's friend and collaborator in the fight against polio, Basil O'Connor). Both, he said in an on-the-record comment, had "after giving the New Deal lip service in 1936, turned around and knifed it in congress." A week before the Maryland primary, he campaigned in the state for Tydings's opponent.[45]

By then, the results were already in from South Carolina, which voted on August 30 for Smith, whose five-term incumbency, stout defense of cotton farming, and demagogic appeals to white supremacy brought him a strong victory. Two weeks later, Maryland decisively returned Tydings, and Georgia gave its vote to George, with Camp finishing third. In New York, O'Connor narrowly lost the Democratic primary, but his defeat could not obscure the other results. The most impressive leader and the canniest operator in American politics had displayed massive failures of judgment.

On November 4, just before the midterm election, Roosevelt went on the air pleading the case for a liberal Democratic Congress. His voice was, as always, strong and golden; more than ever, it possessed an undertone of passion. The Munich conference, at which Britain and France had effectively conceded Czechoslovakia to Hitler, was just five weeks in the past. A few days earlier, Alf Landon had asserted that the New Deal was leading the country toward fascism. The president linked "old-line Tory Republicanism" to both fascism and communism while asserting that the New Deal was the hope of democracy. But with the economy just beginning to recover, even FDR had to sound a little lame when he proclaimed that the business slump had "not become a major economic disaster."[46]

The voters handed the president and the New Deal a stinging rebuke. Democrats still controlled the Senate 69 to 23, with four independent progressives; their House margin was 261 to 164, with four sympathetic independents. But the tide had run mainly against the liberals. The potential for cooperation between the large conservative Democratic bloc on Capitol Hill and the augmented Republican minority was immediately obvious.[47]

THE NEW CONGRESS THAT CONVENED IN JANUARY 1939 WAS LESS INTERESTED in undoing the New Deal than in containing it. In its first session, ending that August, it finally gave the president a much diluted version of his executive reorganization bill. He would use the authority to create an Executive Office of the President, into which he folded the Bureau of the Budget and several other agencies. The legislation also gave the president six new "administrative assistants." But the important quasi-judicial regulatory agencies remained independent. Other executive agencies could be consolidated or reshuffled only subject to congressional veto.

Capitol Hill managed a few last gasps of New Dealism. Congress passed a food stamp welfare plan as a means of disposing of looming mountains of agricultural surpluses; it also sped up Social Security payments and made the program more generous. Nonetheless, an emerging congressional "economy bloc" made significant cuts in relief appropriations. Reacting to the WPA political scandals of 1938, Congress passed the Hatch Act, prohibiting civil servants from engaging in political activity. Even many supportive legislators were in revolt against the peremptory demands Roosevelt had once made freely. By 1939, moreover, the president was primarily concerned with mobilizing congressional support for an activist foreign policy.

The new congressional center of gravity, composed mostly of northern Republicans and southern Democrats, was more skeptical than ever and prone to fund investigations that harassed the administration. With the economy still mired in recession, the New Deal as an ongoing program was sputtering to an end. The Roosevelt presidency seemed likely to follow in the two-term tradition for chief executives.

Roosevelt, like most charismatic leaders, had generated intense emotions. Millions of Americans worshiped him; millions of others quite literally could not bear to speak his name. All but the most vehement haters conceded that he possessed outsized political skills and an imposing personality. What had brought his presidency to a seeming dead end? Both worshipers and demonizers agreed on a common theme: his persistent quest to increase presidential power and probe its limits. Where the admirers saw a leader of the people attempting decisive action in the cause of democracy, the haters perceived a drive toward dictatorship.

Less passionate observers had wavered between the two extremes. The Court-packing controversy, the executive reorganization fight, and the 1938 party purge forced them to take sides. Walter Lippmann provided a vivid example. In the crisis of 1933, he had told Roosevelt to act the dictator and praised him for doing so. But as the sense of existential crisis receded and the continuing Depression became more akin to a dull chronic ache, Lippmann increasingly became a critic, often exposing inner contradictions and palpable fallacies in the administration's rhetoric and programs. Observing politics from a comfortable upper-middle-class perch, he seems to have possessed little sense of the continuing deprivation that characterized the lives of the bottom strata. He had also arrived at a not unrealistic assessment of the false promise of social engineering and observed the horrors being wrought in Europe by Adolf Hitler, Benito Mussolini, and Josef Stalin. In 1937, he published *The Good Society*, a critique of all varieties of planned collectivism and strongman rule. Delivering a lecture at Johns Hopkins University in April 1937, he asserted, "We are faced—now—with the choice between the restoration of constitutional government and a rapid descent into personal government."[48]

Roosevelt had clearly overinterpreted his 1936 mandate, which in terms of percentage of the popular vote was no different from Warren G. Harding's in 1920 and not much more than Herbert Hoover's in 1928. He, like many of his enemies, tended to personalize political differences. Displaying a principled stubbornness in contrast to the facile opportunism so often attributed to him, he really believed in his program and his view of an American society split between the predatory few and the deprived masses. That he was at bottom a democratic leader no one could deny. Nor could one avoid the reality that the New Deal had failed to end the Depression. Still, Roosevelt retained the devotion of millions of Americans whom his programs had helped. The Gallup poll detected marginal drops in his appeal from its 1936 peak but found a majority of the nation behind him, disapproving of a third term yet likely to vote for him if he ran. He risked being remembered as an interesting reformer but largely unsuccessful economic manager. By early 1939, however, new and even more formidable challenges loomed from abroad. FDR was ready to take them on.[49]

PART III

THE WORLD AT WAR

CHAPTER 19

WINDS OF WAR

1933–1939

FRANKLIN ROOSEVELT HAD BECOME PRESIDENT IN 1933 JUST WEEKS AFTER Adolf Hitler had taken power in Germany. At that point Benito Mussolini seemed the strongman of Europe but no threat to American interests. An aggressive, militaristic Japan appeared fixated on conquests in East Asia but unlikely to menace American positions in the Pacific. Well into Roosevelt's second term, the Depression and efforts to restore prosperity at home were his first priorities, whatever the rush of events abroad.

By 1938, the scene had changed so much that John Maynard Keynes ended his response to Roosevelt's brush-off of his deficit-spending advice with an allusion to foreign policy: "The tragedy is that the right-minded show no indication of supporting one another. You will be reluctant to support us; we are reluctant to support France; France is reluctant to support Spain. At long last we shall get together. But how much harm will have been done by then?"[1]

The president did not reply to Keynes's accurate observation that the military and diplomatic challenges were becoming increasingly salient. In facing them, Roosevelt, as he largely had done with domestic issues, blended the realism of his cousin Theodore with the idealistic rhetoric of his World War I leader, Woodrow Wilson. Above all, he moved with the greatest care in a political environment that summarily rejected foreign entanglements.

IN THE 1930S, AMERICANS POSSESSED A FIRM FOREIGN POLICY CONSENSUS: involvement in World War I had been a mistake. The peace arrangements had made a mockery of Wilson's democratic goals. The United States had been tricked into saving the British and French empires. Arms dealers and bankers had promoted the war for their personal profit. Allied nations had defaulted on their war debts. The United States needed to concentrate on its own problems and keep the various European nations at arm's length. Perhaps because this viewpoint was so starkly simple, it permeated all levels of American society and politics. Senator Gerald Nye, a progressive Republican from North Dakota, promoted it as chairman of a special investigating committee that looked into the decision for war in 1917. So did influential authors.[2]

Especially significant to Roosevelt was the nearly unanimous rejection of international involvement by such independent progressive congressmen as George Norris and Robert La Follette Jr. He seems to have understood almost from the beginning of his presidency that the world had become a combustible place and that another great war would surely entangle the United States. But Europe was far away—four or five days by fast ocean liner and not instantly connected electronically until the advent of shortwave radio in the later 1930s.

Hitler and Mussolini might strike those who paid attention as potential adversaries, but Europe was mostly ruled by dictators, and the flare-ups of the 1930s were hard to connect to American interests. The Italian conquest of Ethiopia in 1935? Why get excited over the fate of a primitive nation that still practiced slavery? German and Italian meddling in the 1936–1939 Spanish Civil War? It was a pox-on-both-their-houses conflict between rightist and leftist extremes. The German annexation of Austria in 1938? A unification of German-speaking people accomplished without resistance. The Munich Agreement and Anglo-French acquiescence in the German takeover of the Czechoslovakian Sudetenland? The absorption of yet another predominantly German region. The German move into the rest of Czechoslovakia in 1939? Not a threat to the United States. Mussolini's seizure of Albania in 1939? Who cared?

The few European democracies—the Scandinavian nations, an encircled Czechoslovakia, and a western European fringe consisting of France, Belgium, the Netherlands, Great Britain, and Ireland—fared little better than the authoritarian regimes in the American mind. The two important powers, Britain and France, were both absorbed with domestic problems, struggling to maintain a grip on their large overseas empires, and all but consumed by a common dread of war. Despite their liberal-democratic values, neither country had a particularly close relationship with the United States.

The authoritarian nations were in their terrible way impressive. Mussolini enjoyed recognition as a strongman who had imposed order on an undisciplined nation while carrying through much needed internal development projects. His relationship with Roosevelt was distant but not unfriendly. His deployment of the Italian army to the Brenner Pass had been instrumental in blocking a Nazi takeover of Austria in 1934. Not until 1938 would he be well aware of his subordinate position in the European power structure and let Austria fall without a quibble.[3]

Nazi Germany, far more frightening than Italy, radiated strength and purpose. While Mussolini squandered men and resources on the acquisition of Ethiopia, Hitler constructed the most formidable military establishment on the continent and effectively transformed Italy from rival into junior ally. Most Americans assumed that Nazi persecution of Germany's Jewish population resembled the routine abuse of minorities in many authoritarian countries. Almost none grasped its genocidal potential. Hitler had few American admirers, but his regime laid claim to considerable respect for its growing might.

The fifth major European power, the Soviet Union, had looked inward since the revolution that established it in 1917. Its dictator, Josef Stalin, governed as ruthlessly as Hitler, consolidating power by "purging" any conceivable rival and instituting a system of nearly indiscriminate terror. Yet, in contrast to the Nazis, the Soviet Union officially proclaimed values of egalitarian democracy that belied its lethal totalitarianism. American liberals generally conceded that Stalin's regime was harsh but also admired his efforts at modernizing a backward autocracy while erasing old distinctions of wealth and ethnicity. For many New Dealers and others on the left of American politics, the Soviet Union was, for all its shortcomings, a progressive force with enormous potential. Roosevelt chose his words carefully when he talked about the Soviet enterprise in public, but there is every indication that he shared in the liberal consensus.

The United States also faced westward across the Pacific to Japan, a potential adversary of intermittent concern to Roosevelt since his tenure as assistant secretary of the navy. In 1923, he had written a brief piece for *Asia* magazine, downplaying the possibility of a US-Japanese conflict in the Pacific. He permitted its re-publication eleven years later, albeit likely more as a diplomatic gesture than as a statement of core conviction.[4]

By 1934, Japan had conquered the important Chinese industrial and commercial province of Manchuria and renamed it Manchukuo. The Hoover administration had refused to recognize the new state; its secretary of state, Henry L. Stimson, had reasserted the long-standing US policy that China should be open to trade and commerce with all countries. On this matter at least, Hoover and Stimson spoke for the vast majority of Americans.

Close observers understood that Japan intended to become the dominant power in East Asia. The Japanese had sided with the Allies in World War I and at Versailles had received the German economic concessions in China. The country possessed a formidable navy and rejected any treaty limitations that would keep its fleet inferior to those of Britain and the United States. Aggressive and violent expansionist forces increasingly dominated Japan's internal politics. Peace advocates risked assassination. Jingoist imperialism had wide popular appeal. The Japanese Empire was the industrial powerhouse of East Asia. The Japanese people were among the world's most disciplined, prone to believe that tireless, unrelenting effort could achieve almost any goal. Their emperor, Hirohito, to whom they were fiercely loyal, encouraged a sense of national destiny and allowed himself to be carried along by his aggressive military leaders.[5]

Not long after becoming president, Roosevelt read with interest—and surely with apprehension—a report from US ambassador to Japan Joseph Grew. It painted a stark portrait of an emerging, aggressive great power. The Japanese Empire, including Manchukuo, covered a large area and possessed a population almost as large as that of the United States. The Japanese people were "intelligent, industrious, energetic, extremely nationalistic, war-loving, aggressive and, it must be admitted, somewhat unscrupulous." The Japanese armed forces were "the most complete, well-balanced, co-ordinated and therefore powerful fighting machine in the world today." They considered the United States their most likely potential enemy and possessed an esprit de corps akin to that of Genghis Khan's Mongol hordes. "The force of a nation bound together with great moral determination, fired with national ambition, and peopled by a race with unbounded capacity for courageous self-sacrifice is not easy to overestimate."[6]

The advocates of isolationism were numerous and influential. Strongest in the Midwest and West, they included not just Republicans but many Democrats and independent progressives. Roosevelt himself had to contend with the widespread sense that he was too much like his cousin Theodore: prone to foreign adventures and just perhaps seeing war as a way to stay in power. The Italian invasion of Ethiopia and the Spanish Civil War generated a series of Neutrality Acts from Congress; the president had little choice but to sign them. Addressing the problems widely believed to have dragged the United States into World War I, they aimed to tie the hands of an activist chief executive. They forbade both loans and the sale of arms to warring nations. They further stipulated that American citizens traveled at their own risk on vessels carrying the flag of a belligerent.

Roosevelt understood that the world was dangerously close to an explosion. "These are without doubt the most hair-trigger times the world has gone through in your lifetime or mine," he wrote to his ambassador to Italy, Breckinridge Long, in March 1935. "I do not even exclude June and July, 1914." The apprehension was premature but prescient. The need to keep it private was urgent. Father Charles Coughlin had just blocked American adherence to the World Court. Anything that hinted of international involvement was politically toxic.[7]

In 1936, determined to seek reelection on domestic issues, Roosevelt inoculated himself from charges of internationalist warmongering with a notable speech in Chautauqua, New York. Proclaiming a determination to preserve the nation's neutrality in international conflicts, even at the costs of forfeiting the profits and "false prosperity" that could come from war commerce, he emotionally asserted his resoluteness:

I have seen war. I have seen war on land and sea. I have seen blood running from the wounded. I have seen men coughing out their gassed lungs. I have seen the dead in the mud. I have seen cities destroyed. I have seen two hundred limping, exhausted men come out of line—the survivors of a regiment of one thousand that went forward forty-eight hours before. I have seen children starving. I have seen the agony of mothers and wives. I hate war.

I have passed unnumbered hours, I shall pass unnumbered hours, thinking and planning how war may be kept from this Nation.[8]

ALTHOUGH GENUINE, THE SENTIMENT WAS NO SUBSTITUTE FOR A REALISTIC policy. For Roosevelt's first four years, dealing with the Depression was a necessary first priority. The glimmerings of an international strategy were nonetheless present from the beginning. Its three major points were consolidation of US dominance in the Western Hemisphere, naval expansion, and recognition of the Soviet Union.

Hemispheric dominance in the guise of a "Good Neighbor policy" was subtle and widely misunderstood. On the surface, this was a 180-degree turn away from Uncle Ted's "Roosevelt corollary to the Monroe Doctrine," which had converted the Caribbean Sea into an American lake in which US marines enforced payment of international debt obligations, maintained domestic order, and secured the Panama Canal. Under Wilson, Franklin Roosevelt had managed the policy firsthand as assistant secretary of the navy. If taken aback by its heavy-handedness, he had also boasted of having written the constitution of Haiti. In the 1920s, he and many other Democrats had criticized Republican interventions in the area.

The Hoover administration had in fact already rejected TR's imperialism. FDR, in his inaugural address, assumed ownership of this unacknowledged development by promising that the United States would respect the rights of other nations in the hemisphere. In practice, his Good Neighbor policy consisted primarily of avoiding overt interference but maintaining hegemony in Caribbean countries by negotiating reciprocal trade agreements and supporting friendly dictators. The policy assumed as a matter of course that Latin American political culture was naturally authoritarian. While eschewing military occupations, the administration armed local dictators throughout Central America from Guatemala to Panama. With larger Latin American nations, the norm was accommodation and displays of respect. When the semiauthoritarian revolutionary government of Mexico nationalized US and other foreign oil holdings in 1936, the United States made no protest. Dealings with South American nations promoted hemispheric solidarity.

At the end of 1936, Roosevelt personally attended a US-arranged Inter-American Conference in Rio de Janeiro and also made visits to Argentina and Uruguay, basking at each stop in cheers of "Viva Roosevelt! Viva la democracia!" Five years later, at a small White House dinner, he regaled guests with his memories of riding in a motorcade alongside Brazilian president Getulio Vargas, who acknowledged the cheers, then leaned toward him saying, "Perhaps you've heard that I am a dictator." Roosevelt responded lightheartedly, "Perhaps you've heard that I am one too." Vargas replied, "But I really am!" FDR went on to explain that Brazil, a backward and illiterate nation, had to have a dictator. The tale reflected the instincts of a realist with idealistic sympathies. His international popularity and prestige lent credibility to a strategy that might rightly be characterized as "soft imperialism" but on the whole worked to the advantage of both its objects and the United States.[9]

The US Navy had long been a Rooseveltian hobby. FDR clearly saw it as the nation's first line of defense, far more important than the army, which his administration kept on lean rations for years. Naval construction, unlike an army buildup, did not imply foreign expeditions and provided a lot of jobs. Given a strong White House push, despite sometimes vehement opposition from pacifist and isolationist groups, the navy grew steadily throughout the 1930s. By 1939, it was roughly at quantitative parity with the British Royal Navy, qualitatively second to none, and building rapidly for the possibility of simultaneous action in both the Atlantic and the Pacific.[10]

The United States recognized the Soviet Union toward the end of 1933. The most persuasive rationale for the decision was the simplest: the USSR, shunned since the revolution of 1917, was there to stay and controlled a vast territory with untold natural resources. To this hard fact the administration added the lure of lucrative trade agreements. Privately, Roosevelt and many New Dealers shared the liberal fascination with the Soviet experiment and the sense that, however unlovely it might be in practice, it was working toward a brave new world of progressive equality.

The prospect of trade was not entirely fanciful. Entrepreneurs such as Henry Ford and William Averell Harriman had struck deals with the Communist regime; however, a combination of Russian xenophobia and ideological paranoia that made agreements of any sort difficult and unreliable would disappoint those who expected a plethora of such undertakings. Roosevelt's first ambassador, William C. Bullitt, went to Moscow with high hopes. He and his diplomatic staff quickly found these crushed by the atmosphere of unremitting hostility they encountered from their Soviet counterparts and the not-so-secret police who monitored their every move.[11]

Bullitt was named ambassador to France in 1936. His successor in Moscow, Joseph Davies, a Roosevelt friend since their days together in Woodrow Wilson's Washington, was far more determined to see only the sunny side of life in the USSR. His disposition reflected administration attitudes that an emerging generation of Soviet experts in the Foreign Service found appallingly naive. A few months after Davies's appointment, the State Department, apparently at White House instigation, dismantled its Eastern European Division, a wellhead of anti-Communist sentiment, and packed its head, Joseph F. Kelly, off to Turkey. It presented the move as an economy measure. A young Foreign Service official, Charles ("Chip") Bohlen, saved the division's reference collection of periodicals, newspapers, and other files by arranging for its transfer to the Library of Congress. At the time, Bohlen had the impression that Eleanor Roosevelt and Harry Hopkins were behind the bureaucratic putsch, but many years later he was less certain. The president's involvement, if any, remains unknown.[12]

From a strategic viewpoint, the most urgent motive for recognition of the USSR was the development of a relationship, however tenuous, with a potential ally hostile to both Nazi Germany and imperial Japan. The Soviet Union cared most about access to the technology of an advanced industrial society, sometimes secured through the purchase of needed equipment but often obtained by an ambitious program of industrial espionage, paralleled by spying and political subversion in various administration agencies. The president and his immediate circle seem to have discounted concerns about these efforts. Roosevelt, in fact, supported Soviet attempts in 1938 to contract with American suppliers for sixteen-inch guns, armor plate, and firefighting equipment in the construction of three planned super battleships. He likely saw these as the core of a mighty Russian surface fleet that could face off against the Japanese navy. The US Navy command, however, envisioned the project as a massive transfer of American military technology to a hostile power. The chief of naval operations, Admiral William D. Leahy, fought the project with every resource at his command and ultimately won.[13]

"I DO NOT KNOW THAT THE UNITED STATES CAN SAVE CIVILIZATION BUT AT least by our example we can make people think and give them the opportunity of saving themselves," Roosevelt told his ambassador to Germany, William E. Dodd, at the end of 1935. "The trouble is that the people of Germany, Italy, and Japan are not given the privilege of thinking." Those three nations took the first step toward an alliance by signing the 1936 Anti-Comintern Pact, which affirmed their joint opposition to the spread of Soviet communism. In 1937, Germany sent its army into the hitherto demilitarized area between the Rhine River and the French border.[14]

Japan seemed the most urgent threat to the peace, and most US naval war planning centered on it. The Japanese fleet possessed a rough parity in capital ships, especially aircraft carriers, to that of the United States. Roosevelt had admitted openly in his 1923 *Asia* article that the United States could not defend its major possession in the western Pacific, the Philippines, against a Japanese attack. Still, the Philippines were an important strategic foothold in the region, and American interests, economic and sentimental, were large there.

The islands were scheduled for formal independence in 1944, but the widely held assumption was that they would remain an American protectorate. In 1935, the president assigned retiring army chief of staff Douglas MacArthur to build a Filipino force capable of resisting an outside attack. MacArthur departed Washington with his valued aide, Colonel Dwight D. Eisenhower, accepted the rank of field marshal of the Philippine army, and undertook the slow, tedious process of constructing a modern military culture in a nation-to-be.

In July 1937, the Japanese army launched a full-scale war against China. A deeply divided nation wracked by civil war between a quasi-fascist Nationalist Party and a Marxian Communist movement, China was a venue for numerous Western economic concessions extracted mostly by European nations in the nineteenth century. The United States had its share of business interests there and maintained a small military presence to protect them. Many Americans, moreover, felt a strong sentiment for the Chinese people, fed by American Christian missionary efforts and Pearl Buck's acclaimed novel *The Good Earth*. Roosevelt felt he could not let the brutal Japanese invasion go unchallenged. Japan's developing entente with the emerging axis between Hitler and Mussolini in Europe also worried him.

That October, he delivered his first major foreign policy address at the dedication of a bridge in Chicago, the center of heartland isolationist sentiment. He spoke not far from the offices of the *Chicago Tribune*; the newspaper's owner, Colonel Robert McCormick, had been a class ahead of Roosevelt at Groton, heartedly disliked the president, and loathed the very idea of American engagement outside the Western Hemisphere. The United States and other peaceful nations, Roosevelt declared, had to view with "grave concern and anxiety" the collapse of world order. An epidemic of international lawlessness was spreading. While Roosevelt stopped short of using the word "quarantine"—a characterization coined by Harold Ickes and widely adopted—he clearly suggested that the United States should in some fashion isolate aggressor nations while actively advancing the cause of peace.[15]

The speech drew attention but on close reading was unsatisfactory. What had Roosevelt done other than state his disapproval of aggression? What would a "quarantine" imply? Most observers understood the talk as primarily directed against Japan's war on China, but few expected it to deter the Japanese. Critics depicted the address as a step on the road to war. "Does not Mr. Roosevelt's policy invite the coming of the day when he, too, may have no alternative but resort to arms?" asked the *Chicago Tribune*. The *Portland Oregonian* suggested that the president had "hit upon the idea of becoming aggressive internationally to divert attention from mounting domestic problems." Roosevelt refused to elaborate at a subsequent press conference. The quarantine address was a warning shot fired with a cap pistol.[16]

The Japanese soon displayed their contempt. By December 1937, their forces had overrun Shanghai and were approaching Nanking. From the beginning, they had proclaimed two goals: domination of East Asia and expulsion of Western imperial powers from the region. On December 12, 1937, a Japanese commander, perhaps operating without authorization from Tokyo, launched an air attack on the US gunboat *Panay*, two nearby British gunboats, and some Standard Oil tankers, all on the Yangtze River just east of Nanking. The *Panay* sank in shallow waters; three Americans were killed, eleven wounded. Two of the tankers were destroyed. The British gunboats also went down with loss of life.

Roosevelt made no public statement but let it be known that he had directed Secretary of State Cordell Hull to send directly to the emperor of Japan a protest and a demand for both an apology and reparations; the move implied that the civilian regime could not control its military. The possibility that the incident might lead to war revealed a fundamental split in American opinion that cut across party lines. Republican senator Gerald Nye condemned the president for refusing to withdraw the American military presence in China. Democratic congressman Louis Ludlow of Indiana, a dedicated peace advocate, filed a petition to force a vote in the House of Representatives on a constitutional amendment requiring a national referendum on a declaration of war.[17]

Ludlow quickly got the signatures of a majority of his colleagues. For nearly a month, his amendment dominated discussion of the Far Eastern crisis. Roosevelt denounced it as inconsistent with representative government. The Democratic leadership in the House worked hard to turn signers of the petition around. Most foreign affairs commentators backed the administration. So did the president's 1936 Republican foes Alf Landon and Frank Knox, along with former secretary of state Stimson. Senator Henry Cabot Lodge Jr. of Massachusetts, grandson of the Senator Lodge whom Roosevelt had known in the Wilson years, introduced resolutions that would have effectively nullified the Neutrality Acts. A new isolationist-internationalist narrative that cut deeply across party lines was complicating the old story of conservatism versus progressivism.[18]

On January 10, 1938, the House voted 209 to 188 against consideration of the Ludlow amendment. The minority included one-third of House Democrats, nearly three-fourths of the Republican delegation, and every congressman from the Progressive and Farmer-Labor parties. If eleven congressmen had changed their votes, the administration would have lost. The victory, such as it was, underscored the limits to presidential freedom of action in foreign affairs.[19]

At the beginning of the crisis, Roosevelt had dispatched naval attaches to London for talks with Royal Navy counterparts, raising the possibility of a common military response by the world's two greatest sea powers. Prime Minister Neville Chamberlain privately expressed the hope that at last Britain might get something more than words from the United States. Japan, however, quickly issued multiple apologies and agreed to pay an indemnity eventually fixed at $2.2 million. The administration accepted the settlement on Christmas Day, 1938. The US-British talks subsequently came to nothing. Chamberlain surely put the incident in his mental lessons-learned file.

The Japanese, having taken Nanking and apparently believing that they could subdue an occupied people only through wanton, random terrorism, subjected the residents of the city to a six-week orgy of rape, torture, and killing that shocked the civilized world. By the time they ended their rampage, they had slaughtered perhaps 250,000 Chinese.[20]

THE RESOLUTION OF THE *PANAY* CRISIS AND SUSPENSION OF NAVAL COOPERA-tion talks with Britain confirmed an effective stalemate in American politics between those who wanted the United States to play a strong stabilizing role in an increasingly dangerous world and those who embraced isolation as the only refuge from war. Politically, the mounting world crisis came at the weakest point of Roosevelt's presidency. Having suffered the Court-packing reversal, he now grappled with a serious economic recession and was considering whether to attempt a purge of Democratic conservatives. For the moment, it was impossible to launch an activist foreign policy.

Roosevelt's preferences, expressed most candidly in the quarantine speech, were obvious to all; so were the constraints he felt. "The words may mean little," declared a hopeful *Manchester Guardian* editorial, "but affirmation of a great faith is never futile." *New York Times* foreign policy writer Edwin L. James anticipated the coming year far less optimistically. His summing up of world politics over the previous twelve months, headlined "Democracy Lost in 1937 . . . Totalitarian States, Using Force and Threats of Force Forged Ahead," correctly predicted more of the same for 1938.[21]

By the end of 1939, the Japanese would control most of China's commercial-industrial Northeast and the important Pacific seacoast cities to the south. The interior was far too big for them to occupy and digest. Most of the country's area remained under either Generalissimo Chiang Kai-shek, who established a Nationalist government at Chungking in the South, or the Communist leader Mao Tse-tung at Yenan in the North. Neither Chiang (recognized by the United States and western European nations) nor Mao (recognized by the Soviet Union) was capable of taking the offensive against the invaders. It seemed likely that Japan's expansionist dynamic would, when the time was right, focus on the rich possessions of the United States, Great Britain, France, and the Netherlands to the south and west.

For the moment, most American attention focused on Europe. In Spain, right-wing Falange forces under General Francisco Franco, backed by Italy and Germany, were winning a savage civil war against the left-wing Spanish Republicans, supported far less adequately by the Soviet Union. In realistic geo-political terms, the Spanish conflict was a sideshow, but it equally manifested the great Left-Right ideological rift that divided the Western world. Catholics overwhelmingly favored Franco, a fervent defender of the church's privileged position. Most liberals—the Jews among them were especially visible to critics—backed the republic and either shared in or overlooked the lethal anticlericalism of its partisans. Politically then, Spain divided two core Democratic constituencies. Roosevelt obliquely referred to the German Luftwaffe's April 1937 destruction of the Spanish village of Guernica in his quarantine speech but generally steered clear of the fight.

On March 12, 1938, German troops entered Austria unopposed. A few days later, cheering throngs greeted Adolf Hitler in Vienna. Local Nazis, released from all previous restraints, declared open season on Jews, whom they subjected to public abuse and theft of property. As the democratic leaders of Europe looked on passively, Hitler integrated the once independent nation into the Third Reich. The Führer had established himself as the continent's purpose-driven leader. "He has plans and he has force," *New York Times* correspondent Edwin James commented. "Others have force but no plans." It was not hard, Walter Lippmann ventured, to guess that Hitler would next target Czechoslovakia. Roosevelt's public comments were cautious but firm. Receiving a delegation of young radicals decrying "American militarism" on March 13, he brandished a newspaper headline on the Austrian takeover and warned that some nations did not observe treaties.[22]

The president could do little about an unopposed annexation. Nor did he have much leeway to deal with the refugee crisis it created. Austrian Jews desperately sought entry to the United States. In an era of continuing mass unemployment, most Americans opposed any large-scale immigration from Europe—and perhaps felt especially strongly about Jews. In any case, quotas established by the National Origins Immigration Act of 1924 sharply limited the movement of Europeans to the United States. Roosevelt ordered that the quotas for Germany and Austria be combined and set aside for Jewish refugees, established an advisory committee on immigration, and promoted an international conference on the refugee question that met in Evian, France, that July. The conference could do little more than expose Nazi outrages. Half of all immigrants admitted to the United States after 1936 were Jewish, but hundreds of thousands remained trapped in the Nazi empire.[23]

According to a Gallup poll, nearly 50 percent of Americans felt as early as April 1938 that a war with Germany was likely. They sympathized with England and France by 20–1 margins but also narrowly favored staying out of any future European conflict. Such sentiments—self-contradictory and emotionally wishful—defined the parameters within which Roosevelt had to lead the nation.[24]

That the president had to provide leadership for more than the United States, moreover, was increasingly apparent. By 1938, the only other democratic great powers were France and Britain, the former led by a shifting series of coalition governments, the latter headed by Neville Chamberlain, a humane conservative ill equipped by experience and temperament to manage foreign relations and halfhearted in his preparations for a possible conflict. Roosevelt had clearly become Hitler's nemesis on the world scene. But whereas Hitler had militarized a nation and brought it to the brink of a general war, Roosevelt presided over a country obsessed by the supposed failures of the last conflict and in denial about the dangers of a world dominated by an emerging German-Italian-Japanese alliance.

Speaking in Kingston, Ontario, on August 18, 1938, Roosevelt made clear that his hemispheric strategy looked north as well as south. "The Dominion of Canada is part of the sisterhood of the British Empire. I give to you assurance that the people of the United States will not stand idly by if domination of Canadian soil is threatened by any other empire." At one level, the speech asserted the United States' preeminent influence in the Western Hemisphere. At another, it signaled to London as much as to Ottawa that the United States would permit neither Japanese domination of the eastern Pacific nor German control of the western Atlantic. The pledge itself, sharply criticized in Germany, was noncontroversial in the United States.[25]

The president's next face-off with Hitler came quickly. By September 1938, having rapidly absorbed and digested Austria, Germany was demanding the border portion of Czechoslovakia that Germans called the Sudetenland. The region—heavily German, highly industrialized, and an arms manufacturing center—had become part of the new nation of Czechoslovakia after World War I. Rugged in its terrain and well fortified, it provided a defensible boundary against a German incursion. Without it, Czechoslovakia was fatally exposed.

The German government, which controlled a strong Sudetenland Nazi movement, applied relentless pressure. Hitler saw the Czech project as a test of his will against that of Czechoslovakia's primary guarantors, Neville Chamberlain and French premier Édouard Daladier. He also hoped to lay bare the impotence of Roosevelt and the United States.

The crisis came to a head in September with Germany mobilizing for war despite the palpable reluctance of its people. Chamberlain telegraphed his own impulses by declaring in a radio broadcast that Czechoslovakia was a faraway country of which Britain knew nothing. The irresolute Daladier refrained from any French commitment. Roosevelt, at a low political ebb after the failure of his attempted purge of dissident Democrats, could play no role in the crisis. At the end of September, with Chamberlain and Daladier planning to meet Hitler (now backed by Mussolini) in Munich, the president felt able to do little except send Hitler a public communication pleading for continued negotiation and a peaceful settlement. The debacle that followed—democratic capitulation to Hitler and the first step in the dismemberment of the Czechoslovak state—met at first with a sense of overwhelming relief, followed rather quickly by revulsion and expectation of eventual war in both Britain and the United States. With the absorption of the Sudetenland, Hitler's Third Reich was bigger in terms of area, population, and industrial strength than Kaiser Wilhelm's pre–World War I empire.[26]

Roosevelt had been a minor actor in a humiliating democratic defeat. Yet the growing world crisis enhanced his stature and overshadowed his domestic failures. A majority thought, as one Gallup poll respondent put it, "Maybe I shouldn't be for Roosevelt, but with Europe the way it is, he's the only man for the job." Gallup revealed a brief upward surge in Roosevelt's popularity after his peace plea to Hitler and, more tellingly, also recorded a sense that war with Germany was likely in the future, that the president was the public figure most capable of dealing with Hitler, and that his preparedness program was urgently needed. "You have to carry a big gun," the president told *New York Times* correspondent Anne O'Hare McCormick, "even to sit at peace tables." Privately anticipating continued aggression by Hitler, he told a cabinet meeting that he expected the German leader to demand colonies from Britain and France, that the two countries might agree to hand over Trinidad and Martinique in the Western Hemisphere, and that if they did, he would order the American navy to seize both islands.[27]

One could imagine the ghost of TR looking on approvingly.

Six weeks after the Western surrender at Munich, the Nazis unleashed an astonishing pogrom against the German Jewish community in retaliation for the murder of a minor Reich diplomat in Paris. The ensuing rampage was the most horrifying manifestation of anti-Semitism in Europe since the Middle Ages, involving random mass murder, 20,000 persons arrested and sent to concentration camps, two hundred synagogues and eight hundred Jewish-owned shops destroyed, and a collective fine of $400 million levied against the whole Jewish people. The least of it was the wholesale smashing of windows in Jewish houses, businesses, and places of worship that gave the event its name, *Kristallnacht.*

While the Nazis reveled in their thuggery, shock and anger spread across the democratic world. In Britain, Chamberlain attempted to show statesmanlike restraint in the hope of salvaging his foreign policy. British outrage was nevertheless vehement and stoked by German charges that three leading dissenters in the British Conservative Party—Alfred Duff Cooper, Anthony Eden, and

Winston Churchill—had instigated the Paris assassination. Any thought of colonial transfers to Germany, then under serious consideration, was shelved. The British government's naval building program and enlargement of the army became more urgent than ever.[28]

Roosevelt's response was sharp and to the point. He opened his press conference of November 15, 1938, with a prepared statement: "I myself could scarcely believe that such things could occur in a twentieth-century civilization. . . . I asked the Secretary of State to order our Ambassador in Berlin to return at once for report and consultation." Just a step away from severance of diplomatic relations, Roosevelt's declaration indicated that, as a *Washington Post* editorial put it, "between the United States and Germany a completely irreconcilable cleavage is developing."[29]

But public opinion remained wracked by internal contradictions: Americans saw war as likely, feared it, and hoped against hope to avoid it. The administration's enlargement of the navy, justifiable as a defensive measure, was not terribly controversial. Building a large army, which even in a persistent depression might require conscription, was quite another matter. By the same token, decrying wanton persecution of Jews was one thing; providing refuge was something else. Neither the United States nor any other nation wanted a massive influx of needy immigrants. In London, US Ambassador Joseph Kennedy floated a vague plan for resettlement of German Jews in underpopulated precincts of the British Empire. Quite a few observers suspected that Kennedy proposed the idea to bolster his presidential ambitions by appealing to the growing Jewish constituency within the Democratic Party.[30]

ROOSEVELT UNDERSTOOD THAT HE HAD TO TREAD CAREFULLY. THE UNITED States was already engaged in a war of words with Germany. A scathing attack on the Nazi regime by Harold Ickes drew a formal protest from the German government; the State Department refused to accept it. America was also an arms merchant to Britain and France. In January 1939, newspapers learned that a French pilot had been onboard a new Douglas Aircraft attack bomber that crashed in California. Sales to friendly nations not involved in a state of war were of course within the bounds of neutrality legislation. Still, isolationists were outraged.[31]

Roosevelt held a supposedly secret meeting with the Senate Foreign Relations Committee shortly afterward, hoping to convince his congressional critics that western Europe was vital to American security. One senator promptly leaked to the press that the president had said that America's frontier lay on the

Rhine. Roosevelt labeled the attribution a "deliberate lie," although it surely conveyed the import, if not the precise language, of his remarks.[32]

Just weeks later, Hitler again altered the map of Europe. On March 15, 1939, Germany annexed the western half of the truncated Czech nation, redesignating its constituent provinces by their historical names, Bohemia and Moravia. The remainder of Czechoslovakia became the puppet state of Slovakia. The Nazis also seized the Lithuanian port city of Memel. On March 28, the Spanish Civil War ended with General Franco's capture of Madrid. The following month, Mussolini sent the Italian army to take control of Albania. On the other side of the world, Japanese leaders ostentatiously consolidated their alliance with Germany and Italy. They minced no words in demanding further sacrifices from their people in, as Premier Prince Fumimaro Konoye put it, "emancipating the Far Eastern races from the chains riveted on them before Japan played an important part in the world."[33]

The European events roused even Neville Chamberlain from his state of denial. He and his French counterpart, Édouard Daladier, gave notice that they would go to war if Germany attacked Poland. Roosevelt sent letters directly to Hitler and Mussolini, asking each to pledge not to undertake aggression against thirty listed countries. Hitler treated the communication as a source of comedy. Speaking to the Reichstag, he read off the name of each nation, following each with an emphatic and sarcastic "Nein!" The performance generated peals of laughter from his devoted audience.[34]

By that point, Roosevelt seems to have decided that he had done all he could with the refugee problem. He had personally persuaded Cuban dictator Fulgencio Batista to take in growing numbers of Jewish evacuees, but in June 1939, Cuba denied entry to several hundred Jews aboard the German liner *St. Louis*, rejecting visas they had purchased from a corrupt counsel. Clearly motivated by political considerations, the president refused to allow any of them into the United States. Britain, Belgium, the Netherlands, and France eventually agreed to provide asylum. Many of the *St. Louis* refugees would die in the war that by then seemed just over the horizon.[35]

The summer of 1939 generated a moment of hope. The United States and Great Britain had finally concluded a trade agreement in late 1938. It was popular in the United States, and both sides recognized it as more than a simple economic arrangement. At last the two English-speaking democracies seemed to be coming together.[36]

Nothing symbolized the trend more vividly than the visit of King George VI and Queen Elizabeth to the United States in June 1939. The royal duo excelled at blending the regal grandeur of monarchy with a common touch. The king, a problematic public speaker, was at ease in informal contacts, whether with young men at a Civilian Conservation Corps camp, at the New York World Fair, or at formal receptions meeting with the likes of Senator Ellison D. Smith ("'Cotton Ed' Smith?" he asked). Vice President John Nance Garner pronounced him "a fine feller." The queen, if anything, outdid him in popular appeal. The royal family spent their last weekend in the United States as guests of the Roosevelts at Hyde Park, attending Episcopal services at St. James Church and being driven around the estate by Roosevelt in his specially modified Ford. They, their hosts, and two hundred invited guests consumed hot dogs at a gala picnic lunch. The president delighted in dealing with a monarch on equal terms. That last evening, he and George talked late into the night. At 1:30 a.m., Roosevelt put his hand on the king's knee and said, "Young man, it's time for you to go to bed!"[37]

The royals boarded their train the next day for Canada and the voyage home. The crowd at Hyde Park station saw them off with a rendition of "Auld Lang Syne." As Eleanor remembered it, "We all knew the King and Queen were returning home to face a war." The visit was the beginning of an alliance.[38]

With war probable, Roosevelt pressed Capitol Hill for legislation that would amend the Neutrality Acts to allow the sale of armaments to belligerent nations so long as the buyers paid cash up front and carried the goods away on their own ships. The congressional support was irresolute. The opposition—fueled by Republican partisanship, independent progressive isolationism, and Democrats disaffected by the purge of 1938—was determined.

At the end of June, the administration got a weak bill through the House—it continued the embargo on "arms and ammunition" but allowed cash and carry on other "implements of war"—only to see it stall in the Senate. The showdown came at a White House meeting with Senate leaders on July 18. Supporters and opponents alike told Roosevelt there was no possibility of passage. Senator William Borah of Idaho dismissed a warning by Secretary of State Hull that Europe was at the brink of war. No war was imminent, he airily declared. His sources of information were better than those of the Department of State. Vice President Garner, increasingly distant from a chief unwilling to designate him as a successor, delivered the coup de grâce: "Well, Captain, we may as well face the facts. You haven't got the votes, and that's all there is to it." Soon thereafter Congress adjourned.[39]

Everyone knew Hitler's next targets: at a minimum, the Germanic free city of Danzig and the Polish Corridor to the Baltic Sea; at maximum, the entire country of Poland. His major obstacles were the British-French guarantee of Poland's boundaries and the hostility of the Soviet Union to German expansion eastward. Through the spring and summer of 1939, the British and French engaged in inconclusive discussions with the Soviets, hoping to develop this convergence of interests into an alliance that would contain German aggression. On August 22, Germany announced that Foreign Minister Joachim von Ribbentrop would fly to Moscow to conclude a nonaggression treaty with the Soviet Union. German officials openly boasted that the pact would lead to "the fourth and final partition of Poland." Paris and London began to prepare for the war that now seemed inevitable.[40]

The Germans struck in the early-morning hours of September 1, first with a contrived border incident, then a well-prepared, devastating blitzkrieg into Poland. In Washington, Roosevelt got word of the invasion via a middle-of-the-night phone call from Ambassador Bullitt in Paris. "Well, Bill," he said, "it's come at last. God help us all."[41]

CHAPTER 20

PRIVATE PLANS AND
PUBLIC DANGER

SEPTEMBER 1939–NOVEMBER 1940

ON SUNDAY EVENING, SEPTEMBER 3, 1939, FRANKLIN ROOSEVELT DELIVERED another momentous fireside chat to a national radio audience. His voice strong, serious, and steady, he sent the overriding message that the horror of war compelled American neutrality. "Let no man or woman thoughtlessly or falsely talk of America sending its armies to European fields." He would issue a proclamation of neutrality, but he would not ask Americans to remain neutral in thought. Even a neutral was entitled to the judgment of his conscience. That understood, "I have said not once, but many times, that I have seen war and that I hate war. I say that again and again."[1]

Roosevelt understood the need to address Americans' widespread fear of being drawn once again to the killing fields of northern France. His sentiment was probably sincere, but his strategic calculations were incompatible with his stance. He likely hoped that sending American troops to the European continent would be unnecessary, but like many observers, he worried about Nazi ambitions for influence in the Western Hemisphere. Above all, as he had telegraphed in his Kingston, Ontario, speech of 1938, he saw the British fleet as a potential friendly collaborator in the defense of the hemisphere. Over the next year, events would move more decisively than he could have foreseen on that late-summer evening in 1939, propelling him into a de facto alliance with the beleaguered British and making him a candidate for an unprecedented third presidential term.

Although British prime minister Neville Chamberlain, deeply skepti-cal of Roosevelt's reliability, had shown no interest in a closer relationship, on September 11, 1939, the American president invited him to communicate on matters of mutual interest and assured him that Congress would soon repeal the arms embargo mandated by the Neutrality Acts. He also sent a note to the newly appointed first lord of the Admiralty, Winston Churchill. He wrote, he said, because the two of them had "occupied similar positions in the World War," and he was glad that Churchill was back at the Admiralty. He was surely more motivated by Churchill's well-established position as the foremost critic of Chamberlain's appeasement policy and speculation that he might at some point succeed him. "What I want you and the Prime Minister to know is that I shall at all times welcome it if you will keep me in touch personally with any-thing you want me to know about."[2]

Roosevelt still remembered with some annoyance that Churchill had snubbed him in 1918—Churchill had long forgotten the occasion—but from the beginning the two charismatic personalities felt a reciprocal magnetism that radiated across the Atlantic. Churchill quickly reported the president's letter to the War Cabinet and got its approval to communicate with FDR. Nonetheless, the two men would have found it unimaginable that the president's message was the first of nearly 2,000 that would pass between them over the next five and a half years.[3]

Roosevelt also responded to the outbreak of the war in Europe by press-ing two of the strategic goals he had pursued from the beginning of his presi-dency: defense buildup and hemispheric solidarity. On October 3, he stated in a press conference that, acting under his own authority, he would move ahead with the enlargement of the army and navy by 100,000 men and recommission one hundred World War I–vintage destroyers for patrol duty. He hastily called a hemispheric conference in Panama that proclaimed a wide neutral zone stretching three hundred miles into the Atlantic and Pacific. The proclamation discomfited both Britain and Germany and failed to prevent some significant engagements between them. But it also established a basis for American naval operations well into the Atlantic, showcased US leadership in the Western Hemisphere, and underscored the mission of defending the Panama Canal, a task that enjoyed wide public support.[4]

The Nazi-Soviet pact, the subsequent Soviet occupation of eastern Poland, and the Soviet war on Finland, a nation much admired in the United States as the only one to pay off its World War I debt, rendered the third goal, outreach to the Soviet Union, impossible. In addition, the USSR ordered friendly groups in the United States to denounce any hint that the Americans might aid victims of either Nazi or Soviet aggression. Speaking at Eleanor's behest to a pro-Communist youth group in February 1940, Roosevelt sharply characterized the USSR as "a dictatorship as absolute as any other dictatorship in the world." Newsreel cameras recorded the event for moviegoers all over the country. Though undoubtedly genuine, as future events demonstrated, the sentiment would not prevent Roosevelt from accepting the Soviet Union as an ally.[5]

Britain was already a de facto ally if only because of the joint Anglo-American imperative to maintain control of the Atlantic. Roosevelt's biggest international priority over the next two years was to keep England in the fight. On September 21, the president appeared before a joint special session of Congress and appealed for the sale of weaponry to belligerents on a cash-and-carry basis. He promised to keep American shipping out of war zones and warned US citizens that they traveled on belligerent shipping at their own risk. American interests, he asserted, were best served by reverting to "cash and carry," a traditional practice of open sales to warring nations, "all purchases to be made in cash, and all cargoes to be carried in the purchasers' own ships, at the purchasers' own risk." His sole purpose, he declared, was to keep the country out of the war, but he could not avoid a solemn note: "Darker periods may lie ahead. . . . Destiny first made us, with our sister nations on this Hemisphere, joint heirs of European culture. Fate seems now to compel us to assume the task of helping to maintain in the Western world a citadel wherein that civilization may be kept alive."[6]

His tactical sense was sound. Public opinion surveys revealed widespread fears that a victorious Germany would attack the United States. Just weeks after the start of the war, Gallup found 44 percent of Americans willing to commit American troops against Hitler if the Allies seemed to be losing; a separate survey showed 63 percent convinced that a victorious Reich would make the United States its next target. Cash and carry was a seductive way of addressing the nation's incompatible fears of both involvement and German aggression.[7]

The bill moved through the House of Representatives quickly, then touched off extended debate in the Senate before passing on a 63–30 vote. Roosevelt signed it into law on November 4. The dialogue on Capitol Hill and across the country was impassioned. To a considerable extent, it altered the political divisions created by the New Deal. Some of the anti-Roosevelt voices were familiar: for example, that of Father Charles Coughlin or of Herbert Hoover, who weighed in with a nebulous proposal for the sale of "defensive weapons" only. Others were new on the scene, foremost among them famed aviator Charles A. Lindbergh, who, much impressed by German air power, seems to have possessed some sympathy with Nazi racial theories. He would become Roosevelt's most charismatic critic. Just a few Republicans voted with the administration. Among the independent or Republican progressives in the Senate, Roosevelt got only the vote of George Norris.[8]

For the time being, he had thrown a lifeline to Britain and France. Still, cash and carry rested on the hope that somehow the British-French alliance could stand up against the Nazi juggernaut that had crushed Poland and find a way to defeat Germany before running out of the dollars needed to buy war matériel from the United States.

AS WINTER DESCENDED ON THE CONFLICT, IT WAS POSSIBLE TO BELIEVE THAT the war might become a stalemate. The large and well-equipped French army massed behind the supposedly impregnable Maginot Line at the French-German border. A British Expeditionary Force took up positions farther to the west along the Belgian border. Action was so spotty that observers coined the hopeful phrase "phony war." The phoniness came to an abrupt end on April 9, 1940, when the Germans occupied Denmark without resistance and invaded Norway. Over a three-week period, they beat back British attempts to intervene and compelled Norwegian surrender. The debacle, which revealed the inadequacies of the British military, precipitated the resignation of Chamberlain and his replacement by Churchill on May 10.

That same day, the Nazis launched their offensive against France. The world watched with amazement as German mechanized forces operating with strong air support struck through Belgium, outflanked the Maginot defenses, separated the British army from its French allies, routed the French army at Sedan, and drove toward Paris. On June 15, the invaders paraded through the city. A week later, French officials signed surrender documents at Compiegne in the same railway car in which Germany had accepted defeat in 1918. The capitulation ceded most of the country to German occupation and established a nominally independent French state in the South and West with its capital at Vichy.

The British, also badly routed, managed to evacuate most of their forces and some French units with a remarkable holding action at Dunkirk. Through it all, Churchill prevailed over defeatists within his own government. To his public, he presented the Dunkirk saga, facilitated by civilian volunteers who owned small boats, as a national triumph that displayed England's mettle, but he also freely admitted that evacuations did not win wars. In his first address to the House of Commons as prime minister, he declared, "I have nothing to offer but blood, toil, tears and sweat."

In his first communication to Roosevelt on May 15, he conveyed a wish list of urgent needs: forty or fifty destroyers to patrol British waters against enemy submarines, several hundred fighter planes, antiaircraft guns and ammunition, and steel for Britain's defense plants. He added, "We shall go on paying dollars for as long as we can, but I should like to feel reasonably sure that when we can pay no more, you will give us the stuff all the same."[9]

Roosevelt's reply was vague but not discouraging. He understood the strategic situation. He could not, however, get past the political limitations on his freedom of action. Public opinion polling showed a more intense feeling than ever that a British defeat would place the United States in serious danger. Most Americans supported the sale of armaments. They also strongly backed building up the armed forces and defending the Western Hemisphere, even if that meant higher taxes and military conscription. But the surveys also displayed a continuing revulsion against US entry into the war and hope against hope that England could somehow continue to serve as a bulwark against the Nazi threat. For the next year and a half, the president had to maneuver cautiously within this tangle of contradictory attitudes.[10]

His first, and easiest, priority was a huge enlargement of the military. On May 16, he sent a message to Congress. Stressing, and to some extent exaggerating, the US vulnerability to foreign attack, it called for a supplemental appropriation of $896 million for the army and navy. Stunningly, the message stated a production goal of 50,000 airplanes per year.[11]

On May 26, he delivered a fireside chat. Citing the millions fleeing the Nazi advance in Belgium and France, he characterized America's defenses as strong but warned that much more would be needed. He would call on leaders of private industry to organize an increasing program of military production, but he would neither sacrifice the social gains of the past nor countenance the creation of a new class of war millionaires. He would, he declared, defend the hemisphere and build the nation's defenses "to whatever heights the future may require."

On May 31, with the Nazis sweeping through France, he asked Congress for another $1 billion and authorization to call up the National Guard and army reservists. He warned that critical days lay ahead. It was no longer possible to wait for a war to begin before training and equipping an army.[12]

On June 10 at the University of Virginia, the president delivered a bold commencement address broadcast nationally and carried overseas by the British Broadcasting Corporation. Italy had that very day attacked a France on the verge of collapse. Roosevelt could not resist a contemptuous reference to Mussolini: "On this tenth day of June, 1940, the hand that held the dagger has struck it into the back of its neighbor." He promised all possible aid to the embattled forces of freedom and pledged—"full speed ahead"—a program for America's own defense. "I call for effort, courage, sacrifice, devotion. Granting the love of freedom, all of these are possible."[13]

On June 18, the administration sent to Capitol Hill a plan for a "two ocean navy" capable of controlling both the Atlantic and the Pacific. Congress took only three weeks to authorize the program. In effect, the United States would be building a second navy in itself capable of besting any other navy in the world. From June through September 1940, the administration let contracts for 9 sixteen-inch-gun battleships, 11 aircraft carriers, 14 heavy cruisers, 32 light cruisers, 190 destroyers, and 65 submarines. The battleships would take at least four years from keel laying to commissioning; the rest would come into the line faster.[14]

Only the United States could build at such a rate. Roosevelt had signaled to Germany and Japan that America was going to rule the waves. The effect might be to deter potential enemies or to impel them to strike early and hard.

Plans were also under way for an equally large expansion of the US Army from about 250,000 men to at least 1.25 million and probably many more. Behind all this was a push for a quantum increase in the implements of warfare and the industrial plants to produce them. The entire budget of the United States for fiscal year 1939 (July 1, 1938 to June 30, 1939) had slightly exceeded $8.8 billion. In the six and a half months from January 1, 1940, to July 15, 1940, Congress authorized $20 billion in defense spending alone.[15]

At the end of May, Roosevelt had established an eight-person National Defense Advisory Council. Three of its members—General Motors president William Knudsen, US Steel chairman Edward R. Stettinius Jr., and railway president Ralph Budd—were leading industrialists. Only one labor leader was named, Sidney Hillman. The others were an ideological mix. The pairing of Knudsen and Hillman as cochairs sent a message that the labor-management wars of the 1930s needed to end.[16]

The symbolism was potent, but reality was hard and unyielding. It was bracing to talk of producing 50,000 planes a year and establishing a two-ocean navy, and it was true that US defense-production potential was almost limitless. But in the short term, one bottleneck after another held it back. Defense industries had to compete with increasing consumer demand in an economy at last beginning to recover steadily. Old production facilities needed retooling and new ones needed building. At every step along the way, both labor and management frequently returned the message of reconciliation unopened.

The issues and forces unleashed by the New Deal transferred themselves to the new climate. New Dealers were convinced that a transition to defense production tightly managed by a government they ran would be more effective than a looser, more voluntaristic process overseen by industrial capitalists. Labor unions demanded recognition and a fair share. Strikes disrupted progress; a few were transparently fomented by Communist-influenced unions, whose activists adhered faithfully to the Moscow-imposed line of solidarity with Nazi Germany—until it changed in June 1941. A massive reorientation of a free economy would take time. But time was the enemy.

BRITAIN HAD ESTABLISHED A NATIONAL COALITION GOVERNMENT WITH EQUAL representation from the Labour and Conservative parties. Roosevelt sought something similar. He quietly opened negotiations with his opponents of 1936, Alf Landon and Frank Knox, to bring them into the cabinet as secretary of war and secretary of the navy. Landon saw the offer as a ploy to ease the way to a third term and declined to bite. Knox, who had served with Theodore Roosevelt's Rough Riders in the Spanish-American War, signaled that he would accept the Navy Department if another leading Republican also received a cabinet post. Roosevelt thereupon turned to Henry L. Stimson, secretary of war under William Howard Taft and secretary of state under Herbert Hoover. Stimson, a much respected elder statesman, accepted the president's offer. The administration announced the appointments on June 20, the day before the start of the Republican National Convention.[17]

Knox and Stimson were both critics of the New Deal but ardent supporters of Roosevelt's foreign policy and advocates of a large military manned by conscription. They brought with them a number of Republican lawyers and financiers who would become pillars of a post-1945 foreign policy establishment, among them Robert Patterson, John J. McCloy, Robert Lovett, and James Forrestal. It probably never occurred to Roosevelt that by bringing the corporate and financial community into the war effort, he was at last acting as John Maynard Keynes had advised him to do in February 1938. The defense buildup itself was rapidly becoming an economic stimulus program of Keynesian proportions.[18]

STIMSON AND KNOX WERE APPOINTED ON THEIR SUBSTANTIAL MERITS, BUT the president's bringing them to Washington on the eve of a reelection campaign was hardly coincidental.

George Washington had established the hallowed precedent that no president should serve more than two terms, but Roosevelt long had refused to renounce the possibility of a third. In a climate of peace, voters evaluating him would have grappled primarily with the equivocal record of the New Deal, asking whether its failure to bring economic recovery was more than balanced by its relief efforts and whether the relief programs were primarily political patronage boondoggles or meritorious investments in public goods. By mid-1940, however, the war and a sense of national peril overshadowed all else. The economy was ticking upward as defense industries gathered momentum. A growing sense of national emergency had eclipsed class politics. The president was suddenly the indispensible man as commander in chief.

The Republicans assembled in Cleveland on June 21, stunned by the Stimson-Knox defection and without a clear front-runner. Their leading candidate was Thomas E. Dewey of New York. Just thirty-eight years old, Dewey had made his mark as an aggressive prosecutor who had successfully gone after some of America's most notorious gangsters. He had come within an eyelash of election as governor of New York in 1938. Next in line was Senator Robert A. Taft of Ohio. The son of former president William Howard Taft, elected to the Senate in 1938, he was the intellectual leader of Republicans in the upper house. Senator Arthur Vandenberg of Michigan had ten years of seniority on Taft and enjoyed considerable respect but was a fairly distant third. All had flaws. Dewey was vague on major issues, still simply a district attorney, and notably lacking in warmth. Taft had the demeanor of a cranky accountant. Vandenberg was a standard-issue midwestern senator who had stated an equivocal foreign policy position. None were exciting candidates.[19]

A dark horse swiftly emerged in the person of Wendell Willkie. As head of the New York–based Commonwealth and Southern electric utility corporation, Willkie attracted wide attention as a critic of the Tennessee Valley Authority (TVA) and more generally of New Deal overreach. A Democrat at the beginning of the Depression, he had changed his party registration to Republican in 1938. In the spring of 1940, he took to the pages of *Fortune* magazine with a short manifesto titled "We the People." It eloquently denounced the New Deal for a multitude of sins: pessimism about the nation's future, class warfare, hostility to individual enterprise, overweening government, excessive taxation, reckless social experimentation, and a muddled foreign policy.[20]

A native of Indiana who in many respects looked and sounded like a rustic Hoosier, Willkie possessed a charm that contrasted appealingly with that of the other contenders for the Republican nomination. A successful radio appearance on a popular quiz show had brought him into millions of American homes. Only he among the leading Republican contenders embraced a policy of extending to Britain all-out aid, short of joining the war, although polls showed that as the majority position. He seemed capable of taking on the biggest political personality of them all. Henry Luce's important magazines—*Time*, *Life*, and *Fortune*—promoted his candidacy. So did the flagship newspaper of northeastern Republicanism, the *New York Herald-Tribune*.

His backers packed the convention galleries and subjected the delegates to incessant chants of "We want Willkie." Many delegates were put off by a draft platform that tried to finesse the war issue and dissatisfied by the drab choices the establishment had put in front of them. Renowned old Kansas journalist William White wrote that the rank-and-file attendees were acting "like unwashed Democrats" and running wild.[21]

Willkie gained strength steadily, moving ahead on the fourth ballot and winning the necessary majority on the sixth. After his nomination, he spoke briefly to the convention, warned that the nation was "facing the most crucial test that it ha[d] ever faced in all its long history," and promised a crusading campaign for the preservation of freedom.[22] Here was no Hoover or Landon. Roosevelt probably listened to the acceptance talk and understood that if he ran for a third term, he would confront an opponent whose charisma challenged his own.

THE PRESIDENT REMAINED MUTE BUT DID NOTHING TO ANOINT A SUCCESSOR. He may have once hoped to designate Harry Hopkins, whom he made secretary of commerce in December 1938, but Hopkins had never run for public office and was in precarious health. Two other favored loyalists, Harold Ickes (too old at sixty-six and a former Republican) and Henry Wallace (a former Republican with a reputation as a mystic), were never serious candidates.

Roosevelt's refusal to develop a succession plan discouraged possible candidates and likely provided the most obvious clue to his intentions. A few prominent Democrats—including Vice President John Nance Garner, Secretary of State Cordell Hull, and Postmaster General Jim Farley—were clearly receptive to a convention draft and not hesitant about letting their availability be known. None could wage an active campaign for the nomination, and none could have beaten Willkie. As the president maintained his silence, he allowed Ickes and other lieutenants to work for state convention delegations pledged to him.[23]

As the Democrats assembled in Chicago on July 15, Roosevelt still had not spoken, but most perceptive observers assumed he would be the nominee. The chief string puller was Harry Hopkins, who had come to Chicago early, seemed constantly on the telephone in his hotel suite, and was presumed to be in direct communication with the White House. Other conspirators were the convention's permanent chairman, Kentucky senator Alben Barkley; Roosevelt's most agile loyalist from the Deep South, South Carolina senator James F. Byrnes; and the Democratic boss of Chicago, Mayor Edward J. Kelly. The extent to which any of them was acting on explicit instructions from the White House remains uncertain.[24]

Crunch time came on the second evening of the convention. After the usual partisan speeches, adoption of a platform, and Barkley's stem-winding keynote oration, it was time to call for presidential nominations. At that point, Barkley informed the delegates that he had an additional statement to make at the request of the president:

> The President has never had and has not today any desire or purpose to continue in the office of the President, to be a candidate for that office, or to be nominated by the convention for that office.
>
> He wishes in all earnestness and sincerity to make it clear that all the delegates to this convention are free to vote for any candidate.

After a moment of quiet, bedlam broke out. State delegations formed and marched around the hall with Roosevelt banners, all of them exhorted by a leather-lunged voice that had commandeered the public address system: "We want Roosevelt! The world needs Roosevelt!" The exhorter was Thomas Garry, Chicago's superintendent of sewers, described tongue-in-cheek by a journalist as a "deathless voice echoing down the corridors of time."[25]

The next day, the convention nominated the president on the first ballot, giving him 946 votes to 72 for Farley, 61 for Garner, 9 for Senator Millard Tydings, and 5 for Hull. Roosevelt's longtime New York loyalist Edward Flynn, soon to succeed Farley as chairman of the Democratic National Committee, sensed that most of the delegates "did not support Roosevelt out of any motive of affection or because of any political issues involved, but rather [because] they knew that opposing him would be harmful to their local organizations." Farley, consummate political pro that he was, came to the rostrum and called for the nomination to be made unanimous. Neither Garner nor Tydings followed his lead. Hull, who had indicated no interest in the nomination, remained mute in Washington.[26]

Only the vice presidential selection was left. To many observers' surprise, Hopkins passed the word that Roosevelt wanted Henry Wallace, who as secretary of agriculture had alienated the southern establishment with his tender-minded concern for impoverished (and mostly black) sharecroppers. A registered Republican until 1936, he held no appeal for northern and western organization Democrats. As the president's close aide Samuel Rosenman later recalled it, Roosevelt prized Wallace's militant New Dealism. The president probably also saw him as a candidate who would strengthen the ticket in the increasingly doubtful midwestern farm states. (Willkie's running mate, Senator Charles McNary, was a longtime advocate of agricultural subsidies.) Wallace himself told an interviewer twenty-four years later that he believed the president thought they shared an assumption that war was inevitable.[27]

Many delegates were probably annoyed with Roosevelt's concocted draft but accepted it as either inevitable or necessary for the good of the party. They found neither exigency in Wallace. For a few hours the convention was on the verge of revolt. One anti-Wallace speaker bellowed, "Just because the Republicans have nominated an apostate Democrat, let us not for God's sake nominate an apostate Republican." In Washington, Roosevelt listened to such oratory with mounting irritation. He actually drafted a statement declining the nomination and authorized press aide Steve Early to leak the possibility to the press. Equipped with that threat, Senator Byrnes scurried around the floor, asking anti-Wallace delegates if they wanted to nominate a president or a vice president.[28]

The president called Eleanor, vacationing at Val-Kill, and asked her to fly to Chicago. She arrived late that afternoon, was met by Farley, held an impromptu press conference, stopped briefly at her hotel, and proceeded to the convention. Her speech, brief and graceful, contained praise for Jim Farley and his years of service to the party, a reminder of the president's grave responsibilities in a world of crisis, a warning that he would be unable to conduct a campaign in the usual sense of the word, and an exhortation to give him full support. "You will have to rise above considerations which are narrow and partisan. . . . This is no ordinary time. No time for weighing anything except what we can best do for the country."[29]

The talk calmed the atmosphere, but only a bit. One by one, various vice presidential aspirants withdrew, leaving only Speaker of the House William Bankhead as a serious contender. After a torrent of acrimonious oratory, the delegates swallowed hard and put Wallace over on the first ballot, with 627.7 votes to 327.2. The mood was so surly that the newly minted vice presidential candidate had to pocket his acceptance speech and stay well clear of the convention platform.[30]

Roosevelt accepted his nomination with a nationally broadcast address from the Oval Office. In the convention hall, the rambunctious delegates listened quietly. It was perhaps the most personal speech he had ever delivered, in tone more like a fireside address than convention oratory. In his best strong, commanding voice, he explained that he had eagerly anticipated the relaxation of an honorable retirement but felt compelled as a matter of conscience to accept the call of continued duty. The need to serve the nation at a time of world crisis went beyond party and personal ambition. "All private plans, all private lives, have been in a sense repealed by an overriding public danger."

He told the delegates that he had drafted into the service of the nation numerous men and women to manage the defense program. It would be necessary to draft many ordinary individuals to serve in the army and navy. If the people wanted to draft him, he had no right to refuse. The country faced forces of dictatorial tyranny that posed a mortal threat to a tradition of liberty that ran from England's Magna Carta to the US Declaration of Independence and Constitution. "We face one of the great choices of history . . . the continuance of civilization as we know it versus the ultimate destruction of all that we have held dear." The American people would sustain representative democracy, "asking the Divine Blessing as they face[d] the future with courage and with faith."[31]

The convention with its contrived draft had been, in the words of Robert E. Sherwood, a "dreadful display of democracy at its tawdriest." Eleanor's talk had provided a redemptive note. The president's acceptance transformed what might have seemed an exercise in unbridled personal aggrandizement into a response to a mortal national crisis. The implicit egomania behind its inspirational text could not be wholly concealed, but its call to arms was both necessary and powerful.[32]

RADIO, WHICH HAD DONE SO MUCH TO MAKE ROOSEVELT'S POLITICAL CAREER, greatly facilitated the growing informal alliance between Britain and the United States. By the late 1930s, instantaneous shortwave communication between Europe and the United States had become practical, giving rise to a new breed of newsman who reported events as they happened. Throughout the summer, as Britain came under German attack from the air, radio correspondents described British resistance and resolve in the face of massive bombing. "If the people who rule Britain are made of the same stuff as the little people," Edward R. Murrow told his American audience on August 18, "then the defense of Britain will be something of which men will speak with awe and admiration so long as the English language survives." Churchill's speeches, widely broadcast in the United States, seemed to give assurance that the ruling class would fight to the end and made possible a developing American cobelligerency.[33]

Through the summer, the English showed that they could take it and that the Chamberlain government, for all its failings, had managed to build an air force that could fight off Hitler's vaunted Luftwaffe, then stage its own bombing raids on Berlin. With Germany unable to establish air supremacy, the expected Nazi sweep across the channel never materialized. Enemy bombers, increasingly coming only under cover of darkness, would continue to pound London and many other English cities but fail to destroy the morale of their people.

Britain's greatest need remained the destroyers Churchill had asked for in mid-May. After Roosevelt's third-term nomination, the two leaders groped toward a deal in which the US Navy would send fifty refurbished World War I–vintage destroyers to England in exchange for British naval bases in the Western Hemisphere. The administration leaked the request to the public and orchestrated support for it through the summer, quietly working with the nonpartisan Committee to Defend America by Aiding the Allies, headed by William Allen White. On August 4, General John J. Pershing, revered commander of American forces in Europe during the earlier world war, delivered a dramatic radio address supporting a destroyer transfer.[34]

On September 3, Washington and London announced the deal. In exchange for fifty destroyers, Britain gave the United States ninety-nine-year leases on military bases in eight Western Hemisphere locations, from Newfoundland to Trinidad and British Guiana. Roosevelt, calling the agreement "the most important action in the reinforcement of our national defense that has been taken since the Louisiana Purchase," transmitted formal notification of the deal to Congress and cited a Department of Justice opinion that the transaction could be concluded as an executive agreement that would not require congressional ratification.[35]

The destroyers, built in American shipyards to American specifications, required considerable crew training before the British could make use of them. Given their age, they were second-line craft at best. Still, substantially modernized, they added depth to the British navy. The new American bases, military analysts agreed, would greatly strengthen the nation's grip on the Caribbean and the western North Atlantic. The president was widely believed to have made a good bargain in the interest of hemispheric defense.[36]

The swap represented a problem for Willkie. His most fervent backers supported it, but his partisan imperative was to oppose. He attempted to work both sides of the street, attacking the president for undertaking the transaction without congressional approval or public discussion, while declining to say whether he personally countenanced it. Under pressure to get tougher, he subsequently called the exchange "the most arbitrary and dictatorial action ever taken by any President in the history of the United States," adding, "It does us no good to solve the problems of democracy if we solve them with the methods of dictators."[37]

In addition to sustaining the British effort against Germany, Roosevelt also had to face Japanese moves to take advantage of the European war. After the fall of France, Japan quickly moved south from China into northern French Indochina (North Vietnam) and established military bases there. Vichy France had no alternative but to agree to the de facto occupation. The new Japanese advance threatened to encircle the Chinese Nationalist government and menaced all of Southeast Asia.

On September 26, as Japanese diplomats gathered in Berlin to sign a formal treaty of alliance with Germany and Italy, Roosevelt issued an executive order banning the sale of scrap iron and steel to any country outside the Americas other than Britain. The move was clearly aimed at Japan, which had used large quantities of American scrap for its war industry. For the time being, Roosevelt withheld the one step that would likely lead to military hostilities: an embargo on oil and petroleum products.[38]

By then, Congress had enacted the administration program for a military draft. Just a year earlier, peacetime conscription, unprecedented in American history, would have seemed inconceivable. By the late summer of 1940, it had solid majority support. A bill sponsored by Representative James Wadsworth, a New York Republican, and Senator Edward Burke, a Nebraska Democrat who had bolted the party to support Willkie, moved quickly through Congress with the Republican candidate's support. Roosevelt signed it on September 23 and ordered quick implementation of selective service machinery in every state. It was surely no accident, however, that the first call-up notices would not come until after the election.[39]

Willkie was a formidable campaigner. He accepted the Republican nomination in his hometown of Elmwood, Indiana, recounting the odyssey of a young man who had attended its public schools, worked in its factories, and begun his law practice in its courts. Marketing himself as an independent who happened to be a Republican, he identified himself with his party's progressive tradition. He would not, he declared, be a "pussy-footer." Slamming the New Deal as top-down, class-conscious bureaucratic incompetence, he promised a full economic recovery that would be fair to all.

He generally supported Roosevelt's foreign policies and defense buildup, yet adeptly found differences of detail, which (as with the Destroyer Deal) he elevated to differences in principle. Burly and a bit roughhewn but flashing a ready smile, he aggressively attacked Roosevelt's alleged appetite for personal power. His outgoing, dynamic personality excited Republicans in a way that no candidate since TR had achieved. His voice, characterized by a raspy mid-western twang and a tendency to hoarseness after a day of impassioned speech making, gave him an air of authenticity. The *New York Times*'s early endorsement of his candidacy stunned the administration.[40]

The voting public was clearly intrigued by this new breed of Republican and perhaps let down by the staged draft at the Democratic convention. In August, the Gallup poll showed Willkie in a dead heat with the president for the popular vote and actually leading in the electoral college. By the beginning of September, the White House was receiving alarms from Democratic leaders around the country.[41]

Through the summer, the president had been largely content to confine his public appearances to "inspection trips" of defense plants or installations and otherwise to communicate with the public through his press conferences. He would spend much of the fall away from Washington, mixing partisan campaigning with less political events, such as the dedication of a TVA dam. He continued to profit from the sense that he was better equipped to handle the foreign crisis and probably got a bounce from the Destroyer Deal. By the end of September, he seemed to be pulling away from his opponent, but in October the polls tightened up once again.

Willkie, perhaps sensing that he could not outdo Roosevelt's support for Britain and caught between the interventionists and isolationists in his party, made a last, desperate lunge for victory by emphasizing on the one hand his unconditional commitment to aid England and on the other his unqualified opposition to war with Germany. He would, he asserted, send Britain all the war equipment it needed. But he never would send American troops to Europe. The president, he charged, was both dragging his feet on shipments to Britain and plotting full-scale war.[42]

Willkie's straddling of isolationism and interventionism shrewdly reflected an elemental contradiction in public opinion: a sense of national peril and probable war counterbalanced by a powerful instinct of denial. He made a point of referring to Roosevelt as "the third-term candidate." The issue provided a way to convert Roosevelt's strengths, his personal charisma, oratorical prowess, and maximization of presidential power, into character flaws. The Republican appeal represented the effort to stay in office beyond eight years as an assault on an unwritten constitutional understanding by a president who had effectively declared himself indispensable and was leading the nation toward war. The *Los Angeles Times*, firmly Republican and more conservative, said it all with an editorial cartoon depicting Roosevelt as a maniacal, menacing "Ca3sar."[43]

Through it all, the leader of Roosevelt's core constituency, unionized labor as organized into the Congress of Industrial Organizations (CIO), remained silent. John L. Lewis met with the president at the White House on October 17 and emerged without making an endorsement. A week later he made a nationally broadcast speech backing Willkie. Perhaps he sensed a need to mollify the large Communist constituency in the organization. So long as the Hitler-Stalin pact held, American Communists were monolithically opposed to aiding Britain. Lewis also nursed an intense dislike of Roosevelt. Describing the demonstrably well-fed Willkie as a man who "has worked with his hands, and has known the pangs of hunger," Lewis accused the president of warmongering and an "overweening abnormal and selfish craving for increased power." He made the speech as personal as it could get, declaring that if CIO members voted for Roosevelt, he would resign as the organization's president. Most labor leaders, other than those of the Communist-dominated unions, backed the president. Roosevelt himself must have found being lectured on lust for power by Lewis amusing, but he also knew that having the autocratic CIO leader's backing would have been far better than losing it.[44]

ROOSEVELT, FULLY AS MUCH AS WILLKIE, ATTEMPTED TO STRADDLE THE isolationist-interventionist divide, albeit with a different emphasis. He effectively began his reelection campaign on September 11 with an address to the Teamsters union convention, underscoring his support for labor and his determination to achieve social equity for all working Americans. He repeated an already expressed intention to seize plants and equipment from companies that refused to cooperate with the defense buildup. He assured his audience, "I hate war, now more than ever. . . . We will not participate in foreign wars, and we will not send our army, naval or air forces to fight in foreign lands outside of the Americas, except in case of attack."[45]

On October 23, he began a series of train trips that took him to Philadelphia, New York, and Boston, back to New York for a talk in Brooklyn, and then on to Cleveland, with rear-platform appearances, brief remarks at several other stops, and also a couple of radio talks. On November 4, the day before the election, he delivered a final radio address from Hyde Park. He recalled the economic wasteland of the 1930s, the caring New Deal years, and the economic revival, then moved to the need to defend an imperiled America against rapacious dictators—who, he claimed, had pioneered the techniques of propaganda employed by his opponent—and repeated his determination to avoid an all-out war.[46]

His made his most spectacular appearance on October 28 in New York, spending wearying hours in the open car of a motorcade that traveled fifty-eight miles through the city before an estimated 2 million cheering people. That evening, at the end of a fourteen-hour day, he spoke to a packed house of 22,000 roaring partisans at Madison Square Garden, asserting that he had armed the nation to protect itself over the consistent opposition of a Republican congressional leadership that had displayed only timidity, weakness, and shortsightedness.[47]

Roosevelt surely understood that his most challenging appearance would take place in Boston. Massachusetts had been among the most consistently Republican of states before the Al Smith candidacy of 1928 mobilized its rapidly growing Irish Catholic constituency. Roosevelt had inherited the Smith electoral revolution, but the Irish had scant sympathy for England or for the increasingly close relationship with Britain that the president was fostering. The campaign needed help.

The president summoned Ambassador Joseph P. Kennedy back from London and asked him to deliver a radio speech of endorsement. The gambit was nervy and dangerous. Kennedy, a hero to the state's Irish Americans, was not anti-British, but he was a defeatist who admired Neville Chamberlain and worried about the impact of war on his children. He returned to the United States on October 27, embittered by Roosevelt's consistently bypassing him in dealings with the Churchill government, fully understanding that he lacked the president's confidence, and determined to resign. He would, he told Roosevelt, make the speech but would write it himself without any White House review and pay for the broadcast with family funds. He left the White House with the president uncertain whether he would receive an endorsement and doubtless fuming inwardly.[48]

Two days later, Kennedy delivered his talk on the 114-station CBS radio network. He made clear that he did not favor American participation in the European war and even excused Chamberlain's acquiescence in the Munich Agreement as a way of buying time. But he also endorsed all possible aid to Britain, strongly defended the president against the charge that he wanted war, and supported his preparedness program. He conceded that he and the president had their disagreements but said that on the fundamental issues, there was little space between them. The issue of a third term was insignificant in comparison to the large questions raised by the world crisis. He and his wife were concerned above all with their nine children—"hostages to fortune"—and the world they would inherit. "In the light of these considerations," he concluded, "I believe that Franklin D. Roosevelt should be re-elected President of the United States."[49]

Roosevelt sent a telegram minutes after the speech's conclusion: "We have all just listened to a grand speech many thanks."[50]

The next evening, the president delivered his own nationally broadcast address to a capacity crowd at the Boston Garden. Roosevelt tore into alleged Republican foot-dragging on the nation's defense program and underscored its primary objective: "to keep any potential attacker as far from our continental shores as we possibly can." One key passage dominated the speech:

And while I am talking to you mothers and fathers, I give you one more assurance.

I have said this before, but I shall say it again and again and again:

Your boys are not going to be sent into any foreign wars.[51]

He surely knew that he was making a promise he could not keep. In other speeches, he had followed such declarations with the phrase "except in case of attack." This time, it seemed necessary to be categorical. Anyway, he told Sam Rosenman, "if we're attacked, it's no longer a foreign war." He probably told himself that Willkie had forced him to make the pledge. That same night in Baltimore, the Republican candidate charged that a third term would mean war by April.[52]

Roosevelt cast his ballot on Election Day in Hyde Park, then awaited the returns at Springwood, with Sara, Eleanor, and his sons. (Anna was in Seattle with her husband.) After dining with friends, he kept his own tally sheets in the mansion's smoking room, which was equipped with three news service teletype machines, several radios, and a number of telephones. Harry Hopkins, Sam Rosenman, Henry Morgenthau, Missy LeHand, and his old Poughkeepsie backer, Judge John Mack, all kept the vigil with him. The earliest returns were mixed, but as the evening rolled on, the numbers pointed in the direction of a solid victory. Local Democrats staged an old-fashioned torchlight parade and assembled by the hundreds in front of the Roosevelt home.[53]

By midnight, Roosevelt felt confident enough to address the crowd. A local party leader, Elmer van Wagner, introduced him: "Here's the greatest of them all! Don't ask me—ask Wendell Willkie and John L. Lewis."[54]

THE VICTORY WAS UNEXPECTEDLY DECISIVE. ROOSEVELT TOOK 55 PERCENT OF the popular vote, won the electoral college 449 to 82, and carried thirty-eight of the forty-eight states. Foreign policy issues must have been salient for many of the voters, but something more lay behind them. The president had consolidated the electoral revolution of 1936 in which the Democrats captured the votes of both an immigrant-based working class and increasingly emancipated northern Negroes, voting blocs characterized by high birth rates and a visceral loyalty to their benefactor. By backing unions and providing generous work relief for the unemployed, the New Deal had done what the Socialist Party and other leftists had never achieved. In the words of political analyst Samuel Lubell, it had "drawn a class line across the face of American politics." The primary beneficiaries of the New Deal, voting in the afterglow of an emerging prosperity, registered their enduring loyalty.

The war also played a big part. Many of those same immigrant workers had family roots in nations overrun or threatened by Nazi Germany. Roosevelt seems to have lost the normally Republican-leaning German American vote (as had Woodrow Wilson in 1916) and suffered perceptible losses among Italian Americans. On the other hand, Polish-American precincts voted for him with near unanimity. So did Jewish voters.[55]

More broadly, the electorate as a whole seems to have bought into the president's assertion that the United States could protect itself without becoming an actual combatant. Was that really possible? By the end of 1940, a German invasion of England was unlikely, but only a fantasist could imagine a successful unilateral British assault against the Continent. Roosevelt must have understood that the defeat of Hitler could come only with full American participation in the conflict. Many who voted for him probably understood in their hearts that war was coming.

CHAPTER 21

UNDECLARED WAR

DECEMBER 7, 1940–DECEMBER 7, 1941

IN THE WEEKS AFTER THE PRESIDENTIAL ELECTION, ROOSEVELT MANAGED A few days on the new presidential yacht *Potomac*, a hurried Thanksgiving interlude at Hyde Park, a week and a half in the Caribbean on the Navy cruiser *Tuscaloosa*, and a day at Warm Springs. Even in those comfortable settings, he could not escape a world moving too dangerously to be ignored. Italy, having invaded Greece shortly before the election, met stiff resistance and suffered serious damage to its battle fleet from a British air raid at Taranto. Germany continued its night bombing campaign against England with repeated attacks on London and a devastating pounding of the industrial city of Coventry. The Reich concluded treaties with Hungary and Romania, prior to an expected move against Greece. In North Africa, the British faced a numerically superior Italian army. The German submarine toll against British supply convoys in the Atlantic was enormous, leading to widespread speculation that Britain would request more US destroyers.

When the president left Warm Springs, he told his beloved polios that he hoped to return in a year, "if the world survives."[1]

ON DECEMBER 8, ROOSEVELT GOT A LONG MESSAGE FROM WINSTON CHUR-chill, confirming the urgency both nations faced. Britain, the prime minister declared with more bravado than his nation's depleted resources warranted, was doing its part. But the navy was overstretched, and the U-boat campaign imperiled the Atlantic lifeline to the United States. Most ominously, "The moment approaches when we shall no longer be able to pay cash for shipping and other supplies."[2]

Roosevelt had a quick response, already developed in consultation with Treasury and State Department officials. A month earlier he had told Harold Ickes that first Britain had to exhaust its dollar reserves, but after that, it should be possible to "lease ships or any other property that was loanable, returnable, and insurable."[3]

The president held a press conference on December 17, the day after his return to Washington. A reporter described him sitting at his desk, "his slightly tanned face solemn, his cigarette in its holder tilted upward." There was wide agreement, he declared, "from a selfish point of view of American defense that we should do everything to help the British Empire to defend itself." Some people wanted to repeal the Neutrality Acts, then make a government-to-government loan. Others wanted to make a gift of war matériel. Such solutions were "banal." Why not simply let the US government lend and lease the war equipment, all in pursuit of the best defense of the United States? "What I am trying to do is eliminate . . . the silly, foolish old dollar sign." If your neighbor's house caught on fire, he continued, wouldn't you lend him your garden hose to put it out? If the hose was seriously damaged, the neighbor would gladly replace it or pay for it.[4]

He dodged questions about specifics. A newsman asked whether the president thought "this takes us any more into the war than we are."

"No, not a bit."[5]

In fact, Roosevelt, convinced that Nazi Germany posed a mortal threat to the United States, was determined to deepen American involvement. He clearly believed war was inevitable, that the nation had to prepare for it, and that the United States would need viable allies in the struggle that lay ahead. His task, as historian David Kaiser has put it, entailed "enlisting the nation."[6]

FDR worked closely with Harry Hopkins, who had resigned as secretary of commerce. Functioning without a formal appointment in the administration, a bachelor since the death of his second wife in 1937, and in shaky health, Hopkins had taken an offer of residence in the White House. He was rapidly becoming Roosevelt's closest and most influential adviser. Another important influence was Undersecretary of State Sumner Welles, a superb professional diplomat, a close friend of FDR, and, not least, a fellow Groton man. His closeness to the president was a constant irritant to Secretary of State Cordell Hull.

Sam Rosenman still led the speechwriting team. Two other participants burnished Roosevelt's rhetoric to a high standard: distinguished playwright Robert E. Sherwood and acclaimed poet Archibald MacLeish, whom Roosevelt had appointed Librarian of Congress. Ben Cohen made occasional contributions. So did the old Brains Truster Adolf A. Berle, who had finally come to Washington as an assistant secretary of state.[7]

Roosevelt began his powerful rhetorical offensive with a fireside chat on Sunday, December 29, 1940. The White House had put out word that the speech would make an important national security pronouncement. In New York, movie theaters, normally crowded on a Sunday night, reported unusually low ticket sales. Radio City Music Hall, which carried the audio broadcast of the speech, was packed.[8]

The president did not mince his words. "Never before since Jamestown and Plymouth Rock has our American civilization been in such danger as now." The German-Italian-Japanese pact of September 1940, he asserted, had been undertaken in pursuit of a goal of world domination and directly targeted the United States. Britain and China were in effect protecting the United States by engaging the aggressor nations. Should they fall, control of both the Atlantic and Pacific Oceans might be beyond the power of the American navy. New long-range bombers could endanger the American continent. South America would be far more open to German aggression. "American appeasers" willing to accept peace on Axis terms would lay the United States open to a "new order" characterized by "the concentration camp and the servants of God in chains." He was not, he assured his listeners, asking for war. It was his purpose to avoid war by providing all possible assistance to Britain and to do so with the cooperation of labor and industry united in the common cause. "We must be the great arsenal of democracy."[9]

The State of the Union address followed on January 6, 1941. The message was the same. Continental isolation, a viable policy before 1914, was no longer possible. Democracy was under attack in every part of the world. Continued aloofness could leave the United States as the last refuge of free government in a hostile international environment. The survival of Britain and the British navy was essential to national security. Hostile subversion threatened Latin America. The United States had to respond with a strong defense program and provide the means of resistance to other nations on a lend-lease basis. The cause, he asserted, was greater than national survival. It ultimately involved "the social revolution which is today a supreme factor in the world" and the international struggle for "four essential human freedoms":

The first is freedom of speech and expression—everywhere in the world.

The second is freedom of every person to worship God in his own way—everywhere in the world.

The third is freedom from want . . . everywhere in the world.

The fourth is freedom from fear . . . anywhere in the world.[10]

With the proclamation of the Four Freedoms, Roosevelt gave his war policy a moral significance on a plane with his national security rationale. He neatly combined the outlooks of the two presidents, Theodore Roosevelt and Woodrow Wilson, who had most influenced him. He also laid himself open to the problem that had destroyed Wilson's presidency: the difficulty of achieving millennial goals within a world order that only the relentless application of naked power could create.

Roosevelt next delivered his third inaugural address on January 20, 1941. Once again, on a cold, sunny day in the east portico of the Capitol, he took the oath of office from Chief Justice Charles Evans Hughes. He spoke for only sixteen and a half minutes, not proclaiming a program but making a declaration of the American spirit. Referring to the crisis of 1933, he warned of a looming new emergency, this one precipitated by opponents of democracy who envisioned tyranny and slavery as "the surging wave of the future." The American way—blessed by God and enshrined in such documents as the Mayflower Compact, the Declaration of Independence, the Constitution, and the Gettysburg Address—would meet the challenge, preserve what George Washington called "the sacred fire of liberty," and vindicate the nation's destiny. The inaugural parade that followed was heavy with the latest military hardware.[11]

The reaction in Washington and across the country was one of wary acceptance. The opinion pollsters revealed a public that accepted rearmament and lavish aid to Britain but wanted above all to stay out of the war. Roosevelt clearly understood this dominant current of opinion, respected the limitations it placed on his freedom of action, and played it masterfully.[12]

FIRST NEEDING TO GAUGE BRITAIN'S DETERMINATION AND STAYING POWER, IN January the president dispatched Harry Hopkins to London. Britain's prime minister and the fortitude of its ordinary people won over the initially skeptical emissary. Asked to say a few words at an official dinner in Glasgow, he quoted a passage from the Book of Ruth: "Whither thou goest, I will go; and where thou lodgest, I will lodge: thy people shall be my people, and thy God my

God. Even to the end." He returned to the United States in early March, a firm believer in Churchill and an admirer of the British nation.[13]

In London, Hopkins shared British attention with another prominent American, Wendell Willkie, who had met with Roosevelt before leaving the United States. He came equipped with a message from the president to the prime minister. It was a passage from Henry Wadsworth Longfellow's poem "The Building of the Ship":

> *Sail on, O Ship of State!*
> *Sail on, O Union, strong and great!*
> *Humanity with all its fears,*
> *With all the hopes of future years,*
> *Is hanging breathless on thy fate!*[14]

Traveling as an unofficial visitor, Willkie not only met with Churchill and British officials but had far more opportunities than did Hopkins to visit with ordinary people and share their experiences. He toured bomb shelters during an air raid. Like Hopkins, he received a warm welcome and returned as a firm partisan of the British cause. He would testify before Congress on behalf of the Lend-Lease Bill.[15]

As Congress considered Lend-Lease, American, British, and Canadian military officers engaged in confidential "conversations" in Washington. They aimed to develop a grand strategy should the two countries find themselves allied in a war against Germany and/or Japan. Their primary conclusion, embedded in a March 27 report ("ABC-1"), held that the two powers would give priority to control of the Atlantic and the defeat of Germany. They had thus agreed on the basic design for total war.[16]

Lend-Lease dominated American political debate after its introduction in Congress on January 10 as HR-1776. Given the steady "all aid short of war" public sentiment, congressional approval was all but foreordained. That did not stop the rhetoric from becoming heated. Roosevelt's court-packing critic, Burton K. Wheeler, led the opposition in the Senate. Drawing an analogy to the New Deal agricultural program, he declared that "the lend-lease-give program" would "plow under every fourth American boy." At his regular press conference a few days later, Roosevelt called the remark "the rottenest thing that has been said in public life in my generation."[17]

The Lend-Lease debate effectively terminated FDR's relationship with Joe Kennedy, who had resigned as ambassador to Britain after the presidential election. On January 18, 1941, Kennedy delivered a radio speech arguing for extensive aid to Great Britain but also declaring that the bill in its present form concentrated too much power in the hands of the president. On the morning of January 21, just hours before he was scheduled to testify before the House Foreign Relations Committee, he met with Roosevelt. They had what must have been a strained, if outwardly calm, discussion. In the course of five hours of rambling testimony at the House hearing that afternoon, Kennedy underscored his opposition to the legislation in its present form.[18]

Roosevelt must have been livid, all the more so when he learned that his son-in-law John Boettiger and his daughter Anna had sent Kennedy a supportive note. Kennedy had responded with thanks, complained about attacks by the president's "hatchet men," and lamented that the administration was going to make him "a social outcast." Boettiger forwarded the communication to FDR, who responded with a blistering "memorandum":[19]

> It is, I think, a little pathetic that he worries about being, with his family, social outcasts.
>
> ... [H]e ought to realize of course that he has only himself to blame for the country's opinion as to his testimony.... Most people and most papers got the feeling that he was blowing hot and blowing cold at the same time—trying to carry water on both shoulders.
>
> . . .
>
> The truth of the matter is that Joe is and always has been a temperamental Irish boy, terrificly [*sic*] spoiled at an early age by huge financial success; thoroughly patriotic, thoroughly selfish, and thoroughly obsessed with the idea that he must leave each of his nine children with $1 million apiece when he dies (he has told me that often).
>
> He has a positive horror of any change in the present methods of life in America. To him, the future of a small capitalistic class is safer under a Hitler than under a Churchill. This is sub-conscious on his part and he does not admit it.[20]

Roosevelt's words, dripping with condescension, said as much about him as about Kennedy. They hinted at his sense of belonging to a natural elite, his personal indifference to great wealth, and above all his willingness to use others, accept their favors, and drop them when they had served their purpose.

Lend-Lease cleared Congress on March 11. The president signed the bill ten minutes after it arrived at the White House, then promptly authorized shipments to Britain and Greece. He would, he told a press conference, be requesting large appropriations.[21]

Four days later, riding the crest of a Gallup popularity rating of 72 percent, he delivered a nationally broadcast address to the annual dinner of the White House Correspondents' Association. The humor usually expected at such occasions was brief, the message serious. He called bluntly for national sacrifice in an all-out effort to defend democracy around the world and defeat the Axis powers. The speech recognized the codependency that had emerged between Germany and Japan and came close to a declaration of war against both.[22]

Acting without explicit congressional authorization, Roosevelt had effectively placed the United States in a state of cobelligerency with Britain against the Axis. Moreover, he had suggested generous and idealistic war aims. His actions synthesized the power politics he had learned from Theodore Roosevelt with Woodrow Wilson's millennial goal of constructing a new world order. Details would follow.

The most urgent priority was ensuring that British supply convoys actually made it across a North Atlantic thick with German submarines and surface raiders. On April 10, the United States announced an agreement with the Danish minister in Washington for a US occupation of Greenland. Providing for naval installations, the accord moved the nation's first line of defense far into the North Atlantic. The administration peremptorily dismissed objections from the Nazi-dominated government in Copenhagen and refused to accept its envoy to Washington.[23]

Establishment of a functioning base would take time. The sea lanes remained extremely dangerous. On May 23, Churchill sent Roosevelt an urgent request for US naval convoy support. He attached a list of thirty-four British freighters, many of them loaded with food, weaponry, and ammunition, sunk by enemy action over the previous seven weeks.[24]

That very day, the British navy encountered the deadliest threat yet to the US-British supply line. The new German battleship *Bismarck*, teamed with the heavy cruiser *Prinz Eugen*, had left its port in Norway in search of a Lend-Lease convoy to destroy. One of only two full-scale modern battleships in the German navy, the *Bismarck* represented both the menace and the limitations of German sea power. Heavily armored and equal in its armament to anything in the British navy, it had to be stopped.

On May 24, the *Bismarck* faced off against the World War I–vintage battle cruiser *Hood*, a vessel analogous, as many observers noted, to the British Empire: huge, outdated, and vulnerable. A shell from *Bismarck*'s fifteen-inch guns penetrated *Hood*'s poorly protected ammunition magazine and blew the ship out of the water. Only three of the 1,418 crew members survived. Next, the *Bismarck* exchanged rounds with the new fourteen-inch-gun battleship *Prince of Wales*. The superior German gunnery prevailed again. After serious direct hits and the deaths of several senior officers, *Prince of Wales* threw up a smoke screen and abandoned the fight. It had, however, managed to land a hit on *Bismarck* that caused a serious fuel leak, compelling the ship to head for its port in France. *Prinz Eugen* broke off on its own course toward home base.

King George V, a twin of *Prince of Wales* with just three months of service, took up the chase joined by the older sixteen-inch-gun battleship *Rodney*. An air attack by antiquated torpedo biplanes from the carrier *Ark Royal* appeared at first glance ineffective but managed a hit that jammed *Bismarck*'s rudder, causing the ship to steer uncontrollably in a wide circle and leaving it hopelessly vulnerable. On May 27, after a merciless shelling, *Bismarck*, which its own crew seems to have scuttled, sank beneath the surface. Roosevelt was with Sam Rosenman when he received confirmation from the Navy Department. "There could not have been more satisfaction in his voice," Rosenman recalled a decade later, "if he had himself fired the torpedo that sank her."[25]

That evening, Roosevelt delivered the speech he and Rosenman had been developing. It went farther, he told Churchill, than he had thought possible only two weeks earlier. He spoke from the East Room of the White House before a large audience of diplomats and guests from the other twenty American republics; an estimated 85 million people around the world listened.

Employing references to historic documents ranging from the Magna Carta to the Emancipation Proclamation and casting himself as a defender of the entire Western Hemisphere, the president proclaimed "an unlimited national emergency." Maintaining control of the seas was critical to sustaining the British resistance to Hitler. The navy would extend its "patrol" throughout the Atlantic and do its utmost to insure the delivery of vital supplies to Britain. At home, the government would begin to organize a civilian defense apparatus. It would reject the efforts of "racketeers and fifth columnists" to disrupt the nation's defense program. Capital and labor had to work together in a common cause, facilitated by government mediation as necessary. The nation would defend its ideals, preserve its right to freedom of the seas, place its military forces in strategic positions, and use them without hesitation to repel attack.[26]

A bold assertion of presidential power, the speech heartened the supporters of interventionism and confirmed the fears of its opponents. Roosevelt had in effect issued a declaration of naval war against Germany, utilizing destroyer patrols that were really convoy escorts, working when possible with the British navy but ready to take on enemy U-boats alone. The policy amounted to a quest for an incident that would justify a formal declaration of war. Newspaper editorial commentary was broadly supportive. A post-speech Gallup poll showed 55 percent in favor of convoying shipments to Britain, 38 percent against.[27]

Among the more mainstream Republicans, Willkie tendered unconditional support, but Alf Landon veered toward the isolationist side, and Robert A. Taft dismissed the proclamation of unlimited national emergency as lacking any legal or constitutional standing. The pushback from isolationists was vehement. Burton Wheeler accused Roosevelt of following a line laid down by international bankers, jingoistic journalists, and "elder statesmen who want war but are too old to fight." Senator Gerald Nye labeled him a fearmonger. Republican congressman Hamilton Fish called the fireside chat "a typical Rooseveltian speech to promote further war hysteria and fear."[28]

Sensing an emotional opposition that could draw support from at least a third of the country, Roosevelt reverted to a zigzag course, not unlike a ship trying to evade torpedoes in hostile waters. Responding to charges from his critics, he told a press conference that he would not ask for alterations of the Neutrality Acts and denied any intention of establishing convoys. A step forward, a half step back, the uneasy minuet went on.[29]

THE DAY AFTER HIS FIRESIDE CHAT, ROOSEVELT SENT TO CAPITOL HILL A request for a supplemental defense appropriation of $3.3 billion to fund another 15,000 military aircraft. The process of converting to a war economy, however, remained messy and difficult. At the end of 1940, Roosevelt had scrapped his National Defense Advisory Council and replaced it with an Office of Production Management with William Knudsen as the sole head. Knudsen's authority was nonetheless weak, and the effort continued to sputter.[30]

In early June, Communist leaders of a United Auto Workers local shut down the important North American Aviation aircraft plant in Inglewood, California, despite calls for restraint by the union's national leadership. Just a year before, Franklin Roosevelt's use of troops to break a strike would have been inconceivable. On June 9, citing the national emergency, he sent bayonet-wielding soldiers to end the stoppage and take control of the facility. Military draft authorities announced that they would rescind occupational deferments for striking defense workers, signaling clearly to the nation that the war trumped the old politics of the 1930s.[31]

The New Dealer was giving way to the commander in chief, but that did not necessarily indicate the end of domestic reform. By mid-1941, Negro political activists and intellectuals were openly questioning whether blacks had a stake in the survival of European empires that subjugated people of color around the globe. They also increasingly protested widespread hiring discrimination in the booming defense industries and rigid segregation in the armed forces. On both issues, they had a strong advocate in Eleanor Roosevelt. The president, more dependent than ever on the goodwill of the southern Democratic delegation in Congress, still preferred to soft-pedal racial grievances.

In mid-1941, A. Phillip Randolph, head of the Brotherhood of Sleeping Car Porters and America's most important black labor leader, called for a mass protest march on Washington, threatening to mobilize 10,000 to 25,000 demonstrators. Given the District of Columbia's Upper South, highly segregated character, the potential for violence was real.

Roosevelt's secretaries of the army and navy, along with almost all of his top generals and admirals, advised against using the armed forces as instruments of racial reform. Yet the Negro vote was important to the president, and no fair-minded leader could peremptorily ignore discriminatory segregation. Simple support of the status quo risked social upheaval. After intense negotiations in which Eleanor played a key role, the White House responded on June 25 with an executive order establishing a Fair Employment Practices Committee (FEPC), charged with promoting equitable hiring and promotion procedures in defense industries. It did not, however, abolish segregation in the armed forces. Randolph nonetheless called off the march.[32]

Lacking a congressional mandate and funded parsimoniously from discretionary executive branch appropriations, the FEPC was a timid step forward. It would not prevent several racial riots in the war years that lay ahead, but its presence and mostly educational efforts may have staved off much worse. From his perspective as commander in chief, Roosevelt probably saw it as an expedient that reconciled the long-term thrust of the New Deal with the immediate necessities of the fight against Hitler. The mere establishment of the FEPC moved black civil rights several notches toward the top of the liberal agenda.

ON THE SAME DAY THAT THE PRESIDENT BROKE THE NORTH AMERICAN Aviation strike, the American public learned that a Brazilian ship in the South Atlantic had picked up survivors from the *Robin Moor*, an American merchant vessel bound for Cape Town and sunk by a German submarine. Fomenting a widespread sense of outrage in the United States, Berlin strongly defended its right to sink any ship carrying contraband to the enemy anywhere. In a formal communication to Congress, Roosevelt described the incident as "the act of an international outlaw" and condemned "German plans for universal conquest . . . based upon lawlessness and terror on land and piracy on the sea." Acting on evidence that one of Germany's diplomatic offices in the United States had leaked the sailing date and route of the *Robin Moor*, the president ordered the closing of all German and Italian consulates. Berlin responded with a tit-for-tat shutting of US consulates.[33]

In early July, the president sent American forces to join a British garrison that had already occupied Iceland. The United States gradually replaced the British as the country's controlling force in a light-handed occupation widely accepted by the local population. The frontier of the Western Hemisphere was now at Reykjavik, 2,611 miles from New York and only 833 miles from Glasgow.

By then, the conflict had changed dramatically. On June 21, after mounting evidence of tension between the two allies, Germany launched an all-out offensive against the Soviet Union. Both Roosevelt and Churchill instantly grasped the possibilities of an alliance with the USSR. The prime minister, for years a stern critic of international communism and the Soviet state, put it most memorably to an aide: "If Hitler invaded Hell I would at least make a favorable reference to the Devil in the House of Commons." He quickly opened channels to Moscow.[34]

Roosevelt's attitude toward the USSR and its leader appears always to have been more ambivalent. His belief in the Soviet Union's redeeming, socially transformative qualities existed alongside his realistic understanding of the USSR as a rough dictatorship. At dinner with a few friends on New Year's Day, 1942, FDR remarked, as Joseph Lash recalled, "that Stalin had to rule a very backward people, which he thought explained a good deal," and, moreover, that the Soviet dictator possessed a sense of proportion, illustrated by his sense of humor.[35]

Harry Hopkins, whom Roosevelt had dispatched on a second mission to England in July to establish the agenda for a personal meeting with Churchill, had provided this last insight into Stalin's personality. Gaunt, struggling with severe gastric problems, and prone to bouts of exhaustion, Hopkins completed his work in England, delivered a brief speech to the British people over the British Broadcasting Corporation, and departed for Russia. He carried with him a communication from Roosevelt to Stalin: "I ask you to treat Mr. Hopkins with the identical confidence you would feel if you were talking directly to me. . . . May I express, in conclusion, the great admiration all of us in the United States feel for the superb bravery displayed by the Russian people in the defense of their liberty and in their fight for the independence of Russia."[36]

On the evening of July 30, accompanied by Ambassador Laurence Steinhardt, Hopkins had the first of three meetings with Stalin. Their broad discussions ranged from the Soviet leader's survey of the fight against Germany, to an extensive wish list for aid, to the USSR's precarious relations with Japan. Most important was the personal impression Stalin left. Hopkins saw an absolute ruler, totally in charge, crisp and decisive. "There was no waste of word, gesture, nor mannerism. It was like talking to a perfectly co-ordinated machine." Hopkins left Moscow convinced that the Soviet Union would survive the Nazi onslaught and function as an invaluable ally.[37]

Enduring a harrowing flight in stormy weather, Hopkins returned to Britain on August 2, just in time to join Churchill on a journey across the Atlantic. The next day Roosevelt boarded the presidential yacht *Potomac* off Martha's Vineyard for what was billed as a brief vacation and fishing trip. Kept at its usual distance, the press intermittently managed to catch sight of the president—actually a stand-in who had donned pince-nez glasses—relaxing on deck. After a few days, the reporters saw through the ruse; they began openly discussing Roosevelt's disappearance and speculating that he might be in a secret meeting with Churchill.

On August 5 the president had transferred to the heavy cruiser USS *Augusta*, the flagship of a small but formidable flotilla that moved northeast toward Newfoundland and the American base (acquired in the Destroyer Deal) at Argentia. His party consisted of an emerging elite of wartime commanders and military leaders: Chief of Naval Operations Admiral Harold Stark, Commander in Chief of the Atlantic Fleet Ernest J. King, Director of War Plans Rear Admiral Richmond Kelly Turner, Army Chief of Staff General George C. Marshall, and Chief of the Army Air Corps Major General Henry ("Hap") Arnold. Roosevelt had with him his own military aide, Major General Edwin ("Pa") Watson. Also along were Captain Elliott Roosevelt, who had become a US Army Air Force pilot, and Ensign Franklin D. Roosevelt Jr. Not even informed in advance of the meeting, the secretaries of war and navy remained behind. Roosevelt valued their services but was determined that the war would be his to run and win. Nor did he bring along Secretary of State Hull, whom he also left uninformed in Washington, while he did take Undersecretary Sumner Welles.

The flotilla arrived off Argentia on the morning of August 7. Its party had two days to prepare for a dramatic rendezvous. The president knew, as did Churchill, that the meeting would be less about grand strategy or the details of the American-British relationship and more about the two leaders taking each other's measure.[38]

The personal drama began on August 9. Through the morning mists, *Prince of Wales* entered the harbor, hastily repaired after its confrontation with the *Bismarck* but still bearing scars of the fight, representing in its own way the toughness and sacrifice of the British nation. Shortly after *Prince of Wales* dropped anchor, Churchill, dressed in the blue uniform worn in England on ceremonial occasions by the warden of the Cinque Ports, came aboard the *Augusta* to pay his respects to Roosevelt. To this point, Roosevelt had recognized the Englishman as a dynamic force, not unlike himself, but also harbored doubts about him. As Harold Ickes recorded it, the president had remarked at a cabinet meeting just after Churchill became prime minister that "he supposed Churchill was the best man England had even if he was drunk half of his time." The two of them had an informal private lunch, and Roosevelt found a kindred spirit. In a rare aide-mémoire shared with his distant cousin and close friend Daisy Suckley, he wrote of his British counterpart, "He is a tremendously vital person. . . . I like him—& lunching alone broke the ice both ways."[39]

The next day, Sunday, August 10, Roosevelt transferred to *Prince of Wales* to return Churchill's visit and attend an open-air religious service. Rejecting the plan to wheel him up the deck, FDR insisted on walking to his designated seat. Grasping Elliott's arm, he traversed much of the length of the great ship in front of sailors and marines lined up at attention. Churchill was profoundly impressed by his determination. The service that followed—FDR and Churchill leading American and British sailors in worship and joining in the great, emblematic hymn "Onward Christian Soldiers"—was recorded for British and American newsreels. Providing an aura of sanctification for the meeting, it left an overwhelming impression of warriors from across the seas joined in a crusade against the forces of evil.

The one tangible public product to come out of Argentia was a "joint declaration" of "certain common principles." The eight points that followed rejected any "aggrandizement, territorial or otherwise." It affirmed self-determination in the establishment of national boundaries and types of government, "access on equal terms to the trade and to the raw materials of the world," "improved labor standards, economic advancement, and social security," a peace settlement that would secure freedom from fear and want for all peoples, freedom of the seas, and abandonment of the use of force in international relations. The joint declaration carefully avoided the phrase "war aims," although it would later commonly be described as establishing those. It was neither submitted to nor ratified by either the British parliament or the US Congress. Essentially a press release, it nonetheless had a powerful impact. A British newspaper, drawing a comparison to the Magna Carta, dubbed it the "Atlantic Charter."

Along with the Four Freedoms, the Atlantic Charter illustrated the president's sense that ideals were weapons in the war he was edging the United States toward and that Great Britain and the United States were united in their pursuit. The distinction between power and idealism was, all the same, tenuous. Churchill had his doubts about the Atlantic Charter; many of its propositions, after all, could be used against the British Empire. Still he had little choice but to accept its rhetoric while working to preserve British power in the world.

The military staff meetings were "conversations," yielding perhaps understandings but no firm plans or commitments. Yet the suggestion of alliance and partnership in a combined war effort was overwhelming. There remained, above all, questions about what had been promised orally.

On the latter score, Churchill minced no words in his secret report to the War Cabinet on August 19: the president had promised him that by September 1, the US Navy would escort Lend-Lease convoys as far as Iceland. He assured the cabinet that Roosevelt—"obviously determined" to bring his country into the conflict but doubtful that he could get a declaration of war from Congress—"said that he would wage war, but not declare it, and that he would become more and more provocative." Convoy escorts "were to attack any U-boat which showed itself, even if it were 200 or 300 miles away from the convoy. . . . Everything was to be done to force an 'incident.'" He more than likely described Roosevelt's words accurately. His report foretold the president's behavior in the months to come.[40]

Nonetheless, political reality at home left the president pinned, as Theodore Wilson has put it, "between the horns of isolationist denunciation and interventionist outcry." While FDR and Churchill were conferring, the House of Representatives had voted 203 to 202 to extend the service of army draftees by eighteen months. That slender margin relieved the army of an obligation to send tens of thousands of newly trained men back into civilian life. With only twenty-one Republicans favoring the bill, the vote confirmed an ominous pattern of foreign policy partisanship.[41]

THROUGH ALL THE CLOSE CALLS AND EPOCHAL DEVELOPMENTS, THE PUBLIC Roosevelt appeared more in command than at any time since the spring of 1933. The private Roosevelt dealt as best he could with a disappointing personal life.

Women either devoted to him or at least intent on charming him continued to surround the president. He frequently saw his cousin Daisy Suckley, who gave him the Scottish terrier puppy the world would come to know as Fala. On occasions when Eleanor was away, he had meetings with Lucy Mercer Rutherfurd. Princess Martha of Norway, regal and beautiful, wanting to maximize the president's interest in her country, was another favorite companion.

Missy LeHand remained closer than anyone else until, on the evening of June 4, 1941, she suffered what at first appeared to be a nervous meltdown but was probably a stroke. She lingered for a time in her White House living quarters, was hospitalized, and then eventually returned to 1600 Pennsylvania Avenue. Roosevelt at first visited her regularly, but the war placed increasing limits on his free time. He probably also found it increasingly difficult to deal with the depressing reality of her condition. In 1943, relatives finally moved her back to Massachusetts and saw to her care. Roosevelt acknowledged the debt he felt to her by changing his will to provide that, should he predecease her, half the value of his estate, the legacy he had intended to leave to his children, would be devoted to providing for her medical needs.[42]

The other essential woman in his life was his mother, who provided an emotional connection to a reassuring past, indulged all her son's foibles, and provided unconditional support. She had, as late as the ominous summer of 1939, traveled to Europe, holding an impromptu press conference upon her leave, taking questions in French, and responding fluently. She set foot in the United States just a day before the outbreak of the war. Not long after Missy's collapse, she suffered a minor stroke but recovered well enough to take her customary August at Campobello. Back at Hyde Park, she took on a full-time nurse. In early September 1941, her health deteriorated. Roosevelt rushed to spend a day with her before her death on September 7. Three days later, she was buried in the St. James churchyard, close to her beloved husband. The president wore a black armband in her memory for the next year.[43]

Missy's illness had hung over Roosevelt at Argentia. Sara's illness and death came as he was grappling with the first, albeit anticipated, "incident" stemming from his policy of protecting the convoys to Britain. On September 4, the US destroyer *Greer*, operating just southwest of Iceland on what the administration euphemistically called "the American Neutrality Patrol," underwent attack by a German submarine, which fired torpedoes but failed to score a hit. Although functioning primarily as a supply ship, *Greer*, a recommissioned World War I vessel, had orders to track and report enemy U-boats. It launched depth charges that likewise missed their target.

The administration responded belligerently, never mentioning that *Greer* had relayed the submarine's course to a British plane, which later dropped depth charges, also without effect. On September 11, just a day after the burial of his mother, the president delivered yet another fireside chat. Tough and uncompromising, he insisted that the *Greer* had been attacked without provocation, accused Germany of piracy, and declared that the United States would protect the entire Western Hemisphere. One did not wait for a rattlesnake to strike before crushing it, he declared. The navy would shoot on sight at any German or Italian warship discovered in "waters, the protection of which is necessary for American defense."[44]

The nation reacted much as it had to earlier such declarations: with general approval, yet continued reluctance to wage a real war. It was one thing to strike at Nazi marauders on the high seas and quite another to enter into a full-scale conflict. It did not help that congressional anti-interventionists forced the release of information demonstrating that the attack on *Greer* had come only after the ship had transmitted the German submarine's location to the British.

Other incidents in Icelandic waters followed. On October 17, a German torpedo hit but did not sink the destroyer *Kearney*, with the loss of eleven lives. On October 30, the destroyer *Reuben James* took 115 seamen to a watery grave.[45]

Still, no groundswell developed for a declaration of war. Interventionist Republicans, now reliably led by Wendell Willkie, supported the administration, but a majority of the GOP did not. Vermont senator George Aiken was in line with the bulk of his party when he asserted that the president had broken promises about neutrality and was "personally responsible" for the deaths of American sailors.[46]

Yet the public continued to support the step-by-step measures leading inexorably toward conflict. The administration pressed hard for repeal of the ban on the use of American flag vessels to transport goods to warring nations. In mid-November, Congress complied and also authorized the arming of US merchant ships. Whether the undeclared naval conflict that the nation was willing to fight would lead to full-scale war with Germany remained uncertain.[47]

NAZI GERMANY HAD BEEN THE MAIN OBJECT OF US-BRITISH DISCUSSION AT Argentia, but Japan was also on the agenda. That nation's ultimate goal of dominance, in not only China but the Philippines, French Indochina, British Malaya, and the Dutch East Indies, was no secret.

The administration maintained its support of Chiang Kai-shek's Chinese government as a means of keeping Japan bogged down. In the spring of 1941, Roosevelt quietly sanctioned the formation of an American Volunteer Group, recruited from the US Army Air Force and commanded by retired Captain Claire Chennault. By the beginning of December, Chennault had at least a hundred pilots training in South China and Burma. They would become famous as the Flying Tigers.

Both a sense of national destiny and a severe paucity of natural resources on its home islands motivated Japan's drive to the south. The war in Europe had given the Roosevelt administration an excuse to dry up or severely limit militarily important exports ranging from sophisticated optical equipment to scrap iron and steel. The sanctions failed to deter Tokyo. At the end of July 1941,

Japanese forces occupied southern Indochina, establishing a jumping-off point for operations against other targets in the region.

The administration responded sharply, freezing Japanese assets in the United States, subjecting all commercial transactions between American companies and Japan to government license, and barring Japanese flag vessels from the Panama Canal. The government's refusal to approve sales of strategic resources to Japan quickly became apparent; foremost on the list was the oil that fueled the Japanese war effort. A possible alternative source, the Dutch East Indies, also refused future petroleum sales. The policy was hard to fault as a moral matter. But in practice it meant that peace was now hostage to the ever-falling level of the national Japanese fuel stockpile.

Roosevelt, most of his lieutenants, and a majority of the American people simply did not take Japan seriously. Its civilian industry, in stark contrast to Germany's, seemed capable of producing only textiles, trinkets, and cheap pottery. Its bullying of a weak nation like China and its occupation of defeated France's colony of Indochina were repugnant. Its army, although intensively trained, was equipped mostly with second-rate weaponry. From the perspective of Washington, Japan seemed a nuisance rather than a major threat.

Such estimates were not dead wrong, but they were incomplete. They did not take into account the nation's fanatical sense of solidarity and determination, and they especially underestimated its sea power. The Japanese navy was well equipped, superbly trained, and probably more attuned to the emerging importance of aviation than any other in the world. Its aircraft carrier strength was roughly equivalent to that of the US Navy. Unlike the United States, which had to police both the Atlantic and the Pacific, Japan could concentrate on one ocean. The true two-ocean navy for which Roosevelt had secured appropriations was in the early stages of construction. Although no doubt formidable, the American fleet at Pearl Harbor was less than a sure victor in any encounter, however well prepared it might be for one.

In August, Japanese premier prince Konoye Fumimaro floated the idea of a face-to-face meeting with Roosevelt somewhere in the Pacific, but the proposal lacked specifics, and the administration stalled. Diplomatic contacts continued through the fall, with the president focused on the Atlantic. Japanese leaders fixed on declining oil reserves and the ongoing US naval expansion program that in a year or two would ensure American supremacy in the Pacific.

On October 18, Konoye's government fell. General Tojo Hideki, a militant expansionist, replaced him. Soon American intelligence discerned extensive military preparations for a Japanese offensive toward Southeast Asia. Both Britain and the United States diverted what military assets they could deploy into the Pacific. Churchill ostentatiously sent *Prince of Wales* to Singapore as the flagship of a cobbled-together defensive fleet. The United States began to deploy heavy bombers to the Philippines.

Discussions continued in Washington between the administration and Japanese representatives. Secretary of State Hull floated a proposed three-month modus vivendi that would have resumed limited trade in oil and other commodities. But any arrangement acceptable to the Japanese would look like rank appeasement. Harold Ickes confided to his diary on November 30 that if such an agreement were reached, "I would have promptly resigned from the Cabinet with a ringing statement attacking the arrangement and raising hell generally with the State Department. . . . I believe that the President would have lost the country on this issue." A wide public probably would have agreed with Ickes's reaction. The British and Chinese opposed any such accord. Roosevelt rejected it.[48]

On November 25, in a meeting with Hull, Henry Stimson, Frank Knox, General Marshall, and Admiral Stark, FDR said, as Stimson recorded in his diary, "We are likely to be attacked perhaps as soon as next Monday because the Japanese are notorious for attacking without warning. The question is how to maneuver them into firing the first shot without too much danger to ourselves." It is unclear whether Stimson reproduced Roosevelt's exact words. The fairest interpretation is that the president wanted to avoid any accusation of American aggression.[49]

Hull, receiving the Japanese ambassador on November 26, formally rejected Japanese demands for American abandonment of China, resumption of normal trade relations in all commodities, and facilitation of Japanese designs in Asia. Acting with the president's approval, he responded with a set of equally categorical requirements: Japanese withdrawal from China and Indochina and renunciation of all expansionism. On November 27, the War and Navy Departments sent notices to their commanders in the Philippines (General Douglas MacArthur and Admiral Thomas Hart) and Hawaii (Admiral Husband Kimmel and General Walter Short) to be on alert for a Japanese attack. The messages were explicit war warnings, admonishing the commanders to avoid firing a first shot if possible but to do nothing that might compromise their security.[50]

By the time Hull delivered his demands to Japan, a powerful Japanese task force containing all six of the Imperial Navy's fleet aircraft carriers had left Hitokappu Bay in the Kurile Islands on a circuitous 4,000-mile course that would take it to within 250 miles of Honolulu, Hawaii, and the naval base at Pearl Harbor.

US and British intelligence focused on firm reports of a strong Japanese military buildup in southern Indochina and an attack flotilla moving southward toward Thailand or Malaya. On December 1, Roosevelt instructed Secretary of State Hull and Undersecretary Welles to quiz Japanese ambassador Nomura Kichisaburo on these developments. Meeting with British ambassador Lord Halifax that same day and again on December 3, Roosevelt promised full military support if British possessions came under attack—with the understanding that he might need a few days "to get things into political shape."[51]

He might well have managed it; Gallup polls taken in September and November showed about two-thirds of the electorate willing to risk war with Japan in order to maintain the independence of the Dutch East Indies and Singapore. In any case, aid to Britain against Germany would inevitably spill over into a war in which Britain was fighting Germany's treaty ally, Japan. Revisionist historians would later assert that Roosevelt saw the defense of British interests in Southeast Asia against Japan as a "back door to war," but how could one back Britain in the Atlantic and not in the Pacific? Would Roosevelt have asked for a declaration of war or simply added another undeclared naval war to the one already under way? How valid was the apparent revisionist assumption that a victorious Japan and a crushed Britain would present no significant threat to vital American interests around the world? If George Gallup and his pollsters were correct, a majority of the American people had long since rejected such thinking.[52]

As it was, the president, Winston Churchill, and numerous leading US and British officials retired on the evening of December 6 knowing that war was almost certainly on the horizon.

SUNDAY, DECEMBER 7, WAS A CHILLY AND PLEASANT LATE-AUTUMN DAY IN Washington. Many government officials arose looking forward to attending the last professional football game of the season, the local Redskins versus the Philadelphia Eagles. Those who spent some time with the morning newspapers, however, found them filled with war news and a sense of impending crisis.

Roosevelt faced the day with apprehension. His cousins Mr. and Mrs. Frederick Adams and their children were visiting the White House, but he told Eleanor that he did not see how he possibly could join them for their predeparture lunch. At 12:30 p.m., he met for a half hour or so with the Chinese ambassador. Then he ordered a midday meal for himself and Harry Hopkins in the upstairs study. He and Hopkins were there when the phone rang at 1:40. Secretary of the Navy Knox relayed the report he had just received: Pearl Harbor was under attack.[53]

CHAPTER 22

COMMANDER IN CHIEF OF THE UNITED NATIONS

DECEMBER 1941–JANUARY 1943

ELEANOR DELIVERED THE FIRST PUBLIC WHITE HOUSE RESPONSE TO THE attack on Pearl Harbor. At 6:45 p.m., she read a hastily drafted statement on her regular Sunday NBC radio program:

> I should like to say just a word to the women in the country tonight. I have a boy at sea on a destroyer. For all I know he may be on his way to the Pacific. Two of my children are in coast cities on the Pacific. Many of you all over this country have boys in the services. . . . [Y]ou cannot escape a clutch of fear at your heart, and yet I hope that the certainty of what we have to meet will make you rise above these fears. We must go about our daily business more determined than ever to do the ordinary things as well as we can. . . . Whatever is asked of us, I am sure we can accomplish it. We are the free and unconquerable people of the United States of America.[1]

Franklin delivered his war message to Congress the following afternoon. It called December 7, 1941, "a date which will live in infamy." Emphasizing the "dastardly" nature of the attack on Pearl Harbor and enumerating other Japanese assaults throughout the Pacific, he declared,

No matter how long it may take us to overcome this premeditated invasion, the American people in their righteous might will win through to absolute victory. . . .

Hostilities exist. There is no blinking at the fact that our people, our territory, and our interests are in grave danger.

With confidence in our armed forces—with the unbounding determination of our people—we will gain the inevitable triumph, so help us God.[2]

Both the president and the first lady had made ringing statements designed to unite the American people against a treacherous foe. Eleanor had declared her own children at risk, just like those of Mr. and Mrs. Everybody. Franklin had proclaimed an all-out fight to the finish. A few die-hard isolationists tried to lay blame on Roosevelt, but even Senator Gerald Nye had to admit, "If the facts are as presented, there is only one thing for Congress to do—declare war."[3]

Before the day was out on December 8, Congress had passed a war resolution against Japan with one dissent in the House and a unanimous vote in the Senate. On December 9, Roosevelt delivered a radio address to the nation. He promised an immense war effort fueled by national unity and sacrifice. Reminding the nation that Germany and Italy were Japan's allies, he asserted that those two countries, "regardless of any formal declaration of war, consider themselves at war with the United States at this moment." On December 11, Hitler took the bait and announced that Germany was at war with the United States. Mussolini promptly followed him. Congress quickly reciprocated.[4]

After more than two years of cautious, step-by-step involvement, the United States was finally all-in.

TWO BATTLESHIPS DESTROYED, TWO MORE HEAVILY DAMAGED, ONE MODERately damaged, two requiring light repair, only one immediately serviceable, 188 aircraft destroyed, 2,400 Americans dead: the toll at Pearl Harbor was stunning. The news from Manila was at least equally dispiriting. General MacArthur had ignored standing orders to launch a bombing raid against Japanese bases on Formosa if war broke out. Japanese planes caught his B-17 bomber fleet on the ground ten hours after the Pearl Harbor raid and wiped it out.[5]

In both cases, commanders—Admiral Kimmel and General Short in Hawaii, General MacArthur in the Philippines—had seemingly ignored, or taken very lightly, explicit war warnings. Roosevelt's enemies would spare no effort to pin the blame on him, but he could hardly be faulted for the complacency of his

Pacific admirals and generals. At most, he bore some measure of responsibility for having approved their assignments.

The raid on Pearl Harbor was the spear tip of a far-flung Japanese offensive mainly directed at Malaya, the Dutch East Indies, and the Philippines. The Japanese also attacked two American island bases in the Aleutians and three in the western Pacific: Guam, Wake, and Midway. Only Midway managed to beat back the enemy.

The attack hit the British defense of Malaya hard. On December 10, *Prince of Wales* and the World War I–era battle cruiser *Repulse* had sortied in search of a Japanese attack fleet only to meet a hail of bombs and torpedoes from the air. Both sank with massive loss of life, demonstrating that battle fleets without air support faced disaster. Singapore, the last holdout on the Malay Peninsula, would surrender on February 15, 1942. The British would lose, in all, 130,000 troops killed, wounded, or captured.

There were at least two consolations: the three US aircraft carriers assigned to the Pacific fleet had all been away from Pearl Harbor, and the harbor facilities themselves remained essentially undamaged and instantly useable. Against that, however, was the certainty that the Philippines were in a hopeless position. An attack on Australia was possible. In Russia, the Germans were stalled, but by no means defeated, in front of Moscow and still pushing eastward in the South. The British were at best holding their own in a seesaw North African campaign.

On February 23, a week after the fall of Singapore, with American and Filipino troops retreating in the Philippines, Roosevelt delivered a fireside chat, the first of four that year. The talk was not among his best. At thirty-six and a half minutes, it was too long; for a few minutes a pesky cough marred the delivery. Nevertheless, it effectively summed up the nature and purpose of the war. The president reminded his listeners that the American Revolution too had begun with reverses and been fought through to victory. Asserting that American freedom rested on the establishment of liberty and justice "everywhere in the world," he asked his audience to consult a map of the "whole earth" in order to follow the course of a global war. Millions of Americans would obtain such maps, many of them simple foldouts tacked to the wall of a living room or den.

Roosevelt declared that with peak industrial production, military strength, and the alliance with Britain and the Soviet Union, America could prevail. He correctly denied the destruction of the American fleet at Pearl Harbor while soberly admitting the loss of three battleships; he also claimed, with gross inaccuracy, that the United States had inflicted more aircraft losses on the Japanese than vice versa. Above all, he asserted, the nation needed unity and sacrifice in the common cause. No defeatism! No work stoppages! No special gains or priv-ileges! Quoting Thomas Paine, he affirmed that "tyranny, like hell, is not easily conquered, yet we have this consolation with us, that the harder the sacrifice, the more glorious the triumph."[6]

The talk marked the turning of a historical page. The New Deal and the pol-itics it brought forth—bashing the wealthy, talking redistributionism, aligning the administration with organized labor—were on the shelf. The president was now a semiauthoritarian war leader demanding national unity and a single-minded focus on defeating a mortal challenge from abroad.

DETERMINED TO BE COMMANDER IN CHIEF IN EVERY SENSE OF THE PHRASE, Roosevelt used the title in official directives to his generals and admirals and expected them to employ it when referring to him. He would be the nation's grand strategist, controlling the large outlines of both military and diplomatic operations.

On the military side, he operated in direct contact with his service chiefs of staff: Admiral Ernest J. King, Army General George Marshall, and Army Air Force General Harold ("Hap") Arnold. Marshall was a superb staff officer of great dignity and rectitude, with a penchant for telling truth to power. King was temperamental and something of a bully, but Roosevelt liked his belliger-ent spirit. Arnold presided over an effectively independent air force with firm authority. All three were capable of saying no to their president, who was in turn willing to accept the response if it could be justified.

In July 1942, Roosevelt would appoint as his personal military chief of staff Admiral William D. Leahy, who had served as chief of naval operations from 1937 to 1939, retired, then been brought back to serve as US ambassador to Vichy France. (The president, none too subtly, had sent him to France on a navy cruiser.) Leahy, equally adept at assuming the persona of a gruff com-mander or that of a suave diplomat, would effectively act as chairman of the Joint Chiefs of Staff before the official creation of that post after the war.

Harry Hopkins continued to be Roosevelt's most important advisor without portfolio. His common sense, sound instincts, and undivided personal loyalty overrode his lack of formal qualifications for diplomatic activity. Roosevelt also increasingly relied on William Averell Harriman, a wealthy industrialist and financier who had traveled extensively in the Soviet Union on business ven-tures during the 1920s and lined up behind the National Recovery Adminis-tration during the New Deal. (It did not hurt that, like Roosevelt's man in the State Department, Sumner Welles, Harriman was a Groton product.) From

Argentia to Yalta, Harriman would be present at each of the major wartime conferences Roosevelt attended. Appointed Lend-Lease administrator in Britain in 1941, he was also effectively a "special envoy" to Churchill. In late 1943, the president would make him ambassador to the Soviet Union with a mandate to communicate directly with the White House. He was exhibit A in evidence of Roosevelt's determination to bypass the Department of State and especially to exclude Cordell Hull, whom the president increasingly considered a fusty old relic.[7]

Above all, Roosevelt wanted complete control of the information that came to him. When Winston Churchill visited the United States just after Pearl Harbor, he had installed in the White House a war communications center, replete with detailed maps. Impressed, Roosevelt copied it right down to the name "Map Room." Confidential messages came into the Map Room from army lines and went out through navy lines. The system ensured that only the president would have a complete file.[8]

By virtue of America's wealth, industrial might, and potential military power, Roosevelt was functionally, if not officially, at the head of an improbable coalition in which his two leading partners were Churchill and Stalin. Each had his distinct ideological perspective and concrete objectives. Each understood the necessity of unity. Of the three, Roosevelt was probably alone in believing that this alliance of convenience could stand in a vaguely perceived postwar world.

The president, exhibiting the instincts of his kinsman Theodore, was a man of consummate realism when it came to issues of power. He was also about equally committed to an overriding and unrealistic ideology, essentially derived from the liberalism of Woodrow Wilson. It was embodied in the Atlantic Charter, which, depending on one's perspective, was either a shining statement of principle or a confession of hopeless naiveté. He probably never expected 100 percent implementation of the charter, which he no doubt saw as an important motivational tool for the American war effort. All indications are that he really believed in its principles and envisioned himself, in contrast to his two allies (the Old Tory and the Old Bolshevik), as voicing the aspirations of the common people of the world.

ON DECEMBER 7, 1941, ROOSEVELT'S RELATIONSHIP WITH STALIN WAS STILL IN a very early phase, with only thirteen messages having passed between them. His interaction with Churchill totaled about two hundred communications and the personal meeting at Argentia. Just five days after Pearl Harbor, Churchill, accompanied by an entourage of civilian and military advisers, was aboard the new battleship *Duke of York* on his way to Washington.

Churchill's visit to America, which he code-named ARCADIA, had multiple purposes. The most fundamental, as Chief of the Imperial General Staff Sir Alan Brooke put it, was "to ensure that American help to this country does not dry up." It was also to provide a strong British input into the military strategy of the war. In Brooke's recollection, someone remarked that circumspection had been necessary up to that point in dealing with the United States. Churchill replied, "Oh! That is the way we talked to her while we were wooing her, now that she is in the harem we talk to her quite differently!" Now, the prime minister thought, was the time for a well-prepared Britain to seize control of the direction of the war. Now, he also certainly believed, was the time to personalize the alliance as never before with a display of his outsized ego and rhetorical powers.[9]

During the eight-day voyage to the United States, Churchill began work on four strategy papers, which he would present to Roosevelt. The first, a survey of "the Atlantic Front," focused heavily on a need to clear the enemy from North Africa and secure control of the Mediterranean, the "lifeline" to Suez and Britain's South Asian empire. The second and fourth papers, on "the Pacific Front," conceded the huge temporary advantage of the Japanese and the need to fight a delaying action marked by inevitable losses of territory while the American and British navies built a powerful capability based on aircraft carriers. The third paper, titled "The Campaign of 1943," projected that year as the target date for a major invasion of the European continent, which, assuming large-scale uprisings against the Germans by captive peoples, might bring the war to a quick end. In their large outlines, these documents forecast the course of the war.[10]

The American high command reaffirmed the ABC-1 priority of Germany first but, from the beginning, questioned the British inclination to "peck around the periphery." Senior US officers favored a rapid buildup of American forces in Britain, followed by a direct Anglo-American strike into the heartland of Europe. They actually floated to the skeptical British the possibility of establishing a "lodgment" on the continent that somehow could withstand Wehrmacht counterattacks. The issue was left unresolved.[11]

The talks produced an achievement of great importance: establishment of the Combined Chiefs of Staff, a unified US-British command structure based in Washington. Derived from the American experience of World War I in which the independence of the Allied commands had impeded coordination, the development brought senior American and British officers into a common structure, albeit with US predominance. ARCADIA produced a signature press release. Labeled "Declaration by the United Nations," it had twenty-six signatories, including countries actively at war with Germany or Japan, numerous governments-in-exile, and several Caribbean republics. Released on New Year's Day, 1942, it reaffirmed the principles of the Atlantic Charter, stated a common determination, and produced a name for the alliance: the United Nations.[12]

Churchill spent three weeks in America, leaving a deep impression on both Roosevelt and the larger public. As a guest at the White House, he was both demanding and entertaining. His capacity for alcohol was overwhelming: a tumbler of sherry with breakfast, Scotch and soda at lunch, champagne at dinner, brandy afterward, then more Scotch and soda. As Chief Butler Alonzo Fields remembered it, he once asked for a favor: "I hope you will come to my defense if some day someone should claim that I am a teetotaler." Yet he also worked hard on conference matters and kept in daily touch with London. In private, he generally wore the zippered paramilitary overalls he called a "siren suit."[13]

In public, Churchill charmed a wide audience. He took over a presidential press conference from Roosevelt. Addressing a joint session of Congress, he remarked, "I cannot help reflecting that if my father had been American and my mother British, instead of the other way round, I might have got here on my own." Before the Canadian parliament, he ridiculed the comment of the defeated French general Maxime Weygand in 1940 that Britain would have its neck wrung like a helpless chicken: "Some chicken! . . . Some neck!"[14]

The dynamics of the Roosevelt-Churchill relationship could be grand to watch. The two men at one level sincerely admired each other. All the same, their comradeship was complex and often difficult. Aside from not liking to be upstaged, Roosevelt remained at his core an ideological liberal prone to see Churchill's beloved British Empire as an exploitative enterprise that victimized subjugated peoples around the globe. He had long fixated on Imperial Preference trade policies that he believed excluded American enterprises and products.

On January 13, 1942, the night before the prime minister departed for Britain, Roosevelt could not resist the temptation to haze him at a small White House dinner party. One of the guests, noted author Louis Adamic, recalled the president's words a few years later:

> You know my friend over there doesn't understand how most of our people feel about Britain and her role in the life of other peoples. . . . [W]e're opposed to imperialism—we can't stomach it. . . .
>
> I remember very clearly that when I was seven or thereabouts, in 1889 or '90 and my mother took me to England, and we saw Queen Victoria drive in her carriage down a London street, why, I hated the old woman.

Adamic thought to himself, probably accurately, "He must have said all this to Churchill before. He's using me to rub it in." Churchill, knowing that he had no choice, took it all, jaw clinched, silent and impassive.[15]

The next day, as Churchill departed, Roosevelt's final words to him were "Trust me to the bitter end." At the end of the month, responding to birthday greetings from the prime minister, he said, "It is fun to be in the same decade with you." There is no reason to doubt the sincerity of those statements, but we must remember the president made them after he had established his dominance. That done, he could be a generous and supportive ally. He wrote to Churchill on March 18, "There is no use giving a single further thought to Singapore or the Dutch Indies. . . . Australia must be held and . . . we are willing to undertake that. India must be held, and you must do that; but frankly I do not worry so much about that problem. . . . You must hold Egypt, the Canal, Syria, Iran and the route to the Caucasus. . . . I know you will keep up your optimism and your grand driving force."[16]

IN LATE JANUARY 1942, THE FIRST SIGNIFICANT DETACHMENTS OF US TROOPS arrived in Britain, the small beginnings of a two-and-a-half-year buildup that would transform an insular country into a large and effective invasion base. In late June, General Marshall dispatched his valued aide Major General Dwight D. Eisenhower to London as their commander.

At home, most Americans riveted their attention on the Philippines. MacArthur, in conformity with long-established war plans, fought a delaying action and retreated to the American island fortress of Corregidor, off the tip of the Bataan Peninsula. Relief by sea was impossible. Roosevelt decided that MacArthur, despite his inexplicable unreadiness in the wake of Pearl Harbor, was too famous, and perhaps too politically connected, to sacrifice. In early March, the president ordered him to turn over Corregidor to Major General Jonathan Wainwright and retreat to Australia, where he would assume command of Allied forces in the southwestern Pacific. Wainwright would preside over a determined resistance until finally forced to surrender on May 6. By then some 80,000 already captured American and Filipino soldiers had endured a brutal and homicidal "death march." Word of that atrocity assured that the Pacific War for both sides would become one of extermination.

Having witnessed how World War I had ground Woodrow Wilson down, Roosevelt knew he needed to pace himself. He advised Churchill to follow his example: "Once a month I go to Hyde Park for four days, crawl into a hole and pull the hole in after me. I am called on the telephone only if something of really great importance occurs. I wish you would try it." It was good advice, but the president would learn there was no effective escape from the grueling responsibility of command.[17]

His strongest instinct was to strike back at the enemy as quickly as possible, for morale more than for effect. At his request, the army air force and navy developed a plan to steam a small task force into the Pacific, launch light B-25 bombers about six hundred miles from Tokyo, bomb the city, and then fly to bases in China. Lieutenant Colonel James Doolittle, an already famed aviator widely believed to be, in the words of his copilot, "the best pilot in the Air Force," commanded the operation. Doolittle recruited from the cream of the service's talent. Roosevelt surely recognized the risk he was taking with high-value personnel and deemed it worth the gamble.[18]

On April 18, 1942, Doolittle's squadron, sighted by a Japanese picket ship fifty miles farther from Tokyo than originally planned, took off from the aircraft carrier *Hornet*, dropped its payload on Japan, and made for China. Amazingly, Doolittle and most of the participants survived. They became instant American heroes and lifted the nation's spirits. Where, newsmen asked, had the mission flown from? Roosevelt answered with a big smile and a reference to the mythical realm of James Hilton's *Lost Horizon*: "Shangri-la"![19]

The raid itself was of little material consequence—a few bombs dropped on the Japanese capital hardly amounted to a pinprick—but it delivered a severe blow to Japanese pride and ignited a renewed determination to devote Japan's naval power to the conquest of the western Pacific, from Australia in the South to Midway Island in the East.

Japan faced a US Navy that displayed remarkable resilience. Some three weeks after the Doolittle raid, an American force engaged a Japanese invasion fleet bound for Port Moresby, New Guinea, a position from which Japan could menace Australia. In the ensuing Battle of the Coral Sea, the United States lost one precious aircraft carrier, *Lexington*, and suffered substantial damage to another, *Yorktown*, but still managed to turn back the enemy. Off Midway just a month later, a limping *Yorktown*, along with the carriers *Enterprise* and *Hornet*, defended the island base against a numerically superior Japanese incursion. American naval aviators managed to hit and sink four Japanese carriers. Japan's navy would never recover from the blow. The United States lost only *Yorktown*.

At the beginning of August, the navy landed a division of marines on the island of Guadalcanal in the Solomon chain, initiating a months-long battle that raged on land and sea. In the naval fighting, both sides suffered important losses, but in early 1943 the Allies would secure Guadalcanal. The United States would have only one operational aircraft carrier left in the Pacific, but Australia would be safe and Midway effectively removed from Japanese reach. American ship-yards would replace the carrier losses at a rate the Japanese could not approach. There was every reason to believe that their onslaught had been stopped.

Ten days after the landing on Guadalcanal, a company of marine raiders staged a surprise attack on Makin Island in the Gilberts chain. Their leader, Lieutenant Colonel Evans Carlson, a political radical who enjoyed the friend-ship of the president, took with him as commander of the landing party Major James Roosevelt. Four months short of his thirty-fifth birthday, Jimmy had a medical record that should have disqualified him from combat. In the fighting that followed he was an exemplary leader; at one point, he had a field telephone shot out of his hand. He later received the Navy Cross and an Army Silver Star. One of his men described him to a friend of Eleanor as "a prince." The action inflicted heavy casualties on a small Japanese garrison but was of even less material consequence than the Doolittle raid. All the same, Hollywood used it as the basis for a popular movie, *Gung Ho!* It would be Jimmy's one taste of combat. He was brought stateside and assigned to training duties.[20]

Victory in the Pacific was still a distant prospect, but by the fall of 1942, the United States had taken the offensive. When and where would the European second front appear? And would it be possible to maintain the developing alliance with the Soviet Union?

RUSSIA WAS A DISTANT AND DEMANDING ALLY, SCORNING GENEROUS LEND-Lease assistance as inadequate, harassing US diplomats, and constantly reminding America that the Red Army was battling the Nazis on the eastern front alone. Nonetheless, supporting the USSR's fight against Germany was clearly of prime importance. Instinctively looking to build on the personal rela-tionship Harry Hopkins had established, Roosevelt would consistently strive for a man-to-man bond of confidence and trust with his Soviet counterpart, Josef Stalin. His penchant for dealing with the Russian dictator through special envoys and direct messages frustrated his ambassadors and may have led Stalin to congratulate himself as a shrewd manipulator.[21]

Almost certainly entertaining some illusions about the essential "progres-sivism" of the Soviet Union, Roosevelt and Hopkins were also concerned about the possibility of a separate peace on the eastern front. The USSR and Germany had signed an agreement in 1939; they might conceivably conclude a truce of convenience that would leave Hitler free to transfer the bulk of his forces to the west. The impetus for American deal making with Stalin and the inevitable concessions that would accompany the process began early.

Meeting with Soviet ambassador Maxim Litvinov on March 12, 1942, the president delivered assurance that he would not oppose the USSR's territorial ambitions in eastern Europe, that he had in fact thought it folly to take away from Russia the Baltic states and the eastern half of Poland after World War I. He also remarked that it would be politically unwise to make his commitment public, possibly leaving Litvinov and Stalin wondering whether he was playing them. A year later Roosevelt would tell British foreign secretary Anthony Eden that, as Harry Hopkins summarized it, "he did not like the idea of turning the Baltic States over to Russia and that she would lose a great deal of public opinion in this country." The two statements were not necessarily irreconcilable. The comment to Eden likely reflected political concerns more than personal principle.[22]

On May 29, Soviet foreign minister Vyacheslav Molotov arrived in Washington from London, where he had concluded a treaty with Britain. He stayed at the White House as an honored guest. A servant, unpacking his luggage, found among his belongings black bread, cured Russian sausage, and a loaded revolver. When the Secret Service reported the latter item to Roosevelt, he laughed it off, but he might also have reflected on the paranoia that the items signified.

The talks with Molotov over the next few days were awkward. Palpably uncomfortable with the tedious process of translation between Russian and English, Roosevelt found the doctrinaire Molotov more trying than the cosmopolitan Litvinov. (As Robert Sherwood reflected later, Roosevelt had never before met a doctrinaire Bolshevik.) But he was determined to handle the major issues himself, much as he had done with Churchill. Secretary of State Hull functioned more as an interested bystander than an active participant.[23]

Molotov pushed hard for two objectives: copious Lend-Lease shipments to the USSR and quick establishment of a second front on the European continent in strength sufficient to draw forty German divisions away from the Soviet Union. The first demand was difficult but possible. Throughout the war the United States seldom questioned Soviet Lend-Lease requests and made shipments on terms considerably more generous than those offered the British. In response to the second demand, Roosevelt asked General Marshall to confirm that plans were under development for a second front, then, as the American translator paraphrased it, "authorized Mr. Molotov to inform Mr. Stalin that we expect the formation of a second front this year." In fact, however, American war planners were already beginning to envision the exercise, if attempted at all, as a hopeless "sacrifice play" undertaken to keep the USSR in the war.[24]

On the evening of May 31, Roosevelt wrote to Churchill, "Molotov's visit is, I think, a real success because we have got on a personal footing of candor and as good friendship as can be acquired through an interpreter." On June 12, Hopkins wrote to American ambassador John G. Winant in London, "Molotov's visit went extremely well. He and the President got along famously and I am sure that we at least bridged one more gap between ourselves and Russia." Goodwill, as the Roosevelt-Churchill relationship demonstrated, could lubricate alliances. But Hopkins and his chief seemed to assume that bonhomie could override profound differences in worldview and national interests.[25]

In World War I, it had been possible to transport a huge, semi-prepared army to France and train it further there before finally taking it into combat. In 1942, the Allies would have to attack Hitler's *Festung Europa* from Britain across the treacherous English Channel. The Soviet Union demanded such an operation before the end of the year. American military leaders thought they could comply. The British, more realistic, insisted that lack of landing craft and sufficient numbers of trained troops made an invasion impossible before 1943 at the earliest. On June 9, the most charismatic figure in the British high command, Vice Admiral Lord Louis Mountbatten, met with Roosevelt and Hopkins to survey the war situation. In a wide-ranging discussion, he emphasized the difficulties of an attack across the channel. With the issue still unsettled, Roosevelt invited Churchill to return to the United States for another strategy meeting. The prime minister, accompanied by his military staff, journeyed to America ten days later for the second Washington conference.[26]

The two men talked privately at Hyde Park on June 19 and 20. Roosevelt personally met Churchill at the Poughkeepsie airport, drove him to Springwood, and, just as he had done with the king and queen, motored recklessly around the estate. "On several occasions the car poised and backed on the grass verges of the precipices over the Hudson," Churchill recalled. "I was careful not to take his attention off the driving." Churchill explained to Roosevelt and Hopkins in persuasive detail the impossibility of a quick attack on the continent, arguing instead for a landing in North Africa, where Britain was fighting a tough back-and-forth tank campaign with German general Erwin Rommel's Afrika Corps. That evening, they boarded the presidential train for an overnight trip to Washington.[27]

In a series of intensive meetings over the next five days, the British made their case. The atmosphere shifted precariously between fraternity and hostility. The hot Washington weather did not help. Still, the dour, businesslike Sir Alan Brooke found himself more impressed than he had expected to be by Roosevelt and positively captivated when the president asked if he was related to a Sir Victor Brooke, who had visited Hyde Park some fifty years earlier (Sir Victor was the general's father).[28]

On June 21, while meeting with Roosevelt in the Oval Office, Churchill and Brooke received the news that Britain's eastern Libyan bastion at Tobruk had fallen to the Germans, leaving Egypt and the Suez Canal vulnerable. The president immediately asked, "What can we do to help?" Brooke, years later, recalled "vividly being impressed by the tact and heartfelt sympathy. . . . There was not one word too much or too little." In short order three hundred US Sherman tanks were diverted to the African campaign. Such moments alternated with the dissents of General Marshall, Admiral King, and other American military leaders, who remained convinced that the Allies could hit the Germans directly in Europe and knock them back hard.[29]

When Churchill departed on the evening of June 25, Roosevelt had taken no firm decision. King, anxious to build on the American victory at Midway, advocated a Pacific-first strategy and may have thought he set one in motion by approving plans for the invasion of Guadalcanal. Marshall, Arnold, Eisenhower, and other senior army officers remained wedded to an assault on northern France, although they knew the Germans had twenty-five divisions already stationed in the country and possessed overwhelming advantages with interior lines of transportation and communications. The Combined Chiefs of Staff in Washington continued to do business professionally, but the strategic division limited their effectiveness.

The issue, which Roosevelt let hang too long, had to be resolved. In mid-July, Marshall and Arnold forced the president's hand by joining with King in recommending a shift in emphasis to the Pacific if an invasion of France was to be postponed. Roosevelt, who received their memorandum at Hyde Park, reacted sharply. He demanded a detailed plan, which of course did not exist. Supplied with an admission that it did not, he followed up with a brusque dismissal, telling his service chiefs that they had recommended "exactly what Germany hoped the United States would do" by advocating a diversion of troops to "a lot of islands whose occupation will not affect the world situation this year or next." The proposal would relieve neither Russia nor the embattled Near East. "Therefore it is disapproved as of the present." His signature underscored his authority: "Roosevelt C. in C."[30]

Back in Washington on July 15, he saw Secretary of War Henry L. Stimson, to whom he stated his displeasure with a Chiefs of Staff attitude that amounted to "taking up your dishes and going away." General Marshall followed and later told Stimson that he and the president had had a "thumping argument." Roosevelt's only concession was to send Marshall and Admiral King, accompanied by Harry Hopkins, to London for talks with the British on an early offensive. He gave them a detailed memorandum of instructions that demonstrated the direction in which he was leaning and left them little room for moving away from it. It demanded feasible action for American troops in 1942, expressed doubts about the possibilities for a landing in France, and emphasized the importance of holding the Middle East.[31]

The British had regrouped behind a strong defensive line anchored at El Alamein, just sixty-two miles from Cairo. They seemed likely to beat off further attacks. During the talks that followed in London, the president sent cables prodding his representatives toward the North African plan. Brooke summed up the results in his diary: "A very trying week, but it is satisfactory to think that we have got just what we wanted out of the USA chiefs."[32]

Roosevelt none too subtly had dictated grand strategy to his military Chiefs of Staff. Part of his motivation was no doubt political: a "sacrificial" invasion of France would be bad for him and his party. But it also might be catastrophic for the larger war effort.

He laid out his thinking in a conversation with Harry Hopkins on the evening of July 15. The United States would wage a holding action in the Pacific. Germany was the major threat, the European theater all-important. If an invasion of the continent was not possible, then North Africa and the Middle East were areas of critical urgency. Rommel could not be allowed to drive to Suez, establish German dominance in the Middle East, gain access to important oil supplies, jeopardize the Persian Gulf supply route to the USSR, and conceivably lay the basis for a meeting of triumphant German and Japanese forces in India. These considerations pointed toward a North African enterprise that was doable in short order and carried a high probability of victory.[33]

The president knew full well that, whatever their reservations, his military chiefs could only salute and obey. The normally volatile King, Marshall recalled years later, went along "without a quibble." Marshall himself, fourteen years later, complained to his biographer, "We failed to see that the leader in a democracy has to keep the people entertained." Actually, Roosevelt correctly believed that he had a sounder grasp of the big picture than did King and Marshall. He also expressed hope to his confidants that newspapers would carry banner headlines proclaiming the invasion before the midterm elections.[34]

ALTHOUGH ROOSEVELT AND CHURCHILL FOCUSED MAINLY ON THE SECOND front during their meeting, they also concluded another agreement that they must have understood to be potentially even more important: to pool their research programs on the military development of atomic energy. Albert Einstein had first alerted Roosevelt to the possibility by letter in 1939, but the administration had taken only tentative steps before Pearl Harbor. The British had been more active but lacked the resources for so ambitious a program. Pearl Harbor and the certain knowledge that German physicists were at work on an atomic project unleashed nearly unlimited support for an American-led drive to build an atomic bomb.[35]

In August 1942, the Army Corps of Engineers established a lavishly funded branch called the Manhattan Engineering District, commanded by Brigadier General Leslie Groves. Within a year and a half, Groves presided over a scientific empire based in Los Alamos, New Mexico; Oak Ridge, Tennessee; and Hanford, Washington. University of California physicist J. Robert Oppenheimer, working as his civilian deputy, headed a team of scientists—Americans, British, and émigrés from Nazi-occupied Europe—intent on developing a weapon sure to win the war.

JOSEF STALIN LEARNED OF THE ATOMIC PROJECT THROUGH HIS REMARKABLY productive espionage network in the United States and quickly initiated a Soviet effort. For the moment, however, he had far more urgent priorities.

By mid-August, the German drive through the Ukraine had reached the industrial city of Stalingrad on the west bank of the Volga River. The city was strategically significant; its name made it symbolically vital. The Soviet army poured seemingly endless reinforcements into the struggle. The Wehrmacht pushed forward in urban house-to-house fighting. The ensuing conflagration went on for the rest of the year, devouring men at appalling rates and becoming the decisive battle of not just the eastern front but the entire war.

Churchill assumed responsibility for personally telling Stalin that the second front would have to wait until 1943. Traveling to Moscow by way of Egypt and Iran, he met with the Soviet leader on August 1, accompanied by Roosevelt's special envoy to Britain, Averell Harriman. The atmosphere was made all the more touchy by an Anglo-American decision to suspend northern-route Lend-Lease shipments to the USSR after German submarines and aircraft taking advantage of the Arctic summer's round-the-clock daylight had almost totally destroyed convoy PQ-17.

Stalin did not take the second front postponement lightly. As was becoming a standard pattern of Soviet behavior, he became angry and demanding, accusing the British of cowardice, then relenting when the prime minister promised a massive strategic bombing offensive against German cities. Always wanting more supplies from the West, he was somewhat mollified when his visitors assured him of a southern route that would run through Iran.[36]

The relationship between Roosevelt and Stalin was less volatile but had its own rough edges and uncertainties. The correspondence was polite and businesslike, the relationship lubricated by large quantities of American aircraft, tanks, trucks, and high explosives. But specters hung over it. The biggest was the possibility that, in one fashion or another, the USSR might be forced either to surrender or to make a separate peace. Another was that Stalin might try to play Roosevelt and Churchill against each other.

Roosevelt had faith in the power of his personality. "I think I can personally handle Stalin better than either your Foreign Office or my State Department," he told Churchill on March 18, 1942. "He thinks he likes me better." This at a time when he and Stalin had conducted fewer than two dozen exchanges! He would persist in the belief that he could establish a relationship of trust and friendship with an ally every bit as bloody handed as Hitler and as inflexibly committed to the destruction of liberal capitalism.[37]

ON NOVEMBER 8, 1942, A MOSTLY AMERICAN ALLIED FORCE OF MORE THAN 100,000 troops stormed the beaches of French North Africa. The 35,000 American soldiers who landed at Casablanca under the command of General George S. Patton were transported directly from the United States in the largest amphibious operation in American history. The rest came from bases in Britain. Resistance from the French quickly ceased when the Vichy leader in North Africa, Admiral Jean Darlan, agreed to capitulate in exchange for Allied recognition as the continuing supreme authority. The "Darlan Deal," however justifiable militarily, received wide condemnation in both the United States and Britain as a compromise with fascism, but it gave the Americans most of their objectives with only light casualties. Darlan himself was assassinated shortly thereafter and replaced by a more palatable Frenchman.

On the other side of the continent, the British army, thoroughly reequipped and commanded by General Sir Bernard Montgomery, had begun its own offensive against the Afrika Corps on October 23. By November 8, the British were advancing on Tobruk. It was briefly possible to envision an enemy caught between rapidly advancing irresistible forces and ground to pieces in a relatively quick final battle. Instead, the Germans rushed reinforcements to both African fronts. American forces soon reached the Tunisian border, but from there their advance would become a five-month slugfest. Still, from early on it was a pretty sure thing that the Germans were only buying time in a lost cause.

On New Year's Eve, 1942, Franklin, Eleanor, and a group of their closest friends watched a soon-to-be-released feature film from Warner Brothers titled *Casablanca*. The time had come for another Roosevelt-Churchill conference to make a firm decision on the next move in the war and enjoy a victory lap on conquered territory.[38]

For Churchill, the trip to their destination involved simply a ten-hour flight from Britain. For Roosevelt, given the menacing presence of German submarines in the Atlantic and the still evolving capabilities of transatlantic air transportation, it was an adventure. Supposedly bound for Hyde Park, he left Washington by train for Miami on the evening of January 9, 1943, accompanied by Hopkins, Leahy, numerous other aides, and security personnel. They arrived early on the morning of January 11 and at about 5:00 a.m. transferred to two Pan American Boeing 314 Flying Boats. This was the first time an American president would travel by air while in office. The largest and most advanced passenger planes of the day, the 314s each accommodated a maximum of forty passengers. Fitted with a dining room and separate sleeping area, the planes were luxurious and well heated, but the cabin was unpressurized, limiting the altitude achievable without passenger access to bottled oxygen. Top speed with a good tail wind was two hundred miles per hour.[39]

Twelve hours later, the president's plane came down just north of Venezuela at the American naval base on Trinidad, acquired in the Destroyer Deal of 1940. The travelers had dinner, retired early, and arose at 4:00 a.m. on January 12. Leahy, ill with influenza, had to be left behind. By 5:30, the planes were back in the air again, bound for Belem, Brazil, at the delta of the Amazon River. After a two-and-a-half-hour refueling stop, they took off for an overnight nineteen-hour flight of more than 2,000 miles across the Atlantic to the British base at Bathurst, Gambia, and the US Navy cruiser *Memphis*, which would billet them over the next night. Roosevelt, on the basis of a quick auto ride to the docks, wrote that Bathurst was an "awful, pestiferous hole." On the morning of January 14, the party boarded an Army C-54 transport for a 1,200-mile final hop to, as Roosevelt mockingly called it, "that well-known spot, 'somewhere in North Africa.'"[40]

That afternoon, surely exhausted but exhilarated, he finally arrived at his destination. A trip that fifty years in the future would involve a half-day direct flight of 3,800 miles had consumed five days and traversed approximately 7,300 miles. Two of his sons—Elliott, an air force lieutenant colonel, and Franklin Jr., a navy lieutenant assigned to a destroyer—met him there.

THE MOST IMMEDIATE ISSUE TO BE DECIDED AT CASABLANCA WAS THE NEXT step in the war. The US Joint Chiefs wanted to devote all resources to a buildup in England and to invade France before the end of the year. The British were determined to stay in the Mediterranean, attacking and occupying Sicily, then moving on to either Italy or Greece and the Balkans. They drew on research done for them by a shipload of military and diplomatic officials in direct contact with London. The sessions featured the haughty and imperious manner of General Brooke on the British side and the explosive temper of Admiral King on the American side. The much respected British liaison to the Combined Chiefs of Staff in Washington, Field Marshal Sir John Dill, employed his skill at soothing ruffled egos and finding formulas for agreement to smooth over most of the differences. Roosevelt agreed that control of the Mediterranean was a strategic imperative that required ousting the Germans from Sicily. Italy would be a logical and necessary next step. Beyond that, he was not prepared to support Churchill's enthusiasms.[41]

Roosevelt and Churchill needed to reach agreement on a commander for an emerging Free French military force. Churchill favored Charles de Gaulle; Roosevelt wanted General Henri Giraud. Imposing men with no taint of collaboration with the Germans, both were also impossibly vain, inordinately touchy, obsessed with a sense of their own destinies, and barely able to speak to each other. In the end, there was little to do but cobble together a joint command structure. Giraud, who lacked de Gaulle's political and rhetorical skills, would eventually fade from the scene.[42]

One of Roosevelt's priorities was to appraise the American commander in chief of the North African operation, Eisenhower, now a lieutenant general. They met for the first time on January 15. Roosevelt struck Eisenhower as buoyant and optimistic, expecting a quick end to the military campaign, and prematurely focused on the future of France and its empire. When the president demanded a date for the end of hostilities, Eisenhower "blurted out" May 15— as it turned out just two days later than the final Axis surrender in Tunisia.[43]

Roosevelt's evaluation was mixed. Ike seemed rather "jittery," he told Marshall. Observing that Eisenhower was in a rather difficult position as commander of British officers who held higher rank, Marshall recommended a promotion to four-star status. The president stated firmly that there would be no promotion until the campaign was over and Eisenhower had definitively earned it. (Marshall persisted. On February 11, a week and a half after Roosevelt's return to the United States, Eisenhower received his promotion.)[44]

In a conversation with his aide, Captain Harry Butcher, Eisenhower recalled Roosevelt as believing that he could "dictate the peace" at the end of the war.

"Perhaps lend-lease gives him a feeling Uncle Sam can foreclose on its mortgage," mulled Butcher. "Wonder what luck we will have 'dictating' a peace to Uncle Joe Stalin?"[45]

Josef Stalin hovered over all the deliberations. Ever since Hopkins's report of his first mission to Moscow, Roosevelt had been anxious to meet the Soviet leader. By the beginning of 1943, with Soviet forces clearly on the verge of a crushing victory at Stalingrad, such a rendezvous seemed especially necessary. Stalin declined an invitation to the Casablanca conference, pleading his day-to-day command responsibilities. In fact, at no time during his long tenure as dictator of the Soviet Union would he venture into territory not controlled by Soviet troops. Roosevelt, like most Americans, seems never to have plumbed the implications. Stalin's formal and businesslike correspondence, while thanking the United States for its massive Lend-Lease aid, continually reminded his allies of their pledge to open a second front in Europe. The lack of a face-to-face meeting contributed to an uncertainty about the Soviet-American relationship that would endure for most of the rest of the year.[46]

Roosevelt also was increasingly uncomfortable with the imperialist implications of his alliance with Churchill. Snap impressions from his overnight stopover in Bathurst had deepened his sense of the British Empire as a cruelly exploitative project. Elliott later recalled his observations: the natives in rags, working for one shilling, nine pence and a bowl of rice a day. "Dirt. Disease. Very high mortality rate. . . . Life expectancy—you'd never guess what it is. Twenty-six years. Those people are treated worse than the livestock. Their cattle live longer!" On January 22, the president entertained the sultan of Morocco at dinner. He needled Churchill much as he had done a year earlier in front of Louis Adamic, telling the sultan to beware of European exploiters and promising American aid to modernize his nation.[47]

Elliott later wrote that his father declared, "Don't think for a moment, Elliott, that Americans would be dying in the Pacific tonight, if it hadn't been for the shortsighted greed of the French and the British and the Dutch." The remark, if accurately remembered, was astonishing. How could European imperialism, however deplorable, be held responsible for Japan's own imperial ambitions and loathsome behavior? The emerging breakup of the wartime alliance affected Elliott's recollections, published three years later based on memories formed and notes he took at the time, but they are consistent with other indications of his father's attitude. After the war, the president told Elliott, the empires would become trusteeships under the supervision of a new United Nations Organization that would require European masters to develop educational and health systems, higher standards of living, and an eventual option for independence.[48]

That future was as utopian as anything Woodrow Wilson had ever envisioned. And it lacked elementary perspective. Had the people of Gambia been prosperous and happy before British rule? Had they enjoyed more freedom? The normally tough-minded and realistic Roosevelt condemned Western imperialism in the same categorical fashion on other, mostly private, occasions.[49]

For liberals of the time, living in the fevered atmosphere of a world at war, the rhetoric of a new order of things was intoxicating. Given the sacrificial nature of the war effort, it was perhaps necessary to believe that a new world would transcend the imperfections of the old, that oppressed peoples would universally embrace liberal-democratic virtues. Yet it was also true that when Roosevelt and the wider liberal community talked about the breakup of empires, somehow the Soviet empire, stretching from the Bering Strait to the Baltic Sea and harboring open designs on eastern Europe, seems never to have come to mind. Were the people of Gambia more oppressed than the people of Ukraine? Some questions were best left unasked.

On the last day of the Casablanca meeting, January 24, Roosevelt and Churchill held a press conference. Roosevelt began with a statement about war aims, meandered into a recollection of U. S. ("unconditional surrender") Grant, then announced a policy to which he had secured Churchill's agreement: "The elimination of German, Japanese, and Italian war power means the unconditional surrender by Germany, Italy, or Japan. . . . It does not mean the destruction of the population of Germany, Italy, and Japan, but it does mean the destruction of the philosophies in those countries which are based on conquest and the subjugation of other people." Nazi propagandists would misrepresent the policy as a determination to eradicate the German *Volk*. Perhaps it stiffened Germany's resistance, but it also signaled to the Soviet Union that the Allies were in the fight to the finish. In truth, no one could believe that another "armistice" like that of 1918 would end this war.[50]

At Churchill's insistence, he and Roosevelt drove 150 miles south to Marrakesh, where in earlier days the prime minister had spent time relaxing and painting the Atlas Mountains. That evening, at a villa located outside the city, they had a happy dinner—no one-upmanship, no talk of portentous issues or the hard days ahead. Local servants carried the president to the roof of the villa to view the peaks, illuminated by the setting sun. The next day, Churchill, roused from his sleep and wearing as an overcoat a gaudy robe emblazoned with a large dragon, went to the airport for a final farewell as his friend embarked on the long trip back to America.

Roosevelt returned to the United States by the same route he had taken, pausing briefly in Brazil for a meeting with his favorite Latin American dictator,

Getulio Vargas. On the morning of January 27, 1943, newspapers across the United States filled their front pages with the revelation of his "daring flight" to North Africa, the productive meeting with Churchill, and the goal of unconditional surrender. Early on the evening of January 31, the president was back in the White House, reveling in his triumph but also facing daunting political headwinds at home.[51]

CHAPTER 23

DR. NEW DEAL AT BAY

MOBILIZATION AND MORTALITY, 1942–1944

PEARL HARBOR HAD BROUGHT THE UNITED STATES AT LAST INTO A TOTAL conflict that required mobilization of nearly the entire population, a sharp escalation of economic controls, and conversion of the economy to war production. Demanding widespread sacrifice and utilizing mechanisms of government control and coercion, the process generated widespread resentment of a metastasizing, all-controlling federal bureaucracy. The war had overwhelming popular support, but the way it was run at home kept Roosevelt and his administration constantly on the defensive. Underneath a veneer of national unity, the president's diminishing personal and political resources steadily eroded his leadership.[1]

THE CRISIS IMPACTED VIRTUALLY EVERY AMERICAN HOUSEHOLD. RUBBER AND scrap-metal drives recycled junk into war weaponry. Housewives saved jars of cooking fat that went into the production of explosives. "Hoarders" had to turn in extra automobile tires they had accumulated in expectation of shortages. The auto industry converted wholly to military production. Gasoline was tightly rationed.

Women, once never seen working on factory floors, became a common presence on assembly lines. Negroes also found new opportunities, in part because of the president's Fair Employment Practices Committee but largely because of the ever-tightening supply of white male labor. Social revolutions lurked in these developments. So did widespread resentment of regimentation, shortages, broken families, and all the inconveniences of wartime austerity. The war resoundingly ended the Great Depression and brought full employment to a degree never before experienced, but it was an unsatisfactory, feverish prosperity tinged by the tens of thousands of personal tragedies that accompany any major war and by a scarcity of civilian goods.

The engines of mobilization were new executive agencies with such names as War Production Board, War Manpower Commission, Office of Economic Stabilization, Office of War Mobilization, National War Labor Board, War Food Administration, and Office of War Information. In the main, New Deal liberals seemed to administer those agencies primarily in the business of telling people what they could not have or do. Especially pervasive was the Office of Price Administration, which established a system of price controls, sometimes set detailed standards for consumer products, and issued ration coupon booklets to every man, woman, and child in the nation. Merchants widely evaded price controls despite strong enforcement efforts. The worst offenders might be caught and disciplined, but no federal agency could police the billions of transactions, most of them small, that characterized a continental economy and a population of 130 million people. Few individuals felt guilty about handing over an extra dollar for a prime cut of beef or a pair of scarce nylon stockings.[2]

The selective service system administered a military draft that conscripted 10 million men into the armed forces, providing exemptions primarily to defense workers, productive farmers, and, until manpower shortages enforced revision of the rules, fathers. The draft, though not loved, was widely accepted.

The "tame millionaires" Roosevelt had brought into the administration before Pearl Harbor remained, and new recruits augmented their ranks. Averell Harriman established himself as an indispensible man in foreign policy. Edward R. Stettinius Jr., former chairman of US Steel, would succeed the ailing Cordell Hull as secretary of state at the end of 1944. Dean Acheson returned to the administration as an influential assistant secretary of state. Wall Street banker James Forestall would succeed Frank Knox as secretary of the navy. Two other Wall Streeters, Robert Patterson and John J. McCloy, managed most of the operations of the Department of War for Secretary Henry Stimson.

Major industrialists became heroes of production as they oversaw the manufacture of vast quantities of weaponry and equipment. Their emblematic figure, shipbuilder Henry J. Kaiser, would turn out, in previously unimaginable numbers, the merchant vessels that carried American weaponry across the oceans and made possible the defeat of the Axis. Corporations that had been politically at odds with the New Deal produced jeeps, tanks, and aircraft at unbelievable rates. Seattle's Boeing transformed the agricultural state of Kansas into the major producer of B-17 bombers with a main assembly plant in Wichita. Ford rolled out huge numbers of B-24 bombers and Sherman tanks. Operating out of New Orleans, a small entrepreneur named Andrew Jackson Higgins developed and built the landing craft used to invade Hitler's Fortress Europe.[3]

Given shortages of raw materials and labor, along with the need to either retool civilian assembly plants or build new ones from the ground up, the production process was messy. A generation of Washington lawyers became rich helping industrialists negotiate contracts and obtain vital equipment or raw materials. The kingpin among them was Roosevelt's old aide Tommy Corcoran, who rejected the president's efforts to bring him back to the White House.[4]

Efforts at centralized coordination were at best semieffective. William Knudsen, the onetime shop floor worker who had made General Motors the dominant force in the auto industry, could not accomplish it and was fired as head of the Office of Production Management. Roosevelt created the War Production Board and named Donald Nelson, the head of Sears, Roebuck, as its chairman. Nelson was no more effective. Neither man received the expansive powers an industrial czar required. New Deal liberals, proceeding from the assumption that all big businessmen were morally and intellectually deficient, constantly assailed them.

Roosevelt nearly gave the job to Bernard Baruch, who had run the War Industries Board in World War I. Called to the White House and informed of the president's intentions, Baruch instead endured a rambling conversation that ended without a job offer. The relationship between the two men had always been difficult, despite FDR's willingness to accept large amounts of campaign money and other favors from Baruch. In the end, Roosevelt simply could not bring himself to tender the open-ended mandate the job would have required. He knew, as presidential scholar James MacGregor Burns has expressed it, "that every delegation of power and sharing of authority extracted a potential price in the erosion of presidential purpose, the narrowing of options, the clouding of the appearance of presidential authority, the threat to his reputation for being on top."[5]

Industrial mobilization was an unruly mix of inflated expectations, excessive demands, competing interests, clashing ideologies, and battling egos. But for all the false starts, administrative snarls, and spot shortages of vital materials, the United States produced war equipment in astonishing quantities and gave the Allies the needed edge to achieve victory.

Roosevelt managed the war with structures and attitudes similar to those of the 1930s. Republicans and conservative Democrats viewed the wartime order as essentially the latest incarnation of the New Deal. The president and his loyalists, convinced that a vision of a new and better society at home and abroad must supplement the goal of total victory over Germany and Japan, largely agreed.

By November 1942, with victory in the Pacific at Midway, American progress at Guadalcanal, and the stalled German drives at Stalingrad and El Alamein, the momentum of the war was beginning to shift in favor of the Allies. But that would be more evident in retrospect than it was at the time. More obvious was the chaos and irritation of an unwanted conflict. The Doolittle raid notwithstanding, Pearl Harbor seemed as yet unavenged. On November 3, the nation voted in the congressional elections not knowing that American troops were boarding transports for the invasion of North Africa.

The Republicans scored big gains, winning an additional forty-six seats in the House of Representatives, leaving the Democrats a scant ten-vote majority in that chamber, and gaining nine in the Senate. The conservative coalition that had emerged from the 1938 election was stronger than ever, ready for the most part to give grudging support to the war but deeply skeptical of any initiative aimed at reviving the New Deal at home. For the first time since 1929, many of its representatives spoke more convincingly to the American public than did the president.

Other than the administration itself, the conservatives primarily targeted organized labor, which had grown increasingly dissatisfied with wartime mandates against strikes and strict limitations on wage increases. Most of the unions, however, took and maintained a no-strike pledge. Employers made the situation tolerable by developing such fringe benefits as health insurance, which the government did not count as wage compensation.

There was one big exception to labor's general cooperativeness: John L. Lewis and the United Mine Workers. Lewis's palpable resentment of Roosevelt was coupled with the historic militancy of his workers. They held strong cards in a nation whose heavy industries ran on coal. In 1943, Lewis, prodded by local wildcat strikes, called a series of walkouts that raised the specter of an industrial shutdown. Pitting himself and his union against the administration's wage-control apparatus, he displayed both legitimate concern for the economic difficulties of his men and an ego-driven need to humiliate Roosevelt.[6]

The president sharply condemned the strike, declaring in a fireside chat on May 2, 1943, "Every American coal miner who has stopped mining coal—no matter how sincere his motives, no matter how legitimate he may believe his grievances to be—every idle miner directly and individually is obstructing our war effort." He placed the mines under government seizure, to be managed by Secretary of the Interior Harold Ickes. For the balance of the year and into 1944, intermittent work stoppages continued to hamper the coal industry. Lewis and Ickes cobbled out a deal that stretched government wage guidelines without ostentatiously breaking them. The episode demonstrated that determined labor chiefs willing to accept the hostility of the public could defy Roosevelt with relative impunity.[7]

The labor union movement as a whole came out the loser. In response to the coal strikes, the conservative bloc in Congress pushed through the Smith-Connally labor relations act, which broadened presidential power to seize war industries and provided stiff penalties for unions that engaged in strikes against seized industries. Roosevelt, with an eye to his labor support, vetoed the bill, although it sanctioned powers he had already exercised. Congress overrode the veto.

Other labor actions occurred from time to time. At the end of 1943, the government took over the railroads for a month to head off a strike. A new executive agency, the Office of Economic Stabilization, dealt extensively with labor-management issues. Federal policy supported a "maintenance of membership" arrangement that allowed the mainstream industrial unions to add tens of thousands of members to their rolls. In general, defense workers made good money, enjoyed exemptions from the military draft, accepted as best they could the many inconveniences of wartime life, and had minimal interest in striking. Roosevelt could count on their support.

Corporate management had its counterpart of John L. Lewis in the person of Sewell Avery, the reactionary chairman of Montgomery Ward, the nation's largest catalog retailer. When Avery refused to hold a union representation election, Roosevelt took the advice of Attorney General Francis Biddle and authorized the seizure of the company. Personally directed by Biddle, US Army troops surrounded Montgomery Ward's headquarters in Chicago on April 27, 1944, entered the building, made their way to Avery's eighth-floor office, and carried the sixty-nine-year-old executive out to the sidewalk. Photographs of the aged man adamantly sitting in a sling fashioned from the arms of two sturdy soldiers were, depending on one's point of view, either comical or scandalous evidence of authoritarian rule. Furious at Biddle, Avery resorted to the nastiest epitaph that sprang to mind: "You New Dealer!"[8]

Henry Stimson had prophetically opposed the Montgomery Ward seizure on the grounds of the company's remote significance to the war effort, predicting in his diary that Roosevelt's enemies would use it as evidence that the president was "seeking autocratic power." The symbolism of armed takeover was potent.

The usually supportive *Washington Post* denounced the action as unnecessary. Among Republicans and conservatives, Avery, who might easily have passed for Ebenezer Scrooge in the annual Christmas play, became an instant folk hero. After two weeks, the government relinquished control of the company.[9]

The Montgomery Ward incident was comic but consistent with an ethic of total mobilization. With industry largely brought into line, labor could not be ignored. In January 1944, Roosevelt asked Congress to enact "a national service law—which for the duration of the war, will prevent strikes, and, with certain appropriate exceptions, will make available for war production or for any other essential services every able-bodied adult in this whole Nation." The request had a certain logical consistency but little urgency and no political viability. It died quietly on Capitol Hill.[10]

The decision to herd Japanese Americans into concentration-camp-style "relocation centers" in early 1942, on the other hand, although widely accepted, was a disturbing example of how New Deal liberalism could so easily adopt authoritarian means. Faced with hysteria on the West Coast, Roosevelt agreed to the internment of 110,000 individuals, two-thirds of whom were American citizens born in the United States. The best that could be said for the camps they inhabited over the next two or three years was that they were designed to maintain life and limb under Spartan conditions. By the standards of total war, the Japanese American internment was relatively humane. According to traditional liberal American values, it was a disgrace.[11]

So was the decision to prosecute thirty protofascist publicists and agitators for sedition. After a series of indictments from July 1942 through January 1944, the trial got under way in April 1944. The defendants were a scummy lot; many would have cheerfully heiled Hitler. Roosevelt urged the action on a reluctant Francis Biddle. New Deal liberals, normally scrupulous defenders of civil liberties, by and large approved heartily. The apparent hope for a show trial that would make an example of enemy sympathizers disintegrated quickly. Functioning in an open courtroom and taking advantage of all the opportunities open to them in a liberal society, defense attorneys, forty in all, made a shambles of the proceedings with a barrage of motions, long speeches disguised as legal arguments, and general disorderly behavior. In November 1944, the judge, worn down by the ordeal, died. He was never replaced; the case was eventually dropped after the war.[12]

BEHIND THE HEADLINE-GRABBING EVENTS ON THE HOME FRONT, ROOSEVELT was caught up in more fundamental issues in American politics. These included the future of American liberalism, the character of the Democratic Party, and ultimately the identity of just who would succeed him. The common denominator among all these controversies was the new vice president, Henry Wallace.

The former secretary of agriculture, widely considered a rustic eccentric, broke through the constraints that had limited his public appeal with a widely circulated speech in May 1942 titled "The Price of Free World Victory." Employing messianic rhetoric and calling for a secular millennium, he defined the war as a struggle to the death against satanic forces bent on leading the world into slavery and darkness. The democratic nations had to strive for a "people's revolution" based on Christian ideals that would be the ultimate fulfillment of revolutions from the American in 1776 to the Russian in 1917. The people's revolution would establish a just and enduring peace, end imperialism, achieve global liberty, and above all realize the Rooseveltian goal of freedom from want. "The century on which we are entering—the century which will come of this war—can be and must be the century of the common man," he declared. "The people's revolution is on the march and the devil and all his angels cannot prevail against it. They cannot prevail, for on the side of the people is the Lord."[13]

Roosevelt surely would have avoided evangelical rhetoric, but he essentially agreed with his vice president's manifesto. He may well have considered Wallace a likely successor. He had not reckoned, however, on Wallace's blunderbuss appetite for political combat.

The president had put Wallace in charge of the Board of Economic Warfare (BEW), a special agency primarily concerned with the acquisition of vital raw materials for defense industries. Wallace saw the assignment as a way of pressing an overseas social agenda that would include generous compensation for underpaid workers. But the BEW had to obtain funding from the Reconstruction Finance Corporation and other federal lending agencies long managed by Texas conservative Jesse Jones, who was now also secretary of commerce. Revered by the southern conservative wing of the Democratic Party, Jones dragged his feet on one proposed contract after another. In mid-1943, Wallace issued a public blast charging the secretary with obstructing the war effort. Jones responded sharply.

The episode was, in the estimate of Robert E. Sherwood, "the worst of all the public brawls that marred the record of the Roosevelt Administration and it gave . . . an alarming sense of disunity and blundering incompetence in very high places." The president dissolved the BEW and transferred its functions to the Office of War Mobilization, headed by James Byrnes, a southerner with wide support on Capitol Hill. Wallace remained a hero to most New Deal liberals and a problem for the president who had wanted to advance him.[14]

Wallace was only the most visible spokesman for a liberal bloc determined to bring back a turbocharged version of the New Deal after the war. Publicists and politicians fearful of a reversion to economic depression advocated massive public works programs along lines long advocated by John Maynard Keynes. In Britain, a committee headed by the radical social scientist William Beveridge had drawn up widely hailed plans for a postwar social welfare state. American liberals took it as a model. In 1943, the National Resources Planning Board, an obscure New Deal carryover administered by FDR's uncle, Frederic Delano, issued an annual report advocating a postwar agenda that would include a strong antitrust program, a large-scale economic stimulus, and a comprehensive welfare state.[15]

The liberal Democratic bloc in Congress introduced, but could not pass, legislation to implement the report. The bipartisan conservative coalition swiftly put an end to the board's mischief by zeroing out its annual appropriation. At his last press conference of 1943, Roosevelt responded to a planted question about whether he still "liked" the term "New Deal." Old Dr. New Deal, he said, listing the programs of the 1930s at length, had done a good job of bringing a gravely sick country back from the Depression. Then there had been the "bad accident" of December 7, 1941, which had required a new specialist, Dr. Win-the-War, who was making great progress. When victory came, it would be necessary to carry on with the programs of the past and to pursue goals of an expanded economy, more economic security, more employment, more recreation, more education, more health, and better housing, all with the goal of assuring that the malaise of the Depression would not return.

"Does that all add up to a fourth term declaration?" asked *New York Herald-Tribune* reporter Bert Andrews.

"Oh now—we are not talking about things like that now," the president replied. "You are getting picayune."[16]

Two weeks later in his State of the Union message to Congress, broadcast as a fireside chat, Roosevelt proclaimed an expansive "second Bill of Rights" that effectively restated the planning board's agenda. It asserted rights to "a useful and remunerative job . . . to earn enough to provide adequate food and clothing and recreation . . . to trade in an atmosphere of freedom from unfair competition and domination by monopolies . . . to a decent home . . . to adequate medical care . . . to adequate protection from the economic fears of old age, and sickness, and accident and unemployment . . . to a good education."[17]

The message increased the growing tension between Roosevelt and Congress. FDR escalated hostilities a month later by vetoing a tax bill that failed to contain increases he had requested. The veto message, written in the Treasury

Department at the instigation of Secretary Henry Morgenthau while Roosevelt was resting at Hyde Park, reflected the president's isolation from the prevailing climate of opinion in Washington. It characterized the bill as "providing relief not for the needy but for the greedy."[18]

Legislators, jealous of the congressional power of the purse, took the veto as an insult. The president's opponents played it for all it was worth. So did his friends. Alben Barkley, up for reelection in the fall, announced his resignation as Senate majority leader and declared that the self-respect of Congress demanded an override of the veto. Roosevelt quickly realized he had overreached. Responding with a "Dear Alben" telegram, he asked the senator to reconsider and expressed the hope that if he did resign, the Democratic delegation would promptly reelect him as their leader. Resignation, override, and reelection followed quickly. The incident demonstrated the shakiness of Roosevelt's authority as he contemplated a fourth term.

The rollicking White House over which Roosevelt had presided became emptier as the war progressed. Princess Martha, joined intermittently by her husband, lived in royal style on an estate outside Washington. Roosevelt still saw her frequently. Eleanor, as always, seemed in constant motion. She was often away, speaking across the country, visiting Britain in 1942, and traveling to the South Pacific in 1943. Toward the end of 1943, the recently remarried Harry Hopkins and his wife moved out of the White House, to the considerable annoyance of the president, who had greatly valued Hopkins's twenty-four-hour availability.

The boys were all in military service: Jimmy in California, Elliott in Europe, Franklin Jr. with the navy in the Mediterranean and later the Pacific, and John as a supply officer on an aircraft carrier. Jimmy and Elliott had lived messy civilian lives that verged on personal and financial scandal before the war. They, along with their two younger brothers, compiled distinguished military records that did not prevent sporadic partisan attacks against them.

The children of Roosevelt's associates also put themselves at risk. Henry Morgenthau's son Robert was pulled from the icy waters of the North Atlantic after his ship was sunk on convoy duty. One of Harry Hopkins's sons, Stephen, a marine private, was killed on Kwajalein in the Pacific. Another, Robert, was a combat photographer in the European theater. Hopkins penned a note to General Dwight D. Eisenhower, asking him to disregard Stephen's "bad luck in the Pacific" and allow Robert to participate in the invasion of France. "The war is 'for keeps' and I want so much to have all of my boys where the going is rough." Robert survived the war.[19]

Three cousins with whom the president had varying relationships, the surviving children of Theodore Roosevelt, all managed active military duty. Ted Jr., although not physically fit for combat, cut a swath through North Africa and Normandy as a general who led from the front; he would die of a heart attack in France just after receiving command of a division. The army would award him the Medal of Honor. Archibald managed a combat command in the Pacific. His wife, convinced that he would expend himself as had Ted, lobbied FDR to bring him stateside. He finally was shunted to a staff position with Douglas MacArthur. Kermit, the cousin to whom FDR was closest, wound up posted to Alaska; isolated and prone to depression, he shot and killed himself.

Roosevelt's daughter, Anna, and her husband, John Boettiger, had accepted management of the *Seattle Post-Intelligencer* in what amounted to a peace offering from William Randolph Hearst after the 1936 election. When war came, Boettiger enlisted in the army, serving for a time in Italy. Anna left the newspaper and moved with her children to the White House in early 1944. She quickly established herself as her father's unpaid administrative assistant. In many respects, she was Missy LeHand's successor, single-mindedly devoted to FDR's well-being and managing access to him with a sensitivity far more developed than her mother's. Her husband, called back to the United States, joined her and became an unofficial, sometimes influential, adviser to the president.

Roosevelt got little solace from Eleanor, who remained emotionally estranged from him while continuing to promote the liberal causes she championed. Years later, Anna recalled a telling incident that occurred late one afternoon when she was mixing cocktails for FDR, staff, and a few friends:

> Mother always came in at the end so she would only have to have one cocktail—that was her concession. She would wolf it—she never took it slowly. She came in and sat down across the desk from Father. And she had a sheaf of papers this high and she said, "Now, Franklin, I want to talk to you about this." . . . I thought, Oh, God, he's going to *blow*. And sure enough, he blew his top. He took every single speck of that whole pile of papers, threw them across the desk at me and said, "Sis, you handle these tomorrow morning." I almost went through the floor. She got up. She was the most controlled person in the world. And she just stood there half a second and said, "I'm sorry." Then she took her glass and walked toward somebody else and started talking. And he picked up his glass and started a story. And that was the end of it.

. . . [H]ere was a man plagued with God knows how many problems and right now he had twenty minutes to have two cocktails—in very small glasses. . . . He wanted to tell stories and relax and enjoy himself—*period*. I don't think Mother had the slightest realization.[20]

Daisy Suckley was an increasing presence also. She was often in the company of another Roosevelt cousin, Laura Delano, a fading beauty who dressed with attention-getting garishness and had never married. Both women gloried in Roosevelt's presence.

Miss Suckley bred Scottish terriers as a hobby. She gave Roosevelt a male puppy for Christmas in 1940. The president passed along to him the name he had given to at least one earlier Scottie, Fala. He grew strongly attached to the lively little animal and sensed its value in public relations. By 1943, Fala had become both a devoted companion and a political asset, frequently photographed and featured in newsreels with his master.

One other person was increasingly in Roosevelt's most private life: Lucy Mercer Rutherfurd, whose husband, Winthrop, was in frail health. Using the pseudonym "Mrs. Paul Johnson," she telephoned the president on numerous occasions. White House operators were under orders to put the call through without regard to whatever business occupied Roosevelt. The two often conversed in French for fear of eavesdroppers. From time to time when she visited Washington, they took long drives in the countryside. From June 1941 through March 1945, she visited the White House on at least twenty occasions, always when Eleanor was out of town. Through November 1942, she was "Mrs. Paul Johnson"; after that, she was logged in simply as "Mrs. Rutherfurd." The lack of any recorded visits in 1943 suggests she may have used another name, but it is possible that she was simply overwhelmed in dealing with the fatal illness of her husband, who died in March 1944.[21]

Anna, sensitive to the emotional distance between her parents and solicitous of her father's emotional needs, became a collaborator in the deception. And why not? Grasping the enormous pressures of wartime leadership, she understood his loneliness and need for diversion. And soon she came to realize, far better than Eleanor, that her father was a very sick man.

ACCOMPANYING BRITISH AMBASSADOR LORD HALIFAX TO THE WHITE HOUSE on July 7, 1941, John Maynard Keynes had found himself concerned by the president's shaky health. "He is not a sick man, but he is not exactly a fit one. I thought he was fundamentally weak and tired and using his courage and willpower to keep going." Keynes listed maladies he had been told about: three recent attacks of high fever and chronic sinus trouble. Roosevelt, he noted, refused to use the air conditioning system in his office. (The breeze it generated aggravated his sinuses.) The economist left convinced that Roosevelt was probably suffering, as Keynes himself had, from an undiagnosed streptococcal infection.[22]

A year and a half later, sometime after Roosevelt returned from Casablanca, a young National Broadcasting Company journalist, David Brinkley, attended his first White House press conference. He had anticipated a strong and energetic personality. The reality was "a shock, unnerving . . . a man who looked terribly old and tired. . . . [His] face more gray than pink, his hands shook, his eyes were hazy and wandering, his neck drooped in stringy, sagging folds accentuated by a shirt collar that must have fit at one time but now was two or three sizes too large." When asked what was wrong with the president, Press Secretary Steve Early simply replied, "He's just tired. Running a world war is a hell of a job."[23]

During his first two terms, Roosevelt had seemed healthy and vigorous. His one acknowledged medical problem had been a tendency to sinus infections. On the advice of Woodrow Wilson's personal doctor, Admiral Cary Grayson, he had appointed as White House physician Ross T. McIntire, a navy ear, eye, nose, and throat specialist, whose major duty was daily sinus treatments. Roosevelt had confidence in both McIntire's competence and his commitment to absolute confidentiality regarding the president's health. (He seems to have destroyed Roosevelt's medical records after his death.) By 1938, McIntire was surgeon general of the navy and a rear admiral.[24]

McIntire seems to have succeeded in dealing with Roosevelt's sinuses. The president's other significant health problem during his first two terms appears to have been a badly infected tooth that had to come out. The procedure left him sore and weak for the better part of a month, a long recovery period that may have reflected his underlying fragility.

By the late 1930s, a large, unsightly dark spot had appeared over Roosevelt's left eye. It had developed slowly from a small blemish first apparent in photos taken in 1923. It would be greatly diminished by 1940 and all but gone by 1942. There is no way of knowing whether this was a harmless age spot removed for cosmetic reasons or, as some have speculated, a deadly melanoma that disappeared as it metastasized to other parts of his body. McIntire, responding to a prominent physician who had warned of cancer, characterized it as "very superficial."[25]

In 1941, Roosevelt suffered severe rectal bleeding that McIntire attributed to a bad case of hemorrhoids, a not uncommon problem in the Roosevelt family. His blood count dropped to dangerous levels, requiring medication and at least two transfusions before it stabilized. He does not seem to have experienced another such crisis but remained susceptible to low-grade infections.[26]

Whatever the truth about a possible cancer, by the time he began his third term Roosevelt was clearly beginning to display the effects of progressive cardiovascular disease similar to that which had killed his father. McIntire understood this and took it seriously. Roosevelt's oddly circuitous route to Casablanca in January 1943 probably stemmed from a belief that travel in relatively leisurely installments at low altitude was much safer than the mode employed by his military chiefs: a long direct flight across the Atlantic in a high-altitude C-54 transport plane. McIntire in fact became visibly upset when he learned that a short final hop over the Atlas Mountains would have to ascend to a higher altitude than he considered safe.[27]

Roosevelt appears to have been an active and effective participant at Casablanca, but the long trip exacted a toll. In those final two years after his return from North Africa, Grace Tully observed "the signs of cumulative weariness, the dark circles that never quite faded from under his eyes, the more pronounced shake in his hand as he lit his cigarette, the easy slump that developed in his shoulders as he sat at a desk that was always covered with work."[28]

Why did McIntire fail at the very beginning to consult with a heart specialist? Probably because cardiovascular medicine had not advanced much beyond that available to Roosevelt's father in the 1890s. Doctors knew how to measure blood pressure, for example, but often interpreted readings that are now understood to be dangerously high as evidence of a strong, healthy heart rather than of mortal danger. About the only medication for heart trouble was the recently developed drug digitalis, the proper dosage of which was difficult to determine.

Roosevelt himself seems to have been determined to ignore his symptoms but must have connected his own condition to that of his father. Perhaps he found consolation in recalling that James Roosevelt had lived for ten years after his first heart spasm. Perhaps he was simply in denial.

In those days, many doctors avoided frank conversation with critically ill patients, but it is possible that Roosevelt and McIntire talked honestly and seriously. One can imagine Roosevelt telling his physician he would continue his duties as best he could without regard to his own well-being, like any other soldier in service to his country. Grace Tully, who spent as much time with him as any other person in those years, believed that such was his attitude.[29]

In this spirit Roosevelt departed Washington on November 11, 1943, for his second and third major international conferences of 1943, at Cairo with Chinese Nationalist leader Chiang Kai-shek and at Teheran with Churchill and Stalin. At Teheran on November 28, hosting Stalin and Churchill for dinner, he presided over a spirited discussion of postwar policy toward Germany. Suddenly, as his interpreter Charles Bohlen recalled it, "he turned green and great drops of sweat began to bead off his face; he put a shaky hand to his forehead." Harry Hopkins swiftly had him wheeled out of the room and returned presently with assurances that the president was suffering from indigestion and would be all right. The next day, he seemed fully recovered. The symptoms were compatible with indigestion, but no other diner seems to have been afflicted. The president's malaise may have been a cardiac event. Roosevelt's medical history, as presented to Dr. Howard Bruenn soon afterward, apparently included other such episodes. Back in the United States on December 16, he was superficially in good spirits but at least as worn down by the long journey as he had been by the trip to Casablanca.[30]

Anna was among those who greeted him. Shortly after moving to Washington, she realized that her father was seriously unwell and her mother impervious to his condition. She insisted on a thorough medical examination conducted by specialists and got her way.

In April 1943, McIntire had obtained assignment to the Bethesda Naval Hospital of Dr. Bruenn, a noted young heart specialist who had enlisted in the navy. He may have consulted informally with Bruenn, but Bruenn did not personally examine the president at Bethesda until a year later, on March 27, 1944. He had been given a terse recent medical history. In late December, Roosevelt, just back from Teheran, had come down with influenza that produced "fever, cough, and malaise." He had never fully recovered, suffering "several episodes of what appeared to be upper respiratory infections," as well as "occasional bouts of abdominal distress and distension, accompanied by profuse perspiration." Recently, he had developed a cold with a persistent cough that produced "small amounts of thick, tenacious, yellowish sputum."[31]

Bruenn's examination revealed a normal body temperature (99 degrees) and pulse (72 bpm). The blood pressure was a very high 186/108. (Roosevelt's chart apparently had only a few earlier readings: July 30, 1935: 136/78; April 22, 1937: 162/98; November 30, 1940: 178/88; February 27, 1941: 188/105. They nevertheless revealed a pattern disturbing even to the medical science of those days.) Electrocardiograms, fluoroscopy, and X-rays indicated an enlarged heart and congested pulmonary arteries. Bruenn's diagnosis, which he believed totally surprised McIntire, was "hypertension, hypertensive heart disease, cardiac failure (left ventricular), and acute bronchitis." He recommended a strict treatment regime of one to two weeks in bed with nursing care, the administration of digitalis, a light diet, a program of weight reduction, and sedation as necessary to ensure restful sleep.

"You can't do that," McIntire responded. "This is the President of the United States!" A group consultation with Bethesda staff followed, then a White House meeting with McIntire and two eminent physicians who were honorary consultants to the navy: Dr. James Paulin, a former president of the American Medical Association, and Dr. Frank Leahy, a famed Boston surgeon. Paulin and Leahy read the president's chart and examined him independently. They appear to have concurred with Bruenn's overall diagnosis.

Bruenn himself made it clear that he could not attend a patient if his recommendations were overridden. He got most of what he wanted—very limited activity, a strict diet with weight-loss goals, reduction of tobacco use to six cigarettes a day, lots of sleep, and the use of digitalis as deemed necessary. Thereafter, he saw Roosevelt three or four times a week at the White House and traveled with him when he went outside Washington. Sinus treatments aside, he assumed the role of primary physician. Roosevelt, Bruenn recalled, never asked questions about his condition and made light of it in discussion with others. This was perhaps evidence of denial but more likely a demonstration of fatalism.

In line with Bruenn's prescription, Roosevelt spent a month—April 9 to May 7, 1944—mostly relaxing at Bernard Baruch's imposing estate, Hobcaw, near Charleston, South Carolina. The public was told only that he was on a brief vacation, expected to last about two weeks, somewhere in the South and recovering from a bout with "the grippe." By and large, the press bought the story. FDR's biographer, Ernest Lindley, wrote a widely syndicated column denouncing "misleading rumors" that the president was in ill health.[32]

By then, the invasion of Europe was widely expected, and the American "holding action" against Japan had become a relentless offensive moving from one bloody island battle to another across the vastness of the Pacific toward the Philippines. Dispatches came to Hobcaw from Washington daily. Secretary of the Navy Frank Knox died and was replaced by James Forrestal. The direction of the war was well established and required no command decisions from the White House. Roosevelt's workload, much of which could be managed by the enlarged White House staff he had gotten from the Executive Reorganization Act of 1939, was as light as possible.

One day he started a letter to Daisy Suckley: "A lovely place—plantation for a King. . . . I am really feeling 'no good'—don't want to do anything & want to sleep all the time." He never finished it. He attempted another with the same result. Revealing that he knew he had a cardiac problem, he wrote that his heart was "definitely better—does queer things still."[33]

Guests came down for visits. They included Lucy Mercer Rutherfurd, whose long-ill husband had died earlier in the year. Daisy arrived for a few days in May. Warily noting the forced gaiety at every meal and cocktail hour, she thought Roosevelt's efforts at jolly repartee stressed him. He knew, he told her privately, that "the doctors"—presumably referring to McIntire—were not telling him the whole truth. They couldn't, he assured her, put anything over on him.[34]

The monthlong vacation at Hobcaw did the president some good, but his blood pressure remained ominously high. His weight fell well below the target his doctors had set, betraying a serious lack of appetite. He would have good days and bad days, but his fatigue was chronic, the result of a failing cardio-vascular system that rest could not rejuvenate. After his return to Washington, he met many visitors in his bedroom, customarily spent only two hours a day in the Oval Office, and took long weekends at Shangri-la, his retreat on nearby Catoctin Mountain ridge.

According to a story told secondhand to historian Doris Kearns Goodwin years later, Senator Frank Maloney of Connecticut met with Roosevelt, proba-bly on June 1, 1944. Seating himself in the Oval Office on the other side of the president's desk, he confronted the vacant stare of a man who seemed not to realize a visitor was there. After a moment, he got up and went directly to pres-idential secretary Pa Watson. Unruffled by Maloney's report of the president's condition, Watson replied, "Don't worry. He'll come out of it. He always does." Maloney returned to the Oval Office and found a president who suddenly seemed back to normal. For the next several minutes, they discussed the sen-ator's concerns in a normal and coherent fashion as if nothing had happened.

It is very possible that something like this occurred, although there seems to be no extant firsthand account by Maloney, who died just six and a half months after his only recorded White House visit. Such an event would have been con-sistent with Roosevelt's condition. Neurologist-historian Steven Lomazow has suggested that such episodes—common enough that Watson could say the president always came out of them—were "seizures" or perhaps ministrokes (transient ischemic attacks, or TIAs). TIAs are usually markers on the way to a large-scale event. Whether or not Roosevelt actually experienced TIAs, that he was frequently fatigued to the point of dysfunction is beyond doubt.[35]

On July 12, 1944, Turner Catledge, a distinguished *New York Times* reporter, had a one-on-one meeting with the president. Fully as much as David Brinkley, he was "shocked and horrified" by Roosevelt's condition—emaciated with a "vague, glassy-eyed expression on his face and his mouth hanging open. . . . Repeatedly he would lose his train of thought, stop, and stare blankly at me. It was an agonizing experience." Other callers had similar stories; none felt free to broadcast what they had seen to the public.[36]

Roosevelt, grievously ill with a malady for which there was no cure, was careening toward a medical catastrophe similar to the one that had afflicted Woodrow Wilson a quarter century earlier. Did he recall the visit he and James Cox had made to the White House in 1920 and the terrible impact the sight of the incapacitated president had made on them? Perhaps. But he also knew there was a war to win and a peace to forge. He was determined to be a shaper of history, not an observer or a victim of it.

CHAPTER 24

WAR AND DIPLOMACY

FEBRUARY 1943–JUNE 1944

ON JANUARY 31, 1943, THE DAY ROOSEVELT RETURNED TO WASHINGTON FROM Casablanca, newspapers carried the first stories of the German surrender at Stalingrad. From that point, the Red Army, benefiting from generous American Lend-Lease supplies, would push steadily westward, destroying German forces ruthlessly and compensating for its own enormous losses with a seemingly limitless reservoir of manpower. Most devastatingly, the Russians would win a huge victory at Kursk in July, destroying German armored formations in the greatest tank battle ever waged. After Kursk, Germany could only manage an orderly retreat against an implacable Soviet offensive.

As Roosevelt surveyed the increasingly favorable battle maps, he surely felt that his gamble on the USSR was paying off. He also sensed that to win the peace, the United States had to establish an enduring modus vivendi with Stalin and the Soviet Union. He clearly believed that such an understanding would be far more critical than the relationship with Churchill and a Britain increasingly dependent on US support.

The Anglo-American alliance was also winning victories. In mid-May, the Axis resistance in North Africa collapsed as Allied troops captured Tunis, taking nearly 250,000 prisoners. In July, as the Russians were scoring their massive victory at Kursk, American and British forces invaded Sicily. They would take control of the island in thirty-eight days, during which an internal coup, backed by King Victor Emanuel, deposed Mussolini. Marshal Pietro Badoglio replaced him. On September 8, the new government surrendered unconditionally to the Allies. The Sicilian campaign had eliminated Mussolini and effectively cleared the Mediterranean lifeline to Suez.

In September, British and American forces landed on the Italian boot at Reggio Calabria and Salerno, but the Germans had already taken control of the country. They freed Mussolini from imprisonment and put him at the head of a puppet government. The Allies quickly found themselves in a slow, bloody campaign on a long and mountainous peninsula uniquely suited to defensive warfare.

Just as American military leaders had predicted, the North African and Italian campaigns made a 1943 invasion of northern France (code-named OVERLORD) impossible. So much the better as far as Churchill was concerned. He feared a repetition of the bloody trench stalemate of 1914 to 1918, and he remained determined to restore British hegemony over a region in which he correctly perceived that Stalin had designs of his own. Friendly governments in Italy and Greece were essential to the prime minister's plans. The Americans, from Roosevelt down, were determined that with the Mediterranean secured, the next big move in the war would be across the English Channel into France in the spring of 1944.

From the Russian perspective, the Sicilian campaign was little more than a skirmish, but the US-British accomplishments in the wider war were far from modest. In addition to territorial gains traceable on a map, the two allies, utilizing killer aircraft launched from escort carriers and improved antisubmarine weaponry and tactics, were sweeping German submarines from the North Atlantic. American and British bombers, moreover, were pounding Germany around the clock, creating destructive firestorms and repaying many times over the terror the Luftwaffe had visited on England. And although Europe remained the top priority, US forces in the South Pacific secured Guadalcanal, then moved on against the Japanese in New Guinea, Bougainville, and, by the end of 1943, Tarawa.

BY MID-1943, THE MOMENTUM HAD SHIFTED TO FAVOR THE GRAND ALLIANCE, but only hostility to the Axis united its constituent nations. The United States, Britain, and the Soviet Union had differing outlooks and postwar objectives. If these could not be reconciled, the peace would not be won. Roosevelt saw himself as the American democrat who must serve as the linchpin in an improbable alliance with an old Tory imperialist and an old Bolshevik.

His key target was the Soviet Union. Britain was, to use Winston Churchill's language, "in the harem," dependent on American support. Stalin's communications, always formal and correct and without a trace of the joviality that characterized the president's exchanges with Churchill, pounded constant complaints about the need for more aid and the failure to follow through on the promise of a second front. Roosevelt was anxious to meet one-on-one with the Russian dictator, take his measure, charm him, and above all assure him of American good intentions.

Developments on the eastern front created new difficulties for Roosevelt. In April 1943 the Germans had discovered in western Russia's Katyn Forest the mass graves of some 10,000 Polish army officers, executed with bullets to the back of the head. The Soviet Union denied culpability, blamed the Nazis, and charged the Polish government-in-exile (based in London) of collaborating in the killings. The evidence against the USSR and its dictator was compelling, but neither Roosevelt nor Churchill was willing to risk a rupture with Stalin. They pressured Polish prime minister Wladyslaw Sikorski into withdrawing a request for an independent investigation by the International Red Cross.

Writing to Stalin on April 26, Roosevelt asked him to maintain diplomatic relations with the London Poles, called Sikorski's request for an investigation "a mistake," and offered to help in "looking after any Poles you may desire to send out of Russia." He concluded, "Incidentally, I have several million Poles in the United States, very many of them in the Army and Navy. They are all bitter against the Nazis and knowledge of a complete diplomatic break between you and Sikorski would not help the situation." Stalin's response was unyielding: "It is conceivable that Mr. Sikorski himself has no intention of cooperating with Hitler's gangsters. . . . I do, however, consider that Mr. Sikorski allowed himself to be led by certain pro-Hitler elements. . . . [A]s a result the Polish government, very possibly involuntarily, became a tool in Hitler's hands." That July, as he returned to London after inspecting Polish army forces in the Middle East, Sikorski was killed when his plane crashed on takeoff from Gibraltar. Inevitably, rumors, however improbable, of sabotage circulated.[1]

On May 5, the president suggested a personal meeting with Stalin in Alaska. Stalin responded with demands for more aid and the establishment of a second front in France. He declared that his role as commander in chief of the Red Army and need to visit the front (which he seems never to have done) required his presence in the USSR.[2]

A week after receiving Roosevelt's overture, Stalin recalled to Moscow Maxim Litvinov, his ambassador to the United States and a consistent advocate of close relations with the United States and Britain. In June, he would recall

Ivan Maisky, Soviet ambassador to Britain, and A. Y. Bogomolov, ambassador to the Allied governments-in-exile based in London. At the end of the month, Churchill noted with some trepidation that a Soviet offensive on the eastern front seemed to have halted. "There was now an atmosphere alarmingly reminiscent of that which had preceded the Molotov-Ribbentrop Pact of August, 1939, and the fears of a separate Russo-German Armistice were revived," Robert Sherwood wrote after the war. "It was fortunate that Hitler did not know how bad the relations were between the Allies at that moment, how close they were to the disruption which was his only hope of survival."[3]

Sherwood's account reflected fairly widespread fears, but Stalin was likely just sending a message of dissatisfaction. The underlying reality was that Germany and the USSR shared the existential condition of a scorpion and a tarantula imprisoned in a bottle. A fight to the death was inevitable. This was far from obvious, however, to statesmen in America and Britain.[4]

Roosevelt's push for a Big Two meeting with Stalin exemplified both his grasp of power realities and his naive, but very American, belief that he could transfer to foreign relations the domestic political assets that had served him so well: his personal charm and his skill at transactional politics. There was a certain irony in a patrician president valuing an understanding with a plebian mass murderer over a partnership with the aristocratic Churchill, but the quest had a coherent rationale. Roosevelt understood early on that the United States and the Soviet Union would be the two dominant world powers at the end of the war. Stalin was a ruthless dictator, but dictators were everywhere on the world scene and a fact of life. Ruthlessness was a virtue in waging a remorseless war. (Neither Roosevelt nor Churchill displayed qualms about their murderous bombing offensive against Germany. Roosevelt, in authorizing the Manhattan Project, probably did not fully understand the enormity of its implications but undoubtedly knew he had signed off on development of an unprecedented weapon of mass slaughter.)

The president made the fundamental miscalculation that Stalin was the leader of a traditional power open to pragmatic bargaining with a liberal-capitalist state. To this, he, like many American liberals, seems to have added a conviction that Soviet communism, despite its totalitarian social engineering and the ideological and moral shabbiness of its American Communist Party affiliate, was a progressive force in the world. Stalin, for his part, clearly saw both Roosevelt and Churchill as allies of convenience and future enemies. No matter that Roosevelt did not have Churchill's long and open history of opposition to Bolshevism. The revolutionary Marxist ideology that determined Stalin's view of the world told him that both leaders and their liberal nations were inevitable antagonists. "Churchill is the kind of man who will pick your pocket for a kopeck," he would tell Yugoslav Communist Milovan Djilas in early 1945. "Roosevelt is not like that. He dips in his hand only for bigger coins."[5]

In June, the president told Averell Harriman, who was preparing to leave his position as a "special envoy" in Britain and become US ambassador to the Soviet Union, to float with Churchill the idea of a Roosevelt-Stalin meeting. On June 24, the prime minister wrote to Roosevelt that the world expected the allies to meet and act together. "If this is lost, much is lost."[6]

The president took four days to respond: "I did not suggest to UJ [Uncle Joe] that we meet alone but he told Davies that he assumed (a) that we would meet alone and (b) that he agreed that we should not bring staffs." There would be no military planning, no demands upon the Russians, and an opportunity for a frank exchange of views. "I would want to cover much the same field with him as did [Foreign Secretary Anthony] Eden for you a year ago." At best, one can characterize this response as misleading. Roosevelt's effort at a one-on-one with Stalin signaled how Britain had become the junior partner in the alliance.[7]

Rather than meeting with Stalin, Roosevelt instead had another one-on-one meeting with Churchill, this time at Quebec in August 1943. The prime minister argued for enlarged operations in Italy, the eastern Mediterranean, and ultimately the Balkans, which he misleadingly described as the soft underbelly of Europe. He got only pleasant visits, before and after the meeting, at Hyde Park. Ultimately, the British had to agree that the next major Western military campaign in Europe would be OVERLORD, for which the conference established detailed planning mechanisms and a target date of May 1, 1944. The naming of a supreme commander, everyone understood, would be left to Roosevelt.

AT QUEBEC, ROOSEVELT AND CHURCHILL DECIDED AGAINST A DECLARATION on the future of the British mandate in Palestine. Their discussion reflected interest in the vast oil reserves of the Arab world, reactions to indications that Nazi Germany was pursuing a policy of extermination against European Jews, and concern about an increasing infiltration of militant Zionists bent on transforming Palestine into a Jewish state.

British and American oil companies had already secured drilling rights in the recently established kingdom of Saudi Arabia, ruled by its founding absolute monarch King Abdul Aziz Ibn Saud, a warrior who considered himself the region's protector of Islam and who seemed the Middle East's most important source of stability. British and American diplomats felt an understandable interest in good relations with him.

In 1917, British foreign secretary Arthur Balfour, speaking for the cabinet, had recognized Palestine as a "national home for the 'Jewish people,'" thereby aligning Britain with a relatively small but deeply dedicated Zionist movement. From the beginning, most Arabs were hostile to what they considered an imperial venture. As Nazi power and influence expanded in the 1930s, the numbers of Jewish immigrants to Palestine grew. By the eve of World War II, the mandate was a land of Arabs and Jews, each with distinct communities and their own armed militias. In 1936, Arab anger had erupted into a full-scale revolt, which the British harshly repressed but never fully quashed. When World War II broke out in 1939, Britain, hoping to keep a lid on a difficult situation, forbade further Jewish immigration.

Desperate Jews nonetheless continued to make their way into Palestine, formed armed groups, and engaged in what they considered a war for survival against Arab hostility and British oppression. Their goal was an independent Jewish state. German propagandists appealed to Arabs throughout the Middle East, promising them liberation from Anglo-American-Zionist imperialism. Increasingly, Palestine became a tinderbox in which the British saw themselves resented and attacked by both sides and increasingly viewed the Jewish cause as a noxious distraction.[8]

The strategic significance of the Middle East and the importance of Jews in his political coalition made it impossible for Roosevelt to remain aloof from the situation. Conferring with Zionist leader Chaim Weizmann on June 12, 1943, he was noncommittal but sympathetic and surely aware that he could not summarily dismiss Weizmann's aspirations. Aiming toward strong postwar American influence in the region, he attempted to cultivate Ibn Saud through economic aid and the dispatch of a personal emissary, Lieutenant Colonel Harold Hoskins, an Arabic-speaking Middle Eastern specialist. The king and Hoskins held discussions that coincided with the Quebec conference. The monarch was unyielding in his hostility to a Jewish state and his personal loathing of Weizmann.[9]

Meeting with Hoskins on September 27, Roosevelt floated vaporous hopes that European Jews would be able to return to their homes safely after the war, that those who did not wish to do so could settle in remote portions of South America, and that Palestine might be reorganized as a tri-faith Holy Land under Moslem-Christian-Jewish trusteeship. Only in the turbulence of total war could the last idea have seemed possible.[10]

By late 1943, the difficult issue of Palestine was merging with the grim revelation that German forces were engaging not simply in episodic massacres of Jewish civilians—comprehensible as a by-product of war—but in a systematic effort to eradicate the Jewish population of Europe. The news was mind-numbing both at a rational level—the Nazis committed enormous resources to the project even as they were losing battles on the eastern front—and, in its ghastliness, at an emotional level. On July 28, 1943, Polish emissary Jan Karski briefed Roosevelt himself on what would become known as the Holocaust; he met also with other Washington officials and leading Jews. Some simply could not take in the news. When Karski, accompanied by the Polish ambassador, met with Felix Frankfurter, the Supreme Court justice declared, "I am unable to believe you." The ambassador, a good friend of Frankfurter, objected. The justice replied, "Mr. Ambassador, I did not say that this young man is lying. I said that I am unable to believe him. There is a difference."[11]

If the fact of the Holocaust gained acceptance, the problem of what to do about it remained a quandary. The death camps were located in areas largely beyond the reach of American military power. Roosevelt also had to know about an ugly undercurrent running through the domestic opposition to the war: the assertion that the administration was waging it primarily for the benefit of Jews, often typed as notorious draft dodgers. There was no effective way of striking back at such slanders; an effort to refute them would simply increase their salience.

Did Roosevelt himself have a streak of anti-Semitism? On one occasion, discussing with Alien Property Administrator Leo Crowley a dispute between Crowley and Secretary of the Treasury Henry Morgenthau, he seems to have said, "This is a Protestant country, and the Catholics and Jews are here on sufferance. . . . It is up to both of you to go along with anything I want." Crowley told Morgenthau of the conversation. Both men found the remark upsetting, but it was more likely a bad joke than evidence of deep-seated bigotry.[12]

The best the administration could do was provide whatever it could devise in the way of an escape route for those Jews not yet in the clutches of the Nazis. Here the Department of State was a hindrance. Its top-level officials saw the problem as a matter of neither national interest nor humanitarian necessity. Some, including Roosevelt's old friend from the Wilson administration, Assistant Secretary Breckinridge Long, appear to have acted out of anti-Semitism. Before and during the war, Long misled the president by exaggerating the number of Jews for whom the department had facilitated refuge.[13]

The problem went far beyond a few troublesome functionaries or even a larger public opinion that viewed Jews with scant sympathy. Global total war, producing victims on an unprecedented scale, had a desensitizing impact. The number of Chinese slaughtered, for example, was almost incalculable; Japanese reprisals against those who had sheltered the Doolittle raiders alone were estimated at 250,000 killed. In Europe, the US-British bombing campaign took a large civilian toll at random and without regret. The death camps to which the Nazis transported Jews were in Poland, on the eastern front, a large area of mass slaughter that historian Timothy Snyder has aptly characterized as "bloodlands." It was not that the Allies, who after all were fighting back after an attack, were morally equivalent to the Nazis. The war had its own inexorable logic, chewing up soldiers and civilians in such great numbers that it was easy to lose sight of Hitler's Final Solution.[14]

The leading member of the administration in addressing the Nazi war on the Jews was Morgenthau, whose awareness of his own ethnoreligious identity awakened with the revelations of Nazi genocide. Throughout 1943, he pressed the State Department for action and made Treasury funds available for transportation and bribes to officials in German-occupied Europe. Frustrated by persistent State Department foot-dragging, he pushed for the establishment of a War Refugee Board.[15]

Roosevelt complied on January 22, 1944. The board managed to extricate some thousands of Jews from occupied Europe, albeit against a backdrop of mass murder by the millions. A few of those saved made it to an army internment camp outside Oswego, New York, but public opinion clearly opposed acceptance of large numbers of refugees, Jewish or otherwise, into the United States. The pressure for a national home in Palestine steadily increased.

By mid-1944, Auschwitz in southern Poland had been identified as the major Nazi death camp. A number of Jewish advocates inside and outside the administration called for a bombing attack on it. Some apparently thought it would be possible to make surgical strikes against the gas chambers or the rail lines that fed victims to the camp. The Department of War rejected the proposal. Its arguments were compelling: Auschwitz was in a Soviet area of operations and at the outer limit of American bomber range; identifying the gas chambers from the air would be next to impossible; many prisoners would be killed; rail lines could be quickly repaired; surgical strikes were a fantasy. Many years later, at the age of ninety-one, Assistant Secretary John J. McCloy asserted that Roosevelt had agreed, but the extent to which FDR engaged with the proposal is unclear.[16]

If McCloy's memory was correct, Roosevelt had a firm grasp of military reality. The bombing of Auschwitz, had it occurred, would likely have been condemned by some of the same historians who later advocated it. They would have seen it as a ham-fisted, unintentional contribution to the Nazi war against the Jews. The only way to end the Holocaust was to destroy Nazism. Roosevelt presided over a war effort that was surging toward that goal. Morgenthau doubtless took some solace in the achievements of the War Refugee Board. He also began to think seriously of retribution against the Germans.

BY THE LAST HALF OF 1943, ROOSEVELT HAD DEVELOPED A VISION OF THE postwar world that combined the liberal idealism of Woodrow Wilson with the power-oriented realism of Theodore Roosevelt. From time to time he laid out his ideas to influentials from whom he hoped to garner support or at least acquiescence.

On September 2 and 3, 1943, he met with Archbishop (later Cardinal) Francis Spellman of New York, a prelate of great influence and a conduit to the Vatican. The four great powers—he probably used the phrase "Four Policemen"—would, he told the archbishop, be the controlling force in a new world order. Each would be dominant in its own geographical sphere: China in the Far East; the United States in the Pacific (and presumably the Western Hemisphere); Britain and Russia in Europe and Africa. (The Middle East does not appear to have made its way into his scenario.) There would be a successor organization to the League of Nations, but only the Four Policemen would have decision-making powers. All the rest—a group that would include not simply "small nations" but those of considerable size and resources—would be admitted to a "consultative assembly" with no real power or authority. Germany would be divided into several states and disarmed so thoroughly for forty years that no German would be allowed to learn to fly an aircraft. Yugoslavia would be broken up into its constituent ethnic nations. Russia would keep eastern Poland, with the Polish state receiving territorial compensation from Germany.[17]

To a Catholic prelate, the Soviet Union was the enormous specter in the room. Here, Roosevelt was frank. He believed first of all that he could come to an understanding with Stalin and was better suited to do so than Churchill. The prime minister was an idealist; he was a realist, and so was Stalin. He hoped he could persuade Stalin to settle for predominant influence in Finland, the Baltic states, eastern Poland, and the Romanian province of Bessarabia. Russia had the power to take these anyway; it was best to concede them gracefully. Soviet influence could extend farther, to Austria, Hungary, Croatia, and possibly as far as France, where, wholly misunderstanding the appeal of Charles de Gaulle, FDR thought an independent left-wing Popular Front government might be the best one could expect.

Russia, he said, was an all but unstoppable force on the European continent. The United States and Britain could not fight it. The Soviet capacity for military production was enormous. One could only hope for the development of an enduring friendship and a mellowing of the USSR into a more mixed socialist-capitalist regime. Europe could only accept the inevitable. Spellman paraphrased him as saying, "The European people will simply have to endure the Russian domination." Perhaps in ten or twenty years, the Russians would become less barbarian.

Spellman's summary surely presented a substantially accurate rendition of Roosevelt's thoughts. Given the state of the war in the late summer of 1943, the president's calculations were understandable. He may have discounted the importance of America's vital Lend-Lease aid, which had done so much to enable the mobility with which the Red Army was rolling back the Germans. Nonetheless the Soviets were undeniably moving impressively along an unimaginably broad front, while British and American forces were still pecking at the periphery. Accurately recalling the American isolationist tradition that rejected European involvement at the end of World War I, Roosevelt had reason to doubt that the nation would accept an active US presence on the continent after the end of World War II.

At bottom, despite invoking the phrase "Four Policemen," Roosevelt surely understood that only two nations, the United States and the Soviet Union, would come out of the war with preponderant power. China would remain a disorganized nation, little more than a geographical expression. His thoughts about some balance of American and Soviet influence there remain unknown. Britain would be much diminished, and so would France, a country for which he displayed scant regard. Germany would literally be destroyed. In personal terms, that meant he and Stalin would control the future.

It made sense that he would have more leverage with Stalin than Churchill. Roosevelt, after all, did not have Churchill's anti-Bolshevik baggage and commanded a much greater aggregation of power. Still, he displayed remarkable confidence in his personal presence and in his mistaken sense that Stalin would view personal relationships as transcending ideology.

COULD A FACE-TO-FACE MEETING POTENTIALLY OVERRIDE BOTH STALIN's Marxist theology and his propensity toward totalitarian absolutism? On November 11, Roosevelt, accompanied by Harry Hopkins, Admiral William D. Leahy, and Dr. Ross McIntire, slipped out of Washington for a rendezvous with the new sixteen-inch-gun battleship *Iowa*. His military chiefs—Generals George C. Marshall and Henry ("Hap") Arnold and Admiral Ernest J. King—awaited them. Their first destination was Cairo, where the president would confer with Churchill and Chinese leader Chiang Kai-shek. From there, they would go to Teheran for the long-awaited personal encounter with Stalin, then back to Cairo for further US-British discussions.[18]

The journey was an impressive demonstration of American naval supremacy. The North Atlantic, a death trap for Allied shipping at the beginning of the year, was now clear of the enemy. Three destroyers, twice relieved by three others at prearranged points, escorted the great ship across the ocean. The voyage was tranquil, save for an incident in which one of the destroyers in the midst of an exercise accidentally launched a torpedo in the direction of the *Iowa*. Forewarned, the battleship easily evaded it. Admiral King, reacting volcanically, placed the entire destroyer crew under arrest and planned to court-martial its skipper. The president intervened with a decree of leniency.

On November 17, as the *Iowa* neared Europe, aircraft from an escort carrier close by patrolled the skies. Three British destroyers and a US light cruiser joined the ship two days later as it approached Gibraltar. Transiting the strait, it docked at Oran, Algeria, on the morning of November 20. General Dwight D. Eisenhower, accompanied by Franklin Jr. and Elliott, met the president. The party flew to Tunis, where its members viewed the ruins of ancient Carthage.

That night, after dinner, Roosevelt had a long conversation with Eisenhower. He let the general know that soon he would name a supreme commander for the invasion of western Europe. Surely Eisenhower already knew that the choice was between him and Marshall. If Marshall were chosen, Eisenhower likely would be brought back to Washington as army chief of staff. It was a shame, Roosevelt said, that no one remembered who had been chief of staff of the army during the Civil War. The next evening, after a tour of the recent battle areas and dinner, the president and his party emplaned for Cairo, arriving there at 9:35 a.m. on November 22.[19]

Roosevelt had little time to rest. Churchill quickly called on him to make the case for the British Mediterranean strategy. After Churchill's departure, he met with Chinese Nationalist leader Generalissimo Chiang Kai-shek, accompanied by Madame Chiang. That evening, FDR presided over a working dinner during which Churchill and Lord Louis Mountbatten pitched plans for South Asia operations. Next came a preliminary meeting of US civilian and military officials that lasted until 11:10 p.m. The day foreshadowed the grueling pace the president would endure over the next three weeks.

The Cairo meetings had two key objectives. The first was to settle conclusively the major strategic dispute between the Americans, convinced that the path to victory ran through France, and the British, who remained wedded to further operations in the Mediterranean. The second was to arrive at a strategy against Japan in South Asia and to formulate some sense of what to expect from the Nationalist regime of Chiang Kai-shek.

Churchill eloquently advanced once again the importance of the Mediterranean front. His military chief of staff, Sir Alan Brooke, was equally devoted to it. Both were convinced that Germany, forced back by the Soviet onslaught, would not attempt a defense of the Balkan Peninsula. The Combined Chiefs of Staff met on November 24. The Americans gnashed their teeth as they once again heard Churchill proclaim his undying commitment to the cross-channel operation, then assert that the diversion of two or three divisions to the capture of Rhodes would be inconsequential and would likely bring Turkey into the war. One could be forgiven for wondering just how much the Turks could or would contribute after four years of cautious neutrality. One might suspect that Churchill's real purpose was to restore British influence in the eastern Mediterranean. Churchill would press the enterprise once again at Teheran and then at the second Cairo conference.[20]

The other major problem to address at Cairo was that of China and Chiang Kai-shek, whose Nationalist regime the United States had long recognized as that nation's legitimate government. Here Roosevelt had to confront the hard realization that his long-run vision of China's emergence was valid enough, but the short-run prospects were far more speculative. Despite generous American aid, Chiang's government had been driven to Chungking in China's southern interior, where it held out against the overstretched Japanese. A Communist regime headquartered to the north at Yenan and led by Mao Tse-tung challenged its legitimacy. Chiang himself, although billed as a visionary democratic leader by his backers, was actually best understood as a traditional Chinese warlord who ruled by force, was wary of ambitious lieutenants, and tended to appoint generals more conspicuous for passivity than aggressiveness. Americans who dealt directly with him and his government frequently came away disillusioned with the authoritarian, inefficient, and kleptocratic rule they encountered.

American contacts with Mao's sector were limited. Those with Chiang's were intensive and provided plenty of cause for dissatisfaction. To the frustration of his American military adviser, General Joseph ("Vinegar Joe") Stilwell, who privately referred to him as "Peanut," the Generalissimo displayed little interest in offensives against the Japanese. Those Americans who had some contact with Mao's regime, including some US Foreign Service officials, generally found it preferable to Chiang's and more effective in fighting the Japanese. They seldom stopped to consider that Chiang's area of control was much more strategically important to the invaders and thus under greater pressure from the Japanese. They also tended to give credence to the assertion that Mao's regime, which broadly tolerated free markets during the war, was not really Communist at all and was dedicated to "agrarian reform." The bottom line, not fully perceived by Roosevelt and the other American principals at Cairo, was that both Mao and Chiang sensed that the Japanese had reached their limit and would be gone someday, leaving the fight for China to the two of them. Both husbanded their forces for that eventuality.[21]

Chiang himself was a remote figure to Americans. Not so his wife, Soong May-ling, known to the world as Madame Chiang. Born to a wealthy Christian Chinese family and educated in the United States, Madame Chiang spoke perfect English, was photogenic, and had a forceful personality. Championed along with her husband by Henry Luce's *Time* magazine, a speaker before Congress during long wartime visits to the United States, and a frequent guest at the White House, she was to most Americans the face of the Nationalist regime. Eleanor Roosevelt recalled her as petite and delicate in appearance, eloquent in her invocation of democratic ideals when speaking in the United States, and "as hard as steel." Franklin, surely acquainted with rumors that she had seduced Wendell Willkie (or vice versa), understood that. At a White House dinner party during one of her stays, he took an opportunity to ask her, "What would you do in China with a labor leader like John Lewis?" Eleanor described the response: "She never said a word, but the beautiful, small hand came up very quietly and slid across her throat."[22]

At Cairo, Madame Chiang attended sessions with her husband, who spoke no English. She listened to his translator, then invariably spoke up to say that the gentleman had done an excellent job but had nevertheless failed to capture the Generalissimo's precise meaning, which she then conveyed to the group. The effect was to leave the audience wondering whether they were listening to Chiang's opinions or hers. The only woman in a room of mostly middle-aged men, assertive, trim, and shapely at the age of forty-five, she was the center of attention at every such meeting. Years later, General Brooke recalled her as not conventionally beautiful but "determined to bring into action all the charms nature had blessed her with": "At one critical moment her closely clinging dress of black satin with yellow chrysanthemums displayed a slit which extended to her hip bone and exposed one of the most shapely of legs. This caused a rustle amongst those attending the conference and I even thought I heard a suppressed neigh come from a group of some of the younger members."[23]

Chiang's generals were far less fascinating. The Americans and the British had come with plans for a major offensive in the Bay of Bengal/Burma theater. They discovered that their Chinese counterparts were ciphers, unwilling

to make suggestions or ask questions and clearly not empowered to make commitments. Direct talks between Roosevelt and Chiang were no more satisfactory. Lord Mountbatten, designated supreme Allied commander for the South
Asian theater, commented that Churchill, Roosevelt, and the Combined Chiefs
of Staff were "driven absolutely mad" by their discussions with the Chinese.
Over the next year, primarily British and imperial forces would accomplish the
conquest of Burma.[24]

The conferees issued a Cairo Declaration that reaffirmed their military collaboration and established as their war objective the elimination of all Japanese
conquests since Japan's emergence as a Pacific power in the late nineteenth century, including Formosa (Taiwan), Korea, Manchuria, and numerous Pacific
islands. Press coverage of the conference inevitably trumpeted the participation of Chiang and inflated his staunchness as an ally. Roosevelt himself was
still convinced that China would become a great power at some point after the
war. But he had to be less certain about its immediate future and perhaps more
open to the expectation that the United States might have to share influence in
China with the Soviet Union.[25]

THE PRESIDENT MOVED ON TO HIS LONG-AWAITED MEETING WITH STALIN. THE
Soviet leader had stood firm on his insistence that he could not leave his sphere
of control, rejecting at least ten proposed locations from Fairbanks to Baghdad.
He would settle only for Teheran, firmly in the grip of a Soviet occupation. His
allies would have to come to him. Roosevelt had objected vigorously and per-
sistently, arguing that Teheran, nestled among mountains, presented formidable difficulties of transportation and communications. He likely also protested
on the advice of Dr. McIntire, who remained worried about him flying at high
altitude. His original schedule called for a flight from Cairo to Basra, on the
Persian Gulf, where he would take a train to the Iranian capital. But word of
the meeting at Cairo and the likelihood he would go on to Teheran leaked to
the press. A land trip was risky and unreliable.[26]

On November 27, Roosevelt arose in the middle of the night for a flight to
Teheran. Arriving in mid-afternoon, he was whisked into an armored convoy
that delivered him and his party to the American legation near the center of
the city. He spent most of the rest of the day meeting with advisers. The following morning, he received a message from Stalin, informing him of reports
that Nazi assassins were in the city. Warning that the American compound
was dangerously exposed, Stalin offered him quarters at the Soviet compound,
closer to the edge of the city and safely located next to the British embassy.

Since the Iranian government—and the Soviet occupiers—had failed to provide adequate security for either him or Churchill on the road from the airport, Roosevelt quickly agreed.[27]

He surely realized that the site was probably bugged, and it was indeed riddled with listening devices expertly planted by Sergo Beria, the son of Stalin's feared secret police chief, Lavrenty Beria. What better way to demonstrate trust and confidence in his Soviet partner? And what in any case would they make of comments that the Americans might have made purposely for their ears? On the afternoon of November 28, Roosevelt, Harry Hopkins, Admiral Leahy, and FDR's son-in-law, Major John Boettiger, moved to their new quarters.[28]

The scene was set for an encounter that both leaders had eagerly anticipated. Roosevelt at last had the opportunity to unleash the power of his personality and convince Stalin of his reliability as a partner. One of Stalin's interpreters at Teheran, Valentin Berezhkov, recalled many years later that Stalin, equally intent upon establishing a rapport, had selected the room where they would first meet, had the lighting modulated to minimize the smallpox scars that pitted his face, and wore elevated shoes to make himself appear taller. The two met at 3:00 p.m., one hour before the start of the first conference session, accompanied only by their interpreters, Charles ("Chip") Bohlen for Roosevelt and V. N. Pavlov for Stalin.[29]

Roosevelt spoke first and set the tone of the meeting: "I am glad to see you. I have tried for a long time to bring this about." Stalin responded with similar pleasantries. A brief discussion of the military situation followed, with Stalin emphasizing recent tactical reverses and Roosevelt assuring him of the American desire to divert thirty to forty German divisions to the west. The president followed this with the hope that after the war, a portion of the American-British merchant fleet could be delivered to the Soviet Union with the goal of facilitating mutually beneficial trade relations. He then briefly touched on the meeting with the Chinese at Cairo and made no protest when Stalin remarked that China was very badly led.

Much of the rest of the conversation centered on the future of France, a nation for which neither leader displayed much sympathy. De Gaulle, Stalin asserted, was out of touch with reality. Roosevelt declared that de Gaulle's primary rival, Henri Giraud, had no administrative or political sense. He added that no Frenchman who had taken part in the Vichy government should be allowed to participate in postwar politics. The French ruling classes in general, Stalin declared, were decadent and collaborationist. Roosevelt expressed his disagreement with Churchill that France could quickly return to its status as a major power. They agreed that the time had come to dismantle the French

Empire, focusing especially on Indochina. Stalin, with an eye on the Middle East as well as Southeast Asia, brought up Lebanon.

Roosevelt was motivated by liberal principle, Stalin by the prospect of tactical gain. The Soviet leader's concentration on France doubtless stemmed from the fact that it was the only continental European nation that might be capable of raising a first-class army after the war. Roosevelt saw the end of Western imperialism as a good in itself and one that might provide some trade benefits to the United States. More intriguingly to Stalin, the president went out of his way to indicate disagreement with his capitalist partner Britain and all but invited the exploration of wedges that might be driven between the two nations.

Roosevelt had come to Teheran with no very fixed agenda beyond a meeting of the minds with Stalin. Despite the fact that the encounter came on the heels of an Allied foreign ministers conference that had brought Secretary of State Cordell Hull to Moscow, Hull had been sent back to Washington. Bohlen, the one Department of State official involved in the discussions, was there only as an interpreter. He quickly discerned that the president wanted to practice personal diplomacy, "preferred to act by improvisation rather than by plan," and had made no provision for a record of the conference. Bohlen took it upon himself to construct detailed minutes of the meetings at which he was present.[30]

Roosevelt, who probably would have been happy with no written record, may not have been aware of Bohlen's actions. In any event, he made no objection. Aside from the attack that Dr. McIntire represented as indigestion at dinner on the first evening, the president was in fine form. Bohlen, who remembered him as a pleasant and considerate chief, thought him "the dominating figure at the conference."[31]

Stalin was much the same man Harry Hopkins had met in 1941. He wore a grander uniform, having assumed the rank of marshal of the Soviet Union. He was, as always, firm in stating Soviet interests, calm and deliberate in demeanor, and commanding in presence. He showed himself to be a shrewd military tactician with a grasp of reality that rivaled and perhaps exceeded that of Roosevelt or Churchill. As a negotiator, he maintained a fine line between blunt toughness and hostility.

To the extent that the conference had a goal, it was to nail down the final plans for the defeat of Germany and to arrive at a working outline for the shape of the postwar world. The delegations sat at a large round table, each principal with a translator and two other advisers: Roosevelt, Bohlen, Hopkins, and Harriman; Churchill, Major John Birse (translator), Foreign Secretary Anthony Eden, and General Hastings Ismay; Stalin, Pavlov, Vyacheslav Molotov, and Marshal Kliment Voroshilov.

Churchill, as at Cairo, pressed his plans for further operations in the Mediterranean and the benefits of bringing Turkey into the war. The Americans indicated their skepticism and intention to undertake OVERLORD in the spring. They insisted that the only action in the Mediterranean should be a landing in southeastern France. Stalin demanded the naming of a supreme commander and the setting of a specific date for the invasion. During the second day of the conference, Stalin asked what he called "an indiscreet question": Did the British really believe in OVERLORD? There followed a series of cutting exchanges, with Roosevelt joining in the needling of Churchill. Hopkins later privately visited Churchill and relayed the president's strong belief that the time had come to finalize both the date and the command for the operation. The British gave in, agreeing to a target date of May 1 and the quick appointment of a supreme commander.

Roosevelt met privately with Stalin on November 29 to outline his plan for a new world organization: an assembly, in which all nations would have membership, that could make nonbinding recommendations; an executive committee that would attempt to resolve disputes; and an enforcement mechanism controlled by the Four Policemen. Stalin indicated some skepticism but appeared ready to bring the Soviet Union into any world body that might emerge from the war, especially if he would be in a position to block any action unfavorable to the USSR.

Over dinner that evening—an intimate affair limited to the Big Three, their interpreters, and Elliott Roosevelt, who wandered in uninvited—Churchill and Stalin had the most famous exchange of the conference. Stalin declared that it would be necessary to liquidate the German General Staff and the cohort of perhaps 50,000 German officers who sustained it. Churchill expressed shock: "I would rather be taken out into the garden here and now and be shot myself than sully my own and my country's honour by such infamy." The president offered a "compromise": shoot only 49,000. Elliott arose and delivered an alcohol-fueled speech in favor of Stalin's proposal. Churchill got up and left the room. Stalin hurried after him, assured him it was all a joke, and persuaded him to return.[32]

Perhaps it had all been in good fun. One might remember, however, that Stalin uttered his words just eight months after the discovery of the Katyn Forest Massacre. Quite a prankster, that Stalin.

The conference ended on December 1 to the general satisfaction of all parties. Roosevelt invited Stalin to his quarters for a final tête-à-tête. He told the Soviet leader that because of the upcoming presidential election, he could not publicly express his support for the Soviet acquisition of eastern Poland. For the same reason, he hoped that the Russians would provide him electoral cover in the form of free elections that would endorse the annexation of the Baltic states. Stalin replied that the Baltics had been part of the czarist empire and thereby should belong to the Soviet Union. When the president explained that the American people did not understand that, Stalin recommended that the administration do "some propaganda work."[33]

The Soviet dictator's standoffishness notwithstanding, Roosevelt left Teheran optimistic about future relations. He clearly believed that, as Robert Sherwood put it, Stalin, for all his bluntness, was primarily concerned with legitimate security interests and was "getatable." That a productive partnership lay in the future was easy to believe.[34]

On December 2, the presidential party flew back to Cairo for a final round of British-American conferences. The centerpiece of the endeavor was a meeting with Turkish president Ismet Inonu and his delegation. Held at Churchill's insistence, the conclave was a last-ditch attempt to enlist Turkey in the war and salvage the prime minister's plans for an eastern Mediterranean campaign. It fizzled badly. The Turks were willing to talk but not to commit. General Marshall's stoicism finally cracked. Referring to Churchill's project to capture the island of Rhodes, he shot a profane veto to his British colleagues: "Not one American soldier is going to die on [that] goddamned beach."[35]

The Teheran and Cairo meetings were the pivotal decision-making forums of the war, launching the participants on a trajectory that would largely determine the outcome of the Yalta conference fifteen months in the future. With Churchill's Mediterranean ambitions finally shelved and the cross-channel invasion firmly scheduled, it was up to Roosevelt to name a supreme commander. He moved quickly.

The president had been engaged in more than a sightseeing interlude when he had spent that day in Tunis with Eisenhower. By every measure of loyalty, duty, and capability, Marshall deserved what would be the nation's greatest military distinction. But Marshall, however respected, had never commanded a major combat operation, much less a multinational, multiservice effort. Although greatly admired by his colleagues on the Combined Chiefs of Staff in Washington, he would have to build a new structure of relationships if sent to Europe. Eisenhower, despite some setbacks, had triumphed in North Africa, where he had handled difficult American and British generals, managed political problems, and won the admiration of his troops. He had built a web of goodwill that could not be simply transferred to someone else. Not least, he had a magnetic personality perfectly suited to the leadership of a democratic military effort. Roosevelt doubtless understood all these considerations, especially the power of charisma.

Back in Cairo, FDR saw Ike deliver a report on the Mediterranean theater to the Combined Chiefs of Staff. He dispatched Harry Hopkins to ascertain that Marshall would accept continuance as army chief of staff, then made his decision. He sent for Marshall, told him, "I could not sleep at night if you were out of the country," and dictated a message for him to send to Stalin: "The immediate appointment of General Eisenhower to command of OVERLORD operation has been decided upon." Marshall took the news with scarcely a blink and had the communication transmitted; he kept Roosevelt's handwritten copy and later passed it along to Eisenhower. Roosevelt then flew to Tunis for a meeting with Eisenhower, who still expected to return to Washington as army chief of staff, and said with mock casualness, "Well, Ike, you are going to command OVERLORD."[36]

The pull of OVERLORD was now irresistible, leaving no resources for the eastern Mediterranean and relegating the hard and costly slog up the Italian boot toward Rome to a sideshow.

ROOSEVELT ARRIVED BACK IN WASHINGTON ON DECEMBER 17. THE IMPACT OF a successful Big Three meeting, symbolizing a global alliance and demonstrating the reach of American power around the world, was great. Frank Knox's old newspaper, the *Chicago Daily News*, best described as internationalist-Republican, represented a widespread exultation: "United in war, united in peace—the United Nations!"[37]

The president delivered a radio report to the American people on Christmas Eve. Those who listened closely heard a voice that lacked the richness of earlier years and was interrupted by an occasional cough and throat clearing. Yet, for all its tiredness, it remained commanding and authoritative. Roosevelt reminded his listeners of their nation's strength—10 million men and women in the armed forces, half of them scheduled to be overseas by midsummer and stationed all over the globe—then announced Eisenhower's appointment. Victory, he warned, would require grim sacrifice but was within reach. The personal contacts with Chiang Kai-shek ("a man of great vision, great courage, and a remarkably keen understanding of the problems of today and tomorrow") and Stalin ("a man who combines a tremendous, relentless determination with a stalwart good humor") had cemented the addition of two great nations to the American-British alliance and created the foundation for a new era of global collective security and a lasting peace. He closed the talk with a prayer for America's soldiers, sailors, and airmen—and for the nation's mission in the world.[38]

TEHERAN HAD CONFIRMED THE SOLIDITY OF THE ALLIANCE AND ITS VICTORI-ous trajectory. During the first half of 1944, Allied armies would advance, painstakingly but steadily, staving off Japanese offensives in Burma and China, capturing more strategic Pacific island bases, pushing German forces toward the western boundaries of the Soviet Union, and moving up the Italian Peninsula toward Rome. Even the slippage of the May 1 OVERLORD date would bring no complaint from Stalin.

The long trip to Cairo and Teheran nonetheless took a heavy toll on Roosevelt. He never fully recovered from it. Soon after he was back in Washington, Anna grasped the seriousness of his condition and demanded the services of the young cardiologist Dr. Howard Bruenn. At a time when the burdens of his office demanded a sixty-hour week, the president was told to take his monthlong vacation in the spring of 1944 at Bernard Baruch's southern estate. Once he was back in Washington, the time he could devote to his duties was sharply curtailed. Rumors circulated about his health, but all except an opposition media with scant credibility largely ignored them. His public appearances were few, and he remained capable of gathering his strength for them. The tight White House control of press photos meant that readers of the newspapers and magazines generally saw him, if not at his best, at least as a leader who had aged well and appeared commanding. (The official Teheran photo showed him looking fit, seated between Churchill and Stalin, left leg over right knee, free of the braces he usually wore.)

Late in the spring, he went on the radio to comment on Rome's fall to the Allied armies. He was in great voice, sounding as strong and authoritative as when he had assumed office in 1933. It was the evening of June 5, 1944. He already knew that an Allied invasion fleet was in the English Channel and that he would be on the radio again the next day.[39]

CHAPTER 25

INDISPENSABLE MAN

JUNE 6, 1944–NOVEMBER 7, 1944

Almighty God: Our sons, pride of our Nation, this day have set upon a mighty endeavor, a struggle to preserve our Republic, our religion, and our civilization, and to set free a suffering humanity.

Lead them straight and true; give strength to their arms, stoutness to their hearts, steadfastness in their faith.[1]

ROOSEVELT SPOKE TO THE NATION ON THE EVENING OF D-DAY, JUNE 6, 1944. Nearly twenty-four hours before, the first British and American forces had made their way into Normandy. A three-sentence introduction aside, the entire talk was a five-minute prayer to a God whose commandments aligned with America's cause. Solemn and eloquent, the D-day prayer was of a piece with the first inaugural address of 1933, delivered by a commander in chief still capable of mobilizing the American spirit.

D-DAY WAS A TURNING POINT. DURING THE LAST HALF OF 1944, MILITARY advances in Europe and the Pacific were costly and painful but steady. By the beginning of November, Allied forces in Europe would be pushing the Germans back to their homeland. In the Pacific, US forces would have won bloody battles at Guam and Saipan, effectively destroyed Japanese air and naval power, and begun the reconquest of the Philippines. Victory was in the air—politically more valuable as a prospect than as an accomplished fact that would shift attention to the many hard foreign and domestic issues of an uncertain peacetime.

The objective of winning the war intertwined with that of winning a fourth term. Roosevelt could not resist the lure of presiding over America's greatest military triumph and playing a major role in shaping the peace to follow. On July 11, eight days before the Democratic convention, he released a public letter to Democratic National Committee chairman Robert Hannegan: "All that is within me cries to go back to my home on the Hudson River," but as a good soldier, he would continue in office if the American people commanded him.[2]

Political victory required a difficult tactical retreat: the dumping of the vice president whom Roosevelt had forced on the convention in 1940. Henry Wallace had become the darling of the liberal–New Deal wing of the party. His rhetoric had been instrumental in keeping the New Deal flame alive while Roosevelt busied himself with the war. In the minds of the liberals, he was the heir-apparent to his chief. Yet he had been a failure as an administration liaison to Capitol Hill, disliked not only by the hard-core conservative wing of the party but also by the pragmatic organization politicians who mobilized the northern big-city machine vote.

Who could replace him? The list of usual suspects was uninspiring. James Byrnes had demonstrated strong executive capabilities as head of the Office of War Mobilization, but he would have little appeal in the northern industrial states essential to Democratic victory. A South Carolinian, he was unavoidably a white supremacist; he was also a former Catholic who had left the church to get ahead in the politics of his state.

The list after Byrnes consisted of a number of leading senators with scant national appeal. One slowly came to the surface: Harry S. Truman of Missouri. Truman had achieved national prominence as chair of a special Senate committee investigating waste, fraud, and abuse in national defense; he castigated corporate managers and military procurement officers while avoiding criticism of the president. He had a reliable New Deal voting record but enjoyed friendships with many southern senators. A product of Kansas City's Pendergast machine, he was acceptable to northern organization Democrats. One of his closest associates was party chairman Hannegan, a shrewd St. Louis pol, who held his position largely because of Truman's backing. Truman himself seems to have been uninterested in the vice presidency. Nevertheless, he was emerging as a twentieth-century Missouri Compromise for the number two slot on the ticket.[3]

Wallace sealed his own fate by pressing Roosevelt to send him on a fact-finding mission to Siberia and China. He left Washington on May 20 for travels that took him from Moscow to Chungking. The poorly conceived trip not only deprived him of the opportunity to organize support for his renomination but also highlighted his naiveté, most notably when he let Soviet authorities pass off a Siberian gulag labor camp as a settlement of hardy pioneers. Hannegan and other party leaders convinced the president that Wallace was not worth a party-splitting convention fight.[4]

Wallace did not return to Washington until July 10, just nine days before the Democratic convention. At Roosevelt's request, Harold Ickes and Sam Rosenman met with him, told him that the president had decided against insisting on his renomination, and asked him to announce that he would not be a candidate. Wallace responded that he would discuss his future only with Roosevelt. Later that day, he met with the president for a difficult two-hour talk. Roosevelt said he had received credible warnings that the vice president would cost the ticket as many as 3 million votes. He pretty clearly hoped Wallace would withdraw but would not order him to do so.[5]

The two met again on July 11 and 13. Roosevelt assured Wallace of his personal affection, said he would issue a statement that if he were a delegate he would vote for Wallace, but stopped short of promising to dictate to the convention. As Wallace remembered it, the July 13 meeting ended with a handshake and the president's declaring, "While I cannot put it just that way in public, I hope it will be the same old team."[6]

Roosevelt did not tell Wallace that in an off-the-record dinner meeting with party leaders on July 11, he had, after getting a tepid response to Supreme Court Justice William O. Douglas as a vice presidential possibility, all but acquiesced in the nomination of Truman. He jettisoned the vice president with reluctance but also with a cold, pragmatic evaluation of Wallace's ineptness in his 1943 fight with Jesse Jones and his general ineffectiveness in dealing with congressional leaders.[7]

He also had to deal with Byrnes, for whom he possessed considerable fondness. Roosevelt treated him much as he had Wallace and left him believing he was the president's choice. Byrnes promptly called Harry Truman and asked the senator to place his name in nomination at the convention. Truman, who does not seem to have been aware of his name coming up in Roosevelt's meeting with party leaders, promptly agreed.[8]

Roosevelt had by this point encouraged Wallace, apparently settled on Truman, and encouraged Byrnes. He may have judged it counterproductive to veto any of the possible candidates and likely felt it emotionally painful to do so. He may have been trying to divide the opposition to Wallace. Still, he must have known that after his meeting with Hannegan and the other party leaders, his running mate would be Truman.

What did Roosevelt expect from Truman? He probably thought of the Missourian as a liberal John Nance Garner, a party regular with backing from the northern machines, acceptable to both Negroes and white southerners, and capable of providing reliable information on the pulse of Congress. He almost surely did not see a possible successor. The power of denial overwhelmed any intimation he may have had about being unable to serve out another four years in the White House.

The Democratic convention in Chicago was hectic and disorderly. Roosevelt stayed well clear of it. Traveling in secrecy under wartime censorship rules, he journeyed across the country by train, stopping in Chicago long enough for a final confidential meeting with Bob Hannegan. He arrived in San Diego on the convention's opening day.

Harry Truman came to Chicago planning to deliver a vice presidential nominating speech for Byrnes. Instead he found himself in a hotel room hearing Roosevelt declare via telephone that Truman's refusal to accept the vice presidency would break up the party in the middle of a war. Wallace delivered a stem-winding speech that electrified the delegates and would have resulted in his renomination if the convention had proceeded immediately to a vote. Hannegan countered by releasing a carefully crafted letter in which Roosevelt said, "You have written me about Harry Truman and Bill Douglas. I should, of course, be very glad to run with either of them." With that offhand endorsement, Truman won a close nomination vote from a sharply divided gathering. The president's behavior in *l'affaire Wallace* did him no credit. It displayed the waning judgment of a tired and unwell man beginning to bend under the burdens of leadership.[9]

On the morning of July 20, alone in his railroad car with his son Jimmy, the president had an attack similar to the one he had experienced in Teheran. "For perhaps ten minutes," Jimmy later recalled, "Father lay on the floor of the railroad car, his eyes closed, his face drawn, his powerful torso occasionally convulsed as the waves of pain stabbed him." Yet, although both Doctors McIntire and Bruenn were in the presidential party, they agreed that medical treatment was not necessary.[10]

The malaise passed as suddenly as it had begun. Roosevelt went off to review a military training exercise at nearby Camp Pendleton. That evening, he delivered his nomination acceptance speech by radio from an undisclosed "Pacific Coast naval base." Touting his administration's record in achieving economic recovery and managing a winning war effort, he promised both postwar prosperity and an enduring peace. His voice was strong, but a widely circulated press photo showed him looking worn and haggard. He and Jimmy privately decided to call the event that had felled him a digestive upset. There may have been other such episodes. Writing to Eleanor, FDR simply said, "I got the colly-wobbles." He apparently felt no need to explain the term.[11]

On the evening of July 21, after a day that included a visit with wounded troops at a military hospital, Roosevelt boarded the cruiser USS *Baltimore* for a voyage to Hawaii. He arrived at Pearl Harbor on the afternoon of July 26. For the next two and a half days, he conducted inspections, met soldiers and sailors, and received briefings from General Douglas MacArthur and Admiral Chester Nimitz.

MacArthur greatly resented being called from his headquarters in Australia for what he justly considered a political photo op. All the same, one important issue required a presidential decision. Would the route to Japan run through Taiwan (Nimitz's preference) or the Philippines (MacArthur's imperative)? Despite the mutual wariness that characterized the Roosevelt-MacArthur relationship, the president bought the general's argument. The United States owed the Filipinos as speedy a liberation as possible, and Roosevelt could not have been impervious to the political lift of an American return to the Philippine archipelago just weeks before the election.[12]

On July 29, the president left for the Aleutians, where he visited two bases and made a point of mingling with enlisted men. Two weeks later, he was at Bremerton, Washington, delivering a nationally broadcast speech from the deck of a destroyer to 10,000 shipyard workers. The event was a near disaster. A brisk wind ruffled the pages of his address and rocked the ship. He suffered an onset of sharp angina chest pains, struggled to maintain his footing, and had difficulty following his text. The next day, his train left on the four-day trip to Washington, DC, with its most important passenger under doctor's orders to do nothing but rest.[13]

The pictures and stories quickly followed—of a commander in chief flanked by MacArthur and Nimitz, lunching with enlisted men, and fishing in Alaska with other enlisted men. The White House press operation helpfully calculated the length of the trip at approximately 15,000 miles and reckoned that FDR, during his entire presidency, had logged 306,265 miles in the service of the nation.[14]

BY THE TIME ROOSEVELT RETURNED TO WASHINGTON, HE, HIS LIEUTENANTS, and the larger political world increasingly focused on the new order emerging from the war. It was easy to feel that the future of humankind lay in the balance.

On August 21, a conference to establish a postwar United Nations Organization convened at Dumbarton Oaks in the Georgetown section of Washington. It would adjourn on October 7, having drawn up a plan for an international body not too different from the old League of Nations. Predominant liberal opinion in the United States and Britain held that the League had failed because of American aloofness and that a successor body with full, committed American membership could maintain world peace and stability. Conservative warnings about the inevitability of conflicts among nations had little impact in a country determined to believe that the great sacrifices of total war could lead to an era of total peace.

The Dumbarton Oaks conference revealed rifts between the United States and the Soviet Union. The USSR insisted on the right to veto actions on, and even prevent discussion of, issues in the new organization. Moreover, the USSR asserted that, since Great Britain supported independent memberships for each of its Commonwealth nations, and since the United States could rely on the votes of most Latin American nations, the sixteen Soviet republics should have individual voting status. The conference adjourned with these items unresolved and effectively left to negotiations between Roosevelt, Churchill, and Stalin. A final meeting to establish the new international organization was scheduled for the spring of 1945 in San Francisco.[15]

The most immediately pressing postwar problem was thoroughly predictable and utterly intractable: the future of Poland. The ideals of the Atlantic Charter and the Four Freedoms, reinforced politically by a large Polish American voting bloc that in 1940 had backed Roosevelt by huge margins, required its freedom and independence. In June 1944, the president had welcomed to the White House the Polish prime minister in exile, Stanislaw Mikolajczyk, a genuine democrat who led the Polish Peasants Party. Roosevelt made no promises, but the release of public letters in which the president proclaimed his devotion to the valor of the Polish nation underscored the cordial atmosphere. In fact, he knew that the United States could do little to affect the future of Poland and other eastern European nations and assumed postwar Soviet domination there. At Teheran, he had told Averell Harriman, "I don't care two hoots about Poland."[16]

The USSR had appropriated the eastern half of Poland as its share of the spoils from the Nazi-Soviet pact and clearly aspired to control the entire country at the end of the war. In fact, much of that Soviet-occupied area was not ethnically Polish. At Teheran, both Roosevelt and Churchill had indicated to Stalin that they would not oppose a new eastern Polish boundary along the World War I Curzon Line, which roughly delineated the western border of the 1939

Soviet occupation. Poland would be "compensated" with territory detached from eastern Germany, a move that would likely create lasting German animosity and leave the Poles dependent upon Soviet protection. Moreover, Stalin was determined that the new Poland would have a "friendly" Communist government, based on a regime established by the USSR at Lublin.

By the end of July, the Red Army had advanced across eastern Poland to the Vistula River. Warsaw was on the opposite bank. As the Soviets paused for resupply and reinforcements, lightly armed Polish partisans in the city staged an audacious uprising against the German occupiers. Loyal to the government-in-exile in London, they hoped to establish its claim as a legitimate liberation force. At the beginning, Radio Moscow encouraged the uprising, but Soviet forces on the other side of the river, after their immediate supply needs had been met, did nothing to assist it. Stalin instead shifted divisions to the south to consolidate Soviet control in Hungary and Romania.

In a communication to Churchill and Roosevelt, the Soviet leader characterized the Warsaw insurgents as an irresponsible "handful of criminals." The Russian command on the east bank of the Vistula rejected US and British requests for landing rights and other assistance in efforts to supply the insurgents via airdrops. In the end, only the Royal Air Force made a substantial, if ineffective, attempt and suffered significant losses to German fire. In early September, the remainder of the partisan force surrendered. The episode so incensed George F. Kennan, the number two official at the American embassy in Moscow, that he recommended to Ambassador Harriman threatening cessation of US aid to the Soviet Union. The moral foundation for such a course was undeniable; as a practical matter, its implementation and the consequent break in the alliance were unthinkable. Roosevelt could only watch from afar, recall Stalin's disregard at Teheran for the problem of the Polish American vote in the United States, and hope that the Russian leader's cynicism had not done him much political damage. He surely concluded that Soviet dominance of Poland after the war was inevitable. Perhaps he also wondered what further concessions might be necessary to maintain the US-Soviet relationship.[17]

By then the future of a defeated Germany was the subject of intense discussion within the administration. The United States, Britain, and the Soviet Union had agreed that there would be a postwar military occupation and were in the process of establishing boundaries for their respective zones. The Department of State promoted a plan for the economic and political rehabilitation of Germany within a liberal economic framework. Enlightened and intelligent in principle, the proposal clashed with the bitter feelings engendered by a brutal total war.

No one felt those emotions more deeply than Secretary of the Treasury Henry Morgenthau Jr., motivated especially by what he had learned of the Holocaust. Punishment of German leaders for war crimes, taken for granted by all concerned, was insufficient, Morgenthau argued. The problem was Germany itself and ingrained attitudes of arrogance, authoritarianism, and militarism that defined the German people, who were "beasts."

Even the partition of Germany into several smaller states would not prevent future horrors. The victors had to destroy Germany's capacity to wage war once and for all. The nation had to be irreversibly deindustrialized and made into a "pastoral state" wholly agricultural in its economy and thus incapable of modern warfare. The key to achieving this objective would be the destruction of the German industrial heartland, the Ruhr valley. Its mines should be shut down and its factories leveled. Morgenthau envisioned army engineers flooding and dynamiting "every steel mill, . . . every coal mine, every chemical plant, every synthetic gas business." What to do with all the displaced workers? Feed them, and presumably their families, in army soup kitchens. "Sure it is a terrific problem. Let the Germans solve it. Why the hell should I worry about what happens to their people?"[18]

Roosevelt seemed sympathetic. "We either have to castrate the German people or . . . treat them in such manner that they can't just go on reproducing people who want to continue the way they have in the past," he told Morgenthau.[19]

Secretary of War Henry Stimson was the main opponent to what became known as the Morgenthau Plan. With characteristic (and thoroughly justified) moral indignation, he argued that it could result in the starvation of 30 million people. He was also rightly concerned that Europe as a whole could not recover economically without a strong German industrial sector, and he persisted in his dissent despite sharp criticism from the president.

Roosevelt briefly adopted the Morgenthau Plan and pushed it on Churchill when they met in Quebec from September 11 to 16. Perhaps persuaded by Morgenthau's dubious assertion that the suppression of German heavy industry would pave the way for the resurgence of Britain as Europe's industrial powerhouse, Churchill signed on. The War Cabinet had to ratify the prime minister's assent and later subjected it to skeptical analysis. "In the event," Churchill would write later, "with my full accord, the idea of 'pastoralizing' Germany did not survive."

A similar trend developed in the United States. Word of the Morgenthau Plan leaked to the public. That fall, Republican candidate Thomas Dewey denounced it as a political gift to Hitler worth ten divisions in its potential to inspire a retreating German army to fight on. Roosevelt's own enthusiasm dimmed. Final planning for the occupation of Germany would ultimately fall to the Joint Chiefs of Staff, men motivated more by practical military and administrative considerations than by Morgenthau's fierce anti-Germanism.[20]

A final postwar issue surfaced to public notice: the emerging Soviet hegemony in east-central Europe. Churchill pushed unsuccessfully for another Big Three meeting in late 1944. Roosevelt, focusing his limited energy on his reelection effort, responded that such a conference had to be postponed. Churchill and his cabinet colleagues, feeling a sense of urgency, arranged a bilateral conference with Stalin. The prime minister, Foreign Secretary Anthony Eden, and the rest of the War Cabinet had effectively written off Poland and Czechoslovakia as hopeless cases in which Britain had no pressing interest. Determined to maintain British influence in Greece and Turkey, the keys to the eastern Mediterranean, they hoped to demarcate Soviet and British spheres of dominance in southeastern Europe. Roosevelt disassociated himself from the discussions but arranged to have Ambassador Harriman sit in as an observer.

Accompanied by Eden, Churchill arrived in Moscow on October 9. Meeting with Stalin that evening and perhaps taking advantage of Harriman's inability to attend, he wrote out on a sheet of paper his proposition and passed it over to Stalin:[21]

Rumania

Russia	90%
The Others	10%

Greece

Great Britain	
(in accord with U.S.A.)	90%
Russia	10%

Yugoslavia 50–50%

Hungary 50–50%

Bulgaria

Russia	75%
The Others	25%

The Soviet dictator paused for a moment, then used a blue pencil to make a "large tick" at the top of the paper, which he then pushed to the middle of the conference table. It sat there for a moment before Churchill, assuming that the mark signified agreement, allowed that some might consider the accord cynical and suggested burning it. "No, you keep it," Stalin replied. Whatever their private doubts, he and Eden took Stalin's mark as a serious commitment and clearly tried (with little success) to make the most of it in subsequent discussions with Soviet foreign minister Vyacheslav Molotov.[22]

However obscure the details may have been, there was a widespread understanding in the United States that the Russians had successfully asserted dominance in Poland and that Churchill and Stalin had divided influence in southeastern Europe roughly along the lines of their respective military strengths in that part of the world. Washington-based French journalist Andre Geraud, writing in the New York Times under the pseudonym "Pertinax," accurately described the proposal Churchill had offered. Sophisticates such as Walter Lippmann argued that spheres of influence were a fact of international life, but their reasoning appealed only to other sophisticates. Critics of the administration gained a much wider audience when they denounced the resort to power politics and found Roosevelt guilty by association.[23]

ON AUGUST 18, 1944, ROOSEVELT AND VICE PRESIDENTIAL NOMINEE HARRY S. Truman lunched al fresco at the White House under a great magnolia tree planted more than a century earlier by Andrew Jackson. The president told Truman that he would have to carry the burden of campaigning. Truman, who had not seen Roosevelt face-to-face in more than a year, was shocked by his haggard visage and the trembling of his hand as he attempted to pour cream into his coffee. That did not stop him from telling reporters, "The President looked fine. . . . He's still the leader he's always been and don't let anybody kid you about it." A few weeks later, Truman attended a White House reception with his close friend Eddie McKim. As they left, McKim looked at the White House and said, "You're going to be living in that house before long." Truman replied, "Eddie, I'm afraid I am."[24]

Roosevelt's Republican opponent, Thomas E. Dewey, was a formidable challenger. No longer simply the crime-busting district attorney of 1940, Dewey had won election as governor of New York in 1942. Forty-two years old in 1944 and sporting a dapper mustache, he had the looks of a matinee idol. Ideologically, he was somewhere in the center of his party, conservative enough to criticize New Dealism but receptive to the social mission of government, internationally minded but wary of the Soviet Union. Defeating Wendell Willkie decisively in the Wisconsin presidential primary, he had glided to the nomination. His running mate, Governor John Bricker of Ohio, was a concession to the party's right and, as was the case with Truman among the Democrats, neither an asset nor a liability.

Dewey lacked warmth but exuded energy and competence. Above all, he sought to capitalize on the dissatisfactions of nearly three years of total war. He promised a fresh and energetic administration to replace a tired team. He depicted Roosevelt as running a statist regime that feared peace and a return to mass unemployment. The president could, he asserted, offer nothing beyond a resumption of "the dole." The Republicans, he pledged, would provide jobs for all through a free enterprise economy. Yet, at times he could sound almost New Dealish, advocating the extension of Social Security benefits to such excluded groups as farmers, domestic workers, and the self-employed. He endorsed the principle of publicly provided medical care for those who could not afford it. He assured the nation of his commitment to postwar collective security arrangements to secure the peace but also called for a rapid military demobilization and reliance on a volunteer armed force.

Hard-core conservative and isolationist Republicans had some qualms but found their candidate far preferable to "that man in the White House." If a fair amount of Dewey's rhetoric was facile, it had a visceral appeal to an electorate that had experienced the turmoil of the last four years. In the end, his appeal all came down to one simple maxim: "It's time for a change."[25]

As the campaign got under way, Wendell Willkie was its most prominent wild card. He had staked out positions on domestic policy and international relations that seemed almost Rooseveltian. The title of his 1943 chronicle of a trip that circled the planet, *One World*, alone alienated a critical mass of Republicans. His relationship with the president was cordial but wary. Roosevelt had arranged for Sam Rosenman to meet secretly with Willkie in New York on July 5, just after the Republican convention. Speaking for the president, Rosenman proposed a party realignment in which the progressive wing of the Republican Party would join with liberal Democrats, leaving reactionary Democrats and Republicans to contemplate a conservative alternative. He assured Willkie that the idea had nothing to do with the election.

Willkie, Rosenman recalled, was enthusiastic but unwilling to make any commitments before the November vote. Roosevelt surely hoped to coax an endorsement from him and may have envisioned him as the possible chief executive of the new United Nations Organization. Willkie appears to have been thinking of another shot at the presidency in 1948 and might well have pursued the realignment plan. All such possibilities became moot when he was hospitalized on September 6, purportedly suffering from exhaustion but actually afflicted with serious coronary problems. He died on October 8, having made no endorsement.[26]

While Dewey presided over a relatively united party, the Democrats consisted of three distinct factions in search of a unifying principle: the South, the northern big-city machines, and organized labor. Labor, stronger and more visible than ever, was represented by a new phenomenon, the CIO Political Action Committee (CIO-PAC), headed by Amalgamated Clothing Workers chief Sidney Hillman. The city machines, once massive vote producers, were fading and possessed limited clout at the White House. The South, having for generations supported the Democratic Party as a guarantor of white supremacy, was increasingly restless with administration support for Negro civil rights. The most visible sign of insurgency came in Texas, where a faction calling itself the "regulars" attempted to place independent electors on the Democratic ballot and launched a primary battle against Speaker Sam Rayburn. They reportedly enjoyed the quiet sympathy of Secretary of Commerce Jesse Jones.[27]

As conservatives saw it, the CIO-PAC seemed closer to the president than the machine bosses and raised the specter of labor dominance within the party. Moreover, Hillman espoused a Popular Front liberalism that accepted Communists as coworkers in a common cause, leaving the administration open to charges of Red influence. The Communist Political Association (formerly the Communist Party of the USA) also endorsed Roosevelt. The Republicans, Dewey included, pounded the Communist issue, but it was a simple matter for Roosevelt to disavow Communist backing, which he did in a radio address on October 4. The CIO-PAC nonetheless was an organizational juggernaut that delivered a big vote for the president and the Democratic ticket. The possibility that the Democratic Party might become a labor party seemed real.[28]

In the end the election was all about Franklin D. Roosevelt. The president had just underscored his credentials as a war leader with his travels to Hawaii and the Aleutians, followed by his meeting with Churchill in Quebec. He still had to deal with Republican charges that he was tired, in dire health, and incapable of governing for another four years. However great the degree of personal denial, he knew all too well that the assertions carried a substantial degree of truth and that his efforts needed to be both limited and effective.

He formally opened his campaign on the evening of September 23, as he had four years earlier, with a nationally broadcast speech delivered at Washington's Statler Hotel to delegates at the annual convention of the Teamsters union. For Roosevelt, it mattered a great deal that the Statler was a convenient local venue with a parking garage elevator that greatly simplified the problems of entry and departure. His choice of audience also revealed much about the polarized politics of 1944. The decision to speak to a union gathering reinforced the class appeal symbolized by the CIO-PAC. It also meant lending presidential imprimatur to a labor organization that in many localities had semiopen ties to gangsters, a situation that outraged Republicans but that most Democrats accepted as a fact of life or simply ignored.

However he felt about the Teamsters, the president expressed his delight at being in their presence once again. He started his speech by recognizing their president, Dan Tobin: "Mr. Tobin . . . I should say 'Dan.' I always have." The talk, studded with sarcastic jabs, was tough and masterful. "WELL, here we are together again—after four years. . . . You know I am actually four years older, which is a fact that seems to annoy some people. . . . [T]here are millions of Americans who are more than eleven years older than when we started in to clear up the mess that was dumped in our laps in 1933."[29]

Roosevelt smacked down Republican claims to solicitude for labor and support for social progress. "We have all seen many marvelous stunts in the circus but no performing elephant could turn a handspring without falling flat on his back." He accused the opposition of resorting to the Hitlerite tactic of the Big Lie, indulging in labor baiting, and harboring isolationist tendencies. He professed his dedication to winning the coming peace, globally through the establishment of international machinery, at home through an economic policy that would provide jobs for all.

This was strong stuff, but a single paragraph responding to an improbable story vented on the floor of the House of Representatives by Harold Knutson, an undistinguished Republican congressman from Minnesota, ultimately overshadowed it. Asserting that during FDR's inspection tour of the Aleutians Fala had been left behind on a remote island and a destroyer dispatched at prohibitive cost to retrieve him, the story was of a piece with various complaints and innuendos about the president and his family. Charging that "Republican leaders" had spread this latest attack, Roosevelt ridiculed it: "I don't resent attacks, and my family doesn't resent attacks, *but Fala does resent them*! . . . He has not been the same dog since. I am accustomed to hearing malicious falsehoods about myself. . . . But I think I have a right to resent . . . libelous statements about my dog." The riposte successfully trivialized the Republican campaign. It also underscored the empathy gap between a challenger who could offer cold executive efficiency and an incumbent who, after reminding his audience of the Depression miseries the Republicans had inflicted upon them, lightheartedly proclaimed his affection for his dog.[30]

Roosevelt spent the next four weeks at the White House, gathering his strength for the final push of the campaign. On October 20, he boarded his train for an overnight trip to New York. The next day, he rode in an open car through the four contiguous boroughs of the city, receiving the acclaim of perhaps 3 million residents who lined fifty-one miles of streets, enduring a steady rain and forty-degree temperatures, wearing only his navy cape over his business suit for protection against the elements, and stopping at Ebbets Field to speak at a rally for Senator Robert Wagner. Eleanor and Fala rode alongside him.

Almost everyone realized that the whole point of the excursion was to convince the public that he remained strong and vigorous. Mayor Fiorello La Guardia, who traveled the distance with him, declared that the president had managed the trip better than he. Democratic state chairman Paul Fitzpatrick asserted that Roosevelt had seemed better than four years earlier when campaigning in Buffalo. They were not just reciting expected lines. The president seemed genuinely invigorated by the adulation of the crowds. After about five hours, the motorcade terminated at Washington Square, where the presidential party went to Eleanor's apartment for a late lunch. Roosevelt, whether out of a search for warmth or sheer elation, tossed down two bourbons and napped. He then fortified himself for a major speech with another bourbon and some martinis.[31]

That evening, he delivered a major address to the Foreign Policy Association. Ad-libbing effectively, he was in fine form as he affirmed his commitment to a postwar United Nations association with power to act swiftly against aggressor nations, pledged to preserve the US-British-Soviet alliance, and—in an all but explicit disavowal of the Morgenthau Plan—declared that the Nazi leaders would be punished but the German people would receive fair treatment.[32]

On October 27, after a weekend at Hyde Park and three days back at the White House, he took to the campaign train again for a rear-platform appearance in Wilmington, Delaware, then another cold and rainy motorcade through Philadelphia and Camden past perhaps 1 million people. That evening, he delivered an address to an estimated 50,000 spectators at Shibe Park. Just three days earlier, he reminded the crowd, American forces had fought the largest naval engagement in history, the Battle of Leyte Gulf; his administration, which had begun rebuilding the US Navy a decade earlier in the face of Republican indifference, had made the resulting annihilation of the Japanese fleet possible. Above all, he sent the message that he was the successful commander in chief of a winning war effort.[33]

Then it was on to Chicago, with a rear-platform appearance in Fort Wayne and waves to crowds that had gathered in Gary. On the evening of October 28, Roosevelt's car drove into Soldier Field, where a crowd of 110,000 awaited him, and up a ramp onto a platform in the vicinity of what would have been the fifty-yard line if a football game had been scheduled. From there, he lampooned the Republican assertion that the incompetent, quarrelsome, tired old men in Washington, who somehow were winning the greatest war in history and laying the foundations of a lasting peace, had to go. Rejecting any idea that the New Deal was over, he pledged a continuance of liberal governance, from the Fair Employment Practices Committee to an ongoing farm-support program. Reminding the audience of his economic bill of rights, he promised to "provide America with close to sixty million productive jobs."[34]

One more weekend remained before the election. Roosevelt spent it making appearances in New England, with a final speech in Boston in which he entertained his audience by noting that "a Republican candidate" had in separate speeches on the same day accused him of communism and monarchy. "Which is it?" he asked. "Communism or monarchy? I do not think we could have both in this country."[35]

As usual, he voted in Hyde Park on Election Day, November 7, waited at home for the returns, and received a Democratic torchlight parade. When it arrived at 11:25 p.m., the national trend was already established. "We have partial returns, and they seem to be partial to Hyde Park," he told the crowd. Less than a half hour later, Democratic chairman Hannegan claimed victory. Dewey held out until shortly after 3:00 a.m. before conceding defeat. Roosevelt sent him a telegram of thanks, then, as he was being wheeled to his bedroom, remarked to his aide Bill Hassett, "I still think he is a son of a bitch."[36]

Roosevelt's popular vote margin of more than 3.5 million was the closest of his four presidential elections. The Democrats lost two seats in the Senate but picked up twenty-four in the House. The numbers held little promise for a major legislative program.

A graphic published in the *New York Times* two and a half weeks before the election explained the victory. It displayed responses to three polling questions:

Which man is likely to get the war over in the shortest time? Roosevelt, 44%; Dewey, 22%.

Which man would you rather have represent the United States at the peace conference? Roosevelt, 63%; Dewey, 26%.

Which man do you think would do the best job of running our affairs here in this country? Roosevelt, 46%; Dewey, 43%.[37]

A public almost evenly divided on domestic issues might have opted for a change. On issues of war and peace, the people voted for the commander in chief. At the end of July, Ernest K. Lindley had written a column asking whether the president was indispensable. Roosevelt, he concluded, "is not only experienced but is the repository of information and skills which no other single person has or could have." A majority of Americans agreed.[38]

The champion had won another round. Americans, however, seemed more divided than ever about whether the New Deal remained an attractive foundation for postwar domestic policy, and the new Congress was likely to reflect the view of the skeptics. Roosevelt could look forward to presiding over victory in a war that was almost won, but securing the peace was another matter. Hard tests lay ahead.

CHAPTER 26

THE QUEST FOR A NEW WORLD ORDER

NOVEMBER 8, 1944–APRIL 15, 1945

AT NOON ON JANUARY 20, 1945, A THIN BLANKET OF SNOW COVERED WASHING-ton. The temperature was thirty-four degrees. Franklin Roosevelt's fourth inauguration took place not at the Capitol but at the White House. Suppos-edly reflecting wartime austerity, the choice of venue actually minimized the president's physical effort. A crowd of a few thousand, ranging from foreign diplomats in formal morning dress to ordinary citizens bundled up against the cold, stood on the south lawn. Eleanor, Jimmy, and Anna were among the dignitaries; Elliott, Franklin Jr., and John were away at war. All thirteen of the Roosevelt grandchildren watched from the south portico steps, as did Eleanor's three nieces, the three children of Norway's Princess Martha, and Harry Hop-kins's daughter, Diana. Outgoing vice president Henry Wallace administered the oath of office to his successor, Harry Truman. The president then doffed his navy cape, stood, bareheaded, with Jimmy in marine uniform next to him, and took the oath, his hand on the family Dutch Bible, from Chief Justice Harlan Fiske Stone.[1]

Although not without eloquence, FDR's fourth inaugural address was nota-ble primarily for its six-minute brevity. Perfection might not be achievable, he declared, but America could neither live alone nor gain a lasting peace if it harbored an attitude of suspicion and mistrust toward the rest of the world. Americans had to be "members of the human community." Perhaps the most memorable line was the one he had used in 1926, addressing the Milton Academy: quoting Endicott Peabody, he declared, "The great fact to remember is that the trend of civilization itself is ever upward." The president remained standing through a brief benediction delivered by eminent Catholic social reformer Monseigneur John A. Ryan, followed by the playing of the national anthem. Then, as the band struck up "Hail to the Chief," he waved to the crowd and retreated to the warmth of the White House, where he presided over a buffet luncheon for 250 guests.

Thus began a fourth term in which a tired and sick president would strive to conclude a global war and establish a new world order animated by the liberal values of his old chief, Woodrow Wilson, and underwritten by the military power so valued by his revered cousin Theodore Roosevelt.

THE SCENE PROMOTED AN OPTIMISM ABOUT THE FUTURE THAT SEEMED AMPLY justified by events. In Europe, American and British counterattacks had flattened out the "bulge" lost to a stunning German offensive in the Ardennes a month earlier. On the eastern front, Soviet armies were moving toward Berlin. The war in Europe was almost over. The Pacific conflict would take perhaps another year, but US advances were steady. American troops were just seventy-six miles from Manila. B-29 Superfortress bombers were making devastating strikes on Japan itself.[2]

Roosevelt experienced some chest pain during the ceremony, but he concealed it well. Rumors about his health seemed much overblown after his apparently sturdy appearance in the cold. Briefing reporters, Dr. Ross T. McIntire assured them that aside from perhaps slightly diminished hearing in one ear, "everything's fine. . . . He's carrying a thunder of a lot of work and getting away with it in grand style." Journalists were a bit less ebullient but detected little more than normal ageing. Citing the president's wit and ability to relax, *New York Times* reporter John Crider concluded, "Mr. Roosevelt, even at 63, would be better able to plot an intelligible and constructive course through the wilderness of great problems confronting the country than many men much younger than himself."[3]

Such optimism obscured great uncertainties. The coming end of the world war would be fraught with crises and reconfigurations of power over much of the globe. Maintenance of the Grand Alliance was not a given. The establishment of the world security organization foreshadowed at Dumbarton

Oaks would require a new conceptualization of the global order and perhaps a rethinking of traditional notions of national sovereignty.

Issues at home were also pressing. Military mobilization and the industrial economy it created had absorbed the unemployed and brought 6 million women into the workforce. What would happen when peace broke out and defense plants shut down? Would the overheated full employment of the war revert to the mass joblessness and despair of the Depression? What had Roosevelt intended with his campaign pledge of 60 million jobs? Was another New Deal in the offing? It was almost impossible to find a liberal or progressive who thought that the economy could take care of itself. Conservatives—most Republicans and a sizeable number of Democrats, mostly from the South—recoiled at the thought of yet another New Deal.

Roosevelt's campaign pledge to continue the Fair Employment Practices Committee after the war lent urgency to the issue of race, a secondary concern during the Depression. This reinforced the tendency of Dixie Democrats to ally with GOP conservatives, who might not share their ingrained racism but instinctively distrusted federal intrusions into workplace hiring decisions. Furthermore, the wartime elections had hardened the conservative coalition on Capitol Hill. Domestic economic and racial issues had primarily generated the conservative bloc, which also recoiled from anything smacking of world government and harbored deep suspicion of the Soviet Union.

In this difficult environment, Roosevelt coupled an ambitious domestic agenda with the priority of finding a prominent place for Henry Wallace.

AT HIS PRESS CONFERENCE ON DECEMBER 19, 1944, ROOSEVELT HAD SAID HE would maintain a domestic course "a little to the left of center." On January 6, 1945, he had sent his annual State of the Union message to Congress. Mostly devoted to the war and emerging foreign policy issues, the document concluded with an expansive and unabashedly New Dealish vision of the future. Citing the Economic Bill of Rights enunciated in his 1944 State of the Union address, it called for a full-employment economy, fueled by massive federal funding that would supplement private enterprise in developing "a decent home for every family," a prosperous agricultural sector, urban reconstruction, new TVA-style river valley authorities, a network of airports, and large-scale highway construction. It also advocated a stronger Social Security system, along with "adequate health and education programs." Accompanied by requests for authority to draft nurses for military hospitals and industrial workers for war industries, the message envisioned a statist agenda that went well beyond the New Deal.

It also telegraphed to alarmed conservatives that Henry Wallace would have a high profile in the implementation of the president's agenda.[4]

Wallace retained a fervent following among liberal Democrats. Shortly after the 1944 convention, Roosevelt had sent him a telegram, instructing him to tell his wife that she should not plan on leaving Washington. The president, as a matter of both political calculation and genuine ideological sympathy, wanted to keep him in the administration.

They had met on August 29 for lunch under the White House magnolia tree. As Wallace remembered it, he said just enough to register a sense of grievance even as he reaffirmed his support for the president. Roosevelt responded that he would give Wallace any cabinet post he wanted other than secretary of state; Cordell Hull was "an old dear" and dismissal would break his heart. But he wanted to get rid of some others. First on the list was "Jesus H. Jones." Wallace jumped at the opportunity for revenge against his old antagonist, Secretary of Commerce Jesse Jones. The understanding was reached then and there: Wallace would succeed Jones as secretary of commerce and also inherit Jones's powerful position as head of the Reconstruction Finance Corporation and its subsidiary lending agencies.[5]

Wallace may well have had memories of how Herbert Hoover had used the commerce post to propel himself into the presidency and likely saw himself as a kingpin of postwar economic development. That fall, he had campaigned intensively for Roosevelt. When he rode with the president and Harry Truman in the celebratory procession that marked FDR's return to Washington on November 10, his presence seemed to demonstrate that he would remain an important figure in the administration.

Yet Roosevelt was in no rush to make an appointment. Wallace, deeply concerned by the president's physical deterioration and lack of focus in personal and cabinet meetings, was likely the source of leaks to newspapers that Roosevelt had promised the Commerce Department to him. In the meantime, the president accepted the resignation of "old dear" Cordell Hull, who was in failing health, without offering the post to Wallace. Instead he named Undersecretary Edward R. Stettinius Jr., former chairman of US Steel and far from a stellar choice in the eyes of the liberals. The president and Wallace met again on December 20. Roosevelt confirmed his promise, approved Wallace's ideas for reorganizing the Commerce Department, wandered off into a discussion of astrological predictions that the war would last into 1947, and floated the theory that tropical native workers were healthiest when naked.[6]

On the afternoon of January 19, Roosevelt assured Wallace that he would act after the inauguration. He also mentioned that he would commence a long trip on January 22—he did not tell Wallace he was going to Yalta to meet with Stalin and Churchill—but was certain that Senate confirmation would be routine. In fact, he probably postponed the appointment until the last moment because he knew that the aftermath would be difficult and unpleasant.

On the afternoon of January 20, FDR dictated a communication to be hand-delivered to Jones. Composing the letter was very difficult, he said, "because of our long friendship and splendid relations during all these years and also because of your splendid services to the Government." It was nonetheless necessary to reward Henry Wallace for his own contributions and for his "utmost devotion" in the recent political campaign, a not-so-subtle dig at Jones's own silence about the party revolt in Texas. "There are several ambassadorships. . . . I hope you will have a chance, if you think well of it, to speak to Ed Stettinius." The letter closed with the assurance, "I am very proud of all that you have done during these past years."[7]

The patronizing communication outraged Jones, who had silently endured rumors that he would be dumped. His reply was civil but firm. He thanked Roosevelt for his praise but commented, "It is difficult to reconcile these encomiums with your avowed purpose to replace me." He accepted the president's decision but could not agree that Wallace, "a man inexperienced in business and finance," was qualified to run the Commerce Department or manage the lending agencies. He released both Roosevelt's letter and his response to the press. Many newspapers reprinted them verbatim.[8]

Wallace now faced a major Senate confirmation struggle. On the night of January 22, Roosevelt and the presidential party slipped out of Washington, bound for Yalta, leaving the secretary of commerce designate to fight alone for his political life. A conspiracy theorist might argue that the president intended to rid the administration of both Jones and Wallace. The events more likely revealed the diminished capacity of a sick and distracted chief executive.

As Roosevelt made his way across the Atlantic, the Senate Commerce Committee held sharply contested hearings on the Wallace nomination, listening to testimony from both Jones and Wallace. It became clear that opposition from conservative Democrats and Republicans would defeat the nominee unless Congress separated the lending agencies from the Commerce Department. Senate Majority Leader Alben Barkley and Vice President Truman got a bill through the Senate to accomplish that objective; Sam Rayburn pushed it through the House. It is uncertain whether Roosevelt was either fully informed of these developments or much interested in them. Wallace's confirmation for a much diminished post would come only on March 1, just after Roosevelt's return to the United States.[9]

THE PRESIDENT'S CONCERNS LAY ELSEWHERE. THE INEXORABLE MARCH toward victory in Europe was leaving increasingly urgent problems in its wake. Most of these grew out of the conflict between the Atlantic Charter, with its affirmation of the grand ideal of self-determination, and the realities of armed conquest. The Red Army rolled through eastern Europe leaving a Soviet-dominated sphere of influence in its wake.

Poland was a critical focal point. The Russians had established their own Polish Committee of National Liberation, based in the eastern city of Lublin, and successfully pressured the Czechoslovak government-in-exile to recognize it. The London Poles, still recognized by Great Britain and the United States, resisted Soviet dominance and insisted on Poland's prewar boundaries. Roosevelt and Churchill had agreed to the Curzon Line as Poland's eastern border, effectively conceding to the Soviet Union half of Poland's prewar territory, populated mostly by Ukrainians but including the heavily Polish city of Lwow.

The conflict had no practical solution. In November 1944, during a month-long return to the United States, Averell Harriman had discussed the Polish territorial dispute with Roosevelt. The president suggested with apparent seriousness that Lwow could be made a free city, governed by an international committee, and that Ukrainian peasants would find it a profitable market for their produce. "I tried to tell him that it was impossible," Harriman wrote in his notes of the conversation. "I carried it as far as I could until he became annoyed that I was unwilling to dream with him." The idea, he thought, was of a piece with other Rooseveltian fantasies about personally arbitrating Soviet boundary disputes with Poland and Finland. By then a seasoned observer of Moscow's totalitarian atmosphere, Harriman knew that Soviet leaders would take what they wanted without regard to American qualms. So surely did Roosevelt in soberer moments, but he never gave up hope that he could somehow persuade Stalin to yield to the norms of democratic tolerance and compromise.[10]

Britain, in the meantime, had consolidated its dominance in the Mediterranean. The British gave quiet promises of support to Turkey against possible Soviet efforts to gain control of the Dardanelles. Their armed intervention beat down a Communist insurgency in Greece, from which German forces had withdrawn in the fall of 1944. The use of troops supported by British warships to shell Communist-held working-class areas of Athens drew strong denunciations from American liberals, who demonstrated considerably less concern with Soviet tactics in eastern Europe. Both Harry Hopkins and Roosevelt communicated their qualms to Churchill. For a time in November and December, the US-British alliance seemed on the verge of a crisis, but by the end of the year, the British had put down the Communist bid for power, and Washington was as eager as London to move on to other issues.[11]

Roosevelt's State of the Union message had openly expressed his uneasiness with the situations in Poland and Greece. Calling for a "peoples' peace," it had restated the principles of the Atlantic Charter while also declaring that the United States could not demand 100 percent perfection in their realization. The caution was salutary but less than frank, given Roosevelt's own understanding that the eastern European nations, with the probable exception of Greece, would inevitably fall under Soviet dominance. Few Americans, of Greek descent or otherwise, would strongly object to a British-imposed regime in Greece. A Soviet sphere of influence that extended from Poland and eastern Germany in the north to Albania, Yugoslavia, and Bulgaria in the south would offend most Americans, motivated either by ethnicity or by a simple hatred of communism. Roosevelt surely understood all this, sought to finesse it as best he could, and hoped to convince Stalin of the virtues of restraint in managing his new sphere of influence.

ON THE MORNING OF JANUARY 23, ROOSEVELT AND HIS PARTY BOARDED THE new heavy cruiser USS *Quincy*, which promptly departed on a ten-day voyage to Malta. There Roosevelt would meet with Churchill, then fly to Yalta. His immediate party, the group that dined with him, included Anna, Admiral William D. Leahy, Dr. McIntire, naval aide Vice Admiral Wilson Brown, Appointments Secretary General Pa Watson, Steve Early, James Byrnes, and Ed Flynn. (FDR brought along Byrnes, whose name had been floated for secretary of state after Hull's resignation, and Flynn in recognition of their influence with key Democratic Party constituencies that would need to sign on to any agreements reached at Yalta.) The total American party at the conference itself—diplomats, military leaders, functionaries, and support staff—numbered around 350.

The January crossing of the North Atlantic was about as good as could be hoped. One imagines that the meals were pleasant and the conversation lively. Each night, the president and his party viewed a first-run Hollywood feature film. There is no record of preparatory meetings for the conference. It appears that Roosevelt used the time to rest up for what would surely be a strenuous experience. The extent to which he cracked the briefing books prepared for him is unknown. On February 2, the *Quincy* arrived at Malta, where a conference of the US and British military chiefs was concluding. Harry Hopkins, who had flown across the Atlantic to meet with Churchill, was there waiting, as was the prime minister.[12]

   Roosevelt acknowledged cheering crowds and salutes from British warships
in Valletta Harbor. A photo later cleared for release to the press shows him
sitting across from Churchill in business suit and flat driving cap, appearing
firm-jawed and dominant. In reality, those who met him close up were shocked.
Charles Bohlen, who had gone ahead with Hopkins, summed it up: "He was
not only frail and desperately tired, he looked ill. I never saw Roosevelt look as
bad as he did then." Out of exhaustion, a determination to avoid the appearance of "ganging-up on Stalin," and a sense that American interests diverged
from those of Britain, the president rebuffed Churchill's plea to develop a common negotiating strategy.[13]

   Sometime after 11:00 p.m., he and his party boarded the first aircraft ever
designed for use by the president of the United States. A converted C-54 transport plane equipped with an elevator for Roosevelt's convenience and containing a conference room, it was powerful and luxurious. The president had
given it a whimsical name, *Sacred Cow*. Roosevelt retired immediately. The
plane took off at 3:30 a.m. on February 3. Seven hours and 1,375 miles later, it
landed at Saki in Crimea, where Soviet foreign minister Vyacheslav Molotov
greeted the American and British parties. After lunch and brief ceremonies,
the visitors transferred to a fleet of Lend-Lease Packards for an arduous drive
to Yalta through a frozen, war-devastated landscape. The motorcade crept at
twenty miles per hour along roads lined with Soviet troops, mostly female,
who saluted smartly as it passed. The exhausting journey took nearly five
hours.[14]

   The Russians put the Americans up at Livadia Palace, a former czarist retreat
built in the early twentieth century; it also served as the venue for the plenary
meetings. The British lodged about twelve miles away at Vorontsov Palace, an
imposing mid-nineteenth-century structure. The Russians themselves stayed
about halfway between at Yusupov Palace, built in 1909 for a Russian prince.
All three buildings had accommodated German army officers and been sys-
tematically looted as the invaders retreated. All also reflected a sensibility that
interpreted the phrase "sanitary plumbing" as "chamber pot." The few bath-
rooms with running water were reserved for senior statesmen. Four-star generals and admirals stood in line for more elemental facilities. Bedbugs seemingly
immune to DDT and other pesticides also infested the palaces. Still, the Russians had performed a Herculean task in making them habitable.[15]

   As at Teheran, listening devices expertly placed by Sergo Beria picked up
every word uttered by guests, who, widely suspecting the bugs' presence, had
no alternative but to carry on as if they did not exist.

Never a strong detail man, Roosevelt came to the conference with a few over-riding objectives and a keen sense of his limited bargaining power. He clearly understood that eastern Europe would come under Soviet control and knew he could only hope that the Russians would exercise their dominance lightly. Like many American liberals, he probably thought that Communist regimes, whatever their restrictions on personal liberties, would distribute social benefits equitably and be an improvement over the right-wing dictatorships that had characterized much of the area before the war. As he had been neither willing nor able to block Churchill's moves in Greece, he realized that he could not veto Stalin's domi-nance of areas occupied by the Red Army. He knew also that, once the war was over, there would be an irresistible clamor for demobilization in the United States and a sharp decline in the military power that a president could employ.

His most urgent need was to nail down Soviet participation in the Pacific war. Development of the super bomb under way at Los Alamos was still specu-lative. An invasion of the Japanese home islands could become a long, costly bloodbath. Here, above all, Roosevelt was prepared to concede whatever it took to bring the fighting to an early conclusion. Tens of thousands of American casualties seemingly hung in the balance.

Clearly no starry-eyed idealist in the pursuit of these goals, neither was he as hard-headed as he probably thought. When in human history had three world powers with divergent cultures and ambitions achieved unity of policy and objectives over the long run? Britain and Churchill, sharing a common language and similar traditions with the United States and dependent upon American economic support, could be brought along. The Soviet Union under Stalin was a sworn enemy of bourgeois capitalism and the liberal-democratic institutions that came with it. Its overriding goal of revolution depended on single-minded pursuit of the interests of the Soviet state. Personalities were unimportant; friendship was a bourgeois affectation.

Neither Roosevelt nor Churchill fully grasped this yawning gap in perspec-tives. Both understood practically that much of the world was authoritarian and that one had to deal with dictators, but neither quite apprehended the distinc-tion between run-of-the-mill dictatorships and ideologically driven totalitarian societies. Roosevelt believed the Soviet ruler was amenable to charm and reason. The president and many other policy makers thought that when Stalin was dif-ficult, he was acting under pressure from the Soviet Politburo, whose members actually lived in mortal fear of him. Churchill was more realistic but not with-out his own illusions. He once told Field Marshall Bernard Montgomery, "If only I could dine with Stalin once a week, there would be no trouble at all."[16]

MUCH OF THE WORK OF THE CONFERENCE WAS DONE IN SECOND-ECHELON meetings. American, British, and Soviet military leaders developed the outlines of a planned joint Soviet-US offensive against Japan. The Big Three foreign ministers—Stettinius, Anthony Eden, and Molotov—debated a wide range of issues, many of which they then referred to their superiors, who conferred in eight plenary sessions held from February 4 to 11.

Convening in late afternoon for the first seven plenaries and late morning for a rushed final session, the three leaders sat at a round table, each with two aides on either side and others behind them. Roosevelt usually had Admiral Leahy and Secretary Stettinius to his right. On his immediate left was Bohlen, who served primarily as translator and compiler of a summary of each meeting. The occupant of the fourth seat varied. Averell Harriman was always close to the president, along with Harry Hopkins, who, despite wretched health, attended all but the first plenary. State Department officials H. Freeman Matthews and Alger Hiss (a covert Soviet agent) were also present but exercised little apparent influence.[17]

Each delegation hosted one plenary dinner, a social occasion characterized by groaning-board menus, abundant wine, and a multitude of vodka-fueled toasts. The presence of three special guests, "the girls"—Averell Harriman's daughter, Kathleen; Churchill's daughter, Sarah Oliver; and Roosevelt's daughter, Anna—graced these evenings. At Stalin's dinner on February 8, Sergo Beria's father, Lavrenty Beria, chief of the dreaded secret police, a known killer, rapist, and sexual sadist, attended as a nondiplomatic participant. Stalin sardonically introduced him as "Our Himmler," the Soviet counterpart of the Nazi Gestapo chieftain. Beria seems to have enjoyed chatting up the girls in encounters that provided a revealing contrast of depravity and innocence. Sarah Oliver recounted a conversation in which she recited to him one of the five Russian sentences she had memorized: "Can I have a hot water bottle, please?" He replied, "I cannot believe that you need one! Surely there is enough fire in you!" Kathleen Harriman described him as "little and fat with thick lenses, which give him a sinister look, but quite genial."[18]

At the plenary meetings, Stalin was clearly the dominant figure. He was presiding over a parley on his own turf and commanded an overwhelming military offensive surging into central Europe. He remained much the same man Harry Hopkins had met in 1941: calm, self-possessed, impressive in debate, and confident in the strength of his position. When, in discussion of the new eastern Polish boundary, Churchill argued for a deviation from the Curzon Line in favor of the Polish claim to Lwow, Stalin responded that Lord Curzon, an

Englishman, and Georges Clemenceau, a Frenchman, had agreed on the line after World War I. Should he be less Russian than they?[19]

Churchill displayed the rhetorical talents of an English parliamentarian but could not command the power to be taken seriously. Roosevelt presided over impressive power but was anxious to bring the Russians into the fight against Japan and valued preservation of the alliance as the key to lasting peace. Following the example he had established at Teheran, he played the role of mediator between the Old Tory and the Old Bolshevik.

The conference addressed some relatively trivial problems, such as the list of invitees to the conference that would found the new United Nations Organization (UNO) and the wording of the invitation. Others were moderately important—among them, the disputed Yugoslavian boundary with Italy and Austria and the Soviet interest in making Yugoslavia (led by then compliant Communist Josip Broz Tito) the linchpin of a Balkan federation oriented toward Moscow. One oddity involved UNO representation. Roosevelt had great hopes for the new world security body. He understood it had to be backed by Big Three unity. So long as the great powers, perhaps expanded to include France and China, controlled the organization and agreed on the issues it faced, the UNO could become a powerful force in managing a stable world. Perceiving that Soviet buy-in was essential, he wanted to pin down a commitment at Yalta.

Difficulties emerged quickly. Membership on a UNO Security Council would give the great powers a veto on action resolutions. The Russians demanded a veto on issues to be debated but finally relented. Mindful that the United States would have strong influence over the votes of the Western Hemisphere nations and that Britain would usually be able to muster a bloc vote from the self-governing members of its empire, the Soviet Union renewed the demand made at Dumbarton Oaks for sixteen votes, one for each "independent" Soviet republic. Eventually, Stalin settled for three, one for the USSR as a whole and one each for the Belorussian and Ukrainian republics, which had borne the brunt of the German military offensive. The Soviet dictator even agreed to voting privileges for two US states, an idea dropped after strong negative reaction from leading members of Congress.

Other issues critical in defining the shape of the postwar world included the fate of Poland and the rest of Soviet-occupied eastern Europe, the future of Germany, and the need to bring the USSR into the war against Japan. Poland remained critical to Britain, which had gone to war in response to the German attack upon that nation in 1939, and to the United States, where, as Roosevelt once again reminded Stalin, Polish Americans constituted an important voting bloc. It was also the most prominent test case for implementation of the principles of the Atlantic Charter throughout eastern Europe. Pressed by Roosevelt and Churchill, Stalin promised free elections in which Stanislaw Mikolajczyk's Peasant Party and other democratic forces could participate. Roosevelt declared, "I want this election in Poland to be . . . like Caesar's wife. I did not know her but they said she was pure." Stalin's response was telling: "They said that about her but in fact she had her sins." It was amply clear that Stalin, in full control of the situation on the ground, intended to maintain his grip on the Lublin Poles. The Soviet leader nonetheless consented to a statement that the Polish government would be "reorganized on a broader democratic basis with the inclusion of democratic leaders from Poland itself and from Poles abroad." He issued a similar pledge for Yugoslavia.[20]

The conference communiqué included a general "Declaration on Liberated Europe," citing the Atlantic Charter and promising representative democracy in all the nations freed from Nazi rule. It also made the first formal announcement that Poland would lose its territory east of the Curzon Line (including Lwow) and be compensated with portions of eastern Germany. The democratic generalities glittered impressively, but realists understood that rhetorical gemstones had little value. The hard-nosed Admiral Leahy told Roosevelt, "Mr. President, this is so elastic that the Russians can stretch it all the way from Yalta to Washington without ever technically breaking it." According to Leahy, FDR responded, "Bill, I know it, but it's the best I can do for Poland at this time." He must have privately continued to expect, as he had confided to Archbishop Francis Spellman in September 1943, that the rest of eastern Europe, Greece excepted, would experience the same fate.[21]

The Big Three talked of perhaps a tripartite division of Germany into a primarily Prussian North, a South that fused Bavaria with Austria, and a Ruhr-centered western industrial state. The conference established a committee to explore the question. The public communiqué declared, "Nazi Germany is doomed," but avoided any mention of dismemberment. It did, however, promise an indefinite military occupation, for which the zones had already been drawn, and pledged the destruction of both the Nazi Party and German militarism. Germany, it declared, would have to pay reparations for the damage it had inflicted on the Allies, but no sum was stated. (Stalin had floated the then astounding figure of $20 billion, half of which would go to the Soviet Union. Churchill, citing the post–World War I experience, doubted the Allies could extract one-tenth of that amount.)[22]

Germany, in fact, would be "dismembered." An eastern portion would go to Poland in compensation for that country's involuntary cession to the USSR;

a Soviet zone of occupation would eventually become an East German state; and the US-British-French zones of occupation would become a West German state. The reparations extracted from a destroyed economy would be slim for all the conquerors. Germany's eventual reunification as the quasi-pacifist economic powerhouse of Europe was beyond imagination.

No objective at Yalta was more critical for Roosevelt than pinning down Soviet participation in the war against Japan. He had worked through Averell Harriman to seal a deal with Stalin two months earlier. Stalin had demanded control of the Japanese-held southern half of Sakhalin Island and the Kurile Islands, long-term leases on the Manchurian ports of Port Arthur and Dairen, and another long-term lease on the eastern Manchurian railway link to the Soviet Union. He expected dominance over the sea lanes east of Vladivostok and hegemony in Manchuria.[23]

The Manchurian concessions were technically at the disposal of Chiang Kai-shek, but Roosevelt had no compunction about granting them. Stalin in turn pledged that twenty-five divisions would be transferred to the Manchurian border and ready to attack the Japanese three months after the end of the European war. Critics would later call this a betrayal of Chiang. It was more accurately a recognition that Chiang had, a decade and a half earlier, lost whatever control he might claim over Manchuria and could not stop the Red Army from occupying it. A Roosevelt with a proven atomic bomb at his disposal might have decided Soviet participation in the war against Japan was unnecessary and skipped the whole deal, or he still might have thought the Russians worth mollifying. As it was, he could legitimately feel that he had struck a good bargain and averted American casualties potentially running into the hundreds of thousands. His military leaders agreed. Admiral Leahy said the agreement made the trip worthwhile. Admiral Ernest J. King declared it would save 2 million American lives.[24]

The conference concluded on February 11 in a general mood of amity and optimism. Although the least satisfied of the Big Three, Churchill was far from believing he had participated in a debacle. At the dinner on February 8, Stalin had toasted him as "the bravest governmental figure in the world" for his solitary resistance to Hitler in 1940. Churchill had responded with a tribute to Stalin as "the mighty leader of a mighty country." Roosevelt had called for their continued unity in the objective of giving "every man, woman, and child on this earth the possibility of security and well being."[25]

"We really believed in our hearts that this was the dawn of the new day we all had been praying for and talking about for so many years," Harry Hopkins told Robert Sherwood. "The Russians had proved they could be reasonable and farseeing." He worried only that something might happen to Stalin. "We could never be sure who or what might be in back of him there in the Kremlin."[26]

In the short run, Yalta sealed certain victory in a terrible war. It also revealed contradictions in a foreign policy that stemmed less from Roosevelt's character than from the American mind itself. FDR had inspired the nation by justifying the war with the high-minded ideals of the Four Freedoms and the Atlantic Charter. No less than Woodrow Wilson, he had identified victory with the end of a sordid era of power politics. Yet, in order to defeat the totalitarian threat of Nazi Germany and imperial Japan, he had to strike an alliance with the totalitarian Soviet Union and could do nothing to prevent its dominance over the unfortunate peoples of eastern Europe. Yalta was his final attempt to come to grips with the cunning of a history beyond his control.

AFTER THE FINAL PLENARY SESSION AND LUNCHEON ON FEBRUARY 11, Roosevelt and his party motored eighty miles over winding mountain roads to Sevastopol to board the USS *Catoctin*, a naval communications vessel moored at the Soviet base there. Averell Harriman recalled the trip as tedious and tiring, the vessel as hot and uncomfortable. The visit, he believed, had succeeded in raising the morale of the crew at the expense of the president's health.[27]

After a difficult night, Roosevelt arose early for a relatively short drive to the Saki airport, where he boarded the *Sacred Cow* for a flight to Egypt. There, aboard the *Quincy*, anchored in the Great Bitter Lake of the Suez Canal, he met with Egyptian king Farouk, Ethiopian emperor Haile Selassie, and King Abdul Aziz of Saudi Arabia. His purpose: to continue pursuit of an American presence in a traditional area of British influence. Churchill, informed only at the last minute, was miffed.

The most important audience was with Abdul Aziz, who had the power to grant oil concessions to American companies and the standing to ease the establishment of a Jewish state in the Middle East. On February 14, the American destroyer *Murphy* transported the king from Jeddah to the *Quincy*. The monarch, playing the role of Arab warrior-king to the hilt, was seated on the *Murphy*'s deck in a large gilt armchair, flanked by barefoot Nubian soldiers with drawn sabers. He boarded the *Quincy* accompanied by the royal astrologer, a food taster, a coffee server, and a retinue of slaves, cooks, porters, and scullions. They found much of the cruiser's foredeck covered with oriental carpets upon which had been erected a large tent. The Arabs slaughtered and cooked a sheep on the fantail.

When Roosevelt brought up the subject of Jewish settlement in Palestine, he encountered a cold, stone wall. So far as the king was concerned, the Zionists were European imperialists, and the Arabs had no obligation to atone for the sins of the Nazis. The president, unwilling to damage the larger US-Saudi relationship, backed off. As the king departed, Roosevelt, who in deference to Muslim doctrine had refrained from smoking, took a cigarette from his pocket. When someone suggested that Abdul Aziz might look back and take offense, he said, "Show's over!" or words to that effect. He wrote to Daisy Suckley that the "whole party was a scream." Subsequently, he told a press conference that he had learned more about Palestine at that meeting than he had absorbed in a lifetime. Harry Hopkins privately commented that the remark displayed an utter incomprehension of the problem.[28]

The *Quincy* moved back north to Alexandria, where Churchill, en route to his own meetings with Abdul Aziz, met briefly with the president for a pleasant lunch. Then the ship got under way for a stop at Algiers, where it docked on February 18. There, Hopkins, exhausted and in precarious health, informed the president that he would have to debark, rest a few days, and fly back to the United States for medical treatment. Roosevelt was greatly annoyed; the farewell, Hopkins later told Robert Sherwood, was not pleasant. It added to Roosevelt's distress that his great friend and valued aide, Pa Watson, died from a cerebral hemorrhage as the *Quincy* made its way across the Atlantic.[29]

Churchill, writing several years later of his rendezvous with Roosevelt at Alexandria, described the president as "placid and frail": "I felt that he had a slender contact with life." Sam Rosenman, who boarded the *Quincy* a few days later at Algiers to help write Roosevelt's speech to Congress on the conference, found his chief "listless and apparently uninterested in conversation—he was all burnt out." Not until the day before the ship docked at Newport News did the two men get to work on what was planned as one of the most important speeches of the Roosevelt presidency.[30]

ROOSEVELT DELIVERED THE ADDRESS ON MARCH 1, JUST A DAY AFTER HE HAD returned to the White House from his long journey. The occasion revealed his sharp physical decline. He could no longer stand up with the assistance of braces and had to deliver the talk seated in the well of the House of Representatives. "I hope you will pardon me for this unusual posture," he began, "but I know you will realize it makes it a lot easier for me not to have to carry about ten pounds of steel around on the bottom of my legs; and also because of the fact that I have just completed a fourteen-thousand-mile trip." The legislators responded with applause, but many of them surely realized that he had never before mentioned his handicap in public.[31]

His delivery was unquestionably the worst of his presidency. Whether due to fatigue or some neurological problem, he had trouble following the prepared text, stumbling and ad-libbing so frequently that news reports could not ignore his difficulty. Rosenman, sitting in the gallery, was "dismayed." Still, the president's struggle did not obscure the messages he hoped to get across: the end of the war in Europe was near, the Big Three alliance was strong and durable, any disputes were transient and resolvable, and the new world security organization would preserve and protect an international order based on the Atlantic Charter.[32]

Over the next three weeks, Roosevelt, with the exception of a much needed four-day respite at Hyde Park, worked on a variety of domestic and war issues while maintaining a heavy correspondence with Churchill and Stalin. On Saturday, March 17, he did not get to bed until 1:00 a.m. He seems to have had some assistance from Harry Hopkins, who was in Washington for a time between stays at the Mayo Clinic. (On March 15, Roosevelt, displaying incomprehension of Hopkins's dire health problems, wrote to Churchill, "Harry is getting along well. There is nothing seriously wrong with him and he is getting a good rest.")[33]

FDR took especial interest in State Department planning for the conference to establish the United Nations Organization, scheduled to begin in San Francisco on April 25. Slated to give the opening address, he clearly expected to be the dominating personality there, achieving the mission Woodrow Wilson had botched at Versailles. Yet he displayed a strange detachment about this and other vital matters, including day-to-day reports on the progress of the war and the impending victory in Europe. Some of his aides characterized him as "bored," but surely he was actually displaying symptoms of exhaustion.[34]

When Eleanor was away, he found time to relax with Lucy Mercer Rutherfurd, whom he saw at least five times in March. On March 24, he managed to get away for another four days at Hyde Park. At the beginning of the month, just after his speech to Congress, he had told Vice President Truman (whom he never put in the loop on Yalta or other foreign policy issues), "As soon as I can, I will go to Warm Springs for a rest. I can be in trim again if I can stay there for two or three weeks." Returning to the White House from Hyde Park on March 29, he met with Stettinius, Chip Bohlen, and other diplomats, then left in late afternoon for the Georgia destination that meant so much to him.[35]

ROOSEVELT TOOK WITH HIM TO WARM SPRINGS A SMALL GROUP OF WHITE House staffers, among them Grace Tully, Bill Hassett, and Dr. Howard Bruenn. Reporters representing the three major press services were, as usual, in the party, although forbidden from divulging the president's whereabouts or transmitting any news without clearance. His companions also included Daisy Suckley and Laura Delano. He had told Eleanor they would be with him but did not mention two other guests: Lucy and Madame Elizabeth Shoumatoff, an artist Lucy had commissioned to paint his portrait.

Warm Springs and the Little White House provided a respite. Roosevelt got a lot of sleep, was driven around the countryside—he no longer drove himself—and enjoyed the company and adoration of the ladies. But there was no escape from the routine duties of the presidency, the ongoing war, and continuing friction within the Big Three alliance. A packet came down from Washington by air daily. The president managed to hold his work down to two or three hours a day but never regained his strength. On the day the party arrived at Warm Springs, Hassett took Dr. Bruenn aside and told him despairingly, "He is slipping away from us and no earthly power can save him." Bruenn refused to give up hope but said his patient would have to cut back his schedule even further.[36]

The war news was momentous. American troops had crossed the Rhine, and German resistance in the West was collapsing. In the Pacific, on April 1, American forces landed on Okinawa to begin the last island campaign before the expected invasion of Japan. Final victory in the greatest conflict ever waged was assured.

Nonetheless, the alliance had once again grown precarious. Throughout the month of March, problems piled up, revealing a growing conflict of interests and perspectives between Russia and the West as the impending collapse of Nazism obviated the need for unity. The USSR neglected and mistreated American prisoners of war liberated from German POW camps in Poland. (Neither Roosevelt nor other members of the administration understood that the Soviet government considered its own POWs to be deserters or turncoats.) Stalin refused to admit American military teams behind his lines to assist the Americans and denied the existence of the problem. The president rejected Harriman's urgings for firmer protests.[37]

It became apparent that the Russians had no intention of establishing a more representative Polish government. They refused to find a position for Mikolajczyk or other independent leaders and arrested numerous non-Communists. The same pattern was taking shape throughout eastern Europe.

Near the end of March, Stalin, citing Molotov's need to attend the annual meeting of the Supreme Soviet, notified Roosevelt that the foreign minister would not represent the USSR at the San Francisco conference. Instead, Ambassador Andrei Gromyko would head the Russian delegation. This indication of the low priority the Soviets gave to the new world body came as a shock.

Most astonishingly, Stalin accused his British and American allies of betrayal when they attempted to open negotiations in Bern, Switzerland, for the surrender of the remaining German forces on the Italian front. They aimed, he declared, to achieve a separate peace that would allow Germany to concentrate on its fight with the USSR: "The Germans on the Western front in fact have ceased the war against England and the United States. At the same time, the Germans continue the war with Russia."[38]

Roosevelt's April 4 response, drafted, it seems, primarily by General George C. Marshall in Washington, avoided debate but expressed indignation:

> It is astonishing that a belief seems to have reached the Soviet Government that I have entered into an agreement with the enemy without first obtaining your full agreement.
> ... [I]t would be one of the great tragedies of history if at the very moment of victory now within our grasp, such distrust, such lack of faith should prejudice the entire undertaking after the colossal losses of life, treasure, and materiel involved.
> Frankly, I cannot avoid a feeling of bitter resentment toward your informers, whoever they are, for such vile misrepresentations of my actions or those of my trusted subordinates.[39]

Stalin's reply was a bit more diplomatic than his earlier communication but unyielding. He was equally firm on Poland, insisting that the Russians were proceeding according to the letter of the Yalta agreements.[40]

Roosevelt was in no mood to prolong the argument. On April 11, he messaged Churchill:

> I would minimize the general Soviet problem as much as possible because these problems, in one form or another, seem to arise every day and most of them straighten out as is the case of the Bern meeting.
> We must be firm, however, and thus far our course is correct.[41]

By then, nothing solid had come of the Bern contacts. On the same day, the president sent a conciliatory message to Stalin, stating that Bern had "faded into the past" and admonishing that "minor misunderstandings of this character should not arise in the future." Ambassador Harriman protested that the

Bern issue struck him as a major misunderstanding. The president overruled him. No matter how difficult the Russians might be, he was determined to maintain the alliance he believed necessary to underwrite the United Nations Organization and stabilize the postwar world.[42]

FDR remained weary and increasingly incapable of meeting the demands of his office. Perhaps sometime in 1946, he told his companions, he might retire. Yet he seemed convinced that he could muster the energy to dominate the United Nations conference and establish an international organization that would enforce the peace. He expected to begin work with Grace Tully on his opening address at San Francisco.[43]

Roosevelt had sent his last message to Harriman on the morning of April 12. At about 1:00 p.m. that day, he sat at the table of the Little White House, across from its stone fireplace, reviewing papers Bill Hassett had delivered for his signature. All four ladies—Daisy, Laura, Lucy, and Madame Shoumatoff—were in the room. Suddenly, he said in a low voice, "I have a terrific pain in the back of my head," then slumped forward. Valet Arthur Prettyman, a Filipino servant, and the women managed somehow to get him to the adjacent bedroom. Dr. Bruenn rushed to the house. After two anxious hours, Lucy and Madame Shoumatoff departed for Lucy's home in South Carolina. Soon afterward, Dr. Bruenn made the inevitable announcement.

Daisy later wrote in her diary, "3.35 p.m. Franklin D. Roosevelt, the hope of the world, is dead."[44]

CONDOLENCES POURED IN FROM ALL OVER THE WORLD, BUT THE STRONGEST statements issued from the many thousands of people who lined the railroad tracks and crowded the stations along the way for a glimpse of the train that brought Roosevelt's body back to Washington. They sought one last fleeting contact with the leader who had talked to them directly for twelve years, had seemed to understand them, and supported their aspirations for a better life.

When the train reached Washington on the morning of April 14, President Truman led the delegation that met it. A caisson drawn by six white horses carried the flag-draped casket in a slow one-mile procession to the White House past an estimated half million people. Automobiles conveying the new president and other notables crept along behind. Two military bands played solemn music. Truman later wrote that he would never forget the sight of so many grief-stricken people. He especially remembered "an old Negro woman with her apron to her eyes as she sat on the curb . . . crying as if she had lost her son."[45]

That afternoon six hundred invited guests attended a funeral service at the White House. Harry Hopkins had flown back to Washington from the Mayo Clinic, looking, as Robert Sherwood recalled it, "like death, the skin of his face a dreadful cold white with apparently no flesh left under it." The service, prescribed by Eleanor, was brief and in the spirit of the Roosevelt family's Low Church Episcopalianism: two hymns, a few scripture readings, and a brief eulogy by Bishop Angus Dun, who invoked Roosevelt's admonition that "the only thing we have to fear is fear itself" as a guide for the way in which the American people should face the future.[46]

Many of the notables who attended the funeral boarded a train late that evening for the overnight trip to Hyde Park. The next morning, local villagers, Supreme Court justices, cabinet members, West Point cadets, admirals and generals, President Truman and his family, congressmen, and other political notables gathered around a grave site that lay between the fine old family house and the unpretentious presidential library that Roosevelt had built for his papers a few years earlier. Daisy Suckley held Fala on a leash. FDR's former chief, Josephus Daniels, a month shy of his eighty-fifth birthday, had made the trip from North Carolina. Rosy Roosevelt's elderly widow sat in a large chair next to Eleanor, Anna, and Elliott. (Jimmy was unable to arrive in time from the West Coast. Franklin Jr. and John were on active duty in the Pacific.)

The local seventy-eight-year-old Episcopal minister—looking, a journalist thought, "like a figure from the Old Testament"—presided over the brief service, intoning, as the casket was lowered into the grave, the words to "Now the Laborer's Task Is O'er; Now the Battle Day Is Past." The cadets fired a twenty-one-gun salute, to which Fala responded with three loud barks.[47]

The men of power made their way to the railroad station and the trip back to Washington. Family members were left with complex thoughts and emotions.

Franklin Delano Roosevelt had come full circle, beginning and ending in the one place in the world most important to him.

FDR AND THE AMERICAN CENTURY

IN FEBRUARY 1941, AS CONGRESS DEBATED THE LEND-LEASE BILL, *LIFE* magazine featured an opinion article by its publisher, Henry Luce, titled "The American Century." Consistently skeptical of the New Deal, Luce was also an interventionist-minded Republican convinced that Britain's war was America's, that the isolationist movement was morally bankrupt, and that the fate of the world depended on the triumph of liberal-democratic values most fully developed in the United States.[1]

Isolationists, Luce declared, might see America as the sanctuary of civilized values, but they erred in denying that its destiny was to disseminate them. "The world of the 20th Century, if it is to come to life in any nobility of health and vigor, must be to a significant degree an American Century." The instrument of that destiny had to be the president Luce had so often criticized. "Our job is to help in every way we can, for our sakes and our children's sakes, to ensure that Franklin Roosevelt shall be justly hailed as America's greatest President."

Many self-styled liberals, including a critical mass friendly to the still neutral Soviet Union, dismissed Luce's article as advocacy of cultural and economic imperialism. His call for support of Roosevelt outraged heartland conservative isolationists. In fact, he had stated a truth that both groups denied: American liberal democracy *was* the last best hope of the world, and its greatest tribune *was* Franklin D. Roosevelt.

From the time he was old enough to mount a pony, the boy began his day at Springwood accompanying his father as they rode around the estate, viewing their property and inspecting the work of employees or tenants. The experience was of a piece with the tutors, the foreign travel, the company of notables at home and abroad, the elite schools, and the examples of manhood he saw in his father and his revered cousin Theodore. It left him convinced of his mastery and his mission to lead others. A prominent insurgent legislator at twenty-nine, a dashing assistant secretary of the navy at thirty-two, a vice presidential candidate at thirty-eight, he achieved at an early age an international profile that developed alongside the United States' emergence as a world power.

Roosevelt at a distance seemed to combine virtues of authority, courage, determination, and above all empathy for common people, especially the underprivileged and handicapped. What president had displayed the fortitude he exhibited in his personal fight against polio? What president could begin to match his philanthropic achievements? What president had channeled so much assistance to the downtrodden or tended so strongly to the interests of the blue-collar working class? What president had so clearly made himself the voice of liberal democracy as it faced a global struggle for survival? His death shocked the world and brought special distress to ordinary people, who *knew* that he was great.

Yet the real, flesh-and-blood man, while always charming, was a study in moral ambiguity. His personal relationships were often at variance with the nobility of his achievements. After 1918, his marriage was based on respect more than affection and existed in form only. He possessed little interest in or time for the parenting of his children, all of whom lived lives that might charitably be described as undisciplined. He surreptitiously maintained a relationship with Lucy Mercer for a quarter century after he had promised to break contact with her. Perhaps circumstances made it unavoidable that Missy LeHand, the woman most often at his side for two decades, suffered his neglect after her health broke. But was it impossible to set aside ten minutes a day for her?

Cool calculation rather than friendship or loyalty characterized his ties to most of his aides and political supporters. Even the one for whom he reserved his greatest affection, Louis Howe, he could make the butt of abusive jokes. He summarily cut Tommy Corcoran out of his good graces after the lawyer left his service. He cynically tapped Bernard Baruch and Joseph P. Kennedy for political money and favors while denying them office and influence. They and many others existed, he seems to have believed, to serve him and became dispensable when no longer were of use.

Roosevelt's private shortcomings existed alongside policy failures that, as often as not, remain glossed over. Historians admit, usually sotto voce, that the

New Deal failed to end the Great Depression; for the most part, however, they have little to say about the appalling counterproductiveness of its attempts at a managed economy and prefer to emphasize the relief programs that provided bare sustenance for millions of the needy. These real achievements should not be devalued. Still, six years of the New Deal left the nation impoverished and deprived the world of the economic stimulus an American recovery would have provided.

In the end, Roosevelt's great achievement was his defense of democracy in a world at war. At Yalta, Stalin rightly toasted him for taking a broad conception of his nation's interests and providing the resources that mobilized the Grand Alliance against aggressive fascism. He had in fact taken enormous political risks that revealed a principled approach to democratic leadership and an astute understanding of the stakes of world power. Courageously committing to Britain in 1940, he saved liberal democracy as a force in the world. As a war leader after Pearl Harbor, he displayed an astute grasp of grand strategy beyond the capabilities of his generals and admirals.[2]

Yet he banked on a diplomatic course that attempted to combine Wilsonian idealism (the Atlantic Charter, the Four Freedoms, and a slightly revamped League of Nations) with a "Four Policemen" idea of spheres of influence. Remarkably, he seemed to believe that he could anchor it all by establishing a personal relationship with a Soviet leader committed to a totalitarian version of socialist revolution. At the same time, he pursued the dismantling of a British Empire that, for all its shortcomings, was far more benign than Stalin's. He "gave" Stalin nothing that Stalin could not control anyway, but there is justice in the argument that those concessions weakened the principled foundations of American foreign policy. At best, perhaps there was realism in his realization that the United States could not prevent Soviet domination of eastern Europe. It is unclear how he might have reacted to Soviet ambitions for control of the rest of the continent, but he would not likely have responded as quickly and decisively as his successor, Harry Truman. His private conversation with Archbishop Spellman leaves one with the impression that he was willing to accept Soviet hegemony over all of continental Europe.

The Great Depression and World War II produced numerous "great" leaders. Greatness is not identical with humane virtue. Its characteristics in practice are often unattractive. Among Roosevelt's contemporaries, Winston Churchill, Charles de Gaulle, Adolf Hitler, Josef Stalin, and Mao Tse-tung were all great men in one fashion or another. Churchill could rival Roosevelt as an inspirational rhetorician and undaunted fighter, but Churchill was also an unapologetic imperialist at a time when the sun was setting on imperialism. De Gaulle was vainglorious and in the end petulant. Churchill at Yalta accurately praised Stalin as an indomitable leader who refused to accept defeat and galvanized the mighty Soviet effort against Hitler's war machine. Yet Stalin was a totalitarian sociopath. So were Hitler and Mao. All three possessed enormous egos, experienced and overcame failure, used subordinates callously, sent untold millions to their deaths, impressed their personalities on their times, and changed the course of history.[3]

Roosevelt was a match for them. An American aristocrat born to privilege, he learned the habit of command from his father and combined it with a magnetic charm. From his father's visionary Central American canal project and from Theodore Roosevelt's exploits, he inherited a sense of his destiny to lead and strive for great goals, first as a socially conscious reformer, then as a world statesman. For all his self-indulgence, he displayed courage and determination, whether in coping with the handicap of polio, facing the challenges of the Depression, or dealing with the terrible urgencies of global war.

No one fully understood the causes of the Great Depression or the means by which to end it. But Roosevelt took unprecedented measures to ameliorate widespread suffering and won the devotion of millions of Americans. He excelled in pursuing the national interest against the Nazi juggernaut and a brutal Japanese imperialism. To millions all over the globe, he exemplified the promise of a world governed by a respect for freedom, democracy, and individual opportunity. He left behind a United States that was the greatest power on the planet and disposed to use its might in the pursuit of liberal democratic principles.

We can debate whether Franklin Roosevelt was the greatest of the great men of his time. It is fair to say that, for all his imperfections, he left the most generous and appealing legacy.

ACKNOWLEDGMENTS

It is hard to imagine writing this book without the existence of the Franklin D. Roosevelt Presidential Library and Museum. I am indebted to Robert Clark and his fine archival staff for their invaluable assistance, rendered both on-site and via an excellent online presence. Nor would this study have been possible without the support and facilities of Ohio University, my professional home for nearly five decades. I especially thank my friend and valued colleague, Steven Miner, director of the Contemporary History Institute, for providing office facilities and sharing with me the fruits of his research for his forthcoming major study of the Soviet Union in World War II. Warren F. Kimball, editor of the Roosevelt-Churchill correspondence, generously responded to numerous queries. Mark Stoler helped me develop my thoughts about Roosevelt as commander in chief. I would be remiss if I did not mention my good fortune in three mentors who long ago introduced me to the study of Roosevelt and the New Deal: the late John A. Garraty, William E. Leuchtenburg, and Richard S. Kirkendall. Few students have been more fortunate in their choice of teachers and role models.

Lara Heimert commissioned this book and valiantly critiqued the manuscript. Roger Labrie performed an invaluable line edit, and Jennifer Kelland followed with a thorough and constructive copy edit. My good friend, literary agent, and fellow martini connoisseur, Donald Lamm, provided editorial commentary, moral support, and advice well beyond the essential duties of his profession. I value my connection with him enormously. My wife, Joyce Litton Hamby, took time from her own interests to help with the archival research. She has been a source of aid and comfort in ways at which my dedication can only hint.

NOTES

CHAPTER 1: "THE BEST PEOPLE"

1. Franklin Delano Roosevelt [hereafter FDR] to Sara Delano Roosevelt [hereafter SDR], spring, 1888, in *F.D.R.: His Personal Letters, Early Years* [hereafter *Personal Letters*, I], ed. Elliott Roosevelt (New York: Duell, Sloan and Pearce, 1947), 7.

2. Roosevelt's birth is perhaps most fully described in Kenneth S. Davis, *F.D.R.: The Beckoning of Destiny, 1882–1928* [hereafter *FDR*, I] (New York: G. P. Putnam's Sons, 1972), 51–52.

3. See, e.g., John Sproat, *The Best Men: Liberal Reformers in the Gilded Age* (New York: Oxford University Press, 1968).

4. This and the following paragraphs about the early Roosevelts draw on, among other sources, Davis, *FDR*, I, ch. 1; Geoffrey Ward, *Before the Trumpet: Young Franklin Roosevelt, 1882–1905* (New York: Harper & Row, 1985), 16–21; David B. Roosevelt, *Grandmere: A Personal History of Eleanor Roosevelt* (New York: Warner Books, 2002), 34–35. See also "Franklin Roosevelt's Paternal Ancestry," Franklin D. Roosevelt Presidential Library and Museum [hereafter FDRL], http://www.fdrlibrary.marist.edu/archives/resources/genealogy.html#fdrpaternal.

5. Rita Halle Kleeman, *Gracious Lady: The Life of Sara Delano Roosevelt* (New York: D. Appleton-Century Company, 1935), is a standard source for the early Delanos. On the Leyden of the Pilgrims, see Joke Kardux and Eduard van de Bilt, *Newcomers in an Old City: The American Pilgrims in Leiden, 1609–1620*, 2nd rev. ed. (Leiden: Uitgeverij Burgersdijk & Niermans, 2001), 70–71, 80n55. On the Delanos, in addition to the sources cited above, the following genealogical Web pages have been useful: http://experts.about.com/e/d/de/Delano _family.htm, http://chrisman.org/pedigree/out25.htm, and http://gordonrosalynd.com /green/d181.htm.

6. SDR, as told to Isabel Leighton and Gabrielle Forbush, in *My Boy Franklin* (New York: Ray Long & Richard R. Smith, 1933), 21. This and subsequent paragraphs draw extensively on Ward, *Before the Trumpet*, ch. 2, and Davis, *FDR*, I, 36–44.

7. Ward, *Before the Trumpet*, 30, 31n.

8. This and other business ventures are neatly summarized in Frank B. Freidel, *Franklin D. Roosevelt: The Apprenticeship* (Boston: Little, Brown and Company, 1952), 9–12. On Scott's

designs and their larger role in national politics, see C. Vann Woodward, *Reunion and Reaction* (New York: Doubleday Anchor Books, 1956), esp. 73–80.

9. Lawrence A. Clayton, "The Nicaragua Canal in the Nineteenth Century: Prelude to American Empire in the Caribbean," *Journal of Latin American Studies* 19 (November 1987): 323–352, provides an excellent scholarly overview of the canal issue.

10. Ward, *Before the Trumpet*, 155–156.

11. Ward, *Before the Trumpet*, chs. 4–5; see esp. photos opposite p. 80.

12. Ward, *Before the Trumpet*, 66.

13. Ward, *Before the Trumpet*, 111–112.

14. SDR, *My Boy Franklin*, 139–140, 252–254.

15. SDR, *My Boy Franklin*, 139–140, 252–254.

16. SDR, *My Boy Franklin*, 11–13, 33; FDR to "Papa," June 7, 1890, in Roosevelt, *Personal Letters*, I, 16; Ward, *Before the Trumpet*, 120–122.

17. Clara and Hardy Steeholm, *The House at Hyde Park* (New York: Viking Press, 1950), 86–87.

18. This story is a staple of Roosevelt biographies, e.g., Davis, *FDR*, I, 63.

19. For FDR's private teachers, Ward, *Before the Trumpet*, 150–153, 171–174.

20. FDR to Muriel and Warren Delano, May 30, 1891, in Roosevelt, *Personal Letters*, I, 19–20.

21. SDR, Diary, October 15–31, 1890, SDR Papers, FDRL.

22. Ward, *Before the Trumpet*, 153; SDR, Diary, February 27, 1893.

23. SDR, *My Boy Franklin*, 18.

24. Ward, *Before the Trumpet*, 128, 152–153; FDR to "Mumsy & Pupsy," December 7, 1893, in Roosevelt, *Personal Letters*, I, 24; SDR, Diary, September 1, 1890; SDR, *My Boy Franklin*, 5–6.

25. SDR, *My Boy Franklin*, 17, 27–29. SDR, Diary, June 14, 1895, July 11, 1896. I have been unable to find independent corroboration for the South Kensington Museum episode. The story, which appears in *My Boy Franklin*, may have been related by FDR to Sara's ghostwriter.

26. SDR, *My Boy Franklin*, 35–36.

CHAPTER 2: YOUNG GENTLEMAN

1. SDR, as told to Isabel Leighton and Gabrielle Forbush, *My Boy Franklin* (New York: Ray Long & Richard R. Smith, 1933), 39.

2. John W. Tyler, "Peabody, Endicott," *American National Biography Online* (June 2000 Update), http://www.anb.org, provides a shrewd, brief interpretive sketch of Peabody. Frank D. Ashburn, *Peabody of Groton: A Portrait* (New York: Coward-McCann, 1944), is an admiring and detailed survey.

3. Endicott Peabody, "Academic Influence," in *The Education of the Modern Boy*, ed. Alfred E. Stearns et al. (Boston: Small, Maynard & Company, 1925), 107–138, quote at 113.

4. Harriman quoted in Walter Isaacson and Evan Thomas, *The Wise Men: Six Friends and the World They Made* (New York: Simon & Schuster, 1986), 47. Jerome Karabel, *The Chosen: The Hidden History of Admission and Exclusion at Harvard, Yale, and Princeton* (Boston: Houghton Mifflin Company, 2005), 23–38.

5. Geoffrey Ward, *Before the Trumpet: Young Franklin Roosevelt, 1882–1905* (New York: Harper & Row, 1985), 179–180; Frank B. Freidel, *Franklin D. Roosevelt: The Apprenticeship* [hereafter *FDR*, I] (Boston: Little, Brown and Company, 1952), ch. 3.

6. Peabody, "Academic Influence," 134; "Football Good for Boys," *New York Times* [hereafter *NYT*], October 1, 1898.

7. Endicott Peabody, "School Patriotism," *School Review* (October 1895): 498–506, quotes at 502–503.

8. Elliott Roosevelt, ed., *F.D.R.: His Personal Letters, Early Years* [hereafter *Personal Letters*, I] (New York: Duell, Sloan and Pearce, 1947), 33.

9. FDR to his parents, September 18, 1896, in Roosevelt, *Personal Letters*, I, 35.

10. Ward, *Before the Trumpet*, 182.

11. FDR to his parents, September 20, 1896 (football), May 7, 1897 (baseball), January 9, 12, March 3, 1898 (boxing), April 19, 20, 21, 1899, April 22, 26, May 27, 1900 (baseball), in Roosevelt, *Personal Letters*, I, 36–37, 92–98, 155–157, 183–184, 289–291, 394–395, 400–401.

12. FDR to his parents, March 24, 1897, March 13, 1898, March 23, 1899, in Roosevelt, *Personal Letters*, I, 78–79, 186–187, 282–283.

13. FDR to his parents, March 21, 1897, May 14, 1897, in Roosevelt, *Personal Letters*, I, 76–77, 96–98.

14. Eleanor Roosevelt [hereafter ER], *This I Remember* (New York: Harper & Brothers, 1949), 43.

15. Roosevelt, *Personal Letters*, I, 160–164.

16. FDR to his parents, June 24, 25, 1900, in Roosevelt, *Personal Letters*, I, 410–413.

17. Billings to FDR, n.d., Roosevelt Family Papers Donated by the Children, FDRL, quoted in Geoffrey Ward, *A First-Class Temperament: The Emergence of Franklin Roosevelt* (New York: Harper & Row, 1989), 90n.

18. FDR to his parents, May 28, June 11, 1897, in Roosevelt, *Personal Letters*, I, 105, 114–115.

19. FDR to his parents, April 10, 1900, in Roosevelt, *Personal Letters*, I, 393, 430–431; Ward, *Before the Trumpet*, 195; Freidel, *FDR*, I, 56.

20. SDR, *My Boy Franklin*, 49–52.

21. Last Will and Testament of James Roosevelt, copy in Henry T. Hackett Papers (Box 21), FDRL (available online at http://www.fdrlibrary.marist.edu/psf/box21/A902at01.html). For valuation of assets, see *NYT*, April 22, 1901.

22. SDR to FDR, January 5, 1901, Family Papers (Children), Section II, FDRL.

23. One gets some tangible sense of this process in SDR to FDR, October 11, November 28, 1901, Family Papers (Children), FDRL.

24. On the Harvard of Roosevelt's era, see Karabel, *The Chosen*, 13–23; Bernard Bailyn et al., *Glimpses of the Harvard Past* (Cambridge, MA: Harvard University Press, 1986), esp. 79 (statistics about Jews), 123 (scholarship program); John T. Bethell, "Frank Roosevelt at Harvard," *Harvard Magazine* (November–December, 1996), http://harvardmagazine.com/1996/11/frank-roosevelt-at-harvard; Ward, *Before the Trumpet*, ch. 6.

25. FDR to his parents, January 9, September 28, October 5, 1900, in Roosevelt, *Personal Letters*, I, 370–372, 423, 425.

26. FDR to his parents, October 5, 19, 23, 31, 1900; FDR to SDR, January 21, February 3, 11, 16, 22, March 29, April 20, 27, October 30, November 12, 18, 1901, in Roosevelt, *Personal Letters*, I, 425–465. On Harvard football, see also Craig Lambert and John T. Bethell, "First and 100," *Harvard Magazine* (September–October 2003), http://harvardmagazine.com/2003/09/first-and-100.html.

27. FDR to SDR, April 7, 20, 30, May 24, 1901, and accompanying editor's notes, in Roosevelt, *Personal Letters*, I, 453–458.

28. FDR to his parents, October 31, 1900, in Roosevelt, *Personal Letters*, I, 430–431; Ward, *Before the Trumpet*, 229–230. See also Ward, *A First Class Temperament*, 92–93.

29. FDR to SDR, April 30, May 24, 1901, in Roosevelt, *Personal Letters*, I, 456–458; SDR, *My Boy Franklin*, 58–59.

30. FDR to SDR, November 12, 1901, October 8, 26, November 2, 1902, and accompanying editor's notes, refer to work on the *Crimson*. Roosevelt, *Personal Letters*, I, 453–458, 463–464, 476–479, 481–483.

31. Ward, *Before the Trumpet*, 240.

32. Roosevelt's frenetic activities are well summarized in Ward, *Before the Trumpet*, 237–238, and in numerous letters reproduced in Roosevelt, *Personal Letters*, I.

33. *NYT*, January 3, 1902; FDR to SDR, January 6, 1902, in Roosevelt, *Personal Letters*, I, 467–468.

34. FDR to SDR, November 18, 1901, in Roosevelt, *Personal Letters*, I, 464–465; Ward, *Before the Trumpet*, 230–231.

35. FDR to SDR, October 26, 1902, in Roosevelt, *Personal Letters*, I, 481–482.

36. FDR to SDR, July 24, 1903, in Roosevelt, *Personal Letters*, I, 489–490; Ward, *Before the Trumpet*, 246–247.

37. FDR to SDR, August 3, 5, 12 (two communications), 1903, in Roosevelt, *Personal Letters*, I, 494–502.

38. Ward, *Before the Trumpet*, 239–242. See also Freidel, *FDR*, I, 60–66. FDR quote from *Crimson* editorial, September 30, 1903. See this and other editorials he wrote in Roosevelt, *Personal Letters*, I, 502–503, 506–507 (October 6, 1903), 509 (October 8, 1903), 512–513 (November 2, 1903), 522 (January 9, 1904), and 524–525 (January 26, 1904).

39. Corrine Robinson quoted in Joseph Alsop, *FDR: A Centenary Remembrance* (New York: Viking Press, 1982), 36.

CHAPTER 3: ELEANOR AND FRANKLIN

1. Geoffrey Ward, *Before the Trumpet: Young Franklin Roosevelt, 1882–1905* (New York: Harper & Row, 1985), 252–255.

2. Joseph Alsop, *FDR: A Centenary Remembrance* (New York: Viking Press, 1982), 39.

3. D. A. Steel, "Marie Souvestre," in *Oxford Dictionary of National Biography* (Oxford: Oxford University Press, 2004), accessed online at http://www.oxforddnb.com/index /53/101053508; ER, *This Is My Story* (New York: Harper & Brothers, 1937), ch. 3; Joseph P. Lash, *Eleanor and Franklin: The Story of Their Relationship* (New York: W. W. Norton & Company, 1971), ch. 8; Blanche Wiesen Cook, *Eleanor Roosevelt*, Vol. 1: *1884–1933* [hereafter *Eleanor Roosevelt*, I] (New York: Viking Penguin, 1992), ch. 5.

4. M. Souvestre to ER, July 7, 1902 [English translation], Roosevelt Family Papers (Donated by the Children), Alphabetical File, FDRL; Cook, *Eleanor Roosevelt*, I, 124; ER, *This Is My Story*, 132; Lash, *Eleanor and Franklin*, 147.

5. ER, *This Is My Story*, 100–101, is the major primary source for the next several paragraphs, supplemented by Lash, *Eleanor and Franklin*, chs. 9–13; Cook, *Eleanor Roosevelt*, I, ch. 6; Ward, *Before the Trumpet*, 303–338.

6. ER, *This Is My Story*, 109–111.

7. Lash, *Eleanor and Franklin*, 106–108, 113, 120; Cook, *Eleanor Roosevelt*, I, 154.

8. SDR to FDR, October 8, 1902, Family Papers (Children), Section II.

9. ER, *This Is My Story*, 108–109; Lash, *Eleanor and Franklin*, 135.

10. In addition to the sources already cited, see *NYT*, March 18, 1905, for an account of the wedding.

11. FDR to SDR, June 16, 1905, in *F.D.R.: His Personal Letters, 1905–1928* [hereafter *Personal Letters*, II], ed. Elliott Roosevelt, assisted by James N. Rosenau (New York: Duell, Sloan and Pearce, 1948), 10–11; Geoffrey Ward, *A First-Class Temperament: The Emergence of Franklin Roosevelt* (New York: Harper & Row, 1989), ch. 1 (see 15n for the hotel bill).

12. For Cortina, see FDR to SDR, July 12, 15, 1905, in Roosevelt, *Personal Letters*, II, 32–37, and ER, *This Is My Story*, 130. (However Eleanor felt about Miss Gandy at the time, the two later, by her own account and that of her son Elliott [in a textual note to the July 15 letter cited above], became good friends.) See also Ward, *A First-Class Temperament*, 20–22.

13. Lash, *Eleanor and Franklin*, 146.

14. ER, *This Is My Story*, 127, 162.

15. ER, *This Is My Story*, 142, 151, 157–158, 162–163.

16. Ward, *A First-Class Temperament*, 97–98.

17. ER, *This Is My Story*, 165; Ward, *A First-Class Temperament*, 102.

18. Ward, *A First-Class Temperament*, 98–99.

19. FDR to SDR, September 6, 1907, in Roosevelt, *Personal Letters*, II, 136–138. For full and useful accounts of FDR's law practice, see Kenneth S. Davis, *FDR: The Beckoning of Destiny, 1882–1928* (New York: G. P. Putnam's Sons, 1972), 208–214, and Ward, *A First-Class Temperament*, 70–79.

20. Ward, *A First-Class Temperament*, 70 and n23.

21. Gerald T. Dunne, *Grenville Clark: Public Citizen* (New York: Farrar Straus Giroux, 1986), 21.

22. Dunne, *Grenville Clark*, 21.

CHAPTER 4: INSURGENT PROGRESSIVE

1. Geoffrey Ward, *A First-Class Temperament: The Emergence of Franklin Roosevelt* (New York: Harper & Row, 1989), 81–82.

2. FDR to ER, June 12, 15 (two letters), 1908, in *F.D.R.: His Personal Letters, 1905–1928* [hereafter *Personal Letters*, II], ed. Elliott Roosevelt, assisted by James N. Rosenau (New York: Duell, Sloan and Pearce, 1948), 140–145; Ward, *A First-Class Temperament*, 264–267; Frank B. Freidel, *Franklin D. Roosevelt: The Apprenticeship* [hereafter *Roosevelt*, I] (Boston: Little, Brown and Company, 1952), 80–81.

3. Freidel, *Roosevelt*, I, 390.

4. Ward, *A First-Class Temperament*, 116.

5. Freidel, *Roosevelt*, I, 93.

6. Freidel, *Roosevelt*, I, 91–93; Roosevelt, *Personal Letters*, II, 154–158, contains notes and speech material from the campaign.

7. ER, *This Is My Story* (New York: Harper & Brothers, 1937), 107; Ward, *A First-Class Temperament*, 122n30.

8. Freidel, *Roosevelt*, I, 94; see *NYT*, November 9, 1910, for voting results and analysis.

9. *NYT*, January 1, 1911; ER, *This Is My Story*, 170–171; SDR quote from Ward, *A First-Class Temperament*, 129; SDR to FDR and ER, n.d., Roosevelt Family Papers Donated by the Children, FDRL.

10. FDR, Diary, January 2, 1911, FDR Papers, FDRL; Freidel, *Roosevelt*, I, 100.

11. Twenty-five years later, Eleanor wrote fondly of Grady and Sullivan. One must doubt that her attitude at the time was so benign. See ER, *This Is My Story*, 172. For a quick summary of Murphy's career, see his obituary in *NYT*, April 26, 1924; Nancy Joan Weiss, *Charles Francis*

Murphy, 1858–1924: Respectability and Responsibility in Tammany Politics (Northampton, MA: Smith College, 1968).

12. Kenneth S. Davis, *FDR: The Beckoning of Destiny, 1882–1928* [hereafter *FDR*, I] (New York: G. P. Putnam's Sons, 1972), 248. [From Ernest K. Lindley, *Franklin D. Roosevelt: A Career in Progressive Democracy* (New York: Blue Ribbon Books, 1931), 78.] One is tempted to write this off as a good but apocryphal story. However, it was talked about at the time. See remarks by Thomas Mott Osborne in *NYT*, April 7, 1911 ("Urge College Men to Enter Politics").

13. FDR, Diary, January 3, 1911, FDRL, quoted in J. Joseph Huthmacher, *Senator Robert F. Wagner and the Rise of Urban Liberalism* (New York: Atheneum, 1968), 23.

14. Alfred B. Rollins Jr., *Roosevelt and Howe* (New York: Alfred A. Knopf, 1962), 23–25.

15. Diary, January 1, 1911, FDRL, quoted in Freidel, *Roosevelt*, I, 247. The routine of the insurgency is vividly described in Ward, *A First-Class Temperament*, 134. FDR's quote is from the feature article on him in *NYT*, January 22, 1911.

16. Freidel, *Roosevelt*, I, 104–106; Ward, *A First-Class Temperament*, 137–139.

17. *New York Globe*, February 6, 1911, quoted in Freidel, *Roosevelt*, I, 104.

18. *NYT*, January 22, 1911.

19. Theodore Roosevelt [hereafter TR] to FDR, January 29, 1911, FDRL, in Freidel, *Roosevelt*, I, 108n.

20. Freidel, *Roosevelt*, I, 114–115.

21. *NYT*, April 1, 1911.

22. *NYT*, April 2, 1911.

23. Frances Perkins, *The Roosevelt I Knew* (New York: Viking Press, 1946), 11, 12.

24. Perkins, *The Roosevelt I Knew*, 14; George Martin, *Madam Secretary: Frances Perkins* (Boston: Houghton Mifflin Company, 1976), 98–99, 495–496.

25. Freidel, *Roosevelt*, I, ch. 7; Ward, *A First-Class Temperament*, 153–170; for rejection of appropriations, see *NYT*, June 8, 1911, and clippings in state senator scrapbooks, FDRL, cited in Ward, *A First-Class Temperament*, 814–815; on divorce standards, see *NYT*, September 9, 1911 (editorial).

26. Original speech at FDRL; Freidel, *Roosevelt*, I, 132–133.

27. Freidel, *Roosevelt*, I, 134–135; Davis, *FDR*, I, 270–271.

28. Freidel, *Roosevelt*, I, 136–138.

29. ER, *This Is My Story*, 187–189.

30. FDR to ER, July 2, 1912, in Roosevelt, *Personal Letters*, II, 192.

31. *NYT*, July 13, 18, 30, September 20, October 5, 1912; Rollins, *Roosevelt and Howe*, 53–55.

32. FDR to ER, July 27, August 24, 1912, in Roosevelt, *Personal Letters*, II, 192–196 (including copy of article from *NYT*, August 25, 1912).

33. Rollins, *Roosevelt and Howe*, pt. 1; ER, *This Is My Story*, 192–193.

34. Rollins, *Roosevelt and Howe*, 55–61; Ward, *A First-Class Temperament*, 195.

35. Josephus Daniels, *The Wilson Era: Years of Peace, 1910–1917* (Chapel Hill: University of North Carolina Press, 1944), 69, 124–126; E. David Cronon, ed., *The Cabinet Diaries of Josephus Daniels, 1913–1921* (Lincoln: University of Nebraska Press, 1963), 4; Freidel, *Roosevelt*, I, 155, and interview with Michael Doyle, October 24, 1947, Freidel Oral History Interviews, FDRL.

CHAPTER 5: RIDING IN FRONT

1. E. David Cronon, ed., *The Cabinet Diaries of Josephus Daniels, 1913–1921* (Lincoln: University of Nebraska Press, 1963), 4.

2. "World War 1 at Sea: Rise of the Dreadnought Battleship, 1906 to 1914," Naval-History. Net, http://www.naval-history.net/WW1NavalDreadnoughts.htm.

3. Geoffrey Ward, *A First-Class Temperament: The Emergence of Franklin Roosevelt* (New York: Harper & Row, 1989), 221–222.

4. On Daniels, the best source is Jonathan Daniels, *The End of Innocence* (Philadelphia: J. B. Lippincott Company, 1954); see 54, for "hillbilly" quote. For the characterization of Southern progressivism, see C. Vann Woodward's great work, *Origins of the New South, 1877–1914* (Baton Rouge: Louisiana State University Press, 1951), ch. 9; specific mentions of Daniels at 54, 146, 334–335, 349, 381–382, 475, 480.

5. Michael Kazin, *A Godly Hero: The Life of William Jennings Bryan* (New York: Alfred A. Knopf, 2006); esp. ch. 10.

6. FDR quoted in *NYT*, April 13, 1921. Roosevelt subsequently told versions of this story on several occasions. Frank B. Freidel, *Franklin D. Roosevelt: The Apprenticeship* [hereafter *FDR, I*] (Boston: Little, Brown and Company, 1952), 237n.

7. Daniels, *End of Innocence*, 129.

8. Carroll Kilpatrick, *Roosevelt and Daniels: A Friendship in Politics* (Chapel Hill: University of North Carolina Press, 1952), 11; Cronon, *Cabinet Diaries*, vi, 212–213.

9. FDR to SDR, March 17, 1913, in *F.D.R.: His Personal Letters, 1905–1928* [hereafter *Personal Letters, II*], ed. Elliott Roosevelt, assisted by James N. Rosenau (New York: Duell, Sloan and Pearce, 1948), 199. The reference to a vaccination was not flippant. Washington was in the midst of a smallpox outbreak; both Franklin and Eleanor were inoculated against the disease. *NYT*, March 14, 1913; ER, *This Is My Story* (New York: Harper & Brothers, 1937), 195.

10. Frank B. Freidel, interviews with Charles H. McCarthy, June 8, 1948, and R. H. Camalier, May 28, 1948, FDRL.

11. *NYT*, February 24, 27, April 11, May 25, June 25, 1913. On the Navy League, see http://www.navyleague.org/about_us/history.php. On the position of Daniels, Wilson, and Bryan, see *NYT*, March 2, 10 (editorial), April 12, 21 (editorial), May 25, October 28, December 1, 1913.

12. The early months of the Japanese crisis are detailed in Cronon, *Cabinet Diaries*, 48–72.

13. Freidel, *FDR*, I, 225; *NYT*, May 20, 1913.

14. TR to FDR, May 10, 1913, July 23, 1914, in *The Letters of Theodore Roosevelt*, ed. Elting E. Morison et al. (Cambridge, MA: Harvard University Press, 1954), 7:729, 779; FDR to TR, July 17, 1914, and FDR to Alfred Thayer Mahan, May 28, 1914, FDR Papers (Assistant Secretary of the Navy), FDRL.

15. FDR to Mahan, June 16, July 17, 1914; Mahan to FDR, June 26, 31, August 3, 4, 18, 1914, FDR Papers (Assistant Secretary of the Navy).

16. *NYT*, April 19, 27, 1914.

17. See, e.g., *NYT*, June 22, 1916.

18. *NYT*, January 18, 1914; *Milwaukee Sentinel*, April 27, 1914, cited in Freidel, *FDR*, I, 227.

19. FDR to ER, March 19, July 29, 1913, in Roosevelt, *Personal Letters*, II, 200, 209–210; ER, *This Is My Story*, 234–237; Freidel, *FDR*, I, 167, 169.

20. For the rental agreement, see Anna Roosevelt Cowles to ER, April 7, 1913, Roosevelt Family Papers (Donated by the Children), Family Correspondence, FDRL. For the description of the neighborhood, see Daniels, *End of Innocence*, 77–79, and James Srodes, *On Dupont Circle* (Berkeley: Counterpoint, 2012), chs. 1–2.

21. FDR, Engagement Diary, FDR Papers (Assistant Secretary of the Navy).

22. Anna Roosevelt Halsted, draft article about Lucy Mercer (1966), Anna Roosevelt Halsted Papers, FDRL; SDR to ER and FDR, March 24, 1915, Roosevelt Family Papers

(Donated by the Children), Correspondence, SDR, FDRL; Ward, *A First-Class Temperament*, 358–362; Blanche Wiesen Cook, *Eleanor Roosevelt*, Vol. 1: *1884–1933* (New York: Viking Penguin, 1992), 16, 210.

23. ER, *This Is My Story*, 163.

24. Ward, *A First-Class Temperament*, 312–313, quotes Anna as having been told by her mother that John's birth marked "the end of any marital relationship, period." This seems plausible, but Ward does not cite the source.

25. For pressure from the New York reformers, see *NYT*, April 11, 1913. Roosevelt Papers (Assistant Secretary of the Navy) contains an extensive but highly fragmented correspondence about political patronage. My brief account conforms to the conclusions of Freidel, *FDR*, I, chs. 9–10, and Alfred B. Rollins Jr., *Roosevelt and Howe* (New York: Alfred A. Knopf, 1962), ch. 7.

26. *NYT*, May 23, 1913; Freidel, *FDR*, I, ch. 11; Rollins, *Roosevelt and Howe*, 140–145. See *Washington Post* [hereafter *WP*], October 10, 1913, for an example of the type of labor dispute Roosevelt faced.

27. For the development of FDR's attitudes toward big business in this and the following paragraphs, see esp. Freidel, *FDR*, I, ch. 12. On problems of procuring armor plating and the possibility of expanded government manufacturing, see, e.g., *NYT*, May 17, 21, 22, 25, June 3, July 15, August 24, 28, 29, 30, September 17, 18, 23, 27, October 10, 15, 1913, January 9, 15, March 22, 1914. The development of the issue, culminating in authorization of a government-owned armor manufacturing plant, is traced in Cronon, *Cabinet Diaries*, 81, 83, 96, 126.

28. This and the following paragraph are based on Freidel, *FDR*, I, 272–273; Cronon, *Cabinet Diaries*, 97 (February 5, 1915); *NYT*, March 19, 1909, September 24, 1911, February 18, 21, 1915.

29. FDR to Charles Schwab, February 11, 1915, Roosevelt Papers (Assistant Secretary of the Navy). There is a wonderful story to the effect that Roosevelt dealt with Joseph P. Kennedy at the Fore River shipyard, actually sent marines to seize the ship, and caused Kennedy in consequence to break into tears. Michael Beschloss recounts this story in *Kennedy and Roosevelt* (New York: W. W. Norton & Company, 1980), 44–47, but notes he could find no contemporary verification for it. Roosevelt and Kennedy do seem to have had acrimonious relations during the 1917–1918 period, but even then it does not appear that Roosevelt had to send in the marines.

30. *NYT*, June 15, 17, 1913; Freidel, *FDR*, I, 218–219.

31. *NYT*, January 23, July 22, 23, 24, 1914.

32. FDR to ER, July 19, 1914, in Roosevelt, *Personal Letters*, II, 228–230, 250–252; Rollins, *Roosevelt and Howe*, ch. 8; Daniels, *End of Innocence*, 138–139.

33. *NYT*, September 11, 21, 22, 1914.

34. Frances Perkins, *The Roosevelt I Knew* (New York: Viking Press, 1946), 24–25; Freidel, *FDR*, I, 190–191, 338.

CHAPTER 6: ARMAGEDDON

1. FDR to ER, August 1, 1914, in *F.D.R.: His Personal Letters, 1905–1928* [hereafter *Personal Letters*, II], ed. Elliott Roosevelt, assisted by James N. Rosenau (New York: Duell, Sloan and Pearce, 1948), 232–233.

2. FDR to ER, August 2, 1914, in Roosevelt, *Personal Letters*, II, 237–240.

3. *NYT*, October 22, 1915; *WP*, October 26, 1914; FDR to ER [Wednesday, probably October 21, 1914] in Roosevelt, *Personal Letters*, II, 256–257.

4. *NYT*, December 6, 1914.

5. For Gardner, see *WP*, December 11, 1914, and *NYT*, December 15, 1914; for the testimony, see FDR to SDR, December 17, 1914, and *NYT*, December 17, 1914, article on the testimony reproduced in Roosevelt, *Personal Letters*, II, 261–265.

6. *NYT*, January 31, May 15, November 20, 1915, January 18, 24, March 29, 30, April 14, 1916; *WP*, May 15, 1915, January 15, 18, March 30, April 13, 14, October 8, 1916.

7. This and subsequent paragraphs on President Wilson and his policies draw primarily on the work of Wilson's major biographer, Arthur S. Link, especially *Woodrow Wilson and the Progressive Era* (New York: Harper & Brothers, 1954) and volumes 3 to 5 in his multivolume biography, *Wilson* (Princeton, NJ: Princeton University Press, 1947–1965).

8. FDR to ER [June 10, 1915], in Roosevelt, *Personal Letters*, II, 270–271.

9. FDR to Josephus Daniels, n.d. [1915], in Roosevelt, *Personal Letters*, II, 299.

10. *NYT*, March 30, 1916; *WP*, March 30, 1916; Link, *Woodrow Wilson and the Progressive Era*, 185.

11. See Link, *Woodrow Wilson and the Progressive Era*, chs. 7–8, for a concise account of the preparedness controversy and diplomatic issues. Wilson quote on 185.

12. *WP*, February 12, 1916.

13. Frank B. Freidel, *Franklin D. Roosevelt: The Apprenticeship* [hereafter *FDR*, I] (Boston: Little, Brown and Company, 1952), 262.

14. See *NYT*, August 16, 1916, for provisions of the act. Authoritative data on US battleships is available online at the website of the Naval History and Heritage Command (http://www .history.navy.mil). Joseph L. Morrison, *Josephus Daniels: The Small-d Democrat* (Chapel Hill: University of North Carolina Press, 1966), 83–89, 100–103, covers Daniels's tussles with private industry.

15. FDR to ER, November 9, 1916, in Roosevelt, *Personal Letters*, II, 338–339.

16. Josephus Daniels to Woodrow Wilson with attached memo from FDR, both dated February 10, 1917, and Daniels, Diary, March 13, 1917, in *The Papers of Woodrow Wilson* ed. Arthur S. Link (Princeton, NJ: Princeton University Press, 1983), 41:189–190, 403.

17. FDR, Diary, March 11, 1917, in Freidel, *FDR*, I, 298–299.

18. Barbara Tuchman, *The Zimmermann Telegram* (New York: Viking Press, 1958), provides a full account of this event.

19. Elliott Roosevelt and James Brough, *An Untold Story: The Roosevelts of Hyde Park* (New York: G. P. Putnam's Sons, 1973), 80.

20. FDR to ER, July 25, August 20, 1917, in Roosevelt, *Personal Letters*, II, 352, 358.

21. ER, *This Is My Story* (New York: Harper & Brothers, 1937), 209–210, 253–265; *NYT*, July 17, 1917; FDR to ER, July 18, 1917, in Roosevelt, *Personal Letters*, II, 349.

22. ER, *This Is My Story*, 300–301.

23. ER to Isabella Ferguson, June 21, 1916, quoted in Blanche Wiesen Cook, *Eleanor Roosevelt*, Vol. 1: *1884–1933* (New York: Viking Penguin, 1992), 1:207–208.

24. Jonathan Daniels, *The End of Innocence* (Philadelphia: J. B. Lippincott, 1954), 223.

25. This and the paragraphs that follow rely very heavily on Frank Friedel's penetrating and authoritative account in *FDR*, I, chs. 18–19. On Howe's role, see Alfred B. Rollins Jr., *Roosevelt and Howe* (New York: Alfred A. Knopf, 1962), ch. 10.

26. Camp to FDR, July 25, 1917, FDR Papers, quoted in Freidel, *FDR*, I, 321; FDR to ER, July 16, 25, 26, September 9, 1917, and editor's note (348–349), in Roosevelt, *Personal Letters*, II, 347–349, 352–354, 360–361.

27. The page at http://www.angelfire.com/in/shiphistory/subchasers.html usefully assesses the 110-foot subchasers.

28. On the mine barrage, see "The North Sea Mine Barrage," Doughboy Center, http://www.worldwar1.com/dbc/nsminebr.htm; Byron Farwell, *Over There: The United States in the Great War, 1917–1918* (New York: W. W. Norton & Company, 1999), 73.

29. FDR to Woodrow Wilson, October 29, 1917, in Link et al., *The Papers of Woodrow Wilson*, 44:464–466. The American Churchill was no relation to the English statesman. The two of them met on the Englishman's first lecture tour of America in 1900. The English visitor told his new American acquaintance that he should go into politics. "I mean to be Prime Minister of England; it would be a great lark if you were President of the United States at the same time." Martin Gilbert, *Churchill and America* (New York: Free Press, 2005), 39–40.

30. Freidel, *FDR*, I, 302, 308.

31. Freidel, *FDR*, I, 318–319.

32. Freidel, *FDR*, I, 367n.

33. FDR to ER, August 20, 1918, in Roosevelt, *Personal Letters*, II, 439–440.

34. FDR, Trip Diary, July 20, 1918, in Roosevelt, *Personal Letters*, II, 383.

35. FDR, Trip Diary, July 22, 30, 1918, in Roosevelt, *Personal Letters*, II, 385, 391.

36. Amanda Smith, ed., *Hostage to Fortune: The Letters of Joseph P. Kennedy* (New York: Viking Press, 2001), 411.

37. FDR, Trip Diary, July 30, 1918, in Roosevelt, *Personal Letters*, II, 392–393.

38. FDR, Trip Diary, August 2, 1918, in Roosevelt, *Personal Letters*, II, 409–410.

39. FDR, Trip Diary, August 2, 1918, in Roosevelt, *Personal Letters*, II, 411–412.

40. FDR, Trip Diary, August 4, 1918, in Roosevelt, *Personal Letters*, II, 412–422, quotes at 416, 417.

41. FDR, Trip Diary, August 5, 7, 1918, in Roosevelt, *Personal Letters*, II, 422–432.

42. FDR, Trip Diary, August 10, 11, 1918, in Roosevelt, *Personal Letters*, II, 433–434; Josephus Daniels, Diary, September 3, 1918, in *The Cabinet Diaries of Josephus Daniels, 1913–1921*, ed. E. David Cronon (Lincoln: University of Nebraska Press, 1963), 333.

43. Geoffrey Ward, *A First-Class Temperament: The Emergence of Franklin Roosevelt* (New York: Harper & Row, 1989), 405–407. On the guns themselves, see "United States Navy Railway Batteries," World War I Document Archive, http://www.gwpda.org/naval/wusrw000.htm; "US Navy Railway Guns France 1918," Christopher Eger, http://militaryhistory.suite101.com/article.cfm/us_navy_railway_guns_france_1918; "World War I: About This Creation: 14-Inch Naval Railway Battery Mark I," MOCpages, http://www.mocpages.com/moc.php/12871.

44. Freidel, *FDR*, I, 367–368.

45. Freidel, *FDR*, I, 369; Ward, *A First-Class Temperament*, 408–410; ER, *This Is My Story*, 267–268.

46. TR to FDR, September 23, 1918, FDR Papers (Freidel, *FDR*, I, 369n).

47. Original draft reports, October 16, 21, 1918, FDR Papers, FDRL.

48. Freidel, *FDR*, I, 370; Ward, *A First-Class Temperament*, 417.

49. ER, *This Is My Story*, 272; FDR to H. H. Richards, June 28, 1921, FDR Papers, quoted in Freidel, *FDR*, I, 337.

50. Joseph P. Lash, *Eleanor and Franklin: The Story of Their Relationship* (New York: W. W. Norton & Company, 1971), ch. 21; Joseph Alsop, *FDR: A Centenary Remembrance* (New York: Viking Press, 1982), 67–72. Joseph E. Persico, *Franklin and Lucy* (New York: Random House, 2008), is the most thorough account of the relationship.

51. Ward, *A First-Class Temperament*, 416.

52. Ward, *A First-Class Temperament*, 448–451; Cook, *Eleanor Roosevelt*, I, 254–256.

53. ER, *This Is My Story*, 275; ER to SDR, January 3–9, 1919, in Roosevelt, *Personal Letters*, II, 444–446.

54. ER to SDR, January 11, 1919, in Roosevelt, *Personal Letters*, II, 448–453, quote at 450.

55. ER, *This Is My Story*, 289.

CHAPTER 7: VICTORY IN DEFEAT

1. Geoffrey Ward, *A First-Class Temperament: The Emergence of Franklin Roosevelt* (New York: Harper & Row, 1989), 455–457, excellently describes this incident.

2. This and following paragraphs draw heavily on Frank B. Freidel, *Franklin D. Roosevelt: The Ordeal* [hereafter *FDR*, II] (Boston: Little, Brown and Company, 1954), ch. 2.

3. Arthur S. Link, *Wilson the Diplomatist* (Baltimore: Johns Hopkins Press, 1957), ch. 5; John Milton Cooper, *Breaking the Heart of the World: Woodrow Wilson and the Fight for the League of Nations* (Cambridge and New York: Cambridge University Press, 2010).

4. ER to Isabella Ferguson, quoted in Ward, *A First-Class Temperament*, 464; E. David Cronon, ed., *The Cabinet Diaries of Josephus Daniels, 1913–1921* (Lincoln: University of Nebraska Press, 1963), 497.

5. For Lansing's dismissal and reaction to it, see *NYT*, February 14, 15, 26, 1920.

6. FDR to Mrs. William S. Sims, December 24, 1919, FDR Papers (Assistant Secretary of the Navy). Friedel, *FDR*, II, ch. 3, and Ward, *A First-Class Temperament*, 465–490, 568–574, provide good accounts of these investigations.

7. Sims's memorandum was published in its entirety in *WP*, January 18, 1920; his life and career are nicely summarized in the *American National Biography* sketch by Mark Russell Schulman, most readily available at http://www.anb.org.

8. Sims to FDR, August 26, 1919, FDR Papers (Assistant Secretary of the Navy); *NYT*, February 2, 1920.

9. Ward, *A First-Class Temperament*, 475–478; Cronon, *Cabinet Diaries*, 490–498, esp. entries of February 2, 9, 10, 11, 13, 14, 18, 20, 21, 1920; *NYT*, February 6, 1920; Cronon, *Cabinet Diaries*, 491 (February 5, 1920).

10. *NYT*, June 5, 1920.

11. *New York Sun*, May 22, 1919 For the Dana connection, see Geoffrey Ward, *Before the Trumpet: Young Franklin Roosevelt, 1882–1905* (New York: Harper & Row, 1985), 602; *New York Herald*, November 26, 1919; FDR to Henry M. Heymann, November 26, December 2, 1919, and Heyman to FDR, November 29, 1919, cited in Freidel, *FDR*, II, 51, 55.

12. FDR to Hugh Gibson, January 2, 1920, quoted in Freidel, *FDR*, II, 57.

13. *NYT*, June 29, July 1, 1920.

14. For FDR and Davis, see Freidel, *FDR*, II, 60–61.

15. *WP*, July 12, 1920.

16. Walter Lippmann to FDR, July 8, 1920, and Herbert Hoover to FDR, July 13, 1920, both quoted in Freidel, *FDR*, II, 68n; *NYT*, July 7, 1920 (editorial).

17. Alfred B. Rollins Jr., *Roosevelt and Howe* (New York: Alfred A. Knopf, 1962), 156; James M. Cox, *Journey Through My Years* (New York: Simon & Schuster, 1962), 238.

18. FDR to ER, July 20, 1920, in *F.D.R.: His Personal Letters, 1905–1928* [hereafter *Personal Letters*, II], ed. Elliott Roosevelt, assisted by James N. Rosenau (New York: Duell, Sloan and Pearce, 1948), 495–497; Freidel, *FDR*, II, 73–74; Cronon, *Cabinet Diaries*, 542 (August 3, 1920).

19. *NYT*, August 7, 1920; FDR to Daniels, August 6, 1920, and Daniels to FDR, August 7, 1920, in Roosevelt, *Personal Letters*, II, 489–491; Cronon, *Cabinet Diaries*, 542–543 (August 6, 1920).

20. *NYT*, August 10, 1920. See also Roosevelt, *Personal Letters*, II, 499–508.

21. Freidel, *FDR*, II, 78–79.

22. *NYT*, September 2, 1920. See, e.g., clips from *Philadelphia Record*, September 19, 1920; *Buffalo Evening Times*, September 21, 1920; *Baltimore Sun*, September 29, 1920; 1920 Campaign Clippings File, FDRL.

23. *NYT*, August 14, September 3, 18, 1920.

24. *NYT*, August 19, 1920.

25. Freidel, *FDR*, II, 81–83; *NYT*, September 3, 22, 1920.

26. *NYT*, August 25, 1920.

27. Harold L. Ickes, *The Secret Diary of Harold L. Ickes*, Vol. 1: *The First Thousand Days, 1933–1936* (New York: Simon & Schuster, 1953), 699 (October 30, 1936).

CHAPTER 8: PARALYSIS AND PHILANTHROPY

1. Geoffrey Ward, *A First-Class Temperament: The Emergence of Franklin Roosevelt* (New York: Harper & Row, 1989), 560–575.

2. *NYT*, January 13, 22, March 9, 16, 22, May 1, 15, June 27, July 4, 9, 11, 21, August 6, 1921.

3. Alfred B. Rollins Jr., *Roosevelt and Howe* (New York: Alfred A. Knopf, 1962), 190–191.

4. The short sketch of Missy LeHand by Lois Scharf in *Franklin D. Roosevelt: His Life and Times, an Encyclopedic View*, ed. Otis L. Graham (Boston: G. K. Hall, 1985), 236–237, is useful. Joseph Persico, *Franklin and Lucy* (New York: Random House, 2008), esp. ch. 19, speculatively discusses her relationship with FDR, as does Frank Costigliola, *Roosevelt's Lost Alliances* (Princeton, NJ: Princeton University Press, 2012), 68–78.

5. *NYT*, July 20, 1921.

6. Photograph in the FDRL Archive.

7. The following pages, covering Roosevelt's polio attack and his initial responses to it, rely heavily on the baseline narratives established by Frank B. Freidel, *Franklin D. Roosevelt: The Ordeal* (Boston: Little, Brown and Company, 1954), ch. 6; Ward, *A First-Class Temperament*, chs. 13–14; James Tobin, *The Man He Became* (New York: Simon & Schuster, 2013), chs. 1–4. They also draw on John Gunther, *Roosevelt in Retrospect: A Profile in History* (New York: Harper & Brothers, 1950), ch. 13, especially the long excerpts from the correspondence of doctors Robert Lovett and George Draper (225–227).

8. *NYT*, September 16, 1921.

9. Gunther, *Roosevelt in Retrospect*, 226; Frank B. Freidel, *Franklin D. Roosevelt: The Ordeal* [hereafter *FDR*, II] (Boston: Little, Brown and Company, 1954), 103.

10. James Roosevelt and Sidney Shalett, *Affectionately, F.D.R.: A Son's Story of a Courageous Man* (London: George G. Harrap & Company, 1960), 136–137.

11. ER, *This Is My Story* (New York: Harper & Brothers, 1937), 336–337.

12. Gunther, *Roosevelt in Retrospect*, 229.

13. FDR to S. R. Bertron, November 28, 1922, FDR Papers, 1920–1928.

14. Freidel, *FDR*, II, 187–189; FDR to SDR, March 5, 1923, in *F.D.R.: His Personal Letters, 1905–1928* [hereafter *Personal Letters*, II], ed. Elliott Roosevelt, assisted by James N. Rosenau (New York: Duell, Sloan and Pearce, 1948), 535–536; *Weona II* log, FDR Papers (Family, Business, and Personal), FDRL; Ward, *A First-Class Temperament*, 660–663.

15. *Larooco* logs in Roosevelt, *Personal Letters*, II, 536–544, 552–560, 570–577, 592–609.

16. Freidel, *FDR*, II, 191.

17. Tobin, *The Man He Became*, chs. 10–12; "FDR's Ties to Georgia Introduction," Georgia Info, http://georgiainfo.galileo.usg.edu/FDRvisit.htm.

18. ER, *This I Remember* (New York: Harper & Row, 1949), 27.

19. *Atlanta Journal*, October 26, 1934; FDR to SDR, October 1924, in Roosevelt, *Personal Letters*, II, 567–568.

20. Samuel I. Rosenman, ed., *The Public Papers and Addresses of Franklin D. Roosevelt*, Vol. 3: *The Advance of Recovery and Reform* (New York: Random House, 1938), 487–488; Ward, *A First-Class Temperament*, 722–725; Kenneth S. Davis, *FDR: The Beckoning of Destiny, 1882–1928* [hereafter *FDR*, I] (New York: G. P. Putnam's Sons, 1972), 787.

21. Freidel, interview with ER, September 3, 1952.

22. ER to FDR, May 4, 1926, quoted in Roosevelt, *Personal Letters*, II, 611.

23. David Oshinsky, *Polio: An American Story* (New York: Oxford University Press, 2005), 35–55; "Georgia Warm Springs Foundation, 1940" (report), Disability History Museum, http://www.disabilitymuseum.org/lib/docs/2168.htm. On the policy for indigent clients, see FDR to Frederic A. Delano, August 25, 1931, FDR Papers (Governor of New York).

24. FDR to Anna Roosevelt Cowles, June 29, 1927, Roosevelt Family Papers (Donated by the Children), Family Correspondence, FDRL; ER, *This I Remember*, 44, 367–368.

25. See, e.g., the story on Eugene Murphy, *NYT*, December 22, 1928, and the more typical account of Pauline Murrell, *NYT*, November 24 (news story), 26 (Le Roy Hubbard, letter to the editor), 1932. See also the balanced and intelligent feature story by Diana Rice, *NYT*, September 27, 1931.

26. On fund-raising in general, see, e.g., stories in *NYT*, June 7, 17, November 28, 1930. For the life insurance policy, see *NYT*, October 18, 19, 1930. For Edsel Ford gift, see Ford to FDR, March 15, 1928, Roosevelt Family Papers Donated by the Children, FDRL. See also FDR to Henry Morgenthau Sr., January 29, 1929, and July 10, 1930, FDR Papers (Governor of New York), FDRL, for examples of correspondence with an important donor. On the Foundation payback, see ER, *This I Remember*, 367–368.

27. Frank B. Freidel, interview with ER, September 3, 1952.

28. *WP*, March 19, 1937; William E. Leuchtenburg, *The White House Looks South* (Baton Rouge: Louisiana State University Press, 2005), 36.

CHAPTER 9: THE YOUNG PRINCE RETURNS

1. For St. John the Divine, see *NYT*, January 22, 1925.

2. For examples of FDR's activity with the construction council, see numerous stories in *NYT*, 1923–1928, and Frank B. Freidel, *Franklin D. Roosevelt: The Ordeal* [hereafter *FDR*, II] (Boston: Little, Brown and Company, 1954), 151–158.

3. FDR to Cordell Hull, November 4, 1921, FDR Papers, 1920–1928, FDRL.

4. *NYT*, August 15, 16, 17, 1922; SDR to FDR, August 28, 1922, Roosevelt Family Papers Donated by the Children, Correspondence, SDR, FDRL.

5. *NYT*, June 24, 26, July 13, 1924.

6. James Roosevelt and Sidney Shalett, *Affectionately, F.D.R.: A Son's Story of a Courageous Man* (London: George G. Harrap & Company, 1960), 184–186; *NYT*, June 27, 1924.

7. *NYT*, June 27, 1924.

8. Kenneth S. Davis, *FDR: The Beckoning of Destiny, 1882–1928* [hereafter *FDR*, I] (New York: G. P. Putnam's Sons, 1972), 757.

9. ER, *This I Remember* (New York: Harper & Brothers, 1949), 31–32.

10. Blanche Wiesen Cook, *Eleanor Roosevelt*, Vol. 1: *1884–1933* [hereafter *Eleanor Roosevelt*, I] (New York: Viking Penguin, 1992), 291–299; Joseph P. Lash, *Eleanor and Franklin: The Story of Their Relationship* (New York: W. W. Norton & Company, 1971), 280; SDR to FDR, March 15, 18, 1924, Roosevelt Family Papers Donated by the Children, FDRL.

11. *NYT*, May 25, 1925 (party magazine); June 8, 1925, November 7, 1926; January 5, 1927 (Junior Democratic League); September 28, 1926 (full status for women); December 2, 1927 (women nominees); "Women Must Learn to Play the Game as Men Do," *Red Book* (April 1928), 78–79, 141–142 (reprinted in Allida M. Black, *What I Hope to Leave Behind: The Essential Essays of Eleanor Roosevelt* [Brooklyn, NY: Carlson Publishing, 1995], 195–200).

12. For housing, see *NYT*, November 16, 1924, March 21, April 15, 1926; profile in *NYT*, April 8, 1928 (magazine section); "blacklist invitation" in *NYT*, May 1, 1928.

13. *NYT*, September 5, 1926, January 30, 1928.

14. *NYT*, January 25, April 18, 1928; ER, "Why Democrats Favor Smith," *North American Review* 224 (November 1927), 472–475, in Black, *What I Hope to Leave Behind*, 349–351.

15. This and the following paragraphs about the ER-Cook-Dickerson relationship draw primarily on Cook, *Eleanor Roosevelt*, I, 318–337, 383–384, 397–399, and Lash, *Eleanor and Franklin*, 277–278, 298, 304–308, 475–478.

16. For this and the preceding paragraph, see articles in *NYT*, June 24, July 8, 22, August 10 (magazine section), 1930; also see *Literary Digest*, August 30, 1930 ("The Modern Wife's Difficult Job"), and *Pictorial Review*, December 1931 ("Ten Rules for Success in Marriage"), both in Black, *What I Hope to Leave Behind*, 201–213.

17. See, e.g., FDR to George White, December 5, 1924, General Manuscript Collection, Marietta College Library. White would later become governor of Ohio. Thanks to Professor Irene Neu for providing this example.

18. *NYT*, March 9, 1925.

19. *NYT*, March 10, 22, April 5, 9, 1925; *WP*, March 19, April 5, 1925.

20. FDR to Thomas Pendell, October 2, 1922, FDR Papers, 1920–1928.

21. FDR to James Edgerton, January 27, 1925, FDR Papers, 1920–1928.

22. FDR to Thomas Pendell, September 4, 1922, FDR Papers, 1920–1928.

23. Merrill D. Peterson, *The Jefferson Image in the American Mind* (New York: Oxford University Press, 1962), esp. 330–355.

24. FDR, review of *Jefferson and Hamilton*, in the *New York Evening World*, December 3, 1925, as reprinted in Basil Rauch, ed., *The Roosevelt Reader* (New York: Holt, Rinehart and Winston, 1957), 43–47.

25. FDR to Adolphus Reagan, December 28, 1925, and FDR to George Foster Peabody, December 11, 1925, both in FDR Papers, 1920–1928.

26. On the Mississippi valley flood, see FDR's correspondence with George St. Jean in FDR Papers, 1920–1928, articles in *NYT*, May 13, 19, 1927, and FDR, letter to the editor, *NYT*, August 25, 1927; Freidel, *FDR*, II, 225–226.

27. *Atlanta Constitution*, March 26, 1927, quoted in *NYT*, March 27, 1927.

28. FDR to Lippmann, August 6, 1928, quoted in Freidel, *FDR*, II, 243n. For radio coverage, see *NYT*, June 24, 1928.

29. *NYT*, June 28, 1928. See also Davis, *FDR*, I, 820–823, and Geoffrey Ward, *A First-Class Temperament: The Emergence of Franklin Roosevelt* (New York: Harper & Row, 1989), 784–785.

CHAPTER 10: CHIEF EXECUTIVE

1. Frank B. Freidel, *Franklin D. Roosevelt: The Ordeal* [hereafter *FDR*, II] (Boston: Little, Brown and Company, 1954), 246–247.

2. Ernest K. Lindley, *Franklin D. Roosevelt: A Career in Progressive Democracy* (New York: Blue Ribbon Books, 1931), 16–20.

3. See newspaper commentary in *NYT*, October 3, 1928; *NYT*, October 13, 1928.

4. Lindley, *Franklin D. Roosevelt*, 21; Francis Perkins, *The Roosevelt I Knew* (New York: Viking Press, 1946), 44–45; Samuel I. Rosenman, *Working with Roosevelt* (New York: Harper & Brothers, 1952), 21–22.

5. *NYT*, October 7, 17, 20, 26, 27, 31, November 4, 1928; Samuel I. Rosenman, ed., *The Public Papers and Addresses of Franklin D. Roosevelt*, Vol. 1: *The Genesis of the New Deal, 1928–1932* [hereafter *Public Papers*, I] (New York: Random House, 1938), ch. 1.

6. *NYT*, November 7, 1928.

7. For the final results, see *NYT*, December 4 (Associated Press tally), December 12 (State Board of Canvassers), 1928. The two tallies are nearly identical.

8. ER, interview with Frank Freidel, July 13, 1954, FDRL.

9. *NYT*, April 4, 8, 9, 1929.

10. Edward S. McGuire to FDR, July 16, 1932; FDR to McGuire, July 26, 1932; FDR to Coughlin, July 29, 1932, all in Roosevelt Family Papers Donated by the Children, Political Files, FDRL.

11. This and the following paragraphs on ER and Miller rely heavily on Blanche Wiesen Cook, *Eleanor Roosevelt*, Vol. 1: *1884–1933* (New York: Viking Penguin, 1992), ch. 18, and Joseph P. Lash, *Eleanor and Franklin: The Story of Their Relationship* (New York: W. W. Norton & Company, 1971), 340–342.

12. ER, interview with Frank Freidel, September 3, 1952, FDRL; Kenneth S. Davis, *FDR: The New York Years, 1928–1933* [hereafter *FDR*, II] (New York: Random House, 1985), 32.

13. Perkins, *The Roosevelt I Knew*, 51; ER, interview with Frank Freidel, September 3, 1952, FDRL. See also Elisabeth Israels Perry, *Belle Moskowitz: Feminine Politics and the Exercise of Power in the Age of Alfred E. Smith* (New York: Oxford University Press, 1987).

14. Lash, *Eleanor and Franklin*, 323; Alfred B. Rollins, Jr., *Roosevelt and Howe* (New York: Alfred A. Knopf, 1962), 246; Perkins, *The Roosevelt I Knew*, 53.

15. Rollins, *Roosevelt and Howe*, 252–254.

16. Perkins, *The Roosevelt I Knew*, ch. 3.

17. Farley quoted in Norman Littell to Mrs. Norman Littell, March 30, 1939, Anna Roosevelt Halsted Papers, FDRL.

18. Rosenman, *Public Papers*, I, 75–80; *NYT*, January 2, 1929.

19. Finla G. Crawford, "The Executive Budget Decision in New York," *American Political Science Review* 24, no. 2 (May 1930): 403–408; Bernard Bellush, *Franklin D. Roosevelt as Governor of New York* [hereafter *FDR as Governor*] (New York: Columbia University Press, 1955), 37–57; Rosenman, *Public Papers*, I, 399–348.

20. The following paragraphs on Roosevelt's public power policies draw in general on Bellush, *FDR as Governor*, chs. 9–10; Frank B. Freidel, *Franklin D. Roosevelt: The Triumph* (Boston: Little, Brown and Company, 1956), ch. 8; Davis, *FDR*, II, 88–101; and Rosenman, *Public Papers*, I, ch. 4.

21. Rosenman, *Public Papers*, I, 77–78, 82; FDR to Mackenzie King, June 17, August 20, 1929, in *F.D.R.: His Personal Letters, 1928–1945* [hereafter *PL, 1928–1945*], ed. Elliott Roosevelt (New York: Duell, Sloan and Pearce, 1950), 66, 71. *Forum* article summarized in *NYT*, November 20, 1929; for public service commissioner resignation, see *NYT*, February 6, 1930. See also Samuel I. Rosenman, "Governor Roosevelt's Power Program," *Nation* (September 18, 1929), 302–303.

22. FDR to Frederic Delano, November 22, 1929, in Roosevelt, *PL, 1928–1945*, 90–91; Frederic Delano to FDR, November 25, 1929, FDR Papers (Governor of New York), FDRL.

23. Ernest K. Lindley, "Two Years of Franklin Roosevelt," *Nation* (September 17, 1930),

289–291. Roosevelt's own summary of his achievements can be found in his public letter to Senator Robert F. Wagner, *NYT*, September 11, 1930, and legislative stories in *NYT*, April 9, 1929, April 12 (editorial), 17, 22, 1930.

24. Lindley, "Two Years of Franklin Roosevelt," 289–291.

25. Dr. Leroy Hubbard quoted in *NYT*, January 2, 1929.

26. ER, interview with Frank Freidel, July 13, 1954, FDRL.

27. Lindley, "Two Years of Franklin Roosevelt," 289–291.

28. *NYT*, August 27, 1930.

29. FDR, public letter to Robert F. Wagner, September 9, 1930, in *NYT*, September 11, 1930.

30. Rosenman, *Working with Roosevelt*, 41–47; text of radio speech in *NYT*, October 10, 1930.

31. Freidel, *FDR*, II, 85–88; Curtis Dall to FDR, February 16, 1930, December 30, 1934, Anna Roosevelt Halsted Papers, FDRL. Dall's professional moves can be traced in *NYT*, February 22, 28, December 31, 1930, December 29, 1932, March 29, April 29, July 1, October 24, 1933, December 30, 1934.

32. For this and the following paragraphs about banking issues, see Freidel, *FDR*, II, 92–94, 186–192, and related stories and editorials in *NYT*, March 5, 8, 24, 25, 28, May 15, October 21, 1931, January 7, 10, February 4, 6, March 8, April 24, May 29, 1932.

33. See *NYT*, March 7, 1930, for an account of a Communist hunger march broken up by police. Richard Vedder and Lowell Gallaway, *Out of Work: Unemployment and Government in Twentieth-Century America* (New York: Holmes and Meier, 1993), 77.

34. Perkins, *The Roosevelt I Knew*, ch. 8. See also stories on Perkins's unemployment statistics in *NYT*, February 11, March 11, 22, April 10, June 12, July 26, October 9, 1930, June 11, 1931.

35. Rosenman, *Public Papers*, I, 447–452; Perkins, *The Roosevelt I Knew*, 100–105.

36. *NYT*, August 28, 1930, October 27, November 7, 1931, March 3, 1932; Rosenman, *Public Papers*, I, 453–457.

37. Rosenman, *Public Papers*, I, 457–470; *NYT*, August 29, 1931.

38. Freidel, *FDR*, II, 219–227; Robert E. Sherwood, *Roosevelt and Hopkins: An Intimate History*, rev. ed. (New York: Grosset & Dunlap, 1950), 31–33.

39. *NYT*, March 3, August 1, 12, September 6 (editorial), October 5, 18, 1932; Rosenman, *Public Papers*, I, 470–473.

40. *NYT*, May 28, July 10, August 2, 1932.

41. See *NYT*, January 7, 1932, for the full text of the speech; Rosenman, *Public Papers*, I, 111–125, quote at 124.

CHAPTER 11: DESTINY CALLS

1. FDR to F. W. McLean, January 22, 1932, in *The Public Papers and Addresses of Franklin D. Roosevelt*, Vol. 1: *The Genesis of the New Deal, 1928–1932* [hereafter *Public Papers*, I], ed. Samuel I. Rosenman (New York: Random House, 1938), 623–624.

2. Christopher M. Finan, *Alfred E. Smith: The Happy Warrior* (New York: Hill and Wang, 2002), 266–267; FDR to John Godfrey Saxe, November 3, 1931, in *F.D.R.: His Personal Letters, 1928–1945* [hereafter *PL, 1928–1945*], ed. Elliott Roosevelt (New York: Duell, Sloan and Pearce, 1950), 1:227–228.

3. FDR to Smith, November 10, 1931, in Roosevelt, *PL, 1928–1945*, 1:229; *NYT*, November 16 (editorial), 19, 1931; Clark Howell to FDR, December 2, 1931, in Roosevelt, *PL, 1928–1945*, 1:229–232.

4. *NYT*, February 8, 1932.

5. James Farley, *Behind the Ballots: The Personal History of a Politician* (New York: Harcourt Brace and Company, 1938), 96; *NYT*, February 9, 1932.

6. The Crater-Wagner relationship is documented in *NYT*, September 4, 5, 1930, and Richard J. Tofel, *Vanishing Point: The Disappearance of Judge Crater and the New York He Left Behind* (Chicago: Ivan R. Dee, 2004), 16–17, 88, 106–107. The senator, who was widely acknowledged to be incorruptible, found it necessary to behave as if he had never heard of Crater. The story "Judge Crater Disappearance Possibly Solved," *New York Post*, August 19, 2005, recounts a letter left by the deceased widow of a New York policeman. It asserts that her husband and a fellow officer killed Crater and buried him at Coney Island. When the alleged burial site had been excavated for the construction of the New York Aquarium in the 1950s, it had yielded human remains; there is no way of knowing whether they were Crater's.

7. *NYT*, October 10, 1930; Frank B. Freidel, *Franklin D. Roosevelt: The Triumph* [hereafter *FDR*, III] (Boston: Little, Brown and Company, 1956), 148–150.

8. Walker quote in Kenneth S. Davis, *FDR: The New York Years, 1928–1933* (New York: Random House, 1985), 104.

9. Edward M. House to FDR, April 22, 1931, FDR Papers (Governor of New York); *NYT*, April 21, 29, 1931.

10. Cross to the editor, *Time*, February 17, 1931; Luce to Cross, February 27, 1931; Cross to Luce, March 18, 1931; Luce to Cross, March 26, 1931, FDR Papers (Governor of New York); Freidel, *FDR*, III, 175.

11. FDR to Lee B. Wood, November 30, 1931, FDR Papers (Governor of New York).

12. *New York World-Telegram*, June 21–25, 1932, clippings in FDR Papers (Governor of New York).

13. Lippmann in the *New York Herald-Tribune*, January 8, 1932.

14. *NYT*, February 25, March 1, 2 (editorial), 1932, for Farley and replacement; *NYT*, February 27, 1932; Bernard Bellush, *Franklin D. Roosevelt as Governor of New York* (New York: Columbia University Press, 1955), 269–274; Freidel, *FDR*, III, 256–258.

15. *NYT*, February 26, March 27, 31, April 2, 1932.

16. FDR to Colonel Edward M. House, June 4, 1932, in Roosevelt, *PL, 1928–1945*, 1:280–281.

17. Ernest K. Lindley, *Franklin D. Roosevelt: A Career in Progressive Democracy* (New York: Blue Ribbon Books, 1931).

18. Farley, *Behind the Ballots*, 80–88, quote at 83.

19. *NYT*, April 4, 1932.

20. Farley, *Behind the Ballots*, 72.

21. On the emergence of the intellectual in politics, see Richard S. Kirkendall, "Franklin D. Roosevelt and the Service Intellectual," *Mississippi Valley Historical Review* (December 1962): 456–471.

22. Max Freedman, ed., *Roosevelt and Frankfurter: Their Correspondence, 1928–1945* (Boston: Little, Brown and Company, 1967), 35–97.

23. *NYT*, September 6, 9, 1932. See also Rexford G. Tugwell, *The Brains Trust* (New York: Viking Press, 1968), esp. intro.

24. *New York Evening Journal*, June 2, 1930, clipping in FDR Papers (Governor of New York); FDR to Charles Mitchell, April 14, 1931, FDR Papers (Governor of New York); FDR to the editor, *Montana Standard* (Butte), December 29, 1931, in Roosevelt, *PL, 1928–1945*, 1:246–247; statement by Drs. Samuel Lambert, Russell Hibbs, and Foster Kennedy, April 29, 1931, FDR Papers (Governor of New York); statement by Dr. LeRoy W. Hubbard, May 18, 1932, Roosevelt Family Papers Donated by the Children, Governor Correspondence, FDRL.

25. *NYT*, February 3, 4 (editorial), 1932; Joseph P. Lash, *Eleanor and Franklin: The Story of Their Relationship* (New York: W. W. Norton & Company, 1971), 346–347.

26. Freidel, *FDR*, III, 250–252.

27. *NYT*, April 8, 1932; Rosenman, *Public Papers*, I, 624–627.

28. See *NYT*, April 14, 17, 1932, for Smith speech and reaction.

29. *NYT*, April 17, 18, 1932; Rosenman, *Public Papers*, I, 627–639.

30. *NYT*, April 20, 28, 29, 30, 1932.

31. Rosenman, *Public Papers*, I, 646.

32. *NYT*, May 1, 1932.

33. James Farley to E. M. House, May 13, 1932, FDR Papers (Donated by the Children), Correspondence as Governor, FDRL. See the somewhat speculative but mostly accurate vote map in *NYT*, June 26, 1932.

34. Donald A. Ritchie, *Electing FDR: The New Deal Campaign of 1932* (Lawrence: University Press of Kansas, 2007), 97; *NYT*, June 26, 27, 28, 1932.

35. *NYT*, June 29, 1932.

36. *NYT*, June 30, 1932.

37. Ritchie, *Electing FDR*, 102.

38. Farley, *Behind the Ballots*, 144.

39. Ritchie, *Electing FDR*, 106.

40. Alfred B. Rollins Jr., *Roosevelt and Howe* (New York: Alfred A. Knopf, 1962), 345–346.

41. *NYT*, July 3, 1932.

42. Rosenman, *Public Papers*, I, 647–659.

CHAPTER 12: MUCH TO FEAR

1. This and the following paragraphs on the White House dinner are based on ER, *This I Remember* (New York: Harper & Row, 1949), 61–62; Donald A. Ritchie, *Electing FDR: The New Deal Campaign of 1932* (Lawrence: University Press of Kansas, 2007), 92–94 (photo of FDR and ER at 93); *NYT*, April 27, 28, 29, 1932; Alonzo Fields, Oral History Interview, Hoover Presidential Library (accessed online), 6–9.

2. *NYT*, July 30, 1932; *WP*, July 30, 1932.

3. R. G. Tugwell, *The Brains Trust* (New York: Viking Press, 1968), 357–359.

4. *NYT*, August 17, 1932; *NYT*, September 2, 1932.

5. *NYT*, August 17, 18, 1932.

6. Samuel I. Rosenman, ed., *The Public Papers and Addresses of Franklin D. Roosevelt*, Vol. 1: *The Genesis of the New Deal, 1928–1932* [hereafter *Public Papers*, I] (New York: Random House, 1938), 659–669; *NYT*, July 31, 1932; Tugwell, *The Brains Trust*, ch. 32.

7. Rosenman, *Public Papers*, I, 659–684; *NYT*, August 21, 1932.

8. Rosenman, *Public Papers*, I, 684–692.

9. Ritchie, *Electing FDR*, 127.

10. Rosenman, *Public Papers*, I, 693–711. For Sioux City, see Rosenman, *Public Papers*, I, 756–770.

11. Rosenman, *Public Papers*, I, 742–756; *NYT*, September 24, 1952.

12. Lippmann column, *New York Herald-Tribune*, October 7, 1932, copy in FDR Papers (Governor of New York).

13. *NYT*, October 18, 20, 25, 27, 29, November 5, 1932.

14. For FDR on the bonus, see, e.g., stories in *NYT*, October 15, 18, 1932, and Wayne Westman to the editor, *NYT*, October 27, 1932; for the Hoover comment, see *NYT*, October 29, 1932.

15. Ritchie, *Electing FDR*, 134–148; *NYT*, October 5, 23, 29, November 1, 1932.

16. Rosenman, *Public Papers*, I, 842–855; *NYT*, November 1, 1932.

17. Arthur M. Schlesinger Jr., *The Crisis of the Old Order, 1919–1933* (Boston: Houghton Mifflin Company, 1957), 438–439.

18. *NYT*, February 17, 1933.

19. Raymond Moley, *After Seven Years* (New York: Harper & Brothers, 1939), 138–139.

20. *NYT*, February 14, 1933. See also *NYT*, January 24, 25, February 7, 1933 (articles by James A. Hagerty).

21. Reaction to the cabinet picks is surveyed in *NYT*, February 23 (James A. Hagerty), 26 (Arthur Krock), 1933.

22. *NYT*, January 26, 1933 (James A. Hagerty).

23. *NYT*, December 18, 1932.

24. Linda Lear, "Ickes, Harold LeClair," in *Franklin D. Roosevelt: His Life and Times, an Encyclopedic View*, ed. Otis L. Graham Jr. and Meghan Robinson Wander (Boston: G. K. Hall & Company, 1985), 199–201.

25. Herbert Hoover, "Letter to Franklin D. Roosevelt," February 18, 1933, Teaching AmericanHistory.org, http://teachingamericanhistory.org/library/document/letter-to -franklin-d-roosevelt.

26. Grace Tully, *F.D.R.: My Boss* (New York: Charles Scribner's Sons, 1949), 64.

27. Samuel I. Rosenman, *The Public Papers and Addresses of Franklin D. Roosevelt: The Year of Crisis, 1933* (New York: Random House, 1938), 368; Frances Perkins, *The Roosevelt I Knew* (New York: Viking Press, 1946), ch. 11 and p. 330; FDR to Philip Slomovitz, "Letter on the President's Ancestors," American Presidency Project, March 7, 1935, http://www.presidency .ucsb.edu/ws/?pid=15016.

28. Arthur M. Schlesinger Jr., *The Age of Roosevelt: The Crisis of the Old Order, 1919–1933* (Boston: Houghton Mifflin Company, 1957), 396.

29. Tugwell, *The Brains Trust*, 493.

30. Lewis Gould, *The Modern Presidency* (Lawrence: University Press of Kansas, 2003), 33.

CHAPTER 13: NOTHING TO FEAR

1. FDR, Inaugural Address, March 4, 1933, American Presidency Project, http://www .presidency.ucsb.edu/ws/?pid=14473. The standard published edition of Roosevelt's public papers remains Samuel I. Rosenman's thirteen-volume *The Public Papers and Addresses of Franklin D. Roosevelt* (New York: Random House, 1938–1950). For Roosevelt's presidential years, I have chosen to cite from three rich online depositories: the Franklin D. Roosevelt Presidential Library and Museum (http://www.fdrlibrary.marist.edu), the American Presidency Project at the University of California, Santa Barbara (http://www.presidency.ucsb .edu), and American President at the Miller Center, University of Virginia (millercenter.org). All three provide more comprehensive access to the printed word and in addition have audio of some of FDR's important addresses.

2. Joseph P. Lash, *Eleanor and Franklin: The Story of Their Relationship* (New York: W. W. Norton & Company, 1971), 360.

3. Rexford G. Tugwell, *The Democratic Roosevelt* (Garden City, NY: Doubleday & Company, 1957), 270–271.

4. The best account of this event is in Geoffrey Ward, *A First-Class Temperament: The Emergence of Franklin Roosevelt* (New York: Harper & Row, 1989), xi–xiii.

5. Jean Edward Smith, *FDR* (New York: Random House, 2007), 311.

6. *NYT,* March 9, 1935. Transcripts of this and other FDR press conferences can be found online at the Franklin D. Roosevelt Presidential Library and Museum (http://www.fdrlibrary .marist.edu), the American Presidency Project at the University of California, Santa Barbara (http://www.presidency.ucsb.edu), and American President at the Miller Center, University of Virginia (millercenter.org).

7. For this and subsequent White House conferences, see the White House Usher's Diary, "FDR Day by Day," Franklin D. Roosevelt Presidential Library and Museum, http://www .fdrlibrary.marist.edu/daybyday.

8. Adam Cohen, *Nothing to Fear: FDR's Inner Circle and the Hundred Days That Created Modern America* (New York: Penguin Press, 2009), 77–80; White House Usher's Diary, March 9, 1933, FDRL.

9. Frank B. Freidel, *Franklin D. Roosevelt: Launching the New Deal* [hereafter *FDR*, IV] (Boston: Little, Brown and Company, 1973), ch. 13.

10. For the political use of radio by Baldwin, see Philip Williamson, *Stanley Baldwin: Conservative Leadership and National Values* (Cambridge: Cambridge University Press, 1999), 83–85. There is no evidence that Roosevelt was aware of Baldwin's skill as a radio speaker. Baldwin himself knew of Roosevelt and met his mother at a Downing Street reception in mid-1928.

11. Text and audio are available online at the Franklin D. Roosevelt Presidential Library and Museum (http://www.fdrlibrary.marist.edu), the American Presidency Project at the University of California, Santa Barbara (http://www.presidency.ucsb.edu), and American President at the Miller Center, University of Virginia (millercenter.org).

12. *Public Papers of the Presidents, 1933,* no. 12 (March 10, 1933), online at www.ucsb.edu.

13. The following history of Roosevelt's first months in office draws heavily on the following classic works: Arthur M. Schlesinger Jr., *The Coming of the New Deal* (Boston: Houghton Mifflin Company, 1959); Kenneth S. Davis, *FDR: The New Deal Years, 1933–1937* (New York: Random House, 1986), and Frank B. Freidel, *FDR: Launching the New Deal* (Boston: Little, Brown and Company, 1973).

14. John A. Salmond, "Civilian Conservation Corps," in *Franklin D. Roosevelt: His Life and Times, an Encyclopedic View,* ed. Otis L. Graham and Meghan Robinson Wander (Boston: G. K. Hall & Company, 1985), 62–24; John A. Salmond, *The Civilian Conservation Corps* (Durham, NC: Duke University Press, 1967).

15. Eric F. Goldman, *Rendezvous with Destiny,* rev. ed. (New York: Alfred A. Knopf, 1956), 257.

16. Schlesinger, *Coming of the New Deal,* 268–269.

17. Robert E. Sherwood, *Roosevelt and Hopkins: An Intimate History,* rev. ed. (New York: Harper & Row, 1950), remains the best work on Hopkins, but for the early New Deal, see also Searle R. Charles, *Minister of Relief: Harry Hopkins and the Depression* (Syracuse, NY: Syracuse University Press, 1963). Henry W. Adams, *Harry Hopkins: A Biography* (New York: Putnam Company, 1977), is a sound narrative.

18. Michael J. McDonald, "Tennessee Valley Authority," in Graham and Wander, *Franklin D. Roosevelt,* 420–423, provides an excellent introduction. Among the many works on the TVA, these stand out: Phillip Selznick, *TVA and the Grass Roots* (New York: Harper, 1966); Thomas McCraw, *Morgan versus Lilienthal: A Feud Within the TVA* (Chicago: Loyola University Press, 1970); Thomas McCraw, *TVA and the Power Fight* (Philadelphia: Lippincott, 1971), and Erwin Hargrove and Paul K. Conkin, eds., *Fifty Years of Grass-Roots Bureaucracy* (Urbana: University of Illinois Press, 1984).

19. Richard S. Kirkendall, "Agriculture," in Graham and Wander, *Franklin D. Roosevelt*, 3–4.

20. Shelley Bookspan, "Mortgage Financing," in Graham and Wander, *Franklin D. Roosevelt*, 267–268.

21. William E. Leuchtenburg, "The New Deal and the Analogue of War," in *The FDR Years: On Roosevelt and His Legacy* (New York: Columbia University Press, 1995), 35–75.

22. Freidel, *FDR*, IV, 337.

23. FDR, "Fireside Chat 2: On Progress During the First Two Months," May 7, 1933, American President, http://millercenter.org/president/fdroosevelt/speeches/speech-3299 (audio available).

24. Linda J. Lear, "Public Works Administration," in Graham and Wander, *Franklin D. Roosevelt*, 336–338.

25. Press conference, March 8, 1933, http://www.presidency.ucsb.edu.

26. Text at http://www.presidency.ucsb.edu.

27. Herbert Feis, *1933: Characters in Crisis* (Boston: Little, Brown and Company, 1966), 189.

28. Charles Kindleberger, *The World in Depression, 1929–1939* (Berkeley: University of California Press, 1973), 222–223.

29. Davis, *FDR*, III, 160–162; Freidel, *FDR*, IV, ch. 28; Patricia Clavin, *The Great Depression in Europe, 1929–1939* (New York: St. Martin's Press, 2000), 157–166.

30. *NYT*, July 4, 1933.

31. Keynes article in Donald Moggridge, ed., *The Collected Writings of John Maynard Keynes* (Cambridge: Cambridge University Press, 1971), 21:273–277.

CHAPTER 14: UNLIMITED AMBITIONS, LIMITED ACHIEVEMENT

1. On naval construction, see *NYT*, August 14, 1933, April 26, 1934, and *WP*, December 30, 1933 (F. Britten); for railroad loans, see *NYT*, January 2, 5, 11, February 27, 1934.

2. *NYT*, July 18, 1934 (Arthur Krock).

3. T. H. Watkins, *Righteous Pilgrim: The Life and Times of Harold L. Ickes, 1874–1952* (New York: Henry Holt, 1990), is the standard biography of its subject. See also Harold L. Ickes, *The Secret Diary of Harold L. Ickes*, 3 vols. (New York: Simon & Schuster, 1953–1954).

4. Harold L. Ickes, *The Secret Diary of Harold L. Ickes*, Vol. 1: *The First Thousand Days, 1933–1936* (New York: Simon & Schuster, 1953), 129–130, 152, 154, 162, 207, 218, 227; FDR, "Address at Arthurdale, West Virginia," May 27, 1938, American Presidency Project, http://www.presidency.ucsb.edu/ws/?pid=15647.

5. Arthur M. Schlesinger Jr., *The Coming of the New Deal* (Boston: Houghton Mifflin Company, 1959), 372.

6. Aubrey Williams, "The Gigantic Relief Task," *NYT Magazine*, August 26, 1934, 3.

7. *NYT*, August 6, 1934.

8. John C. Culver and John Hyde, *American Dreamer: The Life and Times of Henry A. Wallace* (New York: W. W. Norton & Company, 2000), 136.

9. Schlesinger, *Coming of the New Deal*, 34; "Unofficial Observer" [John Franklin Carter], *The New Dealers* (New York: Simon & Schuster, 1934), 91–92; *WP*, June 12, 1934; "The Cabinet: Tugwell Upped," *Time*, June 25, 1934, http://www.time.com.

10. *WP*, April 27, 1934 (Raymond Clapper).

11. *WP*, June 12, 1934.

12. Max Freedman, ed., *Roosevelt and Frankfurter: Their Correspondence, 1928–1945* (Boston: Little, Brown and Company, 1967), 7.

13. Culver and Hyde, *American Dreamer*, 126.

14. "Unofficial Observer," *The New Dealers*, 145–148; *NYT*, December 7, 10 (Arthur Krock), 12, 1933.

15. Frances Perkins, *The Roosevelt I Knew* (New York: Viking Press, 1946), 200–201.

16. Perkins, *The Roosevelt I Knew*, 206; "Unofficial Observer," *The New Dealers*, 57.

17. Harold Ickes, "Ickes Hails National Planning," *NYT Magazine*, October 14, 1934, 1–2, 17.

18. "Unofficial Observer," *The New Dealers*, 36.

19. *NYT*, September 13, 14, 1933.

20. *NYT*, August 27, 28, 30, September 6, 1933, January 11, 1934.

21. Alonzo L. Hamby, *For the Survival of Democracy: Franklin Roosevelt and the World Crisis of the 1930s* (New York: Free Press, 2004), 170–171.

22. *NYT*, February 28, 1934.

23. Schlesinger, *Coming of the New Deal*, 133–135.

24. Ellis W. Hawley, *The New Deal and the Problem of Monopoly* (Princeton, NJ: Princeton University Press, 1966), chs. 5–6.

25. Richard Vedder and Lowell Gallaway, *Out of Work: Unemployment and Government in Twentieth-Century America* (New York: Holmes and Meier, 1993), 77.

26. Perkins, *The Roosevelt I Knew*, 240–247; George Martin, *Madam Secretary: Frances Perkins* (Boston: Houghton Mifflin Company, 1976), 331–338; "Recovery: Man of the Year 1933," *Time*, January 1, 1933, www.time.com; Schlesinger, *Coming of the New Deal*, 156. I have arrived at the date for the August 20 meeting by consulting the Day by Day White House appointment calendars online at http://www.fdrlibrary.marist.edu/daybyday. For subsequent developments, see *NYT*, September 10, 11, 1934, and Kenneth S. Davis, *FDR: The New Deal Years, 1933–1937* (New York: Random House, 1986), 412–413.

CHAPTER 15: PRESIDENTIAL GOVERNMENT

1. Dean Acheson, *Morning and Noon* (Boston: Houghton Mifflin Company, 1965), is the main source's for its author's early life. For the paragraph above, see chs. 1–8.

2. Harold L. Ickes, *The Secret Diary of Harold L. Ickes*, Vol. 1: *The First Thousand Days, 1933–1936* [hereafter *Secret Diary*, I] (New York: Simon & Schuster, 1953), 106–107; John Morton Blum, *From the Morgenthau Diaries: Years of Crisis, 1928–1938* [hereafter *Morgenthau Diaries*, I] (Boston: Houghton Mifflin Company, 1959), 57–77, quote at 68.

3. FDR, "Fireside Chat 4: On Economic Progress," October 22, 1933, American President, http://millercenter.org/president/fdroosevelt/speeches/speech-3301.

4. Blum, *Morgenthau Diaries*, I, 70.

5. Acheson, *Morning and Noon*, 193.

6. Max Freedman, ed., *Roosevelt and Frankfurter: Their Correspondence, 1928–1945* (Boston: Little, Brown and Company, 1967), 184; Acheson to Harry S. Truman, August 21, 1956, in *Affection and Trust: The Personal Correspondence of Harry S. Truman and Dean Acheson, 1953–1971*, ed. Raymond H. Geselbracht and David Acheson (New York: Alfred A. Knopf, 2010), 149–150.

7. Acheson, *Morning and Noon*, 165.

8. Acheson, *Morning and Noon*, 211–227.

9. John Maynard Keynes, Open letter to FDR, *NYT*, December 31, 1934; Rexford G. Tugwell, *The Democratic Roosevelt* (Garden City, NY: Doubleday & Company, 1957), 325.

10. William E. Leuchtenburg, *Franklin D. Roosevelt and the New Deal, 1932–1940* (New York: Harper & Row, 1963), 82–84; Arthur M. Schlesinger Jr., *The Coming of the New Deal* (Boston: Houghton Mifflin Company, 1959), 248–252.

11. Charles Kindleberger, *The World in Depression, 1929–1939* (Berkeley: University of California Press, 1973), 236–238; Tugwell, *The Democratic Roosevelt*, 325; "Reciprocal Trade Agreements," in *Franklin D. Roosevelt: His Life and Times, an Encyclopedic View*, ed. Otis L. Graham and Meghan Robinson Wander (Boston: G. K. Hall, 1985), 347–348.

12. William E. Leuchtenburg, *The Supreme Court Reborn: The Constitutional Revolution in the Age of Roosevelt* (New York: Oxford University Press, 1995), ch. 3.

13. Martha Gellhorn to Harry Hopkins, November 11, 1934, Harry Hopkins Papers, FDRL, online at http://newdeal.feri.org/texts/154.htm.

14. *WP*, April 14, 1935; Lyle W. Dorsett, *The Pendergast Machine* (New York: Oxford University Press, 1968); Lyle W. Dorsett, *Franklin D. Roosevelt and the City Bosses* (Port Washington, NY: Kennikat Press, 1977).

15. Ickes, *Secret Diary*, I, 108–109.

16. John C. Culver and John Hyde, *American Dreamer: The Life and Times of Henry A. Wallace* (New York: W. W. Norton & Company, 2000), 153.

17. FDR, Annual Message to Congress, January 3, 1934, American Presidency Project, http://www.presidency.ucsb.edu.

18. Blum, *Morgenthau Diaries*, I, 323–337.

19. Jackson, a talented attorney, would later succeed Cummings as attorney general, then serve thirteen years on the US Supreme Court. He was a devoted follower of Roosevelt and a formidable advocate.

20. *NYT*, March 12, 1934.

21. *NYT*, February 18, March 21, May 25, 1934.

22. Herbert Hoover, *The Challenge to Liberty* (New York: Charles Scribner's Sons, 1934). See the perceptive review by Arthur Krock in *NYT Book Review*, September 30, 1934, 1.

23. *NYT*, August 25, 26, 1934.

24. FDR, "Fireside Chat 6: On Government and Capitalism," September 30, 1934, American President, http://millercenter.org/president/speeches/speech-3303.

25. Anne O'Hare McCormick, "This America: A Re-discovery," *NYT Magazine*, September 9, 1934, 1–2.

26. *NYT*, November 7, 1934.

27. *NYT*, August 24, 1934.

28. *NYT*, November 11, 1934.

CHAPTER 16: TOWARD "A NEW ORDER OF THINGS"

1. A classic contemporary assessment of the Townsend movement and other fringe challenges to the New Deal is "Unofficial Observer" [John Franklin Carter], *American Messiahs* (New York: Simon & Schuster, 1935), serialized in *WP*, May 19–June 10, 1935.

2. *American Messiahs*, *WP*, May 26, 1935.

3. This and the following paragraphs rest heavily on John Franklin Carter's perceptive sketch in *American Messiahs*, *WP*, May 21, 22, 1935.

4. *NYT*, February 5, 19, 1934.

5. *NYT*, April 29, October 28, November 12, 26, 1934.

6. *NYT*, March 4, 1935.

7. *NYT*, March 4, 5, 6 (Arthur Krock), 12, 1935; Press Conference 237, September 11, 1935, *Complete Presidential Press Conferences of Franklin D. Roosevelt*, intro. Jonathan Daniels (New York: Da Capo Press, 1972), 6:150, 157.

8. See, e.g., Walter Lippmann column in the *Los Angeles Times* [hereafter LAT], February 6, 1935.

9. T. Harry Williams, *Huey Long: A Biography* (New York: Alfred A. Knopf, 1970), remains the classic biography of Long. See also T. Harry Williams, *Romance and Realism in Southern Politics* (Athens: University of Georgia Press, 1961).

10. For the patent medicine story, see *Dreamers and Dissenters* (Hearst Documentary Film, no longer in circulation; copy in possession of the author); for Long's belief in his plan, see Williams, *Huey Long*, 695–696.

11. Harold L. Ickes, *The Secret Diary of Harold L. Ickes*, Vol. 1: *The First Thousand Days, 1933–1936* (New York: Simon & Schuster, 1953), 462. Years later, James Farley, *Behind the Ballots: The Personal History of a Politician* (New York: Harcourt Brace and Company, 1938), 249–250, recalled his estimate as 3 million votes.

12. *NYT*, January 5, 1935; text of the speech at American Presidency Project, http://www.presidency.ucsb.edu.

13. Lippmann column, *LAT*, January 6, 1935.

14. FDR to Frankfurter, June 11, 1934, *in Roosevelt and Frankfurter: Their Correspondence, 1928–1945*, ed. Max Freedman (Boston: Little, Brown and Company, 1967), 222. On Brandeis's relationship with FDR and the New Deal, see also Melvin I. Urofsky, *Louis D. Brandeis: A Life* (New York: Pantheon Books, 2009), ch. 28.

15. Press Conference 181, February 6, 1935, *Complete Press Conferences*, 5:98; John C. Culver and John Hyde, *American Dreamer: The Life and Times of Henry A. Wallace* (New York: W. W. Norton & Company, 2000), 155–157; Bernard Sternsher, *Rexford Tugwell and the New Deal* (New Brunswick, NJ: Rutgers University Press, 1964), 203–207.

16. Raymond Clapper column, *WP*, April 19, 1935.

17. Arthur Krock column, *NYT*, June 5, 1934; FDR to Frankfurter, June 11, 1934, in Freedman, *Roosevelt and Frankfurter*, 222; Arthur M. Schlesinger Jr., *The Politics of Upheaval* (Boston: Houghton Mifflin Company, 1960), 405–406; Frances Perkins, *The Roosevelt I Knew* (New York: Viking Press, 1946), 226.

18. *NYT*, June 6, 10, 1934.

19. FDR, "Fireside Chat 7: On the Works Relief Program and Social Security Act," April 28, 1935, American President, http://millercenter.org/president/speeches/speech-3304 (audio available).

20. The gold-clause cases are ably summarized in Schlesinger, *Politics of Upheaval*, 255–260.

21. *NYT*, May 7, 1935.

22. This paragraph and the following description of the argument are based on the news account in *WP*, May 4, 1935. See also Amity Shlaes, *The Forgotten Man* (New York: Harper Collins, 2007), 239–245.

23. *NYT*, May 28, 1935.

24. Bruce Allen Murphy, *The Brandeis-Frankfurter Connection* (New York: Oxford University Press, 1982), 55–56; Schlesinger, *Politics of Upheaval*, 280.

25. Press Conference 209, May 31, 1935, *Complete Presidential Press Conferences of Franklin D. Roosevelt*, intro. Jonathan Daniels (New York: Da Capo Press, 1972), 5:309–337.

26. Press Conference 209, May 31, 1935, *Complete Press Conferences*, 5:309–337.

CHAPTER 17: RENDEZVOUS WITH DESTINY

1. Press Conference 211, June 7, 1935, *Complete Press Conferences*, 5:355.

2. "The Presidency: Home Stretch," *Time*, June 24, 1935, http://www.time.com.

3. "The Congress: Ex-precedent," *Time*, June 3, 1935, http://www.time.com.

4. For the message text, see *NYT*, June 20, 1935; Mark Leff, *The Limits of Symbolic Reform: The New Deal and Taxation, 1933–1939* (Cambridge: Cambridge University Press, 1984), chs. 1–2.

5. NYT, June 21–25, 1936; Leff, *Limits of Symbolic Reform*, ch. 3.

6. *WP*, July 6, 1935; *NYT*, July 6, 1935.

7. See, e.g., *NYT*, June 30 (Arthur Krock), July 10, 14 (Krock), 15, 18, 21, 28 (editorial), 1935); R. L. Duffus, "A Jaded, Harassed Congress Seeks Relief," *NYT Magazine*, August 18, 1935, 3–4; Press Conference, July 17, 1935, *Complete Press Conferences*, 6:32–33. For a classic scholarly account of the "second hundred days," see William E. Leuchtenburg, *Franklin D. Roosevelt and the New Deal, 1932–1940* (New York: Harper & Row, 1963), ch. 7.

8. *NYT*, August 11, 15 (FDR signing statement), 1935; Frances Perkins, "Social Security: The Foundation," *NYT Magazine*, August 18, 1935, 1–2, 15; Long quoted in *NYT*, July 9, 1935. See, more generally, Roy Lubove, *The Struggle for Social Security, 1900–1935* (Cambridge, MA: Harvard University Press, 1968); Daniel Rodgers, *Atlantic Crossings* (Cambridge, MA: Harvard University Press, 1998), esp. ch. 10.

9. See Allan H. Meltzer, *A History of the Federal Reserve*, Vol. 1: *1913–1951* (Chicago: University of Chicago Press, 2003), 463–486, for this and subsequent paragraphs. On Eccles specifically, see *NYT*, November 11, 12 (feature story and editorial), 25, 1934; Marriner S. Eccles, *Beckoning Frontiers* (New York: Alfred A. Knopf, 1951).

10. Arthur M. Schlesinger Jr., *The Politics of Upheaval* (Boston: Houghton Mifflin Company, 1960), 321.

11. *WP*, August 9, 1935.

12. Harry S. Truman, *Memoirs*, Vol. 1: *Year of Decisions* (Garden City, NY: Doubleday & Company, 1955), 150–151.

13. Leff, *Limits of Symbolic Reform*, 138–145.

14. Leff, *Limits of Symbolic Reform*, Table I, 12, 93.

15. The six "major" bills that had failed to clear Congress were the Walsh government contracts bill, requiring federal contractors to abide by the relevant provisions of NRA codes; a shipping subsidies bill; a commodities exchange regulation bill; the World Court protocols; an appropriation for various New Deal agencies; and a food and drug bill, tepidly backed by the administration. *NYT*, August 28, 1935. For Krock quote, see Krock column, *NYT*, August 25, 1935.

16. *NYT*, August 8 (Arthur Krock), 12, 17 (Krock), 28, 1935.

17. *NYT*, July 9 (Arthur Krock), August 2, 1935.

18. For the letters and accompanying story, see *NYT*, September 7, 1935.

19. Harold L. Ickes, *The Secret Diary of Harold L. Ickes*, Vol. 1: *The First Thousand Days, 1933–1936* [hereafter *Secret Diary*, I] (New York: Simon & Schuster, 1953), 423 (August 27, 1935); T. Harry Williams, *Huey Long: A Biography* (New York: Alfred A. Knopf, 1970), 843–847.

20. Williams, *Huey Long*, 862–876.

21. *NYT*, September 10, 11 (Arthur Krock), 1935.

22. Addresses can be accessed in the online version of FDR's Public Papers at the American Presidency Project, http://www.presidency.ucsb.edu.

23. *NYT*, January 4, 5, 1936, for text of the speech and commentary.

24. *NYT*, January 5, 1936.

25. Schlesinger, *Politics of Upheaval*, 472.

26. Schlesinger, *Politics of Upheaval*, 473.

27. For the American Institute for Public Opinion [Gallup] poll and follow-up stories, see *WP*, January 5, 6, 1936.

28. Ickes, *Secret Diary*, I, 524 (January 24, 1936).

29. Leff, *Limits of Symbolic Reform*, 169–185; Schlesinger, *Politics of Upheaval*, 505–509; John Morton Blum, *From the Morgenthau Diaries: Years of Crisis, 1928–1938* (Boston: Houghton Mifflin Company), 305–319.

30. For statistics on work relief, see Donald S. Howard, *The WPA and Federal Relief Policy* (New York: Russell Sage Foundation, 1943), esp. Appendix Table I, 854–855.

31. "The Fortune Quarterly Survey: III," *Fortune* (January 1936): 46–47, 141–157; Ickes, *Secret Diary*, I, 465 (November 9, 1935); Melvin G. Holli, *The Wizard of Washington: Emil Hurja, Franklin Roosevelt and the Birth of Public Opinion Polling* (New York: Palgrave, 2002), 68–75.

32. For the full text of the Republican platform, see *NYT*, June 12, 1936. On Landon generally, see Donald McCoy, *Landon of Kansas* (Lincoln: University of Nebraska Press, 1966).

33. The banner is pictured in Anne O'Hare McCormick, "Republican Party Is Captured by Main Street," *NYT Magazine*, June 14, 1936, 3–4.

34. *NYT*, June 22, 24, 25, 1936.

35. See *NYT*, June 28, 1936, for a description of the speech and its setting; see Schlesinger, *Politics of Upheaval*, 584, for FDR's reaction to his fall.

36. FDR, "Acceptance Speech for the Renomination for the Presidency, Philadelphia, Pa.," June 27, 1936, American President, http://millercenter.org/president/fdroosevelt/speeches /speech-3305 (audio available).

37. *NYT*, June 28, 1936.

38. Samuel I. Rosenman, *Working with Roosevelt* (New York: Harper & Brothers, 1952), 105.

39. *WP*, July 12, 1936; Ickes, *Secret Diary*, I, 640–641.

40. See Ickes, *Secret Diary*, I, 639, for FDR's opinion of Landon; *WP*, July 20, 22, 26, 27, August 1, 14, 15, 1936.

41. FDR, "Fireside Chat 8: On Farmers and Laborers," September 6, 1936, American President, http://millercenter.org/president/fdroosevelt/speeches/speech-3306 (audio available).

42. *WP*, October 18, 1936; see *NYT*, July 9, 10 (editorial), 17, 24, 25, 27, 28 (editorial), August 28, 30, September 4, 6, 11, 15, 21 (editorial), 26, October 17, 18, 28, 1936.

43. Howard, *The WPA*, 854; *WP*, September 11, 1936; *NYT*, October 18, 25, 1936.

44. See *WP*, September 12, 1936, for the progressive conference. For the coalition, see, e.g., Schlesinger, *Politics of Upheaval*, 591–597; Samuel Lubell, *The Future of American Politics*, 3rd rev. ed. (New York: Harper & Row, 1965).

45. Lippmann in *LAT*, October 21, 1936; *WP*, July 20 (editorial), September 12 (Franklyn Waltman), 1936; *St. Louis Post-Dispatch*, September 27, 1936; *The Economist* (October 3, 1936), as summarized in *NYT*, October 13, 1936.

46. Schlesinger, *Politics of Upheaval*, ch. 33.

47. See *WP*, November 1, 1936, for the final Gallup survey; Farley is quoted in *Time*, November 9, 1936, 14.

48. FDR, "Speech at Madison Square Garden," October 31, 1936, American President, http://millercenter.org/president/speeches/speech-3307.

49. *WP*, November 1, 1936.

CHAPTER 18: "PANIC AND LACK OF CONFIDENCE"

1. This and following accounts of the speech draw on the text available at FDR, "Annual Message to Congress," January 6, 1937, American Presidency Project, http://www.presidency.ucsb.edu/ws/?pid=15336.

2. The second inaugural (no audio) can be accessed at either FDR, "Inaugural Address," January 20, 1937, American Presidency Project, http://www.presidency.ucsb.edu/ws/?pid=15349, or FDR, "Second Inaugural Address," January 20, 1937, American President, http://millercenter.org/president/fdroosevelt/speeches/speech-3308.

3. News articles and opinion pieces in *NYT*, January 13, 14, 15, 17, 1937, summarize the reorganization plan and reaction to it. See also the editorial roundup in *WP*, January 17, 1937. An excellent scholarly analysis of the larger political implications of executive reorganization is Sidney M. Milkis, *The President and the Parties* (New York: Oxford University Press, 1993), pt. 1.

4. *WP*, January 5 (news article and column by Franklyn Waltman), 12, 1937.

5. *WP*, January 23, 1937; *LAT*, February 5, 1937 (Walter Lippmann).

6. *NYT*, February 6, 1937.

7. See *NYT*, February 6, 13, 1937, for Wilson veterans and Moley opposition; Lippmann's columns can be followed in LAT, e.g., February 5, 10, 12, 16, 17, 19, 24, 1937. Burt Solomon, *FDR v. The Constitution* (New York: Walker & Company, 2009), is a fine recent account of the controversy.

8. Solomon, *FDR v. The Constitution*, 23; *NYT*, March 2, 1937.

9. Solomon, *FDR v. The Constitution*, 103; *WP*, February 28, 1937 (Robert Albright).

10. *WP*, February 14, 1937.

11. *NYT*, March 5, 1937.

12. FDR, "Fireside Chat 9: On 'Court-Packing,'" March 9, 1937, American President, http://millercenter.org/president/fdroosevelt/speeches/speech-3309 (audio available).

13. *WP*, March 7, 28, 1937.

14. For the text of the Hughes letter, see *NYT*, March 23, 1937.

15. Roger K. Newman, *Hugo Black: A Biography* (New York: Pantheon Books, 1994), esp. chs. 6, 16–17.

16. *NYT*, September 18, 1937; FDR, "Fireside Chat 13: On Purging the Democratic Party," June 24, 1938, American President, http://millercenter.org/president/fdroosevelt/speeches/speech-3314.

17. Ellis W. Hawley, *The New Deal and the Problem of Monopoly* (Princeton, NJ: Princeton University Press, 1966), chs. 11, 14.

18. *NYT*, July 4, 1937.

19. For skepticism about unions in general and the sit-downs in particular, see the Gallup poll results in *WP*, January 19, August 12, September 7, November 14, 20, 1938. Irving Bernstein, *Turbulent Years* (Boston: Houghton Mifflin Company, 1969), ch. 10, provides, almost literally, a blow-by-blow account of steel worker organization. For mainstream reporting on the Memorial Day incident, see *NYT* and *WP*, both May 31, 1937.

20. *Complete Presidential Press Conferences of Franklin D. Roosevelt* [hereafter *Complete Press Conferences*], intro. Jonathan Daniels (New York: Da Capo Press, 1972), 9:280–283, 304–307 (both April 15, 1937).

21. Press Conference, June 29, 1937, *Complete Press Conferences*, 9:467.

22. *WP*, September 4, 1937.

23. Both the WPA employment numbers and AFL unemployment estimates that follow in this chapter are taken from Donald S. Howard, *The WPA and Federal Relief Policy* (New York: Russell Sage Foundation, 1943), Table 1, 845–857.

24. On the Truman-Wheeler investigation and its background, see Alonzo L. Hamby, "'Vultures at the Death of an Elephant': Harry S. Truman, the Great Train Robbery, and the Transportation Act of 1940," *Railroad History* 165 (autumn 1991): 6–36; for FDR's interest, see Harold L. Ickes, *The Secret Diary of Harold L. Ickes*, Vol. 2: *The Inside Struggle, 1936–1939* [hereafter *Secret Diary*, II] (New York: Simon & Schuster, 1954), 249–250 (November 13, 1937).

25. *NYT*, December 21, 1937 (steel industry); Howard, *The WPA*, 855 (unemployment).

26. *NYT*, December 18, 19, 22, 1937; James T. Patterson, *Congressional Conservatism and the New Deal* (Lexington: University Press of Kentucky, 1966), ch. 6; Ickes, *Secret Diary*, II, 260 (December 6, 1937), 339–340 (March 17, 1938).

27. On Keynes's wider public and private life, I have generally followed Robert Skidelsky's *John Maynard Keynes: The Economist as Savior* (New York: Viking Press, 1993) and *John Maynard Keynes: Fighting for Freedom, 1937–1946* (New York: Viking Press, 2001).

28. Keynes to W. W. Stewart, November 14, 1937, and Keynes to the editor, *Times* (London), January 1, 1938, both in *The Collected Writings of John Maynard Keynes*, ed. Donald Moggridge (Cambridge: Cambridge University Press, 1982), 21:426–434.

29. Keynes to Leonard Elmhirst, October 20, 1937, Elmhirst Papers, Dartington Hall, Totnes, Devon, United Kingdom (administered by Devon Record Office, Exeter); Leonard Elmhirst to ER, December 11, 1937, ER Papers, cited in Joseph P. Lash, *Eleanor and Franklin: The Story of Their Relationship* (New York: W. W. Norton & Company, 1971), 468–469.

30. NYT, December 28, 31, 1937; Ickes, *Secret Diary*, II, 282–285 (January 1, 1938); *WP*, December 30 (Franklyn Waltman).

31. Keynes to FDR, February 1, 1938, FDR Papers, PPF 5235, FDRL.

32. Ickes, *Secret Diary*, II, 229 (October 14, 1937), 317 (February 13, 1938).

33. FDR to Keynes, March 5, 1938, FDR Papers, PPF 5235, FDRL; Keynes to FDR, March 25, 1938, in Moggridge, *Collected Writings*, 21:440.

34. FDR, "Fireside Chat 12: On the Recession," April 14, 1938, American President, http://millercenter.org/president/fdroosevelt/speeches/speech-3313 (audio available); for the WPA, see *NYT*, December 19, 1937 (Delbert Clark).

35. On public attitudes toward spending, see Gallup polls published in *WP*, April 1, 17, May 6, June 17, November 20, 25, 1938.

36. FDR, "Annual Message to Congress," January 3, 1938, reproduced in *NYT*, January 5, 1938, and available at American Presidency Project, http://www.presidency.ucsb.edu/ws/?pid=15517.

37. Hawley, *The New Deal and the Problem of Monopoly*, chs. 22–23.

38. NYT, December 16, 1937.

39. Ira Katznelson, *Fear Itself: The New Deal and the Origins of Our Time* (New York: Liveright, 2013), esp. pt. 2, perceptively explores the ambivalence of Southern Democrats toward the New Deal.

40. *NYT*, March 31, 1938.

41. FDR, "Fireside Chat 13: On Purging the Democratic Party," June 24, 1938, American President, http://millercenter.org/president/fdroosevelt/speeches/speech-3314.

42. Patterson, *Congressional Conservatism and the New Deal*, ch. 8.

43. See, e.g., stories in *WP*, June 19 (George Gallup), September 9, 10, November 4, 1938.

44. *NYT*, August 12, 13, 30, 1938.

45. *NYT*, August 17, 1938.

46. FDR, "Radio Address on the Election of Liberals," November 4, 1938, in Public Papers, American Presidency Project, http://www.presidency.ucsb.edu/mediaplay.php?id=15568& admin=32. For Landon speech, see *WP*, November 1, 1938.

47. *WP*, November 10, 1938 (Robert Albright).

48. Lippmann's evolving attitude toward FDR and the New Deal is neatly summarized in Ronald Steel, *Walter Lippmann and the American Century* (Boston: Little, Brown and Company, 1980), 319–326; *WP*, April 22, 1937. A version of Lippmann's talk was printed as his regular column, *LAT*, April 24, 1937.

49. See the Gallup polls in *WP*, January 5, February 13, March 27, April 3, May 1, June 10, July 22, August 3, 7, 14, November 4, 16, 27, December 4, 14, 1938.

CHAPTER 19: WINDS OF WAR

1. John Maynard Keynes to FDR, March 25, 1938, in *The Collected Writings of John Maynard Keynes*, ed. Donald Moggridge (Cambridge: Cambridge University Press, 1982), 21:440.

2. See, e.g., Walter Millis, *The Road to War* (Boston and New York: Houghton Mifflin Company, 1935).

3. FDR to Mussolini, May 14, 1933, in *Franklin D. Roosevelt and Foreign Affairs*, ed. Edgar B. Nixon (Cambridge, MA: Belknap Press of Harvard University Press, 1969), 1:123–124. FDR to Breckenridge Long, June 16, 1933; FDR to Mussolini, July 29, 1937, and accompanying commentary; Mussolini to FDR, November 14, 1936—all in *F.D.R.: His Personal Letters, 1928–1945*, ed. Elliott Roosevelt (New York: Duell, Sloan and Pearce, 1950), 1:352–353, 628, 699–701. See also Mussolini's handwritten letter to FDR, n.d. [probably May 1933], in the Grace Tully Archive—Franklin D. Roosevelt Papers, FDRL.

4. William L. Neumann, "Franklin D. Roosevelt and Japan, 1913–1933," *Pacific Historical Review* 22, no. 2 (1953): 143–153. Roosevelt's article, "Shall We Trust Japan?," was published in *Asia* magazine (March 1923).

5. Herbert P. Bix, *Hirohito and the Making of Modern Japan* (New York: Harper Collins, 2000), esp. chs. 7–9.

6. Cordell Hull to FDR, May 27, 1933, with Joseph Grew to Cordell Hull, May 11, 1933, in Nixon, *Franklin D. Roosevelt and Foreign Affairs*, 1:177–180.

7. FDR to Breckinridge Long, March 9, 1935, and William Bullitt to FDR, May 1, 1935, in Nixon, *Franklin D. Roosevelt and Foreign Affairs*, 2:437–438, 493–495.

8. FDR, "Address at Chautauqua, N.Y.," August 14, 1936, American Presidency Project, http://www.presidency.ucsb.edu/ws/?pid=15097.

9. Louis Adamic, *Dinner at the White House* (New York: Harper & Brothers, 1946), 49.

10. For contemporary discussion of the naval programs, see, e.g., *WP*, January 29, 1938, and *NYT*, January 30, 1938 (H. Baldwin). See *Conway's All the World's Fighting Ships, 1922–1946* (Annapolis, MD: Naval Institute Press, c. 1984), 86–117; "Ship Building, 1933–1945—Roosevelt, Franklin D.," GlobalSecurity.org, http://www.globalsecurity.org/military/systems /ship/scn-1933-roosevelt.htm.

11. George F. Kennan, *Memoirs, 1925–1950* (Boston: Little, Brown and Company, 1967), ch. 3; John Lewis Gaddis, *George F. Kennan: An American Life* (New York: Penguin Press, 2011), chs. 4–5.

12. Charles E. Bohlen, *Witness to History, 1929–1969* (New York: W. W. Norton & Company, 1973), 42–43; see *WP*, June 16, 1937, for Kelly's new assignment.

13. Katherine Sibley, *Red Spies in America: Stolen Secrets and the Dawn of the Cold War* (Lawrence: University Press of Kansas, 2004), ch. 1, esp. 40–42. For information on the planned Soviet battleships, which were never completed, see *Conway's All the World's Fighting Ships*, 325.

14. FDR to William E. Dodd, December 2, 1935, in Nixon, *Franklin D. Roosevelt and Foreign Affairs*, 3:102–103.

15. FDR, "Address at Chicago," October 5, 1937, American Presidency Project, http://www.presidency.ucsb.edu/ws/?pid=15476.

16. For a survey of the press commentary, see *NYT*, October 6, 1937; *Complete Presidential Press Conferences of Franklin D. Roosevelt*, intro. Jonathan Daniels (New York: Da Capo Press, 1972), 10:232, 246–250.

17. *NYT*, January 8 (Anne O'Hare McCormick), September 14 (Gerald Nye), 1938.

18. For FDR's Republican backing, see *NYT*, December 20 (Harold Hinton), 22, 1937.

19. *NYT*, January 11, 1938 (news story and detailed roll call; Arthur Krock column).

20. Iris Chang, *The Rape of Nanking: The Forgotten Holocaust of World War II* (New York: Basic Books, 1997), may exaggerate the killing, but contemporary news reports amply document weeks of indiscriminate slaughter.

21. *Guardian* quoted in *WP*, January 6, 1938 (B. Nover); for James, see *NYT*, January 2, 1938.

22. *NYT*, March 14, 1938 (Edwin James); *LAT*, March 16, 1938 (Walter Lippmann); *WP*, March 13, 1938.

23. Robert N. Rosen, *Saving the Jews: Franklin D. Roosevelt and the Holocaust* (New York: Thunder's Mouth Press, 2006), 58–67.

24. For the Gallup polls, see *WP*, April 6, July 27, September 22, October 2, 1938.

25. For the text of the speech, see *LAT*, August 19, 1938. For the commentary, see *LAT*, August 19, 1938; *WP*, August 19, 20 (Barnet Nover), 1938; *NYT*, August 19, 20 (esp. Anne O'Hare McCormick), 1938.

26. FDR, "Letter to Adolf Hitler Seeking Peace," September 27, 1938, American Presidency Project, http://www.presidency.ucsb.edu/ws/?pid=15544; David Faber, *Munich: The 1938 Appeasement Crisis* (London: Simon & Schuster, 2008), provides accessible coverage of the crisis and its impact. *NYT*, September 25, 1938 (E. Lengyel).

27. For the Gallup poll columns, see *WP*, October 12, 14, 16, November 4, December 28, 1938; Anne O'Hare McCormick, "As Roosevelt Sees His Foreign Policy," *NYT Magazine*, November 13, 1938, 1–2, 20; Harold L. Ickes, *The Secret Diary of Harold L. Ickes*, Vol. 2: *The Inside Struggle, 1936–1939* (New York: Simon & Schuster, 1954), 483–484 (October 9, 1938).

28. See, e.g., *NYT*, November 11, 13, 14, 15, 20 (H. Callender), 1938, and *WP*, November 15 (J. Driscoll; B. Nover), 20 (J. Driscoll), 1938.

29. *NYT*, November 16, 1938; *WP*, November 13, 1938.

30. *NYT*, November 15, 1938; Kenneth S. Davis, *FDR: Into the Storm, 1937–1940* (New York: Random House, 1993), 368–369; Doris Kearns Goodwin, *The Fitzgeralds and the Kennedys: An American Saga* (New York: Simon & Schuster, 1987), 568–571.

31. William L. Langer and S. Everett Gleason, *The Challenge to Isolation: The World Crisis of 1937–1940 and American Foreign Policy* (New York: Harper & Brothers, 1952), 48–49.

32. *Complete Press Conferences*, 13:115.

33. *NYT*, December 31, 1938.

34. Ian Kershaw, *Hitler, 1936–1945: Nemesis* (New York: W. W. Norton & Company, 2000), 189. Newsreel footage of this speech is accessible in numerous film documentaries.

35. Richard Breitman and Allan J. Lichtman, *FDR and the Jews* (Cambridge, MA: Harvard University Press, 2013), 134–139.

36. *WP*, November 22 (W. Lippmann), December 4 (G. Gallup), 1938; *NYT*, December 14, 1938 (N. Chamberlain speech).

37. James MacGregor Burns, *Roosevelt: The Lion and the Fox* (New York: Harcourt Brace and Company, 1956), 393; Conrad Black, *Franklin Delano Roosevelt: Champion of Freedom* (New York: PublicAffairs, 2003), 524; *NYT*, June 9, 11, 1939; *WP*, June 12, 1939; *LAT*, June 10, 1939.

38. Joseph P. Lash, *Eleanor and Franklin: The Story of Their Relationship* (New York: W. W. Norton & Company, 1971), 581.

39. Robert Dallek, *Franklin D. Roosevelt and American Foreign Policy, 1932–1945*, 2nd ed. (New York: Oxford University Press, 1995), 187–192.

40. *NYT*, August 23, 1939.

41. Burns, *Roosevelt: The Lion and the Fox*, 394.

CHAPTER 20: PRIVATE PLANS AND PUBLIC DANGER

1. FDR, "Fireside Chat," September 3, 1939, American Presidency Project, http://www
.presidency.ucsb.edu/ws/index.php?pid=15801 (audio available).

2. Kenneth S. Davis, *FDR: Into the Storm, 1937–1940* (New York: Random House, 1993), 190–193, 492; FDR to Winston Churchill [hereafter WC], September 11, 1939, in *Churchill and Roosevelt: The Complete Correspondence*, Vol. 1: *Alliance Emerging, October 1933–November 1942* [hereafter *Churchill and Roosevelt*, I], ed. Warren F. Kimball (Princeton, NJ: Princeton University Press, 1984), 26–27.

3. Jon Meacham, *Franklin and Winston: An Intimate Portrait of an Epic Friendship* (New York: Random House, 2003), ch. 2.

4. *NYT*, October 3, 4, 5, 1939; *Complete Presidential Press Conferences of Franklin D. Roosevelt*, intro. Jonathan Daniels (New York: Da Capo Press, 1972), 14:207–210.

5. Joseph P. Lash, *Eleanor and Franklin: The Story of Their Relationship* (New York: W. W. Norton & Company, 1971), 604–605.

6. FDR, "Message to Congress Urging Repeal of the Embargo Provisions of the Neutrality Law," September 21, 1939, American Presidency Project, http://www.presidency.ucsb.edu
/mediaplay.php?id=15813&admin=32.

7. For Gallup surveys, see *WP*, September 3, 17, 22, 24, 29, October 4, 1939, and *NYT*, October 15, 1939.

8. *NYT*, October 15, 16, 21, 23, 28, 30, November 3, 4, 5, 1939; on Lindbergh, see Lynne Olson, *Those Angry Days: Roosevelt, Lindbergh, and America's Fight over World War II, 1939–1941* (New York: Random House, 2013).

9. WC to FDR, May 15, 1940, in Kimball, *Churchill and Roosevelt*, I, 37–38.

10. FDR to WC, May 16, 1940, in Kimball, *Churchill and Roosevelt*, I, 38–39; for Gallup polls, see *WP*, May, 19, 24, June 30, 1940.

11. FDR, "Message to Congress on Appropriations for National Defense," May 16, 1940, American Presidency Project, http://www.presidency.ucsb.edu/ws/?pid=15954.

12. FDR, "Fireside Chat," May 26, 1940, American Presidency Project, http://www
.presidency.ucsb.edu/ws/?pid=15959; *NYT*, June 1, 1940.

13. FDR, "Address at University of Virginia," June 10, 1940, American Presidency Project, http://www.presidency.ucsb.edu/ws/?pid=15965.

14. For the text of the May 31 request, see *WP*, June 1, 1940; for the navy request, see *NYT*, June 19, 1940. Naval construction data is from James C. Fahey's *The Ships and Aircraft of the United States Fleet*, Two-Ocean Fleet ed. (New York: Ships and Aircraft, 1941), and *The Ships and Aircraft of the United States Fleet*, Victory ed. (New York: Ships and Aircraft, 1945), both reprinted by the Naval Institute Press in 1976.

15. *NYT*, July 14, 1940 (Hanson Baldwin).

16. *NYT*, May 29, 1940.

17. Donald McCoy, *Landon of Kansas* (Lincoln: University of Nebraska Press, 1966), 430–438; Elting E. Morison, *Turmoil and Tradition: A Study of the Life and Times of Henry L. Stimson* (Boston: Houghton Mifflin Company, 1960), 478–482; Ickes, *Secret Diary*, II, 8, 12, 15–17, 23–24, 180–181; Max Freedman, ed., *Roosevelt and Frankfurter: Their Correspondence, 1928–1945* (Boston: Little, Brown and Company, 1967), 524–530.

18. Jean Edward Smith, *FDR* (New York: Random House, 2007), 450.

19. *WP*, June 16, 1940 (Robert Albright).

20. *NYT*, August 16 (news article; Arthur Krock), 18 (letter from "A Citizen"), 1939; Wendell Willkie, "We the People," *Fortune* (April 1940) (reprinted in *Time*, October 16, 1944, http://www.time.com).

21. The Republican convention is best followed through *NYT* or other leading newspapers, June 24–29, 1940. For White, see *LAT*, June 25, 1940.

22. For the text of Willkie address, see *NYT*, June 29, 1940.

23. Harold L. Ickes, *The Secret Diary of Harold L. Ickes*, Vol. 3: *The Lowering Clouds, 1939–1941* [hereafter *Secret Diary*, III] (New York: Simon & Schuster, 1954), 144, 150–153, 155–157, 167–172.

24. The Democratic convention can be followed in detail through the major newspapers; Ickes, *Secret Diary*, III, 239–269, gives a vivid account from one person's perspective. Samuel I. Rosenman, *Working with Roosevelt* (New York: Harper & Brothers, 1952), ch. 13, is an authoritative view from the perspective of the White House. See Robert E. Sherwood, *Roosevelt and Hopkins: An Intimate History*, rev. ed. (New York: Grosset & Dunlap, 1950), 176–179.

25. For the Barkley statement and convention response, see *NYT*, July 18, 1940.

26. Sherwood, *Roosevelt and Hopkins*, 177.

27. Rosenman, *Working with Roosevelt*, 206; author's interview with Wallace, December 16, 1964.

28. Sherwood, *Roosevelt and Hopkins*, 179; Rosenman, *Working with Roosevelt*, 216–218; *NYT*, July 19, 1940.

29. For text of ER's speech, *NYT*, July 19, 1940.

30. *NYT*, July 19, 1940; *WP*, July 19, 1940.

31. FDR, "Nomination Acceptance Speech," July 19, 1940, American President, http://millercenter.org/president/fdroosevelt/speeches/speech-3318 (audio available).

32. Sherwood, *Roosevelt and Hopkins*, 179.

33. Edward Bliss Jr., ed., *In Search of Light: The Broadcasts of Edward R. Murrow, 1938–1961* (New York: Alfred A. Knopf, 1967), 46.

34. Kimball, *Churchill and Roosevelt*, I, 47–69; Robert Shogan, *Hard Bargain: How FDR Twisted Churchill's Arm, Evaded the Law, and Changed the Role of the American Presidency* (New York: Scribner, 1995), 154–156.

35. FDR, "Message to Congress on Exchanging Destroyers for British Naval and Air Bases," September 3, 1940, American Presidency Project, http://www.presidency.ucsb.edu/ws/?pid=16004; *NYT*, September 4, 1940.

36. *NYT*, September 4, 1940 (Hanson Baldwin; survey of press opinion); *WP*, September 4, 1940; Shogan, *Hard Bargain*, chs. 12–13.

37. *NYT*, September 4, 6, 1940; *WP*, September 4, 1940.

38. David Kaiser, *No End Save Victory: How FDR Led the Nation into War* (New York: Basic Books, 2014), 110–112.

39. See the Gallup polls in *WP*, August 11, 30, 1940, and news items in *WP*, August 11, 18, September 24, 1940. For Willkie's support, see *NYT*, August 29, September 22 (Arthur Krock), 1940.

40. See, e.g., news stories in *NYT*, August 29, 1940, and *WP*, August 2, 18, September 20, 21, 24, 27, 1940. For *NYT* endorsement, see *NYT*, September 19, 1940. On Willkie's campaigning, see *WP*, October 20, 1940 (Robert Albright). See Willkie's acceptance speech at Wendell Willkie, "Address Accepting the Presidential Nomination in Elwood, Indiana," August 17, 1940, American Presidency Project, http://www.presidency.ucsb.edu/ws/?pid=75629.

41. For the Gallup polls, see *WP*, August 4, 25, 1940.

42. *WP*, October 18, 23, 1940.

43. *LAT*, July 18, 1940.

44. *WP*, October 27, 1940; Melvyn Dubofsky and Warren Van Tine, *John L. Lewis: A Biography*, abr. ed. (Urbana: University of Illinois Press, 1986), 258–260.

45. *NYT*, September 12, 1940.

46. This and the following paragraphs draw on FDR's campaign addresses (October 23, 28, 30, November 1, 2, 1940), radio addresses (October 24, 29, November 4, 1940), and rear platform remarks (October 23, November 2, 1940), all at American Presidency Project, http://www.presidency.ucsb.edu.

47. *NYT*, October 29, 1940.

48. Joseph Kennedy, Diary, c. October 30, 1940, in Amanda Smith, *Hostage to Fortune: The Letters of Joseph P. Kennedy* (New York: Viking Press, 2001), 480–482.

49. Smith, *Hostage to Fortune*, 482–489.

50. Smith, *Hostage to Fortune*, 489.

51. FDR, "Campaign Address at Boston, Massachusetts," October 31, 1940, American Presidency Project, http://www.presidency.ucsb.edu/ws/?pid=15887; *WP*, October 31, 1940.

52. Rosenman, *Working with Roosevelt*, 242; *WP*, October 31, 1940.

53. *NYT*, November 6, 1940.

54. *NYT*, November 6, 1940.

55. Samuel Lubell, "Post-Mortem: Who Elected Roosevelt?," *Saturday Evening Post*, January 25, 1941, 9–11, 91–16; Samuel Lubell, *The Future of American Politics*, 3rd rev. ed. (New York: Harper & Row, 1965), 63–68.

CHAPTER 21: UNDECLARED WAR

1. William K. Klingaman, *1941: Our Lives in a World on the Edge* (New York: Harper & Row, 1988), 29.

2. WC to FDR, December 7, 1940, in *Churchill and Roosevelt: The Complete Correspondence* [hereafter *Churchill and Roosevelt*, I], ed. Warren F. Kimball (Princeton, NJ: Princeton University Press, 1984), 1:102–111.

3. Harold L. Ickes, *The Secret Diary of Harold L. Ickes*, Vol. 3: *The Lowering Clouds, 1939–1941* [hereafter *Secret Diary*, III] (New York: Simon & Schuster, 1954), 367.

4. *NYT*, December 18, 1940.

5. Transcript of Press Conference, December 17, 1940, *Complete Presidential Press Conferences of Franklin D. Roosevelt*, intro. Jonathan Daniels (New York: Da Capo Press, 1972), 16:350–365.

6. David Kaiser, *No End Save Victory: How FDR Led the Nation into War* (New York: Basic Books, 2014), ch. 6.

7. Samuel I. Rosenman, *Working with Roosevelt* (New York: Harper & Brothers, 1952), ch. 15, 280.

8. *NYT*, December 30, 1940.

9. FDR, "Fireside Chat," December 29, 1940, American Presidency Project, http://www .presidency.ucsb.edu/ws/?pid=15917 (audio available).

10. FDR, "State of the Union (Four Freedoms)," January 6, 1941, American President, http://millercenter.org/president/speeches/speech-3320 (audio available).

11. FDR, "Third Inaugural Address," January 20, 1941, American President, http://miller center.org/president/fdroosevelt/speeches/speech-3321 (audio available). For descriptions of the event, see *NYT* and *WP*, both January 21, 1941.

12. Compare, e.g., Gallup surveys in *WP*, February 3, 8, March 22, 1941, with those of October 1, 3, 5, 8, 25, 1941, which by and large display consistency of public opinion with an increasingly pro-British trend.

13. Robert E. Sherwood, *Roosevelt and Hopkins: An Intimate History*, rev. ed. (New York: Grosset & Dunlap, 1950), 247; Jon Meacham, *Franklin and Winston: An Intimate Portrait of an Epic Friendship* (New York: Random House, 2003), 94.

14. Meacham, *Franklin and Winston*, 95.

15. *NYT*, January 30, 1941.

16. "United States–British Staff Conversation: Report," ibiblio, http://www.ibiblio.org/pha /pha/pt_14/x15-049.html.

17. *WP*, January 15, 1941; transcript of Press Conference, January 14, 1941, *Complete Press Conferences*, 17:76–77.

18. Joseph P. Kennedy, Diary Notes, January 21, 1941, in *Hostage to Fortune: The Letters of Joseph P. Kennedy*, ed. Amanda Smith (New York: Viking Press, 2001), 524–529; for Kennedy's speech, see *NYT*, January 19, 1941; for congressional testimony, see *WP*, January 22, 1941.

19. Joseph P. Kennedy to John Boettiger, February 10, 1941, in Smith, *Hostage to Fortune*, 529.

20. FDR to John Boettiger, March 3, 1941, Roosevelt Family Papers Donated by the Children, Family Correspondence File, FDRL.

21. Press Conference, March 11, 1941, *Complete Press Conferences*, 17:181–187.

22. FDR, "On Lend Lease," March 15, 1941, American President, http://millercenter.org /president/fdroosevelt/speeches/speech-3322.

23. *NYT*, April 11, 1941.

24. WC to FDR, May 23, 1941, in Kimball, *Churchill and Roosevelt*, I, 192–195.

25. Rosenman, *Working with Roosevelt*, 283.

26. FDR to WC, May 27, 1941, in Kimball, *Churchill and Roosevelt*, I, 196–197. FDR, "Fireside Chat 17: On an Unlimited National Emergency," May 27, 1941, American President, http:// millercenter.org/president/fdroosevelt/speeches/speech-3814 (no audio available). For a photo of the event and the text of the proclamation of national emergency, see *LAT*, May 28, 1941; for the estimated audience size, see *NYT*, May 29, 1941 (Turner Catledge).

27. *WP*, May 28, 1941. For the summary of the editorial commentary, see *LAT*, May 28, 1941; for the Gallup poll, see *WP*, June 15, 1941.

28. *NYT*, May 28, 29, 1941; *LAT*, May 29, 1941; *WP*, May 28, 1941.

29. Press Conference, May 28, 1941, *Complete Press Conferences*, 17:363–370; *NYT*, May 29, 1941.

30. Arthur Herman, *Freedom's Forge* (New York: Random House, 2012), is a spirited account of World War II economic mobilization and Knudsen's travails in Washington; for the OPM, see 127–164.

31. *NYT*, June 7, 8, 10, 1941.

32. Joseph P. Lash, *Eleanor and Franklin: The Story of Their Relationship* (New York: W. W. Norton & Company, 1971), 528–535; Alan Brinkley, *The End of Reform: New Deal Liberalism in Recession and War* (New York: Alfred A. Knopf, 1995), 165–168.

33. The *Robin Moor* story is easily followed in the newspapers. For news and commentary, see, e.g., *NYT*, June 10, 11, 14, 16, 19, 21, 22, 1941; *WP*, June 13, 14, 16, 17, 21, 1941.

34. Joseph P. Lash, *Roosevelt and Churchill: The Partnership That Saved the West, 1939–1941* (New York: W. W. Norton & Company, 1980), 357.

35. Lash, *Roosevelt and Churchill*, 17.

36. Sherwood, *Roosevelt and Hopkins*, ch. 14, quote on 322.

37. Sherwood, *Roosevelt and Hopkins*, 343. Original documents about Hopkins's trip can be accessed online at http://docs.fdrlibrary.marist.edu/PSF/BOX3/folt32.html (directory listing).

38. The definitive account of the ensuing conference is Theodore A. Wilson, *The First Summit: Roosevelt and Churchill at Placentia Bay, 1941*, rev. ed. (Lawrence: University Press of Kansas, 1991).

39. Ickes, *Secret Diary*, III, May 12, 1940, quoted in Meacham, *Franklin and Winston*, 47. The quote, extant in the typescript of the Ickes Diary at the Library of Congress, was omitted from the published version. Geoffrey C. Ward, ed., *Closest Companion: The Unknown Story of the Intimate Friendship Between Franklin Roosevelt and Margaret Suckley* (Boston: Houghton Mifflin Company, 1995), 141.

40. Printed minutes, War Cabinet 84 (41), August 19, 1941, and Typed Secretary's File, August 19, 1941 (available online at "Documents Online," at www.nationalarchives.gov.uk).

41. Wilson, *The First Summit*, 230; *NYT*, August 13, 14 (editorial), 1941.

42. FDR, Last Will and Testament, FDR Papers, FDRL.

43. Geoffrey Ward, *Before the Trumpet: Young Franklin Roosevelt, 1882–1905* (New York: Harper & Row, 1985), describes the French press conference but misdates it as occurring in "the early spring" of 1940. For SDR's return to the United States, see *NYT*, September 1, 1939.

44. FDR, "Fireside Chat 18: On the Greer Incident," September 11, 1941, American President, http://millercenter.org/president/fdroosevelt/speeches/speech-3323.

45. For the *Reuben James*, see *WP*, October 5, 1991 (fifty-year commemorative article).

46. See *LAT*, November 1, 1941, for both Willkie and Aiken.

47. See the Gallup polls in *WP*, October 3, 5, 8, 10, 19, 24, November 22, 1941.

48. Ickes, *Secret Diary*, III, 655 (November 30, 1941). For the details of the modus vivendi, see Gordon Prange, Donald Goldstein, and Katherine V. Dillon, *Pearl Harbor: The Verdict of History* (New York: McGraw-Hill, 1986), 181–184, 653–655.

49. The Roosevelt quote is in Elting E. Morison, *Turmoil and Tradition: A Study of the Life and Times of Henry L. Stimson* (Boston: Houghton Mifflin Company, 1960), 525; Richard N. Current, "How Stimson Meant to 'Maneuver' the Japanese," *Mississippi Valley Historical Review* 40 (June 1953): 67–74.

50. See Prange, Goldstein, and Dillon, *Pearl Harbor*, 651–652 (messages to Hawaii), 657–659 (text of Hull note); for the message to the Philippines, see D. Clayton James, *The Years of MacArthur*, Vol. 1: *1880–1941* (Boston: Houghton Mifflin Company, 1970), 615.

51. FDR, Memorandum to the Secretary of State and the Under Secretary of State, December 1, 1941, FDR Papers, President's Secretary's File, http://www.fdrlibrary.marist.edu /archives/collections/franklin/?p=collections/findingaid&id=502; Waldo Heinrichs, *Threshold of War* (New York: Oxford University Press, 1998), 216–217.

52. See the Gallup poll in *WP*, November 14, 1941.

53. ER, *This I Remember* (New York: Harper & Row, 1949), 232–233; president's appointment calendar, December 7, 1941, at "FDR Day by Day," Franklin D. Roosevelt Presidential Library and Museum, http://www.fdrlibrary.marist.edu/daybyday.

CHAPTER 22: COMMANDER IN CHIEF OF THE UNITED NATIONS

1. ER, see *WP*, December 8, 1941, for text.

2. FDR, "Address to Congress Requesting a Declaration of War," December 8, 1941, American President, http://millercenter.org/president/speeches/speech-3324 (audio available).

3. *WP*, December 8, 1941.

4. FDR, "Fireside Chat," December 9, 1941, American President, http://www.presidency .ucsb.edu/ws/?pid=16056. Samuel I. Rosenman, *Working with Roosevelt* (New York: Harper & Brothers, 1952), 308–313.

5. Roberta Wohlstetter, *Pearl Harbor: Warning and Decision* (Stanford, CA: Stanford University Press, 1962), remains the classic interpretation of its subject, which is nicely summarized in David Kaiser, *No End Save Victory: How FDR Led the Nation into War* (New York: Basic Books, 2014), 326–332. For MacArthur and the Manila debacle, see D. Clayton James, *The Years of MacArthur*, Vol. 2: *1941–1945* (Boston: Houghton Mifflin, 1975), 3–15.

6. FDR, "Fireside Chat," February 23, 1942, American President, http://www.presidency .ucsb.edu/ws/index.php?pid=16224 (audio available).

7. Rudy Abramson, *Spanning the Century: The Life of W. Averell Harriman, 1891–1986* (New York: William Morrow and Company, 1992), esp. chs. 10–15; W. Averell Harriman and Elie Abel, *Special Envoy to Churchill and Stalin, 1941–1946* (New York: Random House, 1975), chs. 8–10.

8. George McKee Elsey, *An Unplanned Life* (Columbia: University of Missouri Press, 2005), 20–21.

9. Field Marshal Lord Alanbrooke, *War Diaries, 1939–1945*, ed. Ales Danchev and Daniel Todman (London: Weidenfeld & Nicholson, 2001), 209.

10. For the full text of all four papers, see Warren F. Kimball, ed., *Churchill and Roosevelt: The Complete Correspondence*, Vol. 1: *Alliance Emerging, October 1933–November 1942* [hereafter *Churchill and Roosevelt*, I] (Princeton, NJ: Princeton University Press, 1984), 294–308.

11. The military aspects of the ARCADIA conference are well summarized in Andrew Roberts, *Masters and Commanders: How Four Titans Won the War in the West, 1941–1945* (New York: HarperCollins, 2009), ch. 2.

12. A copy of the declaration can be found in about any major newspaper of the period for January 2, 1942, or at "Declaration by United Nations (Subscribing to the Principles of the Atlantic Charter, January 1, 1942)," ibiblio, http://www.ibiblio.org/pha/policy/1942.

13. Alonzo Fields, *My 24 Years in the White House* (New York: Coward-McCann, 1961), 81–91.

14. Martin Gilbert, *Winston Churchill: A Life* (New York: Henry Holt and Company, 1991), 714–715.

15. Louis Adamic, *Dinner at the White House* (New York: Harper & Brothers, 1946), 64, 68.

16. Gilbert, *Winston Churchill*, 715; FDR to WC, January 31, March 18, 1942, in Kimball, *Churchill and Roosevelt*, I, 336–337, 420–422.

17. FDR to WC, March 18, 1942, in Kimball, *Churchill and Roosevelt*, I, 420–422.

18. Richard E. Cole, in a television discussion, "A Conversation with Veterans of World War II," hosted by the author, WOUB-TV, November 9, 2000.

19. *NYT*, April 21, 1942.

20. Evans Carlson to FDR, April 29, 1942, and Eleanor Morehouse Herrick to ER, September 24, 1943, both in Roosevelt Papers (General Family Correspondence), FDRL.

21. Mary E. Glantz, *FDR and the Soviet Union: The President's Battles over Foreign Policy* (Lawrence: University Press of Kansas, 2005), chs. 4–5.

22. Glantz, *FDR and the Soviet Union*, 102; Hopkins, notes on FDR conversation with Cordell Hull and Anthony Eden, March 22, 1943, in Robert E. Sherwood, *Roosevelt and Hopkins: An Intimate History*, rev. ed. (New York: Grosset & Dunlap, 1950), 715.

23. Sherwood, *Roosevelt and Hopkins*, 561.

24. George C. Herring Jr., *Aid to Russia, 1941–1946: Strategy, Diplomacy, the Origins of the Cold War* (New York: Columbia University Press, 1973), esp. ch. 2; Sherwood, *Roosevelt and Hopkins*, 563; Rick Atkinson, *An Army at Dawn: The War in North Africa, 1942–1943* (New York: Henry Holt and Company, 2002), 13.

25. FDR to WC, in Kimball, *Churchill and Roosevelt*, I, 503; Sherwood, *Roosevelt and Hopkins*, 577.

26. Kimball, *Churchill and Roosevelt*, I, 508 (editorial note); Sherwood, *Roosevelt and Hopkins*, ch. 25; for Mountbatten's memorandum of the conversation, see 582–583.

27. Sherwood, *Roosevelt and Hopkins*, 589–590; Gilbert, *Winston Churchill*, 722.

28. Alanbrooke, *War Diaries*, 269.

29. Alanbrooke, *War Diaries*, 268–269; Gilbert, *Winston Churchill*, 723.

30. FDR, handwritten draft to Marshall with copies to King and Arnold (July 1942), John L. McCrea Papers, FDRL, online in the "Franklin D. Roosevelt Significant Documents" collection, http://www.fdrlibrary.marist.edu; Forrest C. Pogue, *George C. Marshall: Ordeal and Hope, 1939–1942* (New York: Viking Press, 1966), 340–341; Nigel Hamilton, *The Mantle of Command: FDR at War, 1941–1942* (Boston: Houghton Mifflin Harcourt, 2014), chs. 22–26.

31. Larry I. Bland, ed., *The Papers of George Catlett Marshall*, Vol. 3: *The "Right Man for the Job," December 7, 1941–May 31, 1943* (Baltimore: Johns Hopkins University Press, 1991), 269–278; FDR to Harry Hopkins, George Marshall, and Ernest King, July 16, 1942, in Sherwood, *Roosevelt and Hopkins*, 603–605. This is a revised version of a memorandum written a day earlier (available online at http://docs.fdrlibrary.marist.edu/psf/box3/a39e01.html).

32. Alanbrooke, *War Diaries*, 285 (July 24, 1942).

33. Sherwood, *Roosevelt and Hopkins*, 602–603.

34. Bland, *Papers of George Catlett Marshall*, 3:278; Pogue, *George C. Marshall*, 330.

35. Albert Einstein to FDR, August 2, 1939, FDR Papers (available online at http://www.fdrlibrary.marist.edu/_resources/images/sign/fdr_24.pdf).

36. Gilbert, *Winston Churchill*, 726–729; Harriman and Abel, *Special Envoy*, ch. 7.

37. Kimball, *Churchill and Roosevelt*, I, 421.

38. Kenneth S. Davis, *FDR: The War President, 1940–1943* (New York: Random House, 2000), 757.

39. Raymond Copson, "President Franklin D. Roosevelt Flew to Meet British Prime Minister Winston Churchill for a Summit in Casablanca," *American History* 37 (April 2002), http://www.historynet.com/franklin-d-roosevelt.

40. For FDR's trip diary, see Geoffrey Ward, ed., *Closest Companion: The Unknown Story of the Intimate Friendship Between Franklin Roosevelt and Margaret Suckley* (Boston: Houghton Mifflin Company, 1995), 196–200.

41. Roberts, *Masters and Commanders*, 333–334; see ch. 12 for a good survey of the Casablanca conference.

42. Roberts, *Masters and Commanders*, 310–311, 344.

43. Dwight D. Eisenhower, *Crusade in Europe* (Garden City, NY: Doubleday & Company, 1948), 136–137.

44. Mark Perry, *Partners in Command: George Marshall and Dwight D. Eisenhower in War and Peace* (New York: Penguin Press, 2007), 150; Atkinson, *An Army at Dawn*, 286, 329.

45. Butcher Diary manuscript, February 16, 1943, Dwight D. Eisenhower Papers—Pre-Presidential, Dwight D. Eisenhower Library, Abilene, Kansas. The author gratefully acknowledges Robert Davis's kindness in sharing this material, omitted from the published version of the Butcher Diary.

46. FDR to Stalin, December 2, 8, 1942; Stalin to FDR, December 6, 14, 1942, in *My Dear Mr. Stalin*, ed. Susan Butler (New Haven, CT: Yale University Press, 2005), 101–104.

47. Elliott Roosevelt, *As He Saw It* (New York: Duell, Sloan and Pearce, 1946), 75–76, 109–112. Harry Hopkins's account of the dinner, however, fails to mention any such exchange. Sherwood, *Roosevelt and Hopkins*, 689–690.

48. Roosevelt, *As He Saw It*, 76–77, 115–116.

49. See, e.g., James MacGregor Burns, *Roosevelt: The Soldier of Freedom* (New York: Harcourt Brace Jovanovich, 1970), 590–591.

50. *Complete Presidential Press Conferences of Franklin D. Roosevelt*, intro. Jonathan Daniels (New York: Da Capo Press, 1972), 21:88–89; Roberts, *Masters and Commanders*, 343.

51. See, e.g., *WP*, January 27, 1943.

CHAPTER 23: DR. NEW DEAL AT BAY

1. Two excellent general sources on the "home front" are Richard Pollenberg, *War and Society: The United States, 1941–1945* (Philadelphia: J. B. Lippincott Company, 1972), and John Morton Blum, *V Was for Victory: Politics and American Culture During World War II* (New York: Harcourt Brace Jovanovich, 1976).

2. Eliot Janeway, *The Struggle for Survival* (rpt.; New York: Weybright and Talley, 1976), remains a classic account of the machinery and politics of mobilization.

3. Arthur Herman, *Freedom's Forge* (New York: Random House, 2012), is a spirited and sympathetic survey of the industrial leaders and their accomplishments.

4. FDR to Thomas Corcoran, January 20, 1941, in *F.D.R.: His Personal Letters, 1905–1928*, ed. Elliott Roosevelt, assisted by James N. Rosenau (New York: Duell, Sloan and Pearce, 1948), 1110–1111.

5. James MacGregor Burns, *Roosevelt: The Soldier of Freedom* (New York: Harcourt Brace Jovanovich, 1970), 339, 352.

6. Melvyn Dubofsky and Warren Van Tine, *John L. Lewis: A Biography*, abr. ed. (Urbana: University of Illinois Press, 1986), ch. 18.

7. FDR, "Fireside Chat 24: On the Coal Crisis," May 2, 1943, American President, http://millercenter.org/president/fdroosevelt/speeches/speech-3330.

8. *NYT*, April 28, 1944.

9. Doris Kearns Goodwin, *No Ordinary Time* (New York: Simon & Schuster, 1994), 498; *Chicago Tribune*, April 29, 1944 (roundup of editorial opinion); *NYT*, April 30, 1944 (L. S. Hourne summary of midwestern criticism); *WP*, May 11, 1944 (editorial and Walter Lippmann column).

10. FDR, "State of the Union Radio Address to the Nation," January 11, 1944, American Presidency Project, http://www.presidency.ucsb.edu/ws/?pid=599.

11. Greg Robinson, *By Order of the President: FDR and the Internment of Japanese-Americans* (Cambridge, MA: Harvard University Press, 2001), is a good recent survey.

12. Francis Biddle, *In Brief Authority* (Garden City, NY: Doubleday & Company, 1962), 233–243.

13. For "The Price of Free World Victory" and, more generally, for Wallace in World War II, John Morton Blum, ed., *The Price of Vision: The Diary of Henry A. Wallace, 1942–1946* (Boston: Houghton Mifflin Company, 1973), is indispensable. The speech itself is at 635–640. I have expressed my own thoughts on Wallace and New Deal liberalism during World War II in Alonzo L. Hamby, *Beyond the New Deal: Harry S. Truman and American Liberalism* (New York: Columbia University Press, 1973), chs. 1–2, and "Sixty Million Jobs and the People's Revolution," *Historian* 30 (August 1968): 578–598.

14. Robert E. Sherwood, *Roosevelt and Hopkins: An Intimate History*, rev. ed. (New York: Grosset & Dunlap, 1950), 740.

15. Hamby, *Beyond the New Deal*, 10–12.

16. *Complete Presidential Press Conferences of Franklin D. Roosevelt*, intro. Jonathan Daniels (New York: Da Capo Press, 1972), 22:245–252.

17. FDR, "Fireside Chat 28: On the State of the Union," January 11, 1944, American President, http://millercenter.org/president/fdroosevelt/speeches/speech-3955.

18. For this and the following paragraph, see John Morton Blum, *From the Morgenthau Diaries: Years of War, 1941–1945* (Boston: Houghton Mifflin Company, 1967), 73–78, and contemporary news articles and commentary in *WP*, February 23–28, 1944.

19. David Roll, *The Hopkins Touch: Harry Hopkins and the Forging of the Alliance to Defeat Hitler* (New York: Oxford University Press, 2013), 334–337.

20. Bernard Asbell, ed., *Mother and Daughter: The Letters of Eleanor and Anna Roosevelt* (New York: International Publishing Corporation, 1988), 177.

21. Joseph E. Persico, *Franklin and Lucy* (New York: Random House, 2008), chs. 28–32; White House logs accessed online via "FDR Day by Day," Franklin D. Roosevelt Presidential Library and Museum, http://www.fdrlibrary.marist.edu/daybyday.

22. Robert Skidelsky, *John Maynard Keynes: Fighting for Freedom, 1937–1946* (New York: Viking Press, 2001), 117.

23. David Brinkley, *Washington Goes to War* (New York: Alfred A. Knopf, 1988), 252–253.

24. Steven Lomazow and Eric Fettmann, *FDR's Deadly Secret* (New York: PublicAffairs, 2009), 51–56. This is, despite a tenuous hypothesis that FDR suffered from cancer, the best survey of the state of his health as president. But see also Harry S. Goldsmith, MD, *A Conspiracy of Silence: The Health and Death of Franklin D. Roosevelt* (New York: iUniverse, 2007), which is of special interest because of its reproduction of Dr. Frank Leahy's memorandum on Roosevelt's health.

25. Lomazow and Fettmann, *FDR's Deadly Secret*, ch. 6, quote on 65.

26. Asbell, *Mother and Daughter*, 131–132 (ER to Anna, May 15, 1941), 133 (ER to Anna, June 22, 1941); Howard G. Bruenn, MD, "Clinical Notes on the Illness and Death of President Franklin D. Roosevelt," *Annals of Internal Medicine* 72 (April 1970): 579–591, summarizes relevant information from FDR's medical chart at the time of Bruenn's first examination of the president on March 27, 1944.

27. Sherwood, *Roosevelt and Hopkins*, 671–673.

28. Grace Tully, *F.D.R.: My Boss* (New York: Charles Scribner's Sons, 1949), 273–274. On FDR after the return from Casablanca, see also Geoffrey C. Ward, ed., *Closest Companion: The Unknown Story of the Intimate Friendship Between Franklin Roosevelt and Margaret Suckley* (Boston: Houghton Mifflin Company, 1995), 201–204.

29. Tully, *F.D.R.: My Boss*, 272–273.

30. Charles E. Bohlen, *Witness to History, 1929–1969* (New York: W. W. Norton & Company, 1973), 149–150.

31. For this and the following paragraphs, see Bruenn, "Clinical Notes on the Illness and Death of President Franklin D. Roosevelt," 579–584.

32. *NYT*, April 11, 1944; for Lindley, see *WP*, May 3, 1944.

33. Ward, *Closest Companion*, 295.

34. Ward, *Closest Companion*, 295–296.

35. Goodwin, *No Ordinary Time*, 571. Maloney's only recorded visit to the White House in 1944 was on June 1. He himself would die suddenly, on January 17, 1945. Goodwin's source was Washington economist and gadfly Eliot Janeway. Lomazow and Fettman, *FDR's Deadly Secret*, 151–152.

36. Turner Catledge, *My Life and the Times* (New York: Harper & Row, 1971), 144–146.

CHAPTER 24: WAR AND DIPLOMACY

1. Susan Butler, ed., *My Dear Mr. Stalin: The Complete Correspondence Between Franklin D. Roosevelt and Joseph V. Stalin*, foreword by Arthur M. Schlesinger Jr. (New Haven, CT: Yale University Press, 2005), 123–127; quotes from FDR to Stalin, April 26, 1943, at 126, and from Stalin to FDR, April 19, 1943, at 127.

2. FDR to Stalin, May 5, 1943, in Butler, *My Dear Mr. Stalin*, 128–130.

3. WC to FDR, June 28, 1943, in *Churchill and Roosevelt: The Complete Correspondence*, Vol. 2: *Alliance Forged, November 1942* [hereafter *Churchill and Roosevelt*, II], ed. Warren F. Kimball (Princeton, NJ: Princeton University Press, 1984), 284–285; *WP*, August 22, 1943; Robert E. Sherwood, *Roosevelt and Hopkins: An Intimate History*, rev. ed. (New York: Grosset & Dunlap, 1950), 734.

4. See, e.g., Gerhard L. Weinberg, *A World at Arms: A Global History of World War II* (Cambridge: Cambridge University Press, 1994), 609–611.

5. Milovan Djilas, *Conversations with Stalin*, trans. Michael B. Petrovich (New York: Harcourt Brace & World, 1962), 73.

6. W. Averell Harriman and Elie Abel, *Special Envoy to Churchill and Stalin, 1941–1946* (New York: Random House, 1975), 216–217; WC to FDR, June 25, 1943, in Kimball, *Churchill and Roosevelt*, II, 278–279.

7. FDR to WC, June 28, 1943, and editorial commentary in Kimball, *Churchill and Roosevelt*, II, 283–284.

8. Jeffrey Herf, *Nazi Propaganda for the Arab World* (New Haven, CT: Yale University Press, 2009).

9. Chaim Weizmann, Memorandum, June 12, 1943, in *Foreign Relations of the United States, 1943*, Vol. 4: *The Near East and Africa* [hereafter *FRUS, 1943*, IV] (Washington: US Government Printing Office, 1968), 792–794; Hoskins, Memo of Conversations with Ibn Saud, August 31, 1943, *FRUS, 1943*, IV, 807–810.

10. Hoskins, Memo of Meeting with FDR, September 27, 1943, *FRUS, 1943*, IV, 811–814.

11. Robert N. Rosen, *Saving the Jews: Franklin D. Roosevelt and the Holocaust* (New York: Thunder's Mouth Press, 2006), 293–296.

12. Henry Morgenthau Jr., Presidential Diary, January 27, 1942, *Presidential Diaries of Henry Morgenthau, Jr.* [microfilm] (University Publications of America, 1981), reel 2.

13. Richard Breitman and Allan J. Lichtman, *FDR and the Jews* (Cambridge, MA: Harvard University Press, 2013), 164–168, 173–179, 319–320, for Long.

14. Timothy Snyder, *Bloodlands: Europe Between Hitler and Stalin* (New York: Basic Books, 2010).

15. For this and the following paragraphs, see Breitman and Lichtman, *FDR and the Jews*, chs. 11–14. For Morgenthau's role, see John Morton Blum, *From the Morgenthau Diaries: Years of War, 1941–1945* (Boston: Houghton Mifflin Company, 1967), 207–227.

16. J. W. Pehle to [John J.] McCloy, June 29, 1944, and attached memorandum, American Legation, Bern, to Secretary of State, June 24, 1944, both forwarded to the White House, FDR Papers, online in the "Franklin D. Roosevelt Significant Documents" collection, http://www.fdrlibrary.marist.edu/archives/collections/franklin/?p=collections/findingaid&id=510&q=&rootcontentid=144823#id144823; Breitman and Lichtman, *FDR and the Jews*, 281–288.

17. Robert I. Gannon, *The Cardinal Spellman Story* (Garden City, NY: Doubleday & Company, 1962), ch. 14.

18. For the details of FDR's trip to Cairo and return, see "FDR Day by Day," Franklin D. Roosevelt Presidential Library and Museum, http://www.fdrlibrary.marist.edu/daybyday.

19. Sherwood, *Roosevelt and Hopkins*, 770–771; Eisenhower, in Harry Butcher Diary, December 6, 1943, in Alfred D. Chandler Jr. et al., eds., *The Papers of Dwight D. Eisenhower: The War Years* (Baltimore: Johns Hopkins Press, 1970), 3:1585–1589.

20. Field Marshal Lord Alanbrooke, *War Diaries, 1939–1945*, ed. Alex Danchev and Daniel Todman (London: Phoenix Press, 2001), 475–476; *NYT*, November 21, 1943 (C. L. Sulzberger); Winston S. Churchill, *The Second World War: Closing the Ring* [hereafter *Second World War*, V] (Boston: Houghton Mifflin Company, 1951), 334, 345–346.

21. On Chiang and China in general, see, e.g., Tang Tsou, *America's Failure in China, 1941–1950* (Chicago: University of Chicago Press, 1963), chs. 1–6. A classic account of Stilwell and his discontents is Barbara W. Tuchman, *Stilwell and the American Experience in China, 1911–45* (New York: Macmillan, 1971), chs. 10–16.

22. ER, *This I Remember* (New York: Harper & Row, 1949), 283–284.

23. Lord Alanbrooke, *War Diaries*, 478.

24. Tuchman, *Stilwell and the American Experience in China*, 520.

25. *NYT*, December 2, 1943.

26. On the travel arrangements, see the November 25, 1943, entry at "FDR Day by Day."

27. Churchill, *Second World War*, V, 342–343.

28. Warren F. Kimball, "A Different Take on FDR at Teheran," *Studies in Intelligence* 49, no. 3 (2005), https://www.cia.gov/library/center-for-the-study-of-intelligence/csi-publications/csi-studies/studies/vol49no3/html_files/FDR_Teheran_12.htm.

29. Arthur M. Schlesinger Jr., *Journals: 1952–2000*, ed. Andrew Schlesinger and Stephen Schlesinger (New York: Penguin Press, 2007), 691–692; *Foreign Relations of the United States: The Conferences at Cairo and Teheran, 1943* [hereafter *FRUS: Cairo and Teheran*] (Washington: US Government Printing Office, 1961), 482–484.

30. Charles E. Bohlen, *Witness to History, 1929–1969* (New York: W. W. Norton & Company, 1973), 141–142.

31. Bohlen, *Witness to History*, 142–143.

32. Churchill, *Second World War*, V, 374; Bohlen, *Witness to History*, 152–153.

33. *FRUS: Cairo and Teheran*, 594–596.

34. Sherwood, *Roosevelt and Hopkins*, 798–799.

35. Forrest C. Pogue, *George C. Marshall: Organizer of Victory, 1943–1945* (New York: Viking Press, 1973), 307.

36. Dwight D. Eisenhower, *Crusade in Europe* (Garden City, NY: Doubleday & Company, 1948), 206–207.

37. Alonzo L. Hamby, *The Imperial Years: The United States Since 1939* (New York: Weybright and Talley, 1976), 74.

38. FDR, "Fireside Chat 27: On the Tehran and Cairo Conferences," December 24, 1943, American President, http://millercenter.org/president/speeches/speech-3333 (audio available).

39. FDR, "Fireside Chat 29: On the Fall of Rome," June 5, 1944, American President, http://millercenter.org/president/fdroosevelt/speeches/speech-3334 (audio available).

CHAPTER 25: INDISPENSABLE MAN

1. FDR, "Prayer on D-day," June 6, 1944, American Presidency Project, http://www.presidency.ucsb.edu/ws/?pid=16515 (audio available).

2. *NYT*, July 12, 1944.

3. On Truman's rise in World War II, see Alonzo L. Hamby, *Man of the People: A Life of Harry S. Truman* (New York: Oxford University Press, 1995), chs. 15–16.

4. John C. Culver and John Hyde, *American Dreamer: The Life and Times of Henry A. Wallace* (New York: W. W. Norton & Company, 2000), 330–339.

5. Culver and Hyde, *American Dreamer*, 339–347; Samuel I. Rosenman, *Working with Roosevelt* (New York: Harper & Brothers, 1952), 438–443; John Morton Blum, ed., *The Price of Vision: The Diary of Henry A. Wallace, 1942–1946* (Boston: Houghton Mifflin Company, 1973), 360–367, summarizes the jockeying for the vice presidency from Wallace's viewpoint.

6. Culver and Hyde, *American Dreamer*, 347–351; Blum, *Price of Vision*, 367.

7. David M. Jordan, *FDR, Dewey, and the Election of 1944* (Bloomington: Indiana University Press, 2011), 144–146.

8. Jordan, *FDR, Dewey, and the Election of 1944*, 148–151.

9. See Jordan, *FDR, Dewey, and the Election of 1944*, ch. 16, for the convention and the vice presidential nomination.

10. James Roosevelt and Sidney Shalett, *Affectionately, F.D.R.: A Son's Story of a Courageous Man* (London: George G. Harrap & Company, 1960), 315–316.

11. James Roosevelt's narrative does not include an exact date, but the "FDR Day by Day" utility at the Franklin D. Roosevelt Presidential Library and Museum (http://www.fdrlibrary.marist.edu/daybyday) puts the date of attendance at the military exercise as July 20. For the text of the acceptance speech, see *NYT*, July 21, 1944. See Jordan, *FDR, Dewey, and the Election of 1944*, 171–172, for the photo.

12. Eric Larrabee, *Commander in Chief* (New York: Harper & Row, 1987), 343–348.

13. Steven Lomazow and Eric Fettmann, *FDR's Deadly Secret* (New York: PublicAffairs, 2009), 131–133.

14. *NYT*, August 11, 12, 15, 18, 1944.

15. Fraser J. Harbutt, *Yalta, 1945: Europe and America at the Crossroads* (Cambridge: Cambridge University Press, 2010), 260–269, ably summarizes Dumbarton Oaks.

16. William E. Leuchtenburg, *Franklin D. Roosevelt and the New Deal, 1932–1940* (New York: Harper & Row, 1963), 322; David Reynolds, *Summits: Six Meetings That Shaped the Twentieth Century* (New York: Basic Books, 2007), 110.

17. Stalin to FDR and WC, August 22, 1944, in *My Dear Mr. Stalin*, ed. Susan Butler (New Haven, CT: Yale University Press, 2005), 253–254; Charles E. Bohlen, *Witness to History, 1929–1969* (New York: W. W. Norton & Company, 1973), 167–168; George F. Kennan, *Memoirs, 1925–1950* (Boston: Little, Brown and Company, 1967), 210–211.

18. John Morton Blum, *From the Morgenthau Diaries: Years of War, 1941–1945* [hereafter *Morgenthau Diaries*, III] (Boston: Houghton Mifflin Company, 1967), 355.

19. Blum, *Morgenthau Diaries*, III, 342.

20. Winston S. Churchill, *The Second World War: Triumph and Tragedy* [hereafter *Second World War*, VI] (Boston: Houghton Mifflin Company, 1953), 156–157; Jordan, *FDR, Dewey, and the Election of 1944*, 251.

21. Churchill claimed in his history of World War II that Harriman was at the meeting. Harriman and his coauthor, Elie Abel, state in their *Special Envoy to Churchill and Stalin, 1941–1946* (New York: Random House, 1975), "Harriman's calendar and his messages to Roosevelt leave no room for doubt that the Ambassador was otherwise occupied" (356n).

22. Harbutt, *Yalta, 1945*, 166–179; Churchill, *Second World War*, VI, 226–228; Molotov-Eden talks, October 10, 1944, in Graham Ross, *The Foreign Office and the Kremlin* (Cambridge: Cambridge University Press, 1944), 179–182.

23. On "Pertinax," see *NYT*, October 27, 1944; for Lippmann, see *WP*, October 14, 1944. See also, e.g., *NYT*, October 15 (R. Daniell), 16 (R. LaFollette Jr.), 18 (Norman Thomas), 1944.

24. Hamby, *Man of the People*, 284–285; Jonathan Daniels, *The Man of Independence* (Philadelphia: J. B. Lippincott Company, 1950), 255.

25. See, e.g., Dewey speeches in *NYT*, September 8, 9, 10, 19, 20, 22, 23, 27, 1944, and commentary in *NYT*, September 10 (A. Krock), October 1 (W. Moscow), 1944, and *WP*, September 12 (M. Childs), 13 (E. Lindley), 28 (M. Childs), October 1 (R. Albright), 1944.

26. On FDR to Willkie, August 21, 1944, and editor's note about UN possibility, see Elliott Roosevelt, ed., *F.D.R.: His Personal Letters, 1928–1945* (New York: Duell, Sloan and Pearce, 1950), 2:1531–1533; Jordan, *FDR, Dewey, and the Election of 1944*, 256–260; Richard Norton Smith, *Thomas E. Dewey and His Times* (New York: Simon & Schuster, 1982), 381–384, 411–415; Rosenman, *Working with Roosevelt*, 463–470.

27. See *WP*, July 28, 1944 (Mark Sullivan); Jordan, *FDR, Dewey, and the Election of 1944*, 145, 161, 166; Alan Drury, *A Senate Journal, 1943–1945* (New York: McGraw-Hill, 1963), 176, 198.

28. *NYT*, October 4, 1944; Jordan, *FDR, Dewey, and the Election of 1944*, 295–296, 302, 307–309.

29. FDR, "Address at a Union Dinner, Washington, D.C.," September 23, 1944, American Presidency Project, http://www.presidency.ucsb.edu/ws/?pid=16563.

30. For the Knutson charge, see *NYT*, September 1, 14, 1944, and a rather comical *Chicago Tribune* editorial of September 4, 1944, which seems to say that the rumor was false but should have been true. Smith, *Thomas E. Dewey*, 434.

31. See *NYT*, October 21, 1944, for the motorcade, and Grace Tully, *F.D.R.: My Boss* (New York: Charles Scribner's Sons, 1949), 281–282, for the aftermath.

32. For the text of the speech as delivered, see *NYT*, October 21, 1944.

33. See *NYT*, October 28, 1944, for stories on campaign appearances and the text of the speech.

34. *NYT*, October 29, 1944.

35. Jordan, *FDR, Dewey, and the Election of 1944*, 312.

36. *NYT*, November 8, 1944; Jordan, *FDR, Dewey, and the Election of 1944*, 319–320.

37. *NYT*, October 22, 1944. See also George Gallup in *WP*, November 18, 1944.

38. On Lindley, see *WP*, July 31, 1944.

CHAPTER 26: THE QUEST FOR A NEW WORLD ORDER

1. This and the following paragraphs on the inauguration are based on articles in *NYT* and *WP*, January 20, 21, 1945.

2. The war news summary derives from *NYT*, January 20, 1945.

3. Steven Lomazow and Eric Fettmann, *FDR's Deadly Secret* (New York: PublicAffairs, 2009), 158; *NYT*, January 21, 1945 (John Crider and Associated Press article quoting McIntire). See also Bob Considine in *WP*, January 21, 1945.

4. *NYT*, December 20, 1944; see *NYT*, January 7, 1945, for the text of the message and accompanying stories.

5. John C. Culver and John Hyde, *American Dreamer: The Life and Times of Henry A. Wallace* (New York: W. W. Norton & Company, 2000), 372–373; John Morton Blum, ed., *The Price of Vision: The Diary of Henry A. Wallace, 1942–1946* (Boston: Houghton Mifflin Company, 1973), 381–384.

6. Culver and Hyde, *American Dreamer*, 376–377; Blum, *Price of Vision*, 406–412.

7. FDR to Jones, January 20, 1945, reprinted in *NYT*, January 22, 1945.

8. Jones to FDR, January 20, 1945, reprinted in *NYT*, January 22, 1945.

9. Culver and Hyde, *American Dreamer*, 379–384.

10. W. Averell Harriman and Elie Abel, *Special Envoy to Churchill and Stalin, 1941–1946* (New York: Random House, 1975), 369–370.

11. Fraser J. Harbutt, *Yalta, 1945: Europe and America at the Crossroads* (Cambridge: Cambridge University Press, 2010), 201–202, for Turkey. On Greece, see WC, *The Second World War: Triumph and Tragedy* (Boston: Houghton Mifflin Company, 1953), chs. 18–19, and correspondence in *Churchill and Roosevelt: The Complete Correspondence*, Vol. 3: *Alliance Declining, February 1944–April 1945* [hereafter *Churchill and Roosevelt*, III], ed. Warren F. Kimball (Princeton, NJ: Princeton University Press, 1984), 449–481.

12. For the trip across the Atlantic, see the White House log at "FDR Day by Day," Franklin D. Roosevelt Presidential Library and Museum, http://www.fdrlibrary.marist.edu/daybyday.

13. Photo in Kimball, *Churchill and Roosevelt*, III, [ii]; Charles E. Bohlen, *Witness to History, 1929–1969* (New York: W. W. Norton & Company, 1973), 178–179. See also Robert E. Sherwood, *Roosevelt and Hopkins: An Intimate History*, rev. ed. (New York: Grosset & Dunlap, 1950), 849, for the impression of FDR formed by Admiral Ernest King.

14. See S. M. Plokhy, *Yalta: The Price of Peace* (New York: Viking Press, 2010), 36–39, for the trip to Yalta and for many of the subsequent details in this chapter.

15. Robert Hopkins, "How Would You Like to Be Attached to the Red Army?," *American Heritage* 56 (June–July, 2005), 30–37.

16. David Reynolds, *Summits: Six Meetings That Shaped the Twentieth Century* (New York: Basic Books, 2007), 114.

17. On Hiss, see Allen Weinstein, *Perjury: The Hiss-Chambers Case* (New York: Alfred A. Knopf, 1978).

18. Plokhy, *Yalta*, 232–233.

19. *Foreign Relations of the United States: The Conferences at Malta and Yalta, 1945* [hereafter *FRUS: Yalta*] (Washington: US Government Printing Office, 1955), 669.

20. For the exchange about Caesar's wife, see *FRUS: Yalta*, 854. Subsequent references to the Yalta communiqué are from *NYT*, February 13, 1945, and *FRUS: Yalta*, 968–975.

21. William D. Leahy, *I Was There* (New York: Whittlesey House, 1950), 315–316.

22. *FRUS: Yalta*, 978.

23. For this and the following paragraph, see *FRUS: Yalta*, 378–379, 766–771, 894–897; Harriman and Abel, *Special Envoy*, 396–400.

24. Harriman and Abel, *Special Envoy*, 399; Jon Meacham, *Franklin and Winston: An Intimate Portrait of an Epic Friendship* (New York: Random House, 2003), 317.

25. *FRUS: Yalta*, 797–798.

26. Sherwood, *Roosevelt and Hopkins*, 870.

27. Harriman and Abel, *Special Envoy*, 417.

28. Bohlen, *Witness to History*, 212–213; Allis Radosh and Ronald Radosh, *A Safe Haven: Harry S. Truman and the Founding of Israel* (New York: Harper Collins, 2009), 25–28; FDR to Daisy Suckley, February 18, 1945, in *Closest Companion*, ed. Geoffrey C. Ward (Boston: Houghton Mifflin Company, 1995), 396; Captain Henry Putnam to [White House Map Room], "Comrades in Arms," February 14, 1945, supplied to the author by George M. Elsey; Sherwood, *Roosevelt and Hopkins*, 871–872.

29. Sherwood, *Roosevelt and Hopkins*, 874.

30. Churchill, *Second World War*, 397; Samuel I. Rosenman, *Working with Roosevelt* (New York: Harper & Brothers, 1952), 522.

31. FDR, "Address to Congress on the Yalta Conference," March 1, 1945, American Presidency Project, http://www.presidency.ucsb.edu/ws/?pid=16591; for the text of speech as it appears to have been originally written, see *WP*, March 2, 1945.

32. Rosenman, *Working with Roosevelt*, 527; Steven Lomazow and Eric Fettmann, *FDR's Deadly Secret* (New York: PublicAffairs, 2009), 1–7; *Chicago Tribune*, March 2, 3, 1945; *NYT*, March 2, 1945 (Arthur Krock, William S. White); *WP*, March 2 (editorial; Ernest Lindley), 3 (Barnett Nover), 1945.

33. Kimball, *Churchill and Roosevelt*, III, 569. Sherwood, *Roosevelt and Hopkins*, 528, says the two men never saw each other after Hopkins departed the Quincy at Algiers, but the White House log lists Hopkins as a guest for lunch and dinner on February 28 and March 2 and as a lunch guest on March 17.

34. George Elsey, memos to self, March 27 (2), April 11, 1945, author's possession.

35. For Mrs. Rutherfurd, see March 12, 13, 14, 20, 21, 1945, at "FDR Day by Day," Franklin D. Roosevelt Presidential Library and Museum, http://www.fdrlibrary.marist.edu/daybyday; she may also have been a "motoring" companion on March 19. For the Truman conversation, see Harry S. Truman, *Memoirs*, Vol. 1: *Year of Decisions* (Garden City, NY: Doubleday & Company, 1955), 4.

36. Ward, *Closest Companion*, 402.

37. Harriman and Abel, *Special Envoy*, 419–423.

38. Stalin to FDR, April 3, 1945, in *My Dear Mr. Stalin*, ed. Susan Butler (New Haven, CT: Yale University Press, 2005), 312–313.

39. FDR to Stalin, April 5, 1945, in Butler, *My Dear Mr. Stalin*, 313–315.

40. Stalin to FDR, April 7, 1945, in Butler, *My Dear Mr. Stalin*, 315–317.

41. FDR to WC, April 11, 1945, in Kimball, *Churchill and Roosevelt*, III, 630.

42. FDR to Stalin, April 11, 1945, in Butler, *My Dear Mr. Stalin*, 321; Harriman and Abel, *Special Envoy*, 439–440.

43. Ward, *Closest Companion*, 411–412; Grace Tully, *F.D.R.: My Boss* (New York: Charles Scribner's Sons, 1949), 360–361.

44. Ward, *Closest Companion*, 419.

45. Truman, *Memoirs*, 30; *NYT* and *WP*, April 15, 1945.

46. Sherwood, *Roosevelt and Hopkins*, 881; *NYT*, April 15, 1945.

47. *NYT*, April 16, 1945.

EPILOGUE: FDR AND THE AMERICAN CENTURY

1. Henry R. Luce, "The American Century," *Life* 10 (February 17, 1941): 61–65.

2. *Foreign Relations of the United States: The Conferences at Malta and Yalta, 1945* [hereafter *FRUS: Yalta*] (Washington: US Government Printing Office, 1955), 797–798.

3. *FRUS: Yalta*, 798.

INDEX

Alonzo Hamby is Distinguished Professor of History Emeritus at Ohio University. He is the author of *Man of the People: A Life of Harry S. Truman,* among other books. He lives in Athens, Ohio.